MANAGING TODAY!

Stephen P. Robbins

San Diego State University

Prentice Hall
Upper Saddle River, New Jersey 07458

Acquisitions Editor: David Shafer
Associate Editor: Lisamarie Brassini
Editorial Assistant: Brett Moreland
Editor-in-Chief: James Boyd
Marketing Manager: Sandra Steiner
Production Editor: Louise Rothman
Production Coordinator: Renee Pelletier
Managing Editor: Carol Burgett
Manufacturing Supervisor: Arnold Vila
Manufacturing Manager: Vincent Scelta
Senior Designer: Ann France
Design Director: Patricia Wosczyk
Interior Design: Ann France
Cover Design: Lorraine Castellano
Illustrator (Interior): Dartmouth Publishing, Inc.
Composition: TSI Graphics

Credits and acknowledgments for materials borrowed from other sources and reproduced, with permission, in this textbook appear on pages 564–565.

Library of Congress Cataloging-in-Publication Data

Robbins, Stephen P.,
Managing today! / Stephen P. Robbins.
p. cm.
Includes bibliographical references and index.
ISBN 0-13-233313-9
1. Management. 2. Organizational effectiveness. 3. Personnel management. 4. Management—Problems, exercises, etc. I. Title.
HD31.R5648 1997
658—dc20 96-19873
CIP

Prentice-Hall International (UK) Limited, London
Prentice-Hall of Australia Pty. Limited, Sydney
Prentice-Hall Canada, Inc., Toronto
Prentice-Hall Hispanoamericana, S.A., Mexico
Prentice-Hall of India Private Limited, New Delhi
Prentice-Hall of Japan, Inc., Tokyo
Simon & Schuster Asia Pte. Ltd., Singapore
Editora Prentice-Hall do Brasil, Ltda., Rio de Janeiro

Printed in the United States of America

10 9 8 7 6 5 4 3 2

To Laura Ospanik

BRIEF TABLE OF CONTENTS

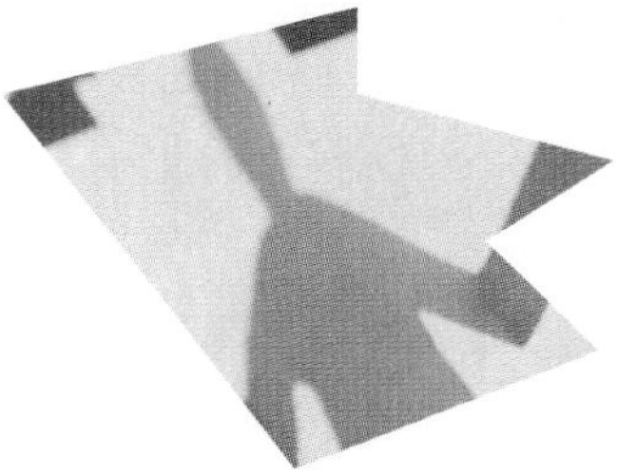

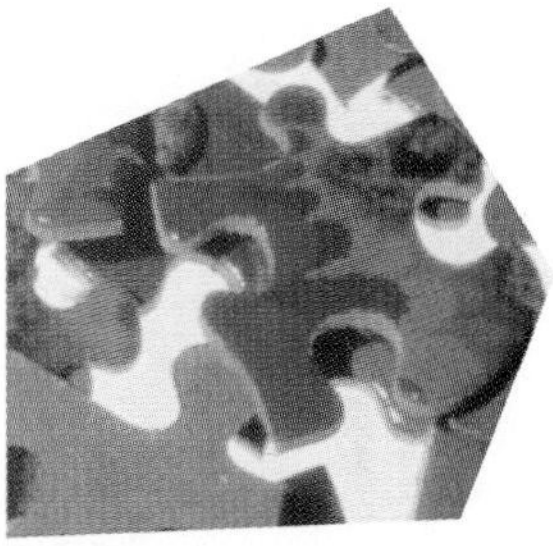

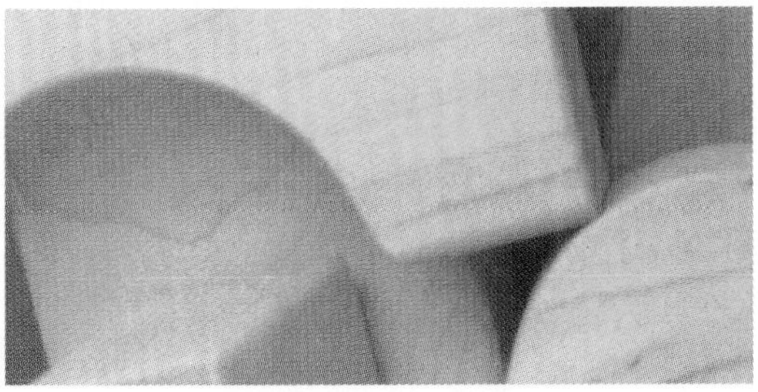

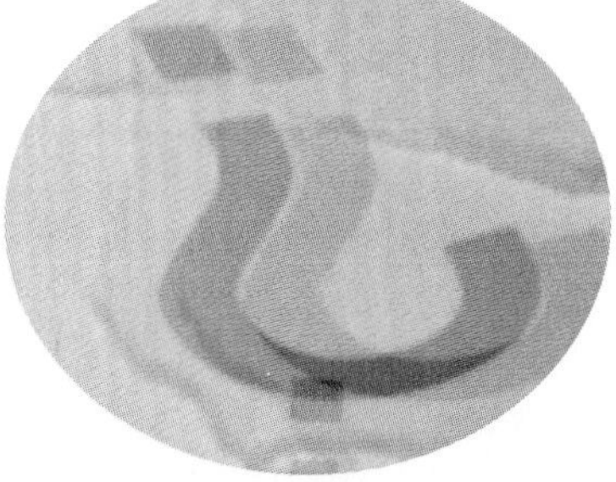

TABLE OF CONTENTS

Chapter 4
ASSESSING THE ENVIRONMENT 96

Chapter 5
PLANNING SYSTEMS 128

Part Four Leading and Empowering People 352

Chapter 12 UNDERSTANDING THE BASICS OF HUMAN BEHAVIOR 352

Chapter 13 WORK MOTIVATION AND REWARDS 384

Part Five
Organizational Renewal 510

PREFACE

I recently counted thirty-three introductory management textbooks on my bookshelf (including my own *Management,* 5th ed., with Mary Coulter, and my *Fundamentals of Management,* with David DeCenzo). All of these thirty-three books are still in print and are being actively marketed by their publishers. So, you might be wondering, why in the world would an author and publisher possibly think there is a need for a thirty-fourth? The answer is that there have been dramatic changes in the field of management in recent years. And these changes have created the need for a textbook that can define and describe what may be called a new "paradigm." This book, *Managing Today!,* reflects what managers and the business press have been acknowledging now for at least a half-dozen years—the economy and workplace have undergone fundamental changes that have significantly reshaped the manager's job. This book immodestly attempts to provide a new paradigm for studying management.

THE "EXPANDING-HOUSE" ANALOGY

For more than thirty-five years, nearly every basic management textbook has used a rigid functional approach ("managers plan, organize, staff, lead, and control") as an organizing framework. When this trend began in the late 1950s, the chapters fit together fairly well and made a comprehensive whole. But while management and organizations have been going through a complete metamorphosis in recent years, most textbook authors have tried to maintain their commitment to this functional approach. In order to appear "contemporary," most authors (myself included) added chapters on topics such as strategy, entrepreneurship, careers, management information systems (MIS), social responsibility, international management, managing conflict, teams, quality, technology, and workforce diversity—force-feeding these topics into the functional paradigm (whether they fit or not!). Then boxes on topics such as globalization, ethics, and management skills were tacked on as "integrative" concepts. The whole thing reminds me of some friends who bought a small two-bedroom, one-bathroom house more than two decades ago and then sporadically, over the years, added several bedrooms, a couple of baths, and an office and converted the garage into a family room. They had no long-term plan. The house just evolved. Today, the house has become a monstrosity. The layout is cumbersome, there is no natural flow from room to room, and little seems to match up properly. It seems to me that most of today's introductory management texts have evolved in precisely the same way. They have become 800+ pages of concepts and issues that no longer fit well together when organized around the traditional functions of planning, organizing, staffing, leading, and controlling. It is time to tear down "the house" and rebuild it from scratch. To carry the analogy to its natural conclusion, *Managing Today!* is my attempt to design and construct a contemporary house on the same lot, using the latest advances in our building technology.

As you will see by glancing through the Table of Contents, *Managing Today!* has not "reinvented the wheel." This book owes a heavy debt to the functional approach, but the functional paradigm does not rigidly drive this book's content. For instance, planning and control issues are discussed together in Part Two; staffing is covered in one chapter in Part Three; Part Four, Leading and Empowering People, has been expanded well beyond what is typically found in an introductory management text; and Part Five reinforces the manager's role in organizational renewal through managing change. In addition, *Managing Today!* presents many contemporary topics that are often overlooked in introductory management texts. These include management competencies, outsourcing, dejobbing, behavioral decision making, decision-making styles, environmental scanning, project management, core competencies, broadbanding compensation, skill-based pay plans, learning styles, visionary leadership, team leadership, ethical leadership, building credibility and trust, coaching, self-directed careers, the development of interpersonal skills, and the learning organization.

ASSUMPTIONS UNDERLYING THIS BOOK

As I was planning this book, I began listing assumptions that I thought reflected management *today* and that could guide me in deciding the book's overall structure, how to organize issues, and what to include and exclude. Let me briefly list those assumptions and then note how they shaped the content of this book.

1. The world of work has changed, and change has become the dominant issue facing every manager.
   Implications. See particularly Chapters 1, 4, and 17.
2. The field of management has gone global, so there is no need to tack on a discussion of globalization. *Management* in the 1990s is synonymous with *global management.*
   Implications. Globalization is integrated throughout and is not emphasized in a single chapter.
3. Similarly, the topics of ethics, diversity, and quality are integrative issues for today's managers and to present them in stand-alone chapters or as boxed themes is inappropriate.

EXHIBIT 1
Integrative Topics (with specific page references)

Chapter	Ethics	Diversity	Quality
1	9-10, 20-21	8-9, 12	10-11, 13
2	48-49	44	33, 48
3	83-84, 87-88	71, 85-86	
4	102, 108, 118-20	116-18	97-98, 107-08, 122
5	142-43		
6	175-77		163
7			
8		248-49	229-30, 231-32, 233
9	274	260-62, 264-65, 273, 276-77, 284	272
10	297	300, 312-13	308
11		346	
12	356	377-79	
13		385-86, 409-10	
14		436-37	
15	455-57, 467-68	464, 466-67	
16	481, 504	482	
17		528-29	

Implications. These topics are integrated throughout the text. The grid in Exhibit 1 provides examples of how ethics, diversity, and quality have been covered *across* chapters.

4. Students' interest in history is minimal, so this subject should not lead their introduction into the field as an early, stand-alone chapter.
   Implications. A detailed historical review—discussed from the perspective of its relevance to practice—is provided in this book as an appendix, where faculty can assign it and students can read it when, or if, they wish.

5. Much of the classical material in management textbooks has little value to today's students except from a historical perspective. For example, autonomous, cross-functional teams contradict scientific management's unwavering belief in division of labor and the separation of management's and labor's responsibilities; and many prescriptions regarding effective organization designs have been made obsolete as a result of changes in information technology.
   Implications. I have limited the discussion on classical principles and emphasized how information technology is reshaping the manager's job.

6. Management is less concerned today with "command and control" than with creating shared visions, empowering employees, and creating self-managed teams.
   Implications. The topics of planning and control are condensed into two chapters (Chapters 5 and 6). There is extensive coverage of leadership, work teams, reward systems, and creating effective cultures.

7. The defining issues in management today are people, technology, globalization, and leadership. These are the issues that determine how organizations are to compete and survive.
   Implications. I have heavily emphasized issues related to organizational behavior (including two chapters, 14 and 15, on leadership). See Chapter 8 on technology. Globalization is integrated throughout.

8. Today's model organizations are no longer the likes of GM, Sears, or IBM. The new models are organizations such as Microsoft, ASEA Brown Boveri, Nucorp Corp., Magna International, Southwest Airlines, and Wal-Mart.
   Implications. The focus of the organization structure discussion is on contemporary designs.

9. Students want material they can apply on their jobs.
   Implications. See the "Building Self-Awareness" boxes and the strong emphasis on skill-building throughout the text.

10. Students want to know what works and what doesn't. They are not interested in the details of research, the historical evolution of our knowledge, or long discourses on competing ideas. "For example, leadership sounds like an applied topic, but its classroom presentation can leave students no better prepared to lead. . . . The business school graduate needs to lead, not trace the history of leadership research. The graduate needs to motivate, not compare and contrast six different theories of motivation." (M. R. Blood, "The Role of Organizational Behavior in the Business School Curriculum," in J. Greenberg, ed., *Organizational Behavior: The State of the Science;* Hillsdale, N.J.: Lawrence Erlbaum, 1994, p. 216).
    Implications: For examples, see Chapters 13, 14, and 15 on motivation and leadership. They downplay names, historical developments, and research methods. They focus on current motivation and leadership issues and draw on the theories to clarify those issues and to provide readers with practical guidelines for applications.

Acknowledgments

I have been fortunate to have a great group of people support me in the development of this book. And here I want to acknowledge their contribution.

Let me start by thanking Marsha Leeman-Conley (National University, Sacramento Campus), Peggy Sue Heath (University of Washington), Forest Jourden (University of Illinois), Kathi Lovelace (Skagit Valley College), Eugene Owens (Western Washington University), and Max Elden (University of Houston, Clear Lake City). These people read a good part of the manuscript during the summer of 1995 and then participated in a one-day focus group. Their suggestions significantly shaped the order of topics and issues covered in the book.

A number of reviewers read all or major parts of this manuscript as it evolved. My thanks to Daniel Kopp (Southwest Missouri State University), Thomas Martin (University of Nebraska at Omaha), Jill Purdy (University of Washington, Tacoma), Sharon Clinebell (University of Northern Colorado), Bob Hatfield (West Virginia State College), Karen Vinton (Montana State University), Steve Thomas (Southwest Missouri State University), Kathi Lovelace (Skagit Valley College), Linda Gibson (Pacific Lutheran University), Glen Miyataki (University of Hawaii at Manoa), Jeff Tschetter (University of Sioux Falls), and Tim Serey (Northern Kentucky University) for their valuable comments.

I also want to single out two friends-colleagues—David DeCenzo at Towson State University and (again) Peggy Sue Heath—who have listened to my frustrations as I tried to get all the pieces in this book to fit and who were kind enough to critically comment on my ideas as they evolved. I particularly relied on Peg to help me sort out and clarify the issues in Chapter 14. Thanks Dave and Peg. This book is a lot better because of your insights.

Finally, I want to acknowledge the people at Prentice Hall who helped make this book a reality. These include David Shafer, Jo-Ann Deluca, Bill Oldsey, Jim Boyd, Nancy Kaplan, Brett Moreland, Crissy Statuto, Tom Nixon, my production editor Louise Rothman, and the book's designer Ann France. Thanks (again!) for all your support.

Stephen P. Robbins

About the Author

Stephen P. Robbins worked for the Shell Oil Company and Reynolds Metals Company before receiving his doctorate from the University of Arizona. Since completing his graduate studies, he has taught at the University of Nebraska at Omaha, Concordia University in Montreal, the University of Baltimore, Southern Illinois University at Edwardsville, and San Diego State University. His research interests have focused on conflict, power, and politics in organizations, as well as on the development of effective interpersonal skills. His articles on these and other topics have appeared in such journals as *Business Horizons,* the *California Management Review, Business and Economic Perspectives, International Management, Management Review, Canadian Personnel and Industrial Relations,* and *The Journal of Management Education.*

In recent years, he has been spending most of his professional time writing textbooks. These include *Organizational Behavior,* 7th ed. (Prentice Hall, 1996); *Essentials of Organizational Behavior,* 5th ed. (Prentice Hall, 1997); *Management,* 5th ed., with Mary Coulter (Prentice Hall, 1996); *Human Resource Management,* 5th ed., with David DeCenzo (Wiley, 1996); *Training in InterPersonal Skills,* 2nd ed., with Phillip Hunsaker (Prentice Hall, 1996); *Fundamentals of Management,* with David DeCenzo (Prentice Hall, 1995); *Supervision Today!* (Prentice Hall, 1995); and *Organization Theory,* 3rd ed. (Prentice Hall, 1990). These books are used at more than a thousand U.S. colleges and universities, as well as hundreds of schools throughout Canada, Latin America, Australia, Asia, and Europe.

In his "other life," Robbins participates in masters' track competition. In 1995 he reaffirmed his title of "the world's fastest human—age 50 and over"—by winning the U.S. national indoor championships at 60 meters and 200 meters; winning the U.S. outdoor nationals at 100-meter and 200-meter; and capturing four gold medals (and setting three world records) at the Eleventh World Veteran Games. At the World Games, he won the 100-meters, 200-meters, and 400-meter dashes, and he anchored the victorious U.S. 4 × 1 relay team. Robbins was named the outstanding age-40-and-over male track and field athlete of 1995 by the Masters Track and Field Committee of USA Track & Field, the national governing body for athletics in the United States.

Managing Today!

PART ONE: Introduction

CHAPTER 1

WELCOME TO THE CHANGING WORLD OF WORK

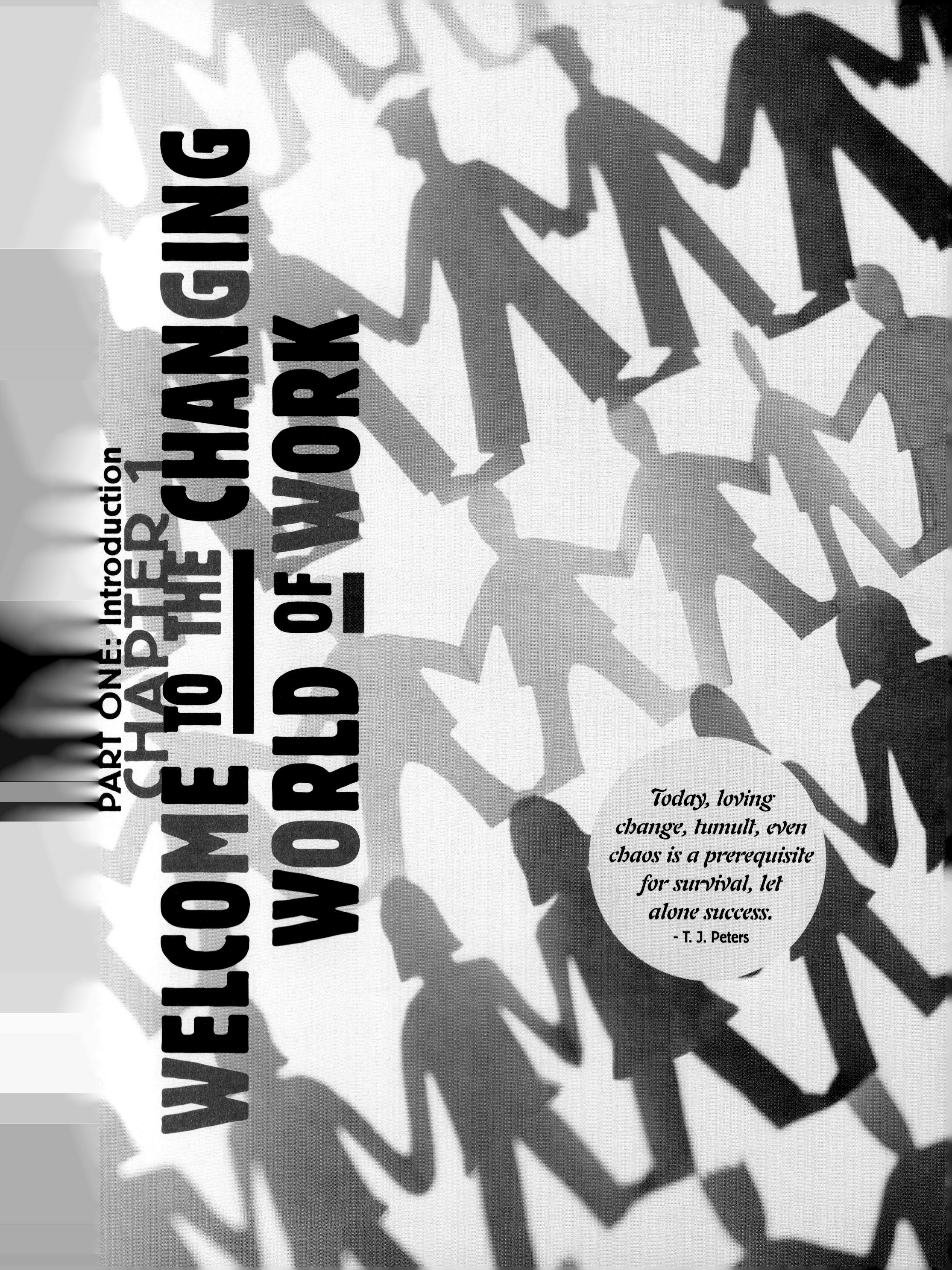

Today, loving change, tumult, even chaos is a prerequisite for survival, let alone success.
- T. J. Peters

LEARNING OBJECTIVES

After studying this chapter, you should be able to:

1. Describe the effects of globalization on the economy and on organizations
2. Explain the three waves in human history and their implications for the economy and organizations
3. Identify the key elements in total quality management
4. Explain why organizations are reengineering work processes
5. Define the contingent work force
6. Explain the bimodal work force
7. Describe what happened to the loyalty-for-job-security arrangement

Duane Hartley, Willow Shire, and Joaquin Carbanel provide us with a window into what managing in the 1990s is like. These three executives, who work for three different companies, share one common characteristic—they're trying to adapt and manage in a corporate world undergoing dramatic changes.[1]

"Right now I'm probably spending 75 percent of my energy on matters that could be called corporate culture. I don't think people really enjoy change, but if they can participate in it and understand it, it can become a positive for them," states 49-year-old Hartley, general manager of Hewlett-Packard's microwave instruments division. He's trying to provide the strong leadership necessary to shift his division toward new products and customers as it weans itself from dependency on creating expensive, high-performance instruments for the defense industry. "We got caught up in the success of the defense industry. And as somebody once put it, 'When you're successful, you forget quickly and learn slowly.' Organizations get successful, then they lose their sense of urgency and end up having to go through some kind of transition to get it back." Hartley is leading his division through that transition as he makes painful layoffs, restructures the work of his group, and carries the message of change to employees. He maintains two offices in two plants, but he's spending an increasing amount of his time walking the plant floors and offices, talking with the troops—sharing information with them and listening. Although the changes at Hewlett-Packard have claimed the jobs of many managers, Hartley thinks he knows why managers fail in times of revolutionary change: "They don't listen. They don't listen to the customers, the market, the field, their own employees. They just flat get out of touch."

Willow Shire, 44, (see photo inset) is corporate vice president at Digital Equipment Corporation, overseeing one of the company's nine major units. She is responsible for selling computer systems to the hospital, pharmaceutical, Social Security, and governmental health industries. Digital has suffered badly from changes in the computer market. For instance, its effort in the mid-1980s to get into the personal computer business flopped, never capturing more than 1 percent of the PC market. And its line of workstations, which made a lot of money for Digital during the 1980s, lost market share to technologically superior products from Sun Microsystems. Between 1991 and 1995, Digital reorganized and cut its work force by more than 25,000 employees. The company now believes its products are more innovative and competitive. Shire's challenge is trying to shore up her employees, most of whom have been beaten down by Digital's past setbacks. At the same time, she realizes that, unless change comes quickly, more staff cuts are inevitable. "Morale is very low," she says, "When I first came here 16 years ago, I was surrounded by intelligent, bright, aggressive, vibrant people who were excited about what they were doing. Now people are tired, frustrated, and frightened." It's in this climate that Shire is attempting to convince her people of the urgency to change past practices. As she says over and over to her employees, "We are out of time. There is no more time. We must return to profitability before too many quarters pass."

Joaquin Carbanel has to be quick on his feet. As the new president of BellSouth Europe, this 42-year-old executive is at the cutting edge of the new global business economy. Cuban by birth, Carbanel was raised in the United States and is a Duke law school graduate. He has had numerous managerial jobs with BellSouth; most included extensive foreign travel. In recent years, for instance, he made three trips to Tel Aviv in 4 months and spent a month commuting between Atlanta and Australia. In 1992, he became president of BellSouth Latin America and was responsible for plotting telecom deals south of the border. In this job, he was round-tripping from Atlanta to South America 2 weeks every month. In his new job, he'll be located in Europe, plotting an expansion strategy for Eastern Europe, but still traveling extensively. What Carbanel has learned in his globetrotting is that he has to constantly adapt his business style to each cultural environment—from Latin America's low-key social wooing to the in-your-face style that's needed in Israel to Australia's wide-open ways. And he's succeeded in making rapid adaptations to these different environments. After a few years as a global manager, he says, "You feel at home wherever you are."

This book is about managing organizations *in times of rapid change.* We are going to show you that the challenges that people like Duane Hartley, Willow Shire, and Joaquin Carbanel face in their jobs are not unique in the 1990s. *Most* organizations recently have reassessed their strategies and restructured themselves to compete more effectively. And an increasing number of organizations are moving to take advantage of global opportunities.

This opening chapter provides you with an overview of the changing world of work. We'll show you how changes in the economy are reshaping organizations and redefining people's jobs. The message of this chapter is simple: The world of work today and in the future is nothing like it was just a decade or two ago.

THE NEW ECONOMY

Let's start by looking at the major changes that are reshaping the economy. These include globalization; technological upheavals, especially in the areas of computers, telecommunications, and information; growth and decline among job sectors; cultural diversity; changing societal expectations; expanding interest in entrepreneurship; and more-fickle, more-demanding customers (see Exhibit 1-1).

Globalization

Twenty or thirty years ago, national borders acted to insulate most firms from foreign competitive pressures. They no longer do. National borders have become nearly meaningless today in defining an organization's operating boundaries. It has become increasingly irrelevant, for instance, to label a company's home country. BMW is supposedly a German firm, but it builds cars in South Carolina. Ford, which is headquartered in Detroit, builds its Mercury Tracers in Mexico. So-called U.S. companies such as Exxon, Gillette, Coca-Cola, and IBM now receive more than 60 percent of their sales from outside the United States.[2] And Mitsubishi of Japan, Siemens of Germany, Nestlé of Switzerland, and Royal Dutch/Shell of the Netherlands are just four examples of the hundreds of multibillion dollar corporations that operate in dozens of countries throughout the world.[3] Even this textbook, published in the United States, is at this very moment being read by students in the United States, Canada, Jamaica, Australia, Singapore, Hong Kong, Malaysia, the Philippines, Great Britain, Sweden, the Netherlands, and across Latin America.

National borders have become nearly meaningless today in defining an organization's operating boundaries.

But globalization doesn't just mean doing business across national borders. It also means expanded competition for almost every type of organization. Today's managers must be aware that they face foreign competitors as well as local and national ones. For instance, since 1972, Dennis Marthell has run a profitable business by processing checks for several major banks in the southeastern United States. In recent years, however, he has found himself competing against firms in the Caribbean. Because of computer technology and overnight delivery services, the Caribbean firms can provide the same services Marthell does but at better prices because of lower labor costs in countries such as Jamaica and Trinidad.

EXHIBIT 1-1
The Changing Economy

Old Economy	New Economy
• National borders limit competition	• National borders are nearly meaningless in defining an organization's operating boundaries
• Technology reinforces rigid hierarchies and limits access to information	• Technological changes in the way information is created, stored, used, and shared have made it more accessible
• Job opportunities are for blue-collar industrial workers	• Job opportunities are for knowledge workers
• Population is relatively homogeneous	• Population is characterized by cultural diversity
• Business is estranged from its environment	• Business accepts its social responsibilities
• Economy is driven by large corporations	• Economy is driven by small, entrepreneurial firms
• Customers get what business chooses to give them	• Customer needs drive business

The two major forces driving globalization have been the search for expanded markets and efforts to reduce costs. If Sony sold its products only in its home country of Japan, its sales potential would be limited. Japan has a population of only 125 million. By going global, Sony has been able to market its products to billions of people. If an organization wants to grow, expanding operations outside its national borders is a logical strategy. Political barriers to this strategy have been lessened in recent years by the creation of multicountry trading blocs. NAFTA (the North American Free Trade Agreement, which unites Canada, the United States, and Mexico), the European Union (which includes fifteen Western European countries), and the Asia-Pacific Economic Cooperation (a group of eighteen Pacific Rim nations that includes NAFTA participants as well as countries such as China, Japan, Australia, and South Korea) are examples of trading blocs that have significantly reduced tariffs and other barriers to cross-national trade among the participating countries. The current world political climate appears to be increasingly moving toward reducing protectionist policies and opening up international trade.

Many organizations have also been motivated to expand beyond their national borders in order to gain cost advantages over rivals. The fact that many North American and European firms manufacture products such as semiconductors and textiles in Southeast Asia can be explained largely in terms of lower labor costs. Very recently, Western companies have been moving into Central Europe to gain access to its low-cost, high-skilled labor force. In 1993, for instance, the average male worker in western Germany earned $33.21 an hour. In Poland, he earned $2.36, and in the Czech Republic, $1.76. German pencilmaker Schwan-Stabilo expects to reduce its product costs 25 percent by moving its manufacturing operations to the Czech Republic.[4]

National borders are becoming increasingly meaningless in defining the boundaries of business. Advances in communication technology and reductions in cross-nation trade barriers have contributed to creating a truly global village.

Technological Changes

We often forget that only 20 years ago, almost no one had a fax machine or a cellular phone; the terms *e-mail* and *modem* were in the vocabulary of, perhaps, a couple of hundred people; computers occupied entire rooms rather than 11 inches of lap space; and *networks* referred to the major providers of television programming. How quickly times have changed.

The silicon chip and other advances in information technology have permanently altered the economies of the world and, as we will demonstrate shortly, the way people work. Digital electronics, optical data storage, more powerful and portable computers, and the ability for computers to communicate with each other are changing the way information is created, stored, used, and shared.

Three Waves: Growth and Decline in Job Sectors

Futurist Alvin Toffler argued that human history can be divided into "waves."[5] The first wave was *agriculture.* Until the late nineteenth century, all economies were agrarian. For instance, in the 1890s, approximately 90 percent of people were employed in agriculture-related jobs. The second wave was *industrialization.* From the late 1800s until the 1960s, most developed countries moved from agrarian societies to ones based on machines. The third wave arrived in the 1970s. It is based on *information.* Toffler and others see these waves as essentially revolutions, in which complete "ways of life" are thrown out and replaced by new ones. The second wave, for instance, totally changed the lives of English villagers as they adjusted to life in English factories.[6] And the third wave is eliminating low-skilled, blue-collar jobs, while, at the same time, it is creating abundant job opportunities for educated and skilled technical specialists, professionals, and other "knowledge workers".

Exhibit 1-2 on page 8 illustrates the changing makeup during the twentieth century of the work force in developed countries like the United States, Canada, the United Kingdom, Germany, France, Italy, and Japan.[7] Before World War I, farmers composed the largest single group in every developed country. Since that time, the proportion of the population engaged in farming has consistently dropped. Now less than 5 percent of the work force is needed to provide our food; in the United States, it's under 3 percent.

The Industrial Revolution destroyed the careers of hundreds of thousands of skilled craftsmen. But it created a new group—blue-collar industrial workers. In 1900, this new group represented about 20 percent of the work force. By the 1950s, industrial workers had become the largest single group in every developed country. They made products such as steel, automobiles, rubber, and industrial equipment. Ironically, "no class in history has ever risen faster than the blue-collar worker. And no class in history has ever fallen faster."[8] Today, blue-collar industrial workers account for less than 20 percent of the U.S. work force, essentially about the same proportion they held in 1900![9] The shift since World War II has been away from manufacturing work and toward service jobs. Manufacturing jobs today are highest, as a proportion of the total civilian work force, in Japan—at 24.3 percent. In the United States, manufacturing jobs make up only 18 percent of the civilian work force. In contrast, services make up 59 percent of jobs in Italy (the lowest percentage of any industrial country) and 72 percent in the United States and Canada.[10]

> **"No class in history has ever risen faster than the blue-collar worker. And no class in history has ever fallen faster."**

Job growth in the past 20 years has been in low-skilled service work (such as fast-food employees, clerks, and home health aides) and knowledge work. This lat-

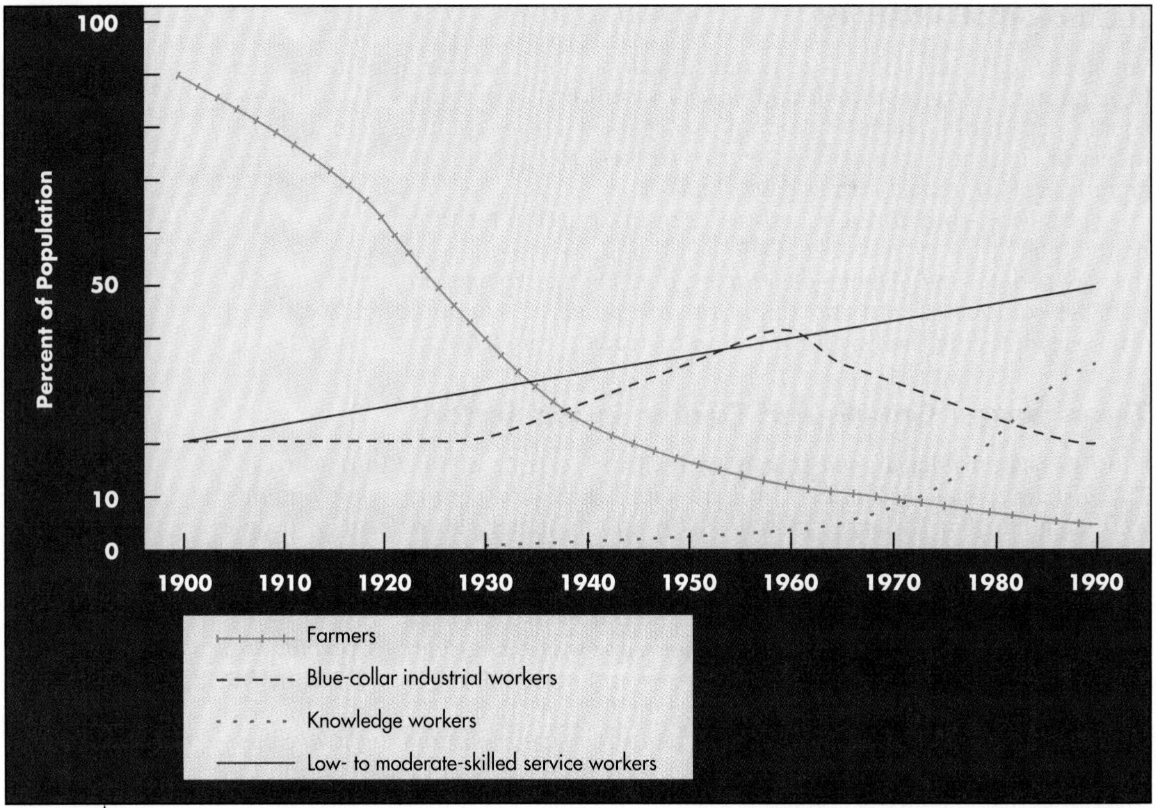

EXHIBIT 1-2
Changing Makeup of the Work Force in Industrialized Countries

Based on T. M. Godbout, "Employment Change and Sectoral Distribution in 10 Countries, 1970–90, *Monthly Labor Review,* October 1993, pp. 3–12; and "Historical Trends, Current Uncertainties," *Monthly Labor Review,* November 1993, p. 8.

ter group includes professionals such as registered nurses, teachers, lawyers, and engineers. It also includes *technologists*—people who work with their hands and with theoretical knowledge.[11] Computer technicians, physical therapists, and medical technicians are examples of jobs in this category. By the year 2000, it's predicted that knowledge workers will make up a third or more of the U.S. work force.[12]

Knowledge workers are at the cutting edge of the third wave. Their jobs are designed around the acquisition and application of information. The economy needs people who can fill these jobs, and they will be paid well for their services. Meanwhile, the number of blue-collar jobs has shrunk dramatically. Many blue-collar workers don't have the education and flexibility necessary to exploit the new job opportunities in the information revolution. They don't have the specific skills to move easily into high-paying technologists' jobs. This situation contrasts with the shift from the first wave to the second. The transition from the farm to the factory floor required little skill, just a strong back and the willingness to work hard.

Cultural Diversity

As recently as 1960, only 32 percent of married women were in the U.S. labor force. Today, that figure is close to 60 percent.[13] By the end of this decade, 61 percent of all working-age women in the United States will have jobs, and women will make up 47 percent of the total work force. Currently, women with children under 6 years of age are the fastest-growing segment of the U.S. work force.[14] This trend of women's joining the work force, incidentally, is taking place worldwide in industrialized nations. The numbers of women in the labor force are rapidly approaching those of men in Great Britain, Canada, Australia, Hong Kong, Singapore, and Japan.

The increased participation rate of women in the work force is not the only diversity issue reshaping the labor pool. Another is multiculturalism. Globalization has been reducing barriers to immigration. In the United States, the proportion of people with Hispanic, Asian, Pacific Island, and African roots has increased significantly over the past two decades. And this trend will continue. Moreover, multiculturalism is not just a U.S. phenomenon. Countries such as Great Britain, Germany, and Canada are experiencing similar changes. Canada, as a case in point, has large populations of people who have recently immigrated from Hong Kong, Pakistan, Vietnam, and Middle Eastern countries. These immigrants are making Canada's population more diverse and its work force more heterogeneous.

Changing Societal Expectations

The 1960s gave us the Beatles, hippies, civil rights legislation, and the women's movement. It also gave us the beginning of heightened expectations for business firms. The term *corporate social responsibility* became an established part of our vocabulary. Business firms would increasingly be judged on how good a citizen they were as well as on how successful they were at making money.

Today, business firms are expected to act as responsible citizens.[15] Society expects corporations, for instance, to contribute to worthy charities, support community programs, and pursue environmentally friendly policies. Executives of these firms are expected to maintain and promote high ethical standards. A recent

IN THE NEWS

So Many Applicants, Yet Employers Can't Fill Jobs

ANDRÉ MILES HAS APPLIED FOR A JOB AT LINCOLN ELECTRIC CO., IN EUCLID, OHIO, THREE TIMES IN THE past 3 years. Each time he's never gotten past a screening interview. Yet Lincoln Electric says it has 200 openings, with basic hourly pay ranging from $8.39 to $20. So why can't Miles get a job? The answer is that Miles's skills don't match Lincoln's needs.

During a recent 18-month period, Lincoln Electric received more than 20,000 job applications. You would understand why when you learned what the typical Lincoln factory worker earns. The average factory worker in the United States makes $19,800 a year. Because pay at Lincoln is tied to productivity and profitability, and because 1994 was a good year for the company, the average Lincoln worker earned $55,614 in 1994!

Despite all these applicants, very few were qualified. Lincoln needs skilled tool-and-die makers, mold makers, and machinists. But only a limited number of applicants could do high school trigonometry or read technical drawings, and most didn't show an aptitude for learning how to operate computer-controlled machines—skills that Lincoln says even entry-level workers need.

Lincoln Electric's problem isn't unique. Many companies are finding it hard to fill factory jobs. "A journeyman welder is like a free agent in baseball," says the executive director of the Economic Development Corp. in Waukesha County, Wisconsin. "We can't find welders, we can't find tool and die makers, we can't find [computer-controlled] machine operators." And these are well-paying jobs. It's not uncommon for an experienced toolmaker to earn $60,000 a year with overtime. But to command those wages, today's factory workers need to use advanced math, have good communication and teamwork skills, and understand the use of computers. Unfortunately, most factory workers looking for jobs don't have those skills.

Source: R. Narisetti, "Manufacturers Decry a Shortage of Workers While Rejecting Many," *Wall Street Journal*, September 8, 1995, p. A1. Reprinted by permission of the *Wall Street Journal*, survey found that Dow Chemical, Exxon, and General Electric were rated negatively by consumers largely because of perceptions about their environmental records or ethical practices.[16] In a globally competitive world, few organizations can afford the bad press or potential economic repercussions associated with being seen as socially irresponsible.

Social responsibility includes a broad range of issues including community relations, employee relations, product development and liability, policies to support women and minorities, and not doing business in countries that abuse human rights. Currently, sensitivity to the environment is receiving a great deal of attention. Business is reassessing its forms of packaging, recyclability of products, environmental safety practices, and the like. "The idea of being environmentally friendly, or 'green,' will have an impact on all aspects of the business—from the conception of products and services to use and subsequent disposal by customers."[17]

"Social responsibility *is* good business."

Corporate executives have gotten the message. Business is accepting society's heightened expectations of its social role. For example, a recent magazine poll of managers found that 76 percent agreed with the statement "Social responsibility *is* good business."[18]

Entrepreneurial Spirit

It's a watershed event in the world of business. People are creating their own businesses at unprecedented rates. It's happening in North America. It's happening in Latin America. It's even taking hold in places such as the Czech Republic, Hungary, Russia, and China. The magnitude of change is impressive: In 1950 there were 90,000 new start-up businesses in the United States; the comparable annual figure today is about 2 million.[19]

Entrepreneurship is the process of initiating a business venture, organizing the necessary resources, and assuming the associated risks and rewards. Because entrepreneurial businesses usually start small, most fall within the definition of a "small business"—one that has fewer than 500 employees.

What explains the increased popularity of individuals' starting their own businesses? There has always been a segment of the population that has wanted to control its own destiny. Such people have long chosen entrepreneurship. But recent changes in the economy have stimulated increased interest in being one's own boss. The downsizing of large corporations has displaced millions of workers and managers. Many of these employees have taken the trauma of being laid off and turned it into a self-employment opportunity, frequently financed in large part by severance pay or an early retirement bonus. Other members of the corporate world have seen colleagues and friends lose their jobs and have concluded that future opportunities in down-sized corporations will be limited. So they have voluntarily cut their corporate ties and chosen self-employment. Another force boosting entrepreneurship is the growing options in franchising. Purchasing a franchise such as Burger King, Merry Maids, Stanley Steamer, or Subway allows an entrepreneur to run his or her own business, but with less risk. Franchises have a lower failure rate than the typical new business because of the marketing, operations, and management support provided by the franchiser.

"The Customer Is King": Quality, Speed, and Low Costs

Henry Ford said his customers could have any color car they wanted "as long as it's black." Stew Leonard, who currently operates the world's largest dairy store in southern Connecticut, says there are only two rules in his business: "Rule 1—The customer is always right. Rule 2—If the customer is ever wrong, reread Rule 1."[20]

Today's economy is being driven by the Stew Leonards of the world. They realize that long-term success can be achieved only by satisfying the customer. For it's the customer who ultimately pays all the bills. And today's customers have more choices than ever and are, therefore, more difficult to please. "We are going to have multiple countries competing in the same businesses," says former vice chairman of Xerox, William F. Glavin. "Fulfilling customer requirements with lower cost will be the driving factor in success."[21] Glavin's viewpoint is widely shared by managers. For instance, a recent survey found that senior executives rated customer satisfaction as the most important issue in determining business success—ahead of financial performance, competitiveness, and marketing.[22]

Customers are demanding quick service, high quality, and value for their money. Mass customization, toll-free service hotlines, the growth of mail order, home shopping via television, discount superstores, and managers who have become obsessed with quality are all responses to more-demanding customers. Even the definition of quality reflects this perspective: Experts in the quality movement emphasize that "quality is what the customer says it is."[23]

THE NEW ORGANIZATION

The economy has been undergoing changes. So, too, have organizations. As the following describes, the underlying theme is that the "new organization" is becoming more flexible and more responsive to its environment.[24] (See Exhibit 1-3.)

Flexibility and Temporariness

Lou Capolzzola worked full-time, for 10 years, at *Sports Illustrated.* He was a photographic lighting specialist. Then his job was eliminated. Well, not really eliminated. Lou was given the choice to continue on as an independent contractor. But

EXHIBIT 1-3
The Changing Organization

Old Organization	New Organization
• Permanent jobs	• Temporary jobs
• Relatively homogeneous work force	• Diverse work force
• Quality is an afterthought	• Continuous improvement and customer satisfaction are critical
• Large corporations provide job security	• Large corporations are drastically cutting overall staff
• If it ain't broke, don't fix it	• Reengineer all processes
• Spread risks by being in multiple sets of businesses	• Concentrate on core competencies
• Hierarchy provides efficiency and control	• Dismantle hierarchy to increase flexibility
• Workdays are defined as 9-to-5	• Workdays have no time boundaries
• Work is defined by jobs	• Work is defined in terms of tasks to be done
• Pay is stable and related to seniority and job level	• Pay is flexible and broadbanded
• Managers alone make decisions	• Employees participate in decision making
• Business decision making is driven by utilitarianism	• Business decision-making criteria are expanded to include rights and fairness

his base pay would be about half what it was as a full-time employee. And he wouldn't be paid most of the overtime pay he previously was entitled to, and he would lose all of his $20,000 a year benefit package and whatever security goes with a full-time, permanent job. Time Warner, the publisher of *Sports Illustrated,* decided it could save money and increase its flexibility by converting a lot of jobs like Lou's into temporary positions.[25]

Time Warner's action is not unique. Many large companies are converting permanent jobs into temporary ones. Eight percent of Delta Air Lines' work force are now temporaries. At McDonnell Douglas, it's 10 percent. And at Apple Computer, 17 percent.[26] Six out of every 10 people who work for the giant British retailer Marks & Spencer are part-timers.[27]

In a world of rapid change, permanent employees limit management's flexibility. A large permanent work force, for example, restricts management's options and raises costs for firms that suffer the ups and downs of market cycles. And this rule applies to all organizations, regardless of where they are located. For instance, the management of firms in Britain, France, and Germany are pursuing the same course. In Britain, 215,000 new part-time jobs were created in 1993, while the number of full-time jobs fell by 287,000.[28]

Workforce Diversity

We described earlier how cultural diversity is changing the makeup of the work force. As organizations become more heterogeneous in terms of gender, age, race, and ethnicity, management has been adapting its human resource practices to reflect those changes. Many organizations today—small ones as well as large ones—have workforce diversity programs. They tend to focus on training employees and modifying benefit programs to make them more "family-friendly."[29]

Training seeks to increase awareness and understanding of diversity. The typical program lasts from half a day to 3 days and includes role playing exercises, lectures, and group experiences. Hewlett-Packard, for instance, has a basic 3-day program.[30] It covers topics such as awareness of attitudes and prejudices, sexual harassment, workers with disabilities, legal issues, corporate objectives, and management responsibilities. In addition, with the work force rapidly graying, age-based stereotypes are becoming an important diversity issue.[31] Hartford Insurance has responded by introducing specific training exercises to increase sensitivity to aging.[32] In one, participants are asked to respond to the following four questions: (1) If you didn't know how old you are, how old would you guess you are? In other words, how old do you feel inside? (2) When I was 18, I thought middle age began at age ______. (3) Today, I think middle age begins at age ______. (4) What would be your first reaction if someone called you an older worker? Answers to these questions are then used to analyze age-related stereotypes.

Family-friendly benefits is a term that encompasses a wide range of work and family programs such as on-site day care, child-care and elder-care referrals, flexible hours, compressed workweeks, job sharing, telecommuting, temporary part-time employment, unpaid leaves of absence, and relocation assistance for employees' family members.[33] With more women working and more two-career couples, family-friendly benefits are seen as a means to help employees better balance their personal lives with work. And studies indicate that helping employees resolve work and family conflicts boosts morale, increases productivity, reduces absenteeism, and makes it easier for employers to recruit and retain first-class workers.[34] For instance, a study at Johnson & Johnson found that absenteeism among employees who used flexible work hours and family-leave policies was on average 50 percent less than for their work force as a whole.[35]

Total Quality Management

You've seen the ad: "At Ford, Quality Is Job 1." Well, Ford isn't alone! In organizations engaged in a wide range of endeavors—for example, Motorola, Xerox, Federal Express, Hospital Corporation of America, Oregon State University, and the U.S. Navy—the goal of improving quality has taken on the appearance of something resembling a religion. The term increasingly used to describe this effort is **total quality management,** or TQM.[36] The TQM movement is largely a response to global competition and more-demanding customers.

Although TQM became popular in the 1980s, its roots go back 30 years earlier. In 1950, an American quality expert, W. Edwards Deming, went to Japan and advised many top Japanese managers on how to improve production effectiveness. Central to his management methods was the use of statistics to analyze variability in production processes. A well-managed organization, according to Deming, was one in which statistical control reduced variability and resulted in uniform quality and predictable quantity of output. His ideas were largely responsible for the incredible success post-war Japan had in creating high-quality products at very competitive prices.

American managers saw what Japanese companies were doing and they responded. The result has been TQM. It's a philosophy of management that is driven by the constant attainment of customer satisfaction through the continuous improvement of all organizational processes.

Exhibit 1-4 summarizes the basic elements of TQM. Notice that the term *customer* in TQM is expanded beyond the traditional definition to include everyone who interacts with the organization's products or service either internally or externally. So TQM encompasses employees and suppliers, as well as the people who buy the organization's products or services.

Although TQM has been criticized by some for overpromising and underperforming, its overall record is impressive.[37] Varian Associates Inc., a maker of scientific equipment, used TQM in its semiconductor unit to cut the time it took to put out new designs by 14 days. Another Varian unit, which makes vacuum systems for computer clean rooms, boosted on-time delivery from 42 percent to 92 percent through TQM. Globe Metallurgical Inc., a small Ohio metal producer, credits TQM for having helped it become 50 percent more productive. And the significant improvements made recently in the quality of cars produced by GM, Ford, and Chrysler can be directly traced to the implementation of TQM methods.[38]

EXHIBIT 1-4
What Is Total Quality Management?

1. Intense focus on the *customer.* The customer includes not only outsiders who buy the organization's products or services but also internal customers (such as shipping or accounts payable personnel) who interact with and serve others in the organization.
2. Concern for *continual improvement.* TQM is a commitment to never being satisfied. "Very good" is not good enough. Quality can always be improved. TQM creates a race without a finish line.
3. Improvement in the *quality of everything* the organization does. TQM uses a very broad definition of quality. It pertains not only to the final product but also to how the organization handles deliveries, how rapidly it responds to complaints, how politely the phones are answered, and the like.
4. Accurate *measurement.* TQM uses statistical techniques to measure every critical variable in the organization's operations. These are compared against standards or benchmarks to identify problems, trace them to their roots, and eliminate their causes.
5. *Empowerment of employees.* TQM involves the people on the line in the improvement process. Teams are used widely in TQM programs as empowerment vehicles for finding and solving problems.

Downsizing

The old rule of thumb was that organizations hired in good times and fired in bad times. Since the late 1980s, that rule no longer seems to apply, at least among large companies. Between 1993 and 1995, for instance, most of the Fortune 500 made drastic cuts in their overall staff. IBM cut staff by 122,000 people, and AT&T by 83,000. General Motors laid off 74,000, Boeing reduced its staff by 61,000, and Sears cut 50,000 jobs.[39]

Downsizing has become a dominant management strategy in the 1990s. It refers to the practice of reducing an organization's size through extensive layoffs. The facts are undebatable—large companies have cut millions of jobs—but management's motivation is not always clear.[40] Critics believe that massive downsizing has become a fad. They say it's a way for management to demonstrate to stockholders that it's serious about keeping costs down. Failure to downsize, when everyone else is doing it, signals to investors that management has gotten soft and lazy. To support their case, the critics point out that many of the companies that downsized did so even though they were experiencing healthy profits. Supporters of downsizing maintain that large-scale staff reductions are necessary to maintain competitiveness in a fast-changing global marketplace. Big corporations overstaffed in the decades when competition was less severe. Downsizing is merely an attempt to get their work forces back in balance.

Downsizing has become a dominant management strategy in the 1990s.

Which is right? Perhaps both. Managers are certainly as susceptible to fads as anybody else, and downsizing does cut costs. But recent evidence suggests that managers are not merely lopping off heads to cut costs.[41] Most organizations are strategically cutting operations that have become overstaffed and, at the same

IN THE NEWS

IBM Has Learned a Lesson: It's Not So Easy to Downsize in Europe

IN 1993, IBM LOST $1.7 BILLION IN ITS EUROPEAN OPERATIONS. IN RESPONSE, MANAGEMENT THREATENED to cut 1,300 jobs at IBM France unless employees agreed to give up their annual bonus and accept management's plan to link pay to company earnings. Instead of accepting the job-saving plan, French unions filed suit and won. "In the United States, we just would have announced the plan, implemented it, and anyone who didn't like it would leave," said an IBM Europe vice president. But as he and the rest of the management team learned, Europe isn't the United States.

Downsizing in Europe is more complicated than in the United States. Strong unions, inflexible labor rules, high unemployment rates, and pro-labor governments make it more difficult for companies to lay off workers there. IBM had to deal with lawsuits over its restructuring in Germany, Italy, and Spain as well as in France.

By the end of 1994, IBM Europe had succeeded in significantly reducing the size of its labor force. But the process was considerably more expensive and took a lot more time than downsizing efforts in the United States.

Source: Based on W. Echikson, "IBM's European Travail," *Fortune,* October 3, 1994, p. 88.

time, are increasing staff in areas that add value. American Airlines, for instance, cut its overall work force by nearly 5,000 workers between 1992 and 1994, but its information services unit added about 2,200 people during the same period.[42]

Reengineering

In times of rapid and dramatic change, it's sometimes necessary for managers to ask: How would we do things around here if we were starting over from scratch? This question expresses the essence of what **reengineering** is about. It asks managers to reconsider how work would be done and the organization structured if they were starting over.[43] Apparently, a lot of managers are asking that question. A recent survey of the largest U.S. industrial corporations found that 83 percent had engaged in reengineering.[44] A similar survey of 600 European companies revealed that 75 percent had implemented at least one reengineering initiative.[45] Even many Japanese firms are replacing their traditional practice of seeking slow and continuous improvements with reengineering efforts. Major companies such as Kao, Kawasaki Steel, Ryoshoku Trading, Seiko Epson, Casio Computer, Fumitsu, and Oki Electric Industry are some of the Japanese companies that have gotten onto the reengineering bandwagon.[46]

The logic underlying reengineering is that organizations develop processes in their early years and then become locked into them despite changing conditions. For instance, most large companies can trace their work practices back to organizing concepts proposed nearly a hundred years ago. Division of labor and the fragmentation of work have been the cornerstones for how all kinds of firms—steel manufacturers, airlines, insurance companies, computer chip makers—have organized work processes. Reengineering argues that, for most firms, these old ways of doing business simply don't work anymore. The old ways are not responsive enough to customers needs and are inefficient. Managers have to rethink what their organization is about and then reinvent the processes for producing and delivering their goods or services.

An accounts payable department at Ford Motor Company illustrates how reengineering can be applied.[47] This unit employed 500 people in a process that had been in place since the 1930s. Ford's purchasing department would send a purchase order to a supplier, and a copy of the purchase order would go to accounts payable. When the supplier shipped the goods and they arrived at Ford, a clerk at the receiving dock would complete a form describing the goods and would send it to accounts payable. Meanwhile, the supplier would send an invoice to accounts payable. The 500 employees in accounts payable spent most of their time straightening out situations in which purchase orders, receiving tickets, invoices, and other documents didn't match.

Ford radically redesigned the entire process. Accounts payable clerks no longer match purchase order with receiving document because the new process eliminated the invoice entirely. In the new process, when a buyer in the purchasing department issues a purchase order to a vendor, that buyer simultaneously enters the order into an on-line database. When goods are received from the supplier at Ford's receiving dock, someone in receiving checks a computer terminal to see whether the received shipment corresponds to an outstanding purchase order in the database. If it does, the clerk at the dock accepts the goods and pushes a button on the terminal keyboard that tells the database that the goods have arrived. The computer then automatically sends a check to the supplier. If the goods do not correspond to an outstanding purchase order in the database, the clerk on the dock refuses the shipment and sends it back to the supplier.

Under the new system at Ford, the receiving dock now handles payment authorization, so most of the accounts payable department's activities are eliminated. Instead of 500 people in that unit, Ford has just 125 people. And in some Ford units, reengineering has resulted in accounts payable departments that have cut their staff by as much as 95 percent.

The prototype of the new organization is one that is undergoing or has undergone reengineering. This dramatic approach to change, in fact, can explain a large part of how many companies have been able to successfully downsize their operations. Reengineering processes have dramatically reduced waste and inefficiencies. And the number of people needed to do the work that remains has been similarly reduced.

Playing to Strengths: Core Competencies

Many organizations in the past thought they could be all things to all people. The growth of conglomerates such as Gulf & Western, ITT, Textron, Rockwell International, TRW, United Technologies, and Litton Industries in the 1960s reflected a belief that the most effective organizations were ones that spread their risks by being in multiple businesses. At one time, for instance, ITT owned Sheraton Hotels, Federal Electric, Grinnel, Rayonier, Continental Baking, Avis, and Eason Oil. Over time, these conglomerates were outperformed by competitors whose strategy was to focus on their unique strengths rather than to "spread the risk".

Today's successful organizations are playing to their strengths. They are focusing on what they do best and what makes them special—their **core competencies**—and are selling off or closing down noncore businesses.[48] Core competencies are the capabilities of an organization that distinguish it from its competitors. They tend to be based on knowledge rather than on current products or assets owned. Examples of capabilities that can be core competencies include superior research and development, a unique technology, manufacturing efficiency, or outstanding customer service. Domino Pizza's strength is not its pizzas. It's the company's super-speedy delivery system. Nordstrom, the Seattle-based retailer, distinguishes itself from its competitors through extraordinary service. Sears has sold off its insurance and brokerage businesses to focus on what it does best—retailing. Similarly, Bausch & Lomb has divested itself of operations, such as making scientific instruments, that at one time generated half the company's sales. Now it concentrates on the businesses it knows—contact lenses, lens-care products, and Ray Ban sunglasses.

Dismantling Hierarchy

The corporation of the 1960s or 1970s sought to own and control as much of its operating activities as possible. Vertically integrated and largely self-sufficient companies such as General Motors, U.S. Steel, and IBM were role models for the world. They owned the manufacturing plants that built their products. To maintain maximum control, they created powerful centralized departments that carefully monitored the decisions of lower-level managers throughout their companies. For similar control reasons, they often bought or merged with the firms that supplied them with raw materials. Support activities such as accounting and maintenance were done by people employed by the corporation.

The above description does not apply to contemporary corporations. Most of today's corporations have aggressively acted to dismantle their hierarchy in order to cut costs, improve efficiency, increase flexibility, and allow them to concentrate on those functions they can do best. Today's corporation is outsourcing functions; partnering with other firms, suppliers, and customers; decentralizing decision making into autonomous units; and replacing independent departments with interdependent teams.

Outsourcing refers to contracting with outside firms to provide resources or services.[49] It is a natural extension of the move to emphasize core competencies. Organizations can focus on their strengths and buy everything else from the outside. Anything can be fair game for outsourcing. A survey of 100 of the largest U.S. corporations found that 77 percent were outsourcing some aspect of their business support services. These include functions such as warehousing, payroll management, tax administration, mailroom operations, and computer systems. The pharmaceutical giant Merck & Company outsources its mail and copier needs to Pitney Bowes. To run its information services, Continental Airlines uses EDS Corp., and General Dynamics uses Computer Sciences Corp. The Presbyterian Medical Center in Philadelphia outsources its food service, environmental services, security, maintenance and engineering, central processing, and transport functions. Keep in mind that outsourcing is not restricted to business services. Three out of ten large U.S. industrial companies now outsource more than half of their manufacturing.[50]

Boeing and Europe's Airbus are competitors, but they have joined forces to do research on developing the next generation of commercial aircraft. Apple Computer relied on Sony's expertise in miniaturization to develop its PowerBook. G & F Industries, a maker of plastic components, has an employee who works full-time, on-site, for high-fidelity systems manufacturer, Bose Corp. These examples illustrate another way in which organizations are reducing their hierarchy. They are developing partnerships with other companies to share expertise and personnel. Like outsourcing, partnering allows firms to do more with less and to benefit from other organizations' core competencies.

ABB (ASEA Brown Boveri), a diversified manufacturer of robotic and power engineering components, has annual sales in excess of $29 billion and employs 240,000 people. But it does this with a very small headquarters staff and by creating lots of autonomous units.[51] Zurich-based ABB has 5,000 business units worldwide, each with its own balance sheet, and a corporate staff that numbers only 200. ABB may be an extreme case, but lots of organizations are creating self-contained and independent units, loosely coordinated by a small headquarters staff. Managers are finding that these structures are more efficient than large centralized organizations, and they can respond faster to customer needs and better foster the entrepreneurial spirit. They provide the economies of large size but with the agility usually found only in smaller organizations.

Teams are another structural device that organizations are rapidly adopting to increase flexibility. A recent survey found that 73 percent of U.S. organizations have at least some employees working in teams, most of which are cross-functional or interdepartmental.[52] Why are teams so popular? Division of labor created overfragmented work tasks. People began to lose sight of the big picture. And coordinating activities between departments became increasingly difficult. Cross-functional work teams break down both horizontal and vertical hierarchical barriers.

The Demise of "9-to-5": The Flexible Workday

Organizations are redefining what we call "the workday." The concept of a "9-to-5" job is essentially a residual of the 1950s, when labor could be measured in an office or factory. Today, especially among professionals and technical specialists, the line is increasingly blurred between work and personal lives.[53] At one time, only doctors were on call 24 hours a day. Now that organizations are pursuing global opportunities and have mobile communication capabilities, employees are increasingly expected to be on call around the clock. Business opportunities in Cape Town, South Africa, may require people in Honolulu to be having phone conversations when most people in Hawaii are sound asleep.

It's the unusual professional that doesn't take work home nowadays. Meanwhile, millions of workers are just staying home, networking their computer to the ones at their employer's offices, and telecommuting. And an increasing number of organizations are keeping their offices open all the time to accommodate the diverse schedules of employees. It's no longer that unusual for employees at Microsoft, Intel, The Princeton Review, and thousands of other organizations to put in 70- or 80-hour weeks, working through the night and on weekends.

Flexible Compensation

The traditional method of compensating people for their work reflected a time of stability. Pay was determined largely by seniority and job level. So the earnings of a grade-3 computer analyst at Chrysler Corp. had to fall between $3,725 and $4,460 a month because that was the pay range for that grade level. The trend in recent years has been to make pay more flexible and to reduce the number of grade levels.

By linking pay to performance variables such as individual productivity and corporate profits, management is able to turn labor expenses into variable rather than fixed costs and consequently has more flexibility in dealing with labor costs. Another, perhaps less desirable, consequence is that employees' pay is less predictable; it can vary significantly from year to year.

In the past, employees typically had to move up in the organization to get major increases in pay. For instance, in our Chrysler example, no matter how much a grade-3 computer analyst contributed to the company, he or she was limited to making no more than $4,460 a month. The latest trend is toward **broadbanding compensation.** This reduces the number of job levels or salary grades into a few wide bands. So, instead of, say, five computer-analyst grade levels, Chrysler might establish two with considerably larger salary ranges. This arrangement allows management considerably more flexibility in linking compensation to individual skills and contributions.

Dejobbing and the Loss of Traditional Job Security

Organizations are eliminating jobs. By that I mean that the whole notion of *jobs,* as we have come to know them, is rapidly becoming obsolete.[54] Before 1800, very few people had a "job." People worked hard raising food or making things at home. They had no regular hours, no job descriptions, no bosses, and no employee benefits. Instead, they put in long hours on shifting clusters of tasks, in a variety of locations, on a schedule set by the sun and the weather and the needs of the day. It was the Industrial Revolution and the creation of large manufacturing companies that brought about the concept of what we have come to think of as *jobs.* But the conditions that created "the job" are disappearing. Customized production is pushing out mass production; most workers now handle information, not physical products; and competitive conditions are demanding rapid response to changing markets.

In a fast-moving economy, jobs are rigid solutions to a fluid problem. In reality, they are no solution at all. Organizations can rewrite a person's job description occasionally, but not every week. When the work that needs doing changes constantly—which increasingly describes today's world—organizations can't afford the inflexibility of traditional jobs, so they are *dejobbing.* That is, they are replacing many of their traditional jobs with part-time and temporary work situations.[55] They are increasingly relying on "hired guns"—members of the **contingent work force** (temporaries, part-timers, consultants, and contract workers)—who join project teams created to complete a specific task. When that task is finished,

In a fast-moving economy, jobs are rigid solutions to a fluid problem.

the team disbands. People then move on to new teams within the organization or join teams in another organization. Some people are working on more than one team at a time.

The dejobbing of work is undermining the security that employees of 20 or more years ago enjoyed. Organizations are increasingly offering people flexibility and autonomy in place of security and predictability.

The dejobbed work force is well under way. For instance, most employees at Boeing, Intel, and Microsoft are typically assigned to a project when they are hired. As the project changes over time, employee responsibilities and tasks change with it. As projects evolve and new projects are developed, employees are added to and dropped from various projects. At any given time, many employees are working on multiple projects, under several team leaders, keeping different schedules, being in various places, and performing different tasks. This model also describes the majority of jobs in advertising, consulting firms, and the largely freelance work force of creative and technical people in the entertainment industry.

The dejobbing process will take time to fully enmesh itself. As a result, it may be more realistic to envision today's work force, and the one in place for the next 15 or 20 years, as made up of three classes of employees that vary in degrees of connectedness to the organization.[56] There will be a small core of permanent employees who have the skills and knowledge that allow the organization to maintain its core competencies. These people will have the security typically associated with what employees had a generation ago when working for a large corporation. A second group will essentially be contract workers. The organization will offer them employment for a specified period of time. This will be the bulk of any organization's work force. As long as their job lasts and their performance is satisfactory, these contracted employees will have full-time work. Finally, a third set of workers will be part-timers. They will work brief periods, on an as-needed basis.

Empowered People

Most organizations that were created before the early 1980s were designed around the notion that there should be a clear division of work and responsibility between management and workers. Managers were to do the planning and thinking, and workers were just to do what they were told. This approach made good sense at the turn of the century, but it doesn't work too well anymore. Most organizations today are redesigning work and jobs so as to let workers make many of the job-related decisions that previously were made exclusively by managers. This transfer of job-related authority and responsibility from managers to workers is called **empowerment.**[57]

What explains this move to empower employees? There are at least three forces at work. First, the work force has changed. Today's workers are far better educated and trained than they were in the early part of this century. In fact, because of the complexity of many jobs, today's workers are often considerably more knowledgeable than their managers about how best to do their jobs. Second, global competitiveness demands that organizations be able to move fast. Companies must be able to make decisions and implement changes quickly. When the people who actually do the work are allowed to make their own job-related decisions, both the speed and quality of those decisions often improve. Finally, there is the effect of dismantling organizational hierarchies. Organizations have eliminated many middle-management positions and have flattened their structures in order to cut costs and improve responsiveness. This process has left many lower-level managers with a lot more people to supervise. A manager who had only six or eight employees to oversee could closely monitor each person's work and micromanage activities. Now that manager is likely to have twenty or thirty people to oversee and can't possibly know everything that is going on. So managers have been forced to let go of some of their authority.

Few organizations have been untouched by the empowerment movement. Its pervasiveness can be seen with a few examples. At a General Electric lighting plant in Ohio, work teams perform many tasks and assume many of the responsibilities once handled by their supervisors. Childress Buick, an automobile dealer in Phoenix, allows their salespeople to negotiate and finalize deals with customers without any approval from management. NCR has instituted a program that cross-trains even part-time employees to do multiple jobs and to take total responsibility for their work.[58] Roger Meade, the chief executive officer of Scitor Corp., a 200-person firm that provides information systems products and services, tells his employees to make all decisions against this simple standard: "Utilize your best judgment at all times. Ask yourself: Is it fair and reasonable? Is it honest? Does it make good business sense in the context of our established objectives? If you can answer yes to all of these, then proceed. Remember, you are accountable against this policy for all your actions."[59]

Social Responsibility and Ethics

As noted earlier, society's expectations of business have changed. Cornelius Vanderbilt's "the public be damned" attitude might have been acceptable in the 1890s, but it certainly is not acceptable in the 1990s. In the 1950s, a Cleveland steel plant could get away with polluting Lake Erie, but it couldn't today. Even the standards in politics have changed. Twenty years ago the public was more tolerant of unethical actions of politicians—for example, profiting from insider information, influence peddling, lying, padding expense accounts, or hiring unqualified friends and relatives. Such practices today are likely to end up on the front page of newspapers and result in full-scale investigations.

One of the ironies of these changing social expectations is shown in Exhibit 1-5. Business firms today are more socially responsible than at any time in the recent past. Yet they continue to be criticized for their lack of social responsibility. What has happened is that society's expectations of what is considered "proper

EXHIBIT 1-5
Rising Societal Expectations

Source: A. B. Carroll, *Social Responsibility of Management,* 1984, p. 14. Reprinted by permission of Prentice Hall, Upper Saddle River, N.J.

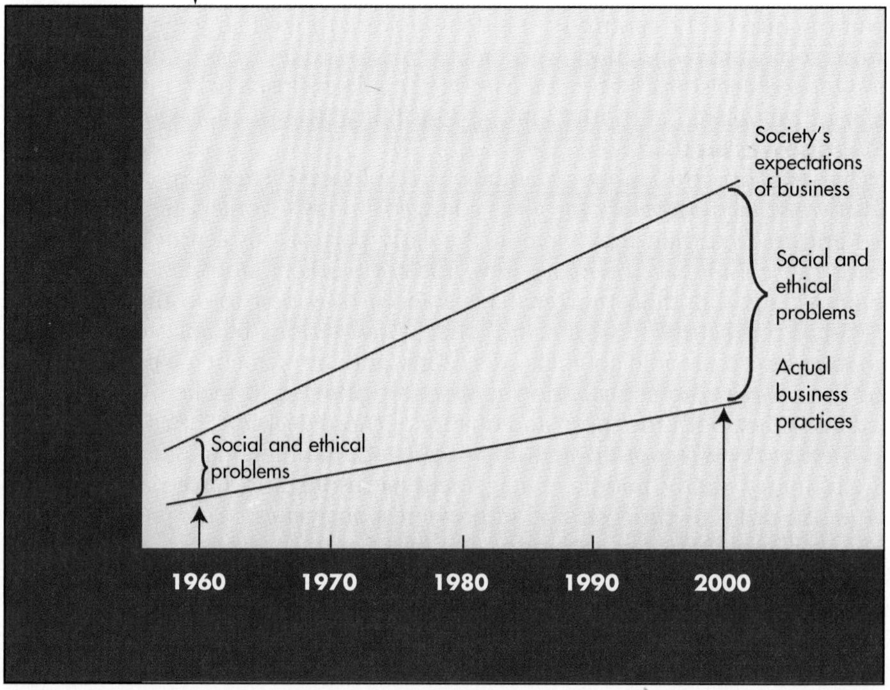

Levi-Strauss is the world's largest apparel maker and is also a model for socially responsible management. For instance, the company has ethical guidelines for doing business with foreign contractors that cover issues from environmental, safety and health requirements to the right of free association.

conduct" have risen faster than the ability of business to raise its standards.[60] So, even though businesses today are more socially conscious, the public's perception is that they still have significant room for improvement.

Most business firms today recognize that their responsibilities go beyond merely obeying the law and earning a competitive financial return for their owners.[61] **Utilitarianism,** which assesses actions in terms of providing the greatest good for the greatest number, no longer is the single criterion by which business decisions can be judged. It prevailed when organizational performance was assessed by narrow goals such as efficiency, productivity, or profit maximization. As managers have become more aware of the number of stakeholders they must satisfy, they have expanded their decision criteria to include respecting and protecting basic rights of individuals (e.g., privacy, speech, due process) and ensuring that rules are enforced fairly and impartially.[62]

Today, companies such as McDonald's, Ben & Jerry's, Timberland Co., Polaroid, and Levi-Strauss have become standardbearers for responsible and ethical practices. McDonald's is well known for its charitable efforts, including support for Ronald McDonald houses. Ben & Jerry's has become the prototype for a socially responsible firm with its efforts to promote world peace, preserve the environment, and support local businesses. Timberland and Polaroid were both recipients of America's Corporate Conscience Awards for 1995—the former for community service and the latter for responsiveness to employees. And Levi-Strauss has won accolades for its progressive human resource policies and proactive stance on setting ethical guidelines for doing business with foreign contractors. For instance, the company voluntarily decided in 1993 not to invest in the booming Chinese market and to phase out contracts with Chinese clothing manufacturers, citing what it termed "pervasive violations of basic human rights" by the Chinese government.[63]

THE NEW EMPLOYEE

How have all these changes in the economy and in organizations redefined *employee?* This section answers that question (see Exhibit 1-6).

EXHIBIT 1-6
The Changing Employee

Old Employee	New Employee
• Low-skilled jobs in manufacturing pay well	• Low-skilled jobs pay poorly
• Receives job security in return for loyalty	• Job security is minimal
• Organization takes responsibility for career development	• Employee is responsible for career development
• Is an individual performer	• Is a team player
• Predictability and stability minimize stress	• Unpredictability and instability heighten stress

The Bimodal Split

As recently as 25 years ago, there were plenty of well-paying manufacturing jobs in industries such as steel, automobiles, and rubber for the high school graduate with minimal skills. A young man in Pittsburgh, for example, could graduate from high school and immediately get a relatively high-paying and secure job in a local steel plant. But those jobs have all but disappeared.[64] A good portion of those manufacturing jobs in industrialized countries have been replaced by automated equipment, reconstituted into jobs requiring considerably higher technical skills, or taken by workers in other countries who will do the same work for a fraction of the wages.

The massive decline of blue-collar manufacturing jobs that pay $25,000 to $35,000 a year in current dollars has created a **bimodal work force.** As shown in Exhibit 1-7, most low-skilled workers are at an income level just a few dollars above the minimum wage. High-skilled workers—professionals and technical or knowledge workers who program computers, conduct laboratory tests, fix office machines, and the like—make up almost a completely separate income group whose pay level is almost three times as high as that of most low-skilled workers. These two separate classes of employees differ on more than just their immediate wage levels. They also differ in their potential for future earnings, their mobility, and their job security. Low-skilled workers face a future of permanent low wages, minimal promotion opportunities, and limited bargaining power with employers. In contrast, the high-skilled group will be able to convert the demand for their skills into financial security and career opportunities.

EXHIBIT 1-7
The Bimodal Work Force

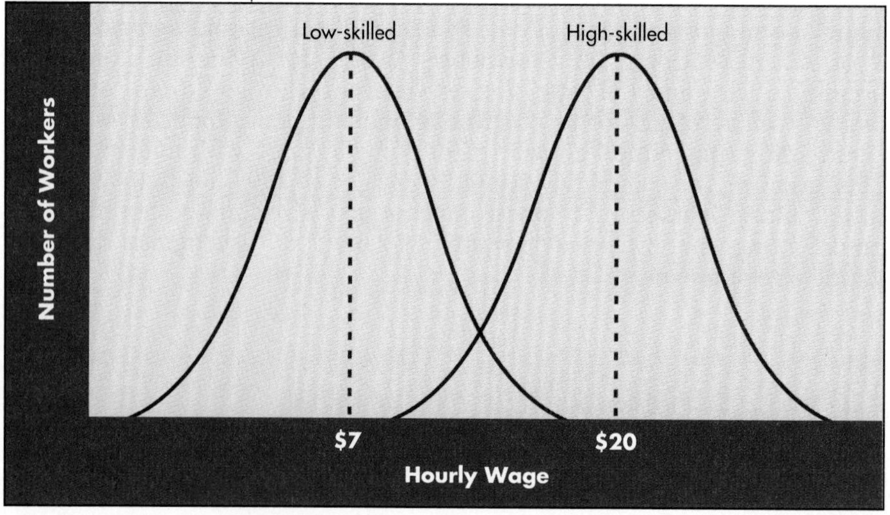

Impermanence

Regardless of skill level, all employees face a world that provides less permanence and predictability than existed 10 or 20 years ago. The unwritten loyalty contract that previously existed between employees and employers has been irrevocably broken.[65]

The unwritten loyalty contract that previously existed between employees and employers has been irrevocably broken.

Downsizing, reengineering, outsourcing, and dejobbing are major reasons why the vast majority of individuals no longer can expect to have career-long employment with a single large organization. The majority of employees have entered the contingent work force.

If the loyalty-for-job-security arrangement is dead, what has taken its place? The new deal essentially says to employees: We don't owe you anything. We make no promises because we don't know what the future holds. But we have shared economic interests. So you have a job here as long as your contribution to the organization's goals exceeds your cost. And employees are responding by reprioritizing their loyalties. As one expert described it, a worker's first loyalty is to his team or project, second to his profession, and only third to the place where he works.[66]

The new deal is both good news and bad news for employees. First the bad news. Paternalism is on its last legs. So, too, is loyalty, as we came to know it. Employers are no longer responsible for your future. The old notion that you joined an organization when you were young, worked hard for a while, built up substantial credits, then coasted into retirement no longer applies. Job security now is almost completely a function of your keeping your skills current and marketable. When or if your "value added" is less than your cost, your employment is in jeopardy. Now the good news. You have choices. You have the right to demand interesting work, the freedom and resources to perform it well, pay that reflects your contribution, and opportunities to learn skills that increase your market value. Moreover, persons who work hard and make a valuable contribution are less likely to have to tolerate working with unproductive colleagues than they would have been in the old more-permanent structure.

Self-Directed Careers

The new compact between employers and employees transfers responsibility for career development from the organization to the employee.[67] So today's employees are becoming more concerned than ever with keeping skills current and developing new skills. They see learning as a life-long process. At one time, a skill learned in youth could provide a living for life. Now technology changes so rapidly that as soon as you have learned something, that "something" becomes obsolete. In this climate, employees are increasingly recognizing that "if you snooze, you lose." There will always be other people out there who are keeping current and who are ready to assume your work responsibilities if you show signs of falling behind.

Some analysts say that workers can expect to change careers—not just jobs, but careers—three or four times during their working lives.[68] If they are right, today's worker must be prepared to go back to school and learn new skills at a minimum of every 5 to 10 years. Since fewer and fewer employers are providing this retraining, most employees will be balancing current work responsibilities with taking courses during their off hours. In the same way that TQM emphasizes continuous improvement, self-directed careers requires continuous training and learning.

Being a Team Player

With work being increasingly organized around teams, employees have had to become team players.[69] This means developing the kind of skills necessary for being

Coping with stress at work is a major issue in the 1990s. Alice Domar, a staff psychologist from a Boston hospital, teaches stress-reduction techniques to employees of the Symmetrix consulting firm in Lexington, Massachusetts.

able to contribute to high-performance teams—especially problem-solving and group decision-making skills and good listening, feedback, conflict resolution, and other interpersonal skills.

Being a team player is a particular challenge for people who have grown up in cultures that encourage and reward individual achievement. They typically find it difficult to think like a team player and to sublimate their personal ambitions for the good of the team. Consequently, team-training programs are popular in companies such as AT&T, Ford, and Motorola (which historically grew and prospered by fostering individual initiative) and among employees raised in the United States, Canada, Great Britain, and Australia (countries that instill individualism in their citizens from an early age).

Coping with Stress

Rapid and unexpected change makes life exciting. It also causes stress. So we shouldn't be surprised to find that stress, burn-out, and the like are among the hottest topics in the new world of work.[70] Downsizing and reengineering have resulted in many employees' having to take on new tasks and, very often, having to work harder. To reduce costs, for instance, companies are frequently increasing overtime among their high-skilled employees. By so doing, the companies don't have to find new workers, train them, or provide additional costly benefits. When you combine reduced job security, pressures to learn new skills, and heightened work loads, you create a workplace that is increasingly stressful on employees.

SUMMARY

(This summary is organized by the chapter-opening learning objectives on page 3.)

1. Globalization has increased competition. Rivals can now come from the other side of the world as well as the other side of town, so organizations must be flexible and responsive if they are to survive. Globalization also creates tremendously expanded opportunities for organizations to offer their products and services worldwide.
2. The first wave was agriculture (up to the 1890s). The second was industrialization (about 1900 to the 1960s). The third wave is information technology (beginning in the 1970s). Today, agriculture represents less than 5 percent of employment in

industrialized countries. Meanwhile, the information age has significantly reduced low-skilled, blue-collar jobs in manufacturing, but it has created abundant opportunities for educated and skilled technical specialists, professionals, and other knowledge workers.

3. The key elements in total quality management are intense focus on the customer; concern for continual improvement in the quality of everything the organization does; accurate measurement; and empowerment of employees.
4. Organizations are reengineering work processes in order to maintain competitiveness. New technologies can bring about dramatic improvements in productivity. Reengineering encompasses looking at all work processes from scratch. It offers opportunities for improvements of far greater magnitude than the traditional approach of incremental change.
5. The contingent work force includes temporaries, part-timers, consultants, contract workers, and others who are employed on a nonpermanent basis.
6. The bimodal work force represents low-skilled workers earning little above minimum wage and high-skilled professional, technical, and knowledge workers who earn solid middle-class wages. The low-skilled workers not only earn low wages, but they have little opportunity to improve their economic status, have restricted mobility, and have weak job security.
7. The loyalty-for-job-security arrangement has been irrevocably broken. Employers need flexibility today, and long-term job security is inconsistent with that objective. As a result, employees are increasingly placing loyalty to their work group and to their profession ahead of loyalty to their employer.

REVIEW AND DISCUSSION QUESTIONS

1. Describe the shift in types of jobs in the work force during the twentieth century.
2. What explains the increased popularity of entrepreneurship in the past 20 years?
3. What is the role of the customer in TQM? In reengineering?
4. How has workforce diversity affected the manager's job?
5. Do you think downsizing is a fad or a permanent organizational strategy? Support your position.
6. How has a focus on core competencies changed the ways in which organizations are structured and managed?
7. What are the implications of outsourcing for large corporations? For small businesses?
8. If organizations "dejob," what employment opportunities might the displaced employees have?
9. What caused the bimodal work force?
10. What kind of things can you do if you accept responsibility for your own career development?

CASE EXERCISE
WHAT HAPPENED TO SEARS ROEBUCK?

In 1972, in terms of stock market valuation, Sears Roebuck was the sixth largest company in the world. In 1982, it had fallen to thirteenth. By 1992, it had dropped to eighty-first. This case is a brief history of the demise of Sears Roebuck.

Sears was born in 1886. It got to the top by outcompeting key competitors such as Montgomery Ward. Its best years were when General Robert E. Wood ran the company—1928 to 1954. During that period it expanded from downtowns to suburban shopping centers. It also solidified its position as America's number one retailer by using its purchasing clout to negotiate highly competitive prices with its suppliers.

As Sears grew and prospered, it developed an amazing mass of procedures to guide decision making. One former executive recounted that the company had a whole library of "bulletins" that spelled out procedures for dealing with almost any problem. "God forbid there should be a problem that comes up for which there isn't a bulletin. That means the problem's *new*!"

Sears's problems can be traced back to the end of General Wood's tenure. Not wanting to retire at age 65, as the rules called for, Wood persuaded his board of directors to give him extensions that lasted more than 9 years, until 1954. At that point, there were several candidates who Wood and the board felt were deserving of the top spot in the company, although most were close to retirement age themselves. The next five CEOs served an average of less than 4 years each. The result: Leadership for the next 20 years took on a caretaker mentality. It was dedicated to maintaining the majesty of Sears. Change was unnecessary; the company believed it had found the formula for success.

What Sears was to learn is that retail customers are a fickle bunch. Before long, Sears's anchor stores in malls were getting tough competition from the specialty shops that fed off the Sears traffic. Stores such as Radio Shack, Victoria's Secret, the Gap, and The Limited were all taking bites out of Sears's hide.

But the critical change for Sears was the surge, in the 1960s, of the discount stores—first Kmart, then Wal-Mart. Sears's first reaction was to ignore the discounters. Sears thought of itself as America's discount store and considered Kmart's customers to be an inferior, unmonied lot. Even when Sears's growth slowed in the early 1970s and Kmart kept expanding, Sears never recognized that there was a major shift going on in retailing. Internal documents indicate that until well into the 1980s management did not even mention Wal-Mart in its analysis of competitors.

In 1973, the Sears Tower in Chicago opened. The skyscraper held the company's headquarters and was an opulent monument to the corporation's greatness. A few years later, Sears expanded its sights on new ventures. To its existing Allstate insurance business, it added stockbroker Dean Witter (a purchase referred to by some as "socks and stocks"). Then Sears bought real estate broker Coldwell Banker to fill out its financial services strategy. Meanwhile, its retailing operations went from one disappointing strategy to another. One year Sears was a general merchandiser, the next year a discounter, the next year a fashion store, and the following year it was a group of specialty boutiques. The company was losing its merchandising magic. Despite all these problems, the company's management was amazingly calm and unconcerned about competitive pressures.

In his 1992 biography, the late Sam Walton, founder of Wal-Mart, summed up what he considered Sears's gravest miscalculation: "One reason Sears fell so far off the pace is that they wouldn't admit for the longest time that Wal-Mart and Kmart were their real competition. They ignored both of us, and we both blew right by them."

Questions

1. What economic factors changed between 1963 and 1993 that might help explain Sears's recent problems? Elaborate on each.
2. Does success breed failures? Is it possible to become large and successful without becoming arrogant and complacent?
3. Have Kmart and Wal-Mart begun to suffer the same disease as Sears? Explain your position.
4. Visit a Sears store or research recent articles on the company. How has it responded to change?

Source: Based on C. J. Loomis, "Dinosaurs?" *Fortune,* May 3, 1993, pp. 36–42; "Sears: In with the New . . . Out with the Old," *Fortune,* October 16, 1995, pp. 96–98; and S. Walton (with J. Huey), *Sam Walton: Made in America* (New York: Doubleday, 1992).

VIDEO CASE EXERCISE
LABOR UNIONS AND THE CHANGING WORKPLACE

ABC NEWS

The new economy is having a major influence on labor unions and their relationship with management.

Caterpillar, Inc., the world's largest manufacturer of construction equipment, has a long history of management/labor conflict. Strikes lasting many months are not unusual at the firm. In spite of record profits, Caterpillar recently asked its workers for wage and benefit concessions. The company says these concessions are necessary if its products are to compete globally. Workers, not surprisingly, aren't excited about having to take cuts.

Other companies with unions have done a better job of treating their employees properly while, at the same time, keeping costs competitive. For instance, Una Dyn, a small firm in Virginia that manufactures machinery used in making plastics, ties employee bonuses to increases in company profits. As a result, employee morale is high and profits have grown. United Airlines has taken another path. It is now majority-owned by its employees. Workers have agreed to accept lower wages in return for company stock and the hope that this stock will appreciate. Additionally, employees are motivated to increase productivity and cut costs to help increase profits and thus create higher stock prices.

The typical labor-union member has suffered badly as a result of changes in the economy. In the past 15 years, college-educated workers have found themselves earning more and enjoying relatively high job security. Meanwhile, those workers with a high school degree or less have been on a downward escalator. And, of course, union members tend to fall into the latter category more often than the former. Government officials believe training will help these less-educated employees. Workers have to update their skills and be retrained. The government believes employees should have the opportunity to engage in lifelong learning.

Questions

1. What is the current status of labor unions in the United States? Explain how this has changed from the 1960s.
2. Why is Caterpillar willing to accept a strike in order to cut labor costs?
3. What options, besides accepting a strike, might Caterpillar's management have pursued to cut costs?
4. What are the advantages and disadvantages to employee ownership?
5. What role, if any, should government play in helping people build job security?
6. What role, if any, do you think business should play in providing its employees with lifelong training and skill development? Should this include training that is in the employee's best long-term interests but is not relevant to the employer's immediate needs?

Source: Based on "The Changing Face of Labor," This Week with David Brinkley; ABC News; aired on September 4, 1994.

SKILL EXERCISE

Identifying Cross-Cultural Differences

The people of Great Britain and the United States speak the same language. But their use of that language varies considerably. Break into groups of four or five. You have 20 minutes to complete this exercise.

Review the following two lists of words. List A is a list of British words and phrases. For each term, write the American word or phrase that means the same thing. List B is a list of American words and phrases. For each term, write the British word or phrase that means the same thing. When you have completed the exercise, your instructor will provide you with the correct answers. Then discuss the implications of this exercise for cross-cultural understanding and managing people from diverse cultures.

Source: Based on G. D. Klein, "Introducing the Largely Land-Locked to Cross-Cultural Differences," *Journal of Management Education,* February 1995, pp. 119–21.

List A		**List B**	
roundabout	fifty "p"	subway	elevator
bonnet	braces	restroom	sweater
boot	"Old Bill"	check in a restaurant	cookie
plasters	queue	police officer	knives, forks, spoons
seven stone	pram	truck	parking lot

NOTES

1. Based on J. Huey, "Managing in the Midst of Chaos," *Fortune,* April 5, 1993, pp. 38–48; and D. Greising, "The Rules of the Game in the New World of Work," *Business Week,* October 17, 1994, p. 102.
2. "U.S. Corporations with the Biggest Foreign Revenues," *Forbes,* July 17, 1995, pp. 274–75.
3. See E. S. Hardy, "The Forbes Foreign Rankings," *Forbes,* July 17, 1995, pp. 226–58.
4. R. Knight, "Sewing Up Central Europe's Work Force," *U.S. News & World Report,* August 29/September 5, 1994, pp. 46–49.
5. A. Toffler, *The Third Wave* (New York: Bantam, 1984).
6. W. Bridges, *JobShift* (Reading, Mass.: Addison-Wesley, 1994), p. xi.
7. This section is based on T. M. Godbout, "Employment Change and Sectoral Distribution in 10 Countries, 1970–90," *Monthly Labor Review,* October 1993, pp. 3–10; "Historical Trends, Current Uncertainties," *Monthly Labor Review,* November 1993, p. 8; K. H. Hammonds, "The New World of Work," *Business Week,* October 17, 1994, pp. 76–87; and J. Greenwald, "The New Service Class," *Time,* November 14, 1994, pp. 72–74.
8. P. F. Drucker, "The Age of Social Transformation," *The Atlantic Monthly,* November 1994, p. 56.
9. Ibid.
10. *Monthly Labor Review,* October 1993, p. 9.
11. Drucker, "The Age of Social Transformation," p. 56.
12. Ibid., p. 62.
13. U.S. Bureau of the Census, *Statistical Abstracts of the United States: 1992* (Washington, D.C.: Government Printing Office, 1991), p. 387.
14. Cited in V. Elliott and A. Orgera, "Competing For and with Workforce 2000," *HR Focus,* June 1993, p. 3.
15. See, for example, R. N. Kanungo and J. A. Conger, "Promoting Altruism as a Corporate Goal," *The Executive,* August 1993, pp. 37–48.
16. J. Martin, "Good Citizenship Is Good Business," *Fortune,* March 21, 1994, pp. 15–16.
17. C. K. Prahalad and G. Hamel, "Strategy as a Field of Study: Why Search for a New Paradigm?" *Strategic Management Journal,* Summer 1994, p. 8.
18. C. Caggiano, "Is Social Responsibility a Crock?" *INC.,* May 1993, p. 15.
19. C. Vesper, *Entrepreneurship and National Policy* (Chicago: Heller Institute, 1983); D. L. Birch, "The Truth about Start-Ups," *INC.,* January 1988, pp. 14–15; and B. O'Reilly, "The New Face of Small Business," *Fortune,* May 2, 1992, p. 82.
20. S. Leonard, "Love That Customer," *Management Review,* October 1987, pp. 36–39.
21. Quoted in J. S. McClenahen, "Can You Manage in the New Economy?" *Industry Week,* April 5, 1993, p. 28.
22. Cited in "A Matter of Priorities," *New York Times,* February 19, 1995, p. F23.
23. A. V. Feigenbaum, quoted in *Boardroom Reports,* April 1, 1991, p. 16.
24. See, for example, "Workplace Trends," *Training,* October 1994, p. 60.
25. C. Ansberry, "Workers Are Forced to Take More Jobs with Few Benefits," *Wall Street Journal,* March 11, 1993, p. A1.
26. Cited in D. Kirkpatrick, "Smart New Ways to Use Temps," *Fortune,* February 15, 1988, p. 110; B. Dumaine, "How to Manage in a Recession," *Fortune,* November 5, 1990, p. 68; and S. Caudron, "Contingent Work Force Spurs HR Planning," *Personnel Journal,* July 1994, p. 54.
27. D. Bentley, "Part Works," *International Management,* July/August 1994, p. 12.
28. Cited in R. Knight, "Gender, Jobs and Economic Survival," *U.S. News & World Report,* September 19, 1994, p. 63.
29. See, for instance, S. E. Jackson, ed., *Diversity in the Workplace* (New York: Guilford Press, 1992); T. Cox Jr., *Cultural Diversity in Organizations* (San Francisco: Berrett-Koehler, 1993); and S. Rynes and B. Rosen, "What Makes Diversity Programs Work?" *HRMagazine,* October 1994, pp. 67–73.
30. "Hewlett-Packard Discovers Diversity Is Good for Business," *Los Angeles Times,* May 17, 1993, p. 16.
31. G. Capowski, "Ageism: The New Diversity Issue," *Management Review,* October 1994, pp. 10–15; and *Valuing Older Workers: A Study of Costs and Productivity,* prepared for the American Association of Retired Persons by ICF Incorporated, 1995.
32. B. Hynes-Grace, "To Thrive, Not Merely Survive," in *Textbook Authors Conference Presentations* (Washington, D.C.: American Association of Retired People, 1992), p. 12.
33. See A. Saltzman, "Family Friendliness," *U.S. News & World Report,* February 22, 1993, pp. 59–66; M. Galen, "Work & Family," *Business Week,* June 28, 1993, pp. 80–88; C. M. Solomon, "Work/Family's Failing Grade: Why Today's Initiatives Aren't Enough," *Personnel Journal,* May 1994, pp. 72–82.
34. Cited in M. A. Verespej, "People-First Policies," *Industry Week,* June 21, 1993, p. 20; and S. Shellenbarger, "Data Gap," *Wall Street Journal,* June 21, 1993, p. R6.
35. M. Galen, "Work & Family," p. 82.
36. See, for instance, R. R. Gehani, "Quality Value-Chain: A Meta-Synthesis of Frontiers of Quality Movement," *The Executive,* May 1993, pp. 29–42; M. Sashkin and K. J. Kiser, *Putting Total Quality Management to Work* (San Francisco: Berrett-Koehler, 1993); D. Greising, "Quality: How to Make It Pay," *Business Week,* August 8, 1994, pp. 54–59; and J. R. Hackman and R. Wageman, "Total Quality Management: Empirical, Conceptual, and Practical Issues," *Administrative Science Quarterly,* June 1995, pp. 309–42.
37. M. Frohman, "Remything Management," *Industry Week,* March 21, 1994, p. 24.
38. See Greising, "Quality: How to Make It Pay;" H. Rothman, "Quality's Link to Productivity," *Nation's Business,* February 1994, pp. 33–34; and M. Maynard, "Big Three Put More Emphasis on Quality, Efficiency," *USA Today,* October 7, 1994, p. B10.
39. "Happy Labor Day," *Time,* September 4, 1995, p. 21.
40. J. A. Byrne, "The Pain of Downsizing," *Business Week,* May 9, 1994, pp. 60–61.
41. J. A. Byrne, "Why Downsizing Looks Different These Days," *Business Week,* October 10, 1994, p. 43.

42. Ibid.
43. M. Hammer and J. Champy, *Reengineering the Corporation: A Manifesto for Business Revolution* (New York: HarperBusiness, 1993); and J. Champy, *Reengineering Management: The Mandate for New Leadership* (New York: HarperBusiness, 1995).
44. Cited in *Business Week,* November 7, 1994, p. 6.
45. Cited in "Business Process Reengineering," *Industrial Management,* September 1994, p. 62.
46. J. Teresko, "Japan: Reengineering vs. Tradition," *Industry Week,* September 5, 1994, pp. 62–70.
47. Hammer and Champy, *Reengineering the Corporation.*
48. G. Hamel and C. K. Prahalad, "The Core Competence of the Corporation," *Harvard Business Review,* May–June 1990, pp. 79–91; and C. Long and M. Vickers-Koch, "Using Core Capabilities to Create Competitive Advantage," *Organizational Dynamics,* Summer 1995, pp. 7–22.
49. This section on outsourcing is based on "Outsourcing," *Fortune,* December 12, 1994, pp. 52–92; S. Lubove, "Fixing the Mix," *Forbes,* April 10, 1995, pp. 86–87; and P. Klebnikov, "Focus, Focus, Focus," *Forbes,* September 11, 1995, pp. 42–44.
50. Cited in T. A. Stewart, "Welcome to the Revolution," *Fortune,* December 13, 1993, p. 76.
51. P. Hofheinz, "Europe's Tough New Managers," *Fortune,* September 6, 1993, p. 114.
52. Cited in "Teams," *Training,* October 1994, p. 62.
53. See, for instance, S. Greengard, "Workers Go Virtual," *Personnel Journal,* September 1994, p. 71.
54. This section is based on W. Bridges, *JobShift: How to Prosper in a Workplace Without Jobs* (Reading, Mass.: Addison-Wesley, 1994).
55. B. Ettorre, "The Contingent Workforce Moves Mainstream," *Management Review,* February 1994, pp. 11–16.
56. See B. O'Reilly, "The New Deal: What Companies and Employees Owe One Another," *Fortune,* June 13, 1994, p. 52.
57. See K. W. Thomas and B. A. Velthouse, "Cognitive Elements of Empowerment: An 'Interpretive' Model of Instrinsic Task Motivation," *Academy of Management Review,* October 1990, pp. 666–81; and J. L. Cotton, *Employee Involvement* (Newbury Park, Calif.: Sage, 1993).
58. T. Catchpole, "Empowering Part-Time Workers," *Industry Week,* March 16, 1992, pp. 18–24.
59. M. A. Verespej, "Roger Meade: Running on People Power," *Industry Week,* October 18, 1993, pp. 13–18.
60. A. B. Carroll, *Social Responsibility of Management* (New York: Macmillan, 1984).
61. See, for example, R. A. Buchholz, *Essentials of Public Policy for Management,* 2nd ed. (Englewood Cliffs, N.J.: Prentice Hall, 1990).
62. G. F. Cavanagh, D. J. Moberg, and M. Valasquez, "The Ethics of Organizational Politics," *Academy of Management Journal,* June 1981, pp. 363–74.
63. J. Impoco, "Working for Mr. Clean Jeans," *U.S. News & World Report,* August 2, 1993, pp. 49–50.
64. See S. Dentzer, "The Vanishing Dream," *U.S. News & World Report,* April 22, 1991, pp. 39–43; A. Bernstein, "The Global Economy: Who Gets Hurt," *Business Week,* August 10, 1992, pp. 48–53; P. T. Kilborn, "For High School Graduates, A Job Market of Dead Ends," *New York Times,* May 30, 1994, p. 1; L. S. Richman, "The New Worker Elite," *Fortune,* August 22, 1994, pp. 56–66; and H. Schachter, "The Dispossessed," *Canadian Business,* May 1995, pp. 30–40.
65. See, for example, S. Sherman, "A Brave New Darwinian Workplace," *Fortune,* January 25, 1993, pp. 50–56; "Jobs in an Age of Insecurity," *Time,* November 22, 1993, pp. 32–39; O'Reilly, "The New Deal"; T. Brown, "Life without Job Security," *Industry Week,* August 15, 1994, pp. 24–32; H. Lancaster, "A New Social Contract to Benefit Employer and Employee," *Wall Street Journal,* November 29, 1994, p. B1; and P. T. Kilborn, "Even in Good Times, It's Hard Times for Workers," *New York Times,* July 3, 1995, p. A1.
66. Cited in C. Rapoport, "Charles Handy Sees the Future," *Fortune,* October 31, 1994, p. 168.
67. See "Career Self-Management," *Industry Week,* September 5, 1994, p. 36; H. Lancaster, "You, and Only You, Must Stay in Charge of Your Employability," *Wall Street Journal,* November 15, 1994, p. B1; B. Filipczak, "You're On Your Own: Training, Employability, and the New Employment Contract," *Training,* January 1995, pp. 29–36; and L. S. Richman, "Getting Past Economic Insecurity," *Fortune,* April 17, 1995, pp. 161–68.
68. Cited in M. Calabresi, J. Van Tassel, M. Riley, and J. R. Szczesny, "Jobs in an Age of Insecurity," *Time,* November 22, 1993, p. 38.
69. This section is based on J. R. Katzenbach and D. K. Smith, *The Wisdom of Teams* (Boston: Harvard Business School Press, 1993), pp. 43–64; and T. D. Schellhardt, "To Be a Star among Equals, Be a Team Player," *Wall Street Journal,* April 20, 1994, p. B1.
70. L. Smith, "Burned-Out Bosses," *Fortune,* July 25, 1994, p. 44; Hammonds, "The New World of Work," B. Baumohl, E. W. Desmond, W. McWhirter, R. Woodbury, and S. Ratan, "We're #1 and It Hurts," *Time,* October 24, 1994, pp. 48–56; and J. Connelly, "Have We Become Mad Dogs in the Office?," *Fortune,* November 28, 1994, pp. 197–99.

CHAPTER 2

MANAGING ORGANIZATIONS AND PEOPLE: WHO, WHAT, AND WHY?

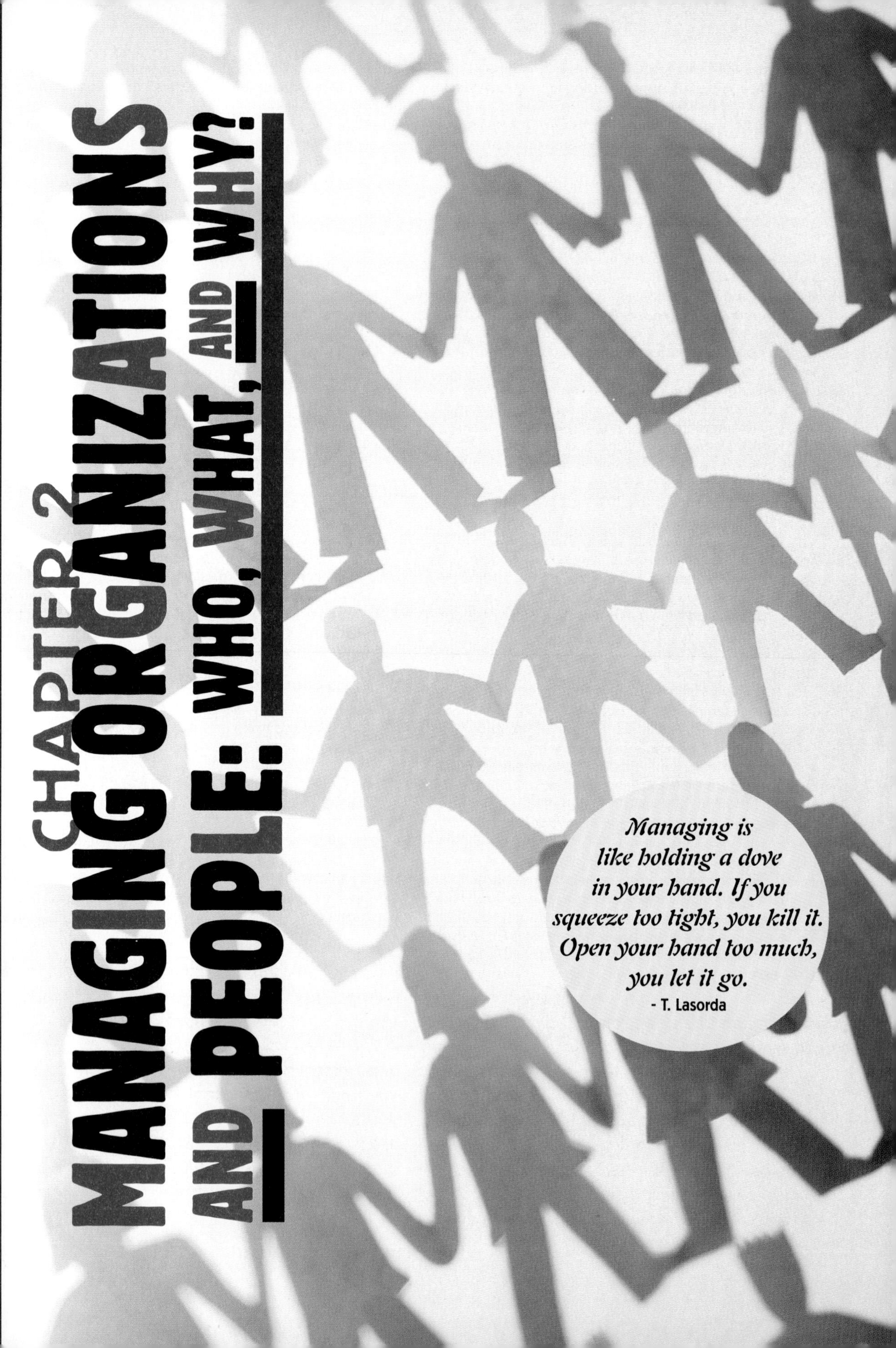

Managing is like holding a dove in your hand. If you squeeze too tight, you kill it. Open your hand too much, you let it go.

- T. Lasorda

LEARNING OBJECTIVES

After studying this chapter, you should be able to:

1. Define who are managers
2. Explain why there are managers
3. Define an organization
4. Contrast management and organizational behavior
5. Describe four management functions
6. Identify four general and six specific skills needed by managers
7. Contrast the managerial role of coach versus boss
8. Explain how chaos and ambiguity can be turned into an opportunity
9. Contrast effectiveness and efficiency
10. Explain why different stakeholders use different criteria to evaluate organizational effectiveness

Kelly Mather and Charlie Farrell probably don't know it, but their jobs represent what many managers' work lives will probably look like in the twenty-first century. Kelly manages a project team for Microsoft, the world's largest software company, at their headquarters just outside Seattle, Washington. Her team of fifteen designers is developing new consumer-software programs. What makes Kelly's managerial job "cutting-edge" is that she is much more a colleague to her team members than a boss. The team assigns tasks to individuals, and Kelly is just one voice among the fifteen. Key operating decisions are analyzed and made by the group. Individual team members are completely responsible for getting their work done on their own schedule. Kelly doesn't even see some of her people for days on end. Microsoft offices are open around the clock, and some of her team members like working nights in contrast to Kelly's preference for days. Even traditional management responsibilities such as performance appraisals are done differently at Microsoft. Although Kelly writes annual performance reviews for each person on her team, the team members also evaluate each other, including Kelly. When asked to describe her job, Kelly said it is "essentially to represent our team at project-manager meetings, fight for resources, share information with my team, offer support and help to team members when they need it, and provide motivation and leadership."

Do you know who the largest private employer in the United States is? If you're thinking of

Exxon, General Motors, or IBM, you're wrong. It's Manpower, Inc., the temporary employment agency. They employ more than 650,000 people. And, although it's true that most of these people perform clerical or low-skilled tasks, there is a growing market for temporary managers. On a typical day, an estimated 125,000 interim executives are on the job in the United States. Charlie Farrell provides an example (see photo inset on previous page). With more than 30 years of management experience, he was hired by a troubled furniture manufacturer as its interim chief executive officer (CEO). His task: To turn the company around. In his 2-year stint as temporary CEO, Farrell reduced the company's product line, improved delivery efficiency, and let a quarter of the company's employees go. Then he, too, moved on.

The jobs performed by managers have undergone a dramatic change in recent years. What most managers do today looks quite a bit different from what managers were doing only 15 years ago. As Kelly Mather is finding at Microsoft, the manager's job is increasingly becoming more like that of a coach than a boss. Similarly, the permanence and stability that jobs offered just a decade ago are disappearing—even for managers. Tomorrow's manager is increasingly likely to be a "hired gun" brought in to solve specific problems.

In Chapter 1 we described how change is reshaping the economy, organizations, and employees' jobs. Those changes, of course, are also radically reshaping the manager's job. In this chapter, we lay the groundwork for understanding who managers are, what they do, and how their jobs are changing. We conclude this chapter with a model of the manager's job. This model shows how Chapters 3 through 17 of this book tie together to capture the challenges and opportunities facing today's and tomorrow's managers.

MANAGERS AND THEIR TERRAIN

Who are *managers?* What differentiates managers from other employees in an organization? And, for that matter, what is an *organization?* We'll answer those questions in this section.

What Is a Manager?

Robert Allen is the chief executive officer (CEO) at AT&T. Michael Walsh is an elementary school principal in Tempe, Arizona. Mary Jean Giroux is a retirement-products supervisor at Canada's London Life Insurance Co. Theresa Gonzalez works as a regional director with the U.S. Internal Revenue Service. And Yong-Chang Chu is a construction foreman with Hong Kong–based Hutchison Whampoa. Despite the fact that these people have jobs with different titles and work in organizations that do very different things, they all have one thing in common—they are **managers.** They all oversee the activities of others. That is, they have people who report to them.

Is everyone who works in an organization a manager? Of course not! For simplicity's sake, we can divide organizational members into two categories: managers and operatives. In contrast to managers, **operatives** are individuals who work directly on a job or task and have *no* responsibility for overseeing the work of others. You are probably most familiar with operative employees because you see them frequently in your everyday life. They cook your hamburgers at Wendy's and sell you stamps at the post office. You also see them on the news putting cars together in a Toyota plant or assembling washing machines on a Whirlpool assembly line. But don't assume that operatives only perform routine jobs for modest pay. Many operatives have highly responsible, important, and high-paying jobs in organizations. For instance, Thad Kennedy is a senior researcher at IBM and earns in excess of $100,000 a year. Yet he's not a manager. Similarly, Joyce Goldberg is a tax specialist with the pharmaceutical giant Warner-Lambert. Al-

though she has no management responsibilities, she's a valuable member of her company's accounting group, earns a salary approaching six figures a year, and enjoys many of the privileges typically associated with managerial positions—an impressive office, an expense account, profit sharing, and minimal restrictions on her daily activities.

Managers make up a significant portion of almost every country's labor force. In the United States, for example, 12.6 percent of the civilian work force are managers.[1] In absolute numbers, that comes to more than 15 million managers! And that's only in the United States. Worldwide, there may be more than 100 million people performing managerial jobs.[2] Clearly this is no insignificant job category.

Managers make up a significant portion of almost every country's labor force.

Why Do We Have Managers?

What would a company such as Eastman Kodak, with its 112,000 employees, look like without any managers? Can you imagine what your local McDonald's might be like without managers?

One of the first words that probably comes to your mind is *chaotic*. If so, you would be right, because one of the things that managers do is give a group or organization direction. They provide formal leadership by clarifying for people what they are supposed to do. They also facilitate coordination. Managers act as a communication conduit by coordinating their unit's activities with the activities of other units in an organization. Still another thing that managers provide is accountability. Organizations reduce ambiguity over performance outcomes by appointing managers who become accountable for achievement of performance goals.

Managers add overhead or additional expense to the operation of any organization. So they must justify their existence by providing "value added"; that is, by creating benefits that exceed their costs. Eastman Kodak, for example, will employ 5,000 or more managers and pay them in excess of half a billion dollars a year (including benefits) because without them Kodak could not accomplish its goals. Similarly, the managers at your local McDonald's hire operating personnel; train them; assign their work schedules; order supplies; ensure that food is prepared appropriately; check to make sure that health, cleanliness, and safety standards are maintained; and handle a wide assortment of problems that can arise. In fact, when you have a bad meal in a restaurant or incur poor service in a retail store, you are likely to comment: "This place is poorly managed." As you will see, good managers make a real difference in the quality of an organization's operations. They can spell the difference between mediocre and excellent service, profits and losses for stockholders of corporations, and winning or losing on the playing field. The success of organizations such as Microsoft, Southwest Airlines, Sony, General Electric, and the Dallas Cowboys football team is largely due to the quality of their management.

How Do We Typically Classify Managers?

As shown by the shaded portions in Exhibit 2-1 on page 34, we typically classify managers as either first-line, middle, or top. Identifying exactly who is a manager and who isn't is not a difficult task, although you should be aware that managers come packaged in a variety of titles. **First-line managers** are the lowest level of management and are frequently called supervisors. In a manufacturing plant, the first-line manager may be called a foreman. On an athletic team, this job carries

IN THE NEWS

The $4.7 Billion Dollar Manager

IF YOU HAVE ANY DOUBT AS TO WHETHER MANAGERS MAKE A DIFFERENCE, CONSIDER THE CASE OF George M. C. Fisher (see photo) and the effect he had on the market value of Motorola and Eastman Kodak stocks one Wednesday in 1993.

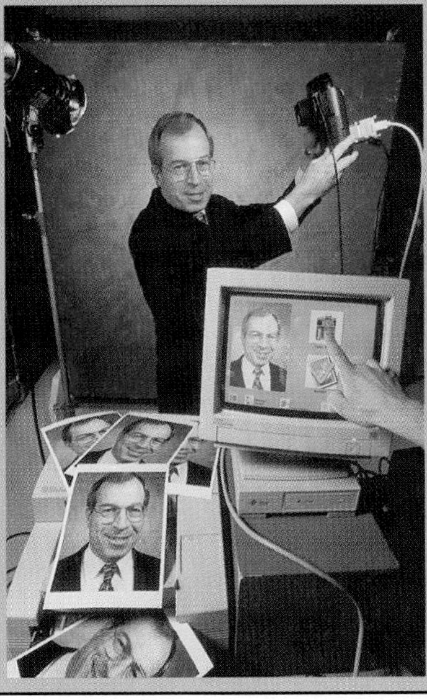

In August 1993, Kodak's board dismissed its chairman, Kay R. Whitmore. The reason? Lackluster financial performance and Whitmore's reluctance to radically change the tradition-bound photographic company. The board then immediately began a search for his replacement. On Wednesday, October 27, the board announced a major coup. It had hired Motorola's chairman, George Fisher, to fill Whitmore's slot.

Fisher seemed a perfect match for Kodak. The 52-year-old executive, who holds a Ph.D. in applied mathematics from Brown University, had been head of Motorola for 3 years and had been instrumental in turning Motorola into a world-class company. The company was one of the first winners of the Baldrige national award for quality; had become widely known for its innovative communications products, including pagers and cellular phones; and generated consistently improving sales and earnings. The appointment of Fisher seemed to fit perfectly with Kodak's efforts to meld its traditional chemical photographic products with the rapidly developing technology of capturing and manipulating electronic images. "George Fisher is an outstanding, proven chief executive with global experience as well as a reputation for keeping costs in line while achieving sales and earnings growth and enhanced shareholder value," said the head of Kodak's search committee.

The stocks of both Motorola and Kodak responded strongly to the board's announcement. Motorola's stock dropped $5.625 per share, or 5.4 percent (a loss in market value of $3.2 billion). Meanwhile, Kodak's stock jumped $4.375 a share, or 13.2 percent (an increase in Kodak's market value of $1.5 billion). This all took place on a day when the overall stock market declined about 0.2 percent.

The stock market doesn't seem to agree with those who argue that one person can't make a difference. On October 27, 1993, at least, the market thought that a change in leadership at Motorola and Kodak justified a combined change in market values for their stocks of $4.7 billion.

Source: Based on J. Holusha, "Motorola's Chairman Will Head Kodak," *New York Times,* October 28, 1993, p. C1.

EXHIBIT 2-1
Classifying Managers

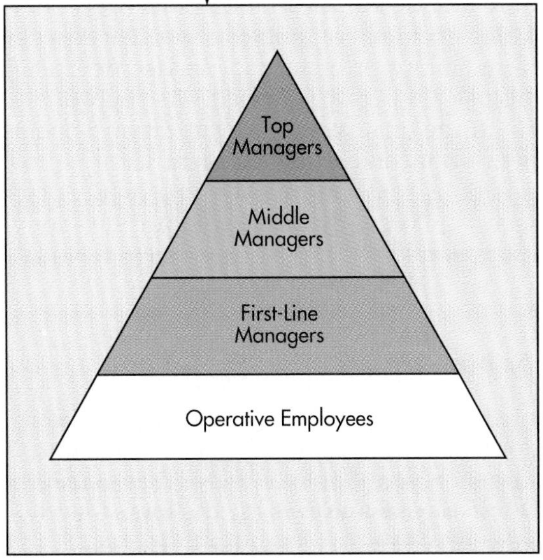

the title of coach. An increasingly popular title for first-line managers in high-tech and professional organizations is project or team leader. Middle managers have titles such as department or agency head, unit chief, district manager, dean, bishop, or division manager. At or near the top of an organization, managers typically have titles such as vice president, president, chancellor, managing director, chief operating officer, chief executive officer, or chairman of the board.

What Is an Organization?

So far, we have thrown around the term *organization* as if we all understood and agreed on what the term means. That may not be the case. For instance, when does a new business become an organization? Can you be a one-person organization? Would you define your family as an organization?

An **organization** is a systematic arrangement of two or more people who fulfill formal roles and share a common purpose. Your college or university is an organization. So are fraternities, government agencies, churches, Eastman Kodak, your neighborhood grocery store, the United Nations, the Toronto Blue Jays baseball team, and the Salvation Army. These are all organizations because they all have three common characteristics.

First, each has a *distinct purpose*. This purpose is typically expressed in terms of a goal or set of goals. Second, each is composed of *people*. Third, all organizations develop a *systematic structure* that defines formal roles and limits the behavior of its members. Development of a structure would include, for example, creating rules and regulations, defining teams, identifying formal leaders and giving them authority over other members, and writing up job descriptions so that members know what they are supposed to do. The term *organization* therefore refers to an entity that has a distinct purpose, includes people or members, and has a systematic structure.

Now we can answer the questions proposed at the beginning of this section. A business becomes an organization when it has formal goals, employs more than a single person, and develops a formal structure that defines the relationships between members. One person alone isn't an organization. And a family is not an organization in the sense that we treat it here. In contrast to a family, an organization is less personal and is designed to accomplish specific tasks rather than to meet personal needs.[3]

Why Do We Have Organizations?

Why do we have organizations? Because they are more efficient than individuals acting independently. This fact can best be understood by looking at two concepts—markets and hierarchies—and demonstrating how they act as alternative ways to coordinate economic activity.[4]

Markets are defined as a means for allocating resources on the basis of bargaining for prices. This, for example, would describe the process you would probably use if you needed to hire someone for a couple of days to paint your house. Because there is competition among painters, the transaction is likely to be perceived as efficient, with both you and the painter feeling that an equitable bargain has been struck.

But markets become too costly, and hence inefficient, when transactions become overly complex or ill defined. Such might be the case if you owned forty or fifty buildings and needed the ongoing services of dozens of painters, electricians, plumbers, and similar tradespeople. What if you happened to be a large chemical manufacturer or owned a dozen new car dealerships? To reduce uncertainty, you would seek the services of accountants, marketing professionals, and personnel specialists, and you would want a sophisticated information system to minimize transaction costs. Under high uncertainty, then, **hierarchies** often become more efficient and replace markets by allocating resources through rules and authority relationships. Rules create job classifications, outline compensation schedules, identify people in authority, determine who can interact with whom, and the like. So hierarchical organizations arise because they reduce costs by establishing rules and coordinating positions that are not found in markets.

Linking Managers and Organizations to Organizational Behavior

Managers work in a place we call an organization. The organization is the "playing field" upon which managers perform. A critical tool of effective managers is the ability to understand and predict the behavior of people in organizations. Why? Look back at our definition of managers. They *oversee the activities of others.* If the key element of management is working with other people, then managers need a solid understanding of human behavior. The field of **organizational behavior** (frequently referred to as just OB) has developed to help us better understand the behavior of individuals and groups. OB is defined as the systematic study of how people behave in organizations. It draws on the disciplines of psychology, sociology, anthropology, and other social sciences, then uses their findings to explain and predict employee performance factors (such as productivity, absenteeism, and turnover) and employee attitudes (such as job satisfaction and organizational loyalty).[5]

The content of this book draws heavily from the field of organizational behavior. For instance, OB research has given us a wealth of insights into how managers can be more effective leaders and offers important suggestions on how to best motivate different types of employees. But *management* isn't synonymous with *organizational behavior.* Rather, OB is a management tool. Just as a knowledge of accounting can help managers more effectively utilize their organization's financial resources, an understanding of organizational behavior can provide insights into how to best utilize an organization's human resources.

MULTIPLE PERSPECTIVES ON WHAT MANAGERS DO

People who study and write about management have long argued over the best way to categorize the manager's job.[6] This debate is not purely academic. If you are going to learn to be an effective manager, you need to understand what the job entails. In this section we review various perspectives on the manager's job.

Management Functions

In the early part of this century, a French industrialist by the name of Henri Fayol (see Appendix A) wrote that all managers perform five functions: They plan, organize, command, coordinate, and control.[7] Today, the use of **management functions** as a way to classify the manager's job is still very popular.[8] Now, however, they are usually condensed to four: planning, organizing, leading, and controlling. Let's briefly define what each of these functions encompasses.

Since organizations exist to achieve some purpose, someone has to define that purpose and the means for its achievement. Management is that someone. The **planning** function encompasses defining an organization's goals, establishing an overall strategy for achieving those goals, and developing a comprehensive hierarchy of plans to integrate and coordinate activities.

Noel Goutard is an effective leader. As CEO of France's Valeo, a $3.8 billion a year auto parts manufacturer, he has changed everything at the company, made "quality, service, and price" the firm's mantra, and significantly increased profits in the ferociously competitive parts market.

Managers are also responsible for designing an organization's structure. This function is called **organizing.** It includes the determination of what tasks are to be done, who is to do them, how the tasks are to be grouped, who reports to whom, and where in the organization decisions are to be made.

Every organization contains people, and it is management's job to direct and coordinate those people. This is the **leading** function. When managers motivate employees, direct the activities of others, select the most effective communication channel, or resolve conflicts among members, they are engaging in leading.

The final function managers perform is **controlling.** After the goals are set, the plans formulated, the structural arrangements delineated, and the people hired, trained, and motivated, something may still go amiss. To ensure that things are going as they should, management must monitor the organization's performance. Actual performance must be compared with the previously set goals. If there are any significant deviations, it is management's job to get the organization back on track. This process of monitoring, comparing, and correcting constitutes the controlling function.

Management Roles

In the late 1960s, Henry Mintzberg undertook a careful study of five chief executives at work. On the basis of diaries kept by these executives and his own observations, Mintzberg concluded that managers perform ten different but highly interrelated roles.[9] The term **management roles** refers to specific categories of managerial behavior. Mintzberg's ten roles can be grouped around three themes: interpersonal relationships, the transfer of information, and decision making (see Exhibit 2-2 on page 38).

Interpersonal Roles All managers are required to perform duties that are ceremonial and symbolic in nature. When the president of a college hands out diplomas at commencement or a factory supervisor gives a group of high school students a tour of the plant, he or she is acting in a *figurehead* role. All managers have a role as a *leader.* This role includes hiring, training, motivating, and disciplining employees. The third role within the interpersonal grouping is the *liaison* role. Mintzberg described this activity as contacting external sources who provide the manager with information. These sources are individuals or groups outside the

EXHIBIT 2-2 Mintzberg's Categories of Managerial Roles

General Role	Specific Role
Interpersonal	Figurehead Leader Liaison
Informational	Monitor Disseminator Spokesperson
Decisional	Entrepreneur Disturbance handler Resource allocator Negotiator

manager's unit, and they may be inside or outside the organization. The sales manager who obtains information from the human resources manager in his or her same company has an internal liaison relationship. When that sales manager has contact with other sales executives through a marketing trade association, he or she has an outside liaison relationship.

Informational Roles All managers will, to some degree, receive and collect information from organizations and institutions outside their own. Typically, they do this by reading magazines and talking with others to learn of changes in the public's tastes, what competitors may be planning, and the like. Mintzberg called this the *monitor* role. Managers also act as a conduit to transmit information to organizational members. This is the *disseminator* role. When they represent the organization to outsiders, managers also perform a *spokesperson* role.

Decisional Roles Finally, Mintzberg identified four roles that revolve around the making of choices. As *entrepreneurs,* managers initiate and oversee new projects that will improve their organization's performance. As *disturbance handlers,* managers take corrective action in response to unforeseen problems. As *resource allocators,* managers are responsible for distributing human, physical, and monetary resources. Last, managers perform as *negotiators* when they discuss and bargain with other groups to gain advantages for their own units.

Management Skills

> **It's not enough to *know about* managing. . . . You need to be prepared to *do it!***

Proponents of the skills perspective argue that it's not enough to *know about* managing organizations and people. You need to be prepared to *do it!* **Management skills** identify those abilities or behaviors that are crucial to success in a managerial position. This approach began with the identification of general skills and then moved to the search for specific skills related to managerial effectiveness.

General Skills There seems to be overall agreement that effective managers must be proficient in four general skill areas.[10] *Conceptual skills* refer to the mental ability to analyze and diagnose complex situations. They help managers see how things fit together and facilitate making good decisions. *Interpersonal skills* encompass the ability to work with, understand, and motivate other people, both individually and in groups. Since managers get things done through other people, they must have good interpersonal skills to communicate, motivate, and delegate. All managers need *technical skills.* These are abilities to apply specialized knowledge or expertise. For top-level managers these abilities tend to be related to knowledge of the industry and a general understanding of the organization's processes and products. For middle and lower-level managers, they are related to the specialized knowledge required in the areas with which they work—finance, human resources, manufacturing, computer systems, law, marketing, and the like. Finally, managers need *political skills*. This area is related to the ability to enhance one's position, build a power base, and establish the right connections. Organizations are political arenas in which people compete for resources. Managers with good political skills tend to be better at getting resources for their group than are managers with poor political skills. They also receive higher evaluations and get more promotions.[11]

Specific Skills Research has identified six sets of behaviors that explain a little bit more than 50 percent of a manager's effectiveness.[12]

1. *Controlling the organization's environment and its resources.* This includes demonstrating, in planning and allocation meetings as well as in on-the-spot decision making, the ability to be proactive and stay ahead of environmental changes. It also involves basing resource decisions on clear, up-to-date, accurate knowledge of the organization's objectives.
2. *Organizing and coordinating.* In this skill, managers organize around tasks and then coordinate interdependent relationships among tasks wherever they exist.
3. *Handling information.* This set of behaviors comprises using information and communication channels for identifying problems, understanding a changing environment, and making effective decisions.
4. *Providing for growth and development.* Managers provide for their own personal growth and development, as well as for the personal growth and development of their employees, through continual learning on the job.
5. *Motivating employees and handling conflicts.* Managers enhance the positive aspects of motivation so that employees feel impelled to perform their work, while eliminating those conflicts that may inhibit employees' motivation.
6. *Strategic problem solving.* Managers take responsibility for their own decisions and ensure that subordinates effectively use their decision-making skills.

Management Competencies

The most recent approach to defining the manager's job has come out of the United Kingdom.[13] It is called the management charter initiative (MCI). Based on an analysis of management functions and focusing on what effective managers should be able to do, rather than on what they know, the MCI sets generic standards of management competence. Currently, there are two sets of standards. Management I is for first-level managers. Management II is for middle managers. Standards for top management are under development.

Exhibit 2-3 on page 40 lists standards for middle management. For each area of competence there is a related set of specific elements that define effectiveness in that area. For instance, one area of competence is recruiting and selecting personnel. Successful development of this competence requires that managers be able to define future personnel requirements, to determine specifications to secure quality people, and to assess and select candidates against team and organizational requirements.

The MCI standards are attracting global interest. The Australian Institute of Management, for example, has already started using the standards, and the Management Development Center of Hong Kong is considering introducing them to help managers become more mobile after China's takeover of Hong Kong. However, despite the generic nature of these standards—the developers of MCI believe that the standards can be applied to management jobs in any industry—there is

EXHIBIT 2-3
Management Charter Initiative Competencies for Middle Managers

Basic Competence	Specific Associated Elements
1. Initiate and implement change and improvement in services, products, and systems	1.1. Identify opportunites for improvement in services, products, and systems 1.2. Evaluate benefits and disadvantages of proposed changes 1.3. Negotiate and agree on the introduction of change 1.4. Implement and evaluate changes in services, products, and systems 1.5. Introduce, develop, and evaluate quality-assurance systems
2. Monitor, maintain, and improve service and product delivery	2.1. Establish and maintain the supply of resources into the organization/department 2.2. Establish and agree on customer requirements 2.3. Maintain and improve operations against quality and functional specifications 2.4. Create and maintain the necessary conditions for productive work
3. Monitor and control the use of resources	3.1. Control costs and enhance value 3.2. Monitor and control activities against budgets
4. Secure effective resource allocation for activities and projects	4.1. Justify proposals for expenditure on projects 4.2. Negotiate and agree on budgets
5. Recruit and select personnel	5.1. Define future personnel requirements 5.2. Determine specifications to secure quality people 5.3. Assess and select candidates against team and organizational requirements
6. Develop teams, individuals, and self to enhance performance	6.1. Develop and improve teams through planning and activities 6.2. Identify, review, and improve developmental activities for individuals
7. Plan, allocate, and evaluate work carried out by teams, individuals, and self	7.1. Set and update work objectives for teams and individuals 7.2. Plan activities and determine work methods to achieve objectives 7.3. Allocate work and evaluate teams, individuals, and self against objectives 7.4. Provide feedback to teams and individuals on their performance
8. Create, maintain, and enhance effective working relationships	8.1. Establish and maintain the trust and support of one's subordinates 8.2. Establish and maintain the trust and support of one's immediate manager 8.3. Establish and maintain relationships with colleagues 8.4. Identify and minimize interpersonal conflict 8.5. Implement disciplinary and grievance procedures 8.6. Counsel staff
9. Seek, evaluate, and organize information for action	9.1. Obtain and evaluate information to aid decision making 9.2. Forecast trends and developments that will affect objectives 9.3. Record and store information
10. Exchange information to solve problems and make decisions	10.1. Lead meetings and group discussions 10.2. Contribute to discussions to solve problems and make decisions 10.3. Advise and inform others

Source: "MCI Launches Standards for First Two Levels," *Personnel Management,* November 1990, p. 13.

Xu Baosheng, an executive at Connecticut's Loctite Corp., is the company's change agent in China. As general manager of Loctite (China) Co. Ltd., he is responsible for bringing contemporary management practices to the company's sealant and adhesive plants in Shandong province.

recognition that national differences can require adjustments. As a case in point, family-run businesses are still common in Italy. So references to *superiors* or *teams* have had to be modified for use with Italian managers.

The Manager as Decision Maker

Almost everything managers do involves making decisions. Selecting the organization's objectives requires making decisions. So, too, do such varied activities as designing the best organization structure, selecting among alternative technologies, choosing among job candidates, or determining how to motivate low-performing employees. In fact, the decision-making process is seen by some commentators as the core of the manager's job.[14] Nobel laureate Herbert Simon, a strong advocate of this position, even went so far as to say that decision making is synonymous with managing.[15]

This decision-making approach looks at the manager's job and addresses such questions as: How do managers identify problems? Are decision makers rational? How do managers make judgments under uncertainty? What general biases surface in the decision-making process? When are groups better for making decisions than individuals? To what degree should managers empower subordinates to make operating decisions?

The Manager as Change Agent

The last approach we'll present is the agent-of-change perspective. This approach answers the question "What do managers do?" by proposing that they bring about change. They are catalysts and assume the responsibility for managing the change process.

The change-agent perspective has evolved through three stages. In its preliminary stage, which began in the 1950s, proponents argued that managers needed to design and execute planned change programs.[16] These intervention programs included attempts to improve interpersonal interactions in organizations, change work processes and methods, and redesign organization structures. The second stage arose in the 1980s and evolved out of efforts to improve quality.[17] It sought to bring about change through continual improvement. The manager's job was to seek out and implement continual incremental changes to improve everything about the organization. Now, in the 1990s, a third view on this perspective has developed. The manager's job is no longer conceived as initiating *incremental* changes. Rather, managers need to implement *quantum,* or radical, change.[18] This theme argues that in a world that is undergoing dramatic change, organizations that attempt to adjust by making only small incremental changes are doomed to fail. Managers, therefore, need to completely reinvent their organizations. They need to start with a blank sheet and rebuild their organizations from scratch. Moreover, this is not a "one-shot" effort. Effective managers will be continually reinventing their organizations to adapt to a changing world.

The manager-as-change-agent perspective is consistent with our discussion, in Chapter 1, on the changing world of work. That is, not only are the economy, organizations, and employee's jobs undergoing change. So, too, is the manager's job. But the manager is on both the receiving end and the giving end. Managers have to adjust to change, and they also must be the catalyst for initiating change within their organizations. Exhibit 2-4 highlights some of the recent changes in the manager's job.

Thriving on Chaos The new economy and new organization do not cause stress only for employees. They have a similar effect on many managers. Reports of high stress levels and job burnout among managers have risen as the work climate has become more chaotic and ambiguous.[19]

Management guru Tom Peters captured the challenge for managers in his best-selling book *Thriving on Chaos: Handbook for a Management Revolution.*[20] In that book he argued that successful managers, in today's unpredictable environment, must be able to thrive on change and uncertainty.

The manager's job is increasingly one of juggling a dozen balls at once, in the dark, on the deck of a boat, during a typhoon! It requires turning an environment of chaotic change into an opportunity—the chance for well-managed organizations to gain a competitive advantage over rivals by being smarter, more flexible, quicker, more efficient, and better at responding to customer needs.

Being a Coach The manager-as-boss model dominated organizations for the first 80 years or so of this century. Managers were assumed to be smarter than their employees and to know each employee's job better than the employee did. It was the boss's job to tell employees what to do, how to do it, and when to do it and to make sure they did it right. Managers made all the relevant decisions, provided direction, gave orders, and carefully controlled activities to minimize mistakes and ensure that the rules were followed.

Today's manager is increasingly more like a coach than a boss.[21] Coaches don't play the game. They create a climate in which their players can excel. They define the overall objectives, set expectations, define the boundaries of each player's role, ensure that players are properly trained and have the resources they need to perform their roles, attempt to enlarge each player's capabilities, offer inspiration and motivation, and evaluate results. Contemporary managers look

EXHIBIT 2-4
The Changing Manager

Old Manager	New Manager
• Operates in climate of predictability and stability	• Thrives on chaos
• The Boss	• The Coach
• Covets authority	• Empowers employees
• Hoards information	• Shares information
• Treats people as all the same	• Is sensitive to differences

much more like coaches than bosses as they guide, listen to, encourage, and motivate their employees.

Empowering Employees Consistent with their coaching role, today's managers are increasingly giving up authority and empowering their employees. As described in our discussion of the new organization, the trend to empowerment has become widespread. Managers are having to adjust their leadership styles to reflect this trend. That is, they are having to expand their leadership options to include empowerment. Empowering employees isn't the only leadership style a manager needs, nor is it the appropriate style for every situation, but those situations in which it is the preferred choice have expanded significantly in recent years.

For most younger managers, the transition to an empowering style has been relatively painless. But that hasn't been the case for many experienced managers. They came of age when effective managers were perceived as "take-charge" people. Letting employees make independent, job-related decisions—even *sharing* decision-making authority with employees—was seen as a sign of weakness. These managers have had difficulty giving up control.[22] In some cases, managers have been unable to give up "being boss" and have subsequently lost their jobs.

Sharing Information Another characteristic of the manager-as-boss model was maintaining control of information. If information is power, then a manager who shared information with employees would increase the employees' power. Managers did not see that outcome as desirable.

But now, individual employees and teams need to make critical, job-related decisions, and to do so they require accurate and up-to-date information. So managers are increasingly sharing with these empowered employees information they used to keep closely guarded. Contemporary managers are acting as conduits. They gather information from horizontal units, upper levels of management, and

IN THE NEWS

Is the Empowerment Trend Eliminating Management Jobs?

[WITH APOLOGIES TO MARK TWAIN] "THE REPORTS OF *MANAGEMENT'S* DEATH ARE GREATLY EXAGGERATED." If you read current business periodicals, you might assume that downsizing, the flattening of organizational hierarchies, and the push to empower employees have dramatically cut the need for managers—especially middle managers. That assumption would be wrong.

The truth is that the managerial ranks of large corporations and other companies remained almost unchanged between 1990 and 1995. And the Bureau of Labor Statistics reports that, for the U.S. work force as a whole, its category of executives, managers, and administrative personnel grew 28.8 percent from the mid-1980s to the mid-1990s. The only actual decline has been in the number of managers per 100 employees. But that decline has been relatively small. There were 11.17 managers per 100 employees in 1995, compared with 11.83 in 1990.

What explains this relative stability among the management ranks? Four forces seem to be at work. First, more and more people in organizations are taking on managerial responsibilities. Many more people are actively involved in the decision-making process, so more people are being elevated to the management category. For instance, rank-and-file employees are increasingly being given management responsibilities such as planning budgets, organizing schedules, hiring team members, and representing the organization to suppliers and customers. Second, the growth of small and medium-sized businesses has expanded the number of management positions. Third, the employee mix is changing. White-collar jobs have grown rapidly as a percentage of the total work force. On average, a group of white-collar workers has historically had far more managers than a group of factory workers of the same size. In addition, as white-collar jobs become more sophisticated, the number of managers required tends to grow. Finally, globalization is also playing an important role. The global expansion of U.S. companies has created more-complex jobs and the need for more upper-level managers.

Source: A. Markels, "Restructuring Alters Middle-Manager Role But Leaves It Robust," *Wall Street Journal,* September 25, 1995, p. A1. Reprinted by permission of the *Wall Street Journal* © 1995 Dow Jones & Co. Inc. All rights reserved worldwide.

external sources; then they share that information with members of their unit. Some organizations have extended information sharing into a corporate philosophy of open-book management.[23] Details on the company's finances are regularly presented to all employees. They learn to analyze and interpret the organization's financial statements and to set budgets for their units. This process, then, becomes the basis for all decision making in each unit. In this system, managers act as advisers and resource persons to help employees get the information they need.

Some managers are having difficulty giving up control of information. They are threatened by sharing power with their staff. Most managers, however, are learning that their unit's performance is enhanced through information sharing. And when their unit does better, they're perceived as more effective managers.

Sensitivity to Differences Workforce diversity requires managers to be increasingly sensitive to differences. The values, needs, interests, and expectations of workers have never been homogeneous. But when the work population was dominated by married white males of European extraction, managers could quite accurately generalize about employees. They could, for instance, assume that "my employees are like me. We prefer similar foods; we have common responsibilities; we celebrate the same holidays; we enjoy similar social and recreational interests." This assumption may never have been true, but the range of variation before the 1970s was considerably narrower than it is today.

The true minority employee in today's work force is a white male who has school-age children and a wife who is not gainfully employed outside the home. Managers now have to understand that it is very difficult for some employees to put in overtime hours without substantial notice, to work weekends, to be gone overnight on business, or to accept a transfer to a new location. Similarly, physical barriers such as narrow doorways or stairs can be troublesome for some employees. Nor can managers assume that all employees share a common understanding of language. In addition, managers have to be sure that employees are sensitive to co-workers who are different. That means being observant of expressions of sexism, racisim, ageism, and more subconscious biases within the work group.

Synthesis and a Look Ahead

Don't let these varied views on the manager's job confuse you. For the most part, they are not in conflict. What they are is just different ways of looking at the same thing. As such, they all have some truths to them. And a close look shows that there is considerable overlap among them. For instance, Mintzberg's decisional roles and the emphasis on conceptual and information-handling skills are all consistent with the view that managers are decision makers. The leading function encompasses Mintzberg's interpersonal roles and the specific skills of motivating employees and handling conflict. The first competency identified in the MCI middle-manager standards—initiate and implement change—is totally consistent with the manager-as-change-agent perspective.

As you read through the chapters in this book, you will see that we draw on all of the various perspectives. Chapter 3 acknowledges the importance of decision making. Chapters 5 and 6 and Parts III and IV—covering planning, control systems, organizing tasks, and leading and empowering people—evolved out of considerations of management functions. In-chapter guidelines on how to apply quantitative decision techniques, competitive intelligence, benchmarking, budgets, control charts, empowering employees, and interpersonal skills are all an effort to help you develop your management skills. Chapters 1 and 17 on the changing world of work and managing change and innovation reflect the belief that managers are catalysts of change. Finally, a review of this text's detailed Table of Contents reveals that almost all of the competencies listed in Exhibit 2-3 on page 40 are touched on within the book's seventeen chapters.

ASSESSING MANAGERIAL EFFECTIVENESS

A primary objective of this book is to help you to be an *effective manager.* In the preceding sections we addressed what a manager is and does, and we used the term *effective* several times. So now we turn to the question: How do we know if a manager is *effective?* In this section, we define managerial and organizational effectiveness, identify the primary organizational stakeholders who judge effectiveness, and review the various criteria they use.

Definitions

Early writers took a somewhat simplistic view when they sought to determine whether a manager was doing a good job. They focused on two concepts: *efficiency* and *effectiveness.*

Efficiency refers to the relationship between inputs and outputs. If you get more output for a given input, you have increased efficiency. Similarly, if you can get the same output from less input, you again increase efficiency. Managers are concerned with the efficient use of input resources—money, people, equipment. So the production manager at a Honda plant who can produce a completed engine with 2.3 hours of labor has a more efficient unit than another production manager whose workers require 2.7 hours of labor to make the same engine.

It is not enough to be efficient. Managers must also be concerned with getting activities completed; that is, they must achieve **effectiveness.** Managers who achieve their organizations' goals are said to be effective. Or, as one management expert put it, "Efficiency means *doing things right,* and effectiveness means *doing the right thing.*"[24] Doing things right means minimizing the cost of resources needed to achieve goals. Doing the right thing means selecting appropriate goals and then achieving them.

"Efficiency means *doing things right,* and effectiveness means *doing the right thing.*"

Is managerial effectiveness the same as organizational effectiveness? No, but the concepts are closely related. Managerial effectiveness is concerned with the achievement of a manager's goals, whereas organizational effectiveness addresses the organization's goals. Yet, because a manager's success is essentially defined in terms of how well his or her organizational unit performs, it is difficult to separate the two concepts. As such, the following discussion is really applicable to both.

Organizational Stakeholders

Effectiveness may sound like a straightforward concept, but it isn't. The problem is that effectiveness, like beauty, is in the eye of the beholder. Different groups judge organizations by different criteria. Employees, for instance, may think that the right thing for an organization to do is to provide workers with good pay and benefits. They would then judge the organization's effectiveness by how well those goals are achieved. In contrast, stockholders typically think that the right thing for an organization to do is to increase stockholder wealth by improving earnings per share. If we want to more fully understand the concept of effectiveness, we need to take a look at the various groups who evaluate managers and organizations.

An organization's **stakeholders** are those groups within or outside the organization that have an interest in it. These typically include employees, customers, management, boards of directors, investors, competitors, suppliers, creditors, media, government agencies, and special interest groups.[25]

Each stakeholder has a set of criteria to which it expects the organization to respond. Unfortunately, because stakeholders have different interests in the organization, the criteria they use for judging the organization's effectiveness also differ.[26] (See Exhibit 2-5.) As you will see shortly, multiple stakeholders and multiple criteria require managers to emphasize different effectiveness criteria to different audiences.

Popular Effectiveness Criteria

In 1983, the head of General Motors announced, with great fanfare, the creation of Saturn Corp. He said Saturn would prove that GM could profitably build a small automobile in the United States that would beat Japanese competition. More than a dozen years have passed since GM created Saturn. So it seems fair to ask: Well, were they successful? The answer is Yes, No, or Maybe.[27] It depends on how you define success. Initial sales were strong. But recent sales figures have been declining. Surveys indicate that Saturn has achieved quality, reliability, and customer satisfaction that are every bit as good as what Japanese auto makers have achieved. But in terms of productivity, costs, and profits, Saturn has been a major disappointment. Saturn is much less productive than comparable Honda and Toyota plants in the United States. GM lost billions of dollars during Saturn's first decade in operation. Saturn broke even in 1993, but only by means of creative accounting. Billions of dollars in Saturn costs were transferred to GM's financial statement.

EXHIBIT 2-5
Common Stakeholders and Their Typical Effectiveness Criteria

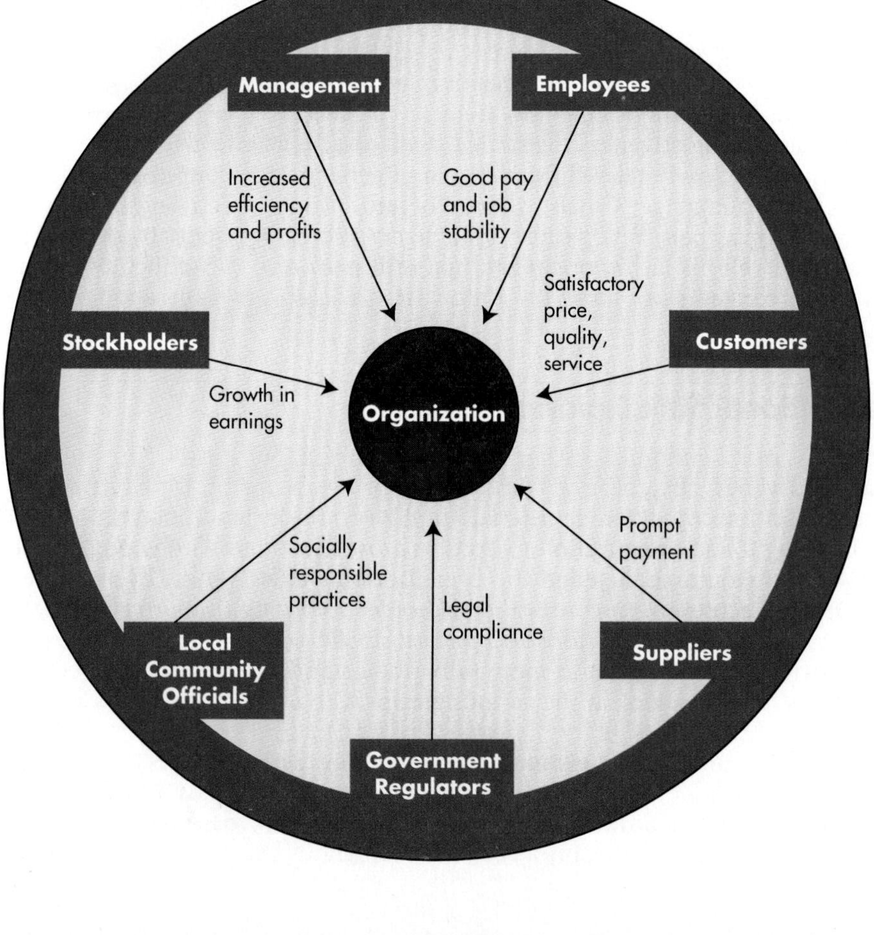

Saturn illustrates the major problem in defining organizational effectiveness. Effectiveness is essentially determined by how well the organization achieves its goals. But we must know *what* goals and *whose* goals.[28] Let's take a brief look at a few of the more popular effectiveness goals or criteria and show how different stakeholders emphasize different criteria.

Financial Measures The best-known criteria for measuring organizational effectiveness are financial measures, especially among profit-seeking business firms. Surveys of large multinational corporations found that, in the late 1960s, the dominant financial goal that these companies sought was maximizing market share. By the mid-1970s, attention shifted to earnings per share. By the early 1980s, return on equity had become the dominant goal. Since the early 1990s, cash flow measures have become the most popular.[29]

Although specific criteria have changed over time, business firms still rely heavily on financial measures to assess how well they're doing. Among publicly held corporations, satisfactory performance on financial criteria is necessary to maintain legitimacy and credibility with investors and lenders.

Productivity Productivity criteria are synonymous with measures of organizational efficiency. The more output an organization can generate from a given input, the more productive it is. A few years back, each Toyota employee produced 57.7 vehicles a year, while his or her Ford counterpart turned out only 16.1 vehicles.[30] Toyota was more productive because it generated more cars per employee.

Examples of efficiency criteria include output per employee labor-hour, costs per patient, and scrap as a percent of steel shipped. Each of those criteria overlaps with financial measures when a criterion such as rate of return on capital or assets is used.

Growth In the 1960s, a popular measure of organizational effectiveness was expansion of payrolls. The more people an organization hired, the more successful many people believed that organization to be. Nowadays it's quite the opposite. Those organizations that can increase production and sales by holding their work force in check or by actually reducing jobs are seen as the most effective.

Growth in payrolls is no longer a valued effectiveness measure, but growth in sales units, total revenues, and net profits continue to have a wide following. In the investment community, high stock prices are frequently justified for firms with modest profits solely on the basis that the firm is expanding and growing rapidly. For instance, in 1995, the stocks of most restaurant chains were selling for about twenty times earnings. But Boston Chicken, Inc., a young company that planned to add more than 300 new locations a year of its Boston Market, was selling at better than fifty times earnings.

Customer Satisfaction As competition has increased for producers of almost every product and service, no organization is safe in taking its customer or client base for granted. This fact of business life explains the recent obsession by management in many organizations with achieving high customer satisfaction.

Studies consistently indicate that it is a lot more expensive to attract new customers than it is to spend whatever is necessary to keep the customers you have. So organizations are doing things such as spending substantial sums of money to train employees who interact with customers, establishing toll-free numbers for customers to get help or register complaints, introducing "no-questions-asked" return policies, and conducting comprehensive after-sale surveys.

As Saturn Corp. has learned, high customer satisfaction is no assurance that an organization will achieve its financial goals. However, the long-term viability of an organization will be severely tested if customers are not satisfied and look to competing organizations to meet their needs. The success of companies such as Nordstrom, L.L. Bean, Lexus, Singapore Airlines, and Federal Express is regularly attributed to their obsession with doing whatever is necessary to satisfy their customers. In addition, many organizations are coming to recognize that building customer satisfaction and loyalty also means not taking short-term financial advantage of customers. Harley Davidson, for instance, sold out its 1995 production capacity of motorcycles by late 1994. Harley's CEO, Richard Teerlink, said his firm could easily have raised prices 10 percent or 15 percent and significantly increased profits, but didn't. Why? "It wouldn't be fair to our customers."[31] Although Harley Davidson is a publicly held company, Teerlink believes that the long-term interests of the company are best served by not exploiting customers.

Quality Closely linked with the criterion of customer satisfaction is the concern for quality. But the goal of quality encompasses internal operations and processes as well as judgments by customers. So the search for quality means cutting out unnecessary steps in the processing of accounts payable, keeping inventory costs down, and maintaining spotless floors in the production areas, as well as ensuring that external customers are satisfied. Part of McDonald's phenomenal success is due to management's commitment to provide high quality at low cost and having restaurants that meet the most stringent standards for cleanliness.

Flexibility A flexible organization is one that can shift resources from one activity to another quickly and easily. In an era of global competition and rapid social, economic, and technological change, the survival of many organizations depends on their ability to adapt quickly. Companies such as the Cable News Network, Charles Schwab, Southwest Airlines, and MCI have succeeded against much larger competitors because they have internal systems that were designed, and employees who were selected and trained, to adapt rapidly to change.

Employee Growth and Satisfaction An organization's employees are its heart and soul. Unfortunately, in recent years, a lot of organizations have lost sight of that fact. Employee loyalty has declined as many employers have laid off workers and undermined the job security of those who remain.[32] Many organizations have considered this a price that has had to be paid in order to increase flexibility and productivity.

There is no question that a number of organizations had overstaffed during the 1970s and 1980s, thus requiring employee cutbacks. But goals such as high quality and improved customer service depend on a well-trained and motivated work force. Therein lies a dilemma: How does an organization achieve high productivity and flexibility while, at the same time, maintaining committed and motivated employees?

Richard Branson, the billionaire founder and head of Virgin Airlines, doesn't think there's a problem. Counter to most executives who say that the customer or profits should come first, Branson says, "Almost 100 percent of running a business is motivating your staff and the people around you. And if you can motivate them, then you can achieve anything. And too many companies have put shareholders first, customers second, staff way last. If you reverse that and you put your staff first, very quickly you find that the customers come first as well, and the shareholders come first, as well."[33]

Social Acceptance Organizations need to be good citizens. When they aren't, they can suffer at the hands of stakeholders such as government agencies, consumer advocate groups, or a critical media. Dow Corning's reputation and financial integrity were severely damaged by its manufacture of defective silicone breast implants. Investigations by newspapers, the U.S. Food and Drug Administration, and congressional subcommittees found company memos indicating that Dow Corning was in such a rush to gets its implants on the market that it either dismissed or short-circuited animal studies showing that silicone leaked from the implants.[34] The company eventually got out of the breast implant business and was required to contribute hundreds of millions of dollars into a fund against future liabilities. In contrast, a company such as Ben & Jerry's Homemade Inc. has gained a strong following for its socially responsible practices and efforts to preserve the environment.

An Integrative Framework

Managers are judged by a diverse set of stakeholders. Moreover, because these stakeholders have different interests, they don't necessarily agree on when managers are doing a good job or when an organization is effective. So what can managers do? How can they satisfy different and even conflicting demands from multiple stakeholders? One answer is that they can prioritize criteria in terms of the power of various stakeholders and emphasize different achievements to different audiences.

The tobacco industry offers an illustration. A study of the major tobacco companies found that the public evaluated the firms in terms of not harming smokers' health, while stockholders evaluated the firms' ability to produce cigarettes efficiently and profitably. Not surprisingly—using such diverse criteria—the public rated the tobacco firms as ineffective, and stockholders rated the same firms as highly effective.[35] Effectiveness of a tobacco company, therefore, can be said to be determined by management's ability to identify the company's critical stakeholders, assess their preference patterns, and satisfy their demands. Stockholders and consumers might be satisfied with tobacco firms, but if the public, through its legislative representatives, outlaws the sales of cigarettes, then the tobacco companies lose and lose big!

The long-term viability of an organization requires that management not overlook the demands of any powerful stakeholder. So management needs to carefully and systematically identify critical organizational stakeholders, assess their relative power, and identify what each expects of the organization. Then management should attempt to satisfy the goals of those stakeholders with the greatest power or, at least, make the effort to persuade those stakeholders that significant progress is being made toward meeting their goals.

The long-term viability of an organization requires that management not overlook the demands of any powerful stakeholder.

Let's apply this integrative framework at Goodyear Tire and Rubber. Goodyear's stakeholders include suppliers of critical petroleum products used in the tire-manufacturing process; officers of the United Rubber Workers union; unionized employees; officials at banks where Goodyear has sizable short-term loans; government regulatory agencies that grade tires and inspect facilities for safety violations; security analysts at major brokerage firms who specialize in the tire-and-rubber industry; mutual fund managers who have large holdings of Goodyear stock; regional tire jobbers and distributors; and purchasing agents responsible for the acquisition of tires at GM, Mack Truck, Caterpillar, and other vehicle manufacturers.

Goodyear's management could evaluate this list to determine the relative power of each. Basically, this means looking at each stakeholder in terms of how dependent on it Goodyear is. Does it have considerable power over Goodyear? Are there alternatives for what this stakeholder provides? How do these stakeholders compare in the impact they have on Goodyear's operations?

Next, Goodyear's management needs to identify the expectations that these stakeholders hold for the organization. What goals does each seek to impose on the

Goodyear's management needs to appease its primary stakeholders, including its employees. Here, Goodyear inspectors check tires at the company's plant in Gasden, Alabama. These workers are likely to evaluate the company's effectiveness by how well they are paid and the job security they are provided.

organization? Stockholders' goals may be in terms of profit or appreciation in the stock's price; the union's may be in acquiring job security and high wages for its members; the U.S. Environmental Protection Agency will want Goodyear's manufacturing plants to meet all minimum air-, water-, and noise-pollution requirements.

Finally, Goodyear's management needs to compare the various expectations, determine common goals and those that are incompatible, assign relative weights to the various stakeholders, and prioritize these various goals for the benefit of the organization as a whole. The resulting preference order, in effect, represents the relative power of the various stakeholders. Goodyear's effectiveness will then be assessed in terms of its ability to satisfy those goals.

One last point: Whether an organization is meeting a stakeholder's goals is not a fully objective determination. Subjective judgments will be made by stakeholders. For instance, suppose that investors are looking for an increase in profits of 15 percent over the previous year, but actual profits rise only 11 percent. If it's crucial to appease these investors, management can take the offensive. It can argue its case for the adequacy of the 11 percent increase. In actual practice, managers are doing this all the time. Like good lawyers, they shape facts and use persuasive language to present the organization in the most favorable light.[36] So when executives are talking to a group of security analysts, the emphasis will be on how successful management has been at improving profitability. When those same executives meet with union officials, they'll emphasize management's efforts to create jobs and improve working conditions. And when those executives have to appear before a local zoning commission to get approval for a plant expansion, the focus will be on what a caring and responsible citizen the company has been in the community.

COMING ATTRACTIONS: A GUIDE TO THE BOOK

If you're going to embark on a journey, it helps to have a plan or guide so you can see where you are going and where you have been. Exhibit 2-6 is your guide to this book. The objectives of this book are to help you understand management and to help you become an effective manager. To achieve either, you need to build management competencies. Those competencies are organized into two groups: knowledge and applicable skills. Knowledge builds understanding. Applicable skills apply that understanding. For the most part, our knowledge base is derived from the management functions: planning, organizing, leading, and controlling. Our skills build from, and elaborate upon, the six specific management skills listed earlier.

Managers and organizations must respond to forces of change, the subject of Chapters 1 and 17. These forces for change operate on the organization by way of the environment to determine the organizational boundaries.

The core of Exhibit 2-6 (and of this book) is made up of three competency areas. Part I—decision and monitoring systems—is covered in Chapters 3 through

EXHIBIT 2-6
Managerial Competencies in a Changing World

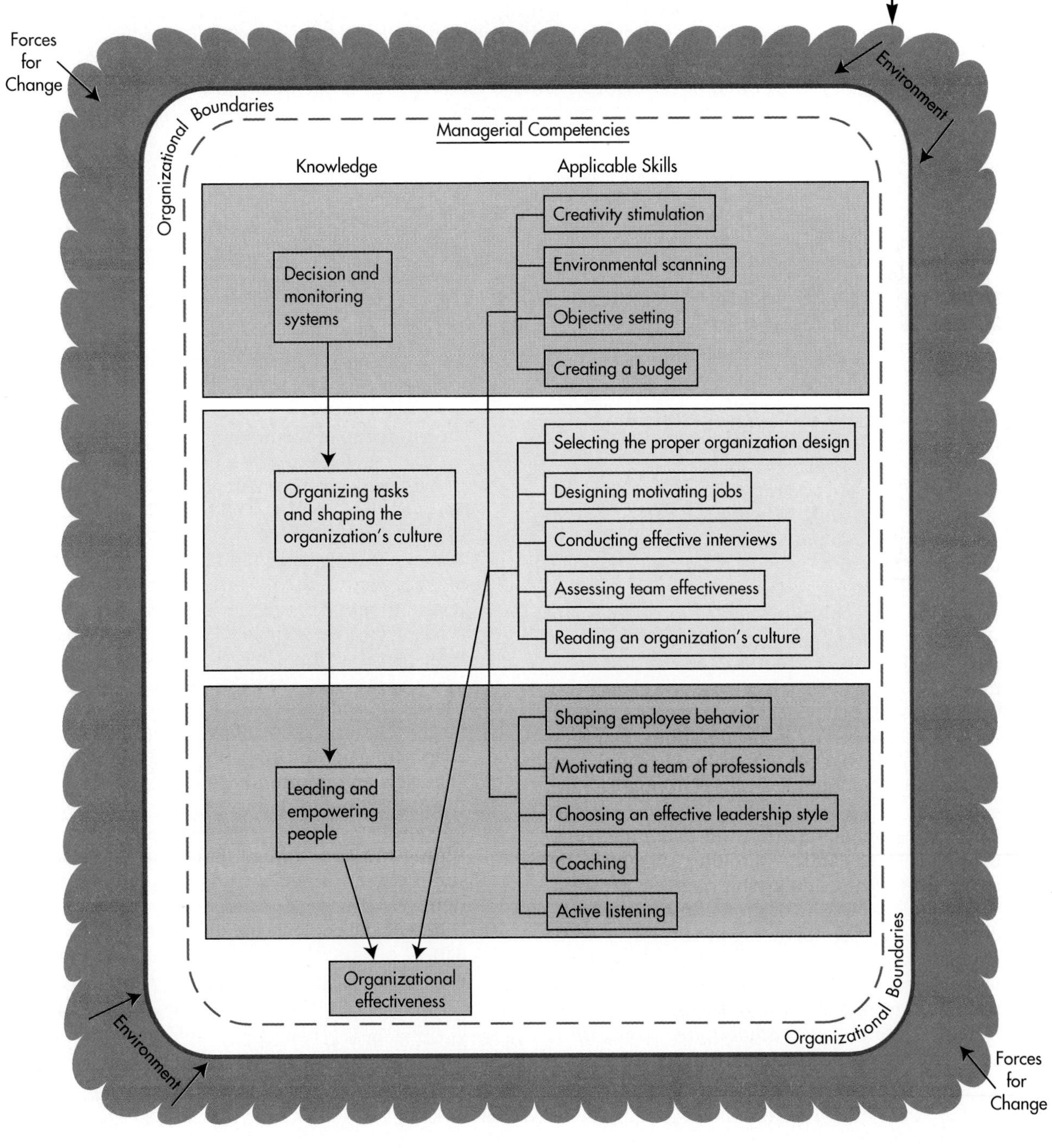

6. Those chapters cover conceptual issues such as making decisions, assessing the environment, creating plans, and developing control systems. Applicable skills presented in Chapters 3 through 6 include creativity stimulation, environmental scanning, objective setting, and budget formulation.

Part III, Chapters 7 through 11, addresses organizing tasks and shaping the organization's culture. You'll learn about organization design, technology and work processes, managing human resources, groups and teams, and the organization's culture. Skills developed in these chapters include choosing the proper organizational structure, designing motivating jobs, conducting effective interviews, assessing team effectiveness, and reading an organization's culture.

Chapters 12 through 16 in Part IV develop your knowledge of leading and empowering people. Applicable skills covered in those chapters include shaping employee behavior, designing motivating workplaces, choosing an effective leadership style, coaching, and active listening.

Note the inclusion of organizational effectiveness in Exhibit 2-6. As we pointed out previously in this chapter, this is the determinant of whether managers are doing a good job. Therefore, managerial competencies are shown as leading to organizational effectiveness.

SUMMARY

(This summary is organized by the chapter-opening learning objectives on page 31.)

1. Managers are individuals who oversee the activities of others. To be a manager, a person needs to have other people report to him or her.
2. Managers give an organizational unit direction, coordinate their unit's activities with the activities of other units, and provide accountability for unit outcomes.
3. An organization is a systematic arrangement of two or more people who fulfill formal roles and share a common purpose. It is designed to accomplish specific tasks rather than to meet personal needs.
4. Organizational behavior (OB) systematically studies how people behave in organizations. Managers use their knowledge of OB to help them work with others and to get high levels of performance from employees.
5. Four management functions are planning, organizing, leading, and controlling. Planning includes goal setting and establishing the organization's strategy. Organizing identifies tasks to be done, who is to do them, how the tasks are to be grouped, who reports to whom, and where in the organization decisions are to be made. Leading refers to directing and coordinating people. Controlling is the process of monitoring, comparing, and correcting performance.
6. Four general skill areas needed by managers are conceptual, interpersonal, technical, and political. Six specific skills are controlling the organization's environment and its resources, organizing and coordinating, handling information, providing for growth and development, motivating employees and handling conflict, and strategic problem solving.
7. Bosses covet authority and control. They tell employees what to do, how to do it, and when to do it, and they make sure they do it right. In contrast, coaches create a climate that supports employee high performance. They guide, listen to, encourage, and motivate their employees.
8. Chaos and ambiguity can be turned into an opportunity because they allow managers who can adapt to gain a competitive advantage. Rapid change is an opportunity for the quick and adept to outsmart or out-maneuver their rivals.
9. Effectiveness is concerned with goal attainment: "doing the right thing." Efficiency is a relationship between inputs and outputs: "doing things right."
10. Different stakeholders use different criteria in evaluating organizational effectiveness because they have different goals and expectations of the organization. Each assesses how well the organization is doing—its effectiveness—in terms of how well it is achieving the goals that satisfy the specific stakeholder's interests.

REVIEW AND DISCUSSION QUESTIONS

1. Can you conceive of an organization of 100 people that has no managers? What problems would you expect it to have?
2. If managers are so important to an organization, why do you think there has been a trend in recent years toward having fewer middle managers and more self-managed teams?
3. Why do you think that managers typically are better paid than nonmanagers?
4. Senior executives in major U.S. corporations routinely earn more than $2 million a year. Are these managers overpaid?
5. American CEOs typically earn two or three times as much as their counterparts in Canada and Europe. Why do you think this is?
6. Contrast markets and hierarchies.
7. Reconcile the four managerial functions, Mintzberg's three role categories, and the four general skills.
8. Introductory university courses often have lecture sections of 200 or more students. Is this practice efficient? Is it effective? Explain.
9. Who are the key stakeholders for (a) IBM, (b) the University of Michigan, and (c) the New York Museum of Modern Art?
10. "For a business firm, the bottom line is profit. You don't need any other measures of effectiveness." Do you agree or disagree with this statement? Support your position.

CASE EXERCISE A
A DAY IN THE LIFE OF CHUCK STONEMAN

Chuck Stoneman really believes in the old cliché "the early bird gets the worm." It's Tuesday morning, and Chuck has already been up for an hour. He spent 20 minutes on his stationary bike, showered, dressed, ate breakfast, and gave the morning newspaper a quick review. As Chuck pulls out of his driveway, he glances at his watch: 5:28 A.M.! It's only a 15-minute drive from Chuck's home to his office, where he's the Omaha plant manager for Lerner Bros. Foods. Lerner Bros. manufactures beef and pork products that are sold as private-label brands at between sixty and seventy-five large supermarket chains.

As Chuck begins the drive, his thoughts float back to last night. He and his wife, Anne, had dinner to celebrate their fifteenth wedding anniversary. They had talked about how they met—on a blind date arranged by mutual friends—and how they had both expected the worst. And they talked fondly of old friends that they hadn't heard from in years. The talk last night made Chuck nostalgic. His mind begins to wander. He's thinking about how he ended up in Omaha, running a processing plant, with 450 people working for him.

Chuck graduated from the University of Illinois with a business degree in 1982. His first and only job was with Lerner Bros. He started as an assistant production scheduler in the Chicago plant. During the next dozen years, he moved through a series of jobs—senior production scheduler, production foreman, shift foreman, and assistant plant manager at the Kansas City operation. In 1994, he was promoted to his current job. An abbreviated organizational chart (see Exhibit 2-7) shows where Chuck is on the "Lerner hierarchy" and the people who immediately report to him. Chuck and Anne like Omaha. It's a great place to raise their two kids, and Anne is finally getting the opportunity to use her degree in statistics as an actuary at Mutual of Omaha.

Chuck is in good spirits this morning. Recent productivity reports showed that Omaha had surpassed both the Kansas City and Birmingham plants and now has the highest per employee labor productivity. For 10 months running, Omaha has been the most profitable of the company's seven plants. Yesterday, in a phone call with his boss, Chuck learned that there was a $23,000 check on its way to him—his semiannual performance bonus. In the past, the largest bonus Chuck had ever gotten was for $8,500.

Chuck is determined to get a lot accomplished today. As usual, he has kept his commitments to a

EXHIBIT 2-7
Excerpt from Lerner Bros. Foods' Organizational Chart

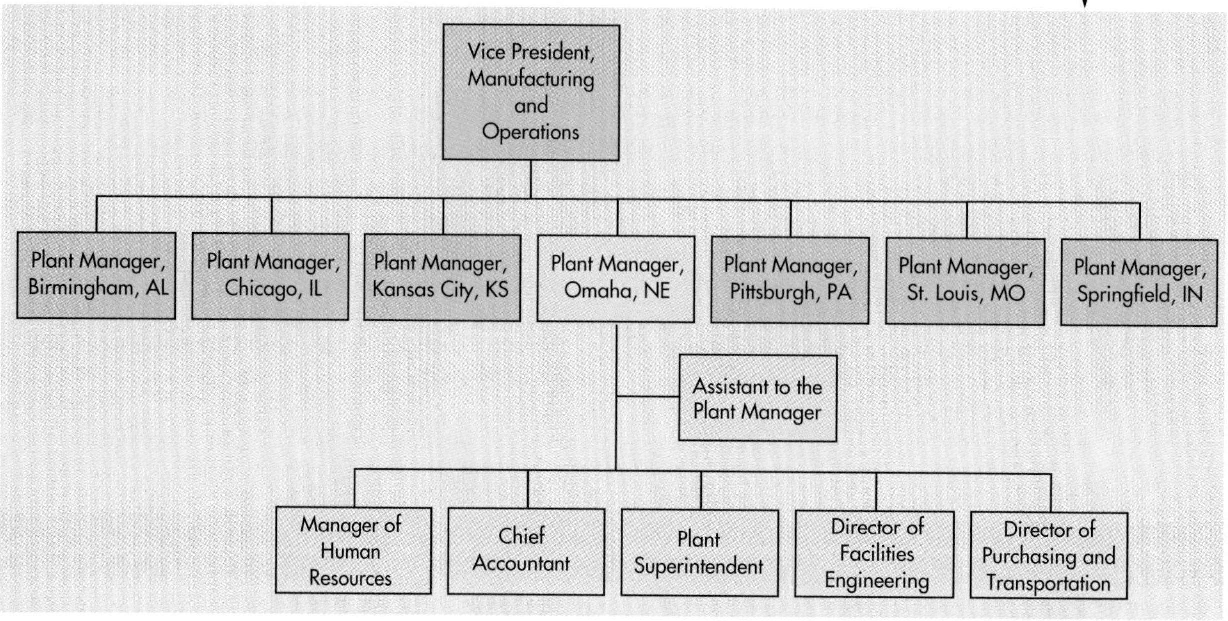

minimum. Except for the 3:30 P.M. staff meeting, his day is open so he can get some important issues resolved. He's going to review the recent internal audit report carefully and rough out his response. He's going to go over the progress on the plant's TQM program. Chuck wants to begin planning next year's capital equipment budget. It's due in less than 2 weeks and he hasn't found time to get to it. Chuck also has other important items on his "to do" list: Talk with the plant superintendent about several employee grievances; write the 10-minute speech he is expected to give at Friday's Chamber of Commerce meeting; and review his assistant's written response to a recent government safety inspection.

Chuck arrives at the plant at 5:45. As he makes his way toward his office, he is intercepted by Beth, the general accounting supervisor. His first reaction: What is she doing here this early in the morning? He soon finds out. Beth tells him that her payroll coordinator didn't show up yesterday. Beth stayed until 10 P.M. last night and got in this morning at 4:30 A.M. to try to meet the payroll deadline. She tells Chuck that there is no way to get this month's payroll data to headquarters on time. Chuck makes a note to talk to the plant's chief accountant and to let his boss, the vice president, know about the problem. Chuck prides himself on keeping his boss informed of any problems. He never likes to have his boss surprised.

Finally, in his office, Chuck notes that his computer is flashing. There are some messages. Reviewing his electronic mail, Chuck finds only one item that needs immediate action. His assistant had worked out next year's vacation schedule for the entire management and professional staff. It must be reviewed and approved. It takes only 10 minutes, but it is another 10 minutes that Chuck hadn't planned on.

The first priority is the capital equipment budget. Chuck uses his computer's spreadsheet program to begin calculating what equipment he needs and what the cost of each item will be. Barely one-third of the way through the project, Chuck gets a call from the superintendent's office. During the night shift, one of the three main conveyor systems went out. Maintenance can overhaul it for a cost of about $45,000. The money isn't in the expense budget. To replace the system will cost about $120,000, and Chuck has already spent this year's capital budget. He arranges a meeting with the superintendent and plant accountant for 10 A.M.

Chuck is back working on the spreadsheet when the plant's transportation director pops into his office. He's having difficulty with rail car scheduling. After 20 minutes of discussion, the two work out a solution. Chuck makes a note to talk with the head of corporate transportation to complain about rail services to his plant. Are the other plants having similar problems? When does the company's rail contract come up again for bidding?

The interruptions in Chuck's day never seem to end. He gets a call from the legal staff at corporate headquarters. They need data to defend the company in a discrimination suit by a former Omaha employee. He transfers the call to his human resources department. Chuck's secretary has a number of letters that need his signature. Suddenly it's 10 o'clock. The accountant and superintendent are outside Chuck's office. The three review the conveyor system problem and rough out some options. They'll present them at this afternoon's staff meeting. It's now 11:15. No sooner does Chuck return to the capital budget than he gets a call from the head of corporate human resources. She spends half an hour updating Chuck on the company's strategy in the forthcoming union negotiations and getting his opinion about issues of particular concern to the Omaha plant. After hanging up, Chuck walks down the hall to his human resource manager's office. They compare notes on the negotiation strategy.

Chuck's secretary reminds him that he's late for his noon lunch with the local head of Omaha's Red Cross drive. He races to his car and arrives 10 minutes late.

By 1:45, Chuck's back at his office. The plant superintendent is waiting for him. The two go over additional modifications in the plant's layout and access areas to meet legal requirements for disabled employees. The meeting runs long because of three phone interruptions. Now it's 3:35. Chuck and the superintendent cross the hall to the conference room. The staff meeting typically runs an hour, but the discussion of labor negotiations and the conveyor system problem prove lengthy. The meeting lasts over 2 hours. As Chuck walks back to his office, he realizes that he has to be getting home. He and Anne are hosting a dinner party tonight for several business and community leaders.

The drive home seems more like an hour than 15 minutes to Chuck. He's frustrated. Twelve hours earlier he was happily anticipating a productive day. With that day now gone, he wonders, "Did I accomplish *anything?*" He knows, of course, that he has, but there was so much more he wanted to get done. Was today unique? Chuck had to admit it wasn't. He starts each day with good intentions and ends each day frustrated. His days are a stream of fragmented activities, with constant unplanned interruptions. Did he plan his day poorly? He isn't sure. He purposely keeps his daily schedule open so that he can communicate with people and be available when they need him. But he wonders if all managers' jobs are characterized by constant interruptions and putting out fires. Will he ever have time for planning and fire prevention?

Questions

1. How do you think Chuck's job compares with the typical manager's job?
2. Evaluate Chuck's activities in terms of a manager's (a) functions, (b) roles, (c) and competencies.
3. Is Chuck *efficient* at his job? Is he *effective?* Explain.
4. What, if anything, could Chuck do to be a better manager?

CASE EXERCISE B
UPS: WHERE EFFICIENCY IS AN OBSESSION

United Parcel Service claims to run "the tightest ship in the shipping business." And they probably do. For decades, UPS has stood as a model of corporate efficiency. It truly "sweats the details." Its management methodically trains its employees to do their jobs as efficiently as possible. For instance, consider the job of a delivery driver—the person who drives that familiar boxy brown truck.

The company's 3,000 industrial engineers have time-studied each driver's route and set standards for each delivery, stop, and pickup. These engineers have recorded every second taken up by stoplights, traffic, detours, doorbells, walkways, stairways, and coffee breaks. Even bathroom stops are put into the standards. All of this information is then fed into company computers to provide detailed time standards for every driver, every day.

To meet their objective of 400 packages to pick up and deliver each day, drivers must follow the engineers' procedures exactly. As they approach a delivery stop, drivers shed their seat belts, toot their horns, and cut their engines. In one seamless motion, they are required to yank up their emergency brakes and push their gearshifts into first. They're now ready for takeoff after their deliveries. The drivers slide to the ground with their clipboards under their right arms and their packages in their left hands. Their keys, teeth up, are in their right hands. They take one look at the package to fix the address in their minds. Then they walk to the customer's door at the prescribed 3 feet per second and knock first to avoid lost seconds searching for the doorbell. After making the delivery, they do the paperwork on the way back to the truck.

UPS's obsession with efficiency has paid off for the company and its employees. UPS is the largest transportation company in the United States. It delivers 10 million packages a day and has annual revenues of $19.6 billion, or twice that of its chief rival, Federal Express. Delivery drivers, who are members of the International Brotherhood of Teamsters union, earn between $40,000 and $50,000 a year and enjoy outstanding benefits and a generous profit-sharing plan.

But UPS is facing challenges to its system. Heated competition is putting pressure on profits, and employees are increasingly complaining about job stress.

In the past, UPS's high labor costs could be offset in part by price increases. But increased competition from nonunion rivals such as Roadway Package Services have made price freezes the norm in the industry. To maintain profitability, UPS has sought to additionally improve efficiency. And employees are increasingly complaining. Some complain about increased workloads. But a bigger problem is the new breed of employee that UPS is hiring—more-skilled and college-educated—to handle delivery jobs that have become more complex. As a result of new technologies introduced by UPS, drivers now have to learn an array of codes and billing systems. More and more packages have special-handling and time-sensitive requirements. These better-educated workers are less tolerant of the company's work rules and controls. So the union has begun to demand limits on driver supervision, workloads, and harassment by managers. In support of these demands, the union claims that UPS employees scored in the ninety-first percentile of U.S. workers for job stress, and that many suffer from anxiety, phobias, and back strain.

UPS's management is considering revising its long-held practices. For instance, the company is using its entire operation in Alabama as a test site for experimenting with giving employees more freedom and responsibility. It is considering eliminating many of its precise measurement practices. And rather than having managers or computers tell the drivers which packages to deliver first and when, the company is allowing the drivers to design their own routes.

Questions

1. Do you think UPS's detailed training and control of employees is inappropriate in the 1990s? Explain your position.
2. Why do you think so few organizations today program employee behavior the way UPS has done?
3. Both the company and the union call UPS drivers "the highest-paid truck drivers in the United States." Doesn't money compensate these drivers for the stress they experience? Explain your position.
4. "If it ain't broke, don't fix it." Should this phrase apply to UPS? Explain.

Source: Based on D. Machalaba, "UPS Gets Deliveries Done by Driving Its Workers," *Wall Street Journal,* April 22, 1986, p. 1; R. Frank, "As UPS Tries to Deliver More to Its Customers, Labor Problems Grow," *Wall Street Journal,* May 23, 1994, p. A1; and R. Frank, "Efficient UPS Tries to Increase Efficiency," *Wall Street Journal,* May 24, 1995, p. B1.

Evaluating the Effectiveness of U.S. Colleges

Every year, *U.S. News & World Report* publishes rankings of U.S. colleges.* These rankings have become well known, and college administrators have begun to pay attention to the results and to the criteria that the magazine uses in establishing the rankings.

The most recent rankings were calculated by asking college presidents, deans, and admissions directors to rate other colleges in their same category (i.e., national universities, national liberal arts colleges, regional universities, regional liberal arts colleges, specialized institutions) on six attributes:

1. Academic reputation. Respondents were asked to rank each institution from a list (for example, 204 national universities were listed) into one of four quartiles based on its reputation.
2. Student selectivity. Determined by applicant acceptance rates, percentage of those accepted who actually enrolled, enrollees' high school class standings, and national aptitude test scores.
3. Faculty resources. Based on student-faculty ratio, percent of full-time faculty with doctorates, percent of part-time faculty, faculty salaries, and class size data.
4. Financial resources. Total expenditures for its education program divided by number of students enrolled.
5. Graduation rates. Average percentage of students who graduated within 6 years of the year in which they enrolled.
6. Alumni satisfaction. Average percentage of a school's living alumni who made a donation to the college during the previous 2 years.

Data for each of the six attributes were converted into percentiles. The highest raw score for any attribute or subattribute was valued at 100 percent. Next, all the other scores were taken as a percentage of that top score and totaled. The six attributes for each institution were then numerically ranked in ascending order and weighted: alumni satisfaction (5 percent), graduation rates (10 percent), financial resources (15 percent), faculty resources (20 percent), and student selectivity and academic reputation (25 percent each). The weighted numbered ranks for each institution were totaled and compared with the weighted totals for all the others in its category. The highest-ranking institution in a given category was the one with the lowest total. Its overall score was converted into a percentile of 100. The totals for the other institutions in the catagory were then translated into a percent of the top score.

The above procedure, in 1994, determined that the top ten rated national universities were Harvard (100.0), Princeton (99.6), Yale (99.4), Massachusetts Institute of Technology (99.1), California Institute of Technology (98.7); Stanford (97.6), Duke (97.5), Dartmouth (96.2), University of Chicago (95.2), and Cornell (94.9).

Class members should form into groups of three to five and answer the following questions.

1. What stakeholders are these rankings legitimizing?
2. What important stakeholders, if any, do you think are being excluded?
3. What is your opinion of the criteria that *U.S. News* has chosen?
4. How might a particular institution improve each of these rankings?
5. What does this exercise tell you about measuring organizational effectiveness?

*See, for example, "America's Best Colleges," *U.S. News & World Report*, September, 1995, pp. 61–67.

NOTES

1. Cited in "Historical Trends, Current Uncertainties," *Monthly Labor Review,* November 1993, p. 8.
2. This calculation is derived as follows. Approximately 6 percent of the total U.S. population (15 million out of 250 million) are managers. The same percentage would yield 38 million managers in Europe, 160 million in Asia, 9 million in the Pacific region, 30 million in Africa, 14 million in South America, 1.5 million in Canada; and 4.5 million in Central America. Given that U.S. organizations may be "overmanaged," I used a conservative estimate of 3 percent of a country or region's population as an estimate of the managerial population.
3. J. J. Macionis, *Sociology,* 5th ed. (Englewood Cliffs, N. J.: Prentice Hall, 1995), p. 188.
4. See O. E. Williamson, *Markets and Hierarchies: Analysis and Antitrust Implications* (New York: Free Press, 1975); and G. Miller, *Managerial Dilemmas* (London: Cambridge Press, 1992).
5. See B. M. Staw, "Organizational Behavior: A Review and Reformulation of the Field's Outcome Variables," in M. R. Rosenzweig and L. W. Porter, eds., *Annual Review of Psychology,* vol. 35 (Palo Alto, Calif.: Annual Reviews, 1984), pp. 627–66.
6. See, for instance, H. Koontz, ed., *Toward a Unified Theory of Management* (New York: McGraw-Hill, 1964); and C. P. Hales, "What Do Managers Do? A Critical Review of the Evidence," *Journal of Management Studies,* January 1986, pp. 88–115.
7. H. Fayol, *Industrial and General Administration* (Paris: Dunod, 1916).
8. See, for instance, S. P. Robbins and M. K. Coulter, *Management,* 5th ed. (Upper Saddle River, N. J.: Prentice Hall, 1996); J. R. Schermerhorn Jr., *Management for Productivity,* 5th ed. (New York: John Wiley, 1996); and J. A. F. Stoner, R. E. Freeman, and D. R. Gilbert Jr., *Management,* 6th ed. (Englewood Cliffs, N. J.: Prentice Hall, 1995).
9. H. Mintzberg, *The Nature of Managerial Work* (New York: Harper & Row, 1973).
10. The first three were originally proposed in R. L. Katz, "Skills of an Effective Administrator," *Harvard Business Review,* September–October 1974, pp. 90–102. The fourth was added by C. M. Pavett and A. W. Lau, "Managerial Work: The Influence of Hierarchical Level and Functional Specialty," *Academy of Management Journal,* March 1983, pp. 170–77.
11. F. Luthans, R. M. Hodgetts, and S. A. Rosenkrantz, *Real Managers* (Cambridge, Mass.: Ballinger Publishing, 1988); and D. A. Gioia and C. O. Longnecker, "Delving into the Dark Side: The Politics of Executive Appraisal," *Organizational Dynamics,* Winter 1994, pp. 47–58.
12. J. J. Morse and F. R. Wagner, "Measuring the Process of Managerial Effectiveness," *Academy of Management Journal,* March 1978, pp. 23–35.
13. "Management Charter Initiative Issues Competence Standards," *Personnel Management,* October 1990, p. 17; "MCI Launches Standards for First Two Levels," *Personnel Management,* November 1990, p. 13; and L. Carrington, "Competent to Manage?" *International Management,* September 1994, p. 17.
14. See, for example, H. A. Simon, *Administrative Behavior* (New York: Macmillan, 1945); E. F. Harrison, *The Managerial Decision-Making Process,* 4th ed. (Boston: Houghton Mifflin, 1995); and M. H. Bazerman, *Judgment in Managerial Decision Making,* 3rd ed. (New York: John Wiley, 1994).
15. H. A. Simon, *The New Science of Management Decision* (New York: Harper & Row, 1960), p. 1.
16. See, for example, K. Lewin, *Field Theory in Social Science* (New York: Harper & Row, 1951); N. Margulies and J. Wallace, *Organizational Change: Techniques and Applications* (Glenview, Ill.: Scott, Foresman, 1973); and W. L. French and C. H. Bell Jr., *Organization Development,* 4th ed. (Englewood Cliffs, N. J.: Prentice Hall, 1990).
17. See, for example, M. Walton, *The Deming Management Method* (New York: Putnam/Perigee, 1986).
18. M. Hammer and J. Champy, *Reengineering the Corporation: A Manifesto for Business Revolution* (New York: HarperBusiness, 1993).
18. P. F. Drucker, *The Effective Executive* (New York: Harper & Row, 1967).
19. L. Smith, "Burned-Out Bosses," *Fortune,* July 25, 1994, p. 44.
20. T. Peters, *Thriving on Chaos: Handbook for a Management Revolution* (New York: Knopf, 1988). See also J. Huey, "Managing in the Midst of Chaos," *Fortune,* April 5, 1993, pp. 38–48.
21. See, for instance, C. D. Orth, H. E. Wilkinson, and R. C. Benfari, "The Manager's Role as Coach and Mentor," *Organizational Dynamics,* Spring 1987, pp. 66–74; and R. D. Evered and J. C. Selman, "Coaching and the Art of Management," *Organizational Dynamics,* Autumn 1989, pp. 16–31.
22. See, for example, J. Weber, "Letting Go Is Hard to Do," *Business Week,* November 1, 1993, pp. 218–19.
23. See, for example, J. Stack, *The Great Game of Business* (New York: Doubleday, 1992); C. Rosen, "Owning Up to Responsibility: Springfield ReManufacturing Corporation," *Hemispheres,* February 1995, pp. 33–37; and S. Gruner, "The Employee-Run-Budget Work Sheet," *INC.,* February 1995, pp. 81–83.
24. M. Keeley, "Impartiality and Participant-Interest Theories of Organizational Effectiveness," *Administrative Science Quarterly,* March 1984, pp. 1–25.
25. See T. Donaldson and L. E. Preston, "The Stakeholder Theory of the Corporation: Concepts, Evidence, and Implications," *Academy of Management Review,* January 1995, pp. 65–91.
26. N. C. Roberts and P. J. King, "The Stakeholder Audit Goes Public," *Organizational Dynamics,* Winter 1989, pp. 63–79.
27. R. R. Rehder, "Is Saturn Competitive?" *Business Horizons,* March–April 1994, pp. 7–15.

28. See M. W. Meyer and V. Gupta, "The Performance Paradox," in B. M. Staw and L. L. Cummings, *Research in Organizational Behavior,* vol. 16 (Greenwich, Conn.: JAI Press, 1994), pp. 309–69.
29. Ibid., p. 322.
30. Cited in T. Moore, "Make-or-Break Time for General Motors," *Fortune,* February 15, 1988, p. 35.
31. Cited in B. Dumaine, "Why Do We Work?," *Fortune,* December 26, 1994, p. 202.
32. B. O'Reilly, "The New Deal: What Companies and Employees Owe One Another," *Fortune,* June 13, 1994, pp. 44–52; and H. Lancaster, "A New Social Contract to Benefit Employer and Employee," *Wall Street Journal,* November 29, 1994, p. B1.
33. From "Richard Branson," *ABC News Business World,* November 22, 1992.
34. S. Fink, "Dow Corning's Moral Evasions," *New York Times,* February 16, 1992, p. F13.
35. R. H. Miles, *Coffin Nails and Corporate Strategies* (Englewood Cliffs, N. J.: Prentice Hall, 1982).
36. C. K. Warriner, "The Problem of Organizational Purpose," *Sociological Quarterly,* Spring 1965, pp. 139–46.

PART TWO: Decision and Monitoring Systems

CHAPTER 3
MAKING DECISIONS

The decision not to decide is still a decision. It's a decision to maintain the status quo.
- Anonymous

LEARNING OBJECTIVES

After studying this chapter, you should be able to:

1. Explain the six-step rational decision-making model and its assumptions
2. Contrast risk with uncertainty
3. Describe three methods for stimulating individual creativity
4. Identify and describe popular quantitative techniques for improving decision making
5. Contrast the conditions favoring individual decisions with those favoring groups
6. Describe actions of the boundedly rational decision maker
7. Identify four decision-making styles
8. Explain how managers can improve their decision making

If there were a Hall of Fame for poor decisions, Andrew Grove (see photo) would easily qualify for induction on the basis of several blunders he and his executive group made in November and December of 1994.[1]

Grove is CEO of Intel Corporation, the world's largest computer chip maker. In late 1993, Intel introduced the powerful Pentium chip. Within a year, these chips had become the brains in more than 4 million personal computers.

In late October 1994, a professor in Virginia discovered a flaw in the Pentium chip. In division problems involving very large numbers, the solution is incorrect. When a trade publication wrote an article on the chip's flaw on November 7, Intel admitted that it had found the flaw 4 months earlier and had corrected it. A small but vocal group of customers and computer industry advocates were not happy with that response. They wanted Intel to replace all the flawed chips. Intel officials approached the issue the way they attacked all large challenges—as an engineering problem. They broke it down into smaller parts, analyzed it rationally, and came to a conclusion. The company announced on November 14 that it had decided it would refuse to guarantee replacement chips for all customers. It would replace faulty Pentium chips, but only if computer owners could demonstrate that they really needed an extra margin of accuracy. The company's position was that the flaw was minor. Most users would encounter an inaccurate answer just once in 27,000 years. Intel's management considered the issue closed.

Then, on December 12, Intel got hit broadside. IBM announced that its own researchers had determined that the Pentium flaw was much more serious than Intel was acknowledging. They said that an average spreadsheet user could experience an error as often as every 24 days. So, effective immediately, IBM was suspending shipments of its personal computers containing the Pentium chip.

IBM's public announcement unleashed a floodgate of criticism. Tens of thousands of people who had bought computers with the Pentium chip were now angry. They wanted replacements regardless of whether they did complex calculations. Intel's reputation was falling fast, and so was its stock. The IBM announcement alone knocked Intel's stock price down by 6.5 percent. Andrew Grove and his senior executive group convened around-the-clock meetings to analyze the problem. They decided to hold their ground. They argued that IBM's "reaction is unwarranted" and repeated their position that the flaw was minor. Grove insisted that the odds were 9 billion to 1 against the Pentium chips' causing a mathematical error. But their stance only escalated criticism. Finally, on December 21, 1994, Intel abruptly changed course and announced that it would replace all flawed Pentium chips for free, no questions asked. The cost to the company to replace all the flawed chips was estimated at between $300 and $400 million. More important, however, was the damage to the company's reputation and the cost of rebuilding public confidence in its products.

How could Grove and his executives have made such blunders? The answer is that Grove responded to the problem like the engineer he is. He treated the flaw as a technical problem, not a consumer problem. From a technical standpoint, logic and reason would argue that there was no need to replace all flawed chips since the flaw affected so few users. What Grove failed to grasp was that the people who bought the flawed chip felt taken advantage of. They had paid for a perfect chip and didn't get one. Grove's position came across as arrogant and uncaring. In this instance, the engineering mentality that Grove so successfully brought to technical problems did him in. As a former Intel vice president concluded, "Andy's analytical approach is his tremendous strength—and at times a weakness. Not everything with human beings is done with the accuracy of electrons."[2]

Making decisions is a critical element of organizational life. In this chapter, we focus on two different approaches to understanding decision making. First we describe how decisions *should* be made. Then, we review a large body of evidence to show you how decisions actually *are* made in organizations. Finally, we present some specific suggestions on how managers can improve their decision-making effectiveness.

HOW SHOULD DECISIONS BE MADE?

There is an irony in the Intel incident we just described. Andrew Grove made his decision the way managers are supposed to. He used a logical and analytical approach to solving his problem. Unfortunately, his analysis failed to identify the problem correctly. Grove's problem was not a chip with a minor and insignificant flaw. His problem was customers who were uncertain whether their computers would do reliable computations. Because he incorrectly defined the issue, he came up with the right solution to the wrong problem. As you will see, good decision making relies as much on proper problem selection as on choosing the right alternative.

Good decision making relies as much on proper problem selection as on choosing the right alternative.

The Rational Decision-Making Process

The optimizing decision maker is **rational.** That is, he or she makes consistent, value-maximizing choices within specified constraints.[3] These choices are made following a six-step model.[4] Moreover, specific assumptions underlie this model.[5]

The Rational Model The six steps in the rational decision-making model are listed in Exhibit 3-1. The model begins by *defining the problem.* A problem exists when there is a discrepancy between an existing and a desired state of affairs.[6] For Andrew Grove at Intel, a problem surfaced when he became aware that there were flaws in the Pentium chip. And, as the Intel example illustrated, the definition of the problem is not always self-evident.[7] Many poor decisions can be traced to the decision maker's overlooking a problem or defining the wrong problem.

Once a decision maker has defined the problem, he or she needs to *identify the decision criteria* that will be important in solving the problem. In this step, the decision maker is determining what is relevant in making the decision. This step brings the decision maker's interests, values, and personal preferences into the process. Identifying criteria is important because what one person thinks is relevant another may not. Also keep in mind that any factors not identified in this step are considered as irrelevant to the decision maker.

The criteria identified are rarely all equal in importance. So the third step requires that the decision maker *weight the previously identified criteria* in order to give them correct priority in the decision.

The fourth step requires the decision maker to *generate possible alternatives* that could succeed in resolving the problem. No attempt is made in this step to appraise these alternatives, only to list them.

Once the alternatives have been generated, the decision maker must critically analyze and evaluate each one. This is done by *rating each alternative on each criterion.* The strengths and weaknesses of each alternative become evident as they are compared with the criteria and weights established in the second and third steps.

The final step in this model requires *computing the optimal decision.* How is this done? By using something called "expected value," which we will describe in the next section. In essence, it requires the decision maker to multiply the expected effectiveness of each choice times the weighting of each criterion times the rating of each criterion for each alternative. The alternative with the highest expected value then becomes the optimal or optimizing choice.

We can use this six-step model to describe how someone *should* make a decision. For instance, take the college-selection decision as an example. If you used the rational model, the process would look something like this. Your graduation from high school creates a problem. What do you do *now?* Let's assume that you've chosen to attend college (versus other, noncollege options). So you begin listing the criteria that will be relevant in your decision. These might include factors such as availability of financial aid, school's reputation, annual cost, degree offerings, geographical location, quality of social life, and the like. After listing these criteria, you weight them in order to prioritize their importance. For instance, using a 1 to 10 scale (with 10 being most important), you might determine that availability of financial aid rates a 10, while quality of social life rates 4. In other words, financial aid is considered 2.5 times as important as social life in your decision. After weighting your criteria, you list all the viable colleges that could possibly be in your decision set. For some people, this list might include

EXHIBIT 3-1
The Six-Step Rational Decision-Making Model

1. Define the problem
2. Identify decision criteria
3. Weight the criteria
4. Generate alternatives
5. Rate each alternative on each criterion
6. Compute the optimal decision

dozens of colleges. Then you need to evaluate each of these college options. The strengths and weaknesses of each alternative become evident when they are compared against the criteria and weights previously established. Finally, if you are following the rational decision model, you will choose the college that scored the highest expected value. And you will have made an optimal decision.

Assumptions of the Model The rational decision-making model we just described contains six assumptions:

1. *Problem clarity.* The problem is clear and unambiguous. The decision maker is assumed to have complete information regarding the decision situation.
2. *Known options.* The decision maker can identify all the relevant criteria and can list all the viable alternatives. Further, the decision maker is aware of all the possible consequences of each alternative.
3. *Clear preferences.* The criteria and alternatives can be ranked and weighted to reflect their importance.
4. *Constant preferences.* The specific decision criteria are constant, and the weights assigned to them are stable over time.
5. *No time or cost constraints.* The rational decision maker can obtain full information about criteria and alternatives because it is assumed that there are no time or cost constraints.
6. *Maximum payoff.* The rational decision maker will choose the alternative that yields the highest perceived value.

Rationality is enhanced by understanding uncertainty and risk, creative problem solving, and quantitative analysis. The following sections review those topics.

Uncertainty and Risk

One of the more challenging tasks facing a decision maker is analyzing alternatives. This analysis is done under one of three sets of conditions. In some cases, decisions are made under the conditions of **certainty.** This means that the decision maker knows in advance the outcome of the decision. For instance, the treasurer of Alcoa recently received $100 million from the sale of bonds but didn't need the money for 6 months. He invested it in 6-month Treasury bills that paid 5.20 percent annual interest. The treasurer was *certain* that when the T-bills matured he would receive $102.6 million. Unfortunately, few decisions are made under conditions of certainty.

A far more typical situation is one of **risk.** By risk, we mean those conditions in which the decision maker is able to estimate the likelihood of alternatives or outcomes. This ability to assign probabilities may be the result of personal experience or secondary information. One of the more visible illustrations of dealing with risk conditions are military leaders who have to make decisions during times of war. For instance, during the Persian Gulf War, General Schwarzkopf had to decide when to begin the ground assault to free Kuwait. Schwarzkopf and his aides calculated probabilities for various scenarios and used those calculations in making the final decision.

A rational approach to evaluating alternatives under risk conditions is the use of expected value. **Expected value** is a concept that allows decision makers to place a monetary value on the positive and negative consequences likely to result from the selection of a particular alternative. It equals the summation of various possible outcomes multiplied by the benefit or cost from each outcome. If you are thinking about opening a small retail business and have narrowed your alternatives down to two locations, you can use expected value to help you make your final choice. As shown in Exhibit 3-2, assume you've calculated two possible outcomes for each store location. You can ascertain that the expected value of locating your store in Palm Beach is $17,500, and in Ft. Lauderdale it is $20,000. On the basis of expected value analysis alone, locating in Ft. Lauderdale is your better choice.

The most difficult condition to make decisions under is **uncertainty.** In this situation, decision makers don't have enough information to be clear about alternatives or to estimate their risk. So what do they do? They rely on their intuition or creativity. Many decisions currently being made in the telecommunications industry fall into this category. For instance, Bert Roberts, head of MCI Communications, has boldly committed his company to spending up to $20 billion through the year 2000 in an attempt to propel MCI into direct competition in nearly every aspect of his industry—from local phone service to cable to wireless communications to computer messaging.[8] Roberts is gambling that he can successfully take on AT&T, the seven Baby Bells, and powerful cable operators such as TeleCommunications Inc.

Creativity

The rational decision maker needs **creativity:** that is, the ability to combine ideas in a unique way or to make unusual associations between ideas.[9] Why is this ability so important? Creativity allows a decision maker to more fully appraise and understand a problem and to see problems others can't see. However, creativity's most obvious value is in helping the decision maker identify all viable alternatives.

Creative Potential Most people have unused creative potential that they can call upon when confronted with a decision-making problem. But to unleash that potential, they have to get out of the psychological ruts most of us get into and learn how to think about a problem in divergent ways.

Most people have unused creative potential that they can call upon when confronted with a decision-making problem.

We can start with the obvious. People differ in their inherent creativity. Einstein, Edison, Picasso, and Mozart were individuals of exceptional creativity. By definition, however, exceptional creativity is scarce. A study of lifetime creativity of 461 men and women found that fewer than 1 percent were exceptionally creative.[10] But 10 percent were highly creative, and about 60 percent were somewhat creative. This result suggests that most of us have creative potential, if we can learn to unleash it.

Methods for Stimulating Individual Creativity Sometimes the simplest action can be very powerful. That seems to be true with stimulating creativity. Evidence indicates that the mere action of instructing someone to "be creative" and to avoid obvious approaches to a problem results in unique ideas.[11] This *direct instruction* method is based on evidence that people tend to accept obvious solu-

EXHIBIT 3-2
Expected Value of Two Retail Locations

Alternative	Possible Outcome	Probability	Expected Value
Ft. Lauderdale	$40,000 profit	0.6	$24,000
	10,000 loss	0.4	(4,000)
			$20,000
Palm Beach	$25,000 profit	0.5	$12,500
	10,000 profit	0.5	5,000
			$17,500

tions, and this tendency prevents them from performing up to their capabilities. So merely hearing or telling yourself that unique alternatives are sought encourages you to be creative and should lead to an increase in unique alternatives.

Another technique is *attribute listing.*[12] In attribute listing, the decision maker isolates the major characteristics of traditional alternatives. Each major attribute of the alternative is then considered in turn and is changed in every conceivable way. No ideas are rejected, no matter how ridiculous they may seem. Once this extensive list is completed, the constraints of the problem are imposed in order to eliminate all but the viable alternatives.

Creativity can also be stimulated by practicing zigzag, or *lateral, thinking.*[13] This is a replacement for the more traditional vertical thinking, in which each step in the process follows the previous step in an unbroken sequence. Vertical thinking is often seen as rational thinking because it must be correct at every step and it deals only with what is relevant. With lateral thinking, individuals emphasize thinking sideways: not developing a pattern but restructuring a pattern. Lateral thinking is not sequential. For example, you could tackle a problem from the solution end rather than from the starting point; then you can backtrack to various beginning states. Lateral thinking doesn't have to be correct at each step. In fact, in some cases, it may be necessary to pass through a "wrong" area in order to reach a position from which a correct path may be visible. Finally, lateral thinking is not restricted to relevant information. It deliberately uses random or irrelevant information to bring about a new way of looking at the problem.

Quantitative Analysis

Students of management typically spend considerable time learning quantitative decision techniques in courses with titles such as "Operations Research," "Decision Sciences," and "Quantitative Methods." These courses are meant to help students develop rational, analytical tools for objectively appraising decision alternatives. In this section, we'll briefly introduce the more popular of these quantitative techniques. Our objective here is simply to make you aware of what they are and what they can generally do, so our discussion will be descriptive rather than technical.

IN THE NEWS

Japan's Struggle to Be Creative

ALTHOUGH JAPANESE COMPANIES HAVE EXCELLED AT IMPROVING EXISTING PRODUCTS AND METHODS, they are rarely innovators. The explanation can be traced to the Japanese culture. The high value that the Japanese place on respect for authority and the preference for consensus over open debate are cultural artifacts that contribute to creating individuals who have difficulty thinking creatively. Similarly, the Japanese education system's emphasis on structure, facts over ideas, and memorization tend to limit individual creativity.

Japanese executives have recently recognized that their companies' growth depends on how effectively they can master the tasks of inventing new products, new markets, and even whole new businesses. Doing so is going to take more independent thinking and organizational improvisation than has existed in the past.

Many companies are introducing creativity training for their managers. For example, Omron Corp., a maker of electronic controls, has started a cram school, in which midlevel managers try to think and plan as if they were nineteenth-century revolutionary warlords, private detectives, or Formula One race car drivers, all in the interest of becoming more creative. Fuji Film asks senior managers to study such offbeat topics as the history of Venice or the sociology of apes. Managers at Shiseido, Japan's largest cosmetic maker, participate in a program of multiple seminars, each of which lasts 3 or 4 days. In these seminars, participants engage in an assortment of unusual exercises designed to stimulate creativity, such as studying the design and function of goldfish, trying to balance eggs on their ends, and analyzing the motions and contortions of dancers to better understand body language.

Source: Based on E. Thornton, "Japan's Struggle to Be Creative," *Fortune,* April 19, 1993, pp. 129–34.

Break-Even Analysis How many units of a product must an organization sell in order to break even—that is, to have neither profit nor loss? A decision maker might want to know the minimum number of units that must be sold to achieve her profit objective or whether a current product should continue to be sold or be dropped from the organization's product line. **Break-even analysis** is a widely used financial decision-making technique that enables decision makers to determine whether a particular sales volume will result in losses or profits.[14]

Break-even analysis is a simplistic formulation, yet it is valuable to decision makers because it points out the relationship between revenues, costs, and profits. To compute the break-even point *(BE),* the decision maker needs to know the unit price of the product being sold *(P),* the variable cost per unit *(VC),* and total fixed costs *(TFC).*

An organization breaks even when its total revenue is just enough to equal its total costs. But total costs has two parts: a fixed component and a variable component. *Fixed costs* are expenses that do not change, regardless of volume. Examples include insurance premiums and property taxes. Fixed costs, of course, are fixed only in the short term because, in the long run, commitments terminate and thus are subject to variation. *Variable costs* change in proportion to output and include raw materials, labor costs, and energy costs.

The break-even point can be computed graphically or by using the following formula:

$$BE = \frac{TFC}{P - VC}$$

This formula tells us that (1) total revenue will equal total cost when we sell enough units at a price that covers all variable unit costs and (2) the difference between price and variable costs, when multiplied by the number of units sold, equals the fixed costs.

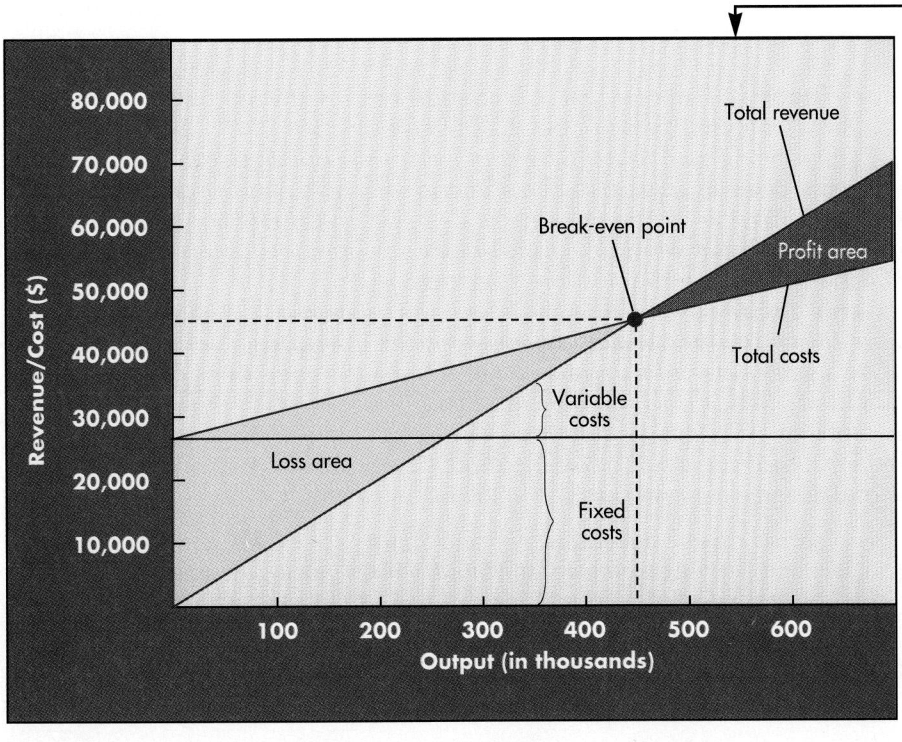

EXHIBIT 3-3
Dave's Copy Center Break-Even Analysis

For example, assume that Dave's Copy Center charges 10 cents per photocopy. If fixed costs are $27,000 a year and variable costs are 4 cents per copy, Dave can compute his break-even point as follows: $27,000/($0.10 – $0.04) = 450,000 copies, or when annual revenues are $45,000. This same relationship is shown graphically in Exhibit 3-3.

Return on Investment Another financial decision tool is **return on investment** (ROI). Among business firms, ROI is a highly popular single criterion by which to measure productivity of assets. By computing profits as a percentage of capital invested, an organization can determine how well the investment is being utilized to generate profits. Thus, ROI can be used to compare firms within industries and between industries.

For example, Checkpoint Systems and Code Alarm are two companies that are both in the electronic security control systems business. In one recent year, Checkpoint had net profits of $1.62 million, while Code Alarm's net profits were a bit lower at $1.54 million. But in terms of return on investment, Code Alarm was much more impressive. Code Alarm's ROI was 6.4 percent against Checkpoint Systems' 1.8 percent.[15] Checkpoint Systems required considerably more investment than did Code Alarm to generate similar profits. As this example illustrates, ROI directs attention away from absolute profits and focuses on how efficient a company is in using its assets.

Marginal Analysis The concept of marginal, or incremental, analysis helps decision makers optimize returns or minimize costs. **Marginal analysis** deals with the additional cost in a particular decision rather than the average cost. For example, Four Seasons Dry Cleaning is a commercial dry cleaner that services hospitals and hotels. Management had the opportunity to take on a new account that would generate approximately $3,000 a month in new business. Using marginal analysis, the operations manager did *not* look at the total revenue and the total cost that would result from the new account. Rather, she assessed what *additional* revenue would be generated by this particular account and what *additional* costs. In this specific case, she turned down the new business because the incremental revenues were less than the incremental costs, and thus would reduce her total profits.

Game Theory Game theory is currently one of the hottest techniques in quantitative analysis. Its major developers won the 1994 Nobel Prize in economics. And it is being used to help decision makers bid on contracts, negotiate labor agreements, develop expansion plans, and make a host of other decisions. For instance, executives at Pacific Telesis recently relied on game theory experts to help the company submit winning bids for wireless communications rights auctioned off by the Federal Communications Commission.[16]

Game theory uses mathematical models to analyze the outcomes that will emerge in multiparty decision-making contexts if all parties act rationally.[17] To analyze a game, the decision maker outlines specific conditions that define how decisions are to be made and then attaches outcome probabilities to every possible combination of player response. The actual analysis focuses on predicting whether an agreement will be reached and, if one is reached, what the specific nature of that agreement will be. The following illustrates how game theory works.

> Say you have two competitors, Ace and Smith. Ace expects Smith to enter the market and is trying to understand Smith's likely pricing strategy. To do so, Ace uses something called a "payoff matrix" (see Exhibit 3-4). Each quadrant in the matrix contains the "payoffs"—or financial impact—to each player for each possible strategy. If both players maintain prices at current levels, they will both be better off: Ace will earn $100 million, and Smith will earn $60 million (quadrant A).

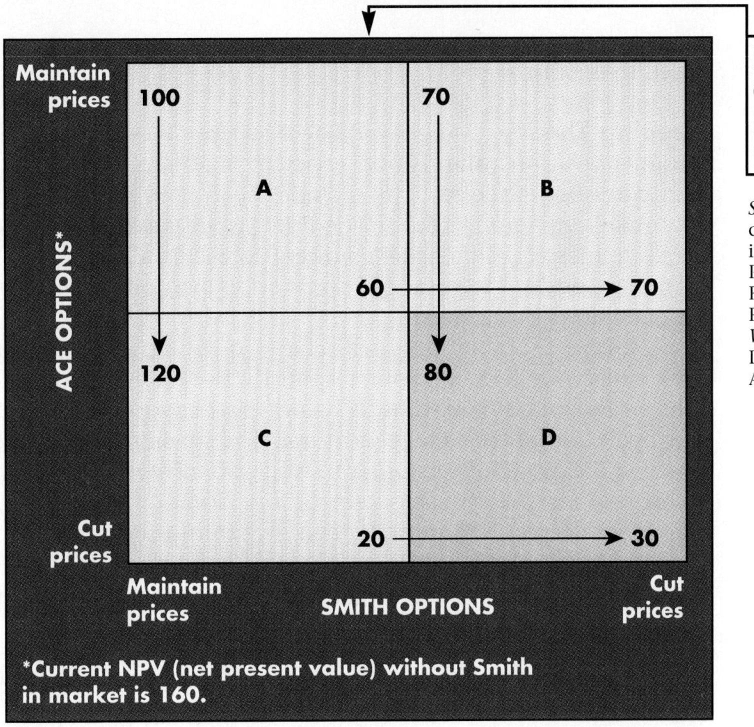

EXHIBIT 3-4
Game Theory Payoff Matrix (in millions of NPV)

Source: McKinsey & Co. Reproduced in F. W. Barnett, "Making Game Theory Work in Practice," *Wall Street Journal,* February 13, 1995, p. A14. Reprinted by permission of the *Wall Street Journal,* © 1995, Dow Jones & Company, Inc. All rights reserved worldwide.

Unfortunately for both Ace and Smith, however, they have perverse incentives to cut prices.

Ace calculates that if he maintains prices, Smith will cut prices to increase earning to $70 million from $60 million. (See arrow moving from quadrant A to quadrant B.) Smith makes a similar calculation that if she maintains prices, Ace will cut. The logic eventually drives them both to quadrant D, with both cutting prices and both earning lower returns than they would with current prices in place. This "equilibrium" is unattractive for both parties. If each party perceives this, then there is some prospect that each will separately determine to try to compete largely on other factors, such as product features, service levels, sales force deployment, or advertising.[18]

Linear Programming **Linear programming** uses graphical or algebraic techniques to optimally solve resource allocation dilemmas. It requires competition between two or more activities for limited resources and assumes a linear relationship in the problem and the objective. For example, if we assume that spending depends on income, then a linear relationship exists when we say that if income goes up 10 percent, spending also increases by 10 percent. Linear programming is especially useful when input data can be quantified and objectives are subject to definite measurement.[19] What kind of problems would these be? Selecting transportation routes that minimize shipping costs, allocating a limited advertising budget among various product brands, making the optimum assignment of personnel among projects, and determining how much of each product to make with a limited number of resources are a few.

For example, assume that an automobile manufacturer that makes both cars and trucks seeks to maximize its profits. Also assume that we know the profit generated by each truck or car produced. If the manufacturer has scarce resources—for example, a given production space and a given number of available labor-hours—and if resources expended to manufacture trucks are at the expense of resources expended to manufacture cars, we could utilize linear programming techniques to determine how many cars and how many trucks should be produced to maximize profit.

Queuing Theory Whenever a decision involves balancing the cost of having a waiting line against the cost of service to maintain that line, it can be made easier with **queuing theory.** This includes such common situations as determining how many gas pumps are needed at gas stations, tellers at bank windows, or check-in lines at airline ticket counters. In each situation, decision makers want to minimize cost by having as few stations open as possible, yet not so few as to test the patience of customers.

A simple example may help clarify queuing theory. Assume that you are a bank supervisor. One of your responsibilities is assigning tellers. You have five teller windows, but you want to know whether you can get by with only one window open during an average morning. You consider 12 minutes to be the longest you would expect any customer to wait patiently in line. If it takes 4 minutes, on average, to serve each customer, the line should not be permitted to get longer than three deep (12 minutes divided by 4 minutes per customer = 3 customers). If you know from past experience that during the morning people arrive at the average rate of two per minute, you can calculate the probability *(P)* that the line will become longer than any number *(n)* of customers as follows:

$$P_n = (1 - \text{arrival rate/service rate}) \times (\text{arrival rate/service rate})^n$$

where n = 3 customers; arrival rate = 2 per minute, and service rate = 4 minutes per customer. Putting these numbers into the above formula generates the following:

$$P_3 = (1 - 2/4) \times (2/4)^3 = (1/2)\ (8/64) = 8/128 = 0.0625$$

What does a P_3 of 0.0625 mean? It tells you that the likelihood of having more than three customers in line during the morning is one chance in 16. Are you willing to live with four or more customers in line 6 percent of the time? If so, keeping one teller window open will be enough. If not, you'll need to add windows and assign additional personnel to staff them.

WHO SHOULD MAKE DECISIONS?

We're not interested in *all* decision making. Our focus is on decisions in *organizations.* Therefore, we need to address the issue of who makes decisions. First, we look at individuals versus groups to learn when one is preferable. Then we look at level in the organization. When should decisions be made by top managers, middle managers, first-level supervisors, or the operating employees themselves?

The Individual versus Groups

The belief—characterized by juries—that two heads are better than one has long been accepted as a basic component of North American and many countries' legal systems. This belief has expanded to the point that, today, many decisions in organizations are made by groups (sometimes also called *teams* or *committees*). But groups aren't always preferable to individuals as decision makers. Let's review the strengths of each.[20]

Strengths of Individual Decision Making A major plus with individual decision making is *speed.* An individual doesn't have to convene a meeting and spend time discussing various alternatives. So when a decision is needed quickly, individuals have the advantage. Individual decisions also have *clear accountability.*

You know who made the decision and, therefore, who is responsible for the decision's outcome. Accountability is more ambiguous with group decisions. A third strength of individual decisions is that they tend to convey *consistent values.* Group decisions can suffer from intragroup power struggles. This disadvantage is best illustrated by decisions of the U.S. Congress. Decisions can vary by as much as 180 degrees from one session to the next, reflecting the makeup of members and their ability to influence their peers on any specific issue. Individuals are not perfectly consistent in their decision making, but they do tend to be more consistent than groups.

Strengths of Group Decision Making Groups generate *more complete information and knowledge.* By aggregating the resources of several individuals, groups bring more input into the decision process. In addition to more input, groups can bring heterogeneity to the decision process. They offer *increased diversity of views.* This opens up the opportunity for more approaches and alternatives to be considered. The evidence indicates that a group will almost always outperform even the best individual. So groups generate *higher-quality decisions.* Finally, groups lead to *increased acceptance of a solution.* Many decisions fail after the final choice is made because people don't accept the solution. Group members who participated in making a decision are likely to enthusiastically support the decision and encourage others to accept it.

Balancing Pros and Cons There are times when decisions are best handled by individuals. For example, evidence indicates that individuals are preferred when the decision is relatively unimportant and does not require subordinate commitment to its success. Similarly, individuals should make the decision when they have sufficient information and when subordinates will be committed to the outcome even if they are not consulted.[21]

Overall, whether individuals or groups should make a decision essentially comes down to weighing effectiveness against efficiency. In terms of effectiveness, groups are superior. They generate more alternatives, are more creative, more accurate, and produce higher-quality decisions than do individuals. But individuals are more efficient than groups. Group efficiency suffers because they consume more time and resources to achieve their solution.

Whether individuals or groups should make a decision essentially comes down to weighing effectiveness against efficiency.

Decision-Making Level

In Chapter 2, we provided a pyramid-shaped figure that identified four organizational levels. They included three levels of management—top, middle, and first-line—plus operative employees. We return to these four levels to ask: At which of these levels should decisions be made? The answer is: It all depends. Let's briefly review what it *depends upon* and which decisions are best made at which level.[22]

Generally speaking, recurring and routine decisions (often referred to as **programmed decisions**) are best handled at lower levels of management. Conversely, nonrecurring and unique decisions (also frequently called **nonprogrammed decisions**) are better handled by top management. Similarly, top management is better qualified to make long-term strategic decisions—such as determining what the organization's business is, the organization's overall strategic direction and objectives, and where to allocate key resources of capital and people. Middle-level managers are best equipped to handle coordinating decisions that have medium-term implications. First-line managers should focus on more routine departmental decisions. They typically make "what" decisions—determining *what* needs to be done. Finally, operative employees are best able to make job-related operating decisions. These are "how" decisions—determining *how* to get the work done.

EXHIBIT 3-5

Source: Non Sequitur, by Wiley, September 4, 1995. © 1995, Washington Post Writers Group. Reprinted with permission.

The above guidelines need to be tempered to reflect the delegating of decision-making authority to lower levels in the organization. In all but the smallest organizations, top management cannot make all the decisions. There would be too many to make. Decision making would become incredibly slow and laborious, bogged down at the top. So managers push decisions down to lower levels. Even strategic decisions may filter down to middle and lower-level managers for ideas. These managers might even actively participate in evaluating alternatives and choosing a final course of action. But the final responsibility for strategic decisions stays with top management. Similarly, first-line managers might share their decision-making authority with operating employees, but the first-line managers remain responsible for the outcome.

Two recent trends are significantly influencing who makes decisions in organizations. First, middle management positions are being reduced in many large organizations.[23] Middle managers historically existed to channel information between upper management and operating departments. They gathered information, processed it, interpreted it, and passed it either up or down. Computerized management information systems, however, now allow top executives to bypass middle management and communicate directly with supervisors, project teams, and individual employees. So many of the decisions previously made by middle managers are now either being made by top managers or being pushed down to the lowest levels. The second relevant trend is toward empowering operating employees with decision authority.[24] As noted in the previous chapter, individuals and teams are increasingly being given greater discretion over work-related decisions. In contrast to 10 or 20 years ago, many of the decisions that had been the province of managers have been turned over to employees. As a result, having effective decision-making skills is becoming increasingly important for all employees—not just for managers.

HOW ARE DECISIONS ACTUALLY MADE IN ORGANIZATIONS?

Are decision makers in organizations rational? Do they carefully assess problems, identify all relevant criteria, use their creativity to identify all viable alternatives, and painstakingly evaluate every alternative to find an optimizing choice? In some situations they do. When decision makers are faced with a simple problem having few alternative courses of action, and when the cost of searching out and evaluating alternatives is low, the rational model provides a fairly accurate description of the decision process.[25] But such situations are the exception. Most decisions in the real world do not follow the rational model.[26] For instance, people are usually content to find an acceptable or reasonable solution to their problem rather than an optimizing one.[27] So decision makers generally make limited use of their creativity. Choices tend to be confined to the neighborhood of the problem symptom and to the neighborhood of the current alternative.[28] Moreover, even though an increasing number of decision makers are aware of and capable of using quantitative analysis, they rarely do.[29] And when they do, it's a good bet that it's to objectively support decisions that were made subjectively. As one expert in decision making recently concluded: "Most significant decisions are made by judgment, rather than by a defined prescriptive model."[30] The following reviews a large body of evidence to provide you with a description of how most decisions in organizations are actually made.

Most decisions in the real world do not follow the rational model.

Bounded Rationality

When you considered which college to attend, did you look at *every* viable alternative? Did you carefully identify all the criteria that were important in your decision? Did you calculate the expected value of each alternative against the criteria in order to find the optimum college? I expect the answer to all those questions is No. Well, don't feel bad. Most people chose their college in the same way you did. Instead of optimizing, they "satisficed."

When faced with a complex problem, most people respond by reducing the problem to a level at which it can be readily understood. They do so because the limited information-processing capability of human beings makes it impossible to assimilate and understand all the information necessary to optimize. So people *satisfice;* that is, they seek solutions that are satisfactory and sufficient.

Because the capacity of the human mind for formulating and solving complex problems is far too small to meet the requirements for full rationality, individuals operate within the confines of **bounded rationality.** They construct simplified models that extract the essential features from problems without capturing all their complexity.[31] Individuals can then behave rationally within the limits of the simple model.

How does bounded rationality work for the typical individual? Once a problem is identified, the search for criteria and alternatives begins. But the list of criteria is likely to be far from exhaustive. The decision maker will identify a limited list made up of the more conspicuous choices. These are the choices that are easy to find and that tend to be highly visible. In most cases, they will represent familiar criteria and tried-and-true solutions. Once this limited set of alternatives is identified, the decision maker will begin reviewing them. But the review will not be comprehensive—not all the alternatives will be evaluated carefully. Instead, the decision maker will begin with alternatives that differ only in a relatively small degree from the choice currently in effect. Following along familiar and well-worn paths, the decision maker will proceed to review alternatives only until he or she identifies an alternative that is "good enough"—one that meets an acceptable level of performance. The first alternative that meets the "good enough" criterion ends the search. So the final solution represents a satisficing choice rather than an optimum one. (See Exhibit 3-6 on page 74.)

One of the more interesting aspects of bounded rationality is that the order in which alternatives are considered is critical in determining which alternative is se-

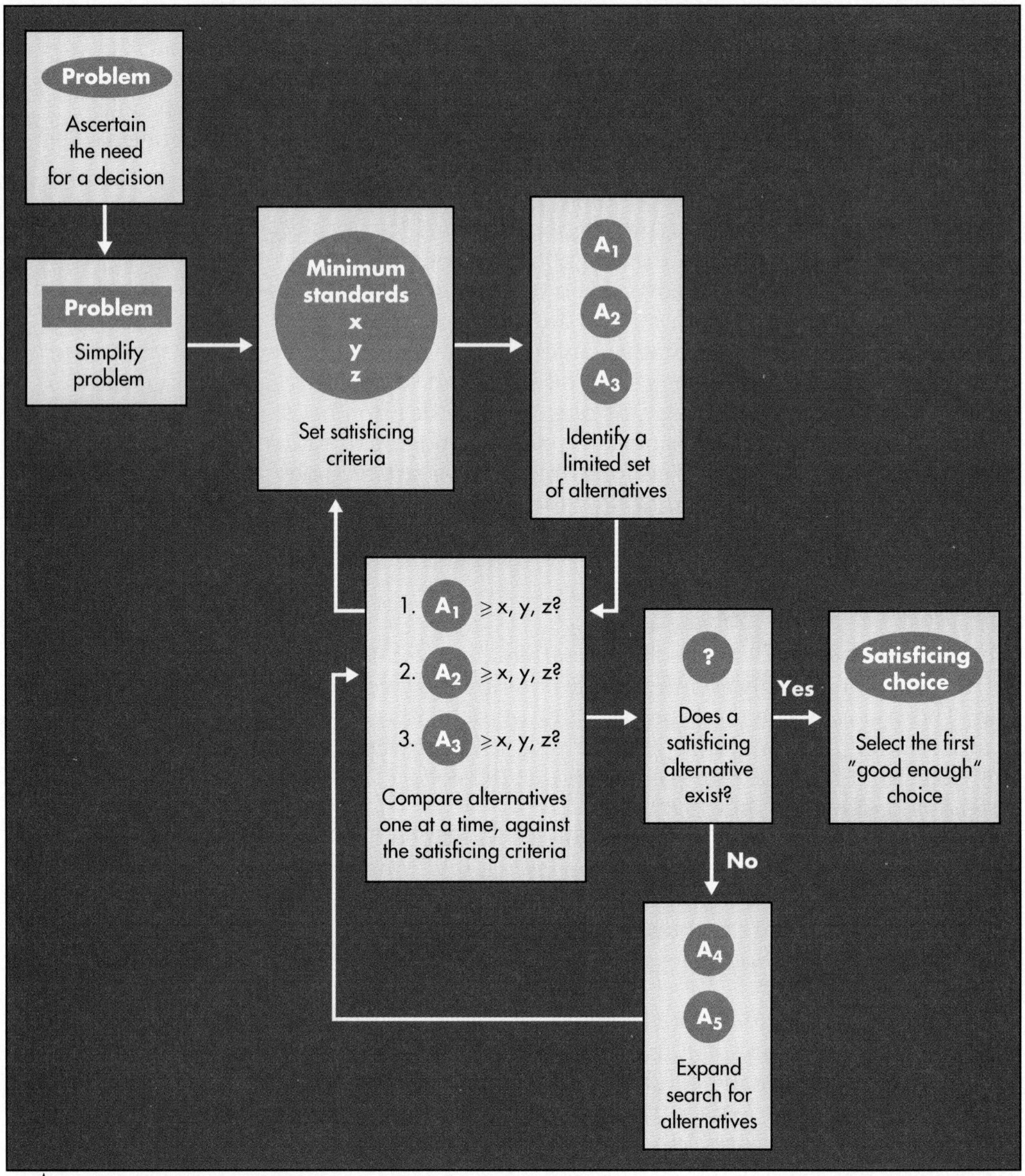

EXHIBIT 3-6
A Model of Bounded Rationality

lected. Remember, in the fully rational optimizing model, all alternatives are eventually listed in a hierarchy of preferred order. Since all alternatives are considered, the initial order in which they are evaluated is irrelevant. Every potential solution gets a full and complete evaluation. But this isn't the case with bounded rationality. If a problem has more than one potential solution, the satisficing choice will be the *first acceptable* one the decision maker encounters. Because decision makers use simple and limited models, they typically begin by identifying alternatives that are obvious, ones with which they are familiar, and those not too far from the status quo. Those solutions that depart least from the status quo and meet the decision criteria are most likely to be selected. A unique and creative alternative may present an optimizing solution to the problem, but it is unlikely to be chosen because an acceptable solution will be identified well before the decision maker is required to search very far beyond the status quo.

Intuition

"Sometimes you've just got to go with your gut feeling," the manager said as he tried to explain how he chose between two qualified job applicants. Was this manager wrong to use his "gut feeling"? Is using gut feelings a sign of being a poor manager? Does it necessarily result in an inferior outcome? The anwer to all these questions is No. Managers regularly use their intuition, and it may actually help improve decision making.[32]

Managers regularly use their intuition, and it may actually help improve decision making.

Definition First, let's define what we mean by intuitive decision making. There are several ways to conceptualize intuition.[33] For instance, some consider it a form of extrasensory power or sixth sense, and some believe it is a personality trait that a limited number of people are born with. For our purposes, we'll define **intuitive decision making** as an unconscious process created out of distilled experience. It doesn't necessarily operate independently of rational analysis; rather, the two complement each other.

Research on chess playing provides an excellent illustration of how intuition works.[34] Novice chess players and grand masters were shown an actual, but unfamiliar, chess game with about twenty-five pieces on the board. After 5 or 10 seconds, the pieces were removed and each player was asked to reconstruct the board. On average, the grand master could put twenty-three or twenty-four pieces in their correct squares, whereas as the novice was able to replace only six. Then the exercise was changed. This time the pieces were placed randomly on the board. Again, the novice got only about six correct, but so did the grand master! The second exercise demonstrated that the grand master didn't have any better memory than the novice. What he did have was the ability, based on the experience of having played thousands of chess games, to recognize patterns and clusters of pieces that occur on chessboards in the course of games. Studies further show that chess pro-

The game of chess relies heavily on intuitive decision-making skills. Garry Kasparov recently received considerable attention when he challenged an IBM computer to a chess match.

fessionals can simultaneously play fifty or more games in which decisions must be made in only seconds and exhibit only a moderately lower level of skill than when playing one game under tournament conditions, in which decisions often take half an hour or longer. The expert's experience allows him or her to recognize a situation and draw upon previously learned information associated with that situation to quickly arrive at a decision. The result is that the intuitive decision maker can decide rapidly with what appears to be very limited information.

Image Theory **Image theory** offers a comprehensive explanation of how most people use intuition in making decisions.[35] The theory is quite complex, so we'll extract its key elements and show you how people use it to make decisions such as: Should I adopt a certain course of action?

There are three basic elements to image theory: images, tests, and frames. Decision makers are guided by three different views, called **images.** One image represents a decision maker's basic *principles,* or values. The second represents the *goals,* or ends, to which a decision maker aspires. The third image represents the *plans,* or means for achieving those goals.

There are two *tests* by which decisions are made. The *compatibility test* determines whether an alternative fits with your principles and existing goals. The *profitability test* compares potential consequences of one alternative against those of other alternatives. The object of the compatibility test is to screen out the unacceptable. The object of the profitability test is to seek the best option.

Frames refers to the context of a decision or how information is presented. The proverbial question "Is the glass half-empty or half-full?" is a framing issue. Framing is important because image theory argues that the context in which decisions occur gives them meaning and that past successes and failures in the same or similar contexts provide guidance about what to do about the current decision. So framing allows the decision maker to draw on his or her intuition to decide what to do this time.

The proverbial question "Is the glass half-empty or half-full?" is a framing issue.

Given the above concepts and definitions, here's what image theory proposes. (See Exhibit 3-7.) Decision making is essentially an automatic and intuitive process, requiring a minimal amount of thinking. Individuals make adoption decisions on the basis of a simple two-step process. First an option needs to pass the compatibility test. Does it fit with the decision maker's principles, goals, and plans? If it does, and no other competing candidates also fit, this option is adopted. This, incidentally, is synonymous with a satisficing choice. If the option fails the compatibility test, it is rejected. Most decisions do not go any further than this step. That is, there is only one alternative being considered, and either it's "good enough" or it isn't! In cases where there are multiple alternatives and two or more pass the compatibility test, a second step is necessary. This is the more complex and deliberative profitability test. But both these tests are influenced by the decision maker's frame. That is, he or she assesses information in the context of past experiences. So framing tends to taint objectivity. It encourages decision makers to rapidly size up a decision situation, then quickly develop and assess an alternative on the basis of their intuition.

Problem Identification

Problems don't come with flashing neon lights identifying them as problems. And one person's *problem* is another person's *acceptable status quo.* So how do decision makers identify and select problems?

Problems that are visible tend to have a higher probability of being selected than ones that are important.[36] Why? We can offer at least two reasons. First, it's easier to recognize visible problems. They are more likely to catch a decision

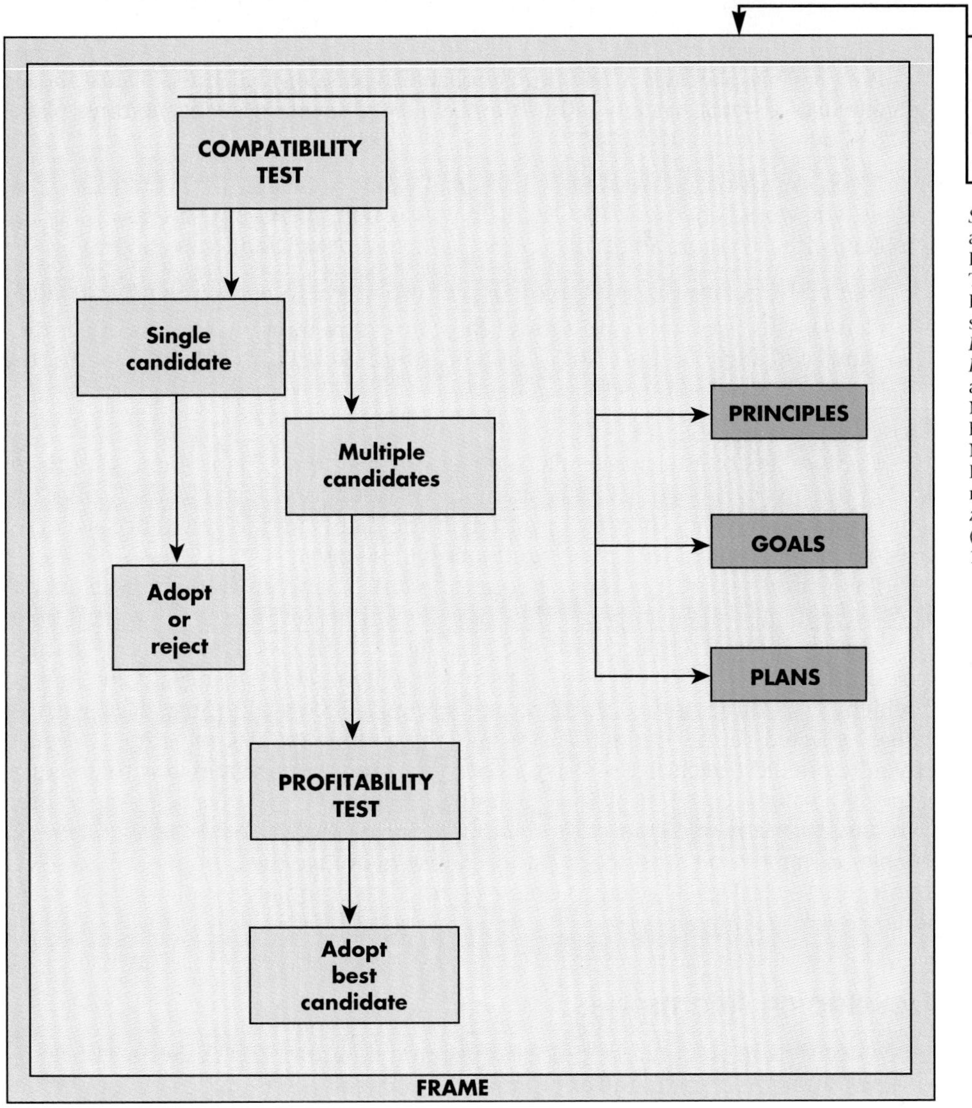

EXHIBIT 3-7
Image Theory Applied to Adoption Decisions

Source: Based on T. R. Mitchell and L. R. Beach, "'. . . Do I Love Thee? Let Me Count . . .' Toward an Understanding of Intuitive and Automatic Decision Making," *Organizational Behavior and Human Decision Processes,* October 1990, p. 11; and L. R. Beach and T. R. Mitchell, "Image Theory: A Behavioral Theory of Decision Making in Organizations," in B. M. Staw and L. L. Cummings, eds., *Research in Organizational Behavior,* vol. 12 (Greenwich, Conn.: JAI Press, 1990), p. 13.

maker's attention. This tendency explains why politicians are more likely to talk about the "crime problem" than the "illiteracy problem." Second, remember that we are concerned with decision making in organizations. Decision makers want to appear competent and "on top of problems." This desire motivates them to focus on problems that are visible to others.

Don't ignore the decision maker's self-interest. If a decision maker faces a conflict between selecting a problem that is important to the organization and one that is important to the decision maker, self-interest tends to win out.[37] Self-interest also is related to the issue of visibility. It is usually in a decision maker's best interest to attack high-profile problems. It conveys to others that things are under control. Moreover, when the decision maker's performance is later reviewed, the evaluator is more likely to give a high rating to someone who has been aggressively attacking visible problems than to someone whose actions have been less obvious.

Finally, when a problem is identified it is also framed. And framing has a large bearing on how the problem will be approached. For instance, consider the following problem.[38] A large car manufacturer has recently been hit with economic difficulties; it appears as if three plants will have to be closed and 6,000 employees laid off. The vice president of production has been exploring alternative ways to avoid this crisis. She has developed two plans:

Plan A: This plan will save one of the three plants and 2,000 jobs.

Plan B: This plan has a one-third probability of saving all three plants and all 6,000 jobs, but it has a two-thirds probability of saving none of the three plants and none of the 6,000 jobs.

If you were the vice president, which plan would you choose? If you're like most people, you would choose A. We'll explain why in a moment. But let's reconsider the problem with two more alternative plans. Which of *these* would you choose?

Plan C: This plan will result in the loss of two of the three plants and 4,000 jobs.

Plan D: This plan has a two-thirds probability of resulting in the loss of all three plants and all 6,000 jobs, but it has a one-third probability of losing none of the three plants and none of the 6,000 jobs.

Most people choose Plan D.

The two sets of alternative plans are exactly the same. Plans A and C both result in the loss of 4,000 jobs and the saving of 2,000 jobs. Plans B and D offer the same probabilities—a 1-in-3 chance that all the plants and jobs will be saved and a 2-in-3 chance that all the plants and jobs will be lost.

The reason people typically choose differently between these options is that they were framed differently in terms of gains and losses. And a substantial body of evidence indicates that decision makers tend to be risk-averse when facing a positively framed problem and risk-seeking when facing a negatively framed problem.[39] If you're offered the choice of *losing* $1,000 or taking a gamble with an equal expected value, you're likely to take the gamble (be risk-seeking). However, if you're offered the choice of *being given* $1,000 or taking a gamble with an equal expected value, you'll probably take the $1,000 (be risk-averse). Apparently, avoiding the pain of certainly or possibly losing $1,000 is the deciding factor. So problems framed to emphasize positive gains encourage decision makers to select conservative choices, whereas problems framed to emphasize potential losses encourage risk-seeking choices.

Developing Alternatives

Since decision makers rarely seek an optimum solution, but rather a satisficing one, we should expect to find a minimal use of creativity in the search for alternatives. And that expectation is generally on target.

Efforts will be made to try to keep the search process simple. It will tend to be confined to the neighborhood of the current alternative. More complex search behavior, which includes the development of creative alternatives, will be resorted to only when a simple search fails to uncover a satisfactory alternative. Or, in image theory terms, one satisfactory alternative frequently exists that meets the compatibility test. So this is chosen, and the decision maker rarely needs to go to the profitability test.

Rather than formulating new and unique problem definitions and alternatives, with frequent journeys into unfamiliar territory, most decision makers, the evidence indicates, practice decision making that is incremental rather than comprehensive.[40] This means that decision makers avoid the difficult task of considering all the important factors, weighing their relative merits and drawbacks, and calculating the expected value for each alternative. Instead, they make successive limited comparisons. This branch approach simplifies decision choices by comparing only those alternatives that differ in relatively small degree from the choice currently in effect. This approach also makes it unnecessary for the decision maker to thoroughly examine an alternative and its consequences; one need investigate only those aspects in which the proposed alternative and its consequences differ from the status quo.

What emerges from the above description is a decision maker who takes small steps toward his or her objective. It acknowledges the noncomprehensive nature of choice selection; in other words, decision makers make successive comparisons because decisions are never made forever and written in stone, but rather they are made and remade endlessly in small comparisons between narrow choices.

Implementing Solutions

"Good decisions" often fail because of poor implementation. So, in addition to understanding how decisions are made, we need to know something about how they are implemented.[41] Interestingly, the rational decision-making model speaks little to this issue. It essentially assumes that the people who have to carry out a decision will enthusiastically endorse and support it. That, of course, is an idealistic assumption.

In practice, three sets of variables will largely determine the success of a solution's implementation—leadership, communication, and political support. Leaders make choices about how decisions will be made. The popularity in recent years of the use of participative decision making, empowerment, and self-managed teams reflects the belief that people are most likely to support decisions in which they actively participated.[42]

People need to understand the reasons underlying decisions that will affect them. Major changes can be particularly disruptive for employees. Change brings uncertainty and ambiguity. Opening channels of communication and explaining why a decision was made and how it will affect people will go a long way toward lessening resistance and increasing support.

Failure to gain political support for a decision often leads to its downfall.[43] People with power can use it to support or undermine a decision. So successful implementation requires support from individuals and groups who have the power to thwart the decision if they do not agree with it. One of the most potent techniques that powerful people use to stymie a decision they don't like is to do nothing. This is what happens in the U.S. Congress when a bill "dies in committee." Many an organizational decision has died because it lacked political support among those who had to carry it out.

Making Choices

We've already noted that biases can creep into decisions. For instance, positively framed problems lead to different choices than negatively framed problems. But there are other biases. In order to avoid information overload, we rely on **heuristics,** or judgmental shortcuts, in decision making.[44] There are two common categories of heuristics—availability and representativeness. Another bias that decision makers confront is the tendency to escalate commitment to a failing course of action.

Availability Heuristic A lot more people suffer from fear of flying than fear of driving a car. The reason is that many people think that flying is more dangerous than driving. It isn't, of course. With apologies ahead of time for this graphical example, if flying on a commerical airline were as dangerous as driving, the equivalent of two 747s filled to capacity would have to crash every week, killing all aboard, to match the risk of being killed in a car accident. But the media give a lot more attention to air accidents, so we tend to overstate the risk in flying and understate the risk in driving.

This illustration is an example of the **availability heuristic,** which is the tendency for people to base their judgments on information that is readily available to them. Events that evoke emotions, that are particularly vivid, or that have occurred recently tend to be most available in our memory. As a result, we tend to be prone to overestimating unlikely events such as an airplane crash. The availability heuristic can also explain why managers, when doing annual performance appraisals, tend to give more weight to recent behaviors of an employee than to those of 6 or 9 months ago.

Representative Heuristic Literally millions of inner-city, African-American boys in the U.S. talk about the goal of playing basketball in the NBA. In reality, they have a better chance of becoming medical doctors than they do of playing in the NBA. But these kids are suffering from a **representative heuristic.** They tend to assess the likelihood of an occurrence by drawing analogies and seeing identical situations where they don't exist. They hear about some boy from their neighborhood 10 years ago who went on to play professional basketball. Or they watch NBA games on television and think that those players are like them. We all are guilty of using this heuristic at times. Managers, for example, frequently predict the performance of a new product by relating it to a previous product's success. Or they hired three graduates from the same college who turned out to be poor performers, so they predict that a current job applicant from that college won't be a good employee.

Escalation of Commitment Another bias that creeps into decisions in practice is a tendency to escalate commitment when a course of action represents a decision stream (a series of decisions).[45] **Escalation of commitment** is an increased commitment to a previous decision despite negative information. For example, a friend of mine had been dating a woman for about 4 years. Although he admitted that things weren't going too well in the relationship, he informed me that he was going to marry the woman. A bit surprised by his decision, I asked him why. He responded: "I have a lot invested in the relationship!" Similarly, another friend was explaining why she was working on a doctorate in education even though she disliked teaching and didn't want to continue her career in education. She told me she really wanted to be a software programmer. Then she hit me with her escalation of commitment explanation: "I already have a master's in education and I'd have to go back and complete some deficiencies if I changed to work on a degree in software programming now."

It has been well documented that individuals escalate commitment to a failing course of action when they view themselves as responsible for the failure. That is, they "throw good money after bad" to demonstrate that their initial decision wasn't wrong and to avoid having to admit they made a mistake. Escalation of commitment is also congruent with evidence that people try to appear consistent in what they say and do. Increasing commitment to previous actions conveys consistency.

Escalation of commitment has obvious implications for managerial decisions. Many an organization has suffered large losses because a manager was determined to prove that his or her original decision was right by continuing to commit resources to what was a lost cause from the beginning. In addition, as we'll elaborate on in our discussion of leadership in Chapters 14 and 15, effective leaders are perceived as consistent. So managers, in an effort to appear effective, may be motivated to be consistent even when switching to another course of action may be preferable. In actuality, effective managers are those who are able to differentiate between situations in which persistence will pay off and situations where it won't.

Individual Differences

Put Chad and Sean into the same decision situation and Chad almost always seems to take longer to come to a solution. Chad's final choices aren't necessarily always better than Sean's, he just is slower in processing information. In addition, if there's an obvious risk dimension in the decision, Sean seems consistently to prefer a riskier option than does Chad. What this description illustrates is that we all bring personality and other individual differences to the decisions we make. Two of these individual variables seem particularly relevant to decision making in organizations—an individual's decision-making style and level of moral development.

Decision-Making Styles The decision-styles model identifies four different individual approaches to making decisions.[46] It was designed to be used by managers and aspiring managers, but its general framework can be used by any individual decision maker.

The basic foundation of the model is the recognition that people differ along two dimensions. The first is their *way of thinking*. Some people are logical and rational. They process information serially. In contrast, some people are intuitive and creative. They perceive things as a whole. Note that these differences are above and beyond the general human characteristics—specifically, bounded rationality and image theory—discussed earlier. The other dimension addresses a person's *tolerance for ambiguity*. Some people have a high need to structure information in ways that minimize ambiguity, whereas others are able to process many thoughts at the same time. When these two dimensions are diagrammed, they form four styles of decision making: directive, analytic, conceptual, and behavioral (see Exhibit 3-8).

People using the *directive* style have low tolerance for ambiguity and seek rationality. They are efficient and logical. But their efficiency concerns result in their making decisions using minimal information and assessing few alternatives. Directive types make decisions fast, and they focus on the short run.

The *analytic* type has a much greater tolerance for ambiguity than do directive decision makers. This trait leads to the desire for more information and consideration of more alternatives than is true for directives. Analytic managers would best be characterized as careful decision makers with the ability to adapt or cope with new situations.

Individuals with a *conceptual* style tend to be very broad in their outlook and consider many alternatives. Their focus is long-range, and they are very good at finding creative solutions to problems.

The final category—those with a *behavioral* style—characterizes decision makers who work well with others. They are concerned with the achievements of peers and subordinates. They are receptive to suggestions from others and rely heavily on meetings for communicating. This type of manager tries to avoid conflict and seeks acceptance.

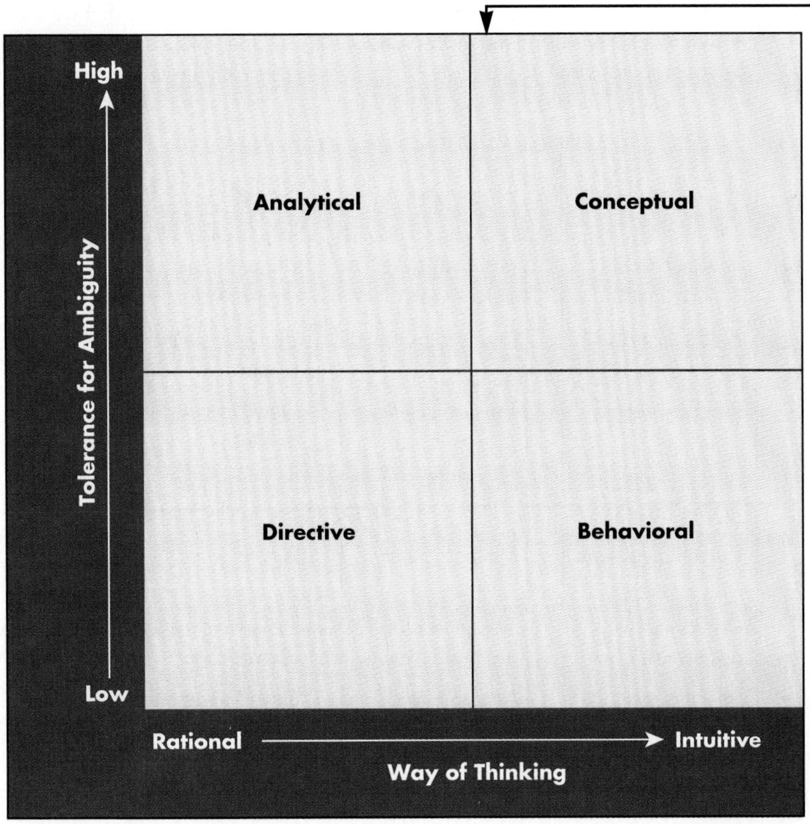

EXHIBIT 3-8
Decision-Style Model

Source: A. J. Rowe, J. D. Boulgarides, and M. R. McGrath, *Managerial Decision Making,* Modules in Management Series (Chicago: SRA, 1984), p. 18.

Although these four categories are distinct, most managers have characteristics that fall into more than one. So it's probably best to think in terms of a manager's dominant style and his or her backup styles. Some managers rely almost exclusively on their dominant style; more flexible managers can make shifts depending on the situation. (You can determine your own dominant decision style by doing the self-assessment exercise in the Building Self-Awareness box, below.)

BUILDING SELF-AWARENESS • BUILDING SELF-AWARENESS

WHAT'S YOUR DECISION-MAKING STYLE?

INSTRUCTIONS:

1. Use the following numbers to answer each question:
   8 = when the question is MOST like you
   4 = when the question is MODERATELY like you
   2 = when the question is SLIGHTLY like you
   1 = when the question is LEAST like you
2. Rate the four answers to each question by inserting one of those numbers into each box in columns I–IV.
3. DO NOT repeat any number in a given row. For example, the numbers you might use to answer a given question could read across as 8 2 1 4, BUT NOT 8 8 1 4.
4. In answering the questions, think of how you NORMALLY act in your work situation.
5. Use the first thing that comes to your mind when answering the question. Your responses should reflect how you feel about the questions and what you prefer to do, not what you think might be the right thing to do.
6. There is no time limit in answering the questions, and there are no right or wrong answers.
7. Score the questions using the instructions given in Appendix B. Your score reflects how *you see yourself,* not what you believe is correct or desirable. This assessment is related to *your work situation.* It covers *typical decisions* that you make in your work environment.

	I	II	III	IV
1. My prime objective is to:	Have a position with status	Be the best in my field	Achieve recognition for my work	Feel secure in my job
2. I enjoy jobs that:	Are technical & well defined	Have considerable variety	Allow independent action	Involve people
3. I expect people working for me to be:	Productive and fast	Highly capable	Committed and responsive	Receptive to suggestions
4. In my job, I look for:	Practical results	The best solutions	New approaches or ideas	Good working environment
5. I communicate best with others:	On a direct one-to-one basis	In writing	By having a group discussion	In a formal meeting
6. In my planning, I emphasize:	Current problems	Meeting objectives	Future goals	Developing people's careers
7. When faced with solving a problem, I:	Rely on proven approaches	Apply careful analysis	Look for creative approaches	Rely on my feelings
8. When using information, I prefer:	Specific facts	Accurate and complete data	Broad coverage of many options	Limited data that are easily understood

(continues)

WHAT'S YOUR DECISION-MAKING STYLE? continued

	I	II	III	IV
9. When I am not sure about what to do, I:	Rely on intuition	Search for facts	Look for a possible compromise	Wait before making a decision
10. Whenever possible, I avoid:	Long debates	Incomplete work	Using numbers or formulas	Conflict with others
11. I am especially good at:	Remembering dates and facts	Solving difficult problems	Seeing many possibilities	Interacting with others
12. When time is important, I:	Decide and act quickly	Follow plans and priorities	Refuse to be pressured	Seek guidance or support
13. In social settings, I generally:	Speak with others	Think about what is being said	Observe what is going on	Listen to the conversation
14. I am good at remembering:	People's names	Places we met	People's faces	People's personalities
15. The work I do provides me:	The power to influence others	Challenging assignments	Achievement of my personal goals	Acceptance by the group
16. I work well with those who are:	Energetic and ambitious	Self-confident	Open-minded	Polite and trusting
17. When under stress, I:	Become anxious	Concentrate on the problem	Become frustrated	Am forgetful
18. Others consider me:	Aggressive	Disciplined	Imaginative	Supportive
19. My decisions typically are:	Realistic and direct	Systematic or abstract	Broad and flexible	Sensitive to the needs of others
20. I dislike:	Losing control	Boring work	Following rules	Being rejected

Turn to page 560 for scoring directions.

Source: **A. J. Rowe, R. Mason, and K. Dickel, *Strategic Management and Business Policy* (Reading, Mass.: Addison-Wesley, 1982), p. 217. Reprinted by permission of Dr. Alan J. Rowe.**

Business students, lower-level managers, and top executives tend to score highest in the analytic style. That's not surprising, given the emphasis that formal education, particularly business education, gives to developing rational thinking. For instance, courses in accounting, statistics, and finance all stress rational analysis.

In addition to providing a framework for looking at individual differences, focusing on decision styles can be useful for helping you understand how two equally intelligent people, with access to the same information, can differ in the ways in which they approach decisions and in the final choices they make.

Level of Moral Development

Moral development is relevant because many decisions have an ethical dimension. An understanding of this concept can help you see how different people apply different ethical standards to their decisions.

There is a substantial body of research that confirms the existence of three levels of moral development, each comprising two stages.[47] At each successive

EXHIBIT 3-9
Stages of Moral Development

Level	Stage Description
Principled	6. Following self-chosen ethical principles even if they violate the law
	5. Valuing rights of others and upholding absolute values and rights regardless of the majority's opinion
Conventional	4. Maintaining conventional order by fulfilling obligations to which you have agreed
	3. Living up to what is expected by people close to you
Preconventional	2. Following rules only when doing so is in your immediate interest
	1. Sticking to rules to avoid physical punishment

Source: Based on L. Kohlberg, "Moral Stages and Moralization: The Cognitive-Developmental Approach," In T. Lickona, ed., *Moral Development and Behavior: Theory, Research, and Social Issues* (New York: Holt, Rinehart & Winston, 1976), pp. 34–35.

stage, an individual's moral judgment grows less and less dependent on outside influences. The three levels and six stages are described in Exhibit 3-9.

The first level is labeled *preconventional.* At this level, individuals respond to notions of right or wrong only when there are personal consequences involved, such as physical punishment, reward, or exchange of favors. Reasoning at the *conventional* level indicates that moral value resides in maintaining the conventional order and the expectations of others. In the *principled* level, individuals make a clear effort to define moral principles apart from the authority of the groups to which they belong or society in general.

Research on these stages of moral development allows us to draw several conclusions.[48] First, people proceed through the six stages in a lock-step fashion. They gradually move up a ladder, stage by stage. They don't jump steps. Second, there is no guarantee of continued development. Development can terminate at any stage. Third, the majority of adults are at stage 4. They are limited to obeying the rules and laws of society. Finally, the higher the stage a manager reaches, the more he or she will be predisposed to make ethical decisions. For instance, a stage 3 manager is likely to make decisions that will receive approval by his or her peers; a stage 4 manager will seek to be a "good corporate citizen" by making decisions that respect the organization's rules and procedures; and a stage 5 manager is more likely to challenge organizational practices that he or she believes to be wrong.

Organizational Constraints

The organization itself constrains decision makers. Managers, for instance, shape their decisions to reflect the organization's performance evaluation and reward system and organizationally imposed time constraints. Previous organizational decisions also act to constrain current decisions.

Performance Evaluation Managers are strongly influenced in their decision making by the criteria by which they are evaluated. If a division manager believes that the manufacturing plants under his responsibility are operating best when he hears nothing negative, we shouldn't be surprised to find that his plant managers spend a good part of their time ensuring that negative information doesn't reach him. Similarly, if a college dean believes that an instructor should never fail more than 10 percent of her students—to fail more reflects on the instructor's ability to teach—we should expect that new instructors, who want to receive favorable evaluations, will decide not to fail too many students.

Reward Systems The organization's reward system influences decision makers by suggesting to them which choices are preferable in terms of personal payoff. For example, if the organization rewards risk aversion, managers are likely to make conservative decisions. From the 1930s through the mid-1980s, General Motors consistently gave out promotions and bonuses to those managers who kept a low profile, avoided controversy, and were good team players. The result was that GM managers became very adept at dodging tough issues and passing controversial decisions on to committees.

System-Imposed Time Constraints Organizations impose deadlines on decisions. For instance, department budgets need to be completed by next Friday. Or the report on new product development has to be ready for the executive committee to review by the first of the month. A host of decisions have to be made quickly in order to stay ahead of the competition and keep customers satisfied. And almost all important decisions come with explicit deadlines. These conditions create time pressures on decision makers and often make it difficult, if not impossible, to gather all the information they might like before having to make a final choice. The rational model ignores the reality that, in organizations, decisions come with time constraints.

Historical Precedents Rational decision making takes an unrealistic, closed-system perspective. It views decisions as independent and discrete events. But that isn't the way it is in the real world! Decisions aren't made in a vacuum. They have a context. In fact, individual decisions are more accurately characterized as points in a *stream of decisions.*

Decisions made in the past are ghosts that continually haunt current choices. For instance, commitments made in the past constrain current options. We can use a social situation as an example. The decision you might make after meeting "Mr. (or Ms.) Right" is more complicated if you're married than if you're single. A prior commitment—in this case, the marriage vow—constrains your options. In a business context, Eastman Kodak is a good example of a firm that has had to live with its past mistakes.[49] Starting in the early 1970s, Kodak's management concluded that the days of silver halide photography were numbered. They predicted that other technologies, such as electronic photography, would soon replace it. But instead of approaching the problem deliberately, Kodak management panicked. They took off in all directions. Today, virtually all of Kodak's problems can be traced to the decisions made and not made since then. Government budget decisions also offer an illustration of our point. It is common knowledge that the largest determining factor of the size of any given year's budget is last year's budget.[50] Choices made today, therefore, are largely a result of choices made over the years.

Decisions made in the past are ghosts that continually haunt current choices.

Cultural Differences

The rational model does not acknowledge cultural differences. But Arabs, for instance, don't necessarily make decisions the same way that Canadians do. Therefore, we need to recognize that the cultural background of the decision maker can significantly influence selection of problems, depth of analysis, the importance placed on logic and rationality, whether organizational decisions will be made autocratically by an individual manager or collectively in groups, time orientation, and belief in the ability of people to solve problems.[51] Differences in time orientation help us understand why managers in Egypt will make decisions at a much slower and more deliberate pace than their American counterparts. Although rationality is valued in North America, it isn't valued everywhere in the world. A North American manager might make an important decision intuitively, but he or she knows that it's important to appear to proceed in a rational fashion. This is because rationality is highly valued in the West. In countries such as Iran, where rationality is not deified, efforts to appear rational are not necessary.

Some cultures—the United States is one—emphasize solving problems; others, such as Thailand and Indonesia, focus on accepting situations as they are. Because problem-solving managers believe they can and should change situations to their benefit, American managers might identify a problem long before their Thai or Indonesian counterparts would even recognize it as such.

Decision making by Japanese managers is much more group-oriented than in the United States. The Japanese value conformity and cooperation. So before Japanese CEOs make an important decision, they collect a large amount of information, which is then used in consensus-forming group decisions.

WHAT CAN MANAGERS DO TO IMPROVE THEIR DECISION MAKING?

If you're a manager, what can you do to become a more effective decision maker? Here are a few suggestions.

Analyze the Situation

You can improve your decision-making effectiveness by assessing the decision context, including the national culture you're operating in, the characteristics of your organization's culture, and your organization's political climate. *National culture* is a key variable in determining whether you should use groups and the importance you should place on rationality. In countries that score high on individualism, you should expect much more resistance to group decision processes than in highly collectivist cultures. Great care needs to be shown in relying on group decision-making practices in individualistic countries such as the United States, Sweden, Italy, France, England, Canada, and Australia. In contrast, managers and employees alike will be willing to accept group decision making in such countries as Greece, Japan, Mexico, Singapore, and Venezuela.

As previously noted, rationality is widely accepted among Western cultures, but it's not a universal standard. So if you're in a country that doesn't value rationality, don't feel compelled to follow the rational decision-making model or even to try to make your decisions appear rational. In fact, you may be more effective by purposely avoiding the appearance of following rational processes.

Organizational cultures differ in terms of the importance they place on factors such as risk, the use of groups, reliance on formalized procedures, and the need for decisions to closely follow the chain of command. Adjust your decision style to ensure that it's compatible with the organization's culture.

Finally, don't ignore the organization's *political climate*. Don't confuse optimization and pragmatism. The "best" choice is not necessarily the one that can be implemented successfully. So, after deciding what's optimally best, make sure it can pass the reality test. Will others find it acceptable, and can it be realistically implemented? If not, show flexibility and adapt the decision to increase the likelihood that it will be accepted.

Be Aware of Biases

We all bring biases to the decisions we make. Unfortunately, however, we typically don't recognize what our biases are. And we fail to differentiate situations in which biases cause minimal problems from those in which they can have a catastrophic impact. If you understand the biases influencing your judgment, you can begin to change the way you make decisions to reduce those biases.

Combine Simplified Rational Analysis with Intuition

Don't forget that rational analysis and intuition are not conflicting approaches to decision making. By using both, you can actually improve your decision effectiveness. As you gain managerial experience, you should feel increasingly confident in imposing your intuitive processes on top of your rational analysis.

Match Decision-Making Style to Job Requirements

Don't assume that your specific decision style is appropriate for every job. Just as cultures differ, so too do jobs within an organization. And your effectiveness as a decision maker will increase if you match your decision style to the requirements of the job.

All management jobs aren't alike. Managing a group of creative copywriters in an advertising agency, for instance, is different from supervising clerical personnel in a retail store. If you're a directive style of decision maker, you'll be more effective working with people whose jobs require quick action. This style, for instance, would match up well with managing stockbrokers. An analytic style would work well managing accountants, market researchers, or financial analysts. A conceptual style fits well with managing corporate planners, forecasters, or creative types. And jobs that require managers to spend a large portion of their time as a team leader are compatible with individuals who use a behavioral style.

Your effectiveness as a decision maker will increase if you match your decision style to the requirements of the job.

Use Creativity-Stimulation Techniques

We all have the tendency to get in mental ruts. We see a problem that we've confronted before and quickly scan our memory for how we handled it in the past. Unless our previous experience was memorably negative, we tend to handle the problem the same way we did before. In many cases, this approach is perfectly satisfactory. If nothing else, it makes life a lot simpler. We don't have to invent a totally new solution to solve an old problem. The downside, however, is that there might be a far better solution available if only you'd take the time to search for it.

You can improve your overall decision-making effectiveness by searching for novel solutions to problems. Your inspiration for finding them can be as elementary as telling yourself to think creatively and to specifically look for unique alternatives. In addition, you can practice the attribute-listing and lateral-thinking techniques described earlier in this chapter.

Apply Ethical Decision Guides

Your decisions should consider ethical implications. Although there is no simple credo that will ensure that you won't err in your ethical judgments, the following questions can help guide you. Ask yourself these questions when making important decisions or ones with obvious ethical implications.[52]

1. How did this problem occur in the first place?
2. Would you define the problem differently if you stood on the other side of the fence?
3. To whom and to what do you give your loyalty as a person and as a member of your organization?
4. What is your intention in making this decision?
5. What is the likelihood that your intentions will be misunderstood by others in the organization?
6. How does your intention compare with the probable result?
7. Whom could your decision injure?
8. Can you discuss the problem with the parties who will be affected before you make the decision?
9. Are you confident that your position will be as valid over a long period of time as it seems now?
10. Could you disclose your decision to your boss or your immediate family?
11. How would you feel if your decision was described, in detail, on the front page of your local newspaper?

IN THE NEWS

Ursula Burns's Style Fits Her Job at Xerox

IN 1991, XEROX'S CHAIRMAN AND CEO, PAUL ALLAIRE, RECOGNIZED THE NEED TO CHANGE HIS COMPANY'S strategy and its corporate structure. Xerox needed to take its mechanical product lines digital and give customers the ability to do everything from standard copying to sophisticated desktop publishing on a single machine. To handle this transition, he decided to shift Xerox's structure from one organized around functional areas such as marketing and engineering to one organized around agile, autonomous business teams. This change would additionally require a different type of manager. The reorganization, which took place in 1992, proved a major boost to the career of Ursula Burns.

Burns joined Xerox in 1984. An engineer by training, her first job at Xerox was developing business plans. Her nimble mind and strong communication skills caught the attention of higher-ups, and she was given increased responsibilities. She was promoted to systems-engineering manager on the design team for the 5100 office copier in 1988. In the early 1990s, she became executive assistant to Allaire. And after the 1992 reorganization, Burns was promoted to vice president and general manager for fax machines and color copiers.

Burns's style is well matched to Xerox's current requirements. It needs entrepreneurial leaders who foster personal initiative, push decision making down the line, and get more done with fewer resources. Burns is that type of leader. She has been described as having "an ability to work up, down and across the organization" and "the courage to change things that need to be changed. . . . She has a great sense of urgency."

In her new job, Burns immediately made some tough and unpopular decisions in order to turn around her group's fax business, which had been losing money for years. And her efforts have paid off. After only 1 year, she had the fax business profitable, with revenues up 20 percent.

Source: Based on A. Gabor, "The Making of a New-Age Manager," *Working Woman*, December 1994, pp. 18–27.

SUMMARY

(This summary is organized by the chapter-opening learning objectives on page 61.)

1. The six-step rational decision-making model is (1) define the problem; (2) identify the decision criteria; (3) weight the decision criteria; (4) generate possible alternatives; (5) rate each alternative on each criterion; and (6) compute the optimal decision. The assumptions of this model include: the problem is clear and unambiguous; all options are known; preferences are clear and constant; there are no time or cost constraints; and the decision maker will choose the maximum payoff.
2. Risk assumes that a decision maker can estimate the likelihood of alternatives or outcomes. With uncertainty, no probabilities can be estimated, so the decision maker must rely on intuition or creativity.
3. Three methods for stimulating individual creativity are direct instruction, attribute listing, and lateral thinking.
4. Popular quantitative techniques include break-even analysis (identifies profit or loss at various sales volumes); return on investment (measures productivity of assets); marginal analysis (compares the additional cost in a particular decision rather than average cost); game theory (mathematical models that analyze multiparty decision contexts); linear programming (for optimally solving resource allocation problems); and queuing theory (for calculating waiting lines).
5. Individual decision making is best when decisions are relatively unimportant, subordinate commitment isn't necessary for success, sufficient information is available, and speed is important.
6. The boundedly rational decision maker simplifies the problem, creates a limited set of satisficing criteria that a solution must meet, reviews a limited set of familiar options, and chooses the first solution that meets the satisficing criteria.
7. There are four decision making styles: directive, analytic, conceptual, and behavioral.
8. Managers can improve their decision making by: modifying the process to reflect national culture, the organization's culture, and the organization's political climate; recognizing biases; using both rational and intuitive processes; matching their style to the job; using creativity-stimulation techniques; and by applying ethical guides.

REVIEW AND DISCUSSION QUESTIONS

1. What is rationality? Are decision makers rational?
2. Relate how the type of decision changes with levels of management.
3. What is image theory?
4. What is a decision frame? How does it affect problem selection?
5. What is a heuristic? Describe two common categories.
6. Why might a manager escalate commitment to a losing cause?
7. Describe the six stages in the level of moral development model. At what stage are most people?
8. How do historical precedents influence a decision?
9. On the basis of your decision style, what type of job fits you best? Explain.
10. Describe an ethical dilemma you have faced. How did you resolve it?

CASE EXERCISE A
TIME WARNER: THE FLAP OVER RAP

During the summer of 1995, Time Warner's management found itself under attack for its promotion of so-called gangsta rap music. William Bennett, a secretary of education in the Reagan administration, said this music is "not fit for human consumption" and openly asked Time Warner executives, "Are you folks morally disabled?" Republican senator Bob Dole called it "nightmares of depravity." C. DeLores Tucker, head of the National Political Congress of Black Women, speaking at a Time Warner shareholders' meeting, called the company "devoid of social conscience and citizen responsibility."

What was all the fuss over? The lyrics of gangsta rap artists such as Snoop Doggy Dogg, Tupac Shakur, Dr. Dre, and the Geto Boys. These lyrics are said to be violent and sexually degrading. On this point, there seems to be little debate. They graphically describe scenes of gunplay, sex, drug use, and violence, often referring to women as "ho's" and "bitches." The genre of gangsta rap differs from the broader category of rap, in which political and educational themes predominate.

Time Warner has received more attention from gangsta rap critics than have other music companies for several reasons. First, it's big. The company is the world's largest media and entertainment conglomerate. Second, it owns 50 percent of Interscope Records, a leading label for rappers. This link gives Time Warner a 16.4 percent of the rap market. The market leader, the Bertelsmann Music Group (with an 18.5 percent share), is a German-based company, and is seen as being somewhat outside the influence of U.S. politicians and pressure groups. Third, the standards of taste at Warner Music labels have at times seemed extraordinarily lax. For instance, when one of its divisions rejected a Geto Boys album because of its explicit lyrics about mutilating women and having sex with dead bodies, the album was immediately distributed by another Warner label. Fourth, Time Warner's management has been vocal in defending its actions as consistent with protecting artists' creative freedom. And, finally, some say Time Warner has been singled out for criticism by Republicans because of its past financial support and favoritism of Democratic candidates.

Advocates of gangsta rap say its lyrics are cautionary tales depicting real life in the inner city. Its detractors say that its lyrics are exaggerated fantasies advocating brutality and misogyny.

Time Warner's management has consistently defended the company's raunchy rap music on the grounds of freedom of expression. In 1992, when Time Warner was under fire for releasing Ice-T's violent rap song "Cop Killer", the company's CEO, Gerald Levin, described rap as a legitimate expression of street culture, which deserves an outlet. "The test of any democratic society," Levin stated, "lies not in how well it can control expression but in whether it gives freedom of thought and expression the widest possible latitude, however controversial or exasperating the results may sometimes be." But Levin acknowledges a concern with balancing creative freedom and social responsibility. On this point, he has recently launched a drive to develop industrywide standards for the distribution and labeling of potentially objectionable music. In addition, Time Warner feels that Bennett—the leader in this campaign against the company—is using the issue for personal recognition and publicity. Said the head of Time Warner's music group, when Bennett spoke at the company's annual meeting, "He came in with no information and no credentials to discuss any of this intelligently. I guess he thought he was the self-appointed marshal riding in on a white horse to be the arbiter of morals."

The bottom line for Time Warner is whether it should censor what it distributes. One entertainment industry executive says, "There is no such thing as a little censorship." But can a firm like Time Warner be socially responsible without imposing some censorship guidelines? If the company severs its ties to gangsta rap music, it risks a backlash in the creative community. If it holds firm to distributing this music, the company becomes a lightning rod for a Republican crusade against the erosion of traditional values in society.

Questions

1. Are the production and sale of gangsta rap music by Time Warner consistent with rational decision making?
2. What insights from the chapter's discussion of how decisions are actually made in organizations can explain the behavior of Time Warner's management?
3. Use the ethical decision guides presented in this chapter to assess Time Warner's position.
4. Do you think Time Warner's management is socially irresponsible? Consider your answer in terms of the company's various stakeholders.

Source: Based on M. Landler, "Time Warner Seeks a Delicate Balance in Rap Music Furor," *New York Times,* June 5, 1995, p. A1; R. Zoglin, "A Company under Fire," *Time,* June 12, 1995, pp. 37–39; and R. S. Dunham, "Gunning for the Gangstas," *Business Week,* June 19, 1995, p. 41.

CASE EXERCISE B
THE DENVER INTERNATIONAL AIRPORT DEBACLE

The new Denver International Airport (DIA) opened on February 28, 1995, 16 months later than planned and at a cost of $4.2 billion, about twice the original estimate. Supporters and critics can argue about whether DIA is a giant white elephant or a modern marvel. But almost everyone agrees that it is a striking example of poor decision making and planning.

The city's previous airport, Stapleton International, was just 10 minutes from downtown Denver. Many experts state that Stapleton could have been expanded and modernized to meet Denver's growing needs. It was efficiently handling just over 32 million passengers a year when it was closed down to make way for DIA. Critics of DIA say that the new airport is too far from downtown (18 miles northeast), too ornate and complex, and too costly. Not only is DIA costing taxpayers a bundle in interest on its bonds, but travelers are having to bear a large part of the cost. Just weeks before DIA's opening, Continental Airlines and United Airlines, the major air carriers hubbing in Denver, announced they were raising prices by $40 a ticket to cover the extra costs of operating at the new airport. Many experts now believe that the added costs of flying into and out of Denver may significantly reduce passenger traffic. Salt Lake City is already promoting its nearby ski slopes as being cheaper to get to.

How did DIA come to be? Here's the essence of the story. Federico Pena became mayor of Denver in 1983 on a platform that opposed building a new airport. He supported expanding Stapleton. However, officials in adjacent Adams County wanted a new airport so that they could get a share of the tax revenue Denver was realizing on the airport hotels, restaurants, and concessions. In addition, a number of Denver businesspeople saw a new airport as a financial opportunity. Pena listened, and plans for a new airport were in the works within a year. A site was identified northeast of the city. The airport would cover 53 square miles—twice the size of Manhattan! Not surprisingly, announcement of the site set off a land boom. One 39-acre parcel located near the new airport changed hands three times in 2 years, tripling in value from $1.5 million to $4.3 million. Obviously, a lot of people were going to make a ton of money off this airport.

To proceed, the city needed voters' support to get the project under way and to approve $3.3 billion in bonds to fund the airport. Getting voters' support wasn't going to be easy, especially since many people saw no need for the project. So the city began a vigorous campaign to win voter support. Although not clear at the time, it has since become evident that millions of dollars were funneled into the pro-airport campaign by companies and individuals who expected to benefit greatly from the project. For example, a law firm that eventually worked on the bond sale gave $30,000; a home builder with land near the airport contributed $131,000; and U.S. West gave $200,000, an investment that paid off when it later won a $24 million contract to wire the new airport. In addition, facts and figures were manipulated to make it appear that the need for the airport was more pressing than it was. For instance, a city-hired consultant forecast 100 million passengers a year at the new airport within 30 years; that figure included a number of best-case-scenario assumptions. And city officials appear to have purposely failed to disclose construction setbacks and other questions about the airport project for fear that disclosing them would have made selling the airport bonds more difficult.

The most publicized problem at DIA had to be the airport's computerized, integrated baggage system. The state-of-the-art system—with 22 miles of track, 10,000 motors, 14 million feet of wire, and 100 souped-up IBM AT computers to run it—was designed to move any bag to any carousel or load point in less than 10 minutes. It was nice in theory, but the system had continual problems. Initially, no baggage-system builders bid on the project. They thought the system was too complex and that there was insufficient time to design it and get the bugs out. One insider said, "The city got caught in a trap. They were lulled into believing they'd find companies to build the system. They were shocked when they were told it couldn't be done." Eventually, one firm, BAE Automated Systems, agreed to take on the project, under very specific contractual terms. Almost immediately, however, the city began modifying many key terms and reneging on others. For instance, they wanted outside stations to be relocated and a baggage platform to be added. The previous promise of unrestricted access for BAE equipment was broken. Airlines also began requesting changes. United, for example, decided to cut one of the two track loops in its concourse.

The baggage system was identified as the primary reason for the airport's delayed opening. But closer analysis found that that was just the most visible problem. Other problems that contributed to the delay included faulty power supplies, poor communications systems, incomplete security and fire protection systems, and a lack of passenger information systems. These problems contributed to the city's estimate that every month of delay had cost $33 million.

Questions

1. What does this case say about the politics of decision making?
2. "Government and business decisions are different. Political factors apply to the former, but not the latter." Do you agree or disagree? Discuss.
3. Does this case illustrate the escalation-of-commitment phenomenon? Explain.

Source: Based on G. Rifkin, "What Really Happened at Denver's Airport," *Forbes ASAP,* August 29, 1994, pp. 111–14; S. J. Hedges, B. Duffy, and A. Martinez, "A Taj Mahal in the Rockies," *U.S. News & World Report,* February 13, 1995, pp. 48–53; B. D. Ayres Jr., "Mistake or Modern Marvel? Denver Airport Set to Open," *New York Times,* February 19, 1995, p. Y12; and M. Charlier, "Denver's New Airport Braces for Takeoff," *Wall Street Journal,* February 27, 1995, p. A7B.

SKILL EXERCISES

Creativity Stimulation

1. Take out a couple of sheets of paper. You have 20 minutes to list as many medical or health-care-related jobs as you can that begin with the letter *r*. For example: radiologist, registered nurse, rheumatologist. If you run out of listings before the time expires, it's OK to quit early.

   When the exercise is complete: (a) Identify the range (most to fewest) of how many jobs class members were able to list. (b) Identify unusual or novel jobs that no more than one student in class listed.
2. List on a piece of paper some common terms that apply to both *water* and *finance*.[53] How many were you able to come up with? Compare your list with the lists of others in your class.

NOTES

1. This opening vignette is based on J. Markoff, "In About Face, Intel Will Swap Flawed Pentium Chip for Buyers," *New York Times*, December 21, 1994, p. A1; J. Markoff, "Intel's Crash Course on Consumers," *New York Times*, December 21, 1994, p. C1; J. Carlton, "Humble Pie: Intel to Replace Its Pentium Chips," *Wall Street Journal*, December 21, 1994, p. B1; and J. Castro, "When the Chips Are Down," *Time*, December 26, 1994–January 2, 1995, p. 126.
2. R. D. Hof, "The Education of Andrew Grove," *Business Week*, January 16, 1995, p. 61.
3. See H. A. Simon, "Rationality in Psychology and Economics," *The Journal of Business*, October 1986, pp. 209–24; and A. Langley, "In Search of Rationality: The Purposes behind the Use of Formal Analysis in Organizations," *Administrative Science Quarterly*, December 1989, pp. 598–631.
4. For a review of the rational model, see E. F. Harrison, *The Managerial Decision-Making Process*, 4th ed. (Boston: Houghton Mifflin, 1995), pp. 75–113.
5. J. G. March, *A Primer on Decision Making* (New York: Free Press, 1994), pp. 2–7.
6. W. Pounds, "The Process of Problem Finding," *Industrial Management Review*, Fall 1969, pp. 1–19.
7. R. J. Volkema, "Problem Formulation: Its Portrayal in the Texts," *Organizational Behavior Teaching Review* 11, no. 3 (1986–87), pp. 113–26.
8. M. A. Verespej, "Gutsy Decisions of 1994," *Industry Week*, January 23, 1995, pp. 38–42.
9. T. M. Amabile, "A Model of Creativity and Innovation in Organizations," in B. M. Staw and L. L. Cummings, eds., *Research in Organizational Behavior*, vol. 10 (Greenwich, Conn.: JAI Press, 1988), p. 126.
10. Cited in C. G. Morris, *Psychology: An Introduction*, 9th ed. (Upper Saddle River, N. J.: Prentice Hall, 1996), p. 344.
11. M. A. Colgrove, "Stimulating Creative Problem Solving: Innovative Set," *Psychological Reports* 22 (1968), pp. 1205–11.
12. See M. Stein, *Stimulating Creativity*, vol. 1 (New York: Academic Press, 1974).
13. E. deBono, *Lateral Thinking: Creativity Step by Step* (New York: Harper & Row, 1971).
14. See, for example, S. Stiansen, "Breaking Even," *Success*, November 1988, p. 16.
15. From *Standard & Poor's*, June 24, 1994.
16. R. Koselka, "Playing Poker with Craig McCaw," *Forbes*, July 3, 1995, pp. 62–64.
17. M. Bazerman, *Judgment in Managerial Decision Making* (New York: John Wiley & Sons, 1994), p. 124.
18. F. W. Barnett, "Making Game Theory Work in Practice," *Wall Street Journal*, February 13, 1995, p. A14.
19. For details on using linear programming, see E. E. Adam Jr. and R. J. Ebert, *Production and Operations Management*, 5th ed. (Englewood Cliffs, N. J.: Prentice Hall, 1992), pp. 192–210.
20. This section is based on N. R. F. Maier, "Assets and Liabilities in Group Problem Solving: The Need for an Integrative Function," *Psychological Review*, April 1967, pp. 239–49; G. W. Hill, "Group versus Individual Performance: Are N+1 Heads Better Than One?" *Psychological Bulletin*, May 1982, pp. 517–39; R. A. Cooke and J. A. Kernaghan, "Estimating the Difference between Group versus Individual Performance on Problem-Solving Tasks," *Group & Organization Studies*, September 1987, pp. 319–42; and L. K. Michaelsen, W. E. Watson, and R. H. Black, "A Realistic Test of Individual versus Group Consensus Decision Making," *Journal of Applied Psychology*, October 1989, pp. 834–39.
21. V. H. Vroom and A. G. Jago, *The New Leadership: Managing Participation in Organizations* (Englewood Cliffs, N. J.: Prentice Hall, 1988).

22. Based on A. L. Delbecq, "The Management of Decision-Making within the Firm: Three Strategies for Three Types of Decision-Making," *Academy of Management Journal*, December 1967, pp. 329–39; P. F. Drucker, *Management: Tasks, Responsibilities, Practices* (New York: Harper & Row, 1974), pp. 449–50, 465–80; and H. A. Simon, *The New Science of Management Decision*, rev. ed. (Englewood Cliffs, N. J.: Prentice Hall, 1977), pp. 45–49.
23. R. Zemke, "The 'New' Middle Manager," *Training*, August 1994, pp. 42–46.
24. J. Pfeffer, *Competitive Advantage through People: Unleashing the Power of the Work Force* (Boston: Harvard Business School Press, 1994).
25. D. L. Rados, "Selection and Evaluation of Alternatives in Repetitive Decision Making," *Administrative Science Quarterly*, June 1972, pp. 196–206.
26. See, for example, March, *A Primer on Decision Making*, pp. 8–25; and A. Langley, H. Mintzberg, P. Pitcher, E. Posada, and J. Saint-Macary, "Opening Up Decision Making: The View from the Black Stool," *Organization Science*, May–June 1995, pp. 260–79.
27. J. G. March and H. A. Simon, *Organizations* (New York: John Wiley & Sons, 1958).
28. H. A. Simon, *Administrative Behavior*, 3rd ed. (New York: Macmillan, 1976).
29. See, for instance, T. B. Green, W. B. Newsom, and S. R. Jones, "A Survey of the Application of Quantitative Techniques to Production/Operation Management in Large Corporations," *Academy of Management Journal*, December 1977, pp. 669–76; D. J. Isenberg, "How Senior Managers Think," *Harvard Business Review*, November–December 1984, pp. 81–90; Y. Kathawala, "Application of Quantitative Techniques in Large and Small Organizations in the United States: An Empirical Analysis," *Journal of Operations Research*, July 1988, pp. 981–89; and S. S. K. Lam, "Applications of Quantitative Techniques in Hong Kong: An Empirical Analysis," *Asia Pacific Journal of Management*, October 1993, pp. 229–36.
30. Bazerman, *Judgment in Managerial Decision Making*, p. 5.
31. See Simon, *Administrative Behavior*, 3rd ed., and J. Forester, "Bounded Rationality and the Politics of Muddling Through," *Public Administration Review*, January–February 1984, pp. 23–31.
32. See K. R. Hammond, R. M. Hamm, J. Grassia, and T. Pearson, "Direct Comparison of the Efficacy of Intuitive and Analytical Cognition in Expert Judgment," *IEEE Transactions on Systems, Man and Cybernetics*, SMC-17, 1987, pp. 753–70; W. H. Agor, ed., *Intuition in Organizations* (Newbury Park, Calif.: Sage, 1989); and O. Behling and N. L. Eckel, "Making Sense Out of Intuition," *The Executive*, February 1991, pp. 46–47.
33. Behling and Eckel, "Making Sense Out of Intuition," pp. 46–54.
34. As described in H. A. Simon, "Making Management Decisions: The Role of Intuition and Emotion," *The Executive*, February 1987, pp. 59–60.
35. See L. R. Beach, *Image Theory: Decision Making in Personal and Organizational Contexts* (Chichester, England: Wiley, 1990); L. R. Beach and T. R. Mitchell, "Image Theory: A Behavioral Theory of Decision Making in Organizations," in B. M. Staw and L. L. Cummings, eds., *Research in Organizational Behavior*, vol. 12 (Greenwich, Conn.: JAI Press, 1990), pp. 1–41; and T. R. Mitchell and L. R. Beach, "'. . . Do I Love Thee? Let Me Count . . .' Toward an Understanding of Intuitive and Automatic Decision Making," *Organizational Behavior and Human Decision Processes*, October 1990, pp. 1–20.
36. See, for example, M. D. Cohen, J. G. March, and J. P. Olsen, "A Garbage Can Model of Organizational Choice," *Administrative Science Quarterly*, March 1972, pp. 1–25.
37. See J. G. Thompson, *Organizations in Action* (New York: McGraw-Hill, 1967), p. 123.
38. Bazerman, *Judgment in Managerial Decision Making*, pp. 54–55.
39. A. Tversky and D. Kahneman, "The Framing of Decisions and the Psychology of Choice," *Science*, January 1981, pp. 453–63.
40. C. E. Lindholm, "The Science of 'Muddling Through,'" *Public Administration Review*, Spring 1959, pp. 79–88.
41. See J. Pfeffer, "Understanding Power in Organizations," *California Management Review*, Winter 1992, p. 37.
42. See, for instance, C. E. Larson and F. M. J. LaFasto, *TeamWork* (Newbury Park, Calif.: Sage, 1989); and J. L. Cotton, *Employee Involvement* (Newbury Park, Calif.: Sage, 1993).
43. See J. Pfeffer, *Organizational Design* (Arlington Heights, Ill.: AHM Publishing, 1978).
44. A. Tversky and D. Kahneman, "Judgment under Uncertainty: Heuristics and Biases," *Science*, September 1974, pp. 1124–31.
45. See B. M. Staw, "The Escalation of Commitment to a Course of Action," *Academy of Management Review*, October 1981, pp. 577–87; and D. R. Bobocel and J. P. Meyer, "Escalating Commitment to a Failing Course of Action: Separating the Roles of Choice and Justification," *Journal of Applied Psychology*, June 1994, pp. 360–63.
46. A. J. Rowe, J. D. Boulgarides, and M. R. McGrath, *Managerial Decision Making*, Modules in Management Series (Chicago: SRA, 1984), pp. 18–22.
47. L. Kohlberg, *Essays in Moral Development: The Philosophy of Moral Development*, vol. 1 (New York: Harper & Row, 1981); and L. Kohlberg, *Essays in Moral Development: The Psychology of Moral Development*, vol. 2 (New York: Harper & Row, 1984).
48. See, for example, J. Weber, "Managers' Moral Reasoning: Assessing Their Responses to Three Moral Dilemmas," *Human Relations*, July 1990, pp. 687–702; and S. B. Knouse and R. A. Giacalone, "Ethical Decision-Making in Business: Behavioral Issues and Concerns," *Journal of Business Ethics*, May 1992, pp. 369–77.
49. S. N. Chakravarty and A. Feldman, "The Road Not Taken," *Forbes*, August 30, 1993, pp. 40–41.
50. A. Wildavsky, *The Politics of the Budgetary Process* (Boston: Little, Brown, 1964).
51. N. J. Adler, *International Dimensions of Organizational Behavior*, 2nd ed. (Boston: Kent Publishing, 1991), pp. 160–68; F. Kluckhohn and F. L. Strodtbeck, *Variations in Value Orientations* (Evanston, Ill.: Row, Peterson, 1961); G. Hofstede, *Cultures and Organizations: Software of the Mind*

(New York: McGraw-Hill, 1991); and G. Hofstede, "Cultural Constraints in Management Theories," *The Executive,* February 1993, pp. 81–94.

52. Adapted from L. L. Nash, "Ethics without the Sermon," *Harvard Business Review,* November–December 1981, p. 81.

53. D. A. Whetton and K. S. Cameron, *Developing Management Skills,* 2nd ed. (New York: HarperCollins, 1991), p. 182. Common answers: banks, currency, solvent, washed up, liquid assets, deposits, float a loan.

CHAPTER 4
ASSESSING THE ENVIRONMENT

Don't overlook the importance of worldwide thinking. A company that keeps its eye on Tom, Dick, and Harry is going to miss Pierre, Hans, and Yoshio.

-A. Ries

LEARNING OBJECTIVES

After studying this chapter, you should be able to:

1. Define the environment
2. Explain the importance of environmental scanning and identify four environmental-scanning techniques
3. Describe the typical benchmarking process
4. Describe how managers can reduce environmental uncertainty
5. Identify and describe the five dimensions for analyzing national cultures
6. Compare the classical and socioeconomic views on social responsibility
7. Contrast social responsibility and social responsiveness
8. Define ISO 9000 and its implications for management practice

In school, you'd probably be in big trouble if you sought out the student with the best grades and intentionally tried to copy his or her work. It might surprise you to learn, then, that one of the hottest and fastest-spreading techniques in business encourages companies to do essentially that. A company tries to identify the best practices of its competitors or of those firms recognized as industry leaders, compares itself against those firms, and copies those things that the competition does better. The technique is called *benchmarking*. And one of its strongest proponents is the Xerox Corporation.[1]

In 1979, Xerox undertook what is widely regarded as the first benchmarking effort in the United States. It was a response to aggressive competition from Japanese firms. Xerox had seen its market share in the copy machine business drop from 49 percent to 22 percent. Moreover, Xerox's management couldn't figure out how Japanese manufacturers could sell midsize copiers in the United States for considerably less than Xerox's production costs. So management decided to investigate the costs and processes used by Japanese competitors such as Canon. Using public sources, consultants, tours of Japanese factories, and contacts at its own Japanese joint venture, Fuji-Xerox, management found that its Japanese rivals were light-years ahead of Xerox in efficiency. Management then began analyzing the data it had collected to identify performance gaps and to determine the cause of differences. Interestingly, Xerox also looked outside the copier industry to find outstanding practices at other successful companies. For instance, Xerox Business Systems' Logistic and Distribution group benchmarked the warehousing and distribution systems used by catalogue merchandiser L.L. Bean.

Using what it learned from other companies, Xerox implemented a comprehensive restructuring of its manufacturing processes as well as its transportation, warehousing, and inventory management systems. The results from these benchmarking efforts have been nothing less than spectacular. Xerox reduced manufacturing costs by 50 percent, reduced product development cycles by 25 percent, and increased revenue per employee by 20 percent. Today, Xerox's products and services are widely considered to be of world-class quality.

Xerox's experience with benchmarking is an example of how management can improve linkages between the organization and its environment. Effective management requires scanning the environment for opportunities, keeping close contact with key constituencies such as customers and competitors, and making proactive efforts to positively shape the environment so as to make it more favorable for the organization. As you'll see in this chapter, the organization-environment relationship is a two-way street. The environment influences, shapes, and constrains organizations. But there are strategies management can pursue that allow the organization to also exert some control on its environment.

DEFINING THE ENVIRONMENT

An organization's **environment** is composed of the institutions and forces that are outside the organization and can affect the organization's performance. As noted in Chapter 2, the environment typically includes suppliers, customers, competitors, unions, government regulatory agencies, and public pressure groups.

Every organization's environment is different. The exact nature of an organization's environment at any given time depends on the "niche" that the organization has staked out for itself with respect to the range of products or services it offers and the markets it serves. Ferrari and Toyota both manufacture cars. But they appeal to very different customers. Nucor and Bethlehem Steel both produce steel, but because Bethlehem's employees are unionized and Nucor's aren't, labor unions are not part of Nucor's environment. Similarly, San Francisco State University is a state-supported institution. Stanford University is private. As a result, the California state legislature is a key environmental constituent of SFSU but not of Stanford. On the other hand, wealthy alumni are a much more powerful environmental force at Stanford than at SFSU. Why? Because SFSU depends on the state for much of its funding, whereas Stanford relies heavily on alumni contributions.

The key thing to understand about an organization's environment is that it creates potential uncertainty. Some organizations are fortunate to face relatively certain or static environments—few forces in their environment ever change. There are, for example, no new competitors, no new technological breakthroughs by current competitors, and little activity by public pressure groups to influence the organization. Other organizations face dynamic environments—rapidly changing government regulations affecting their business, new competitors, difficulties in acquiring raw materials, continually changing product preferences by customers, and so on. Ideally, management would prefer to operate in a static environment. There would be no uncertainty, and decision making would be simple and highly accurate. But there are few static environments nowadays. Environmental uncertainty characterizes the world that most organizations currently face. And since uncertainty is a threat to an organization's effectiveness, management will try to limit environmental uncertainty through activities such as market research, advertising, lobbying, benchmarking, forecasting, and creating joint ventures with other firms.

The key thing to understand about an organization's environment is that it creates potential uncertainty.

Recent research has helped clarify what is meant by environmental uncertainty. It has been found that there are three key dimensions to any organization's environment. They are labeled capacity, volatility, and complexity.[2]

The *capacity* of an environment refers to the degree to which it can support growth. Rich and growing environments generate excess resources, which can buffer the organization in times of relative scarcity. Abundant capacity, for example, leaves room for an organization to make mistakes; scarce capacity does not. In 1996, firms operating in the multimedia software business had relatively abundant environments, whereas those in the full-service brokerage business faced relative scarcity.

The degree of instability in an environment is captured in the *volatility* dimension. A high degree of unpredictable change creates a dynamic environment in which it is difficult for management to predict accurately the outcomes of various decisions. At the other extreme is a stable environment. The accelerated changes in Eastern Europe and the ending of the Cold War had dramatic effects on the U.S. defense industry in the early 1990s. The environment of major defense contractors such as McDonnell Douglas, Lockheed Martin, General Dynamics, and Northrop moved from relatively stable to dynamic.

Finally, the environment needs to be assessed in terms of *complexity:* that is, the degree of heterogeneity and concentration among environmental elements. Simple environments are homogeneous and concentrated. The tobacco industry is one example, because there are relatively few players. It is easy for firms in this industry to keep a close eye on the competition. In contrast, environments characterized by heterogeneity and dispersion are called complex, a term that aptly describes the current environment in the on-line computer data-services business. Every day there seems to be another "new kid on the block" with whom established data-services firms have to deal.

Exhibit 4-1 summarizes our definition of the environment along its three dimensions. The arrows in this figure indicate movement toward higher uncertainty. So organizations that operate in environments characterized as scarce, dynamic, and complex face the greatest degree of uncertainty. Why? Because they have little room for error, high unpredictability, and a diverse set of elements in the environment to constantly monitor.

EXHIBIT 4-1
Three-Dimensional Model of the Environment

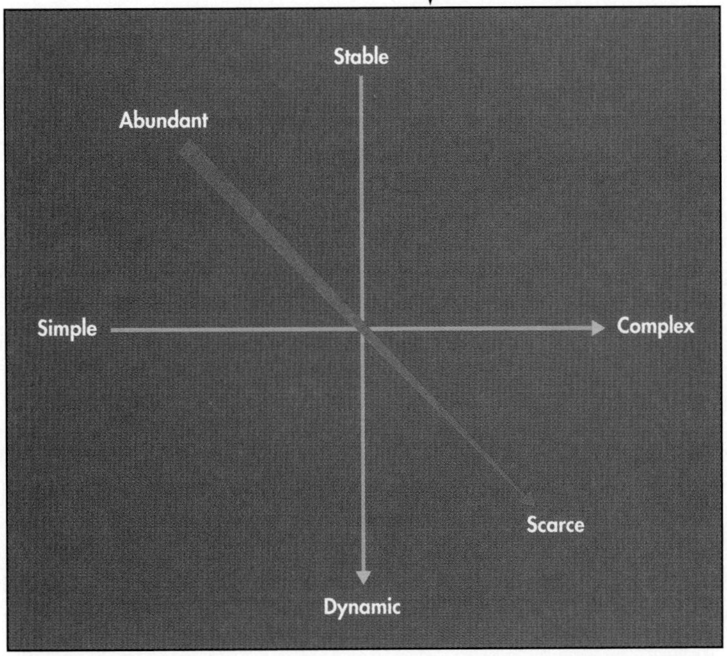

MAJOR SOURCES OF ENVIRONMENTAL UNCERTAINTY

In Chapter 2, we identified key stakeholders that organizations need to satisfy. In this section, we revisit the concept of stakeholders. But this time, we look at only *external* stakeholders and specifically assess how each creates uncertainty for management.

Customers

Customers' tastes and preferences change. And those changes represent uncertainty to management and organizations. In the 1980s, for instance, conspicuous consumption was in. Manufacturers and retailers of expensive designer clothes, jewelry, and luxury automobiles did well. But the purchase of high-status items went out of fashion in the early 1990s. Suddenly, consumers were looking for value. This change in consumer preference was good news to firms such as Wal-Mart, Levi-Strauss, and Ikea. It was bad news, however, for Rolls-Royce, Rolex, and Ralph Lauren.

Competitors

In a static environment, competitors offer the same products and services at the same prices today that that they did yesterday and that they will tomorrow. Unfortunately for managers, competitors change strategies. They introduce new products, for instance, with improved features. Motorola, as a case in point, is continually bombarded by Intel's introduction of ever more powerful microprocessors.

Organizations also face the possibility that new competitors will surface. That is, the players will change. Ten years ago, cable companies could concentrate their attention on other cable rivals. Not today. Telephone companies and firms that sell home-satellite dishes are aggressive competitors for cable service.

Suppliers

Organizations depend on raw materials, labor, and capital to operate. If availability of those resources is restricted, if their prices increase, or if their quality suffers, the ability of the organization to continue operating can be threatened.

Paper manufacturers did very well in 1995. Demand was strong, plants were running at full capacity, and manufacturers were able to push through big price increases. But the price increases created serious problems for newspaper publishers. The cost of news pulp rose more than 40 percent during the year. In addition, supplies were often interrupted. Many newspapers actually had to reduce the size of their daily editions in order to preserve their paper stock.

All organizations rely on people to accomplish goals. They're dependent, therefore, on the availability of labor inputs. The growth of many software companies, in recent years, has been restricted solely because of the limited supply of high-caliber software engineers. Of course, labor uncertainty is most visible when a firm's work force is unionized, because a strike can cut off the organization's labor supply. For instance, when a coalition of Hyundai unions recently called a general strike against nine Hyundai companies in Ulsan, South Korea, 60,000 of its workers refused to come to work and caused a complete shutdown of Hyundai plants.[3]

In addition to materials and labor, organizations need capital to operate. Capital can come from internally generated profits, investors who buy equity in the firm, or lenders who loan the organization money. Highly profitable and well-regarded companies have no trouble obtaining money to operate. And they can secure funds at favorable terms. Other companies, however, depend on suppliers, banks, and other financial institutions for capital. To the degree that those sources withhold support, they create uncertainty for management.

Government

Government creates uncertainty for organizations through changes in regulations, the degree to which it enforces regulations, and through its actions that can create economic and political instability.

The Americans with Disabilities Act (ADA) became law in the United States in 1992. In ADA's first year, complaints against companies averaged 1,200 a month. Half of those charges were for wrongful discharge, and another 22 percent were for failure to accommodate an individual to an existing job.[4]

In September 1994, Microsoft announced that it was buying Intuit, the leader in personal financial software, for $1.5 billion. But by the end of 1995, the deal was dead. The reason: The U.S. Department of Justice, concerned about past practices of Microsoft that Justice claimed restricted competition, sought to block the deal using U.S. antitrust laws.[5]

In January 1991, the U.S. Congress added a 10 percent luxury tax on boats costing more than $100,000. This action dramatically cut sales of high-priced boats. Industry sales dropped from $18 billion to under $11 billion, and many small boat builders went out of business. Sales rebounded after August 1993, when Congress repealed the luxury tax, but it was too late for some firms.[6]

Economic and political actions of governments can also play havoc with organizations. In early 1995, for example, when the Mexican government devalued the peso relative to the dollar, it created problems for every global firm operating in Mexico. For instance, 2,600 workers at the Ciudad Juarez plant of French giant Thomson Consumer Electronics walked off the job to protest the 40 percent cut in the value of their wages caused by the peso's devaluation.[7] Along similar lines, no business operating in Hong Kong can ignore the ramifications of the colony's return to Chinese rule in 1997.[8]

Media

You've probably heard this joke before: What's the worst thing a secretary can say to his or her boss? "Mike Wallace and the camera crew from *60 Minutes* are here and would like to talk with you."

The bold headline in the *Arizona Daily Star* read, "Econo Lube Cited in 68 Bureau Complaints."[9] The article then proceeded to describe how the Better Business Bureau had received an unusually high number of claims for poor workmanship, unnecessary repairs, incomplete work, and excessive bills at six Econo Lube shops in Tucson. This publicity seriously damaged the company's local reputation and resulted in a significant loss of business.

The above examples illustrate how television, newspapers, and other media create uncertainty for organizations by their power to influence consumers and regulatory agencies. Unflattering exposés on national television programs or in publications such as the *Wall Street Journal* or *Fortune* magazine have caused dramatic declines in a company's stock, derailed plans to sell new securities, precipitated legal action and multimillion-dollar fines, and even resulted in an occasional corporate bankruptcy. On the other hand, favorable media publicity can do just the opposite. A positive review of Apple's PowerBook 5 series in several computer magazines, for instance, accelerated demand and forced management to increase production of these portable computers.

Special Interests

Organizations are vulnerable to bad publicity, boycotts, and consumer pressures from special interest groups. We can highlight a few examples. Mothers Against Drunk Drivers attacks beer manufacturers such as Miller's and Anheuser-Busch for advertising to young people. The American Association of Retired Persons lobbies restaurants and cinemas to offer senior discounts. The Christian Coalition promotes its pro-life agenda by picketing in front of facilities that perform abortions. Meanwhile, women's groups boycott Domino's Pizza because its owner, Tom Monaghan, financially supports pro-life advocates.

IN THE NEWS

Activists Protest New Wal-Mart Stores

AGING SOCIAL ACTIVISTS FROM THE 1960S AND 1970S ARE RALLYING AROUND A NEW CAUSE: STOPPING Wal-Marts from being built in their communities. To these activists, Wal-Mart stands for everything they dislike about American society—mindless consumerism, paved landscapes, and homogenization of community identity.

Wal-Mart is the world's largest retailer. Its current strategic plan is to expand from its traditional rural locations to more densely populated settings. But it is running into some very aggressive action to restrict its growth plans. Listen to what some of these activists are saying:

"We've lost a sense of taste, of refinement—we're destroying our culture and replacing it with . . . Wal-Mart," states an Ohio high school teacher.

"I really hate Wal-Mart," says a self-employed clothing designer. "Everything's starting to look the same, everybody buys all the same things—a lot of small-town character is being lost. They disrupt local communities, they hurt small businesses, they add to our sprawl and pollution because everybody drives farther, they don't pay a living wage—and visually, they're atrocious."

A former Vietnam protester who now helps coordinate anti-Wal-Mart campaigns across the United States, Canada, and Puerto Rico helped keep Wal-Mart out of Greenfield, Massachusetts, by rousing citizens' with newspaper ads. One read: "You can't buy small-town life at a Wal-Mart. You can only lose it there." Another former Vietnam protester persuaded three television newscasts and a daily paper to cover an anti-Wal-Mart rally in Litiz, Pennsylvania.

There are at least forty organized groups actively opposing proposed or anticipated Wal-Mart stores in communities such as Oceanside, California; Gaithersburg, Maryland; Quincy, Massachusetts; East Lampeter, Pennsylvania; Lake Placid, New York; and Gallatin, Tennessee.

These anti-Wal-Mart efforts have had some success in curtailing the discount retailer's expansion plans. Opponents have delayed some stores and led Wal-Mart to drop plans in Greenfield, Massachusetts, and two other towns in that state, as well as in Bath, Maine; Simi Valley, California; and Ross and West Hempfield, Pennsylvania.

Nathan Wallace-Senft of North Bennington, Vermont, protests the opening of the first Wal-Mart store in Vermont.

Source: B. Ortega, "Aging Activists Turn, Turn, Turn Attention to Wal-Mart Protests," *Wall Street Journal,* October 11, 1994, p. A1. Reprinted by permission of *Wall Street Journal,* © 1994, Dow Jones & Co., Inc. All rights reserved worldwide.

ENVIRONMENTAL SCANNING

Maria Iriti, who runs a glass company in Massachusetts, put in a bid of $18,000 to repair stained glass windows in a church. She won the bid but lost a bundle. She later found out that the next lowest bid had come in at $76,000. Iriti learned a valuable lesson from her mistake. She now keeps a folder on each competitor, socializes with them at trade shows, and has friends write to competitors for price lists and brochures.[10]

Managers in both small and large organizations are increasingly turning to **environmental scanning** to anticipate and interpret changes in their environment.[11] The term, as we'll use it, refers to screening large amounts of information to detect emerging trends, monitoring the actions of others, and creating a set of scenarios.

The importance of environmental scanning was first recognized (outside of the national security community) by firms in the life insurance industry in the late 1970s.[12] Life insurance companies found that the demand for their product was declining. Yet all the key environmental signals they were receiving strongly favored the sale of life insurance. The economy and population were growing. Baby boomers were finishing school, entering the labor force, and taking on family responsibilities. The market for life insurance should have been expanding. But it wasn't. What the insurance companies had failed to recognize was a fundamental change in family structure in the United States.

Young families, who represented the primary group of buyers of new insurance policies, tended to be dual-career couples who were increasingly choosing to remain childless. The life insurance needs of a family with one income, a dependent spouse, and a houseful of kids are much greater than those of a two-income family with few, if any, children. That a multibillion-dollar industry could overlook such a fundamental social trend underscored the need to develop techniques for monitoring important environmental developments.

ENVIRONMENTAL-SCANNING TOOLS

There are four main environmental-scanning techniques: competitive intelligence, scenario development, forecasting, and benchmarking.

Competitive Intelligence

One of the fastest-growing tools of environmental scanning is **competitive intelligence.**[13] It seeks basic information about competitors. Who are they? What are they doing? How will what they're doing affect us? As Maria Iriti learned the hard way, accurate information on the competition can allow managers to *anticipate* competitor actions rather than merely *react* to them.

One expert on competitive intelligence emphasizes that 95 percent of the competitor-related information an organization needs to make crucial strategic decisions is available and accessible to the public.[14] In other words, competitive intelligence isn't organizational espionage. Advertisements, promotional materials, press releases, reports filed with government agencies, annual reports, employment want ads, newspaper reports, and industry studies are examples of readily available sources of information. Specific information on your industry and competitors is increasingly available through electronic databases. Managers can literally tap into a wealth of competitive information through purchasing access to databases sold by companies such as Nexus and Knight-Ridder. Trade shows and the debriefing of your own sales force can be other good sources of information on competitors. Many firms even regularly buy competitors' products and have their own engineers break them down to learn about new technical innovations.

If you're in any segment of the computer business, the annual Comdex trade show in Las Vegas is a dream come true for engaging in competitive intelligence.[15] Computer firm representatives, many posing as customers, eavesdrop on conversations, examine competitors' products, and elicit information about pricing, performance, shipping dates, what chips are used, and who supplies key components. For instance, at a recent Comdex show, Michael Dell of Dell Computer moved quickly from exhibit to exhibit, checking out new products and grabbing brochures. In an interview, Dell revealed that his competitive intelligence tactics at Comdex a few years earlier had helped convince him that the notebooks he had on the drawing board weren't competitive with products already on the showroom floor. So he scrapped his plans and started over from scratch.

Scenario Development

Extensive environmental scanning is likely to reveal issues and concerns that could affect an organization's current or planned operations. They are not likely to be equally important, so it's usually necessary to focus on a limited set—say, three or four—that are most important and to develop scenarios based on each.

A **scenario** is a consistent view of what the future is likely to be. For instance, in 1996, President Clinton was actively seeking to increase the national minimum wage in the United States. At the time, it was $4.45 an hour. The proposals being discussed ranged from $5.00 to $5.75 an hour. McDonald's management was aware of these proposals because of their scanning activities. In response, they created a multiple set of scenarios to assess the possible consequences of new minimum-wage legislation. What, for example, would be the implications for the company's labor supply if the minimum were raised to $5.00 an hour? To $5.50 an hour? Different assumptions lead to different outcomes. The intention of this exercise is not to try to predict the future, but to reduce uncertainty by playing out potential situations under different specified conditions.[16] In McDonald's case, they developed a set of scenarios ranging from optimistic to pessimistic in terms of the minimum-wage issue. The company was then prepared to initiate changes in its strategy if new legislation passed.

Forecasting

Environmental scanning creates the foundation for forecasts. Information obtained through scanning is used to form scenarios. These, in turn, establish parameters for **forecasts,** which are predictions of outcomes.

Types of Forecasts Probably the two most popular outcomes for which management is likely to seek forecasts are future revenues and new technological breakthroughs. However, virtually any component in the organization's environment can be the focus of forecasting attention.

Mitsubishi Corporation's sales level drives purchasing requirements, production goals, employment needs, inventories, and numerous other decisions. Similarly, the University of Michigan's income from tuition, donations, grants, and state appropriations will determine course offerings, staffing needs, salary increases for faculty, and the like. Both of these examples illustrate that predicting future revenues—**revenue forecasting**—is a critical activity for both profit and not-for-profit organizations.

Where does management get the data for developing revenue forecasts? Typically, it begins with historical revenue figures. For example, what were last year's revenues? This figure can then be adjusted for trends. What revenue patterns have evolved over recent years? What changes in social and economic factors or actions of rivals might alter the pattern in the future? Answers to questions such as these provide the basis for revenue forecasts.

You probably haven't given much thought to the subject of college textbooks, but it's a fairly good bet that texts, as you know them, will soon look very different. College textbook publishers know that change is in the air, but there is little agreement among decision makers at these firms as to what form the content will take and when these changes are likely to be realized. CD-ROM technology, for instance, could permit students to purchase interactive texts on disks. Some "books" are already being produced in this format. The major barrier to CD-ROM texts is the high cost of the hardware needed to play them. The faster the price of this hardware declines, the sooner most students will own computers with CD-ROM players. But CD-ROM is only one technological alternative among many. Another option could be nonpaper texts that are bought directly from publishers through on-line services. Some publishers think the future might have students purchasing digital "books" by downloading texts on their personal computers via modem hookup to the publisher's central data bank. You could call the publisher's toll-free number, use your credit card for payment, and then download the texts you need for your courses onto your personal computer. You could do all this in just minutes, and you would never have to step inside a bookstore. The point of these scenarios is that technology is very likely to change textbook publishing sometime in the near future. Those publishers that can accurately forecast when the market will be ready for these changes, what format the changes will take, and their specific structure, will be able to score big in the market.

Technological forecasting attempts to predict changes in technology and the time frame in which new technologies are likely to be economically feasible. The rapid pace of technological change has seen innovations in lasers, biotechnology, robotics, and data communications dramatically change surgery practices, pharmaceutical offerings, the processes used for manufacturing almost every mass-produced product, and the practicality of networked computers and cellular telephones. Few organizations are exempt from the possibility that technological innovation might dramatically change the demand for their current products or services. Those organizations that do a better job of technological forecasting will have a leg up on their competitors.

Forecasting Techniques Forecasting techniques fall into two general categories: quantitative and qualitative. **Quantitative forecasting** applies a set of mathematical rules to a series of past data to predict future outcomes. These techniques are preferred when management has sufficient "hard" data from which to work. **Qualitative forecasts,** on the other hand, use the judgment and opinions of knowledgeable individuals. Qualitative techniques typically are used when precise data are scarce or difficult to obtain. Exhibit 4-2 on page 106 lists some of the better-known quantitative and qualitative forecasting techniques.

Forecasting Effectiveness In the early 1980s, when Alain Gomez became chairman of Thomson Group, the state-owned French conglomerate, he decided to take advantage of the growing trend toward a unified Europe to build a powerful, European high-tech company.[17] His strategy was based on forecasts of a continued worldwide defense buildup and a rapid movement to a European Union. Unfortunately for Gomez and his company, his forecasts missed the mark. Just as he had all the pieces in place to dominate world defense and consumer electronics markets, the environment changed. The Cold War started winding down, and military budgets around the world began shrinking. Powerful U.S. defense companies also began competing harder for shares of the diminished market. Meanwhile, movement toward greater European unity stalled, and what progress had

EXHIBIT 4-2
Forecasting Techniques

Technique	Description	Example
Quantitative		
Time-series analysis	Fits a trend line to a mathematical equation and projects into the future by means of this equation	Predicting next quarter's sales of Dove Bars based on 3 years' of previous sales data
Regression models	Predicts one variable on the basis of known or assumed other variables	Predicting level of sales for Marlboro cigarettes on basis of different advertising outlays
Econometric models	Uses a set of regression equations to simulate segments of the economy	Predicting change in sales of Hatteras yachts as a result of changes in tax law
Economic indicators	Uses one or more economic indicators to predict a future state of the economy	Using change in gross domestic product to predict discretionary income
Substitution effect	Uses a mathematical formulation to predict how, when, and under what circumstances a new product or technology will replace an existing one	Managers at Banca Inbursa of Mexico predicting the effect of ATMs on the employment of bank personnel
Qualitative		
Jury of opinion	Combines and averages the opinions of experts	Executives polling all of Sony's purchasing agents to predict future price increases in various raw materials
Sales-force composition	Combines estimates from field sales personnel of customers' expected purchases	Predicting next year's sales of GE industrial lasers
Customer evaluation	Combines estimates from established customers of expected purchases	Surveys of major retailers to determine types and quantities of Nintendo games desired

been made in creating a single market allowed Asian competitors to initiate aggressive price wars in consumer electronics. The result: Thomson's defense revenues have been steadily declining, and its consumer electronics group has become a money loser. We can generalize from the Thomson example. In spite of the importance of forecasting to effective decision making and planning, managers have had mixed success in forecasting events and outcomes accurately.[18]

The more dynamic the environment, the greater the uncertainty and the more likely management is to develop inaccurate forecasts.

Forecasting techniques are most accurate when the environment is static. The more dynamic the environment, the greater the uncertainty and the more likely management is to develop inaccurate forecasts. Forecasting has a relatively unimpressive record in predicting nonseasonal turning points such as recessions, unusual events, discontinuities, and the actions or reactions of competitors.

Although forecasting has a mixed record, there are some things managers can do to improve forecasting effectiveness.[19] First, they should rely on simple forecasting techniques. They tend to do as well as, and often better than, complex methods that tend to mistake random data for meaningful information. Second, they need to compare every forecast with "no change." A no-change forecast is very accurate approximately half the time. Third, they should not rely on any single forecasting method. Accuracy is increased by using several models and averaging them, especially for longer-range forecasts. Fourth, they should not assume that they can accurately identify turning points in a trend. What is typically perceived as a significant turning point is most often an unusual random event. Finally, accuracy declines with expanding time frames. By shortening the length of forecasts, managers can improve their accuracy.

Benchmarking

We opened this chapter by illustrating how Xerox used benchmarking to significantly improve its competitive position against Japanese rivals in the copy machine market. In this section, we describe the benchmarking process in detail and show how it has helped managers keep on top of the best practices used by competitors and others.

Benchmarking is the practice of comparing, on some measurable scale, the performance of a key business operation in-house vis-à-vis a similar operation in other organizations.[20] It is an essential element in any organization's TQM (total quality management) program. The basic idea underlying benchmarking is that management can improve quality by analyzing and copying the methods of the leaders in various fields. And because benchmarking focuses on practices outside an organization, it is appropriately classified as an environmental-scanning tool.

The typical benchmarking process follows four steps (see Exhibit 4-3):

1. The organization forms a benchmarking planning team. The team's initial task is to identify what is to be benchmarked, identify "best practices" used by other organizations, and determine data collection methods. To maximize efficiency, the team should benchmark only functions or processes that are critical to their organization's success.
2. The team collects data internally on its own operations and externally from other organizations. Teams often err in paying too little attention to self-assessment—to uncover performance gaps, they must first understand and measure their own processes.

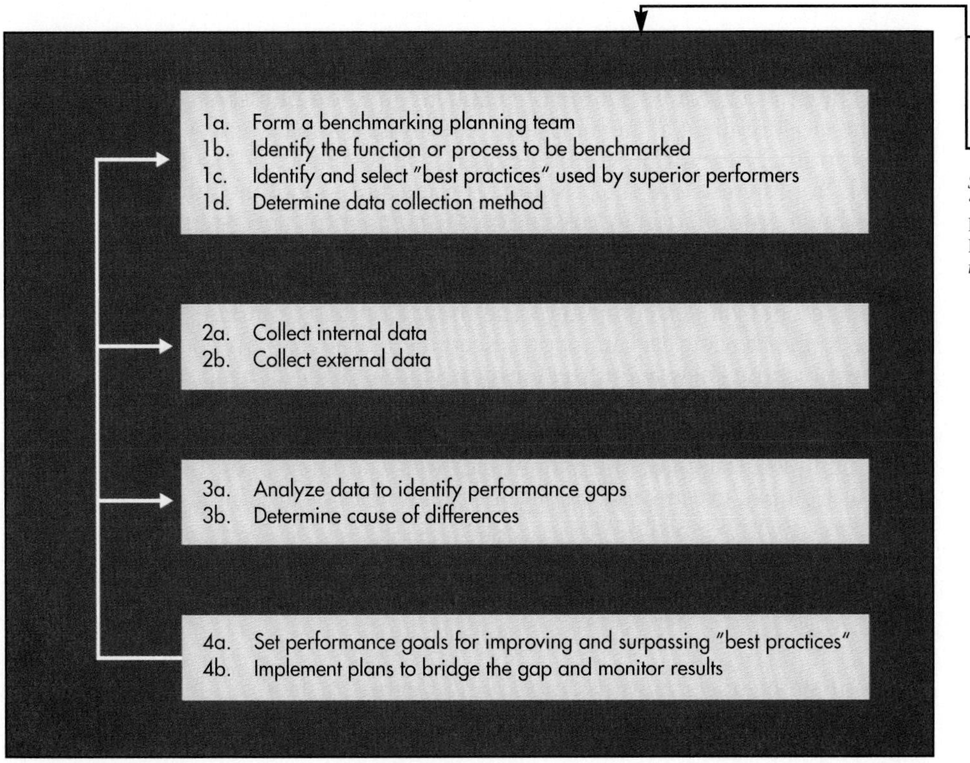
1a. Form a benchmarking planning team
1b. Identify the function or process to be benchmarked
1c. Identify and select "best practices" used by superior performers
1d. Determine data collection method
2a. Collect internal data
2b. Collect external data
3a. Analyze data to identify performance gaps
3b. Determine cause of differences
4a. Set performance goals for improving and surpassing "best practices"
4b. Implement plans to bridge the gap and monitor results

EXHIBIT 4-3
The Benchmarking Process

Source: Based on Y. K. Shetty, "Aiming High: Competitive Benchmarking for Superior Performance," *Long Range Planning,* February 1993, p. 42.

3. The data are analyzed to identify performance gaps and to determine the cause of differences.
4. An action plan is prepared and implemented that will result in meeting or exceeding the standards of others.[21]

Let's look at a few functions and processes that have been identified as "best practices" for benchmarking. Xerox has identified a long list of best-practice companies covering a variety of areas. They use Toyota and Komatsu for their manufacturing operations; American Express for billing and collection; AT&T and Hewlett-Packard for research and product development; L.L. Bean, Hershey Foods, and Mary Kay Cosmetics for distribution; Procter & Gamble for marketing; and Deere & Co. for computer operations.[22] To improve its ability to empty its planes of passengers and baggage and ready the plane for another flight, Southwest Airlines benchmarked the pit crews at Indy 500 car races. IBM used the operations of Las Vegas casinos to find ways to reduce the risk of employee theft.[23] And Giordano Holdings Ltd., a Hong Kong–based manufacturer and retailer of mass market casual wear, borrowed its "good quality, good value" concept from Marks & Spencer; used The Limited to benchmark its point-of-sales computerized information system; and modeled its simplified product offerings on McDonald's menu.[24]

ETHICAL ISSUES IN ENVIRONMENTAL SCANNING

When environmental scanning relies exclusively on data readily available to the public, there's little debate about its propriety. But what about practices such as hiring competitors' employees, planting spies in rival firms, or lying to gain competitive information?[25] Consider the following situations, and *you* judge whether environmental scanning is ethical or not.

Texas Instruments hires a senior engineering executive from Intel. The new executive is well qualified for the position, but so were a dozen or more other candidates. They, however, did not work for Intel, and they did not have up-to-date knowledge of what new microchip products Intel was developing. Is it unethical for TI, one of Intel's primary microchip competitors, to hire this executive? Is it acceptable to hire this executive but unacceptable to question him about Intel's plans?

The vice president at a major book publishing company encourages one of her editors to interview for an editorial vacancy at a competing book publisher. The editor is not interested in the position. The sole purpose of the interview will be to gain as much information as possible on the competitor's near-term publishing list and relay that information back to the vice president. Is going to such an interview unethical? Is asking a subordinate to engage in this intelligence mission wrong?

At a recent Comdex computer trade show, Compaq Computer sent a senior executive to the Hewlett-Packard booth. Keeping his badge in his pocket, he never let on how much he knew about the business, and, to conceal his position, he wore a sweater and slacks instead of a business suit. He asked numerous questions of the H-P sales representative about a specific new product. The sales rep explained how it was built, who supplied the communication technology, and H-P's future plans. Has this Compaq executive been deceitful? Has he done anything wrong?

STRATEGIES FOR MANAGING THE ENVIRONMENT

Environmental uncertainty is, in varying degrees, a fact of life for most managers.[26] Although managers would prefer to operate in a completely predictable and autonomous environment, almost all organizations face some uncertainty, and many environments are quite dynamic. Is there anything managers can do to reduce uncertainty? The answer is Yes. Managers and organizations are not totally captive to their environment. In this section, we'll briefly review strategies for managing the uncertainties presented by various forces in the environment.

Managers and organizations are not totally captive to their environment.

Classifying Strategies

In very simplistic terms, managers have two general strategies they can take in their attempt to lessen environmental uncertainty. They can respond by adapting and changing their actions to fit the environment, or they can attempt to alter the environment to fit better with the organization's capabilities. The former approach we call **internal strategies,** and the latter **external strategies.**[28]

When management selectively cuts prices or recruits executives from its competitors, it is making internal adjustments to its environment. The environment doesn't change, but the fit between the organization and the environment is improved. The result is that the organization's dependence on the environment is reduced.

External strategies are designed to actually *change* the environment. If competitive pressures are cutting an airline's profitability, it can merge with another airline to gain a synergistic network of routes. If changes suggested in a federal tax reform proposal threaten a small life insurance company, it might use its membership in a trade association to lobby against those changes.

Internal Strategies

The following internal strategies demonstrate actions that almost any organization can take to better match its environment and, in so doing, lessen the impact of the environment on the organization's operations.

Changing Domains Although there are few environments with *no* uncertainty, astute management can change domains to shift the organization into a niche with *less* uncertainty! Safeco Insurance of California provides an example of changing domains. California has given Safeco's balance sheet a couple of heavy "jolts" in recent years. First was the San Francisco earthquake, followed a few years later by an even larger earthquake in Los Angeles. After absorbing hundreds of millions of dollars in losses, Safeco's management decided to stop writing earthquake insurance in California.

When faced with an unfavorable environment, management chose to change its business focus to areas with less environmental uncertainty. Managers in many firms have pursued this strategy when faced with a hostile environment. They have, for instance, staked out a niche that has fewer or less-powerful competitors or that has barriers, such as high entry costs, economies of scale, or regulatory approval, to keep other competitors out. Or they have moved to a domain where the environment is more favorable because, for instance, there is little regulation, there are numerous suppliers, there are no unions, or public pressure groups are less powerful. Unfortunately, because there aren't many opportunities for organizations to become unregulated monopolies, most decisions to change domains substitute one set of environmental uncertainties for another.

Recruitment During the heyday of the Cold War—from the 1950s through the 1980s—major defense contractors such as McDonnell Douglas and Northrop Grumman regularly recruited high-ranking officers when they retired from military service. Why? These officers had information and contacts that could significantly improve the defense firms' likelihood of securing lucrative government contracts.

The governor of Tennessee retires and is immediately hired as president of the University of Tennessee. Why? You can bet it wasn't because he was the most knowledgeable about academic administration or the problems facing higher education. He was selected because the board thought he was the best candidate for dealing with the university's primary uncertainty—obtaining increased funding from the state.

The practice of selective hiring to reduce environmental uncertainty is widespread. For instance, corporations hire executives from competing firms to acquire information about their competitor's future plans. High-tech firms entice scientists from competitive firms with large salary increases and stock options to gain the technical expertise held by their competition. However, the greatest media attention tends to be reserved for private organizations that recruit former government officials. Business and legal firms regularly hire such officials, often at exorbitant salaries, to acquire their favorable ties with influencial decision makers and their knowledge of government operations. The major New York and Washington law firms, for instance, are full of former influential members of Congress and high-ranking presidential appointees.

Buffering In early 1995, with paper prices escalating and shortages developing, book publisher Simon & Schuster didn't sit idly by. Managers placed massive orders with paper suppliers—for quantities three or four times the amount typically ordered. Their strategy was to use stockpiled inventory to reduce the possibility of running out of paper and to cushion the blow from higher prices.

Buffering reduces the possibility that the organization's operations will be disturbed by reduction of supplies or depletion of outputs. On the input side, buffering is evident when organizations stockpile raw materials and supplies, use multiple suppliers, or engage in preventive maintenance. Buffering at the output level allows fewer options. The most obvious method is through the use of inventories. If an organization creates products that can be carried in inventory without damage, then maintaining warehouse inventories allows the organization to produce its goods at a constant rate regardless of fluctuation in sales demand. Toy manufacturers such as Mattel and Fisher-Price, for example, typically ship most of their products to retailers in the early fall for selling during the Christmas season. These manufacturers, of course, produce their toys year-round and merely stockpile them for shipping during the fall.

Smoothing Hertz will rent you a full-size car in Chicago on a weekday for $59 a day. But Hertz will rent you that same car on a Saturday or Sunday for only $42 a day. Why the difference in price? Hertz's management is smoothing demand. Business people are heavy users of rental cars, and their primary demand is during the week. Rather than have the cars sit idle on weekends, Hertz cuts prices to attract nonbusiness customers.

Smoothing seeks to level out the impact of fluctuations in the environment. Organizations that use this technique, in addition to car rental agencies, include telephone companies, retail stores, magazines, and sports teams.

The heaviest demand on telephone equipment is by business between the weekday hours of 8 A.M. and 5 P.M. Telephone companies have to have enough equipment to meet peak demand during this period. But the equipment is still there during the rest of the time. So they smooth demand by charging the highest prices during their peak period and low rates during the evenings and on weekends. Managers of retail clothing stores in North America know that their slowest months are January (after the Christmas "blitz") and August (before the "back-to-school" blitz). To reduce this "trough" in the revenue curve, they typically run their semiannual sales at these times of the year. Magazine publishers give you a substantial discount—often 50 percent or more off newsstand prices—if you become a mail subscriber. As a subscription holder, you are now a guaranteed customer for the length of your subscription. Finally, we observe that sports teams usually give fans reduced prices when they buy season tickets covering all the home games. Even if the team has a very poor win-loss record, management has assured itself of a certain amount of income.

Rationing The Mesa Grill in New York City requires reservations. Moreover, you have to call before 2 P.M. on the day of your reservation to confirm; otherwise, it will be canceled. The manager of the Mesa Grill has only a fixed number of seats in his restaurant, and he wants to be as certain as possible that every one is filled. His reservation system essentially rations those seats.

When uncertainty is created by way of excess demand, management may consider **rationing** products or services: that is, allocating output according to some priority system. In addition to restaurants, examples of rationing can be found in many organizations. Hospitals, for instance, often ration beds for nonemergency admissions. And when a disaster strikes—fire, flood, earthquake, plane crash—beds are made available only to the most serious cases. The U.S. Postal Service resorts to rationing, particularly during the peak Christmas rush. First-class mail takes priority, and lesser classes are handled on an "as-available" basis. Have you ever called a mail-order firm or the ticket office for a major airline? If you have, you probably heard something like: "Currently all our agents are busy. But please hold. Your call will be answered in the order in which it was received." This is an illustration of management's rationing the time of their telephone agents.

Geographic Dispersion Japanese car manufacturers Toyota, Nissan, and Honda have all built plants in the United States. So, too, have German manufacturers BMW and Mercedes. By building plants in the United States, these companies have lessened their dependence on fluctuating currency rates and have reduced potential criticism that they are making profits in the United States but not creating jobs.

Environmental uncertainty sometimes varies with location. There is clearly more political uncertainty for a business firm operating in Iran than for one operating in Switzerland. To lessen location-induced uncertainty, organizations can move to a different community or operate in multiple locations.

Historically, unions were strongest in the northeastern United States and weakest in the South. Many business firms responded by moving their operations to the South. In so doing, they reduced one uncertainty—union-induced strikes or walkouts—from their environment. One of the major advantages of being a global company is that it spreads risk and uncertainty. Christies International PLC is a British firm, but it runs auctions in New York, Paris, Geneva, Sydney, and Tokyo as well as London. By globally dispersing its operations, Christies is less vulnerable to economic recessions in any one country.

External Strategies

Now we turn to strategies that directly seek to change the environment to make it more favorable for an organization. These include everything from the use of advertising to shape consumer tastes to illegal agreements with a rival to restrict competition.

Advertising Wrigley, the chewing gum maker, advertised its products in the United States throughout World War II. What's interesting about this fact is that the company didn't sell chewing gum in the United States during those years! All its output was being bought by the military for use by service personnel overseas. But Wrigley's management wanted to be sure that civilian demand for its products would still be there when the war was over. So it continued its advertising campaigns.

Nestlé, the giant Swiss consumer products firm, spends hundreds of millions of dollars each year to promote Kit Kat candy bars, Friskies pet food, Carnation ice cream, Buitoni pasta, and dozens of other Nestlé products. Through extensive advertising, Nestlé's management seeks to reduce competitive pressures, stabilize demand, and allow it the opportunity to set prices with less concern for the response of its competitors.

The organization that can build brand loyalty reduces uncertainty. Advertising, then, is a device that management uses to lessen its dependence on fickle consumers and new alternatives offered by the competition.

Maybe the classic example of advertising's creating a following and sustaining demand for a product over time is Bayer aspirin. The content of aspirin is the same regardless of brand name. Yet Bayer AG, the aspirin's maker, has convinced a significant segment of the aspirin-buying public that Bayer's "pure aspirin" is superior to its rivals' aspirin and so a price from two to five times higher than that of generic brands is justified.

Contracting A major soap manufacturer—whose products are household names—contracts to sell 10,000 cases a month of its standard detergent to discount operator Price/Costco, that will be sold under Price/Costco's private label. This strategy assures the soap manufacturer of a certain amount of sales and reduces its dependency on the fluctuating preferences of consumers. Similarly, KLM Airlines contracts with Royal Dutch Shell to buy fuel on a fixed-term contract, thus reducing KLM's susceptibility to fluctuations in availability and price.

Contracting protects the organization from changes in quantity or price on either the input or the output side. We see this strategy used when management agrees to a long-term fixed contract to purchase materials and supplies or to sell a certain part of the organization's output.

Coopting Look at the makeup of the board of directors of any major corporation. External members are likely to be prominent names from finance, politics, the media, and industry. The selection of external board members is not a random process. Astute management chooses individuals who can reduce uncertainty for their organization.[28]

Managers resort to **coopting** uncertainties when they absorb those individuals or organizations in the environment that threaten their organization's stability. If an organization's primary need is capital, expect to find a high percentage of directors from banks, insurance companies, mutual funds, and other financial institutions. Regulated industries such as public utilities are overseen by government agencies, and these industries respond by disproportionately loading their boards with lawyers. Following this theme, you can expect organizations facing labor uncertainties to appoint union officers to their boards; those vulnerable to public sentiment to appoint board members who are consumer advocates, prominent women, or minority spokespersons; those whose legitimacy is in question to include on the board winners of the Nobel Prize, prominent military heroes, or similarly accomplished individuals.

Coalescing Du Pont and Phillips joined forces to develop, produce, and sell optical-storage disks. Caterpillar and Mitsubishi teamed up to manufacture giant

IN THE NEWS

Joining Up with the Dream Team

In January 1995, David Geffen, Jeffrey Katzenberg, and Steven Spielberg announced the creation of Hollywood's newest studio. Each has been incredibly successful in his own right. Geffen became a billionaire from the record business. Katzenberg led Disney's resurgence in animation. And Spielberg, of course, is the genius behind such money-making films as *E.T.: The Extra Terrestrial, Jaws, Jurassic Park,* and *Schindler's List.* Now they've founded DreamWorks as a vehicle to make movies, interactive games, animated films, and records.

The three co-founders have put in an estimated $100 million of their own money and control two-thirds of the company. But they're spreading the risk. Why put up all your own money if you don't have to? And these three *don't have to!* With their company barely 4 months old, and not having produced a single product, the DreamWorks' founders had entrepreneurs as well as entertainment, financial, and software companies lining up to throw money and deals at them.

Paul Allen, co-founder of Microsoft, invested $500 million and got himself 18.3 percent of DreamWorks. Independently, Microsoft committed about $100 million both as an investment and to begin a joint venture that will create multimedia software.

Capital Cities/ABC/Disney has put $100 million into a joint venture to produce TV shows with DreamWorks. Bankers Trust and Chemical Bank are assembling a $1 billion credit line. Samsung and Bell Atlantic are considering paying the co-founders $900 million for a one-third interest in the company. Silicon Graphics wants DreamWorks to help them develop a futuristic, digitalized studio. MCA wants to distribute DreamWorks' records, movies, and videos. And DreamWorks is talking to three pay-movie channels—Encore!, Home Box Office, and Showtime—about cable distribution deals. "All you do is look at their track record," says Encore! Chairman John Sie. "How can you lose?"

DreamWorks founders (from left) David Geffen, Jeffrey Katzenberg, and Steven Spielberg.

Source: Based on R. Grover, "They're Stuffing Money through the Studio Gates," *Business Week,* March 6, 1995, p. 38; and K. Maney, "DreamWorks and Microsoft Join Forces," *USA Today,* March 23, 1995, p. B1.

earthmovers. Lufthansa is working with Deutsche Telekom on a multimedia program to speed aircraft repairs. Suzuki is manufacturing GEOs, and General Motors is distributing them under the Chevrolet nameplate. These are examples of **coalescing**—combining with one or more other organizations for the purpose of joint action. It includes mergers, joint ventures, and cooperative (though illegal) agreements to fix prices or split markets.

Mergers and joint ventures are legal means for organizations to manage their environment. They frequently reduce environmental uncertainty by lessening interorganizational competition and dependency. For instance, Chevron's acquisition of Gulf Oil created one less player in the big-oil game. In contrast, while illegal cooperative activities for managing the environment are certainly not condoned here, we do need to acknowledge their existence. For example, many states make it illegal for real estate agents to conspire to set a fixed sales commission rate. Yet within these states, agents' commissions almost never deviate from the 6 or 7 percent "norm." Selling real estate requires cooperation among many agents. Most use multiple-listing services, which create the opportunity for implicit cooperative agreements to develop. Moreover, any agent who undercuts the norm will find other agents uncooperative. The result is that the real estate sales industry essentially operates with fixed prices.

Lobbying Since 1991, Microsoft's competitors have been ganging up to attack what they believe are unfair practices by the software giant. Apple Computer, Novell, Lotus Development, Oracle, Sun Microsystems, Sybase, Borland International, and America Online have lobbied the U.S. Federal Trade Commission and the Department of Justice to restrain Microsoft's allegedly monopolistic practices.[29] Microsoft's position is that it has done nothing wrong and that these competitors are merely looking for government to do what these firms have been unable to do in the free market. To the degree that Microsoft's competitors succeed in influencing government in restraining Microsoft and reducing its control of the software industry, these competitors will have effectively reduced environmental uncertainty.

Lobbying—using influence to achieve favorable outcomes—is a widespread practice used by organizations to manage their environment. For instance, many companies and industry groups have formed political action committees (PACs). These PACs are a major source of funds for political candidates. And organizations that seek particular advantages can direct money through PACs to those candidates who will support their interests. In addition, trade and professional associations actively lobby on behalf of their members. The Tobacco Institute and the National Rifle Association fight hard in Washington and in state capitals to reduce uncertainties that might affect tobacco and gun interests, respectively. Some organizations also use the power of the government to stabilize relationships in an industry. Doctors, chiropractors, and other professionals lobby state licensing boards to restrict entry, regulate competition, and keep their professions more stable.

Applications

Success in managing the environment requires managers to analyze the source of uncertainty and then select a strategy that the organization can effectively implement. Exhibit 4-4 presents some responses managers can make to reduce environmental uncertainty. The strategic actions listed are only examples. They do not purport to be *all* or the *only* options available to management.

The U.S. tobacco industry illustrates how firms can use some of the strategies in the preceding section to manage their environment. The major area of uncertainty facing this industry has been government regulation—at the local, state, and federal levels. Since the late 1960s, several tobacco firms have responded by expanding their domain through diversification. R.J. Reynolds Industries purchased Nabisco Brands and became RJR Nabisco. Philip Morris bought General Foods and Kraft. These merged companies are now more food companies than cigarette manufacturers. Meanwhile, the Liggett Group changed domains by selling off its tobacco division to a British firm.

Another response of tobacco firms has been to spend heavily on lobbying. They have fought hard to defeat any legislation that has sought to limit smoking in public areas and at the workplace. Individual tobacco firms and the Tobacco Institute (which is supported by tobacco companies) have also contributed funds for research on the relationship between smoking and cancer. The companies realize that it is statistically unlikely that the research will "prove" that smoking causes cancer, thus giving the tobacco firms more data to cloud the controversy. Moreover, if such research is unfavorable to tobacco interests, the researchers

EXHIBIT 4-4
Matching Sources of Uncertainty with Strategic Actions

Source	Examples of Strategic Actions
Government	Lobby for favorable treatment Recruit former government officials Relocate to a different governmental jurisdiction
Competitors	Advertise to build brand loyalty Select a less competitive domain Merge with competition to gain larger market share
Unions	Negotiate a long-term collective-bargaining agreement Build facilities in countries with a large, low-cost labor supply Appoint prestigious union officials to board of directors
Suppliers	Use multiple suppliers Inventory critical supplies Negotiate long-term contracts
Financial institutions	Appoint financial executives to board Establish a line of credit to draw upon when needed Use multiple financial sources
Customers	Advertise Use a differentiated price structure Change domain to where there are more customers
Special interest groups	Appoint critics to board Engage in visible activities that are socially conscious Use trade association to counter criticism

Source: Adapted from S. P. Robbins, *Organization Theory: Structure, Design, and Applications*, 3rd ed. (© 1990), p. 377. Reprinted by permission of Prentice Hall, Upper Saddle River, N. J.

have no strong motivations to publicize their findings widely. Why kill the goose that lays the golden eggs?

Finally, tobacco firms have aggressively used advertising to protect their interests. In the late 1980s, this advertising focused on selling the position that tobacco companies were not trying to convert nonsmokers; rather, they were trying to get current smokers to switch to their brand. This approach was probably best exemplified in the Carlton ad campaign that merely stated, in very large typeface, "IF YOU SMOKE, please try Carlton." In more recent years, tobacco ads have been specifically directed at countering the strong antismoking forces. Emphasis in these ads has been on framing the decision to smoke as a "right" and laws to restrict smoking as an attack on individual freedom.

CONTEMPORARY ORGANIZATION-ENVIRONMENT ISSUES

We close this chapter by addressing four current issues that deal with the organization-environment interface. First, we consider how managers need to adjust their actions when dealing with people from different national cultures. Second, we look at how organizations can become more socially conscious and responsive. Third, we describe what some managements are doing to more effectively "satisfy the customer." And finally, we discuss the rise of global quality standards and their implications for management practice.

Adjusting Management Practices to Different National Cultures

When Corning and giant Mexican glass manufacturer Vitro created a joint venture in 1991, it seemed a blessed union.[30] By 1994, the honeymoon was over. Corning gave back Vitro's $130 million investment and called off the joint venture. The reason for failure illustrates the challenges of merging different national cultures. Business in Mexico is done on a consensus basis, is sensitive to the concerns of others, and often is slow by U.S. standards. Corporate style is also more formal in Mexico than in the United States.

Employees at Corning and Vitro took a different approach to work, reflected in everything from scheduling to decision making to etiquette. Corning managers were sometimes left waiting for important decisions about marketing and sales because in the Mexican culture only top managers make them, and at Vitro those people were busy with other matters. The Mexicans frequently thought Corning moved too fast; the Americans felt Vitro was too slow. The Mexicans sometimes saw the Americans as too direct, while Vitro managers, in their dogged pursuit of politeness, often seemed to the Americans as unwilling to acknowledge problems and faults. Executives at the two firms even responded to the failure of their venture differently. Corning people openly discussed what went wrong and tried to learn from the experience. Their counterparts at Vitro were reluctant to criticize anyone and wanted to focus on positive aspects of the venture.

The United States and Mexico share a common border, but their cultures are different. Therefore, it is difficult for them to work together or to manage individuals from the other's culture. But this fact is generalizable to interactions between people from many different nations. So we ponder these two questions: How do cultures differ? And what are the implications of these differences to management practice?

Cultural Differences The most comprehensive and accepted framework for analyzing national cultures identifies five dimensions along which they can differ:[31]

1. *Power distance.* The degree to which people in a country accept that power in institutions and organizations is distributed unequally. Ranges from relatively equal (low power distance) to extremely unequal (high power distance).
2. *Individualism versus collectivism.* Individualism is the degree to which people in a country prefer to act as individuals rather than as members of groups. Collectivism is the opposite, or the equivalent of low individualism.
3. *Quantity of life versus quality of life.* Quantity of life is the degree to which values such as assertiveness, the acquisition of money and material goods, and competition prevail. Quality of life is the degree to which people value relationships and show sensitivity and concern for the welfare of others.[32]
4. *Uncertainty avoidance.* The degree to which people in a country prefer structured over unstructured situations. People with high uncertainty avoidance prefer structured situations. In countries that score high on uncertainty avoidance, people have a higher level of anxiety, which manifests itself in greater nervousness, stress, and aggressiveness.
5. *Long-term versus short-term orientation.* People in long-term countries look to the future and value thrift and persistence. A short-term orientation values the past and present and emphasizes respect for tradition and fulfilling social obligations.

Exhibit 4-5 provides a summary of how ten countries rate on these five dimensions. For instance, not surprisingly, most Asian countries are more collectivist than individualistic. On the other hand, the United States ranked highest among all countries surveyed on individualism.

EXHIBIT 4-5
Examples of Cultural Dimensions

Country	Power Distance	Individualism*	Quantity of Life†	Uncertainty Avoidance	Long-Term Orientation††
China	High	Low	Moderate	Moderate	High
France	High	High	Moderate	High	Low
Germany	Low	High	High	Moderate	Moderate
Hong Kong	High	Low	High	Low	High
Indonesia	High	Low	Moderate	Low	Low
Japan	Moderate	Moderate	High	Moderate	Moderate
Netherlands	Low	High	Low	Moderate	Moderate
Russia	High	Moderate	Low	High	Low
United States	Low	High	High	Low	Low
West Africa	High	Low	Moderate	Moderate	Low

Source: Adapted from G. Hofstede, "Cultural Constraints in Management Theories," *The Executive,* February 1993, p. 91.
* A low score is synonymous with collectivism.
† A low score is synonymous with high quality of life.
††A low score is synonymous with a short-term orientation.

Implications for Management Practice A country's score on the five cultural dimensions can go a long way toward helping you understand what management practices are considered normal and desirable in a specific country. For instance, a high power distance society accepts wide differences in power in organizations. Employees show a great deal of respect for those in authority. Titles, rank, and status carry a lot of weight. When negotiating in high power distance countries, companies find that it helps to send representatives with titles at least as high as the title of those with whom they are bargaining. In contrast, low power distance societies play down inequalities as much as possible. Superiors will still have authority, but employees are not fearful or in awe of the boss.

Performance evaluation and reward systems look different in countries that score high on individualism than in high-collectivism countries. As might be expected, managers in high-individualism countries emphasize and reward individual contribution. Managers in high-collectivist societies tend to stress being part of the work group and to evaluate and reward groups of employees rather than any specific individual.

Countries that score high on quantity of life almost all have strong capitalistic economic systems. They value materialism and achievement. Managers in these countries encourage competition among individuals and teams. Organizations in these countries also tend to place high importance on status differences between managerial levels, pay differentials, performance bonuses, and other visible material symbols.

Employees in high uncertainty avoidance countries are threatened by uncertainty and ambiguity. So organizations in these countries tend to create mechanisms to provide security and reduce risk. Their organizations are likely to have formal rules and there will be little tolerance for deviant ideas and behaviors. In organizations in countries with high uncertainty avoidance, employees demonstrate relatively low job mobility, and lifetime employment is a widely practiced policy.

Managers in long-term orientation countries are likely to focus on the future. They feel comfortable with implementing change, pursuing new markets, and introducing new policies and practices. In short-term cultures, the emphasis is on preserving traditional ways of doing things and respecting historical precedents. Managers are expected to support and maintain those traditions.

In summary, there is substantial evidence that national cultures differ in terms of the fundamental values held by the majority. These values, in turn, shape employee expectations and managerial practices. Effective managers, therefore, realize the need to modify their behavior when dealing with people from different cultures or when managing in a country significantly different in values from the one in which they grew up.

Social Responsiveness

An increasing number of business firms are finding that *doing good* and *doing well* are not mutually exclusive goals.

An increasing number of business firms are finding that *doing good* and *doing well* are not mutually exclusive goals. Take a look at the following examples:[33]

- Rhino Records rewards employees who engage in charitable activities. For instance, workers who contribute 16 hours of personal time each year in community service can take Christmas week off with pay. Nearly all of Rhino's 100 employees participate in this program.
- If you telephone the Kentucky Fried Chicken restaurant on Kuala Lumpur's Jalan Ipoh, you'll get a recorded message. That's because all twenty workers are deaf. Hiring the hearing-impaired is part of the company's policy to help people in the area who normally have difficulty finding work.
- Under IBM's Community Service Assignment Program, employees can take a 1-year leave of absence, at full pay, to work with eligible nonprofit organizations. Since the program was created in 1971, more than 1,000 IBM employees have taken part.
- Workers at the clothing company Esprit of Australia are given time off work to engage in philanthropic activities in the community. The average employee gets involved in about three projects a year.
- After Hurricane Andrew, which hit southern Florida and did tens of billions of dollars in damage, building materials retailer Home Depot reduced its prices for exterior plywood in its south Florida stores, foregoing millions in profits. Its competitors raised prices an average of 100 percent!
- Hanna Andersson, a children's clothing mail-order company in Portland, Oregon, asks customers to recycle its products. Any used piece of the company's clothing that isn't torn or stained can be sent back, and 20 percent of the returned item's original price will be applied to the customer's next purchase. The company washed and donated 107,000 garments to needy children over a 9-year period.

Classical versus Socioeconomic View Not every manager or organization accepts that business has a responsibility to the larger society in which it operates. You can put the issue of social responsibility into perspective once you understand the underlying debate. Two polar positions capture the essence of that debate. On one side, there's the classical—or purely economic—view that management's only social responsibility is to maximize profits. On the other side stands the socioeconomic position, which holds that management's responsibility goes well beyond making profits to include protecting and improving society's welfare.

The most outspoken advocate of the classical view is economist and Nobel laureate Milton Friedman.[34] He argues that most managers today are professional managers, which means they don't own the businesses they run. They are employees, responsible to the stockholders. Their primary charge is therefore to conduct the business in the interests of the stockholders. And what are those interests? Friedman says that the stockholders have a single concern: financial return.

According to Friedman, when managers take it upon themselves to spend their organization's resources for the "social good," they undermine the market mechanism. Someone has to pay for this redistribution of assets. If socially responsible actions reduce profits and dividends, stockholders are the losers. If wages and benefits have to be reduced to pay for social action, employees lose. If prices are raised to pay for social actions, consumers lose. If higher prices are rejected by the market and sales drop, the business might not survive—in which case, *all* the organization's constituencies lose.

The socioeconomic view counters that times have changed and with them so have society's expectations of business. This view is best illustrated in the legal formation of corporations. Corporations are chartered by governments. The same government that creates a charter can take it away. So corporations are not independent entities, responsible only to stockholders. They also have a responsibility to the larger society that creates and sustains them.

According to proponents of the socioeconomic perspective, a major flaw in the classicists' view is their time frame. Supporters of the socioeconomic view contend that managers should be concerned with maximizing financial returns over the *long run*. To do that, they must accept some social obligations and the costs that go with them. They must protect society's welfare by *not* polluting, *not* discrimininating, *not* engaging in deceptive advertising, and the like. They must also play an affirmative role in improving society by involving themselves in their communities and contributing to charitable organizations.

Proponents of the socioeconomic position also point out that the classical view flies in the face of reality. Modern business firms are no longer merely economic institutions. They lobby, form political action committees, and engage in other activities to influence the political process for their benefit. Society accepts and even encourages business to become involved in its social, political, and legal environment. That might not have been true 30 or 40 years ago, but it is the reality of today.

From Obligations to Responsiveness In order to provide more clarity to this debate, we will differentiate three related concepts: social obligation, social responsibility, and social responsiveness.[35] This discussion should help you see how different organizations actually handle the question: How socially active should we be?

As Exhibit 4-6 depicts, social obligation is the foundation of business's social involvement. A business has fulfilled its **social obligation** when it meets its economic and legal responsibilities and no more. It does the minimum that the law

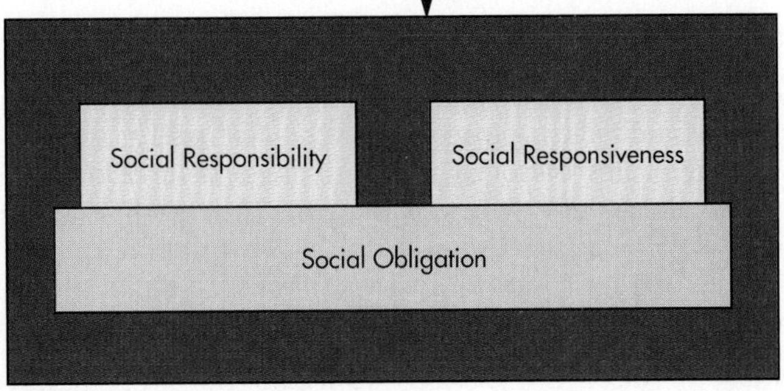

EXHIBIT 4-6
Levels of Social Involvement

Massachusetts-based Web Industries is proving that doing good and doing well can go hand-in-hand. The company hires former prisoners (pictured in photo), opens its books to workers, and distributes stock to employees. Web Industries continues to significantly increase revenues each year while, at the same time, achieving record-setting profits.

requires. A firm pursues social goals only to the extent that they contribute to its economic goals. In contrast to social obligation, both social responsibility and social responsiveness go beyond merely meeting basic economic and legal standards.

Social responsiveness refers to the capacity of a firm to adapt to changing societal conditions. As such, it's guided by social norms. Organizations that are socially responsive scan the environment to identify changing mores and attitudes. Then management modifies its practices to align with the prevailing standard.

Social responsibility adds an ethical imperative to do those things that make society better and *not* to do those that could make it worse. It's a business firm's efforts, beyond those required by the law and economics, to pursue long-term goals that are good for society. Note that social responsibility views business as a moral agent. In its effort to do *good* for society, it must differentiate between right and wrong.

A U.S. company that meets pollution control standards established by the federal government or doesn't discriminate against employees over the age of 40 in promotion decisions is meeting its social obligation and nothing more. The law says that the company may not pollute or practice age discrimination. Consider, on the other hand, Du Pont, which now provides on-site child-care facilities for employees; Procter & Gamble, which declares that Tide "is packaged in 100 percent recycled paper"; and the world's largest tuna canner, whose head says, "StarKist will not purchase, process, or sell any tuna caught in association with dolphins." These firms are being socially responsive. Why? Pressure from working mothers and environmentalists make their practices pragmatic. If these same companies had provided child care, offered recycled packaging, or sought to protect dolphins back in the early 1970s, they would have been accurately characterized as socially responsible.

Advocates of social responsiveness believe that the concept replaces philosophical discourse with pragmatism. They see it as a more tangible and achievable objective than social responsibility. Rather than assessing what is good for society in the long term, a socially responsive management scans the environment, identifies the prevailing social norms, and then changes its social involvement to respond to changing societal conditions.

Calibration supervisor Donna Voshell, with quality assurance manager Doug Grossenbaugh, led the ISO 9000 certification effort for office-equipment maker Canon Virginia.

Satisfying the Customer

It's a truism that organizations can't exist without customers. It's ironic, then, that during the 1970s and 1980s, a lot of managers seemed to take this critical constituency for granted. Instead of focusing on doing what was necessary to keep customers satisfied, managers became obsessed with financial numbers. Business organizations weren't treated as producers of products and services. Rather, they were seen as bundles of assets that were to be bought, sold, merged, leveraged, or closed down—whichever would increase their value the most. During those decades, organizations were dancing to the tunes played by financial institutions and markets. In the 1990s, as we noted in Chapter 1, managers have increasingly returned the customer to his or her rightful place as the primary determinant of an organization's success.

A 1993 *Fortune* list of companies that prided themselves on their customer-service record and turned that commitment into solid profits includes Home Depot, Toyota's Lexus, Singapore Airlines, Southwest Airlines, Banc One, Hertz, Dell Computer, Four Seasons Hotels, USAA Insurance, MCI, Federal Express, United Parcel Service, and the Grateful Dead.[36] The Grateful Dead rock band? Yep!

The Grateful Dead broke up in 1995 when lead guitarist Jerry Garcia died. But until then, they were consistently ranked among the highest-paid entertainers in the world.[37] Though they'd had only one hit record in 20 years, they continued to sell out stadiums, performing the same program. In 1993, for instance, the Dead was the top touring act in the United States and Canada, raking in more than $50 million from tickets and merchandise sales. A large part of this success can be explained by the attention that Grateful Dead Productions (GDP) gave to its customers. Grateful Dead fans were better served than the fans of any other musical artist or group. GDP's fan-club operations maintained a database of 90,000 names. Each fan received a copy of the *Grateful Dead Almanac,* a combination newsletter and product catalogue. The Dead made it easy for their ardent fans to keep track of scheduled performances—two hotlines, one for each coast, described tours and other appearances by band members. But it was the band's ticketing system that was probably the service most appreciated by customers. Grateful Dead Ticket Sales distributed up to half of all Dead concert tickets directly to fans. In addition to the hotlines and a line dedicated to ticketing instructions, there was still another line to exclusively handle ticket problems. The Dead is the only band ever to have run such an extensive ticket-service operation.

Quality and ISO 9000

In today's global economy, ISO 9000 is becoming the world standard for quality management. If a company wants to be able to convey to its customers that its products meet the highest quality standards, they can obtain ISO 9000 certification. And companies throughout the world are doing just that.[38]

In today's global economy, ISO 9000 is becoming the world standard for quality management.

What is **ISO 9000?** It's a certificate attesting that an organization's factory, laboratory, or office has met quality management requirements determined by the International Organization for Standardization in Geneva. It's a way of demonstrating process quality and consistency. Certification doesn't focus on end products. A company, for instance, can meet ISO 9000 standards and still make shoddy products (although it's not likely). Meeting the standards means that an organization is following rigid procedures for inspecting production processes, updating engineering drawings, maintaining machinery, calibrating equipment, training workers, and dealing with customer complaints. ISO 9000 standards are becoming to quality what generally accepted accounting principles have become to financial data. They are becoming an internationally recognized system for documenting quality procedures.

Getting a certificate is not an easy process. For most firms it takes between 18 months and 2 years. But when they get it, their quality standards have instant global credibility. And for some firms, meeting ISO 9000 standards is becoming an absolute necessity to do business. For instance, British Telecom, Du Pont, Eastman Kodak, General Electric, Hewlett-Packard, Motorola, and Philips Electronics are among the big-name companies that insist that their suppliers adopt ISO 9000.

IPL Inc., a 500-worker plastics fabricator in Quebec, Canada, spent 2 years and about $350,000 for its certificate. But its efforts translated into new contracts with General Motors, Bell Canada, and Frigidaire Canada. Those companies knew that IPL could be depended upon to manufacture quality products. "Once you're certified," says IPL's quality manager, "customers know you can contract to perform at a high level of quality." Tadao Okabe, president of Canon Virginia, Inc., offered a similar analysis. Since his company achieved ISO certification, it's no longer necessary for a customer such as Hewlett-Packard "to come to this plant to check all the details of our quality-control systems, again and again."

The number of companies meeting ISO 9000 standards is expanding rapidly as certification is increasingly being regarded as the price of entry into international markets. In 1994, there were about 40,000 ISO 9000-registered companies worldwide. Canada, for instance, expects to increase the number of companies with certificates to 7,500 in 1998 from about 500 in 1993.

SUMMARY

(This summary is organized by the chapter-opening learning objectives on page 97.)

1. The environment is composed of those institutions or forces that are outside the organization and potentially can affect the organization's performance, including customers, competitors, suppliers, government, media, and special interest groups.

2. Environmental scanning is important if managers are to be aware of changing tastes of customers, future actions of competitors, and similar changes taking place in their environment. Four environmental-scanning techniques are competitive intelligence, scenario development, forecasting, and benchmarking.

3. The typical benchmarking process is made up of four steps: (1) forming a planning team; (2) collecting internal and external data; (3) analyzing data to identify performance gaps and the cause of differences; and (4) preparing and implementing an action plan.

4. Managers can reduce environmental uncertainty by adapting to the environment through internal strategies such as changing domains, recruitment, buffering, smoothing, rationing, or geographical dispersion. They also can attempt to alter the environment through external stategies such as advertising, contracting, coopting, coalescing, or lobbying.
5. The five dimensions for analyzing national cultures are (1) power distance, which is a measure of power distribution; (2) preference for individual versus collective activities; (3) quantity versus quality of life, which contrasts values of materialism against concern for others; (4) uncertainty avoidance, which measures preference for structure; and (5) long-term versus short-term orientation.
6. The classical view of social responsibility argues that management's only responsibility is to maximize profits. The socioeconomic view says that management's responsibility goes well beyond making profits to include protecting and improving society's welfare.
7. Social responsibility portrays business as a moral agent, deciding what is right and wrong for society. Social responsiveness is pragmatic—managers scan the environment, identify changing mores and attitudes, and modify organizational practices to align with the prevailing standards.
8. ISO 9000 is a certificate attesting that an organization's processes have met universal quality standards. By achieving these standards, management makes it easier for its firm to compete globally because other firms interpret the standards as reducing their environmental uncertainty as related to quality.

REVIEW AND DISCUSSION QUESTIONS

1. Define and describe the three dimensions of environmental uncertainty.
2. Who are external stakeholders?
3. What are forecasts, and how accurate are they?
4. Is environmental scanning unethical? Explain.
5. Contrast internal and external strategies for managing the environment.
6. How does the United States rate on the five national culture dimensions?
7. How might managing in China be different from managing in the United States?
8. "The business of business is business." What does this statement mean to you? What are its implications for socially conscious management?
9. Are most business firms socially responsible? Explain your answer.
10. Why might a small firm producing electronic components seek ISO 9000 certification?

CASE EXERCISE A
ANDY JEHL GETS TRANSFERRED TO MEXICO

Andy Jehl joined Ford Motor Co. in 1986, after a short stint as a management consultant. His original assignment at Ford was as a productivity analyst at company headquarters in Detroit. From there he was transferred to a Mazda plant outside Toledo, Ohio (Ford owns a major portion of Mazda and frequently interchanges personnel). At Mazda, Andy began as a production supervisor. Two promotions later, Andy was assistant plant superintendent.

In the fall of 1995, Andy was informed of his next assignment, effective January 1, 1996. He was to become plant manager at the large Ford plant in Hermisillo, Mexico. Andy had mixed feelings about this assignment. It was a high-profile and coveted position within the company. But he didn't know much about Mexico and had little idea what it would be like to manage a labor force of people from a different culture. Andy grew up in Connecticut, and his total knowledge of Mexico and its people came from a couple of vacations in Cancun and Cabo San Lucas.

To prepare for his new assignment, Andy went to the local university library to see if he could get a quick education on Mexican culture. He found an informative article that discussed the struggle many U.S. executives have in adjusting to the Mexican workplace.* The following highlights some of the facts presented in the article:

- Many U.S. managers have considerable difficulty understanding the motivations and values of Mexican staff members. Many become exasperated when they can't find ways to encourage their Mexican colleagues and employees to work according to what they perceive as "commonly accepted" professional standards.
- Mexicans tend to accept the inherent worth of friends and colleagues without demanding specific performance or achievement. Americans, on the other hand, believe that one demonstrates integrity or dignity through action. Americans view performance situations in terms of winner and losers, and the one who wins is obviously the "better person." For the Mexican, the individual is special, whether the winner or not.
- Americans believe that all people are created equal. A person shouldn't look for any special favors or exemptions from the rules. No one is above the law. Rules, policies, and procedures are sometimes overlooked by the Mexican worker. Given the belief in the uniqueness of each individual, it stands to reason that people, rather than abstract principles or concepts, should be respected. Americans' insistence on "playing by the rules" is often received with amused, yet polite, disregard by Mexicans. Following the rules is often considered the most ineffective way to get things done.
- There is a strong tendency in Mexico to shun open confrontation because of fear of losing face and having to acknowledge disagreements. Negative or disappointing information is either withheld or modified to avoid being offensive or irritating. In contrast, Americans place great emphasis on stating the facts, regardless of the impact.
- Within Mexican society, there is a tendency to respect those in power. Title and position are usually sufficient to enforce authority. Americans believe respect is earned, not given.
- When a U.S. executive agrees to do something, it is a matter of personal honor and professional integrity to fulfill that commitment. For many Mexicans, a commitment is more of an intention to do something than a firm decision. A commitment is a statement of a desirable outcome, not a promise to fulfill an agreed-upon arrangement.
- Mexicans and Americans have a different perception of time. For Mexicans, there is a loose notion of what being "on time" means, interruptions are handled without undue stress, and there is little expectation that plans will proceed in a logical order. In the U.S. culture, appointments and deadlines are scheduled tightly and respected as much as possible; interruptions are annoying and inefficient; and "on time" literally means "on time."

As Andy read the article, he pondered some of the challenges that awaited him in Hermisillo.

Questions

1. How would you describe Mexican culture using the five-dimension framework presented in this chapter?
2. What changes, if any, do you think Andy will have to make in his management style and practices to be effective in his new assignment?

*M.I. Erlich, "Making Sense of the Bicultural Workplace," *Business Mexico,* August 1993, pp. 16–18.

CASE EXERCISE B
AMERICAN EAGLE AND THE GROUNDING OF THE ATR-42 AND ATR-72

On October 31, 1994, American Eagle Flight 4184 was preparing to land at Chicago's O'Hare airport. The weather was poor—drizzle at 10,000 feet and the temperature near freezing. Suddenly, the plane flipped on its side in a 70 degree roll. Within seconds, the plane—an ATR-72 made by a French-Italian consortium—slammed into a bean field near Roselawn, Indiana. All sixty-eight people on board were killed.

On December 9, 1994, the Federal Aviation Administration (FAA) banned the ATR-72 and its sister plane, the ATR-42, from flying in conditions in which ice is likely to build up on their wings. The FAA made this decision after extensive tests on the plane, which showed that control of the plane could be lost in certain foul-weather conditions.

American Eagle is a commuter division of American Airlines. It is also the largest user of the ATR commuter plane in the United States. Of the 153 ATRs affected by the FAA ruling, American Eagle operated seventy-one of them.

The FAA's decision had a major influence on American Eagle's operations in Chicago. The airline, which serves about 30 Midwestern cities from its Chicago hub, was forced to cancel 290 flights in and out of O'Hare on the first day of the ban. The ATR dilemma also acted as the straw that broke the camel's back for American Eagle's hub in Raleigh-Durham, North Carolina. This mostly commuter hub had been consistently losing money and relied heavily on ATR equipment. The company announced the immediate cancellation of about half of its daily flights in Raleigh-Durham and said it would permanently eliminate flights in and out of the airport within 30 days. American Eagle employed 778 people at the Raleigh-Durham International Airport.

Questions

1. How does this case illustrate the influence of the environment on American Eagle?
2. What, if anything, could environmental scanning have done to help American Eagle anticipate problems with the FAA?
3. If you were head of American Eagle, what could you do to minimize the effect on your company of the FAA decision?
4. Would you characterize the actions you took in question 3 as socially responsible? Socially responsive? Explain.

Source: Based on A. Bryant, "Two Types of Planes Grounded by F.A.A. in Icy Conditions," *New York Times,* December 10, 1994, p. A1; A. Bryant, "Flights Canceled after Commuter Planes Are Banned," *New York Times,* December 11, 1994, p. Y14; and S. J. Hedges, P. Cary, and R. J. Newman, "Fear of Flying: One Plane's Story," *U.S. News & World Report,* March 6, 1995, pp. 40–46.

SKILL EXERCISE

Environmental Scanning

Tina Irwin owns Friendship Cards, a small firm that designs greeting cards and sells them directly to retailers. Last year, her company had sales of a little over $300,000. She employs three full-time people and another five on a part-time basis. Because Friendship is small, Tina makes almost all key managerial decisions.

Tina has an idea for a new line of cards that combine humor and environmental issues. She knows that none of her competitors—which include Hallmark, American Greetings, and dozens of small producers like herself—have yet introduced a line exactly like what she has in mind. But she doesn't know what her competitors have planned for the coming card season. Tina is very sensitive to her competitors' actions because most are much larger than she is and command considerably more clout with retailers. Her existence depends on filling niches that competitors pass over.

If you were Tina, what sources would you utilize to find out what your competitors have planned for the coming season? Would your sources be different if you wanted to assess your competitors' plans for a year or more ahead? Be specific in your answer, and identify what information you would expect to get from each source.

NOTES

1. Based on Y. K. Shetty, "Aiming High: Competitive Benchmarking for Superior Performance," *Long Range Planning,* February 1993, pp. 39–44.
2. See G. G. Dess and D. W. Beard, "Dimensions of Organizational Task Environments," *Administrative Science Quarterly,* March 1984, pp. 52–73; E. A. Gerloff, N. K. Muir, and

W. D. Bodensteiner, "Three Components of Perceived Environmental Uncertainty: An Exploratory Analysis of the Effects of Aggregation," *Journal of Management,* December 1991, pp. 749–68; and O. Shenkar, N. Aranya, and T. Almor, "Construct Dimensions in the Contingency Model: An Analysis Comparing Metric and Non-Metric Multivariate Instruments," *Human Relations,* May 1995, pp. 559–80.

3. L. Nakarmi, "Showdown at Hyundai," *Business Week,* July 19, 1993, p. 19.
4. "The ADA Scorecard," *INC.,* January 1994, p. 11.
5. A. Cortese, "Microsoft and Intuit May Not Do It," *Business Week,* March 6, 1995, p. 6.
6. Cited in P. Mao, "Why Warren Luhrs Gave Up Ocean Racing," *Forbes,* March 13, 1995, pp. 120–21.
7. "Peso's Plunge Spurs Walkout at Factory in Northern Mexico," *New York Times,* February 1, 1995, p. A11.
8. N. McGrath, "Prospering in a Sea of Change," *Asian Business,* November 1994, pp. 28–30.
9. L. Brooks, "Econo Lube Cited in 68 Bureau Complaints," *Arizona Daily Star,* March 5, 1995, p. B1.
10. M. Robichaux, "'Competitor Intelligence': A Grapevine to Rivals' Secrets," *Wall Street Journal,* April 12, 1989, p. B2.
11. See S. C. Jain, "Environmental Scanning in U.S. Corporations," *Long Range Planning,* April 1984, pp. 117–28; L. M. Fuld, *Monitoring the Competition* (New York: John Wiley & Sons, 1988); E. H. Burack and N. J. Mathys, "Environmental Scanning Improves Strategic Planning," *Personnel Administrator,* April 1989, pp. 82–87; and A. C. Bluedorn, R. A. Johnson, D. K. Cartwright, and B. R. Barringer, "The Interface and Convergence of the Strategic Management and Organizational Environment Domain," *Journal of Management,* Summer 1994, pp. 211–19.
12. W. L. Renfro and J. L. Morrison, "Detecting Signals of Change," *The Futurist,* August 1984, p. 49.
13. See, for instance, B. D. Gelb, M. J. Saxton, G. M. Zinkhan, and N. D. Albers, "Competitive Intelligence: Insights from Executives," *Business Horizons,* January–February 1991, pp. 43–47; L. Fuld, "A Recipe for Business Intelligence," *Journal of Business Strategy,* January–February 1991, pp. 12–17; R. S. Teitelbaum, "The New Role for Intelligence," *Fortune,* November 2, 1992, pp. 104–07; S. Caudron, "I Spy, You Spy," *Industry Week,* October 3, 1994, pp. 35–40; and T. A. Stewart, "The Information Wars: What You Don't Know Will Hurt You," *Fortune,* June 12, 1995, pp. 119–21.
14. Cited in Robichaux, "'Competitor Intelligence'", p. B2.
15. S. McCartney, "'Go to IBM's Booth. Avoid Recognition. Skulk,'" *Wall Street Journal,* November 17, 1994, p. B1.
16. See, for instance, M. Werner, "Planning for Uncertain Futures: Building Commitment through Scenario Planning," *Business Horizons,* May–June 1990, pp. 55–58; and P. J. H. Schoemaker, "Scenario Planning: A Tool for Strategic Thinking," *Sloan Management Review,* Winter 1995, pp. 25–39.
17. W. Echikson, "When You Can't Control History," *Fortune,* December 13, 1993, p. 170.
18. See, for example, A. B. Fisher, "Is Long-Range Planning Worth It?" *Fortune,* April 23, 1990, pp. 281–84; and P. Schwartz, *The Art of the Long View* (New York: Doubleday/Currency, 1991).
19. P. N. Pant and W. H. Starbuck, "Innocents in the Forest: Forecasting and Research Methods," *Journal of Management,* June 1990, pp. 433–60.
20. See S. Greengard, "Discover Best Practices through Benchmarking," *Personnel Journal,* November 1995, pp. 62–73.
21. See M. J. Spendolini, *The Benchmarking Book* (New York: AMACOM, 1992); J. Main, "How to Steal the Best Ideas Around," *Fortune,* October 19, 1992, pp. 102–06; and T. B. Kinni, "Measuring Up," *Industry Week,* December 5, 1994, pp. 27–28.
22. Shetty, "Aiming High," p. 43.
23. "Benchmarkers Make Strange Bedfellows," *Industry Week,* November 15, 1993, p. 8.
24. A. Tanzer, "Studying at the Feet of the Masters," *Forbes,* May 10, 1993, pp. 43–44.
25. This section is partially based on M. Galen, "These Guys Aren't Spooks. They're 'Competitive Analysts'," *Business Week,* October 14, 1991, p. 97; and McCartney, "Go to IBM's Booth."
26. W. R. Dill, "Environment as an Influence on Managerial Autonomy," *Administrative Science Quarterly,* March 1958, pp. 409–43.
27. S. P. Robbins, *Organization Theory: Structure, Design, and Applications,* 3rd ed. (Englewood Cliffs, N.J.: Prentice Hall, 1990), pp. 361–77.
28. See, for instance, J. Pfeffer, "Size and Composition of Corporate Boards of Directors: The Organization and Its Environment," *Administrative Science Quarterly,* March 1972, pp. 218–28; and M. S. Mizruchi and L. B. Stearns, "A Longitudinal Study of the Formation of Interlocking Directorates," *Administrative Science Quarterly,* June 1988, pp. 194–210.
29. B. R. Schlender and D. Kirkpatrick, "The Valley vs. Microsoft," *Fortune,* March 20, 1995, pp. 84–90.
30. A. DePalma, "It Takes More Than a Visa to Do Business in Mexico," *New York Times,* June 26, 1994, p. F5.
31. See G. Hofstede, *Culture's Consequences: International Differences in Work-Related Values* (Beverly Hills, Calif.: Sage, 1980); G. Hofstede, *Cultures and Organizations: Software of the Mind* (New York: McGraw-Hill, 1991); and G. Hofstede, "Cultural Constraints in Management Theories," *The Executive,* February 1993, pp. 81–94.
32. Hofstede called this dimension *masculinity versus femininity;* but I have changed it because of the strong sexist connotation in his choice of terms.
33. Based on "At Your Service," *Business Ethics,* October 1992, p. 30; E. E. Spragins, *"Making Good," INC.,* May 1993, pp. 114–22; D. James, "Heir to a Style That Is Yet to Be Understood," *Business Review Weekly,* October 10, 1994, p. 68; and N. McGrath, "Drawing Morals from Morality," *Asian Business,* March 1995, pp. 20–26. See also D. L. Boroughs, "The Bottom Line on Ethics," *U.S News & World Report,* March 20, 1995, pp. 61–66.
34. M. Friedman, *Capitalism and Freedom* (Chicago: University of Chicago Press, 1962); and "The Social Responsibility of Business Is to Increase Its Profits," *New York Times Magazine,* September 13, 1970, p. 33.
35. This discussion is based on S. L. Warwick and P. L. Cochran, "The Evolution of the Corporate Social Performance Model," *Academy of Management Review,* October 1985, pp. 758–69; D. J. Wood, "Corporate Social Perfor-

mance Revisited," *Academy of Management Review,* October 1991, pp. 703–08; D. L. Swanson, "Addressing a Theoretical Problem by Reorienting the Corporate Social Performance Model," *Academy of Management Review,* January 1995, pp. 43–64; and M. B. E. Clarkson, "A Stakeholder Framework for Analyzing and Evaluating Corporate Social Performance," *Academy of Management Review,* January 1995, pp. 92–117.
36. See, for example, P. Sellers, "Companies That Serve You Best," *Fortune,* May 31, 1993, pp. 74–88.
37. L. Brokaw, "The Dead Have Customers, Too," *INC.,* September 1994, pp. 90–92.
38. See, for instance, R. Henkoff, "The Hot New Seal of Quality," *Fortune,* June 28, 1993, pp. 116–20; J. Southerst, "The Gold Standard," *Canadian Business,* December 1993, p. 27; A. Zuckerman, *ISO 9000 Made Easy: A Cost-Savings Guide to Documentation and Registration* (New York: AMACOM, 1994); and "ISO 9000 Series Vital for Smaller Korean Firms," *Business Korea,* August 1994, pp. 34–35.

CHAPTER 5
PLANNING SYSTEMS

I look to the future because I'm going to spend the rest of my life there.
- C. Kettering

LEARNING OBJECTIVES

After studying this chapter, you should be able to:

1. Explain the benefits that can accrue from planning
2. Describe the value of SWOT analysis
3. Contrast cost-leadership, differentiation, and focus strategies
4. Identify the elements in successful strategy implementation
5. Explain what is unique about the concept of project management
6. Define entrepreneurship
7. Describe the personality characteristics of an entrepreneur
8. Explain why an organization's stated objectives might not be its real objectives
9. Describe the steps in a typical MBO program for individual employees

When Jeff Frasier took over the chairmanship of Unilever Australia in February 1992, he faced some real challenges.[1] Sales of the packaged-goods maker were flat. After all, consumers can buy only so much margarine, laundry detergent, and hair-care products. And Unilever's brands—such as Continental soup, Pond's skin-care products, Bushells tea, and Omo laundry detergent—were being confronted with aggressive competition from other big-brand companies such as Procter & Gamble, as well as lower-priced generic and house brands offered by retailers. Frasier needed to expand his company's sales. His analysis led to the creation of a 3-year growth plan based on a strategy of product innovation.

Frasier's environmental analysis and internal evaluation led him to three conclusions. First, sales growth couldn't come through higher prices. Low inflation and consumer resistance to price increases prevented all packaged-goods manufacturers from increasing their prices. Second, Unilever Australia's big market shares in many categories and the absence of competitors that could be bought out eliminated the option of growth through acquisition. And third, export opportunities were limited. Unilever companies in Europe, Asia, and the United States were already well entrenched in those markets.

Jeff Frasier and his executive team decided that Unilever Australia's best chance for increasing sales and market share would be through internal product innovation. "Innovation is the only way our products will continue to be dynamic and continue to secure the allegiance of consumers. Other elements, such as efficient manufacturing, distribution, and logistics, are givens. Innovation is what will differentiate our products and generate growth," said Frasier. "We must generate organic growth, which means a constant focus on product innovation. Innovation is our first priority, our second priority and, if anyone is in doubt, our third priority."

After 3 years, Frasier was getting mixed results. Market share had risen in several categories, including tea, margarine, soup, laundry detergent and skin-care products. And new products such as Drive Power Liquid detergent, Surf concentrated laundry detergent, Magnum ice cream, and a range of potato products under the Continental brand were being well received by consumers. But overall sales and profits were up only a few percentage points. So Frasier and his executive team were reassessing their plans and looking for new ways to better implement their growth-through-innovation strategy.

Successful managers, like Jeff Frasier, rely on plans to guide their organizations. In this chapter, we present the essential elements that you need to know about creating plans and formulating an organizational strategy.

WHAT IS PLANNING?

What do we mean by the term *planning*? As we stated in our description of management functions in Chapter 1, planning encompasses defining an organization's goals, establishing an overall strategy for achieving those goals, and developing a comprehensive hierarchy of plans to integrate and coordinate activities. It is concerned, then, with *ends* (what is to be done) as well as with *means* (how it is to be done).

Planning can be further defined in terms of whether it is informal or formal. All managers engage in planning, but it might be only the informal variety. For instance, when I asked the owner-manager of a door-manufacturing firm whether he did planning or not, he answered: "Yeah, I have a rough vision in my mind of where we're going." This is an example of informal planning.

The primary factors that differentiate formal from informal planning are the extent of written documentation and a multiyear time frame.[2] Formal plans typically are written down and cover at least 3 years into the future. So when we use the term *planning* in this chapter, we're implying *formal* planning. We'll assume that specific objectives are formulated, that they cover a period of years, that they are committed to writing, and that specific action programs exist for the achievement of those objectives.

TYPES OF PLANS

The most popular way for managers to classify plans is by their breadth—*strategic* versus *operational*—and by their time frame—*short-*, *intermediate-*, and *long-term*. As we will show, these planning classifications are not independent of one another. For instance, there is an overlapping relationship between strategic and long-term plans.

Strategic versus Operational Plans

Plans that apply to the entire organization, that establish the organization's overall objectives, and that seek to position the organization in terms of its environment are called **strategic plans.** Those that specify the details of how the overall objectives are to be achieved are called **operational plans.** At Unilever Australia, for example, the strategic plan focuses on finding growth opportunities in a relatively stagnant market. Unilever's operational plans offer the details on how that growth is going to be achieved.

Strategic and operational plans differ in their time frame and their scope.[3] Operational plans tend to cover shorter periods of time. For instance, an organization's monthly, weekly, and day-to-day plans are almost all operational. Strategic plans tend to include an extended time period—usually 5 years or more. They also cover a broader area and deal less with specifics. Operational plans have a narrower and more limited scope.

Generally speaking, the higher a manager is in an organization, the more he or she is involved with strategic plans. Conversely, the focus of most lower-level managers is on operational plans. So almost all of Jeff Frasier's planning for Unilever Australia is of the strategic variety. On the other hand, Unilever's factory supervisors and department managers spend their planning time working on monthly or quarterly budgets, weekly schedules, and other forms of operational plans. But this generalization between level in the organization and type of planning needs to be qualified to reflect the size of the organization. For owner-managers of small businesses and for entrepreneurs, the difference between strategic and operational plans is essentially academic because they'll typically be working on both types of plans simultaneously.

Short-, Intermediate-, and Long-Term Plans

Financial analysts traditionally describe investment returns as *short-, intermediate-,* and *long-term.* The short term covers less than 1 year. The intermediate term covers from 1 year up to 5 years. And any time frame beyond 5 years is classified as long-term. Managers have adopted the same terminology to describe plans.

Why is time frame important in classifying plans? The answer lies in the **commitment concept.** The more current plans affect future commitments, the longer the time frame for which managers need to plan. So the commitment concept states that plans should extend far enough to see through those commitments that are made today. Planning for too long or too short a period is inefficient.

The more current plans affect future commitments, the longer the time frame for which managers need to plan.

Why do executives at large public utilities such as Hydro Quebec or Arizona Public Service develop plans that cover 50 years or more into the future, whereas the managers of convenience marts typically have no formal plans that extend beyond a year or two? These differences don't have to do with the quality of management. They have to do with the future impact of the decisions that these managers currently make. The decision to build a hydroelectric plant entails an investment of hundreds of millions or even billions of dollars that will take decades to recoup. The convenience store turns over its entire inventory every 2 weeks and may have only a 1-year renewable lease.

The commitment concept can also provide insights into why the length of the planning horizon tends to increase at ever higher levels of management. The decisions that top management typically make imply a greater commitment of resources and contain greater uncertainty than do those of lower-level management. To justify this resource commitment and to help reduce uncertainty, top management engages in long-term planning. A supervisor, on the other hand, rarely makes decisions that commit the organization well into the future. So the plans developed by supervisors tend to be of the short-term variety.

PLANNING IN AN UNCERTAIN ENVIRONMENT

Harlan Accola swears by the value of planning. His firm, American Images, is in the aerial photography business.[4] It started in 1980, but by 1986 it was on the verge of bankruptcy. Today his business has fifty-four employees, has annual sales of nearly $5 million, and generates profits of over $300,000 a year. What happened? According to Accola, "We grew too fast and it was simply from lack of planning." Now American Images has identified its unique market niche, introduced formal planning sessions, sets annual sales goals, conducts monthly planning meetings, and generates comprehensive weekly reports on performance.

Harlan Accola has turned religious about planning, but not all managers are so enthusiastic. In fact, formalized planning has come under increased criticism in recent years. In this section, we outline the potential benefits of planning, describe the primary arguments that critics have made, and review the research evidence to determine whether planning actually enhances an organization's performance.

Why Managers Plan

Why should managers plan? We can propose at least four reasons. Planning gives direction, reduces the impact of change, minimizes waste and redundancy, and sets the standards to facilitate control.

Planning establishes coordinated effort. It gives direction to managers and nonmanagers alike. When all concerned know where the organization is going and what they must contribute to reach the objective, they can begin to coordinate their activities, cooperate with each other, and work in teams. A lack of planning can foster "zigzagging" and thus prevent an organization from moving efficiently toward its objectives.

By forcing managers to look ahead, anticipate change, consider the impact of change, and develop appropriate responses, planning reduces uncertainty. It also clarifies the consequences of the actions managers might take in response to change.

Planning also reduces overlapping and wasteful activities. Coordination before the fact is likely to uncover waste and redundancy. Further, when means and ends are clear, inefficiencies become more obvious.

Finally, planning establishes objectives or standards that facilitate control. If we are unsure of what we are trying to achieve, how can we determine whether we have achieved it? In planning, we develop the objectives. And, as we illustrate in the next chapter, the control process compares actual peformance against the objectives, identifies any signficiant deviations, and takes the necessary corrective action. Without planning, there can be no control.

Criticisms of Planning

Formalized and strategic planning became popular in the 1960s. And it still is. There's an intuitive appeal to planning—"the plannning urge remains powerful because it is so tied up with man's notion of himself as an intelligent and rational creature. Everybody makes plans."[5] But critics of planning are accumulating. The following summarizes the major arguments that have recently been offered against formalized and strategic plannning.

Planning creates too much rigidity.[6] Formalized planning systems lock people and organizational units into specific goals with specific time periods. The plans assume that conditions will remain relatively stable during that time period, which is almost never the case.

You can't plan for change in a turbulent environment.[7] Most organizations face dynamic, changing, and unpredictable environments. "Setting oneself on a predetermined course in unknown waters is the perfect way to sail straight into an iceberg."[8] Turbulence can be turned into an opportunity for those flexible enough to seize it. But if you're locked into formal plans, every unpredictable change is seen only as a problem.

Systems can't replace intuition and creativity.[9] Formalized strategic planning systems tried to do for management what Frederick Taylor (see Appendix A) and scientific management tried to do for production work—program and routinize it.

But formal procedures will never be able to forecast discontinuities. Developing strategy is a complex and demanding task that depends as much, if not more, on intuition and creativity as on formal analysis. Most successful strategies are visions, not plans. Pedestrian thinkers can't become incisive merely by following some systematic strategic framework.

Planning focuses management's attention on competing within today's industry structure rather than on competing for tomorrow's.[10] Strategic planning has directed too much attention on how to position products and businesses within existing industry structures. The real attention should be toward changing the industry's rules or creating tomorrow's industries. The inability of many managers to look ahead for ways to reinvent their industries has led to both costly blunders and monumental catch-up costs.

Planning reinforces successful organizations to become overly preoccupied with the factors responsible for their success, setting up the conditions that can lead to failure.[11] Ironically, success breeds failure. Managers in successful organizations tend to develop perceptual biases that encourage them to maintain the status quo. Since managers are most likely to assess and change their views of the world when they run into problems, long-term success provides little opportunity for managers to evaluate or change their strategic framework. They tend to become overconfident and more entrenched in the strategy they have created.

Looking at the Bottom Line: Does Planning Improve Organizational Performance?

Does planning pay off? Who's right—the proponents of planning or the critics? Let's look at the evidence. Dozens of studies have been undertaken to test the relationship between planning and organizational performance.[12] Contrary to arguments made by critics, the overall evidence is generally positive. In fact, the evidence allows us to draw the following conclusions. First, generally speaking, formal planning is associated with increased growth in sales and earnings, higher profits, higher return on assets, and other positive financial results. Second, the *quality* of the planning process and the appropriate *implementation* of the plans probably contribute more to high performance than does the *extent* of planning. Third, managers have learned to build in flexibility by creating contingency plans covering alternative scenarios and by treating planning as an ongoing process rather than a once-a-year activity. This approach counters the tendency for planning to become overly rigid. Fourth, consistent with our discussion of decision making in Chapter 3, no planning system or strategic framework can substitute for creative and intuitive insight. Well-conceived strategies are unlikely to evolve from mediocre minds using sophisticated frameworks. But an *absence* of strategic planning is also no evidence that management has a creative vision. Finally, in those studies in which formal planning hasn't led to higher performance, the environment is typically the culprit. When strong government regulations, powerful labor unions, and similar environmental forces constrain management's options, planning will have less of an impact on an organization's performance than when those constraints are weak. Why? Because management will have fewer choices for which planning can propose viable alternatives. For example, planning might suggest that General Motors should produce some of its key parts in Asia in order to keep costs down. But if GM's U.S. labor contracts specifically forbid transferring the manufacturing of these parts outside the United States, the value of the company's planning effort is significantly reduced. Dramatic shocks from the environment can also undermine the best-laid plans. The rapid and unexpected rise in bond interest rates in 1994 undermined the formal plans previously developed by administrators in Orange County, California. The county's assets were heavily invested in bond-sensitive options that collapsed in value as interest rates rose; the result was a loss to the county of over $1 billion. In conditions of such environmental uncertainty, there is no reason to expect that planners will necessarily outperform nonplanners.

THE PLACE TO START: DEFINING AN ORGANIZATION'S PURPOSE

The good statements of an organization's purpose are short, clear, and easy to understand. For instance, Rubbermaid states that it wants "to be the leading world-class creator and marketer of brand-name, primarily plastic products which are creatively responsive to global trends and capable of earning a leading market share position."[13] Haworth, Inc., a manufacturer of office furniture with annual sales of more than $800 million, simply says that the company seeks "to be world class in the eyes of our customers at creating well-designed, effective, and exciting work environments."[14] What are we talking about? We're referring to the **mission statement** or vision that defines an organization's purpose and answers questions such as What business are we in? and What are we trying to accomplish? It also provides important guidance to both managers and employees. Gary Simmons, president of Healthtex, a children's-clothing company, says his firm's mission statement has been valuable for getting different groups of people within the company to focus on a strategic direction.[15]

A recent survey found that more than 50 percent of large companies have formal mission statements.[16] And an increasing number of small firms are realizing

Rubbermaid's mission statement gives direction to managers and employees alike when it states that the company seeks "to be the leading world-class creator and marketer of brand-name, primarily plastic products which are creatively responsive to global trends and capable of earning a leading market share position."

© 1993 Rubbermaid Inc., Wooster, Ohio 44691-6000.

MISSION

Our mission is to be the leading world-class creator and marketer of brand-name, primarily plastic products which are creatively responsive to global trends and capable of earning a leading market share position. We will achieve this mission by creating the best value available for the consumer, commercial, and industrial markets.

We will think, plan, experiment, operate and manage strategically. We will monitor, interpret and respond to changing trends to pursue the following avenues of growth:

- Continuous Value Improvement – Make our products a better value

WE WILL ACHIEVE THIS MISSION BY CREATING THE BEST VALUE AVAILABLE.

- Market Penetration – Sell more of our current products
- Product Enhancement – Revitalize our current products
- Product Line Extensions – Expand present product lines
- New Product Lines – Add lines to strengthen current market positions
- New Markets – Enter markets where strengths can provide a better value
- New Technology – Aggressively utilize new materials and processes
- Global Expansion – Think and compete internationally
- Service – Make our products easy to buy, easy to handle and easy to sell
- Franchising – Create businesses with partners
- Licensing – Leverage our and our partners' brand names
- Acquisitions – Add complementary businesses
- Joint Ventures and Alliances – Capitalize upon synergistic expertise
- Retailing – Utilize our retail outlet to learn and expand globally
- Rubbermaid Resources – Utilize the full resources of Rubbermaid

that the time required to thrash out a written mission statement is worth the effort.[17] When key people in the organization sit down and attempt to define what the company is about, they are forced to clarify and find common agreement on what the organization's values are and what differentiates it from other organizations. And when complete, the finalized product provides focus and direction for all organizational members.

No organization can be all things to all people. As we'll discuss in the next section, every organization has its strengths and weaknesses. The best managers are able to capitalize on the strengths in order to make their organization more effective. And a clear mission statement can help in this process. How? By focusing on those strengths that give the organization its competitive advantages. Rubbermaid's management, for instance, understands that its company's strength lies in producing plastic products, marketed under their brand name, where they can be the market leader. This statement may not seem to give the organization much focus, but it actually does. Even if management saw opportunities in steel products, or in selling to large retailers who would sell Rubbermaid products under the retailer's house brand, or in competing in markets where others would have a larger market share, Rubbermaid's mission statement would deter pursuing those opportunities. It's not that some company couldn't make money by following those strategies, it's just that they don't play to Rubbermaid's strengths.

EXHIBIT 5-1

THE IMPORTANCE OF STRATEGIES
ALL COMPANIES NEED A STRATEGY SO THE EMPLOYEES WILL KNOW WHAT THEY DON'T DO.
COMPANY WITH NO STRATEGY
UH-OH... WHAT SHOULD I DO?
RRRRING
S.Adams
COMPANY WITH A STRATEGY
WE DON'T DO THAT.

Source: S. Adams. *Dilbert* reprinted by permission of United Feature Syndicate, Inc.

CREATING A STRATEGY

Sanyo Electric and Sharp Corp. are two Japanese companies, of similar size, with partly overlapping product lines. But they are worlds apart in corporate strategy, and that difference has resulted in very different levels of performance.[18]

Both companies make computers, minidisk players, TVs, and refrigerators. Sanyo thrived until the mid-1980s selling low-end products in overseas markets. But it never developed a quality image and was slow in new product introductions. Sanyo has tried to be a low-cost producer, but its prices have often been higher than those of its rivals. In contrast, Sharp has a more focused strategy. It emphasizes using key devices such as color liquid crystal displays to produce distinctive products that stand out in mature markets. Sharp is so good at focusing its research and development that it often develops more new products each year than a competitor such as Hitachi, which spends nearly five times as much. Sharp's management is also good at keeping personnel costs down. Its sales per employee, for example, are about 30 percent higher than Sanyo's. These differences show themselves on the bottom line. In the most recent fiscal year, Sanyo reported a loss of $11.7 million, while Sharp earned $269 million.

The Sharp-Sanyo comparison illustrates the value and importance of a well-thought-out strategy. In this section, we describe four general or grand strategies, an overall framework for approaching strategy, and some specific strategy applications.

Types of Strategies

Enterprise Rent-A-Car, outdoor clothier Patagonia, Inc., and drug producer Marion Merrell Dow (MMD) are successful, profitable companies. In recent years, however, each seems to be going in a different direction.[19] Enterprise is rapidly expanding its operations and is now number one in the United States—bigger than Hertz Corp. Patagonia's management is content to maintain the status quo. Meanwhile, MMD is cutting staff and downsizing its operations. The different directions of these companies can be explained by the fact that their managements have chosen different grand strategies.[20]

Growth The pursuit of growth has long had appeal to managers, especially in North America. If bigger is better, than biggest is best! In our terms, a growth strategy means increasing the level of the organization's operations. Typical measures of growth would be expanding revenues, adding employees, and increasing market share. Popular means for achieving growth include aggressive direct expansion, development of new products or services, mergers and acquisitions, joint ventures, and expansion into global markets.

Enterprise has pursued aggressive direct expansion by capitalizing on its niche in the low-budget insurance-replacement market. Its growth has come mainly at the expense of the fragmented collection of independents that compete for insurance-replacement dollars. Barnes & Noble's growth has been fueled by the development of superstores that provide entertainment and coffee as well as books. When Chemical Bank absorbed Manufacturers Hanover Trust, it chose the merger route to growth. Union Carbide has been able to grow in a highly capital-intensive industry, despite limited funds, by using joint ventures. For instance, it is doubling the size of its ethylene glycol plant in Alberta, Canada, by taking on partners from Japan and Taiwan, and building a $2 billion glycol and polyethylene plant in Kuwait in partnership with the Kuwait Petroleum Corp. And Bausch & Lomb is expanding its optics business by moving into new markets in China, India, and Poland.

Stability Not every organization deifies growth. Some managers see their organization's future as being best assured through the pursuit of a stability strategy. A stability strategy is characterized by an absence of significant change.

Why would management choose a stability strategy? For Patagonia, management purposely chose to halt growth for environmental reasons. "Everything we make pollutes. Polyester, because it's made from petroleum, is an obvious villain, but cotton and wool are not any better. To kill the boll weevil, cotton is sprayed with pesticides so poisonous they gradually render cotton fields barren; cotton fabric is often treated with formaldehyde. Wool relies on large flocks of sheep that denude fragile, arid areas of the earth."[21] The number of styles offered in Patagonia's catalogue has been cut by 30 to 40 percent, and those styles are now available in only half the colors. In addition, Patagonia's customers receive new catalogues only twice, rather than four times, a year.

WD-40 represents a more traditional pursuit of stability. The company's highly profitable niche product, a petroleum-based lubricant, has had its own unique niche and little competition since the 1950s, so management has little interest in changing the status quo.[22] Management is perfectly happy keeping its good thing going.

Downsizing As we've pointed out numerous times, many organizations—particularly large corporations—have been downsizing their operations. These include firms such as General Dynamics, Mobil Oil, Eastman Kodak, Chase Manhattan Bank, Olivetti, R.R. Donnelly, and Marion Merrell Dow.

MMD offers a good example of why a company would pursue a downsizing strategy.[23] MMD enjoyed growth throughout the 1980s, but then two things happened. First, several high-profile products suffered market declines. The public became concerned about possible adverse side effects from Seldane, its popular antihistamine. And there was a sharp drop in demand for its Nicoderm antismoking patches. But the bigger problem was the rise of managed-care services and mail-order prescriptions. To better compete, MMD's management reduced its work force by 1,300 people.

Combination A combination strategy is the simultaneous pursuit of two or more of the preceding strategies. This option recognizes that units of large organizations are often going in different directions. Raychem, for instance, is a plastics and electronics company that had become heavily dependent on the defense industry. As the defense business declined, Raychem's management responded by closing plants, selling businesses, and terminating 8 percent of its work force in its electronics group. At the same time, however, Raychem was expanding its commercial plastics business to take advantage of new technologies it had developed.[24]

SWOT Analysis

The essence of any strategic-planning effort is referred to as **SWOT analysis** because it requires managers to assess the organization's *s*trengths, *w*eaknesses, *o*pportunities, and *t*hreats in order to identify a niche that the organization can exploit. Because an organization's environment, to a large degree, defines management's options, a successful strategy will be one that aligns well with the environment. So we begin by assuming that management has an accurate grasp of what is taking place in its environment and is aware of important trends that might affect its operations (see Chapter 4).

The essence of any strategic-planning effort is referred to as SWOT analysis.

Then it is ready to identify internal strengths and weaknesses and external opportunities and threats. It will then be able to specify a niche that the organization can exploit.

Identify External Opportunities and Threats Management also needs to evaluate what it has learned from its environmental scanning in terms of opportunities that the organization can exploit and threats that the organization faces.[26] Keep in mind that the same environment can present opportunities to one organization and pose threats to another in the same industry because of their different resources. Consider the European market for computers. The environment has recently been characterized by cutthroat competition and aggressive price cutting.[27] More efficient producers such as Apple, Motorola, Matsushita, and Compaq have used their leaner cost structures to significantly increase their European market shares. Meanwhile, companies such as Olivetti and Groupe Bull, which are burdened with heavy overhead costs, have lost market share and absorbed huge operating losses. So what an organization considers an opportunity or a threat depends on the resources it controls.

Identify the Organization's Strengths and Weaknesses After analyzing the environment, management needs to look inside its organization.[25] What skills and abilities do the organization's employees have? What is the organization's cash position? Has it been successful at developing new and innovative products? How do consumers perceive the organization and the quality of its products or services?

This step forces management to recognize that every organization, no matter how large and powerful, is constrained in some way by the resources and skills it has available. A small automobile manufacturer, such as Alfa Romeo, cannot start making minivans simply because management sees opportunities in that market. Alfa Romeo does not have the resources to successfully compete in the minivan market against the likes of Chrysler, Ford, Toyota, and Nissan. Similarly, managers of a six-person computer software firm with annual sales of less than $2 million might see a huge market for on-line services. But their minimal resources limit their ability to act on this opportunity. In contrast, Microsoft's management was able to create the Microsoft Network because it had the access, people skills, name recognition, and financial resources to pursue this market.

Analysis of the organization's resources should lead management to a clear assessment of its organization's strengths and weaknesses. Then management can identify the organization's **distinctive competence,** or the unique skills and resources that determine the organization's competitive weapons. Black & Decker, for instance, bought General Electric's small appliance division—which made coffeemakers, toasters, irons, and the like—renamed them, and capitalized on Black & Decker's reputation for quality and durability to make these appliances far more profitable than they had been under the GE name.

Choosing a Niche Exhibit 5-2 illustrates the objective of SWOT analysis. A successful analysis identifies a niche in which the organization's products or services can have some competitive advantage. The area in which the opportunities in the environment overlap with the organization's resources represents the niche wherein the organization's opportunities lie.

A Strategic Framework

How do managers actually choose a specific strategy for their organization? For instance, how do they achieve growth if that is their grand strategy? There are a number of frameworks available for managers to follow.[28] The most widely ac-

EXHIBIT 5-2
Using SWOT Analysis to Identify the Organization's Niche

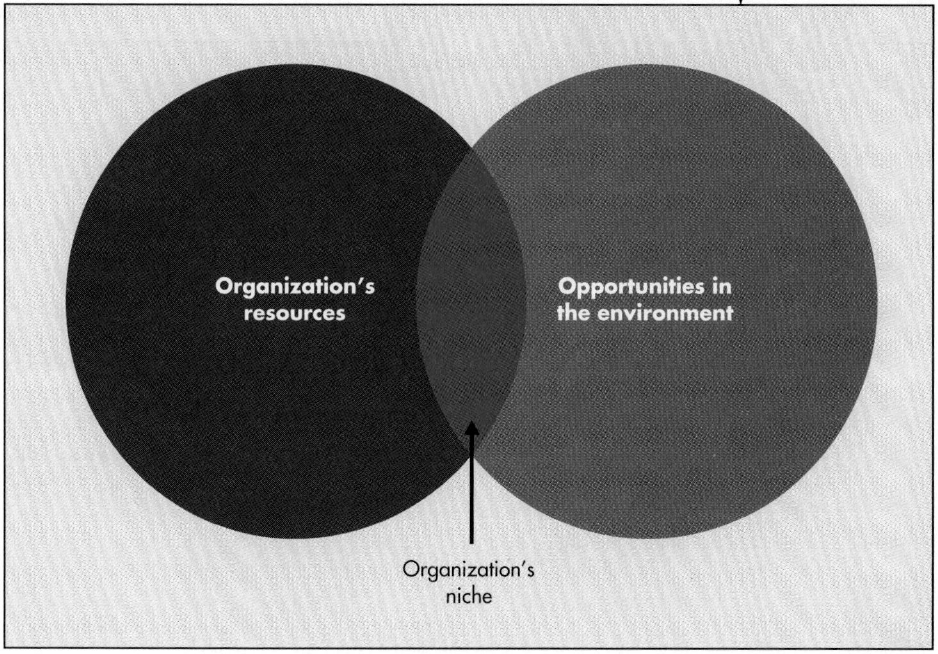

cepted and validated framework has been developed by Michael Porter of Harvard University.[29]

Porter proposes that no firm can successfully perform at an above-average level by trying to be all things to all people. Management, therefore, must select a strategy that will give its organization a **competitive advantage.** This is a capability or circumstance that gives an organization an edge over its rivals. For instance, Home Depot has proved to be very competitive in every market it has entered because of its broad selection of merchandise and commitment to service. These qualities, which are highly valued by customers, make it difficult for rivals to compete against Home Depot.

Porter has identified three strategies from which management can choose: cost-leadership, differentiation, and focus. Which one management chooses depends on the organization's strengths and its competitors' weaknesses. According to Porter, management should avoid a position in which it has to slug it out with everybody in its industry. Management's objective should be to put its organization's strength where the competition isn't.

When an organization sets out to be the low-cost producer in its industry, it is following a **cost-leadership strategy.** Success with this strategy requires that the organization be *the* cost leader and not merely one of the contenders for that position. In addition, the product or service being offered must be perceived as comparable to that offered by rivals, or, at least, it must be acceptable to buyers.

How does a firm gain such a cost advantage? Typical means include efficiency of operations, economies of scale, technological innovations, low-cost labor, or preferential access to raw materials. Examples of firms that have used this strategy successfully include Price/Costco and Gallo wines.

The firm that seeks to be unique in its industry in ways that are widely valued by buyers is following a **differentiation strategy.** The list of attributes by which an organization can differentiate itself would include high quality, speed, state-of-the-art design, technological capability, expert advice, convenience, breadth of selection, extraordinary service, or an unusually positive brand image.

IN THE NEWS

Bombardier: From Snowmobiles to Jet Aircraft

WHEN LAURENT BEAUDOIN BECAME CEO OF BOMBARDIER IN 1966, THE COMPANY HAD ONLY ONE MAJOR product—the Ski-Doo snowmobile—and annual sales of $15 million. Today the company still makes snowmobiles, but it also makes high-tech railcars and jet planes. And Bombardier's annual sales now exceed $3.4 billion. The road that Beaudoin has taken his company over during the past 30 years provides a good illustration of opportunistic strategy setting.

Bombardier CEO Laurent Beaudoin

Bombardier faced a major turning point in 1973. The energy crisis wiped out all but 4 of the 100 snowmobile manufacturers. Beaudoin decided that his company's future lay in diversification. The company's core competency that could give it a competitive advantage was efficient production of engine-based transportation equipment. First, the company successfully bid to make 423 subway cars for Montreal. That initial contract led to building subway cars for New York, double-deck Superliner cars for Amtrak, and monorail cars for Walt Disney World. Today, Bombardier has one-third of the North American market for mass transit equipment and five plants in Europe. Next, the company made a number of strategic acquisitions. It bought Canadair, a maker of large business jets. To develop synergy in the business jet market, it bought two other plane makers that were losing money—Boeing's de Havilland unit and Learjet—and pooled their resources with Canadair. Beaudoin anticipates that new products from his aerospace group over the next few years will fuel significant growth for his company. It has already created the fifty-seat Regional Jet for the fast-growing commuter carriers, and it has a backlog of forty-two plane orders. The final link in Bombardier's strategy has been expansion into global markets. In 1994, over 40 percent of company sales came from Europe and Asia. And that number should increase over the next couple of years. The company has recently won contracts to manage China's largest passenger-rail factory and to build a 20-mile light-rail system in Kuala Lumpur, Malaysia.

Beaudoin has made Bombardier a global force in three related industries: rail and mass-transit equipment; aerospace, including business and regional jets; and consumer products such as snowmobiles and watercraft. Moreover, the company has successfully transferred what it has learned in its North American markets to become a world player.

Source: Based on W. C. Symonds, "Bombardier's Blitz," *Business Week*, February 6, 1995, pp. 62-66.

The key is that the attribute chosen must be different from those offered by rivals and significant enough to justify a price premium that exceeds the cost of differentiating.

There is no shortage of firms that have found at least one attribute that allows them to differentiate themselves from competitors. Intel (technology), Maytag (reliability), Mary Kay cosmetics (distribution), L.L. Bean (service), Armani (prestige brand), McKesson drugs (delivery system), Porsche (high performance), and Nike (innovation) are a few.

The first two strategies sought a competitive advantage in a broad range of industry segments. The **focus strategy** aims at a cost advantage (cost focus) or differentiation advantage (differentiation focus) in a narrow segment. That is, management will select a segment or group of segments in an industry (such as product variety, type of end buyer, distribution channel, or geographical location of buyers) and tailor the strategy to serve them to the exclusion of others. The goal is to exploit a narrow segment of a market. Of course, whether a focus strategy is feasible depends on the size of a segment and whether it can support the additional cost of focusing. Stouffer's used a cost-focus strategy in its Lean Cuisine line to reach calorie-conscious consumers seeking both high-quality products and convenience. Similarly, National University in San Diego appeals to busy working students who need flexibility by offering its courses in intense, 1-month terms. This is an example of a differentiation-focus strategy.

IMPLEMENTING A STRATEGY

A well-designed strategy means little if it isn't effectively implemented. In this section, we briefly review the factors that determine implementation success.

Characteristics of Successful Strategy Implementation

The consulting firm of McKinsey & Co. has developed a "checklist" for successful strategy implementation.[30] This **7-S model** provides a useful summary of the key factors that managers need to address (see Exhibit 5-3).

- *Strategy.* Management obviously must begin by having the right strategy. The strategy needs to reflect an accurate assessment of the environment, particularly the current and future actions of rivals.
- *Superordinate goals.* This factor translates the strategy into overarching goals that unite the organization in some common purpose. It is typically synonymous with the organization's mission statement.
- *Skills.* This refers to the organization's core competencies. What does the organization do best? The strategy chosen must be congruent with the organization's inherent skill resources.
- *Structure.* Strategy determines structure. The organization's structural design is a vehicle to help the organization achieve its goals. If the organization's strategy changes, so too typically does its structure.
- *Systems.* Systems also need to align with, and support, the strategy chosen. Systems include all the formal policies and procedures such as capital budgeting, accounting, and information systems.
- *Style.* Top management acts as a role model. Its substantive and symbolic actions communicate to everyone in the organization what the priorities are and the organization's true commitment to the strategy.

EXHIBIT 5-3
The 7-S Model

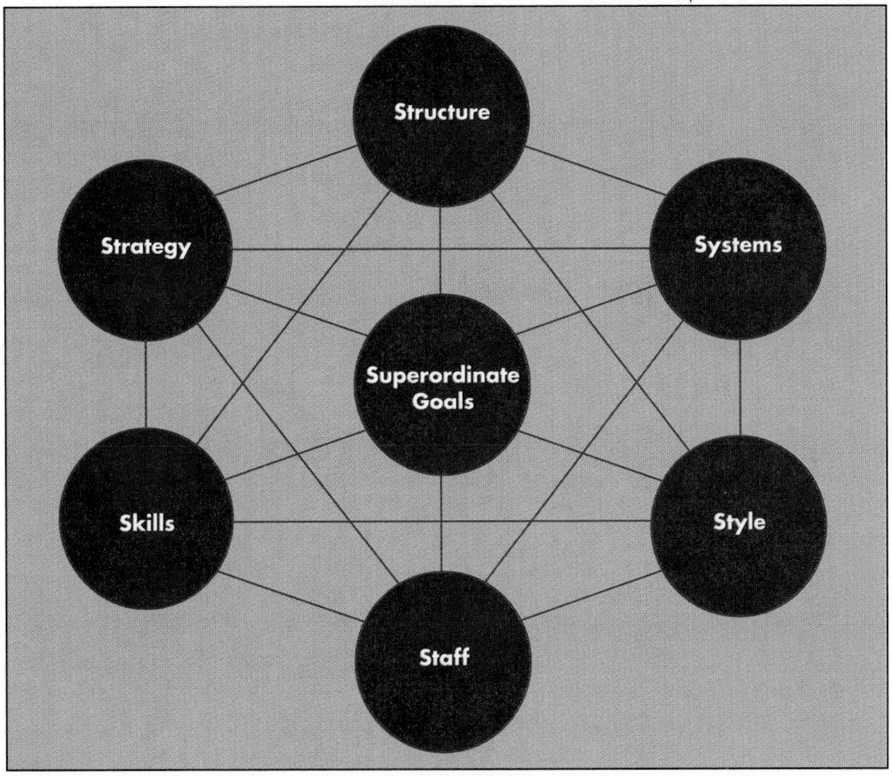

Source: H. Waterman Jr., T. J. Peters, and J. R. Phillips, "Structure Is Not Organization," Reprinted from *Business Horizons,* June 1980. Copyright © 1980 by the Foundation for the School of Business at Indiana University. Used with permission.

- *Staff.* It is people who execute a strategy. The organization's selection process and training programs need to support the strategy by ensuring that the right people are hired and that employees have the abilities and skills to carry out the strategy.

The Importance of Sustaining a Competitive Advantage

Long-term success with any strategy requires that its competitive advantage be sustainable. That is, it must resist erosion by the actions of competitors or by evolutionary changes in the industry. Sustaining a competitive advantage is no simple task.

Technology changes, as do tastes of customers. Most important, some advantages can be imitated by competitors. Management needs to create barriers that make imitation difficult or that reduce competitive opportunities. Many of the techniques for managing the environment, discussed in the preceding chapter, tend to create barriers for rivals. For example, the use of patents and copyrights reduces opportunities for imitation. When there are strong economies of scale, reducing price to gain volume is a useful tactic. Tying up suppliers with exclusive contracts limits their ability to supply rivals. And encouraging government policies that impose import tariffs can limit foreign competition.

Southwest Airlines provides an excellent illustration of how to effectively sustain a competitive advantage.[31] Southwest has consistently made money, in an industry that lost $12 billion over the past 5 years, by pursuing a cost-leadership strategy. It has no meals, no reserved or first-class seats, no computerized reservation systems, no baggage transfers to other airlines, and it uses standardized aircraft and reusable boarding passes. It costs Southwest 7.1 cents per available seat–mile to operate. Comparable figures for American, Delta, TWA, and USAir are 10.6, 9.1, 8.5, and 10.1, respectively. But Southwest recently faced aggressive price competition from major carriers and low-cost copycats such as Reno Air, Kiwi, and Shuttle by United. So what did Southwest do? It took advantage of the excellent relationship it has with its employees to persuade its 2,000-strong pilots' union to accept an unprecedented 10-year contract that provides no wage increases in the first 5 years and then only three 3 percent increases in the second 5 years. In exchange, the pilots will be granted options to acquire as many as 1.4 million shares of Southwest stock each year during the life of the contract. And what's the bottom line? This deal virtually assures Southwest of maintaining its cost advantage over rival airlines.

Southwest Airlines provides an excellent illustration of how to effectively sustain a competitive advantage.

ETHICS OF STRATEGY: HOW FAR IS TOO FAR?

The selection of an organizational strategy is not value-free. Some people, for instance, might consider it unethical for a large company with abundant financial resources to sell its products at little or no profit to drive out marginally financed rivals. An arguably more interesting ethical issue has recently surfaced in the creation of so-called folksy brands by major consumer-product firms.[32]

Have you heard of Dave's, a new discount cigarette? A recent brochure about the product read, "Down in Concord, North Carolina there's a guy named Dave. Dave is an entrepreneur who believes in the value of homemade products and the concept of offering folks quality cigarettes at the right price." A promotional brochure for the cigarettes promises, "Dave guarantees 'If you don't like 'em, I'll eat 'em.'"

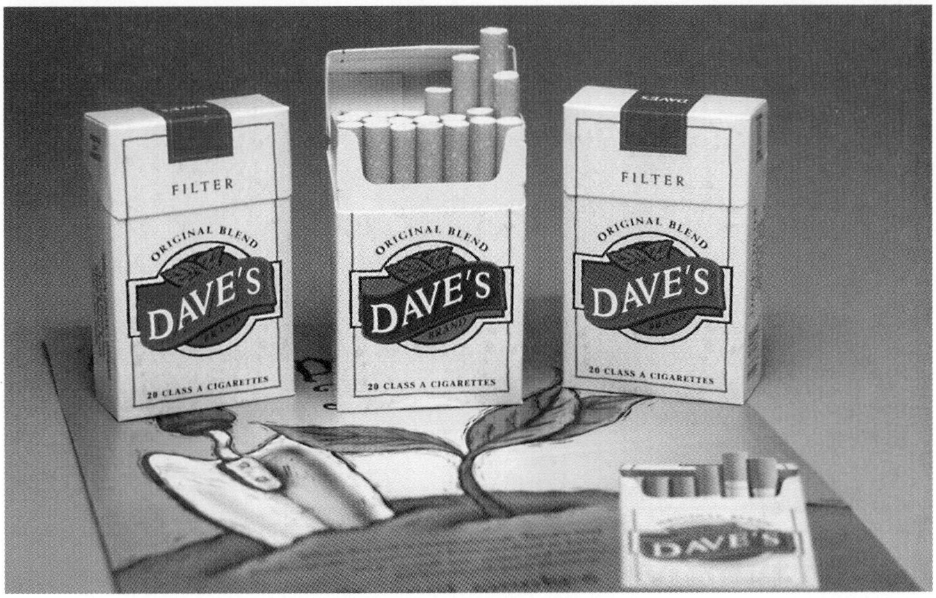

Dave's Cigarettes are marketed as if they're produced by a small entrepreneur in Concord, North Carolina. In reality, they're made by tobacco giant Philip Morris.

Look closely at those ads or the package that Dave's come in. The only organizational reference is Dave's Tobacco Co. Well, there really is no Dave's Tobacco Co.! It's a creation of Philip Morris, the $60 billion conglomerate that makes Marlboro, Merit, Parliament, Virginia Slims, and other brand-name cigarettes. Is Philip Morris just having a little fun, or is it trying to deceive the public? You make the call.

Philip Morris's management is trying to respond to those consumers who are not predisposed to buy big national brands. Dave's image—from his aw-shucks demeanor to his yellow '57 pickup—is designed to be reverse chic. E&J Gallo Winery followed this strategy in the 1980s with its Bartles & Jaymes wine coolers.

A marketing consultant points out that for this strategy to work, not only does the product have to convey cutting-edge hipness to urbanites without turning off mainstream America, but "it is incumbent on the marketer to make sure consumers don't figure [the strategy] out." The vice president of corporate affairs at Philip Morris says, "We certainly have never tried to keep it a secret—we're obviously claiming Dave's as our product. I think people will see the whimsy in the positioning, and while there might be a few people who might take exception, overall consumers will understand it."[33] But Philip Morris isn't publicizing its tie to the brand. Is this *whimsy* or *lying* to the public?

PROJECT MANAGEMENT: A TOOL FOR THE '90S

Managing a production department at Chrysler's Windsor, Ontario, minivan plant is different from managing a design team at Chrysler's Technology Center in Auburn Hills, Michigan. The former involves an ongoing process. The latter, however, is an example of project management. In this section, we briefly describe project management and why it has become so popular in recent years.

A **project** is a one-time-only set of activities with a definite beginning and ending point in time.[34] Projects vary in size and scope—from a NASA space shuttle launch to arranging a wedding. **Project management** is the task of getting the activities done on time, within budget, and according to specifications.[35]

More and more organizations are using project management. Why? Because it fits well with a dynamic environment and the need for flexibility and rapid response. Organizations are increasingly undertaking projects that are somewhat unusual or unique, have specific deadlines, contain complex interrelated tasks requiring specialized skills, and are temporary in nature. These types of projects don't lend themselves well to the standardized operating procedures that guide routine and continuous organizational activities.

In the typical project, team members are temporarily assigned and report to a project manager. This manager coordinates the project's activities with other departments and reports directly to a senior executive. But the project is seen as temporary. It exists only long enough to complete its specific objectives. Then it's wound down and closed up; members move on to other projects, return to their permanent departments, or leave the organization.

The essential features of the project planning process have been summarized as follows:[36]

- Define the project's objectives
- Identify activities and the resources needed to achieve them
- Establish sequencing relationships for activities
- Make time estimates for activities
- Determine project completion time
- Compare project schedule objectives
- Determine resource requirements to meet objectives

The planning process begins by clearly defining the project's objectives. This step is necessary because the manager and team members need to know what's expected. All activities in the project and the resources needed to accomplish them must then be identified. That is, what labor and materials are needed to complete the project? This task is often time-consuming and complex because the project is unique, so there aren't the history and experience that typically exist in planning most tasks.

IN THE NEWS

A New Species: The Project Manager

AS MIDDLE MANAGERS DISAPPEAR, A NEW TYPE OF MANAGER IS EVOLVING TO TAKE THEIR PLACE IN THE management chain. This is the project manager.

Says William Dauphinais, a partner at Price Waterhouse: "Project management is going to be huge in the next decade." Project management is "the wave of the future," says a General Motors in-house newsletter.

Project management has been around for a long time in industries such as construction and movie making. Now it has expanded into almost every type of business. For instance, one of the last places you would expect to find project management is the mortgage business. But the Federal National Mortgage Association, which processes more than $1 billion in mortgage purchases every day, uses it. Says Fannie Mae's chief information officer, "Automation and empowerment take away the need to have managers oversee the day-to-day work. Everything has become projects. This is the way Fannie Mae does business today."

The temporary nature of projects makes managing them different from, say, overseeing a production line and preparing a weekly tally of costs on an ongoing basis. The one-shot nature of the work makes project managers the organizational equivalent of a hired gunman. There's a job to be done. It has to be defined—in detail, with much haggling. And the project manager is responsible for how it's done.

A real challenge is managing people who are still linked, authority-wise, to their permanent department. Janine Coleman is a project manager for AT&T's global business communications systems, which installs equipment for large corporate clients. Says Coleman, "The company tells the client, 'We assign you a project manager, and she's in charge.' If it fails, it's my fault. But does this put real authority there? No. If a VP won't go along, it's up to the project manager to get him to."

Source: T. A. Stewart, "The Corporate Jungle Spawns a New Species: The Project Manager," *Fortune,* July 10, 1995, pp. 179-80.

Once the activities have been identified, their sequential relationship needs to be determined. That is, what activities must be completed before others can begin? And which can be undertaken simultaneously? This step typically is done using flowchart-type diagrams.

Next, the project activities need to be scheduled. The manager estimates the time required for each activity and then uses these estimates to develop an overall project schedule and completion date. Then the project schedule is compared with the objectives, and adjustments are made. For example, if the project time estimate is too long, the manager can assign more resources to critical activities so they can be completed faster. Several of the scheduling techniques used in project planning are described in Chapter 6.

ENTREPRENEURSHIP: A SPECIAL CASE OF STRATEGIC PLANNING

You've heard the story dozens of times. With only an idea and a few hundred dollars, someone starts what eventually becomes a multimillion-dollar business. For Cherrill Farnsworth, it's getting to be a habit. At age 44, she's already working on her fifth start-up company![37]

Farnsworth has a talent for exploiting opportunities. In 1974, she spotted her first. After her husband was transferred from Indianapolis to Houston, she noticed that people had no way to get downtown from her northwestern suburb. Despite opposition from major bus operators, she secured a bus line franchise. After 2 years, she sold it for a profit. "I realized at that point what value you could get by working hard and creating something new—especially if there's no competition," Farnsworth says. Her next three ventures leased equipment—luxury vehicles, office equipment, and oil field equipment. Then, in 1984, she identified another opportunity. Magnetic resonance imaging machines were beginning to appear. "The equipment seemed to have so much merit," she says. But many hospitals couldn't afford the $1.5 million to $2 million it would cost to buy their own MRI machines. The hospitals knew that offering MRI services could be profitable, but they couldn't borrow to buy the machines because Medicare had not yet approved reimbursements from insurers for the service. Thus the seed was planted for her current company, TME, which provides MRI services for hospitals. She convinced a set of investors that there was money to be made—big money—in her idea. Today her company operates twenty imaging centers in nine U.S. states, serving thirty-six hospitals and four universities. TME employs 164 people and is adding about eighteen a year. Annual revenues are up to $28 million and growing at about 30 percent a year.

Yla Eason's three-year-old son told her "he wanted to be like He-Man but he said he couldn't because He-Man was white." That comment sparked the entrepreneurial spirit in Eason, a Harvard business school graduate. Unable to find an African-American super-hero for her son, she decided to create a line. Her Olmec Toys now sells 31 dolls for children of color and has sales of more than $5 million a year.

Strategic planning tends to carry a "big business" bias. It implies a formalization and structure that fits well with large, established organizations that have abundant resources. But the primary interest of many people is not in managing large and established organizations. Like Cherrill Farnsworth, Phil Knight of Nike, or Dave Thomas of Wendy's, they're excited about the idea of starting their own businesses from scratch. In this section, we'll demonstrate that entrepreneurship is actually just a special case of strategic planning.

What Is Entrepreneurship?

There is no shortage of definitions of entrepreneurship.[38] Some, for example, apply the term to the creation of any new business. Others focus on intentions, claiming that entrepreneurs seek to create wealth, which is different from starting a business merely as a means of income substitution (i.e., working for yourself rather than working for someone else). When most people describe entrepreneurs, they use adjectives such as *bold, innovative, venturesome,* and *risk-taking.* They also tend to associate entrepreneurs with small business. We'll define **entrepreneurship** as a process by which individuals pursue opportunities, fulfilling needs and wants through innovation, without regard to the resources they currently control.[39]

It's important not to confuse managing a small business with entrepreneurship. Why? Because not all small business managers are entrepreneurs.[40] Many don't innovate. A great many managers of small businesses are merely scaled-down versions of the conservative, stability-seeking individuals who staff many large corporations and public agencies.

Can entrepreneurs exist in large, established organizations? The answer to that question depends on one's definition of entrepreneur. The noted management guru Peter Drucker, for instance, argues that they can.[41] He describes an entrepreneurial manager as someone who is confident of his or her ability, who seizes opportunities for innovation, and who not only expects surprises but capitalizes on them. He contrasts that with what he calls a "trustee type" of manager who feels threatened by change, is bothered by uncertainty, prefers predictability, and is inclined to maintain the status quo.

Drucker's use of the term *entrepreneurial,* however, is misleading. By almost any definition of good management today, his entrepreneurial type would be preferred over his trustee type. Moreover, the term **intrapreneurship** is now widely used to describe the effort to create the entrepreneurial spirit in large organizations.[42] Yet intrapreneurship can never capture the autonomy and riskiness inherent in true entrepreneurship. Because intrapreneurship takes place within a large organization, all financial risks are carried by the parent company; rules, policies, and other constraints are imposed by the parent; intrapreneurs have to report to bosses or superiors; and the payoff for success is not financial independence but rather career advancement.[43]

Are You an Entrepreneurial Type?

Does entrepreneurship lie in your future? An increasing proportion of new business graduates, as well as experienced managers who have lost their jobs in large companies as a result of downsizing, are pursuing entrepreneurial opportunities.[44] In this section we look at the personality characteristics of entrepreneurs and other factors related to entrepreneurial pursuits.

Three factors . . . profile the entrepreneurial personality—a high need for achievement, a strong belief that you can control your own destiny, and a desire to take only moderate risks.

The Entrepreneurial Personality One of the most researched topics in entrepreneurship has been the question of what, if any, psychological characteristics entrepreneurs have in common. Some common characteristics have been found: hard work, self-confidence, optimism, determination, and a high energy level.[45] But three factors regularly sit on the top of most lists and profile the entrepreneurial personality—a high need for achievement, a strong belief that you can control your own destiny, and a desire to take only moderate risks.[46]

The research allows us to draw a general description of entrepreneurs. They tend to be independent types who prefer to be personally responsible for solving problems, for setting goals, and for reaching those goals by their own efforts. They value independence and particularly don't like being controlled by others. While they're not afraid to take chances, they're not wild risk takers either. They prefer to take calculated risks in which they feel they have some control over the outcome.

The evidence on entrepreneurial personalities leads us to two obvious conclusions. First, people with this personality makeup are not likely to be contented, productive employees in the typical large corporation or government agency. The rules, regulations, and controls that these bureaucracies impose on their members frustrate entrepreneurs. Second, the challenges and conditions inherent in starting one's own business mesh well with the entrepreneurial personality. Starting a new venture, which they control, appeals to their desire to determine their own destinies and their willingness to take risks. But because entrepreneurs believe that their future is fully in their own hands, they perceive the risk as moderate, whereas nonentrepreneurs often see it as high.

Other Factors Related to Being an Entrepreneur Besides certain personality characteristics, other forces have been found to be associated with becoming an entrepreneur.[47] Entrepreneurship tends to flourish in supportive environments. American culture, for instance, places a high value on being your own boss and achieving personal success. These cultural values help explain the wide popularity of entrepreneurial activities in the United States. In contrast, in other countries—including Ireland and Norway—less value is placed on personal achievement and a greater stigma is attached to failure. In addition, some areas of a country often become pockets of entepreneurial subcultures. In the United States, the Route 128 area surrounding Boston; Silicon Valley and northern San Diego County in California; Austin, Texas; and the Research Triangle area in North Carolina are examples of communities that encourage and support entrepreneurs.

Supportive parents seem to play an important part in influencing the entrepreneurial tendencies of their offspring. Entrepreneurs typically have parents who encouraged them to achieve, be independent, and take responsibility for their actions.

Entrepreneurs usually have role models whom they have attempted to emulate. Seeing someone else do something innovative and succeed makes innovation and success seem more realistically achievable. Not surprisingly, given this evidence, one or both parents of entrepreneurs tend to have been self-employed or entrepreneurial themselves.

A final variable related to entrepreneurial activity is previous entrepreneurship. Past behavior is the best predictor of future behaviors. Since it's generally easier to start a second, third, or fourth venture than it is to start the first one, beginning an entrepreneurial business tends to be a recurring activity for certain individuals, as we saw in the case of Cherrill Farnsworth. TME is her fifth start-up venture.

EXHIBIT 5-4
Comparing Entrepreneurs and Traditional Managers

Characteristic	Traditional Managers	Entrepreneurs
Primary motivation	Promotion and other traditional corporate rewards such as office, staff, and power	Independence, opportunity to create, financial gain
Time orientation	Achievement of short-term goals	Achievement of 5- to-10-year growth of business
Activity	Delegation and supervision	Direct involvement
Risk propensity	Low	Moderate
View toward failures and mistakes	Avoidance	Acceptance

Source: Based on R. D. Hisrich, "Entrepreneurship/Intrapreneurship," *American Psychologist,* February 1990, p. 218.

How Entrepreneurs and Traditional Managers Differ

Exhibit 5-4 summarizes some key differences between entrepreneurs and traditional managers in large organizations. The latter tend to be custodial, whereas entrepreneurs actively seek change by exploiting opportunities. When searching for these opportunities, entrepreneurs often put their personal financial security at risk. The hierarchy in large organizations typically insulates traditional managers from these financial wagers and rewards them for minimizing risks and avoiding failures.

In addition, as shown in Exhibit 5-5, entrepreneurs approach strategy differently than typical bureaucratic managers do. Their key strategic questions may focus on the same general areas—resources, structure, control, and opportunity—but they address those questions in a different order, from a different perspective, and with a different emphasis.

The entrepreneur's strategic emphasis is driven by perception of opportunity rather than by availability of resources.[48] The entrepreneur's inclination is to monitor the environment closely in search of opportunities. The resources at his or her disposal take a back seat to identifying an idea that can be capitalized upon.

Once an opportunity is spotted, the entrepreneur begins to look for ways to take advantage of it. Because of his or her personality makeup, the entrepreneur is confident that the opportunity can be exploited. Moreover, the entrepreneur is not afraid to risk financial security, career opportunities, family relations, or psychic well-being to get the new venture off the ground. Entrepreneurs tend to ignore the hard statistics against success—about 60 percent of new businesses aren't around after 6 years.[49] The entrepreneur who sees an opportunity has the confidence and determination to believe that he or she will be on the winning side of those statistics.

Only after the entrepreneur has identified an opportunity and a way to exploit it does he or she begin to feel concerned about resources. But the entrepreneur's priorities are first to find out what resources are needed and then to determine how they can be obtained. This order is in contrast to that of the typical bureaucratic managers, who focus on the resources that are at their disposal. Entrepreneurs are often able to make imaginative and highly efficient use of very limited resources. Finally, when the resource obstacles have been overcome, the entrepreneur will put together the organizational structure, people, systems, marketing plan, and other components necessary to implement the overall strategy.

EXHIBIT 5-5
The Order of Strategic Questions

Typical Bureaucratic Manager	Typical Entrepreneur
What resources do I control?	Where is the opportunity, and how do I capitalize on it?
What structure determines our organization's relationship to its market?	What resources do I need?
How can I minimize the impact of others on my ability to perform?	How do I gain control over those resources?
What opportunity is appropriate?	What structure is best?

Source: Used by permission of *Harvard Business Review;* an excerpt from "The Heart of Entrepreneurship" by H. H. Stevenson and D. E. Gumpert, March–April 1985, pp. 86–87. Copyright © 1985 by the President and Fellows of Harvard College; all rights reserved.

OBJECTIVES: THEIR USE AND MISUSE IN PLANNING

Creating an organization's strategy tends to be an exercise restricted to top-level managers. Similarly, entrepreneurial planning is restricted to people who are starting up new businesses. But one element of planning permeates just about every manager's job—from CEOs to project managers and first-line supervisors. That's setting objectives.

Objectives or goals (we use the terms interchangeably), refer to desired outcomes for individuals, groups, or entire organizations. In this section we present the key concepts you need to know in order to use objectives effectively.

Organizations Have Multiple Objectives

At first glance, you might assume that each organization has a singular objective—business firms want to make a profit; not-for-profit organizations want to provide a service efficiently. But closer examination demonstrates that all organizations have multiple objectives. Businesses also seek to increase market share, develop new products, move into new markets, satisfy employee welfare, and be responsible citizens.[50] For instance, Haworth, Inc., the office furniture manufacturer, states that in addition to seeking a fair return on investment, the company's objectives include complete customer satisfaction, the pursuit of quality, and employee development.[51]

Or consider the objectives of a church. A church provides a "road to heaven through absolution." But it also assists the underprivileged in its community and acts as a place for church members to congregate socially.

No one measure can evaluate effectively whether an organization is performing successfully. And because organizations seek to satisfy multiple constituencies, it's only logical that they also have multiple objectives.

Real versus Stated Objectives

Allstate says, "Our goal is to be known by consumers as the best insurer in America." Bell Atlantic's annual report states that the company is "responding to the imperative of global competition with greater personal responsibility and the power of teamwork." Southern Illinois University's catalogue says that it "emphasizes a commitment to quality education."

The statements you find in an organization's charter, annual report, mission statement, brochures, public relations announcements, or in public statements made by managers are **stated objectives.** They are official announcements of what an organization says—and what it wants various constituencies to believe—are its objectives. However, they are often conflicting and excessively influenced by what society believes organizations *should* do.

The conflict in stated goals exists because organizations respond to a vast array of constituencies or stakeholders. And, as we noted in Chapter 2, these stakeholders typically evaluate the organization by different criteria. As a result, management is forced to say different things to different audiences. For example, in the summer of 1995, as part of a U.S. effort to force the Japanese to open their markets to U.S. products, President Clinton imposed a short-lived 100 percent tariff on thirteen luxury automobile models sold by the Japanese.[52] This tariff put executives at Lexus, Infiniti, Acura, Mazda, and Mitsubishi in an unpleasant situation as they sought to get the tariff lifted. To Clinton, trade officials, and legislators, the auto executives were saying that the tariff would throw many U.S. workers out of work and that dealerships would go out of business. At the same time, attempting to reassure their dealers, owners, and potential customers, these same executives were saying that they were committed to the U.S. market for the long haul and would provide financial support to their dealers. These Japanese auto executives had explicitly presented themselves in one way to the government and another way to their dealers and the public. Was one true and the other false? No. Both were true, but they were in conflict.

The objectives we described previously from Allstate, Bell Atlantic, and Southern Illinois University all contain considerable ambiguity and social desirability. And these organizations' objectives are not unique. Stated objectives tend to be vague, and they are more likely to represent management's public relations skills than to act as meaningful guides to what the organization is actually seeking to accomplish. What executives, for example, would admit that their organization sought "mediocrity," "to meet minimal quality standards," or "to treat our employees as disposable resources"?

The fact is that an organization's stated objectives are often quite irrelevant to what actually goes on in that organization.[53] In a corporation, for instance, one statement of objectives is issued to stockholders, another to customers, and still others to employees and to the public.[54]

The overall objectives stated by top management should be treated for what they are: "fiction produced by an organization to account for, explain, or rationalize to particular audiences rather than as valid and reliable indications of purpose."[55] The content of objectives is substantially determined by what constituencies want to hear. Moreover, it is simpler for management to state a set of consistent, understandable objectives than to explain a multiplicity of objectives. If you want to know what an organization's **real objectives** are, closely observe what members of the organization actually do. Actions define priorities. The university that proclaims the objectives of limiting class size, facilitating close student-faculty relations, and actively involving students in the learning process, and then puts its students into lecture halls of 300 or more, is not unusual. Nor is the automobile service center that promotes high-quality, low-cost repairs and then gives mediocre service at high prices. An awareness that real and stated objectives can deviate is important, if for no other reason than because it can help you explain what might otherwise seem to be management inconsistencies.

The Value of Objectives

The previous discussion shouldn't be interpreted as a blanket indictment of stated objectives. Overall organizational objectives might be more style than substance, but unit objectives and those established for individual employees are more substance than style. For instance, there is an overwhelming amount of evidence to demonstrate that people perform better with goals than without them.

The case for the value of objectives was proposed nearly 30 years ago.[56] Known as **goal-setting theory,** it claimed that specific goals increase performance; that difficult goals, when accepted, result in higher performance than do easy goals; and that feedback leads to higher performance than does the lack of feedback. The evidence strongly supports those three claims.[57]

Specific hard goals produce a higher level of output than does a generalized goal of "do your best." The specificity of the goal itself seems to act as an internal stimulus and encourages people to strive to meet the goal. If factors such as ability and acceptance of the goals are held constant, the evidence also demonstrates that the more difficult the goal, the higher the level of performance. Of course, it's logical to assume that easier goals are more likely to be accepted. But once an employee accepts a hard task, he or she will exert a high level of effort until the goal is achieved, lowered, or abandoned. Finally, people will do better when they get feedback on how well they are progressing toward their goals because feedback helps to identify discrepancies between what they have done and what they want to do.

From Concepts to Skills: Management by Objectives (MBO)

How do you apply goal-setting theory? You implement a management by objectives (MBO) program.[58] MBO converts overall organizational objectives into specific objectives for organizational units and individual members. It provides a process by which objectives cascade down through the organization. The organization's overall objectives are translated into specific objectives for each succeeding level—division, department, individual—in the organization. When in place, MBO creates a hierarchy of objectives that links objectives at one level to those at the next level.

The following eight-step process captures the essential features of an MBO program. You can improve your employees' performance by helping them set goals using this process.

1. *Identify an employee's key job tasks.* Begin by defining what it is you want your employee to accomplish. This definition is derived from your unit's goals. When all the employees in your unit achieve their individual goals, your unit should achieve its overall goals.
2. *Establish specific and challenging goals for each key task.* This step should include both quantity and quality dimensions of performance. Examples: To deliver the project within 3 percent of budget; To process all telephone orders within 24 hours of receipt; To keep returns to less than 1 percent of sales.
3. *Specifiy the deadline for each goal.* Putting a realistic deadline on each goal reduces ambiguity. Example: To deliver the project within 3 percent of budget by November 1, 1999.
4. *Have the employee actively participate.* Having employees participate in defining goals increases acceptance of goals. However, the request for participation must be sincere. Employees need to believe that you are truly interested in their input.
5. *Prioritize goals.* Presumably, employees have multiple goals. Prioritizing encourages employees to take action and expend effort on each goal in proportion to its importance.
6. *Rate goals for difficulty and importance.* Goals should not be chosen because they're easy to achieve. By rating goals for their difficulty and importance, individuals can be given credit for trying difficult goals, even if they don't fully achieve them.
7. *Build in feedback mechanisms to assess goal progress.* Feedback lets employees know whether or not their level of effort is sufficient to attain the goal. Feedback should be frequent.
8. *Link rewards to goal attainment.* Goal progress or attainment should be reinforced by performance-based rewards. These rewards should reflect goal difficulty as well as goal outcomes.

The Downside of Objectives

Despite the strong evidence linking specific goals and high employee performance, not everyone enthusiastically endorses the value of objectives. The loudest critic was undoubtedly the late quality guru W. Edwards Deming.[59] He argued that specific numerical goals do more harm than good. Since people tend to focus on the goals by which they will be judged, Deming claimed quantitative goals encourage employees to direct their effort toward quantity of output and away from quality. In addition, people treat specific goals as ceilings rather than as floors. They set a goal, achieve it, and then tend to rest on their laurels. So specific goals tend to limit people's potential by deterring efforts for continual improvement. At the other extreme, overly demanding goals, especially when unilaterally dictated from above, put pressure on individuals to cheat or misrepresent data in order to achieve the goals. For instance, a recent investigation of Bausch & Lomb found division managers engaging in numerous questionable practices—such as inflating revenues by faking sales, shipping products that were never ordered, and forcing distributors to take unwanted merchandise—largely because the company's CEO insisted that managers achieve double-digit annual growth objectives and fired those who didn't.[60]

Specific goals tend to limit people's potential by deterring efforts for continual improvement.

These criticisms of specific goals are potentially correct. But they can be overcome.[61] One answer is for managers to ensure that employees have multiple goals and that they address quality of output as well as quantity. A production worker or team should be evaluated on number of rejects as well as on total output. Similarly, assessing the number of complaints registered against service employees adds a quality goal to their performance evaluation. Another solution is to treat goal setting as an ongoing activity. Goals should be regularly reviewed and updated. Further, individuals should be rewarded for setting difficult goals even if they aren't fully achieved. Goals are more likely to limit individual effort when people believe they'll be punished for not reaching them. So employees should be encouraged to set ambitious goals that stretch their capabilities, and they should not be made to fear repercussions if they fail.[62]

SUMMARY

(This summary is organized by the chapter-opening learning objectives on page 129.)

1. Planning gives direction and coordinates effort, reduces uncertainty and the impact of change, reduces overlapping and wasteful activities, and establishes objectives or standards that facilitate control.
2. SWOT analysis matches the internal strengths and weaknesses of the organization with opportunities and threats in the environment. Its value lies in finding opportunities in the environment that can be exploited with the distinctive competencies possessed by the organization.
3. Cost-leadership strategies seek to be the lowest-cost operator, while still providing an adequate product or service. A differentiation strategy allows an organization to charge more, but the higher price must be justified by customers in terms of value added. A focus strategy is a narrowly segmented cost-leadership or differentiation strategy.
4. Successful strategy implementation encompasses: (1) the choice of a correct strategy; (2) superordinate goals to unite organizational members; (3) a strategy that is congruent with the organization's core competencies or skills; (4) a supportive structure; (5) supportive systems; (6) top management style that provides substantive and symbolic commitment to the strategy; and (7) a staff with the ability and skills to carry out the strategy.
5. Project management involves specific programs that are temporary in nature and that have definitive deadlines. Planning and scheduling are critical to the success of each project.
6. Entrepreneurship is a process by which individuals pursue opportunities, fulfilling needs and wants through innovation, without regard to the resources they currently control.
7. Entrepreneurs have a high need for achievement, a strong belief they can control their own destiny, and a desire to take only moderate risks.
8. Stated and real objectives may differ because organizations try to satisfy multiple stakeholders who evaluate the organization using different criteria. In addition, organizations are under pressure to state objectives that are socially desirable. These factors often lead to stated objectives that differ significantly from what the organization is actually doing.

9. The steps in an MBO program would include: identify an employee's key job tasks; establish specific and challenging goals for each key task; specify the deadline for each goal; have employees participate; prioritize goals; rate goals for difficulty and importance; build in feedback; and link rewards to goal attainment.

REVIEW AND DISCUSSION QUESTIONS

1. Contrast strategic and operational plans.
2. What is the commitment concept, and why is it important?
3. What arguments can you make against formalized and strategic planning?
4. What is the relationship between planning and organizational performance?
5. What is the link between assessing the environment and formulating a strategy?
6. How do entrepreneurs and traditional managers differ?
7. What is goal-setting theory?
8. What criticisms have been made against the use of specific objectives?
9. "Business firms have one and only one objective—to maximize profit." Do you agree or disagree? Support your answer.
10. If stated objectives are often "fiction produced by an organization," what value is there in a formal mission statement that defines an organization's purpose?

CASE EXERCISE
BURGERWORLD

When Todd Richman graduated from the University of Connecticut in 1988, he turned his part-time job at McDonald's into a full-time one. Starting off as assistant manager in Hartford, he quickly became a manager and then a district supervisor.

One day, in spring of 1995, Todd saw a For Sale sign on a piece of property he passed every day on his way to work. The property was on a major street with high traffic volume. He envisioned the site as an ideal location for a fast-food hamburger restaurant. Todd thought that this vacant property might be "opportunity knocking." Maybe it was time to strike out on his own. But instead of working through a major franchisor—such as McDonald's or Burger King—Todd wanted to go it alone. He figured the big money and future would be in creating his own chain.

With money from a small trust fund left to him by a grandfather and financial help from his parents, Todd opened BurgerWorld in June 1996. As Todd quickly found out, in contrast to buying a franchise, he had to build his business from scratch. He had to, for example, oversee the design and the internal layout of his building, create the menu, find suppliers, select uniforms, hire staff, and develop procedures and systems.

Questions

1. Contrast Todd's planning efforts for BurgerWorld with how planning might have been done if Todd had bought a McDonald's franchise.
2. Build a strategic plan that Todd might use for his new business. Begin with a mission statement.

VIDEO CASE EXERCISE
FORD'S GLOBAL STRATEGY

Is the world ready for a global car? Are there national preferences for cars or can one standardized vehicle meet the diverse needs of people from, say, Singapore, Sweden, Mexico, France, and the United States? Ford Motor Company is betting that "one size can fit all."

Ford is spending $6 billion to develop its new world car. Called the Ford Contour or Mercury Mystique in the United States, it will be called a Mondeo in Europe. With a few local variations, Ford plans to sell the same car in 70 countries.

The logic of Ford's strategy isn't much different from that of McDonald's: Sell one basic product all over the world, and keep the quality high and consistent. Modifications to the product, from one country to the other, will be minor. For instance, exterior sheet metal will vary. And Europeans prefer a tighter shifting feel, while Americans prefer a softer suspension. Ford's new system of flexible manufacturing will allow global consumers to have all kinds of choices, but the basic chassis of the car will be identical around the world.

Ford seeks to take advantage of economies of scale. It costs much less to design and produce one basic car than to create a unique product for each market. The global strategy acknowledges that distance and borders no longer impede production. Because of communication technology, Ford designers in Kansas City and Germany can work together just as if they were in the same room. By producing a global car, Ford can take advantage of low-cost suppliers, regardless of where they are located. The new car will have seats that are made in Kansas City, rubber trim from Spain, and dashboard circuitry from Europe.

The risks in Ford's strategy go beyond merely considering customer taste. This strategy requires a very different type of organizational structure than that used by most large corporations. The trend today is toward decentralized decision-making, allowing managers in distant locations the autonomy and discretion to respond to their customer's unique needs. Yet Ford is consolidating its operations into one global bureaucracy. With the world car, is Ford putting too many eggs in one basket?

Questions

1. Describe Ford's global strategy.
2. What, if anything, is unique in this strategy relative to key competitors such as GM or Toyota?
3. Describe the downside risks in this strategy.
4. What potential problems do you see for management in implementing a global strategy?

Source: Based on "Ford's Global Automobile Strategy," World News Tonight; ABC News; aired September 15, 1994.

SKILL EXERCISES

Objective Setting

You worked your way through college while holding down a part-time job bagging groceries at a Grand Union supermarket. When you graduated, you decided to accept a job with Grand Union as a management trainee. Five years have passed, and you've gained wide experience in operating a large supermarket. Sixteen months ago, you became an assistant store manager. Last week, you made store manager at another location. You report to Frank Sullivan, the area manager, who is reponsible for fourteen stores.

One of the things you liked about the Grand Union chain was that it gave its managers a great deal of autonomy in running the stores. The company provided very general policies to guide its managers. The concern was with the bottom line; for the most part, how you got there was your own business.

You want to establish an MBO-type program in your store. You like the idea that everyone should have clear goals to work toward and then should be evaluated against those goals. That system might just eliminate excuses like "I didn't know what was expected of me" or "But I tried my best."

Your store employs ninety people, although, except for the managers, most work only 20 to 30 hours a week. You have five people reporting to you: an assistant manager and grocery, produce, meat, and bakery managers. The only highly skilled jobs belong to the butchers. Other, less-skilled jobs include cashiering, shelf stocking, cleanup, and grocery bagging.

Specifically describe how you would go about setting objectives in your new position, including examples of objectives for jobs such as cashier and bakery manager.

NOTES

1. N. Shoebridge, "Unilever's Big Cleanup," *Business Review Weekly,* September 19, 1994, pp. 76–79.
2. See, for instance, M. A. Lyles, I. S. Baird, J. B. Orris, and D. F. Kuratko, "Formalized Planning in Small Business: Increasing Strategic Choices," *Journal of Small Business Management,* April 1993, pp. 38–50.
3. R. Ackoff, "A Concept of Corporate Planning," *Long Range Planning,* September 1970, p. 3.
4. J. Finegan, "Everything According to Plan," *INC.,* March 1995, pp. 78–85.
5. P. Foster, "By-the-Book Brilliance," *Canadian Business,* May 1994, p. 78.
6. H. Mintzberg, *The Rise and Fall of Strategic Planning* (New York: Free Press, 1994).
7. Ibid.
8. H. Mintzberg, "The Strategy Concept II: Another Look at Why Organizations Need Strategies," *California Management Review,* Fall 1987, p. 26.
9. Mintzberg, *The Rise and Fall of Strategic Planning.*
10. G. Hamel and C. K. Prahalad, *Competing for the Future* (Boston: Harvard Business School Press, 1994).
11. D. Miller, "The Architecture of Simplicity," *Academy of Management Review,* January 1993, pp. 116–38.
12. See, for instance, J. A. Pearce II, K. K. Robbins, and R. B. Robinson Jr., "The Impact of Grand Strategy and Planning Formality on Financial Performance," *Strategic Management Journal,* March–April 1987, pp. 125–34; L. C. Rhyne, "Contrasting Planning Systems in High, Medium and Low Performance Companies," *Journal of Management Studies,* July 1987, pp. 363–85; J. A. Pearce II, E. B. Freeman, and R. B. Robinson Jr. "The Tenuous Link between Formal Strategic Planning and Financial Performance," *Academy of Management Review,* October 1987, pp. 658–75; D. K. Sinha, "The Contribution of Formal Planning to Decisions," *Strategic Management Journal,* October 1990, pp. 479–92; and C. C. Miller and L. B. Cardinal, "Strategic Planning and Firm Performance: A Synthesis of More Than Two Decades of Research," *Academy of Management Journal,* December 1994, pp. 1649–65.
13. Cited in Rubbermaid's "Philosophy, Management Principles, Mission, and Objectives," April 1993.
14. S. Nelton, "Put Your Purpose in Writing," *Nation's Business,* February 1994, p. 62.
15. Ibid., p. 63.
16. G. Fuchsberg, "'Visioning' Missions Becomes Its Own Mission," *Wall Street Journal,* January 7, 1994, p. B1.
17. Nelton, "Put Your Purpose in Writing," pp. 61–64.
18. G. Eisenstodt, "Unidentical Twins," *Forbes,* July 5, 1993, p. 42; and D. Hulme, "The Sharp End of Innovation," *Asian Business,* February 1995, pp. 6–7.
19. G. Burns, "It Only Hertz When Enterprise Laughs," *Business Week,* December 12, 1994, p. 44; "Sustainability, Not Growth, at Patagonia," *At Work,* May/June 1993, p. 1; and R. Henkoff, "Getting beyond Downsizing," *Fortune,* January 10, 1994, pp. 58–60.
20. See T. T. Herbert and H. Deresky, "Generic Strategies: An Empirical Investigation of Typology Validity and Strategy Content," *Strategic Management Journal,* March–April 1987, pp. 135–47.
21. "Sustainability, Not Growth, at Patagonia," p. 20.
22. "How to Be Happy in One Act," *Fortune,* December 19, 1988, p. 119.
23. Henkoff, "Getting beyond Downsizing."
24. Ibid.
25. J. B. Barney, "Looking Inside for Competitive Advantage," *Academy of Management Executive,* November 1995, pp. 49–61.
26. See S. E. Jackson and J. E. Dutton, "Discerning Threats and Opportunities," *Administrative Science Quarterly,* September 1988, pp. 370–87.
27. J. Rossant, "Olivetti Tries to Stagger to Its Knees," *Business Week,* March 22, 1993, p. 19.
28. See, for instance, R. E. Miles and C. C. Snow, *Organizational Strategy, Structure, and Process* (New York: McGraw-

Hill, 1978); M. E. Porter, *Competitive Strategy: Techniques for Analyzing Industries and Competitors* (New York: Free Press, 1980); D. C. Hambrick, I. C. Macmillan, and D. L. Day, "Strategic Attributes and Performance in the BCG Matrix: A PIMS-Based Analysis of Industrial Product Businesses," *Academy of Management Journal,* September 1982, pp. 510–31; and M. Treacy and F. Wiersema, *The Discipline of Market Leaders* (Reading, Mass: Addison-Wesley, 1995).

29. Porter, *Competitive Strategy;* M. E. Porter, *Competitive Advantage: Creating and Sustaining Superior Performance* (New York: Free Press, 1985); E. Mosakowski, "A Resource-Based Perspective on the Dynamic Strategy-Performance Relationship: An Empirical Examination of the Focus and Differentiation Strategies in Entrepreneurial Firms," *Journal of Management,* Winter 1993, pp. 819–39; A. Miller and G. G. Dess, "Assessing Porter's (1980) Model in Terms of Its Generalizability, Accuracy, and Simplicity," *Journal of Management Studies,* July 1993, pp. 553–82.
30. R. H. Waterman Jr., T. J. Peters, and J. R. Phillips, "Structure Is Not Organization," *Business Horizons,* June 1980, pp. 14–26.
31. B. O'Brian, "Southwest Wins Pilots' Accord Offering No Wage Boost in First Five of 10 Years," *Wall Street Journal,* November 18, 1994, p. A2; "Southwest's New Deal," *Fortune,* January 16, 1995, p. 94; and D. Jones, "Low-Cost Carrier Still Challenges Industry," *USA Today,* July 10, 1995, p. 5B.
32. This section is based on S. L. Hwang, "Philip Morris Makes Dave's—But Sh! Don't Tell," *Wall Street Journal,* March 2, 1995, p. B1.
33. Ibid.
34. E. E. Adam Jr. and R. J. Ebert, *Production & Operations Management,* 5th ed. (Englewood Cliffs, N.J.: Prentice Hall, 1992), p. 333.
35. See, for instance, J. W. Weiss and R. K. Wysocki, *5-Phase Project Management* (Reading, Mass: Addison-Wesley, 1992), p. 3.
36. This discussion is based on R. S. Russell and B. W. Taylor III, *Production and Operations Management* (Englewood Cliffs, N.J.: Prentice Hall, 1995), p. 827.
37. C. Burck, "The Real World of the Entrepreneur," *Fortune,* April 5, 1993, pp. 64–65.
38. See, for example, J. B. Cunningham and J. Lischeron, "Defining Entrepreneurship," *Journal of Small Business Management,* January 1991, pp. 45–61.
39. Adapted from H. H. Stevenson, M. J. Roberts, and H. I. Grousbeck, *New Business Ventures and the Entrepreneur* (Homewood, Ill: Irwin, 1989).
40. See, for instance, T. M. Begley and D. P. Boyd, "A Comparison of Entrepreneurs and Managers of Small Business Firms," *Journal of Management,* Spring 1987, pp. 99–108.
41. P. F. Drucker, *Innovation and Entrepreneurship* (New York: Harper & Row, 1985).
42. G. Pinchot III, *Intrapreneuring: Or, Why You Don't Have to Leave the Corporation to Become an Entrepreneur* (New York: Harper & Row, 1985).
43. K. H. Vesper, *New Venture Strategies* (Englewood Cliffs, N.J.: Prentice Hall, 1980), p. 14.
44. See, for instance, J. P. Kotter, *The New Rules: How to Succeed in Today's Post-Corporate World* (New York: Free Press, 1995).
45. J. A. Hornaday, "Research about Living Entrepreneurs," in C. A. Kent, D. L. Sexton, and K. H. Vesper, eds., *Encyclopedia of Entrepreneurship* (Englewood Cliffs, N.J.: Prentice Hall, 1982), p. 28.
46. R. H. Brockhaus, "The Psychology of the Entrepreneur," in Kent, Sexton, and Vesper, eds., *Encyclopedia of Entrepreneurship,* pp. 41–49; and M. Oneal, "Just What Is an Entrepreneur?," *Business Week/Enterprise 1993,* November 1, 1993, pp. 104–12.
47. This section is based on R. D. Hisrich, "Entrepreneurship/Intrapreneurship," *American Psychologist,* February 1990, pp. 209–22.
48. H. H. Stevenson and D. E. Gumpert, "The Heart of Entrepreneurship," *Harvard Business Review,* March–April 1985, pp. 85–94.
49. Cited in "More Small Businesses Succeeding," *USA Today,* May 8, 1989, p. E1.
50. See Y. K. Shetty, "New Look at Corporate Goals," *California Management Review,* Winter 1979, pp. 71–79.
51. Nelton, "Put Your Purpose in Writing," p. 62.
52. J. Bennet, "A Case of Nerves at the High End," *New York Times,* June 24, 1995, p. Y17.
53. See, for instance, C. K. Warriner, "The Problem of Organizational Purpose," *Sociological Quarterly,* Spring 1965, pp. 139–46; and J. Pfeffer, *Organizational Design* (Arlington Heights, Ill.: AHM Publishing, 1978), pp. 5–12.
54. Warriner, "The Problem of Organizational Purpose."
55. Ibid.
56. E. A. Locke, "Toward a Theory of Task Motivation and Incentives," *Organizational Behavior and Human Performance,* May 1968, pp. 157–89.
57. G. P. Latham and G. A. Yukl, "A Review of Research on the Application of Goal Setting in Organizations," *Academy of Management Journal,* December 1975, pp. 824–45; E. A. Locke, K. N. Shaw, L. M. Saari, and G. P. Latham, "Goal Setting and Task Performance," *Psychological Bulletin,* January 1981, pp. 125–52; A. J. Mento, R. P. Steel, and R. J. Karren, "A Meta-Analytic Study of the Effects of Goal Setting on Task Performance: 1966–1984," *Organizational Behavior and Human Decision Processes,* February 1987, pp. 52–83; M. E. Tubbs, "Goal Setting: A Meta-Analytic Examination of the Empirical Evidence," *Journal of Applied Psychology,* August 1986, pp. 474–83; P. C. Earley, G. B. Northcraft, C. Lee, and T. R. Lituchy, "Impact of Process and Outcome Feedback on the Relation of Goal Setting to Task Performance," *Academy of Management Journal,* March 1990, pp. 87–105; E. A. Locke and G. P. Latham, *A Theory of Goal Setting and Task Performance* (Englewood Cliffs, N.J.: Prentice Hall, 1990); and D. E. Terpstra and E. J. Rozell, "The Relationship of Goal Setting to Organizational Profitability," *Group & Organization Management,* September 1994, pp. 285–94.
58. This section is based on S. P. Robbins and P. L. Hunsaker, *Training in InterPersonal Skills: TIPS for Managing People at Work,* 2nd ed. (Upper Saddle River, N.J.: Prentice Hall, 1996), pp. 52–57.

59. W. E. Deming, *Out of the Crisis* (Cambridge, Mass: MIT Center for Advanced Engineering Study, 1986).
60. M. Maremont, "Blind Ambition," *Business Week,* October 23, 1995, pp. 78–92; and M. Maremont, "Judgment Day at Bausch & Lomb," *BusinessWeek,* December 25, 1995, p. 39.
61. See, for instance, P. P. Carson and K. D. Carson, "Deming versus Traditional Management Theorists on Goal Setting: Can Both Be Right?" *Business Horizons,* September–October 1993, pp. 79–84.
62. S. Tully, "Why to Go for Stretch Targets," *Fortune,* November 14, 1994, pp. 145–58.

CHAPTER 6

EVALUATING PERFORMANCE THROUGH CONTROL SYSTEMS

Why is there so much month left at the end of the money?

- Anonymous

LEARNING OBJECTIVES

After studying this chapter, you should be able to:

1. Describe the steps in the control process
2. Identify the various behavioral control devices available to managers
3. Describe the objectives of the EOQ model
4. Contrast data and information
5. Trace the evolution of modern MIS
6. Contrast incremental and zero-base budgets
7. Explain the steps in creating a PERT network
8. List the steps in developing a control chart

Before January 1995, Nicholas Leeson was just a 28-year-old "successful trader" in Singapore for one of Britain's oldest (233 years old!) and most respected investment banks—Barings PLC. But in a period of only a few weeks in early 1995, this young man single-handedly lost more than $1 billion of Barings' money—nearly twice its available capital—and brought about the collapse of the firm. How he was able to do this is a case study in what happens when an organization has inadequate controls.[1]

Leeson (shown in white shirt in photo) began his career at Barings in 1989, in their London office, as a back-office clerk. He learned about derivatives—a complex product based on heavily leveraged options—and used his knowledge to gain promotions within the investment bank. He ended up trading for Barings in their Singapore office. His specialty was buying and selling Japanese stock index futures and options on the Osaka and Singapore exchanges, making profits out of the price differentials between the two markets. By 1994, Leeson was bringing in more than $30 million of profits for his firm. That compared with a profit of $1.6 million in 1992, the year Leeson arrived in Singapore.

Everything was working out fine for Leeson until December 1994. He decided to wager that the Japanese Nikkei index would not drop below 19,000 points on March 10, 1995. It seemed a safe bet since the Japanese economy was rebounding from a 2-year recession. But on January 17, 1995, a massive earthquake hit Kobe, Japan. The Nikkei index dropped more than 7 percent in a week. To cover his losses, Leeson gambled hundreds of millions more of Barings' money that the Nikkei would stabilize at 19,000. It didn't, resulting in the billion-dollar loss.

This debacle could have been prevented by proper controls. As early as the summer of 1994, Barings' management was advised by its internal auditors that there were potential problems with Leeson's operation in Singapore. The auditors were particularly concerned that Leeson was both trader and manager, which allowed him to settle his own trades. At most banks, those two jobs are split because allowing a trader to confirm his own transactions and write checks makes it simpler to hide risks. Barings' management did nothing to correct the situation. It trusted Leeson and didn't want to interfere with his highly profitable trading. This trust continued in spite of obvious signs that Leeson was risking increasingly large amounts of the firm's money. For instance, just 4 weeks before the bank's collapse, it took out an $850 million loan so it could continue to fund Leeson's activities.

Barings' management assumed that Leeson was hedging his bets to protect the firm's huge exposure—a staggering $29 billion in future and option contracts. But he wasn't. And because Leeson operated with virtually no supervision and was responsible for settling his own trades, the control mechanisms that would typically expose the risks that he was taking were absent. As the head of futures trading at Barclays Bank PLC said about Leeson's activities, "You can't stop someone from going berserk, but you can have a system to catch it in 24 hours."[2] Unfortunately for Barings, it didn't have such a system in its Singapore office.

As the Barings case vividly illustrates, inadequate controls can literally bring down an organization. Regardless of how thoughtful and insightful management is in developing plans, there is no guarantee that people in the organization are carrying them out properly. For example, objectives give people specific direction. However, just stating objectives or having subordinates accept your objectives is no guarantee that the necessary actions will be accomplished. The effective manager, therefore, needs to follow up to ensure that the actions that others are supposed to take and the objectives they are supposed to achieve are, in fact, being taken and achieved.

In this chapter, we describe the control process, identify those elements in the organization that management seeks to control, demonstrate the role of computerized information systems in control, discuss the downsides of controls, and present some basic control tools for effective management.

THE CONTROL PROCESS

Control is the process of monitoring activities to ensure that they are being accomplished as planned and of correcting any significant deviations. Managers can't really know whether their units are performing properly until they've evaluated what activities have been done and have compared the actual performance with the desired standard.[3]

It helps to think of the **control process** as consisting of three separate and distinct steps: (1) *measuring* actual performance, (2) *comparing* actual performance against a standard, and (3) taking *managerial action* to correct deviations or inadequate standards (see Exhibit 6-1).

Notice from Exhibit 6-1 that the control process assumes that standards of performance *already* exist. These standards are the specific objectives against which progress can be measured. If managers use MBO, then objectives are, by definition, tangible, verifiable, and measurable. In such instances, these objectives are the standards by which progress is measured and against which it is compared. If MBO isn't practiced, then standards are the specific performance indicators that management uses. In either case, keep in mind that planning must precede the setting of controls because it is in planning that the standards are established.

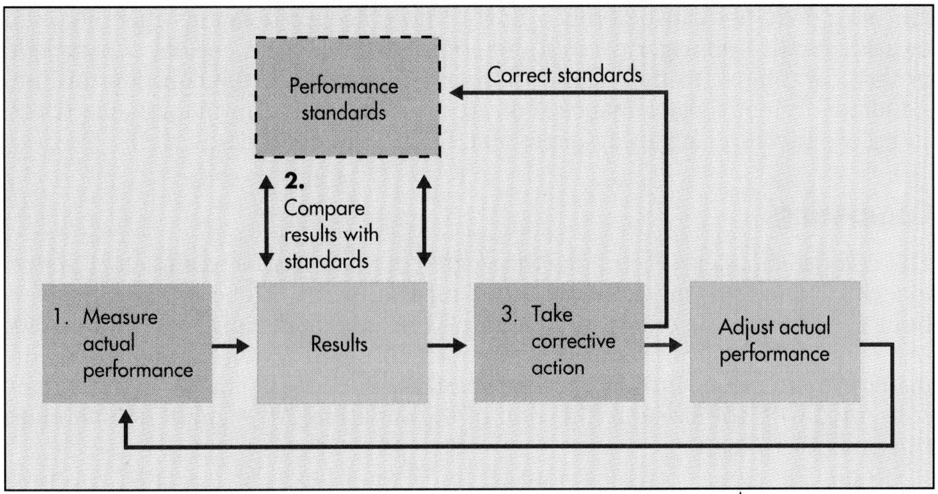

EXHIBIT 6-1
The Control Process

Measuring

To determine what actual performance is, a manager must acquire information about it. The first step in control, then, is measuring. Let's consider *how* we measure and *what* we measure.

The most frequently used sources of information for measuring actual performance are personal observation, statistical reports, oral reports, written reports, and computer-accessed databases. The effective manager tends to use multiple sources, recognizing that different sources provide different types of information. Personal observations obtained by walking around and talking with employees, for instance, can be a rich source of detailed performance data. A manager can pick up important clues about potential problems from an employee's facial expression or casual comment that might never be evident from reviewing a statistical report. On the other hand, statistical reports typically contain more comprehensive and objective data.

What we measure is probably more critical to the control process than *how* we measure it. Selecting the wrong criteria can have serious dysfunctional consequences. Besides, what we measure determines, to a great extent, what people in the organization will attempt to excel at.[4]

What we measure determines, to a great extent, what people in the organization will attempt to excel at.

Some control criteria are applicable to any management situation. For instance, because all managers, by definition, direct the activities of others, criteria such as employee attendance or turnover rates can be measured. Most managers have budgets for their area of responsibility set in monetary costs. Keeping costs within budget is therefore a fairly common control measure. Any comprehensive control system, however, needs to recognize the diversity of activities among managers. A production manager in a manufacturing plant might use measures of the quantity of units produced per day, number of units produced per labor-hour, or percent of units rejected by customers because of inferior quality. The manager of an administrative department in a government agency might use number of orders processed per hour or average time required to process service calls. Marketing executives often use measures such as percent of market captured, average dollar value per sale, or number of customer visits per salesperson.

The performance of some activities is difficult to quantify. It is more difficult, for instance, for an administrator to measure the performance of a research chemist or an elementary school teacher than of a person who sells life insurance.

But most activities can be broken down into objective segments that allow for measurement. A manager needs to determine what value a person, department, or unit contributes to the organization and then convert the contribution into standards. When a performance indicator can't be stated in quantifiable terms, subjective measures are always preferable to having no standards at all.

Comparing

The comparison step determines the degree of variation between actual performance and the standard. Some variation in performance can be expected in all activities; it is therefore critical to determine the acceptable range of variation (see Exhibit 6-2). Deviations in excess of this range become significant and receive the manager's attention. In the comparison stage, managers should be particularly concerned with the size and direction of the variation. An example should make this process clearer.

Todd Cruz is new-car sales manager for Dixon Jeep-Eagle in Seattle, Washington. The first week of each month, Todd prepares a report based on sales from the previous month, classified by model. Exhibit 6-3 displays both the standard and actual sales figures for the month of July.

Should Todd be concerned about the July performance? Sales were a bit higher than he had originally targeted, but does that mean that there were no significant deviations? Even though overall performance was generally quite favorable, several models might deserve Todd's attention. However, which models deserve attention depends on what Todd believes to be *significant*. How much variation should Todd allow before he takes corrective action?

The deviation on several models is very small and undoubtedly not worthy of special attention. These include the Grand Wagoneer and Summit. Is the shortfall for Vision significant? That's a judgment Todd must make. Talon sales were 30 percent below Todd's goal. Sales performance for this model needs attention. Todd should look for the cause of the shortfall. In this case, Todd attributed the lower sales to price cuts by competitors on comparable models. If this decline in Talon sales is more than a temporary slump, Todd will need to reduce his orders with Chrysler and lower his inventory stock.

Understating sales goals can be as troublesome as overstating them. For instance, is the popularity of the Jeep Wrangler and Grand Cherokee a 1-month aberration, or are these models increasing their market share? As our example illustrates, both overvariance and undervariance require managerial attention.

EXHIBIT 6-2
Defining an Acceptable Range of Variation

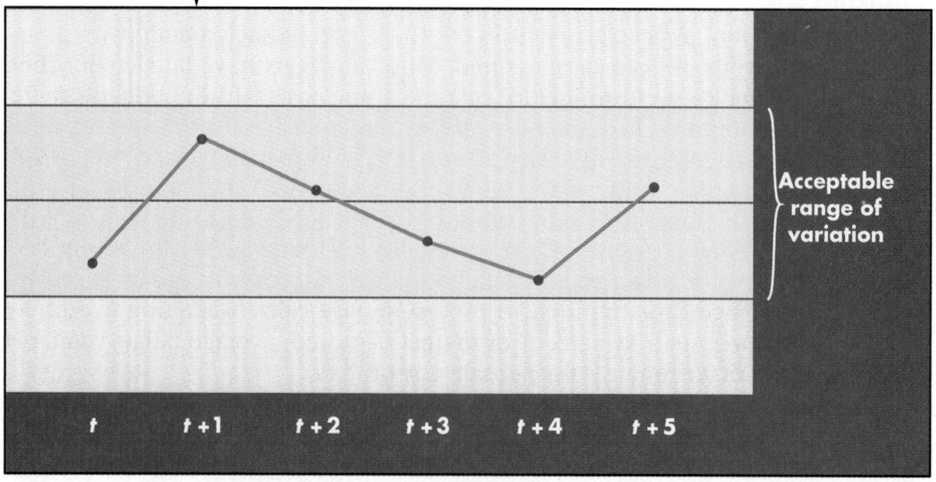

Model	Standard	Actual	Over (under)
Wrangler	8	13	5
Cherokee	11	11	0
Grand Cherokee	10	14	4
Grand Wagoneer	6	7	1
Talon	13	9	(4)
Vision	10	8	(2)
Summit	4	3	(1)
Total	62	65	3

EXHIBIT 6-3
Dixon Jeep-Eagle's July Sales Performance (in number of units sold)

Taking Managerial Action

The third and final step in the control process is taking managerial action. Managers can choose among three courses of action: They can do nothing; they can correct the actual performance; or they can revise the standard. Because doing nothing is fairly self-explanatory, let's look more closely at the latter two.

IN THE NEWS

Granite Rock Believes in Measurement

"MEASUREMENT IS WHAT IT'S ALL ABOUT," SAYS VAL VERUTTI, QUALITY-SUPPORT MANAGER FOR GRANITE Rock Co. in Watsonville, California. "If you set goals and lofty ideals, without means of measuring, you're just kidding yourself. You've got to have ways of finding out if improvements really are improvements."

Granite Rock's business—it manufactures construction materials—isn't the sophisticated and complex type of business you typically think of when you think of a company obsessed with quality. But Granite Rock takes quality very seriously. Seriously enough for the 386-employee firm to have won a Malcolm Baldrige National Quality Award.

The company has identified sixty-six baseline goals it uses as measures of its performance. These baseline goals are the specific action areas that Granite Rock focuses on that support the company's nine corporate objectives. "This is what makes the corporate objectives come alive," says the firm's CEO.

Management attaches great importance to selecting the right information to be tracked because that information "organizes the quality process for the entire company," says one manager. For instance, the company measures the cubic yards and tons of material moved per hour. It measures not just its profit performance but also its market share. It checks the reliability of its technical data by having its own laboratory's measurements monitored by outside labs. And, because customers indicate through surveys that on-time delivery is their highest priority, management carefully measures its on-time performance.

Granite Rock CEO Bruce Woolpert (foreground) with driver Paul Bush.

Source: Based on M. Barrier, "Learning the Meaning of Measurement," *Nation's Business*, June 1994, pp. 72–74.

Correct Actual Performance If the source of the variation has been deficient performance, managers will want to take corrective action. Examples of such corrective action might include a change in strategy, reorganization, or providing employees with training.

A manager who decides to correct actual performance has to make another decision: Should he or she take immediate or basic corrective action? **Immediate corrective action** corrects problems at once and gets performance back on track. **Basic corrective action** asks how and why performance has deviated and then proceeds to correct the source of deviation.

It's not unusual for managers to rationalize that they don't have time to take basic corrective action and therefore must be content to perpetually "put out fires" with immediate corrective action. Effective managers, however, analyze deviations and, when the benefits justify it, take the time to permanently correct significant variances between standard and actual performance.

In our example of Dixon Jeep-Eagle, Todd Cruz might take basic corrective action on the negative variance for the Talon. He might increase advertising for this model, run a price-cutting promotion, offer bonuses to his salespeople to encourage them to push this model, or reduce future orders with the manufacturer.

Revise the Standard It is possible that the variance is a result of an unrealistic standard—that is, the goal may be too high or too low. In such cases it is the standard that needs corrective attention, not the performance. In our example, Todd Cruz might need to raise the standard for the Grand Cherokee to reflect its increasing popularity. Athletes revise their standards when, for example, they adjust their performance goals upward during a season if they achieve their season goal early.

The more troublesome problem is the revising of a performance standard downward. If an employee or unit falls significantly short of reaching its target, the natural response is to shift the blame for the variance to the standard. Students, for example, who make a low grade on a test often attack the grade cutoff points as too high. Rather than accept the fact that their performance was inadequate, students argue that the standards are unreasonable. Similarly, salespeople who fail to meet their monthly quota may attribute the failure to an unrealistic quota. It may be true that standards are too high, resulting in a significant variance and acting to demotivate those employees being assessed against it. But keep in mind that if employees or managers don't meet the standard, the first thing they are likely to attack is the standard itself. If you believe the standard is realistic, hold your ground. Explain your position, reaffirm to the employee or manager that you expect future performance to improve, and then take the necessary corrective action to turn that expectation into reality.

WHAT MANAGERS SEEK TO CONTROL

> **Most control efforts are directed at one of four areas: human behavior, finances, operations, or information.**

What do managers control? Most control efforts are directed at one of four areas: human behavior, finances, operations, or information.

Human Behavior

It may sound manipulative, but managers seek to control their employees' behavior. Remember, managers accomplish goals by working through other people. They depend on these people to achieve their unit goals. And they are accountable for the results, or lack of results, that these people achieve. To ensure that employees are performing as they're supposed to, managers rely on a wide range of behavioral control devices.

The following discussion briefly identifies some of the more powerful behavioral control mechanisms available to managers.

Selection The hiring process offers managers an opportunity to impose controls. How? By identifying and selecting people whose values, attitudes, and personality fit with what management desires. If, for example, managers want only employees who are assertive and risk-taking, individuals who don't have those qualities can be screened out of the job applicant pool.

New-Employee Orientation Once new employees are hired, they are given an initial orientation. In some organizations, this may be several weeks of formal training. In others, it may be nothing more than a brief talk with an immediate supervisor. However, even the most informal orientation typically includes implicit communication by managers to the new employee on what behaviors the organization considers acceptable and unacceptable. So the new-employee orientation acts to fine-tune behavioral expectations of individuals who have already been selected because they appear to fit into the organization.

Mentoring Some organizations have formal mentoring programs for new employees. Mentors act as guides and role models for new employees—showing them "the ropes to skip and the ropes to know." For instance, when mentors show protégés how to do certain tasks or provide insight into job behaviors that can get them into "trouble with the big boss," they are contributing to standardizing the protégé's behavior. The selection of formal mentors should not be random. Managers should judiciously select mentors who will convey to new employees the attitudes and behaviors it wants these new employees to exhibit.

Goals As described in Chapter 5, goals guide and constrain employees by clarifying what behaviors are likely to lead to goal attainment. Once employees accept specific goals, the goals then direct and limit employee behavior.

Job Design The way jobs are designed determines, to a large degree, the tasks the jobholder does, the pace of the work, the people with whom he or she interacts, and similar activities. For example, assembly-line work tends to constrain behavioral options far more than do traveling sales positions. The latter jobs give employees considerable autonomy, thus allowing them greater control over their daily activities. So managers can influence employee behavior by the way they design their employees' jobs.

Formal Regulations Almost all organizations have formal rules, policies, job descriptions, and other regulations that define acceptable practices and constrain behavior. These can range from a short list of Do's and Don'ts to large and detailed policy manuals. The more formal regulations management creates, the greater the visibility of those regulations, and the more managers require employees to adhere to them, the greater control regulations will have over employees.

Direct Supervision On a day-to-day basis, managers oversee employees' work, identify deviant employee behavior, and correct problems as they occur. The manager who spots an employee taking an unnecessary risk when operating his or her machine may point out the correct way to perform the task and tell the employee to do it the correct way in the future. In so doing, the manager constrains the employee's behavioral options.

Training Most organizations encourage or even require employees to undergo training in order to keep their skills current. These formal training programs teach employees desired work practices and, in so doing, act to shape the employees' on-the-job behaviors.

Performance Appraisal Managers formally assess the work of their employees through performance appraisals. An employee's recent performance is evaluated. If performance is positive, the employee's behavior can be rewarded. If performance is below standard, managers can seek to correct it or, depending on the nature of the deviation, discipline the employee. Performance appraisals become control devices because employees tend to behave in ways so as to look good on the criteria by which they will be appraised.

Organizational Rewards Rewards such as pay increases, promotions, desirable job assignments, and recognition awards act as reinforcers to encourage desired behaviors and to extinguish undesirable ones. So by the choices managers make in terms of the critieria they reward—for example, loyalty, dependability, risk-taking, openness, deceitfulness, collegial support—they encourage or discourage certain behaviors.

Finances

Business firms seek to earn a profit. Not-for-profit organizations seek efficiencies through cost control. In pursuit of these objectives, managers of these organizations introduce financial controls. These include budgets, the use of financial ratios, and audits.

Budgets Few of us are unfamiliar with budgets. Most of us learned about them at an early age, when we discovered that unless we allocated our "revenues" carefully, we would consume our weekly allowance before half the week was out.

A **budget** is a numerical plan for allocating resources to specific activities. Budgets provide managers with quantitative standards against which to measure and compare resource consumption. And, by pointing out deviations between standard and actual consumption, they become control devices.[5] As shown in Exhibit 6-4, the typical manager is most likely to use budgets to control revenues, expenses, profits, cash usage, and capital expenditures.

The popularity of budgets as a financial control mechanism lies largely in their applicability across different countries, types of organizations, and functions and levels within organizations. We live in a world in which almost everything is expressed in monetary units. Dollars, pesos, yen, marks, francs, and the like are used as a common denominator within a country. Controlling monetary allocations is as important to hospitals and school districts as it is to business firms. And budgets make a useful common denominator for controlling activities in a research lab as well as a production department. Budgets seem to be one device that most managers, regardless of level in the organization, use on a regular basis.

EXHIBIT 6-4
Popular Types of Budgets

Revenue budgets. Project future sales. Determined by multiplying estimated sales volume by sales price.

Expense budgets. List the primary activities undertaken by a unit and allocate a monetary value to each.

Profit budgets. Used by separate units of an organization that combines revenue and expense budgets to determine the unit's profit contribution.

Cash budgets. Forecast how much cash an organization will have on hand and how much it will need to meet expenses.

Capital expenditure budgets. Estimate investments in property, buildings, and major equipment.

Financial Ratios Exhibit 6-5 summarizes some of the most popular **financial ratios** used in organizations. Taken from the organization's financial statements (the balance sheet and income statement), they compare two significant figures and express them as a percentage, or ratio. Because you undoubtedly have encountered these ratios in introductory accounting and finance courses, or you will in the near future, we needn't elaborate on them. We mention them, however, to remind you that managers use such ratios as internal control devices for monitoring how efficiently the organization uses its assets, debt, inventories, and the like.

Audits An **audit** is a formal verification of an organization's accounts, records, operating activities, or performance. Audits can generally be characterized as either external or internal.

An *external audit* is a verification of an organization's financial statements by an outside and independent accounting firm. The organization creates its own financial statements using its own accountants. The external auditor's job is then to review the various accounts on the financial statements in respect to their accuracy and conformity with generally accepted accounting practices.

For publicly held corporations, the primary purpose of the external audit is to protect stockholders. The external audit's value to management, in terms of a control device, is generally indirect because the audits are meant only to verify that which management already knows. They are an indirect control device, however, in the sense that their existence serves as a deterrent against abuses or misrepresentations by those who develop the financial statements.

EXHIBIT 6-5
Popular Financial Ratios

Objective	Ratio	Calculation	Meaning
Liquidity test	Current ratio	$\frac{\text{Current assets}}{\text{Current liabilities}}$	Tests the organization's ability to meet short-term obligations
	Acid test	$\frac{\text{Current assets} - \text{inventories}}{\text{Current liabilities}}$	Tests liquidity most accurately when inventories turn over slowly or are difficult to sell
Leverage test	Debt-to-assets	$\frac{\text{Total debts}}{\text{Total assets}}$	The higher the ratio, the more leveraged the organization
	Times-interest-earned	$\frac{\text{Profits before interest and taxes}}{\text{Total interest charges}}$	Measures how far profits can decline before the organization is unable to meet its interest expenses
Operations test	Inventory turnover	$\frac{\text{Sales}}{\text{Inventory}}$	The higher the ratio, the more efficiently inventory assets are being used
	Total asset turnover	$\frac{\text{Sales}}{\text{Total assets}}$	The fewer assets used to achieve a given level of sales, the more efficiently management is using the organization's total assets
Profitability	Profit margin on sales	$\frac{\text{Net profit after taxes}}{\text{Total sales}}$	Identifies the profits that various products are generating
	Return on investment	$\frac{\text{Net profit after taxes}}{\text{Total assets}}$	Measures how efficiently assets generate profits

The *internal audit,* as its name implies, is done by members of the organization. It encompasses verifying the financial statements, just as the external audit does, but additionally includes an evaluation of the organization's operations, procedures, and policies, plus recommendations for improvement. So, in terms of control, the internal audit is a more comprehensive evaluation. It goes beyond merely verifying financial statements, seeks to uncover inefficiencies, and offers suggested actions for their correction.

Operations

The success of an organization depends to a large extent on its ability to produce goods and services effectively and efficiently. Operations control is designed to assess how effectively and efficiently an organization's transformation processes are working. That is, how effective and efficient the organization is in turning inputs into outputs.[6]

Operations control typically encompasses monitoring production activities to ensure that they're on schedule; assessing purchasing's ability to provide the proper quantity and quality of supplies needed at the lowest cost possible; monitoring the quality of the organization's products or services to ensure that they meet preestablished standards; and making sure that equipment is well maintained.

Scheduling When managers engage in **scheduling,** they determine what activities have to be done, the order in which they are to be done, who is to do each, and when they are to be completed. As such, scheduling involves both planning and control of operational activities. When they focus on prioritizing activities, then they are planning devices. When they are used to determine whether work is being completed on time, then they become control devices.

One of the simplest and best illustrations of a scheduling technique is something called the **Gantt chart.**[7] It was developed early in this century by Henry Gantt. The Gantt chart is essentially a bar graph with time on the horizontal axis and activities to be scheduled on the vertical axis. The bars show output, both planned and actual, over a period of time. The Gantt chart visually shows when each task is supposed to be done and compares that with the actual progress on each. It is a simple device that allows managers to detail easily what has yet to be done to complete a job or project and to assess whether the project is ahead of, behind, or on schedule.

Exhibit 6-6 depicts a Gantt chart that was developed by a production manager at Simon & Schuster publishers. Time is expressed in months across the top of the chart. The major activities are listed down the left side. The planning comes in deciding what activities need to be done to get the book finished, the order in which they need to be done, and the time that should be allocated to each activity. Where a box sits within a time frame reflects its planned sequence. The shading represents actual progress. The chart becomes a control device when the manager looks for deviations from the plan. For instance, in Exhibit 6-6, the production manager has given her team 9 months to go from getting the manuscript copyedited to having bound copies complete. But after 3 months (reporting date), she has two control problems. The people responsible for selecting photos and getting permissions for their use are a full month behind schedule. Similarly, the galley proofs are 2 weeks behind schedule. If the book is to be completed on time, the production manager is going to have to take some immediate action to pick up lost time on those two activities.

Purchasing It has been said that human beings *are* what they eat. Metaphorically, the same applies to organizations. Their processes and outputs depend on the inputs they "eat." It's difficult to make quality products out of inferior inputs.

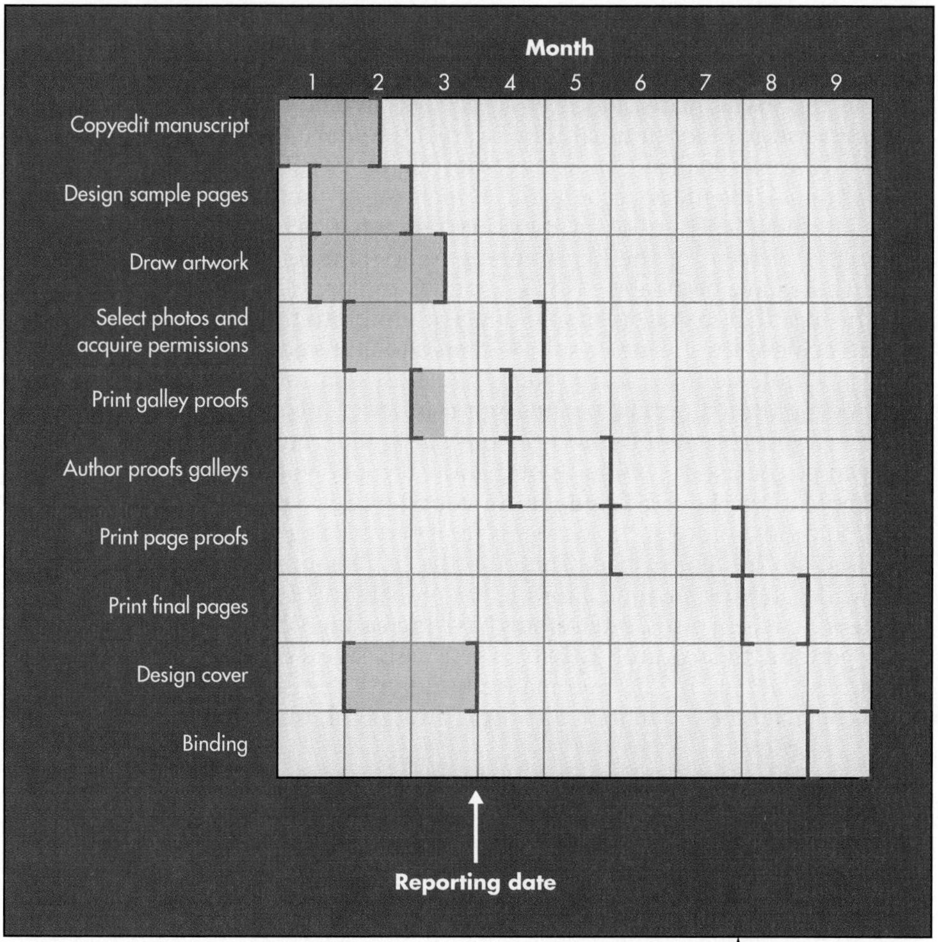

EXHIBIT 6-6
A Gantt Chart for Book Production

Highly skilled leather workers need quality cowhides if they're going to produce high-quality wallets. Gas station operators depend on a regular and dependable inflow of certain octane-rated gasolines from their suppliers in order to meet their customers' demands. If the gasoline isn't there, they can't sell it. If the gasoline is below the specified octane rating, customers may be dissatisfied and take their business elsewhere. Management must therefore monitor the delivery, performance, quality, quantity, and price of inputs from suppliers. Purchasing control seeks to ensure availability, acceptable quality, continued reliable sources, and, at the same time, reduced costs.

What can managers do to facilitate control of inputs? They need to gather information on the dates and conditions in which supplies arrive. They need to gather data about the quality of supplies and the compatibility of those supplies with operations processes. Finally, they need to obtain data on supplier price performance. Are the prices of the delivered goods the same as those quoted when the order was placed?

This information can be used to rate suppliers, identify problem suppliers, and guide management in choosing future suppliers. Trends can be detected. Suppliers can be evaluated, for instance, on responsiveness, service, reliability, and competitiveness. In recent years, an increasing proportion of manufacturers have reduced the number of vendors they deal with.[8] The reason? It is easier to monitor relations and develop close ties with only two suppliers than it is with twenty-two. Specific purchasing-control techniques range from the simple to the very complex. The following discussion briefly describes several of these techniques.

In the 1800s, economist Vilfredo Pareto found that 80 percent of the wealth was controlled by only 20 percent of the population. Managers typically find that just a few of their employees cause most of their problems. This concept, the vital few and the trivial many, has been applied to inventory control. It's called the **ABC system.** It is not unusual for a company to have thousands of items in inventory. However, evidence indicates that roughly 10 percent of the items in most organizations' inventory account for 50 percent of the annual dollar inventory value. Another 20 percent of the items account for 30 percent of the value. The remaining 70 percent of the items appear to account for only 20 percent of the value. These have been labeled as A, B, and C categories, respectively. Consistent with the idea that managers should direct attention to those areas where their effort can achieve the greatest result, A items should receive the tightest control, B items moderate control, and C items the least control. A items, for example, might be monitored weekly, B items monthly, and C items quarterly.

When you ordered checks from the bank, did you notice that the reorder form was placed about two-thirds of the way through your supply of checks? This is a simple example of a **fixed-point reordering system.** At some preestablished point in a process, the system is designed to "flag" the fact that the inventory needs to be replenished. The objective is to minimize inventory carrying costs while, at the same time, limiting the probability of *stocking out* of the inventory item. In recent years, retail stores have increasingly been using their computers to perform this control activity. Their cash registers are connected to store computers, and each sale automatically adjusts the store's inventory record. When the inventory of an item hits the critical point, the computer tells management to reorder.

One of the most sophisticated and well-known quantitative techniques for managing purchasing and inventories is the **economic order quantity (EOQ) model.** The EOQ model seeks to balance four costs involved in ordering and carrying inventory: the purchase costs (purchase price plus delivery charges less discounts); the ordering costs (paperwork, follow-up, inspection when the item arrives, and other processing costs); carrying costs (money tied up in inventory, storage, insurance, taxes, and so forth); and stockout costs (profits foregone from orders lost, the cost of reestablishing goodwill, and additional expenses incurred to expedite late shipments). As shown in Exhibit 6-7, the objective of the EOQ model is to minimize the total costs of two of these four costs—carrying costs and ordering costs. As the amount ordered gets larger and larger, average inventory increases, and so do carrying costs. But placing larger orders means fewer orders and thus lowers ordering costs. The lowest total cost—and thus the most economic order quantity—is reached at the lowest point on the total cost curve. A detailed mathematical equation is available for specifically identifying the optimal order quantity.[9]

Information

The quality of any managerial decision is largely dependent on the quality of information that the manager has at his or her disposal. This principle is illustrated in the well-worn computer phrase GIGO (garbage in, garbage out). In today's increasingly complex world, where the ability to make quick and intelligent decisions is an absolute necessity for survival, information control has gained significantly enhanced importance.

Managers in the city of Mississauga, Ontario, for instance, are using their computerized executive information system (EIS) to keep costs down.[10] The EIS gives the city's commissioners and managers the key information they need, when they need it, displayed in a user-friendly format. A sophisticated software program analyzes data that individual managers have deemed critical to their specific jobs and then the system delivers the analyses to the manager's computer

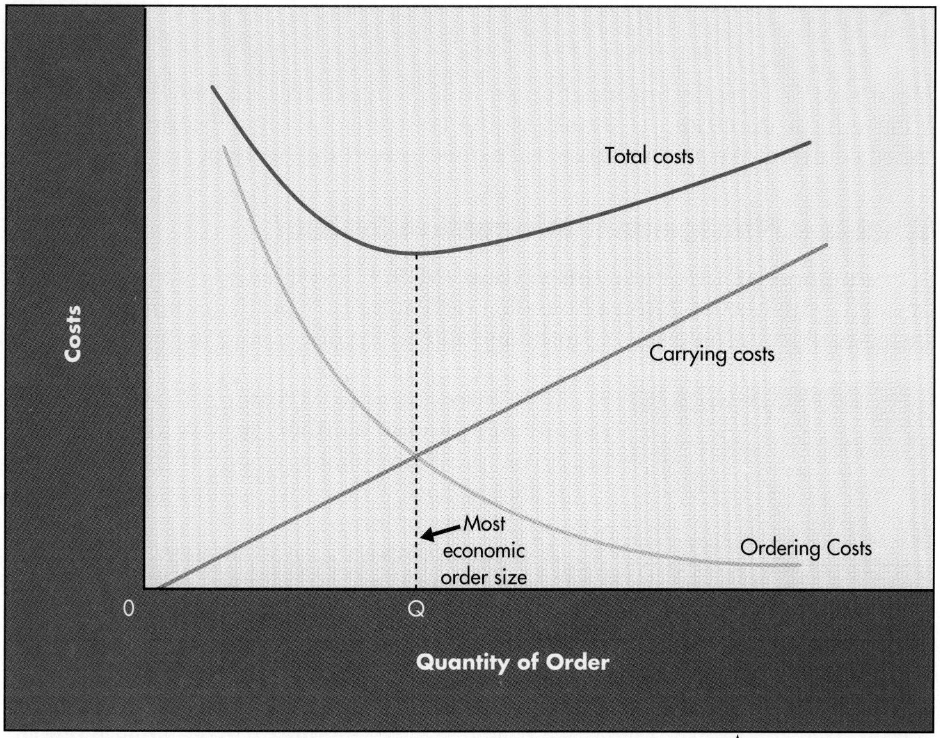

EXHIBIT 6-7
Determining the Most Economic Order Quantity

screen in an easy-to-read graphics and text format. Managers can find out at any point in time exactly what they have spent and how much they have left. This information allows them to react instantly to financial changes. The system, which has been in place for just 3 years, has enabled the city to operate for the past 2 years without increasing taxes.

Today, information control is typically subsumed under the topic of management information systems. Because this issue is now so important to almost every manager's daily activities, let's proceed to a discussion of how management information systems are changing control systems in organizations.

Mississauga mayor Hazel McCallion and executive assistant John Wright know what they want—a city that runs like a business.

HOW MIS IS CHANGING CONTROL SYSTEMS

What is MIS? How has information control changed over the past 30 years? And what ethical implications should we be concerned about regarding computer-based controls? We answer those three questions in this section.

What Is a Management Information System?

A **management information system (MIS)** is a system used to provide management with needed information on a regular basis.[11] In theory, this system can be manual or computer-based, although all current discussion, including ours, focuses on computer-supported applications.

An MIS focuses specifically on providing management with *information,* not merely *data.*

The term *system* in MIS implies order, arrangement, and purpose. Further, an MIS focuses specifically on providing management with *information,* not merely *data.* These two points are important and need elaboration.

A library provides a good analogy. Although it can contain millions of volumes, a library doesn't do users much good if they can't *find* what they want *quickly.* That's why libraries spend a lot of time cataloguing their collections and ensuring that volumes are returned to their proper locations. Organizations today are like well-stocked libraries. There is no lack of data. There is, however, a lack of ability to process that data so that the right information is available to the right person when he or she needs it.[12] A library is almost useless if it has the book you want, but either you can't find it or the library takes a week to retrieve it from storage. An MIS, on the other hand, has organized data in some meaningful way and can access the information in a reasonable amount of time. **Data** are raw, unanalyzed facts, such as numbers, names, or quantities. But as data, these facts are relatively useless to managers.[13] When data are analyzed and processed, they become **information.** An MIS collects data and turns them into relevant information for managers to use. Exhibit 6-8 summarizes these observations.

EXHIBIT 6-8
MIS Makes Data Usable

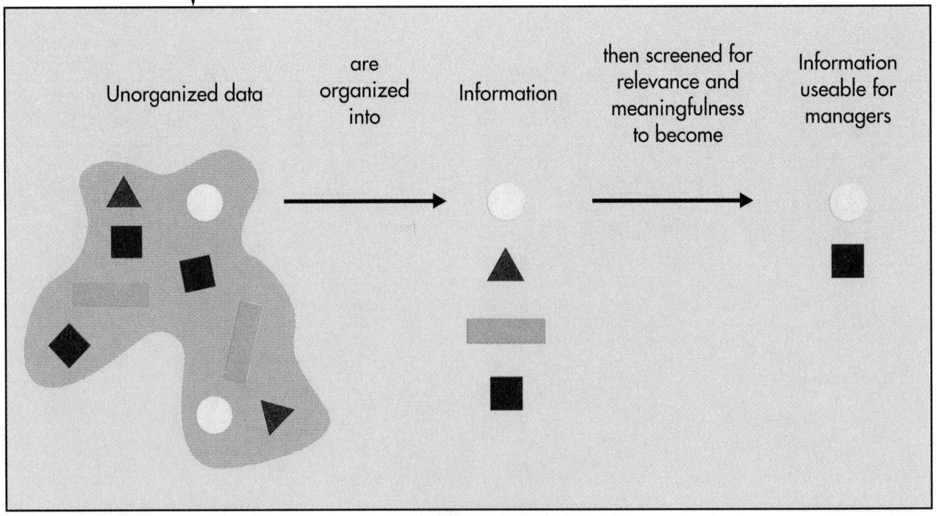

The Evolution of MIS

Exhibit 6-9 describes the four-stage evolution of modern MIS. Beginning in the mid-1960s, it reflects extraordinary changes. In fact, only in stages 3 and 4 has MIS reached its full potential as an integrated and coordinated information system.

Stage 1: Management-Focused Data Processing Beginning around 1965, organizations began to convert the centralized data processing systems that had been created for accounting and clerical activities to providing support information for management and operational personnel. Information systems were redesigned specifically to help managers in diverse functions to make better decisions. Not only were managers in the accounting area involved with information control, but so were managers in purchasing, human resources, marketing, engineering, research and development, and production and operations.

Managers of every type began to see how computers could help them do their jobs better and more efficiently. Computers could accumulate and analyze large quantities of data that could never be analyzed economically on a manual basis. Marketing executives, for instance, could now not only review weekly sales reports broken down by each salesperson, but they also could have those data analyzed by product groups. If the sales of a particular product line suddenly dropped, computer-generated information could alert management quickly and allow for rapid corrective action.

The major constraint on managers during stage 1 was that managers were dependent on others for information access and control. Computer-generated reports, for the most part, were produced by MIS specialists who worked in departments with titles like Data Systems or Information Systems. When managers had an information control problem, they had to go to the MIS specialists for a solution.

Stage 2: Decentralized End-User Computing By 1980, centralized data processing was being rapidly replaced by decentralized systems in which part or all of the computer logic functions were performed outside a single, centralized computer. In stage 2, managers became end users, personal computers became overwhelmingly popular, and data systems departments evolved into information support centers.

When a manager becomes an **end user,** he or she takes responsibility for information control.[14] It is no longer delegated to some other department or staff

EXHIBIT 6-9
The Evolution of Management Information Systems

Stage	Approximate Time Period	Description
1. Management-focused data processing	1965–1979	Direct support for management and operational functions
2. Decentralized end-user computing	1980–1985	Personal computers under the direct control of users
3. Fixed-location interactive networks	1986–1995	Linking of individual end users at their fixed work locations
4. Mobile interactive networks	1996–	Linking of individual end users through mobile personal communicators

assistant. As end users, managers had to become knowledgeable about their own needs and the systems that were available to meet those needs, and they had to accept responsibility for their systems' failures. If they didn't have the information they wanted, there was no one to blame but themselves.

A major explanation of why end-using computing became popular was the creation of powerful, low-cost personal computers. By the 1980s, a $5,000 desktop personal computer could do tasks that 15 years earlier required a roomful of equipment that cost millions of dollars.

With decentralized data processing and user-friendly software, the need for centralized data systems departments declined. Most remade themselves into support centers that could help managers become more effective end users. For instance, they could help managers select appropriate software as well as create executive information systems like the one put into place in the city of Mississauga, Ontario.

Stage 3: Fixed-Location Interactive Networks The third stage of MIS development built on communication software packages to fully achieve the *system* objective of MIS. In stage 3, the emphasis was on creating and implementing mechanisms to link end users. By means of an interactive network, a manager's computer can communicate with other computers.[15]

Networking interconnects computer hardware. By networking, the user of a personal computer can communicate with other users, turn the computer into a terminal and gain access to an organization's mainframe system, share the use of sophisticated printers, and tap into outside databases.

Networks are reshaping the manager's job. Electronic mail, for instance, is lessening the manager's dependence on the telephone and traditional mail delivery service.[16] Networks permit some employees, including managers, to **telecommute**—to do their jobs at home and connect to the workplace by means of a personal computer. Networks also enable managers to monitor their subordinates' work closely. For employees who perform their tasks on a terminal, software packages are available that can summarize, in detail, each employee's hourly productivity, error rate, and the like.

We also should not overlook the effect that networks are having on interorganizational communications. Interorganizational networks are widening the scope of database management. If you want to know what other companies are doing in regard to strategic planning, for instance, you can get your answer through a computer search of outside databases. Companies such as Dow Jones, Mead Corporation, and Knight-Ridder have developed extensive databases that are available on a fee basis. On-line services such as Prodigy, CompuServe, and America Online also provide easy access to massive databases to anyone with a personal computer and a modem.

Stage 4: Mobile Interactive Networks Computer technology has recently progressed to a fourth stage. Managers can now network into other computers while maintaining complete mobility. This ability has become possible through personal digital assistants (PDAs), or personal communicators.[17] These palm-sized communicators are combining phone, fax, and computing capability in a completely portable package. They allow users to enter information and commands by writing with a special pen instead of tapping on a keyboard. They feature special software that makes it easy to keep track of appointments and schedules. And they can incorporate faxes, modems, and cellular phones so that users can communicate in a multitude of ways, anytime and anywhere.

Imagine how the PDA is going to change the way managers do things. A marketing executive finds herself in an airport and her flight is canceled. She pulls out her PDA, taps into an on-line database of airline schedules, and books a ticket on an alternative flight. Then she unhooks the communicator's pen, scrawls out the

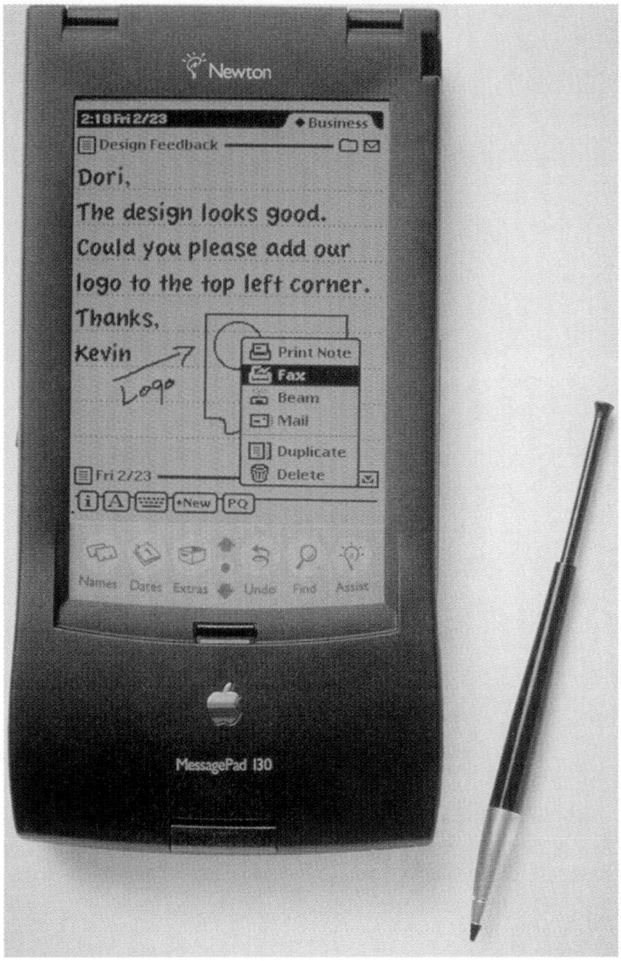

Wireless personal digital assistants, like Apple's Newton, allow managers to easily communicate with people above and below them in their organization, as well as with outside suppliers and customers.

schedule change on the device's screen and faxes it to her secretary. After a 5-minute walk to her new boarding gate, she retrieves several messages from her company's electronic mail network. Finally, as she hears the last call for boarding her flight, she phones one of her field staff representatives to ensure that a key customer's order has been received.

Although PDAs are currently in the early stage of development, they are likely to be as common as cellular phones in just a few years. And when that day comes, managers will be able to easily communicate with people above and below them in their organization, as well as with outside suppliers and customers. Moreover, PDAs will allow managers to monitor and control activities to a degree that was never thought possible just a decade ago.

Ethical Implications of Computer-Based Controls

Computerized information controls create opportunities for ethical abuses that were never possible a decade or two ago.[18] Consider the following actual examples.

The U.S. Internal Revenue Service's internal audit group monitors a computer log that shows employee access to taxpayer's accounts. This monitoring activity allows management to check and see what employees are doing on their computers.[19]

The mayor of Colorado Springs, Colorado, read the electronic mail messages that City Council members sent to each other from their homes. He defended his actions by saying he was making sure that e-mail was not being used to circum-

IN THE NEWS

He Sees All, He Knows All

EVERY REVOLUTION BRINGS WITH IT CERTAIN LOGISTICAL PROBLEMS. REENGINEERING, FOR EXAMPLE, BY flattening management structures, has created a rather simple operational problem. How do senior executives stay in touch with, and in control of, their businesses? They no longer want, nor can they afford, armies of middle managers to compile information, answer questions, and pass instructions up and down the corporate ladder. And they don't need them. Technology can do the job for them.

A new generation of software, called enterprise support systems (ESS), is changing the way executives work. ESS provides information on everything going on within the organization. The UCS Group, the $300 million retailing arm of Imasco Ltd. known as United Cigar Stores, is finding out just how useful an ESS can be. Every day any of its thirty senior or middle managers can log onto its system and check sales at any of its 476 stores. A marketing executive might pull up a weekly or monthly sales summary and check it against the company's business plan. If sales are off target, he can then "drill down" through the data to find the division, region, or district in which sales are weak. He can cross-reference by store type or by product line to see if, perhaps, it is cigarette sales at hotel locations in Ontario that are causing the problem. He can even search by promotion, to find out, for example, if a two-pack cigarette discounting program is dragging down revenue instead of boosting it.

"It's a very powerful tool," says Jim Booth, UCS's vice president and chief information officer. "Upper management has had difficulty staying in touch, obtaining accurate, timely data. Now the information is much closer at hand."

Source: M. Stevenson, "He Sees All, He Knows All," *Canadian Business*, Spring 1994, pp. 30–35.

vent his state's "open meeting" law that requires most council business to be conducted publicly.[20]

American Express has an elaborate system for monitoring telephone calls. Daily reports are provided to supervisors that detail the frequency and length of calls made by employees, as well as how quickly incoming calls are answered.[21]

Management at Midland Bank's branch in Newark, New Jersey, have defined forty-eight everyday tasks that employees do, and each task has a spot on every employee's computer screen. Every time workers complete a task, they make a record of it by touching the appropriate box on the screen. Custom software then tabulates reports for management that classify which tasks people do and exactly how long it takes to do them.[22]

The above examples illustrate a growing trend. Technology is increasing the capability of managers to monitor employees, and managers seem to be taking advantage of this new-found capability. Electronic monitoring systems "provide managers with access to their employees' computer terminals and telephones, allowing managers to determine at any moment throughout the day the pace at which employees are working, their degree of accuracy, log-in and log-off times, and even the amount of time spent on bathroom breaks."[23] In 1990, more than 10 million American workers were subject to electronic monitoring.[24] Sales of computer monitoring software were more than $175 million in 1991 and were projected to have exceeded $1 billion by 1996.[25]

Managers typically defend their actions in terms of ensuring quality, productivity, and proper employee behavior. An IRS audit of its southeastern regional offices, as a case in point, found that 166 employees took unauthorized looks at the tax returns of friends, neighbors, and celebrities.

When does management's need for information about employee performance cross over the line and interfere with a worker's right to privacy? For example, is any action by management acceptable as long as employees are notified ahead of time that they will be monitored? And what about the demarcation between monitoring work and nonwork behavior? When employees do work-related activities at home during evenings and weekends, does management's prerogative to monitor employees remain in force? Answers to questions such as these have become increasingly relevant as technology has redefined management's ability to monitor the most minute details of employees' behavior.

THE DOWNSIDE OF CONTROLS

Managing without controls is abdication of responsibility. Because managers are accountable for the actions of the people in their unit and the overall performance of that unit, it is imperative that proper controls are established to ensure that activities are being accomplished as planned. But controls can produce unproductive behaviors.[26] Consider the following examples.

Larry Boff called the Dallas Fire Department's emergency number to get immediate help for his stepmother, who was having trouble breathing.[27] The nurse-dispatcher, Billie Myrick, spent 15 minutes arguing with Boff because he wouldn't bring his stepmother to the phone. He repeatedly told Myrick that his stepmother was in the bedroom and couldn't speak. Myrick insisted that she was required to talk to the person in question so she could determine if the situation was a true emergency. Boff insisted that his stepmother was unable to speak on the phone and pleaded with Myrick to send an ambulance. Myrick continually responded that she could not send an ambulance until she spoke to Boff's stepmother. After getting nowhere for 15 minutes, Boff hung up the phone. His stepmother was dead.

Three managers at a big General Motors truck plant in Michigan installed a secret control box in a supervisor's office to override the control panel that governed the speed of the assembly line.[28] The device allowed the managers to speed up the assembly line—a clear violation of GM's contract with the United Auto Workers union. When caught, the managers explained that, while they knew what they had done was wrong, the pressure from higher-ups to meet unrealistic production goals was so great that they felt the secret control panel was the only way they could meet their targets. As described by one manager, senior GM executives would say, "I don't care *how* you do it—*just do it.*"

Did you ever notice that the people who work in the college registrar's office often don't seem to care much about the problems of students? They become so fixated on ensuring that every rule is followed that they lose sight of the fact that their job is to *serve* students, not to *hassle* them!

These examples illustrate what can happen when controls are inflexible or control standards are unreasonable. People lose sight of the organization's overall goals.[29] Instead of the organization running the controls, sometimes the controls run the organization.

Because any control system has imperfections, problems occur when individuals or organizational units attempt to look good exclusively in terms of the control devices. The result is dysfunctional in terms of the organization's goals. More often than not, this dysfunctionality is caused by incomplete measures of performance. If the control system evaluates only the quantity of output, people will tend to ignore quality. Similarly, if the system measures activities rather than results, people will spend their time attempting to look good on the activity measures. For instance, public employment agencies exist to match up workers searching for jobs with employers who have job vacancies. But when agency interviewers were evaluated by the number of employment interviews they conducted, they focused on activities rather than results. The interviewers emphasized the number of interviews they conducted rather than the number of clients they placed in jobs.[30]

To avoid being reprimanded by managers because of the control system, people can engage in behaviors that are designed solely to influence the information system's data output during a given control period. Rather than actually performing well, employees can manipulate measures to give the appearance that they are performing well. Evidence indicates that the manipulation of control data is not a random phenomenon. It depends on the importance of an activity. Organizationally important activities are likely to make a difference in a person's rewards; therefore, there is a great incentive to look good on those particular measures.[31] When rewards are at stake, individuals tend to manipulate data to appear in a favorable light by, for instance, distorting actual figures, emphasizing successes, and suppressing evidence of failures. On the other hand, only random errors occur when the distribution of rewards is unaffected.[32]

Failure to design flexibility into a controls system can create problems more severe than those the controls were implemented to prevent.

Our conclusion is that controls have both an upside and a downside. Failure to design flexibility into a controls system can create problems more severe than those the controls were implemented to prevent.

CONTROL TOOLS

We conclude our discussion of control systems by describing three control tools that can help you be a more effective manager. These are budgets, PERT network analysis, and control charts.

Budgets

We briefly introduced budgets earlier in this chapter in our discussion of financial controls. Because almost every manager is involved in expense budgets, we'll focus on them. You should be aware of the difference between incremental and zero-base budgets, the advantages to bottom-up budgeting, the growing popularity of activity-based budgeting, and the steps in preparing a budget. In this section, we look at those four topics.

Incremental versus Zero-Base Budgets The traditional budget is incremental in nature. It develops out of the previous budget. In the **incremental budget,** each period's budget begins by using the last period as a reference point. Then adjustments are made to individual items within the budget.

The major problems with the incremental approach are that it tends to hide inefficiencies and waste, encourages continual increases, and hinders change. Inefficiencies tend to grow because, in the typical incremental budget, nothing ever gets cut. Each budget begins with the funds allocated for the last period—to which are added a percentage for inflation and requests for new or expanded activities. So this approach to budgeting often provides money for activities long after the need is gone. And because incrementalism builds on the past, this type of budget also tends to constrain bold or radical changes.

An alternative, which directly deals with the incremental budget's limitations, is the **zero-base budget (ZBB).** With the ZBB, the entire budget begins from scratch, and each budget item must be justified. No reference is made to previous appropriations.[33] The major advantage of the ZBB is that all programs, projects, and activities going on within every unit of the organization are assessed in terms of benefits and costs. The primary drawbacks to ZBB include increased paperwork and preparation time, the tendency of managers to inflate the benefits of activities they want funded, and the negative effect on intermediate- and long-term planning. On this last point, for example, when departmental budgets have to be completely justified every year, the potential for dramatic ups and downs in funding can create chaos for managers and make intermediate and long-term planning almost impossible.

Most organizations rely on incremental budgeting. But the zero-base approach is increasingly appealing. ZBB is particularly relevant when organizations are developing new strategies, undertaking a significant reorganization, or introducing similar organizationwide change programs.[34] Under these conditions, ZBB will lessen the likelihood that outdated or less important activities will continue to receive their prior level of funding.

Top-Down versus Bottom-Up Budgeting Another choice that has to be made on budgets is where it will initially be prepared.[35] **Top-down budgeting** originates at the upper levels of the organization. Budgets are initiated, controlled, and directed by top management. This approach assumes that top management is best able to allocate resources among alternative uses within the organization. These budgets are then given to middle-level and lower-level managers whose responsibilities are to carry them out. This method has the advantage of simplifying the budgeting process and focusing on the organization's overall strategy and goals. However, the top-down approach has some huge disadvantages. It assumes that top management has comprehensive data on all activities within the organization. This assumption is rarely valid, especially in relatively large organizations. Since operating personnel and lower-level managers have no input into their budgets, the top-down approach also does nothing to build support and commitment for budgets.

Most organizations today have moved to **bottom-up budgeting,** in which the initial budget requests are prepared by those who must implement them. Then they are sent up for approval to higher levels of management, where modifications may be suggested. Differences are negotiated, and the process is followed upward until an organizationwide budget is developed.

Essentially, the bottom-up approach to budgeting has the opposite advantages and disadvantages of top-down budgeting. Because lower-level managers are more knowledgeable about their needs than are managers at the top, they are less likely to overlook important funding requirements. And a very important advantage is that lower-level managers are much more likely to enthusiastically accept and try to meet budgets they had a hand in shaping.

Activity-Based Budgeting **Activity-based budgeting** allocates costs for producing a good or service on the basis of the activities performed and services employed.[36] Instead of concentrating on the cost of such budget items as salaries, supplies, or insurance, activity-based budgeting focuses on the processes integral to an organization's operations. In addition, activity-based budgeting redirects the budget's focus from departmental costs to organizational processes. Unlike cost-based budgets, which prompt managers to play numbers games with costs, activity-based budgets force managers to focus on what work needs to be accomplished in the organization and how that work contributes to the overall strategy.

Activity-based budgeting is a natural complement to reengineering and TQM efforts. Why? Because it helps management distinguish between those actions that add value for customers and those that do not. Take, as an example, the response of a senior bank executive to this new form of budgeting. His primary complaint about traditional cost-based budgeting was that it left him with very little understanding of the business the bank was in. "As a manager, I can begin [now] to look at . . . performance and I can target improvements, because I now have names to attach" to the actions. "What I'm doing is moving from a cost-control perspective to a cost-reduction perspective."

The Budget Process If you were a new manager and were asked to submit your first budget, what would you do? The following steps provide some guidance.[37] They assume a bottom-up approach.

1. *Review the organization's overall strategy and goals.* Understanding your organization's strategy and goals will help you focus on where the overall organization is going and your unit's role in that plan.
2. *Determine your unit's goals and the means to attain them.* What activities will you do to reach your departmental goals and help the organization achieve its overall goals? What resources will you require to achieve these goals? Think in terms of things such as staffing requirements, workloads, and the materials and equipment you'll need. This is also your opportunity to formulate new programs and propose new responsibilities for your unit.
3. *Gather cost information.* You'll need accurate cost estimates of those resources you identified in step 2. Old budgets may be of some help. But you'll also want to talk with your immediate manager, colleagues, and key subordinates and to use other contacts you have developed inside your organization and out.
4. *Share your goals and cost estimates with your manager.* Your immediate manager typically will need to approve your budget, so his or her support is necessary. Discuss your goals, costs estimates, and other ideas with your immediate manager *before* you include them in your budget. Preliminary discussion will assure that your goals are aligned with the goals of the unit above yours and will build consensus for your proposed submission.
5. *Draw up your proposed budget.* Once your goals and costs are in place, constructing the actual budget is fairly simple. But be sure to show the linkage between your budget items and your unit's goals. You need to justify your requests. And be prepared to explain and sell your budget to your immediate manager and others on the management team. Assume that there will be other managers competing for some of the same resources that you want.
6. *Be prepared to negotiate.* It is unlikely that your budget will be approved exactly as you submitted it. Be prepared to negotiate changes that senior management suggests and revise your original budget. Recognize that there are politics in the budget process, and negotiate from the perspective of building credits for future budgets. If certain projects aren't approved this time, use this point in the budget process to build support for them in the next budget period.
7. *Monitor your budget.* Once your budget has been approved and implemented, you will be judged on how well you carry it out. Set variance targets that include both percentages and dollars. For instance, you might set a decision rule that says you will investigate all monthly variances of 15 percent or larger if the actual dollar variance is $200 or more.
8. *Keep superiors informed of your progress.* Keeping your immediate manager and other relevant parties advised on how close you are to meeting your budget is likely to help protect you if you exceed your budget for reasons beyond your control. Also, do not expect to be rewarded for underspending your budget. In incremental budgets, underspending only means that you will be allocated fewer funds in the next budget period!

PERT Network Analysis

PERT is an acronym for *p*rogram *e*valuation and *r*eview *t*echnique. It is an important scheduling technique that is widely used by project managers. A Gantt chart can help you schedule simple work projects. But what would you do if you had to manage a large project such as a reorganization, a cost-reduction campaign, or the development of a new product that requires coordinating inputs from marketing, production, and product design personnel? Such projects require coordinating hundreds of thousands of activities, some of which must be done simultaneously and some of

PERT is an important scheduling technique that is widely used by project managers.

which cannot begin until earlier activities have been completed. For instance, if you're overseeing the construction of a building, you obviously can't have your people start to erect walls until after the foundation has been laid. PERT was developed to help manage such complex projects.

Definition The **program evaluation and review technique** (more typically called just **PERT** or PERT network analysis) was originally developed in the late 1950s for coordinating the more than 3,000 contractors and agencies working on the *Polaris* submarine weapon system.[38] This project was incredibly complicated; hundreds of thousands of activities had to be coordinated. PERT is reported to have cut 2 years off the completion date for the *Polaris* project.

The PERT network is a flowchart-like diagram that depicts the sequence of activities needed to complete a project and the time or costs associated with each activity. With a PERT network, a manager must think through what has to be done on a given project, determine which events depend on one another, and identify potential trouble spots. PERT is a valuable control tool because it makes it easy to compare the effects alternative actions will have on scheduling and costs. Thus PERT allows managers to monitor a project's progress, identify possible bottlenecks, and shift resources as necessary to keep the project on schedule.

To understand how to construct a PERT network, you need to know three terms: *events, activities,* and *critical path.* Let's define these terms, outline the steps in the PERT process, and then develop an example.

Events are end points that represent the completion of major activities. **Activities** represent the time or resources required to progress from one event to another. The **critical path** is the longest or most time-consuming sequence of events and activities in a PERT network.

The PERT Process Developing a PERT network requires a manager to identify all key activities needed to complete a project, rank them in order of dependence, and estimate each activity's completion time. This process can be translated into five specific steps.

1. *Identify every significant activity* that must be achieved for a project to be completed. The accomplishment of each activity results in a set of events or outcomes.
2. *Ascertain the order* in which these events must be completed.
3. *Diagram the flow* of activities from start to finish, identifying each activity and its relationship to all other activities. Use circles to indicate events and arrows to represent activities. The result is a flowchart diagram called the **PERT network.**
4. *Compute a time estimate* for completing each activity. This computation is done with a weighted average that employs an *optimistic* time estimate (t_o) of how long the activity would take under ideal conditions, a *most-likely* estimate (t_m) of the time the activity normally should take, and a pessimistic estimate (t_p) that represents the time that an activity should take under the worst possible conditions. The formula for calculating the expected time (t_e) is then

$$t_e = \frac{t_o + 4\,t_m + t_p}{6}$$

5. Finally, using a network diagram that contains time estimates for each activity, *determine a schedule* for the start and finish dates of each activity and for the entire project. Any delays that occur along the critical path require the most attention because they delay the entire project. That is, the critical path has no slack in it; therefore, any delay along that path immediately translates into a delay in the final deadline for the completed project.

An Application As we noted, most PERT projects are quite complicated and may be composed of hundreds of thousands of events. Such complicated computations are best done with a computer using specialized PERT software.[39] But for our purposes, let's work through a simplified example.

Charley Williams is the production supervisor in the casting department at a Reynolds Metals aluminum mill in upstate New York. Charley has proposed and received approval from corporate management to replace one of the massive furnaces that are part of his responsibilities with a new, state-of-the-art electronic furnace. This project will seriously disrupt operations in his department, so he wants to complete it as quickly and as smoothly as possible. He has carefully separated the entire project into activities and events. Exhibit 6-10 outlines the major events in the furnace modernization project and Charley's estimate of the expected time required to complete each activity. Exhibit 6-11 depicts the PERT chart Charley created on the basis of the data in Exhibit 6-10.

Charley's PERT chart tells him that if everything goes as planned, it will take 21 weeks to complete the modernization program. This figure is calculated by tracing the chart's critical path: A-C-D-G-H-J-K. Any delay in completing the events along that path will delay the completion of the entire project. For example, if it took 6 weeks instead of 4 to get construction permits (event B), this delay would have no effect on the final completion date. Why? Because Start-B + B-E + E-F + F-G equals only 11 weeks, whereas Start-A + A-C + C-D + D-G equals 17 weeks. However, if Charley wanted to cut the 21-week time frame, he would give attention to those activities along the critical path that could be speeded up.

Control Charts

Control charts are a tool that grew out of the quality movement.

Control charts are a tool that grew out of the quality movement.[40] When a manager wants to ensure that a process is being done within an acceptable quality range, control charts can be of valuable assistance.

EXHIBIT 6-10
A PERT Network for the Furnace Modernization Project

Event	Description	Expected Time (in weeks)	Preceding Event
A	Approve design	8	None
B	Get construction permits	4	None
C	Take bits on new furnace and its installation	6	A
D	Order new furnace and equipment	1	C
E	Remove old furnace	2	B
F	Prepare site	3	E
G	Install new furnace	2	D, F
H	Test new furnace	1	G
I	Train workers to handle new furnace	2	G
J	Final inspection by company and city officials	2	H
K	Bring furnace on line into production flow	1	I, J

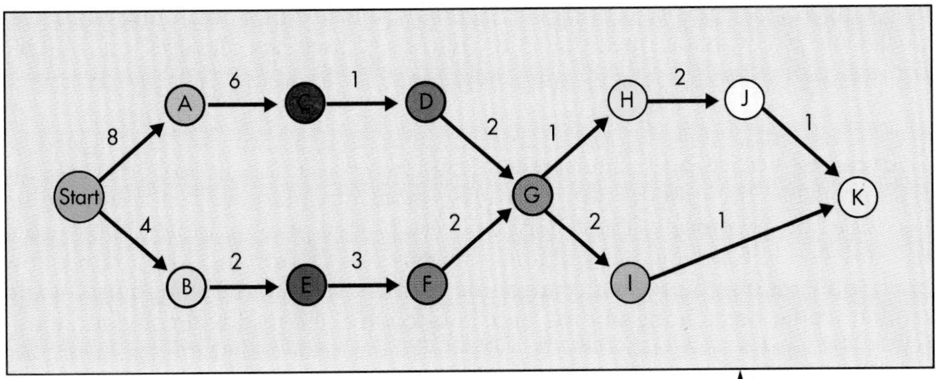

EXHIBIT 6-11
PERT Chart for Furnace Modernization Project

As shown in Exhibit 6-12, **control charts** are diagrams that show plottings of results over a period of time, with statistically determined upper and lower limits. For instance, Coca-Cola samples its 2-liter bottles after they have been filled to determine their exact quantity and then plots the data on a control chart. This process tells management when the filling equipment needs adjustment. As long as the process variables fall within the predefined limits, as shown in Exhibit 6-12, the system is said to be "in control." When a point falls outside the limits, then the variation is unacceptable.

Types of Control Charts There are two basic types of control charts. One measures *attributes* and the other measures *variables.* **Attribute charts** measure a product characteristic in terms of whether it is good or bad. You might use this approach to judge the quality of a bicycle's paint color or the physical appearance of potato chips. **Variable charts** measure a characteristic such as length, weight, or volume on a continuous scale. So the measurement involves a range rather than a dichotomy. Variable charts require the setting of a standard and an accept-

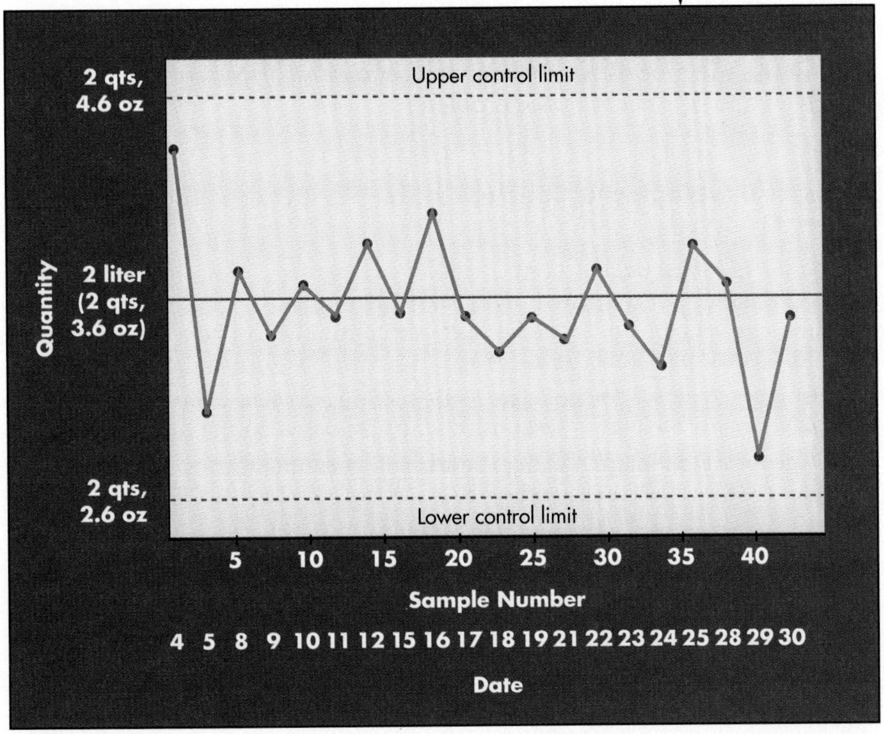

EXHIBIT 6-12
Control Chart for 2-Liter Diet Coke Bottles

able range of deviation around that standard. Our example of filling bottles at Coca-Cola is a variable measure. The following discussion focuses on variable control charts.

Sources of Variation There are two sources of variability in any process—one is controllable, the other is not. **Chance causes** of variation are due to random variations in the process. These exist in every process and are impossible to control unless you fundamentally change the process. For instance, no matter how finely tuned a photo-processing machine is, there will still be some minute and random variations among photographs. But control charts are directed at identifying **assignable causes.** These are due to nonchance variations and, thus, are capable of being identified and controlled.

Calculating Variablity A basic knowledge of a few statistical concepts is needed to create a control chart and calculate variability. First is the **central limit theorem.** This states that a sampling distribution approaches normality as the size of the sample increases. Second is the concept of a **normal distribution.** This assumes that variations from a standard follow a bell-shaped curve. When a college instructor gives out grades that are 10 percent each of As and Fs, 20 percent each of Bs and Ds, and 40 percent Cs, she is grading "on a curve" that follows a normal distribution. Third is the term **standard deviation.** This is a measure of variability in a group of numerical values. In a normal distribution, most of the measures will be close to the mean or average. But there will be some deviation. The *typical* difference from the mean is the standard deviation. In a normal distribution, approximately 68 percent of a set of values will fall between +1 and -1 standard deviation from the mean. Ninety-five percent will fall in the range of +2 and -2 standard deviations.

In developing a control chart, you define the upper and lower limits by the degree of deviation you are willing to accept. Typically, managers will set the limits at three standard deviations. This means that 99.7 percent of the mean values sampled should lie between the control limits (see Exhibit 6-13). When a sample average falls outside the limits, that is, above the upper control limit or below the lower limit, the process is very likely out of control. This result should then initiate a search for the cause of the problem.

Steps in Developing a Control Chart The five actual steps that need to be followed to develop a control chart can be summarized as follows.[41]

1. *Gather historical data.* A control chart is constructed from historical data; future performance is compared with past performance. You need two distinctly different data sets, one to construct the control chart and a second to reflect the most recent performance.
2. Using the data for control chart construction, *calculate a process average and upper and lower control limits.* The control limits are based on the sampling distribution.
3. *Draw the control chart,* placing the variable measurement on one axis and the sequence of samples on the other axis.
4. *Plot the current or most recent sample average* on the chart.
5. *Interpret the chart* to see if (a) the process is in control and no action is required; (b) the process is out of control and a cause should be sought, or (c) the process is in control but trends are occurring that should alert you to possible nonrandom conditions.

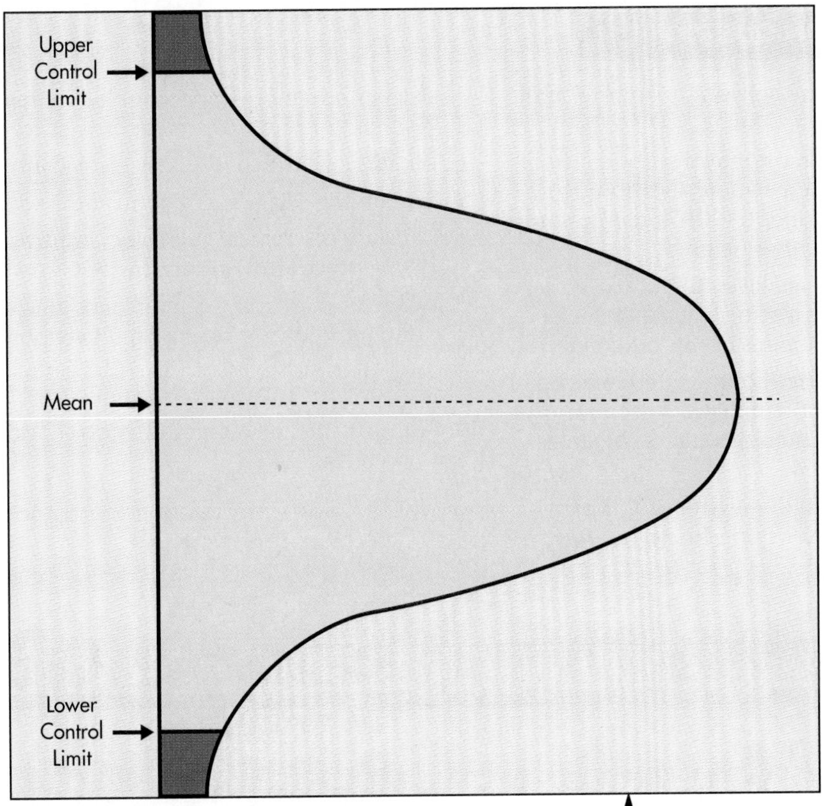

EXHIBIT 6-13
A Control Chart Using Three Standard Deviations as Limits

SUMMARY

(This summary is organized by the chapter-opening learning objectives on page 159.)

1. The control process consists of three separate and distinct steps: (1) measuring actual performance; (2) comparing actual performance against a standard; and (3) taking managerial action to correct deviations or inadequate standards. The control process assumes that standards of performance already exist.
2. The following behavioral control devices are available to managers: selection, new-employee orientation, mentoring, goals, job design, formal regulations, direct supervision, training, performance appraisal, and organizational rewards.
3. The economic order quantity (EOQ) model seeks to balance four costs involved in ordering and carrying inventory: purchasing, ordering, carrying, and stockout.
4. Data are raw, unanalyzed facts. Information is data that have been analyzed and processed. Managers rely on information, not on data, to make decisions.
5. Modern MIS can be separated into four stages: (1) management-focused data processing, in which centralized MIS units provided reports to management; (2) decentralized end-user computing, in which managers took responsibility for information control; (3) fixed-location interactive networks, when computers became linked and able to communicate with each other; and (4) mobile interactive networks, in which personal digital assistants allow information access and communication in multiple ways, anytime and anywhere.
6. Incremental budgets begin by using the last period as a reference point. Zero-base budgets create each new budget from scratch, and every item must be justified. Incremental budgets tend to limit bold or radical changes by reinforcing the past.
7. The five steps in creating a PERT network are: (1) identify all significant activities and events; (2) determine the order that events must be completed; (3) diagram the flow of activities from start to finish; (4) compute a time estimate for completing each activity; and (5) determine a schedule for the start and finish dates for each activity and for the entire project.
8. The steps in developing a control chart are: (1) gather historical data; (2) calculate a process average and upper and lower control limits; (3) draw the control chart; (4) plot the current or most recent sample average on the chart; and (5) interpret the chart.

REVIEW AND DISCUSSION QUESTIONS

1. What is the relationship between planning and control?
2. What critieria would be most effective for controlling (a) a stockbroker in a remote location; (b) a production supervisor; and (c) the membership sales office for a prominent museum?
3. A department manager achieves his unit's goals, yet spends only 70 percent of his allocated budget. Discuss the pluses and minuses of this outcome.
4. Specifically explain how each of the following controls human behavior: (a) employee selection; (b) mentoring; (c) goals; (d) training; and (e) organizational rewards.
5. What problems do you think might occur if a division manager is judged solely on his or her financial performance—for example, on return on investment or profit per dollar of sales revenue?
6. What is a Gantt chart? Why is it a control tool?
7. Explain the ABC system of inventory control.
8. Contrast the typical manager's control options in 1996 with control options in 1956.
9. When do electronic surveillance devices such as computers, video cameras, and telephone monitoring step over the line from "effective management controls" to "intrusions on employee rights"?
10. Contrast the advantages of control against its disadvantages.

CASE EXERCISE
WOULD YOU WANT TO WORK FOR RON EDENS?

Ron Edens runs a company called Electronic Banking System Inc. EBS, located outside Baltimore, Maryland, provides outsourcing clerical services. It handles the clerical tasks involved in processing donations for groups such as Mothers Against Drunk Driving, Greenpeace, and the National Organization for Women. Most of Edens' employees earn $6 an hour or less doing repetitive tasks such as opening envelopes or recording donation data on a computer. Ron Edens is especially proud of the control system he has created to closely monitor his employees.

Walking around EBS, you see long lines of people sitting at spartan desks, slitting open envelopes, sorting contents, and filling out "control cards" that record how many letters they have opened and how long it has taken them. These letter openers must process three envelopes a minute. Nearby, other workers tap keyboards, keeping pace with a quota that demands 8,500 strokes an hour. Jobs are highly specialized and involve extensive repetition. Letter openers only open envelopes and sort contents. Workers in the audit department just compute figures. Data-entry clerks punch in the information that the others have collected.

The workroom is silent. Talking is forbidden. The windows are covered. Coffee mugs, personal photos, and other adornments are barred from workers' desks. Edens wants to remove anything that might distract his workers from the job at hand. For example, commenting on the blocked windows, Edens says, "I don't want them looking out—it's distracting. They'll make mistakes."

In his office upstairs, Edens sits before a TV monitor that flashes images from eight cameras posted throughout the plant. "There's a little bit of Sneaky Pete to it," he admits, using a remote control to zoom in on a document atop a worker's desk. "I can basically read that and figure out how someone's day is going." In addition, his system's software generates daily reports recording the precise number of keystrokes tapped by each data-entry worker and the number of errors made by each worker.

The work floor at EBS resembles an enormous classroom in the throes of exam period. Desks point toward the front, where a manager keeps watch from a raised platform. Other supervisors are positioned toward the back of the room. "If you want to watch someone," Edens explains, "it's easier from behind because they don't know you're watching." There's also a black globe hanging from the ceiling, in which cameras are positioned.

At EBS, workers handle thousands of dollars in checks and cash. That's one reason, Edens says, for the cameras. It can help deter would-be thieves. But Edens concedes that tight observation also helps EBS monitor productivity and weed out workers who don't keep up. "There are multiple uses," Edens says of surveillance.

Edens is unapologetic about his control system, including the rule that forbids all talk unrelated to the completion of each task. "I'm not paying people to chat. I'm paying them to open envelopes," he says.

Edens offers considerable insight into his philosophy of management when he says, "We don't ask these people to think—the machines think for them. They don't have to make decisions." His words could have come directly out of the mouth of Frederick Taylor. In fact, EBS is living proof that today's technology can allow managers to monitor workers more closely than a turn-of-the-century foreman with a stopwatch ever could.

Questions

1. What kind of people do you think Edens is able to find to work in his firm? (Clue: Think in terms of matching individual personalities and job preferences with the work climate at EBS.)
2. List both the advantages and the disadvantages you see in Edens's control system.
3. What ethical issues, if any, would you be concerned about at EBS and why?

Source: Based on T. Horwitz, "Mr. Edens Profits from Watching His Workers' Every Move," *Wall Street Journal,* December 1, 1994, p. A11.

VIDEO CASE EXERCISE

CONTROLS (OR LACK OF CONTROLS) IN THE U.S. FEDERAL GOVERNMENT

ABCNEWS

The U.S. federal government takes a lot of heat for its inefficiencies. But perhaps that heat is justified! As examples, consider the federal government's practice of handing out annual bonuses and the way the U.S. Army mishandles stored military equipment.

Business firms typically use bonuses as a way to stimulate employee performance. The U.S. government seems to hand bonuses out regardless of performance. Moreover, those recommending the bonuses don't always seem to know why they made their recommendations. In one recent year, senior federal administrators paid or recommended to be paid more than $650 million in bonuses to their employees.

Manuel Lujan was Secretary of the Interior in the Bush administration. A memo went out under his signature just before he left his position recommending presidential merit bonuses for 12 senior officials in his department. Yet, Lujan says, "I had nothing to do with it. In fact, I'd already left town" when the memo went out. Actually, he didn't even sign the memo. Every year, every Cabinet officer submits a list of names to the president for consideration for meritorious service. Lujan was merely following routine. The memo was signed by an auto pen!

One of those on Lujan's list was Dean Bibles, director of the Interior's Bureau of Land Management (BLM) in Oregon. A department peer group recommended he receive a $20,000 bonus, largely due to his success in eliminating the backlog of reforestation problems in Oregon. But the department's own inspector general questions this "success." He says the peer group "apparently declared that they now have no backlog . . . We think it is not right. We think that they still have the same backlog." Lujan admitted he didn't know whether BLM eliminated the backlog. He just allowed his name to be affixed to a recommendation!

The management of U.S. Army depots shows another example of poor controls. These depots repair and store military equipment. They are supposed to protect the equipment from deterioration and theft. But an inspection of four of the 10 depots in the continental United States found ruined equipment at all four. At Corpus Christi, Texas, for instance, helicopter parts that had been left outside were corroded by the salt air from the Gulf of Mexico or stolen from unfenced and unguarded areas. Similarly, 70 percent of the diesel engines stored at the Tooele Repair Depot near Salt Lake City had rusted out, were no longer salvageable, and had to be scrapped. According to Senator John Glenn, a member of the Governmental Affairs Committee, "inventory control and control of this whole process [at the Army depots] has been very, very lax."

Questions

1. Do you think it's fair to generalize that controls in government are inferior to those in business? Explain.
2. How do you evaluate the performance of a senior-level government administrator?
3. Bonuses are typically used to increase employee performance. Why don't they seem to work in the federal government?
4. What, if anything, can be done to improve control over stored military equipment?

Source: Based on "Washington Waste," Prime Time Live; ABC News; aired March 18, 1993.

SKILL EXERCISE

Creating a Budget

You have recently been appointed as advertising manager for a new monthly health and diet magazine, *Fitness 1,* being developed by the Magazine Division at Hearst Corporation. You were previously an advertising manager on one of the company's established magazines. You will report to the new magazine's publisher, Molly Tymon.

Estimates of first-year subscription sales for *Fitness 1* are 125,000. Magazine-stand sales should add another 40,000 a month to that number. But your concern is with developing advertising revenue for the magazine.

You and Molly have set a goal of selling advertising space totaling $6 million during *Fitness 1*'s first year. You think you can do this with a staff of about ten people.

Since this is a completely new publication, there is no previous budget for your advertising group. You've been asked by Molly to submit a preliminary budget for your group.

Write up a report, not to exceed three pages in length: (1) Describe in detail how you would go about this assignment. For example, where would you get budget categories? Whom would you contact? (2) Present your best effort at creating a budget for your department.

NOTES

1. Based on N. Bray and M. R. Sesit, "Barings Was Warned Controls Were Lax But Didn't Make Reforms in Singapore," *Wall Street Journal,* March 2, 1995, p. A3; P. Dwyer and W. Glasgall, "The Lesson from Barings' Straits," *Business Week,* March 13, 1995, pp. 30–32; and A. Salpukas, "Barings Trader Questions Monitoring by His Superiors," *New York Times,* September 11, 1995, p. C4.
2. Dwyer and Glasgall, "The Lesson from Barings' Straits," p. 32.
3. For a thorough review of control systems, see W. H. Newman, *Constructive Control: Design and Use of Control Systems* (Englewood Cliffs, N.J.: Prentice Hall, 1975). See also A. Globerson, S. Globerson, and J. Frampton, *You Can't Manage What You Don't Measure: Control and Evaluation in Organizations* (Brookfield, Verm.: Gower Publishing, 1991); and R. Simons, *Levers of Control* (Boston, Mass.: Harvard Business School Press, 1995).
4. See, for instance, E. E. Lawler III and J. G. Rhode, *Information and Control in Organizations* (Pacific Palisades, Calif.: Goodyear, 1976).
5. See Ramsey and Ramsey, *Budgeting Systems* (1975).
6. See R. S. Russell and B. W. Taylor III, *Production & Operations Management,* (Englewood Cliffs, N.J.: Prentice Hall, 1995).
7. W. Clark, *The Gantt Chart: A Working Tool of Management* (New York: Ronald Press, 1922).
8. T. M. Rohan, "Supplier-Customer Links Multiplying," *Industry Week,* April 17, 1989, p. 20.
9. See, for instance, Russell and Taylor, *Production & Operations Management,* pp. 591–601.
10. J. Hampton, "Friends of the People," *Canadian Business,* November 1994, p. 43.
11. J. T. Small and W. B. Lee, "In Search of an MIS," *MSU Business Topics,* Autumn 1975, pp. 47–55.

12. H. A. Simon, *Administrative Behavior,* 3rd ed. (New York: Free Press, 1976), p. 294.
13. J. C. Carter and F. N. Silverman, "Establishing an MIS," *Journal of Systems Management,* January 1980, p. 15.
14. See G. L. Boyer and D. McKinnon, "End-User Computing Is Here to Stay," *Supervisory Management,* October 1989, pp. 17–22.
15. See, for example, B. Filipczak, "The Ripple Effect of Computer Networking," *Training,* March 1994, pp. 40–47.
16. "Electronic Mail: Neither Rain, Nor Sleet, Nor Software . . . ," *Business Week,* February 20, 1989, p. 36.
17. See, for example, J. Teresko, "Tripping Down the Information Superhighway," *Industry Week,* August 2, 1993, pp. 32–40; G. Brockhouse, "I Have Seen the Future . . . ," *Canadian Business,* August 1993, pp. 43–45; and C. Newsome, "Executives Can Work on the Move," *Asian Business,* January 1996, pp. 51–55.
18. See, for instance, T. L. Griffith, "Teaching Big Brother to Be a Team Player: Computer Monitoring and Quality," *The Executive,* February 1993, pp. 73–80; and J. Smolowe, "My Boss, Big Brother," *Time,* January 22, 1996, p. 56.
19. G. Bylinksy, "How Companies Spy on Employees," *Fortune,* November 4, 1991, pp. 131–40.
20. J. Markoff, "The Snooping Mayor," *New York Times,* May 4, 1990, p. B1.
21. J. Rothfeder, "Memo to Workers: Don't Phone Home," *Business Week,* January 25, 1988, pp. 88–90.
22. J. R. Hayes, "Memo Busters," *Forbes,* April 24, 1995, pp. 174–75.
23. J. R. Aiello and K. J. Kolb, "Electronic Performance Monitoring and Social Context: Impact on Productivity and Stress," *Journal of Applied Psychology,* June 1995, p. 339.
24. Ibid.
25. Cited in Bylinksy, "How Companies Spy on Employees," p. 140.
26. See, for instance, Lawler and Rhode, *Information and Control in Organizations;* B. J. Jaworski and S. M. Young, "Dysfunctional Behavior and Management Control: An Empirical Study of Marketing Managers," *Accounting, Organizations and Society,* January 1992, pp. 17–35; and S. Kerr, "On the Folly of Rewarding A, While Hoping for B," *The Executive,* February 1995, pp. 7–14.
27. Based on a tape recording made by the Dallas Fire Department and made available under the Texas Open Records Act.
28. Cited in A. B. Carroll, "In Search of the Moral Manager," *Business Horizons,* March–April 1987, p. 7.
29. See, for instance, Jaworski and Young, "Dysfunctional Behavior and Management Control," pp. 17–35.
30. P. M. Blau, *The Dynamics of Bureaucracy,* rev. ed. (Chicago: University of Chicago Press, 1963).
31. Lawler and Rhode, *Information and Control in Organizations,* p. 108.
32. J. D. Thompson, *Organizations in Action* (New York: McGraw Hill, 1967), p. 124.
33. P. A. Pyhrr, "Zero-Base Budgeting," *Harvard Business Review,* November–December 1970, pp. 111–18; and M. Dirsmith and S. Jablonski, "Zero Base Budgeting as a Management Technique and Political Strategy," *Academy of Management Review,* October 1979, pp. 555–65.
34. See, for instance, J. V. Pearson and R. J. Michael, "Zero-Base Budgeting: A Technique for Planned Organizational Decline," *Long Range Planning,* June 1981, pp. 68–76.
35. N. C. Churchill, "Budget Choice: Planning vs. Control," *Harvard Business Review,* July–August 1984, pp. 150–64.
36. J. Thomas, "As Easy as ABC," *Chilton's Distribution,* January 1994, p. 40; and J. S. McClenahen, "Generally Accepted Practice?" *Industry Week,* November 6, 1995, pp. 13–14.
37. See R. N. Anthony, J. Dearden, and N. M. Bedford, *Management Control Systems,* 5th ed. (Homewood, Ill.: Irwin, 1984), chapters 5–7.
38. See Russell and Taylor, *Production and Operations Management,* p. 830.
39. For a discussion of software and application to a project for restructuring a large retail chain, see P. A. Strassmann, "The Best-Laid Plans," *INC.,* October 1988, pp. 135–38.
40. See, for instance, M. Sashkin and K. J. Kiser, *Putting Total Quality Management to Work* (San Francisco: Berrett-Koehler, 1993), pp. 12–15.
41. Adapted from Russell and Taylor, *Production & Operations Management,* pp. 153–172

PART THREE: Organizing Tasks and Shaping the Organization's Culture

CHAPTER 7

ORGANIZATION DESIGN: THE EFFICIENCY-FLEXIBILITY DILEMMA

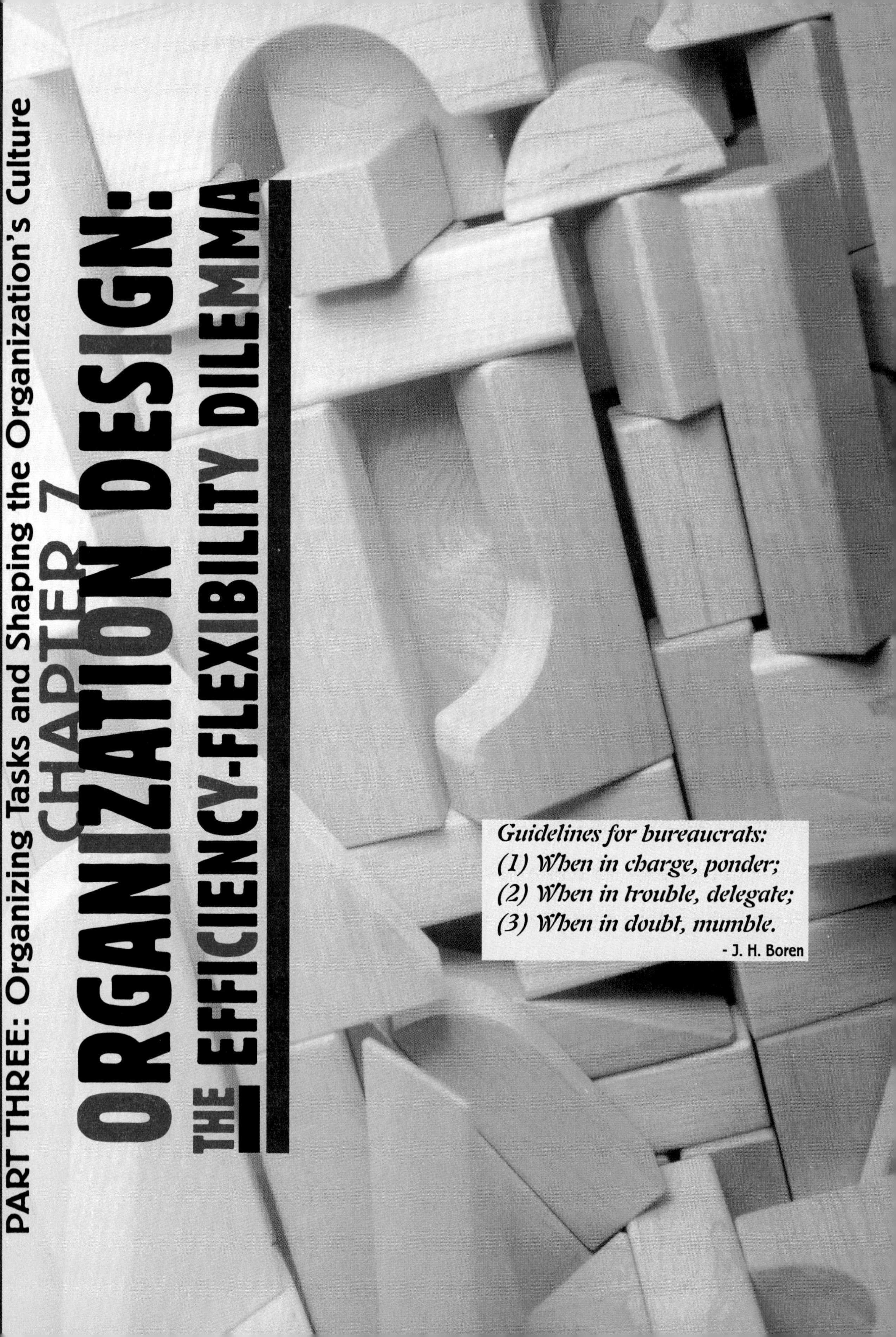

Guidelines for bureaucrats:
(1) When in charge, ponder;
(2) When in trouble, delegate;
(3) When in doubt, mumble.
- J. H. Boren

LEARNING OBJECTIVES

After studying this chapter, you should be able to:

1. Define the six key elements of organization structure
2. Contrast mechanistic and organic designs
3. Identify the four contingency variables that explain structural differences
4. Explain how environmental uncertainty affects an organization's structure
5. Describe the bureaucracy and its strengths
6. Explain the advantages and disadvantages of a matrix structure
7. Describe the virtual organization and its strengths
8. Identify the characteristics of a boundaryless organization and this structure's appeal

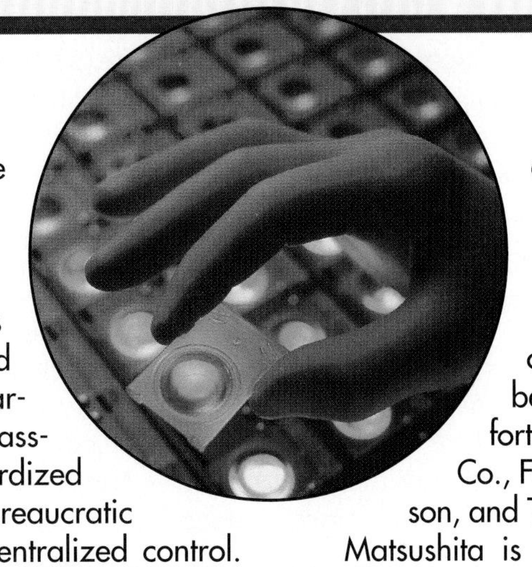

Until less than a decade ago, managers in both large and small organizations sought to emulate the structural designs of companies such as General Motors and IBM. They strove to create hierarchical organizations with mass-production efficiencies, standardized rules and regulations, and bureaucratic qualities that provided tight, centralized control. That design is no longer the standard. The environmental changes described in Chapters 1 and 4, combined with breakthroughs in computer-based communication technologies, have led to revolutionary changes in the design of organizations.[1] Nowadays, it seems as if every organization is undergoing, or recently has undergone, restructuring.

Managers are restructuring their organizations to make them more flexible and more responsive to continuously changing conditions. They are flattening hierarchies, decentralizing decision making, and blurring structural boundaries by teaming up with other organizations to create strategic alliances and other forms of interdependencies. Large organizations are breaking up into multiple, autonomous units that take on characteristics of small organizations. These trends can be seen in recent restructuring efforts at Matsushita Electric Industrial Co., Ford Motor Co., Johnson & Johnson, and Toshiba Corp.

Matsushita is the world's largest consumer-electronics company. But it was burdened by a plodding, heavily centralized bureaucratic structure. To better compete, new management has recently slashed bureacracy and decentralized decision making.[2] For instance, an entire layer of management at corporate headquarters, which traditionally oversaw the company's forty-four divisions, has been eliminated and the people reassigned. To make the heads of operating divisions more entrepreneurial, the company has given them full responsibility for product development, production, and finance. In effect, each division now "owns" its factories and sales offices and has its own balance sheet.

Similarly, Ford is currently undergoing the most sweeping restructuring in the company's 91-year history.[3] The new organization, dubbed "Ford 2000," has so far dramatically cut levels of management, combined separate operations on two continents, and reshuffled responsibilities for more than 4,000 high-level managers.

Johnson & Johnson, which "may have mastered the art of decentralized management better than any other company in the world,"[4] is modifying its structure. J&J is essentially 168 small, autonomous companies—making everything from Tylenol to contact lenses (see photo on p. 191). But it wants to get more global synergy among its subunits. Consistent with J&J's decentralized culture, senior management is relying heavily on lower-level management to create the coordinating mechanisms to gain that global synergy.

Meanwhile, Toshiba, a major competitor of Matsushita, has taken a different structural approach than its rival to improve its competitiveness.[5] It is developing a network of high-tech partners. By stretching its structural boundaries and creating alliances with companies such as Apple Computer, LSI Logic, Ericsson, Motorola, Samsung, Siemens, and Olivetti, Toshiba is reducing its risks while, at the same time, it is gaining access to state-of-the-art electronic technologies.

No topic in management has undergone more change in the past decade than the area of organization design. The reason is quite simple—the environment has become considerably more chaotic. In times of relative environmental stability, organizational effectiveness tends to focus on achieving high efficiency. How do you achieve high efficiency in a stable environment? Through standardization. So organizations created rigid structures, with lots of rules and regulations and tight controls. Rigid structures, however, are unable to respond rapidly to change. In dynamic times, they become vulnerable to more-flexible competitors. GM, for instance, found itself being regularly beaten in the marketplace by the likes of nimbler competitors such as Ford, Toyota, and Honda. And IBM was losing market share to new upstarts such as Compaq, Dell, and Gateway 2000. The message was clear—rigid bureaucratic structures could be a real handicap in a dynamic environment. To meet and beat their rivals, managers have had to aggressively redesign their structures in ways that can make their organizations more adaptive. As a case in point, recent evidence indicates that more than 75 percent of large companies have significantly altered their structures since 1990 to make them more flexible.[6]

In this chapter, we'll describe the key structural dimensions that managers control, show how those dimensions can be combined to create different structural options, and discuss the conditions that favor different options. We'll also present a description of how organization designs have evolved from efficiency machines to structures that seek balance between efficiency and the need for flexibility.

WHAT IS ORGANIZATION STRUCTURE?

An **organization structure** defines how job tasks are formally divided, grouped, and coordinated. For instance, Johnson & Johnson has historically grouped activities into semiautonomous companies organized around products and has allowed managers of those companies considerable decision-making latitude.

There are six key elements that managers need to address when they design their organization's structure: work specialization, departmentalization, chain of command, span of control, centralization and decentralization, and formalization.[7] Exhibit 7-1 presents each of those elements as an answer to an important structural question. The following sections describe the six elements of structure.

Work Specialization

Early in this century, Henry Ford became rich and famous by building automobiles on an assembly line. Every Ford worker was assigned a specific, repetitive task. For instance, one person would put on the right front wheel, and someone else would install the right front door. By breaking jobs up into small standardized tasks that could be performed over and over again, Ford was able to produce cars at the rate of one every 10 seconds while using employees who had relatively limited skills.

Ford demonstrated that work can be performed more efficiently if employees are allowed to specialize. Today we use the term **work specialization,** or *division of labor,* to describe the degree to which tasks in the organization are subdivided into separate jobs.

The essence of work specialization is that an entire job is not done by one individual; it is broken down into steps, and each step is completed by a different person. Individuals specialize in doing part of an activity rather than the entire activity.

By the late 1940s, most manufacturing jobs in industrialized countries were being done with high work specialization. Management saw this as a means to make the most efficient use of its employees' skills. In most organizations, some tasks require highly developed skills; others can be performed by unskilled personnel. If all workers were engaged in each step of, say, an organization's manufacturing process, all would have to have the skills necessary to perform both the most demanding and the least demanding jobs. The result would be that, except when performing the most skilled or highly sophisticated tasks, employees would be working below their skill levels. And, since skilled workers are paid more than unskilled workers and their wages tend to reflect their highest level of skill, it represents an inefficient usage of organizational resources to pay highly skilled workers to do simple tasks.

Managers also looked for other efficiencies that could be achieved through work specialization. Employee skills at performing a task successfully increase through repetition. Less time is spent in changing tasks, in putting away one's tools and equipment from a prior step in the work process, and in getting ready for another. Equally important, training for specialization is more efficient from the organization's perspective. It is easier and less costly to find and train workers to do specific, repetitive, limited tasks than to find and train workers to do all the tasks. This is especially true of highly sophisticated and complex operations. For example, could Cessna produce one Citation jet a year if one person had to build the en-

EXHIBIT 7-1
Six Key Questions That Managers Need to Answer in Designing the Proper Organization Structure

The Key Question Is	The Answer Is Provided By
1. To what degree are tasks subdivided into separate jobs?	*Work specialization*
2. On what basis will jobs be grouped together?	*Departmentalization*
3. To whom do individuals and groups report?	*Chain of command*
4. How many individuals can a manager efficiently and effectively direct?	*Span of control*
5. Where does decision-making authority lie?	*Centralization and decentralization*
6. To what degree will there be rules and regulations to direct employees and managers?	*Formalization*

tire plane alone? Not likely! Finally, work specialization increases efficiency and productivity by encouraging the creation of special inventions and machinery.

For much of the first half of this century, managers viewed work specialization as an unending source of increased productivity. And it probably was. Because specialization was not widely practiced, its introduction almost always generated higher productivity. But, by the 1960s, evidence was increasing that a good thing can be carried too far. The point had been reached in some jobs at which the human diseconomies from specialization—such as boredom, fatigue, stress, low productivity, poor quality of work, increased absenteeism, and high turnover—more than offset the economic advantages (see Exhibit 7-2). In such cases, productivity could be increased by enlarging, rather than narrowing, the scope of job activities. In addition, a number of companies found that employees who were given a variety of activities to do, allowed to do a complete job, and put into teams with interchangeable skills often achieved significantly higher output and were more satisfied with their jobs than were specialized employees.

For much of the first half of this century, managers viewed work specialization as an unending source of increased productivity. And it probably was.

Most managers today see work specialization as neither obsolete nor an unending source of increased productivity. Rather, managers recognize the economies it provides in certain types of jobs and the problems it creates when it is carried too far. McDonald's, for example, uses high work specialization to efficiently make and sell hamburgers and fries, and medical personnel in most health maintenance organizations are highly specialized. On the other hand, companies such as the Saturn Corporation and Aetna Life and Casualty have had success by broadening the scope of jobs and reducing specialization.

Departmentalization

Once you have divided jobs up through work specialization, you will need to group the jobs together so that common tasks can be coordinated. The basis on which jobs are grouped is called **departmentalization.**

Historically, one of the most popular ways to group activities is by *function* performed. A manufacturing manager might organize his or her plant by separat-

EXHIBIT 7-2
Economies and Diseconomies of Work Specialization

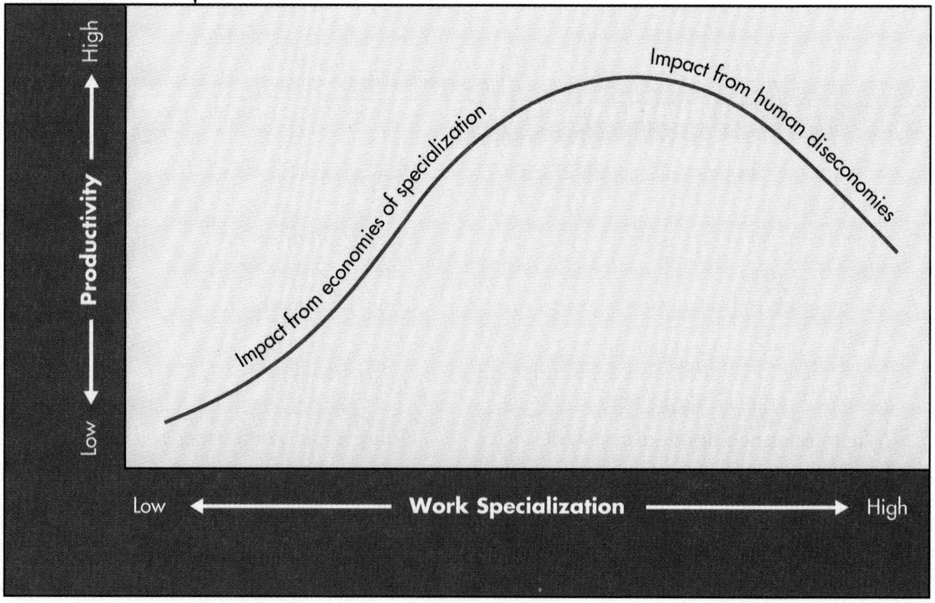

ing engineering, accounting, manufacturing, personnel, and purchasing specialists into common departments. Of course, departmentalization by function can be used in all types of organizations, but the functions change to reflect the organization's objectives and activities. A hospital might have departments devoted to research, patient care, accounting, and so forth. A professional football franchise might have departments entitled Player Personnel, Ticket Sales, and Travel and Accommodations. The major advantage to this type of grouping is obtaining efficiencies from putting like specialists together. Functional departmentalization seeks to achieve economies of scale by placing people with common skills and orientations into common units.

Tasks can also be departmentalized by the type of *product* the organization produces. This is essentially the structural foundation at Johnson & Johnson. Each of J&J's 168 companies focuses on a narrow set of products (e.g., baby oil, artificial optic lenses, blood-testing machines, adhesive bandages). The head of each company is responsible for everything having to do with his or her product line. Each, for example, has his or her own manufacturing and marketing group. The advantage of the product grouping is that it increases accountability for product performance, since all activities related to a specific product are under the direction of a single manager. If an organization's activities were service- rather than product-related, each service would be autonomously grouped. For instance, an accounting firm could have departments for tax preparation, management consulting, auditing, and the like. Each department would offer an array of related services under the direction of a service manager.

Another way to departmentalize is on the basis of *geography* or territory. The sales function, for instance, may have western, southern, midwestern, and eastern regions. Each of these regions is, in effect, a department organized around geography. If an organization's customers are scattered over a large geographical area, then this form of departmentalization can be valuable.

At a Reynolds Metals aluminum tubing plant in upstate New York, production is organized into five departments: casting, press, tubing, finishing, and inspect, pack, and ship. This is an example of *process* departmentalization because each department specializes in one specific phase in the production of aluminum tubing. The metal is cast in huge furnaces; sent to the press department, where it is extruded into aluminum pipe; transferred to the tube mill, where it is stretched into various sizes and shapes of tubing; moved to finishing, where it is cut and cleaned; and finally arrives in the inspect, pack, and ship department. Since each process requires different skills, this method offers a basis for the homogeneous categorizing of activities.

Process departmentalization can be used for processing customers as well as products. If you've ever been to a state motor vehicle office to get a driver's license, you probably went through several departments before receiving your license. In one state, applicants must go through three steps, each handled by a separate department: (1) validation, by motor vehicles division; (2) processing, by the licensing department; and (3) payment collection, by the treasury department.

A final category of departmentalization is to use the particular type of *customer* the organization seeks to reach. The sales activities in an office supply firm, for instance, can be broken down into three departments to service retail, wholesale, and government customers. A large law office can segment its staff on the basis of whether they service corporate or individual clients. The assumption underlying customer departmentalization is that customers in each department have a common set of problems and needs that can best be met by having specialists for each.

Large organizations often combine many of the forms of departmentalization that we have described. A major Japanese electronics firm, for instance, organizes each of its divisions along functional lines and organizes its manufacturing units around processes; it departmentalizes sales around seven geographical regions; and it divides each sales region into four customer groupings. Two general trends, however, seem to be gaining momentum in the 1990s. First, customer departmentalization is growing in popularity. In order to better monitor the needs of customers and to be better able to respond to changes in those needs, many organizations have given greater emphasis to customer departmentalization. Xerox, for example, has eliminated its corporate marketing staff and placed marketing specialists out in the field.[8] This arrangement allows the company to better understand who their customers are and to respond faster to their requirements. The second trend is that rigid functional departmentalization is being complemented by teams that cross over traditional departmental lines. As tasks have become more complex and more-diverse skills are needed to accomplish those tasks, management has turned to cross-functional teams.

Chain of Command

Twenty years ago, the chain-of-command concept was a basic cornerstone in the design of organizations. As you will see, it has far less importance today. But contemporary managers should still consider its implications when they decide how best to structure their organizations.

The **chain of command** is an unbroken line of authority that extends from the top of the organization to the lowest echelon and clarifies who reports to whom. It answers questions for employees such as "Who do I go to if I have a problem?" and "Who am I responsible to?"

You can't discuss the chain of command without discussing two complementary concepts: *authority* and *unity of command*. **Authority** refers to the rights inherent in a managerial position to give orders and expect the orders to be obeyed.[9] To facilitate coordination, the organization gives each managerial position a place in the chain of command and each manager a degree of authority in order to meet his or her responsibilities. The **unity of command** principle helps preserve the concept of an unbroken line of authority. It states that a person should have one and only one superior to whom he or she is directly responsible. If the unity of command is broken, a subordinate might have to cope with conflicting demands or priorities from several superiors.

The concepts of chain of command, authority, and unity of command have substantially less relevance today because of advancements in computer technology and the trend toward empowering employees.

Times change and so do the basic tenets of organization design. The concepts of chain of command, authority, and unity of command have substantially less relevance today because of advancements in computer technology and the trend toward empowering employees. Just how different things are today is illustrated in the following excerpt from a recent article in *Business Week:*

> Puzzled, Charles Chaser scanned the inventory reports from his company's distribution centers one Wednesday morning in mid-March. According to the computer printouts, stocks of Rose Awakening Cutex nail polish were down to three days' supply, well below the three-and-a-half week stock Chesebrough-Pond's Inc. tries to keep on hand. But Chaser knew his Jefferson City (Missouri) plant had shipped 346 dozen bottles of the polish just two days before. Rose Awakening must be flying off store shelves, he thought. So Chaser turned to his terminal next to the production line and typed in instructions to produce 400 dozen more bottles on Thursday morning.
>
> All in a day's work for a scheduling manager, right? Except for one detail: Chaser isn't management. He's a line worker—officially a "line coordinator"—one of hundreds who routinely tap the plant's computer network to track shipments, schedule their own workloads, and generally perform functions that used to be the province of management.[10]

A low-level employee today can access information in seconds that, 20 years ago, was available only to top managers. Similarly, computer technology increasingly allows employees anywhere in an organization to communicate with anyone else without going through formal channels. Moreover, the concepts of authority and maintaining the chain of command are increasingly less relevant as operating employees are being empowered to make decisions that previously were reserved for management. Add to this the popularity of self-managed and cross-functional teams and the creation of new structural designs that include multiple bosses, and the unity-of-command concept takes on less relevance. There are, of course, still many organizations that find they can be most productive by enforcing the chain of command. There just seem to be fewer of them nowadays.

Span of Control

How many subordinates can a manager efficiently and effectively direct? This question of **span of control** is important because, to a large degree, it determines the number of levels and managers an organization has. All things being equal, the wider or larger the span, the more efficient the organization. An example can illustrate the validity of this statement.

Assume that we have two organizations, both of which have approximately 4,100 operative-level employees. As Exhibit 7-3 illustrates, if one has a uniform span of four and the other a span of eight, the wider span would have two fewer levels and approximately 800 fewer managers. If the average manager made $40,000 a year, the wider span would save $32 million a year in management salaries! Obviously, wider spans are more efficient in terms of cost. However, at some point wider spans reduce effectiveness. That is, when the span becomes too large, employee performance suffers because supervisors no longer have the time to provide the necessary leadership and support.

EXHIBIT 7-3
Contrasting Spans of Control

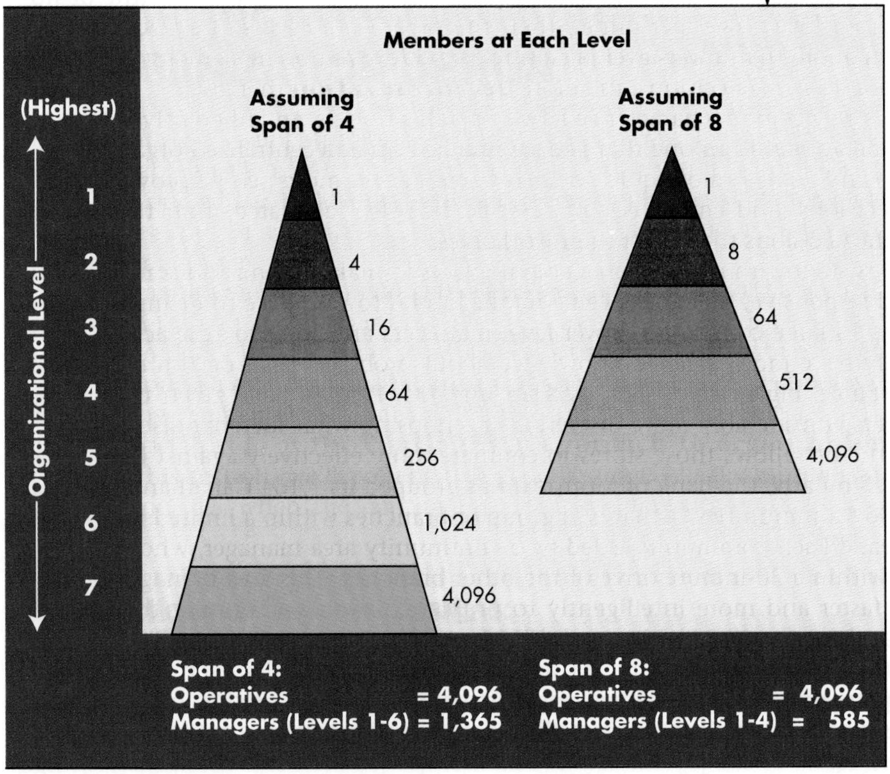

formalization, a limited information network (mostly downward communication), and little participation by low-level members in decision making.

In the mechanistic structure, work specialization creates jobs that are simple, routine, and standardized. Further specialization through the use of departmentalization increases impersonality and the need for multiple layers of management to coordinate the specialized departments. There is also strict adherence to the unity-of-command principle. This ensures the existence of a formal hierarchy of authority, with each person controlled and supervised by one superior. Narrow spans of control, especially at increasingly higher levels in the organization, create tall, impersonal structures. And, as the distance between the top and the bottom of the organization expand, top management tends to impose rules and regulations. Why? Because top managers can't control lower-level activities through direct observation and ensure the use of standard practices, so they substitute high formalization.

In its ideal form, the mechanistic organization becomes an *efficiency* machine, well oiled by rules, regulations, routinization, and similar controls. This organizational form tries to minimize the impact of personalities, human judgments, and ambiguity because these are seen as imposing inefficiencies and inconsistencies. Although there exists no pure form of the mechanistic organization in practice, almost all large corporations and government agencies as recently as 25 or 30 years ago had most of these mechanistic characteristics. And a number of large organizations today still have many mechanistic properties.

The **organic organization** is a direct contrast to the mechanistic form. It is a highly adaptive form that is as loose and flexible as the mechanistic organization is rigid and stable. The organic structure is flat, uses teams to cut across functional departments and hierarchical levels, has low formalization, possesses a comprehensive information network (utilizing lateral and upward communication as well as downward), and actively involves all employees in decision making.

Rather than having standardized jobs and regulations, the organic structure's *flexibility* allows it to change rapidly as needs require. The organic form has divi-

EXHIBIT 7-4
Mechanistic vs. Organic Designs

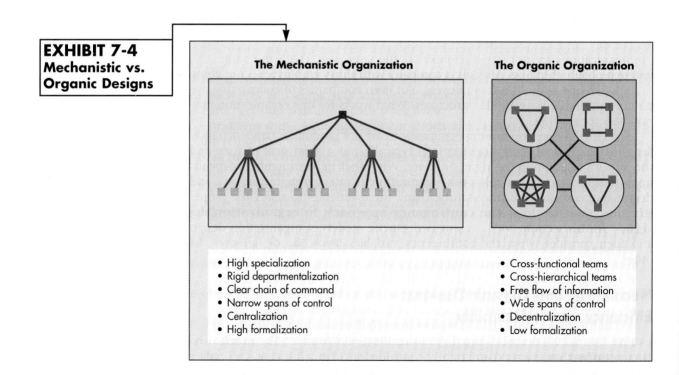

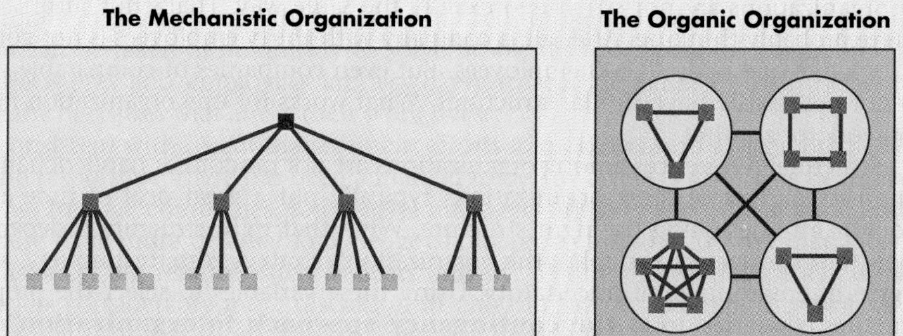

- High specialization
- Rigid departmentalization
- Clear chain of command
- Narrow spans of control
- Centralization
- High formalization

- Cross-functional teams
- Cross-hierarchical teams
- Free flow of information
- Wide spans of control
- Decentralization
- Low formalization

sion of labor, but the jobs people do are not standardized. Employees are highly trained and empowered to make job-related decisions. And organic structures tend to rely heavily on teams. The net effect is that employees in this form require a minimal degree of formal rules and little direct supervision—their high skills, training, and the support provided by other team members tend to make high formalization and tight managerial controls unnecessary.

With these two models in mind, we're now prepared to address the question: Why are some organizations structured along more mechanistic lines while others lean toward organic characteristics?

Strategy

An organization's structure is a means to help management achieve its objectives. Since objectives are derived from the organization's overall strategy, it's only logical that strategy and structure should be closely linked. More specifically, structure should follow strategy. If management makes a significant change in its organization's strategy, the structure will need to be modified to accommodate and support this change.[18]

Most current strategy-structure frameworks focus on three strategy dimensions—innovation, cost minimization, and imitation—and the structural design that works best with each.[19]

To what degree does an organization introduce major new products or services? An **innovation strategy** does not mean a strategy merely for simple or cosmetic changes from previous offerings but rather one for meaningful and unique innovations. Obviously, not all firms pursue innovation. This strategy may appropriately characterize 3M Co., but it certainly is not a strategy pursued by the publisher of *Reader's Digest*.

An organization that is pursuing a **cost-minimization strategy** tightly controls costs, refrains from incurring unnecessary innovation or marketing expenses, and cuts prices in selling a basic product. This would describe the strategy pursued by Wal-Mart or the sellers of generic grocery products.

Organizations following an **imitation strategy** try to capitalize on the best of both of the previous strategies. They seek to minimize risk and maximize opportunity for profit. Their strategy is to move into new products or new markets only after viability has been proved by innovators. They take the successful ideas of innovators and copy them. Manufacturers of mass-marketed fashion goods that are knockoffs of designer styles follow the imitation strategy. This label also probably characterizes such well-known firms as IBM and Caterpillar. They essentially follow their smaller and more innovative competitors with superior products, but only after their competitors have demonstrated that the market is there.

Exhibit 7-5 (p. 202) describes the structural option that best matches each strategy. Innovators need the flexibility of the organic structure, whereas cost minimizers seek the efficiency and stability of the mechanistic structure. Imitators combine the two structures. They use a mechanistic structure in order to maintain tight controls and low costs in their current activities, while, at the same time, they create organic subunits in which to pursue new undertakings.

Organization Size

A quick glance at the organizations we deal with regularly in our lives would lead most of us to conclude that size would have some bearing on an organization's structure. The more than 800,000 employees of the U.S. Postal Service, for example, do not neatly fit into one building or into several departments supervised by a couple of managers. It's pretty hard to envision 800,000 people being organized

EXHIBIT 7-5
The Strategy-Structure Thesis

Strategy	Best Structural Option
Innovation	Organic: A loose structure; low specialization, low formalization, decentralized
Cost minimization	Mechanistic: Tight control; extensive work specialization, high formalization, high centralization
Imitation	Mechanistic and organic: Mix of loose with tight properties; tight controls over current activities and looser controls for new undertakings

in any manner other than one that contains a great deal of specialization and departmentalization, uses a large number of procedures and regulations to ensure uniform practices, and follows a high degree of decentralized decision making. On the other hand, a local messenger service that employs ten people and generates less than $300,000 a year in service fees is not likely to need decentralized decision making or formalized procedures and regulations.

There is considerable evidence to support the idea that an organization's size significantly affects its structure.[20] For instance, large organizations—those typically employing 2,000 or more people—tend to have more specialization, more departmentalization, more vertical levels, and more rules and regulations than do small organizations. But the relationship is not linear. Rather, size affects structure at a decreasing rate; the impact of size becomes less important as an organization expands. Why? Essentially, once an organization has around 2,000 employees, it is already fairly mechanistic. An additional 500 employees will not have much impact. On the other hand, adding 500 employees to an organization that has only 300 members is likely to result in a shift toward a more mechanistic structure.

Technology

The term **technology** refers to how an organization transforms its inputs into outputs. Every organization has at least one technology for converting financial, human, and physical resources into products or services. The Ford Motor Co., for instance, predominantly uses an assembly-line process to make its products. Colleges, on the other hand, may use a number of instruction technologies—the ever-popular formal lecture method, the case analysis method, the experiential exercise method, the programmed learning method, and so forth.

The initial interest in technology as a determinant of structure can be traced to the mid-1960s and the work of Joan Woodward.[21] Her research, which focused on production technology, was the first major attempt to view organization structure from a technological perspective.

Woodward studied nearly 100 small manufacturing firms in the south of England to determine the extent to which organization-design principles such as unity of command and span of control were related to firm success. She was unable to derive any consistent pattern from her data until she segmented her firms into three categories based on the size of their production runs. The three categories, representing three distinct technologies, had increasing levels of complexity and sophistication. The first category, *unit production,* comprised unit or small-batch producers that manufactured custom products such as tailor-made suits and turbines for hydroelectric dams. The second category, *mass production,* included large-batch or mass-production manufacturers that made items such as refrigerators and automobiles. The third and most technically complex group, *process production,* included continuous-process producers such as oil and chemical refiners.

Woodward found that (1) distinct relationships existed between these technology classifications and the subsequent structure of the firms and (2) the effectiveness of the organizations was related to the "fit" between technology and structure.

For example, the number of vertical levels increased with technical complexity. The median number of vertical levels for firms in the unit, mass, and process categories were three, four, and six, respectively. More important, from an effectiveness standpoint, the more successful firms in each category clustered around the median for their production group. But not all the relationships were linear. As a case in point, the mass-production firms scored high on formalization, whereas the unit and process firms rated low on this structural characteristic. Woodward found that imposing rules and regulations was impossible with the nonroutine technology of unit production and unnecessary in the highly standardized process technology.

After carefully analyzing her findings, Woodward concluded that specific structures were associated with each of the three categories and that successful firms met the requirements of their technology by adopting the proper structural arrangements. Within each category, the firms that most nearly conformed to the median figure for each structural component were the most effective. She found that there was no one best way to organize a manufacturing firm. Unit and process production were most effective when matched with an organic structure, whereas mass production was most effective when matched with a mechanistic structure.

Since Woodward's initial work, numerous studies have been carried out on the technology-structure relationship. And these studies generally demonstrate that organization structures adapt to their technology.[22] The details of those studies are quite complex, so we'll go straight to "the bottom line" and attempt to summarize what we know. The common theme that differentiates technologies is their *degree of routineness*. By this we mean that technologies tend toward either routine or nonroutine activities. The former are characterized by automated and standardized operations. Nonroutine activities are customized. They include such varied operations as furniture restoring, custom shoemaking, and genetic research.

What relationships have been found between technology and structure? Although the relationship is not overwhelmingly strong, we find that routine tasks are associated with taller and more departmentalized structures. The relationship between technology and formalization, however, is stronger. Studies consistently show routineness to be associated with the presence of rule manuals, job descriptions, and other formalized documentation.

Environmental Uncertainty

As we described in Chapter 4, an organization's environment is composed of those institutions or forces that are outside the organization and potentially affect the organization's performance. The environment has acquired a large following as a key determinant of structure.

Why should an organization's structure be affected by its environment? Because of environmental uncertainty. Again, as noted in Chapter 4, some organizations face relatively static environments, while other organizations face very dynamic environments. Static environments create significantly less uncertainty for managers than do dynamic ones. And since uncertainty is a threat to an organization's effectiveness, management will try to minimize it. One way to reduce environmental uncertainty is through adjustments in the organization's structure.[23]

There is substantial evidence that relates the degrees of environmental uncertainty to different structural arrangements. Essentially, the more scarce, dynamic, and complex the environment—that is, the greater the environmental uncertainty—the greater the need for flexibility. Hence, the organic structure will lead to higher organizational effectiveness. Conversely, in abundant, stable, and simple environments, the mechanistic form will be the structure of choice.

Explaining the Increasing Popularity of the Organic Structure

Why are managers increasingly restructuring their organizations and trying to make them more organic? The answer substantially lies in the contingency approach to organization design.

The most powerful force driving the restructuring of organizations toward the organic form is, arguably, increased environmental uncertainty.

The most powerful force driving the restructuring of organizations toward the organic form is, arguably, increased environmental uncertainty. Global competition, accelerated product innovation by all competitors, and increased demands from customers for higher quality and faster deliveries are examples of dynamic environmental forces that confront today's managers. Mechanistic organizations tend to be ill-equipped to respond to such rapid environmental change.

An argument can be made that the other contingency variables are also increasingly favoring the organic structure. For the first two-thirds of this century, most large corporations chose to pursue cost minimization or imitation strategies. They tended to leave innovation to the little guys. But many of those "little guys" became hugely successful, took business away from the big companies, and became big companies themselves. The result? Large and small companies alike increasingly have been pursuing innovation strategies. Consistent with a dynamic environment and the need to innovate, large organizations have also been breaking themselves up into smaller and more flexible subunits. Instead of being one large company, management is creating a bunch of autonomous minicompanies. Finally, increased competition and demand by customers for more-customized products and services is requiring organizations to rely more heavily on nonroutine technologies. In aggregate, then, these forces—more innovation strategies, smaller-sized units, and the expanded use of nonroutine technologies—when combined with increased environmental uncertainty, explain why managers are restructuring their organizations to make them more organic.

THE EVOLUTIONARY APPROACH TO ORGANIZATION DESIGN

The contingency approach to organization design provides a basic theoretical framework for labeling structures and explaining why organizations are structured differently. But placing organizations into only two categories—mechanistic and organic—fails to capture the nuances and realities of today's organizations. A more practical approach to understanding organization design today is to consider it in an evolutionary context.

Twenty years ago, most large organizations were designed around high specialization, extensive departmentalization, narrow spans of control, and centralized decision making. They looked like pyramids, with the people on top making all the decisions and tightly controlling the actions of those below them. Today, the pyramid is being challenged by structures that more closely resemble domes, networks, wheels, clusters, and pancakes.[24]

In this section, we present seven structural designs. We start with the simple structure—the form that almost all new organizations begin with and that continues to be widely used by managers of small business firms.

The Simple Structure

What do a small grocery store, a software design firm run by a hard-driving entrepreneur, and a new furniture-manufacturing company have in common? They probably all utilize the **simple structure.**[25]

IN THE NEWS

Motorola: The Best-Managed Company in the World?

Henry Conn, vice president in charge of research at the consulting firm A.T. Kearney declares, "Motorola is the best-managed company in the world. Nobody else is even close." Those are strong words, but he may be right. Between 1992 and 1993, Motorola sales increased 27.5 percent, and profits surged 127 percent. In 1994, sales and profits increased another 31.1 percent and 52.6 percent, respectively. Pretty impressive performance for a $22-billion corporation!

Less than a decade ago, Motorola was a slowly declining American electronics company. New management, however, decided to remake Motorola into a world-class leader in innovation and quality. And it has obviously succeeded. Motorola is now a world leader in the manufacturing of cellular telephones, pagers, two-way radios, semiconductors and other electronic and wireless communication products. The company's fanatic pursuit of six-sigma quality—3.4 mistakes per million—has led to numerous quality awards.

Motorola has succeeded where most large firms have failed. It has dramatically increased sales and profits in a rapidly changing and competitive environment. One major reason for its success is that, despite its size, Motorola's management has restructured the company to be highly adaptive and flexible. The essence of this structure is the creation of autonomous business units, decentralized decision making, the breaking down of organizational boundaries, obsessive attention to customer needs, extensive reliance on teams, the use of flexible manufacturing processes, and management's encouragement of candid internal debate. For instance, at the company's Arlington Heights, Illinois, cellular equipment plant, self-directed teams (see photo) hire and fire their co-workers, help select their supervisors, and schedule their own work. In addition, the Arlington Heights plant has created dozens of teams that cross over traditional department lines to handle issues such as improving quality, cutting costs, reducing cycle time, and meeting customer expectations.

Source: Based on R. Henkoff, "Keeping Motorola on a Roll," *Fortune,* April 18, 1994, pp. 67–78; and "The Fortune 500 Largest U.S. Corporations," *Fortune,* May 15, 1995, p. F1.

This team at Motorola's Boynton Beach, Fla., paging plant is just one of the 4,300 teams that the company relies on to achieve its extraordinary record for quality products.

In structural terms, the simple structure has a low degree of departmentalization, wide spans of control, authority centralized in a single person, and little formalization. It is a "flat" organization—with typically only two or three vertical levels, a loose body of employees, and one individual in whom the decision-making authority is centralized.

The simple structure is most widely practiced in small businesses in which the manager and the owner are one and the same. This structure, for example, is illustrated in Exhibit 7-6 (p. 206)—an organization chart for a 2-year-old software-design firm in the Boston area. Kevin Jordan owns and manages the firm. Although Kevin employs five full-time people, he "runs the show."

The strength of the simple structure lies in its simplicity. It's fast, flexible, and inexpensive to maintain, and accountability is clear. It is an ideal structure for small organizations and new start-ups. Its major weakness is that it is difficult to maintain in anything other than small organizations. It becomes increasingly inadequate as

The one common technological thread that makes the boundaryless organization possible is networked computers. They allow people to communicate across intraorganizational and interorganizational boundaries.[50] Electronic mail, for instance, enables hundreds of employees to share information simultaneously and allows rank-and-file workers to communicate directly with senior executives. And interorganizational networks now make it possible for Wal-Mart suppliers such as Procter & Gamble and Levi-Strauss to monitor inventory levels of laundry soap and jeans, respectively, because P&G and Levi's computer systems are networked to Wal-Mart's system.

The boundaryless organization has the potential to create a major shift in our living patterns. In a boundaryless world, people will be free to work where they want. Many, of course, will still prefer metropolitan areas because of the cultural options they provide. But as smaller communities such as Jackson, Wyoming; Taos, New Mexico; Prescott, Arizona; Blacksburg, Virginia, Saint Tropez, France; and Hamilton, Bermuda, combine assets such as good weather, scenery, outdoor activities, moderate cost of living, proximity to a major university, or favorable tax climates, with diverse cultural amenities, people are likely to gravitate away from traditional job centers.

The boundaryless organization has the potential to create a major shift in our living patterns.

SUMMARY

(This summary is organized by the chapter-opening learning objectives on page 191.)

1. The six key elements of organization structure are (1) work specialization, the degree to which tasks in the organization are subdivided into separate jobs; (2) departmentalization, the basis by which jobs are grouped together; (3) chain of command, an unbroken line of authority that extends from the top of the organization to the lowest echelon and clarifies who reports to whom; (4) span of control, the number of subordinates directly reporting to a manager; (5) centralization/decentralization, where decision making is concentrated; and (6) formalization, the degree to which jobs are standardized.
2. Mechanistic structures are rigid. They are characterized by high specialization, departmentalization, narrow spans of control, high formalization, and centralized decision making. Organic structures are the opposite. They are flexible and adaptive. They have wide spans of control, fewer levels of vertical hierarchy, fluid communications, decentralized decision making, and low formalization.
3. The four contingency variables that explain structural differences are the organization's strategy, size, technology, and degree of environmental uncertainty.
4. The greater the degree of environmental uncertainty, the more susceptible an organization is to shocks from the environment. Since management does not like uncertainty, it tries to reduce it. One means for reducing uncertainty is through the organization's structure. If uncertainty is high, a flexible and adaptive structure is better at allowing the organization and its members to respond quickly.
5. The bureaucracy is characterized by highly routine operating tasks achieved through specialization, very formalized rules and regulations, tasks that are grouped into functional departments, centralized authority, narrow spans of control, and decision making that follows the chain of command. It is effective and efficient when the organization's technology is routine and standardized. It also matches up well with a stable environment, where there is little change.
6. The advantages of the matrix are that it facilitates coordination across functional specialties, provides for clear responsibility for all activities related to a product or project, and facilitates the efficient allocation of specialists. Its primary disadvantages are increased confusion and ambiguity, the tendency to foster power struggles, and increased stress for organizational members.
7. The virtual organization has a small permanent staff who oversee operations, focus on the organization's core competencies, and coordinate relations with external constituencies. This structure relies heavily on outsourcing for noncore functions. The strength of this structure is that it provides tremendous flexibility for management. It facilitates using the resources of other organizations to allow the virtual organization to do more with less.

8. The boundaryless organization seeks to eliminate the chain of command, have limitless spans of control, and replace departments with empowered teams. It attempts to break down horizontal boundaries, vertical boundaries, barriers to external constituencies, and barriers created by geography. Its primary appeal is to allow large organizations to behave like small ones. They become closer to customers and suppliers and reduce communication barriers between levels in the organization and between functional units.

REVIEW AND DISCUSSION QUESTIONS

1. Contrast how the typical large corporation is organized today against how it was organized in the 1960s.
2. Why isn't work specialization an unending source of increased productivity?
3. In what ways can management departmentalize?
4. What is the relationship between span of control and vertical levels of hierarchy?
5. Contrast the value of formalization for management with its value for employees.
6. Summarize the strategy-structure relationship.
7. When would the simple structure be the preferred organization design?
8. How could management of a large bureaucracy maintain their efficiencies but also increase the organization's flexibility?
9. What could management do to make a bureaucracy more like a boundaryless organization?
10. Would you rather work in a bureaucracy or a virtual organization? What are the implications of your answer to your career plans?

CASE EXERCISE A
HOW WAL-MART BEAT KMART

Go back to 1987 and compare Kmart and Wal-Mart. At that time, Kmart had the advantage and the momentum. Kmart had almost twice as many discount stores, 2,223 to 1,198. It also had a big advantage in sales volume—$25.63 billion versus $15.96 billion. So how, in less than 10 years, could Kmart get blown away by Wal-Mart?

Back in 1987, the two chains had a lot in common. They sold the same products and sought each other's customers. They were even founded in the same year—1962. But by 1995, Kmart provided little competition for the Big W. Wal-Mart sales were nearly three times that of Kmart. And Kmart's market share of total discount sales had dropped to 22.7 percent from 34.5 percent. Meanwhile, Wal-Mart's had soared to 41.6 percent from 20.1 percent!

The two prime players in this battle were Sam Walton, the founder of Wal-Mart, and Joseph Antonini. Antonini started as an assistant manager at Kmart in 1964 and was appointed CEO in 1987. As you'll see, their leadership, or lack of same, had a lot to do in explaining why Wal-Mart won the battle.

When Antonini took over as head of Kmart, he inherited some stores that were as old as 17 years, with broken fixtures and cheap displays. His predecessors had also failed to develop a sophisticated computerized information system. But Kmart had strong urban locations. In contrast, Wal-Mart stores were newer, often twice as large as otherwise comparable Kmarts, and located in rural areas outside small towns. Sam Walton had great respect for Kmart. He wrote in his autobiography, "So much about their stores was superior to ours that sometimes I felt like we couldn't compete." In contrast, Antonini showed no fear of Wal-Mart. He reportedly dismissed Wal-Mart executives as "snake-oil salesmen."

Antonini focused on his strength: marketing and merchandising. He invested heavily in national television campaigns. He sought to build Kmart's image and store loyalty. Meanwhile, Sam Walton focused obsessively on keeping costs down. He invested tens of millions of dollars in a companywide computer system linking cash registers to headquarters, enabling him to quickly restock goods selling off the shelves. He also invested heavily in trucks and distribution centers, around which he located his stores. These moves allowed Wal-Mart to closely control costs. Walton believed that price would prove more important toward building customer loyalty than any other factor.

Kmart tried to bolster its growth by diversifying into other retailing operations. It bought the Sports Authority sporting-goods chain, OfficeMax office-supply stores, and Borders bookstores. At the same time, Walton was taking precisely the opposite approach. He was "betting the ranch" on discount retailing. He started Sam's Club, a deep-discount, members-only retailer, and he opened Supercenter stores, which combined discount merchandise and groceries.

By 1990, Wal-Mart was running out of small towns to conquer and began its assault on Kmart's turf. In response, Kmart spent heavily on renovating, enlarging, and replacing its oldest and shabbiest stores. Antonini figured that diversifying and stressing Kmart's image would give Kmart a competitive advantage against Wal-Mart. [Especially now that Wal-Mart would have to pay the high property costs, just as Kmart did, associated with locating in urban areas.]

Wal-Mart's information system eventually proved to be the "knife" that did the greatest damage to Kmart. Wal-Mart's far superior distribution, inventory, and scanner systems meant that customers almost never encountered depleted shelves or price-check delays at the cash register. Kmart's customers, in contrast, were continually disappointed—merchandise was regularly out of stock. In a frantic attempt to catch up, Antonini spent a fortune on a sophisticated information system only to find that his employees woefully lacked the training and skill to plan and control inventory. Kmart's cash registers often had out-of-date information and would charge customers the wrong prices.

In March 1995, Antonini threw in the towel. Under heavy pressure from stockholders, he was forced to resign.

Questions

1. Analyze this case from a strategy-structure perspective.
2. Analyze this case from a technology-structure perspective.
3. Analyze this case from an environment-structure perspective.

Source: C. Duff and B. Ortega, "How Wal-Mart Outdid a Once-Touted Kmart in Discount-Store Race," *Wall Street Journal*, March 24, 1995, p. A1. Reprinted by permission of the *Wall Street Journal* © 1995 Dow Jones & Co., Inc. All rights reserved worldwide.

CASE EXERCISE B
HOME DEPOT, INC.

Revenues at Home Depot, Inc. climbed by 36 percent a year in the 5 years ending in 1994. Profits during this same period grew at a rate of 44 percent a year. Home Depot's management intends to maintain this growth record by following what it calls its "distinct waves" strategy.

Home Depot's management sees their problems as akin to those faced by an army in times of war: seizing the right territory, maintaining supply lines, controlling occupied terrain, and planning offensives. The first wave is to "plant the flag"—putting three or four stores on the perimeter of a designated city. Each store typically serves 100,000 households that have median incomes of $45,000. And 75 percent of those households are owner-occupied. Once the initial stores reach combined sales of about $50 million, the second wave fills in the territory with new outlets designed to make Home Depot dominant over 3 to 5 years.

Wave three begins when sales surpass Home Depot's average of $400 per square foot or when growth lags behind the inflation rate. At that point, management figures a store is getting too crowded, so it engages in what it calls "cannibalizing." It will close a thriving store and open two smaller ones to improve the shopping experience for customers.

This strategy has worked well so far. In 1994, for instance, the company's goal was to expand by 25 percent, to 330 stores. In actuality, the chain grew to 340 locations. By 1998, Home Depot aims to add another 460 stores to bring the chain's total outlets to 800.

Questions

1. How is strategy driving structure at Home Depot?
2. Do you think it is possible for a company like Home Depot to be both big *and* flexible? Explain.

Source: Based on W. Zellner, "Go-Go Goliaths," *Business Week*, February 13, 1995, pp. 64–70.

SKILL EXERCISE

Selecting the Proper Organization Design

Kitchen Stuff is growing like crazy. And Anne Turrin isn't sure how to control the monster she has created. Anne started Kitchen Stuff out of her three-room Milwaukee apartment in 1991. It was to be a mail-order business that carried everything people would need for their kitchens. She used her savings and a $10,000 loan from her parents to fund her first catalogue. That catalogue contained only twenty pages and generated sales of $65,000. Today, the Kitchen Stuff catalogue is a slick 170 pages and is expected to bring in revenues in excess of $10 million.

The Kitchen Stuff operations comprise essentially three functions: buying/ordering, warehousing, and taking orders. Until 1993, Anne and her sister ran the whole business out of Anne's apartment. Then she hired her first real employee to handle telephone orders. Recently Anne moved her business into a 6,000-square-foot warehouse in a suburb of Milwaukee. She and her sister do all the buying, although the task has become far too cumbersome for the two to handle by themselves. Anne plans to add at least two additional full-time buyers. Anne also recognizes that her staff of six telephone operators are overburdened. She plans to triple the size of this group over the next 6 months. But by doing so, she realizes that she will not be able to directly oversee everything anymore. Her managerial demands are now pushed beyond her ability. Finally, the warehouse itself is grossly understaffed. Currently, one person is responsible for all shipping. He is assisted by four college students who work part-time.

In 1991, Kitchen Stuff had two employees. At the time this was written, it had nine full-time employees (including Anne and her sister) and four part-timers. Anne runs everything and makes all the decisions. Within 6 months, the company will very likely employ twenty-five to thirty people. Anne realizes that she will not be able to single-handedly manage the firm as it moves to this new level. Moreover, if Anne succeeds in reaching her 5-year plan, Kitchen Stuff will be doing more than $50 million a year and employing between sixty and seventy-five people by the year 2000.

If you were Anne, what organization design options would you consider viable? Which one would you choose? Why?

NOTES

1. R. L. Daft and A. Y. Lewin, "Where Are the Theories for the 'New' Organizational Forms? An Editorial Essay," *Organization Science,* November 1993, pp. i–vi.
2. B. R. Schlender, "Matsushita Shows How to Go Global," *Fortune,* July 11, 1994, pp. 159–66; and R. Neff, "Tradition Be Damned," *Business Week,* October 31, 1994, pp. 108–10.
3. O. Suris, "Retooling Itself, Ford Stresses Speed, Candor," *Wall Street Journal,* October 27, 1994, p. B1.
4. B. O'Reilly, "J&J Is on a Roll," *Fortune,* December 26, 1994, pp. 178–92.
5. B. R. Schlender, "How Toshiba Makes Alliances Work," *Fortune,* October 4, 1993, pp. 116–20.
6. Cited in T. Lester, "Balancing Act," *International Management,* September 1994, p. 30.
7. See, for instance, R. L. Daft, *Organization Theory and Design,* 5th ed. (St. Paul, Minn.: West Publishing, 1995).
8. J. H. Sheridan, "Sizing Up Corporate Staffs," *Industry Week,* November 21, 1988, p. 47.
9. For a discussion of authority, see W. A. Kahn and K. E. Kram, "Authority at Work: Internal Models and Their Organizational Consequences," *Academy of Management Review,* January 1994, pp. 17–50.
10. J. B. Treece, "Breaking the Chains of Command," *Business Week/The Information Revolution 1994,* (Special Issue), p. 112.
11. See, for instance, L. Urwick, *The Elements of Administration* (New York: Harper & Row, 1944), pp. 52–53.
12. J. S. McClenahen, "Managing More People in the '90s," *Industry Week,* March 20, 1989, p. 30.
13. J. R. Brandt, "Middle Management: Where the Action Will Be," *Industry Week,* May 2, 1994, p. 31.
14. A. Ross, "BMO's Big Bang," *Canadian Business,* January 1994, pp. 58–63.
15. J. B. Levine, "For IBM Europe, 'This Is the Year of Truth,'" *Business Week,* April 19, 1993, p. 45.
16. See, for instance, G. Schreyogg, "Contingency and Choice in Organization Theory," *Organization Studies,* no. 3(1980), pp. 305–26; and H. L. Tosi Jr. and J. W. Slocum Jr., "Contingency Theory: Some Suggested Directions," *Journal of Management,* Spring 1984, pp. 9–26.
17. T. Burns and G. Stalker, *The Management of Innovation* (London: Tavistock, 1961); and J. A. Courtright, G. T. Fairhurst, and L. E. Rogers, "Interaction Patterns in Organic and Mechanistic Systems," *Academy of Management Journal,* December 1989, pp. 773–802.

18. The strategy-structure thesis was originally proposed in A. D. Chandler Jr., *Strategy and Structure: Chapters in the History of the Industrial Enterprise* (Cambridge, Mass.: MIT Press, 1962). For an updated analysis, see T. L. Amburgey and T. Dacin, "As the Left Foot Follows the Right? The Dynamics of Strategic and Structural Change," *Academy of Management Journal,* December 1994, pp. 1427–52.
19. See R. E. Miles and C. C. Snow, *Organizational Strategy, Structure, and Process* (New York: McGraw-Hill, 1978); D. Miller, "The Structural and Environmental Correlates of Business Strategy," *Strategic Management Journal,* January–February 1987, pp. 55–76; and D. C. Galunic and K. M. Eisenhardt, "Renewing the Strategy-Structure-Performance Paradigm," in B. M. Staw and L. L. Cummings, eds., *Research in Organizational Behavior,* vol. 16 (Greenwich, Conn.: JAI Press, 1994), pp. 215–55.
20. See, for instance, P. M. Blau and R. A. Schoenherr, *The Structure of Organizations* (New York: Basic Books, 1971); D. S. Pugh, "The Aston Program of Research: Retrospect and Prospect," in A. H. Van de Ven and W. F. Joyce, eds., *Perspectives on Organization Design and Behavior* (New York: John Wiley, 1981), pp. 135–66; R. Z. Gooding and J. A. Wagner III, "A Meta-Analytic Review of the Relationship between Size and Performance: The Productivity and Efficiency of Organizations and Their Subunits," *Administrative Science Quarterly,* December 1985, pp. 462–81; and A. C. Bluedorn, "Pilgrim's Progress: Trends and Convergence in Research on Organizational Size and Environments," *Journal of Management,* Summer 1993, pp. 163–92.
21. J. Woodward, *Industrial Organization: Theory and Practice* (London: Oxford University Press, 1965).
22. See C. Perrow, "A Framework for the Comparative Analysis of Organizations," *American Sociological Review,* April 1967, pp. 194–208; J. D. Thompson, *Organizations in Action* (New York: McGraw-Hill, 1967); J. Hage and M. Aiken, "Routine Technology, Social Structure, and Organizational Goals," *Administrative Science Quarterly,* September 1969, pp. 366–77; and C. C. Miller, W. H. Glick, Y. Wang, and G. P. Huber, "Understanding Technology-Structure Relationships: Theory Development and Meta-Analytic Theory Testing," *Academy of Management Journal,* June 1991, pp. 370–99.
23. F. E. Emery and E. Trist, "The Causal Texture of Organizational Environments," *Human Relations,* February 1965, pp. 21–32; P. Lawrence and J. W. Lorsch, *Organization and Environment: Managing Differentiation and Integration* (Boston: Harvard Business School, Division of Research, 1967); M. Yasai-Ardekani, "Structural Adaptations to Environments," *Academy of Management Review,* January 1986, pp. 9–21; and Bluedorn, "Pilgrim's Progress."
24. R. Tomasko, "Toppling the Pyramids," *Canadian Business,* May 1993, pp. 61–65; N. K. Austin, "Reorganizing the Organization Chart," *Working Woman,* September 1993, pp. 23–26; and J. A. Byrne, "The Horizontal Corporation," *Business Week,* December 20, 1993, pp. 76–81.
25. This discussion is based on H. Mintzberg, *Structure in Fives: Designing Effective Organizations* (Englewood Cliffs, N.J.: Prentice Hall, 1983), pp. 157–62.
26. S. Baker, "Can Nucor Forge Ahead—And Keep Its Edge?" *Business Week,* April 4, 1994, p. 108.
27. See, for example, C. J. Loomis, "Dinosaurs?" *Fortune,* May 3, 1993, pp. 36–42; and R. E. Hoskisson, C. W. L. Hill, and H. Kim, "The Multidivisional Structure: Organizational Fossil or Source of Value?" *Journal of Management,* Summer 1993, pp. 269–98.
28. See, for instance, the interview with E. Lawler in "Bureaucracy Busting," *Across the Board,* March 1993, pp. 23–27.
29. C. K. Bart, "Gagging on Chaos," *Business Horizons,* September–October 1994, pp. 26–36.
30. B. Harrison, *Lean and Mean: The Changing Landscape of Corporate Power in the Age of Flexibility* (New York: BasicBooks, 1994).
31. See, for instance, K. Knight, "Matrix Organization: A Review," *Journal of Management Studies,* May 1976, pp. 111–30; L. R. Burns and D. R. Wholey, "Adoption and Abandonment of Matrix Management Programs: Effects of Organizational Characteristics and Interorganizational Networks," *Academy of Management Journal,* February 1993, pp. 106–38; and R. E. Anderson, "Matrix Redux," *Business Horizons,* November–December 1994, pp. 6–10.
32. P. Dwyer, "Tearing Up Today's Organization Chart," *Business Week,* November 18, 1994, pp. 81–82.
33. See, for instance, S. M. Davis and P. R. Lawrence, "Problems of Matrix Organization," *Harvard Business Review,* May–June 1978, pp. 131–42.
34. J. Flynn, "An Ever-Quicker Trip from R&D to Customer," *Business Week,* November 18, 1994, p. 88.
35. Dwyer, "Tearing Up Today's Organization Chart," p. 82.
36. S. A. Mohrman, S. G. Cohen, and A. M. Mohrman Jr., *Designing Team-Based Organizations* (San Francisco: Jossey-Bass, 1995).
37. M. Kaeter, "The Age of the Specialized Generalist," *Training,* December 1993, pp. 48–53.
38. L. Brokaw, "Thinking Flat," *INC.,* October 1993, p. 88.
39. W. E. Halal, "From Hierarchy to Enterprise: Internal Markets Are the New Foundation of Management," *The Executive,* November 1994, pp. 69–83.
40. Ibid.
41. Cited in *At Work,* May–June 1993, p. 3.
42. M. F. R. Kets de Vries, "Making a Giant Dance," *Across the Board,* October 1994, pp. 27–32.
43. W. C. Symonds, "Frank Stronach's Secret? Call It Empower Steering," *Business Week,* May 1, 1995, pp. 63–65.
44. H. Kahalas and K. Suchon, "Managing a Perpetual Idea Machine: Inside the Creator's Mind," *The Executive,* May 1995, pp. 57–66; and N. Alster, "Making the Kids Stand on Their Own," *Forbes,* October 9, 1995, pp. 49–56.
45. S. Woolley, "Who Says the Conglomerate Is Dead?" *Business Week,* January 23, 1995, pp. 92–93.
46. See S. Tully, "The Modular Corporation," *Fortune,* February 8, 1993, pp. 106–16; E. A. Gargan, "'Virtual' Companies Leave the Manufacturing to Others," *New York Times,* July 17, 1994, p. F5; D. W. Cravens, S. H. Shipp, and K. S. Cravens, "Reforming the Traditional Organization: The Mandate for Developing Networks," *Business Horizons,* July–August 1994, pp. 19–27; M. Landler, "It's Not Only Rock 'n' Roll," *Business Week,* October 10, 1994, pp. 83–84; R. T. King Jr., "The Virtual Company," *Wall Street Journal,* November 14, 1994, p. R12; J. W. Verity, "A Company That's 100% Virtual," *Business Week,* November 21, 1994, p. 85; F. Meeks, "'I Don't Want to Manage People,'" *Forbes,* March 13, 1995, pp. 146–50; R. E. Miles and C. C. Snow, "The New Network Firm: A Spherical Structure Built on a Human Investment Philosophy," *Organizational Dynamics,* Spring 1995, pp. 5–18; and G. G. Dess, A. M. A. Rasheed, K. J. McLaughlin, and R. L. Priem, "The New

Corporate Architecture," *Academy of Management Executive,* August 1995, pp. 7–20.
47. "Why Every Business Will Be Like Show Business," *INC.,* March 1995, pp. 64–78.
48. "GE: Just Your Average Everyday $60 Billion Family Grocery Store," *Industry Week,* May 2, 1994, pp. 13–18.
49. See L. Grant, "The Management Model That Jack Built," *Los Angeles Times Magazine,* May 9, 1993, pp. 20–22 and 34–36; J. A. Byrne and K. Kerwin, "Borderless Management," *Business Week,* May 23, 1994, pp. 24–26; P. LaBarre, "The Seamless Enterprise," *Industry Week,* June 19, 1995, pp. 22–34; and R. Ashkenas, D. Ulrich, T. Jick, and S. Kerr, *The Boundaryless Organization: Breaking the Chains of Organizational Structure* (San Francisco: Jossey-Bass, 1995).
50. See J. Lipnack and J. Stamps, *The TeamNet Factor* (Essex Junction, Verm.: Oliver Wight Publications, 1993); J. R. Wilke, "Computer Links Erode Hierarchical Nature of Workplace Culture," *Wall Street Journal,* December 9, 1993, p. A1; and T. A. Stewart, "Managing in a Wired Company," *Fortune,* July 11, 1994, pp. 44–56.

CHAPTER 8

TECHNOLOGY AND THE DESIGN OF WORK PROCESSES

I have a 9-to-5 job—
9 A.M. on Monday to
5 P.M. on Sunday.

J. Robbins

LEARNING OBJECTIVES

After studying this chapter, you should be able to:

1. Explain how technology can improve productivity
2. Describe the advantages of computer-aided design
3. Identify why management might consider introducing flexible manufacturing systems
4. Define and describe the three key elements in reengineering
5. Explain how information technology is providing managers with decision support
6. Identify the five key dimensions in a job
7. Describe how managers can design individual jobs to maximize employee performance
8. Explain how flextime, job sharing, and telecommuting increase organizational flexibility

Brenda French (see photo inset) is using technology to totally reinvent her business.[1] Starting in 1978, French had built French Rags into a $10 million a year business manufacturing women's knitwear. From an outsider's perspective, the business looked healthy. Her garments were being sold at leading department stores such as Neiman Marcus, Bonwit Teller, and Bloomingdale's. But French knew otherwise. Retailers were slow in paying for merchandise, and the long wait for payment put pressures on her limited financial resources. In addition, she was frustrated by department store buyers who were often choosing to sell just a few of her styles, sizes, and colors. She felt that her knitwear product line was reaching only a small percentage of its potential.

Her financial and distribution problems were solved, and her business completely reshaped, by two isolated events in 1989. First, a friend introduced her to a man who was an expert in knitting equipment and who just happened to have acquired a German-made Stoll computerized knitting machine. The sleek Stoll knitting machine uses thousands of precisely angled needles to do things the old-fashioned way—one stitch at a time—while churning out garments at a breathtaking pace. This one machine could produce as many garments as two dozen of French's hand knitters could in the same amount of time. Second, French's cash crunch had forced her to cut back production and sell only to the few stores who were willing to pay cash on delivery. One loyal customer, frustrated by not being able to buy her favored French Rags garments, called French on the phone. On learning of French's money problems, the customer said, "You bring your clothes to my house, and I know twenty

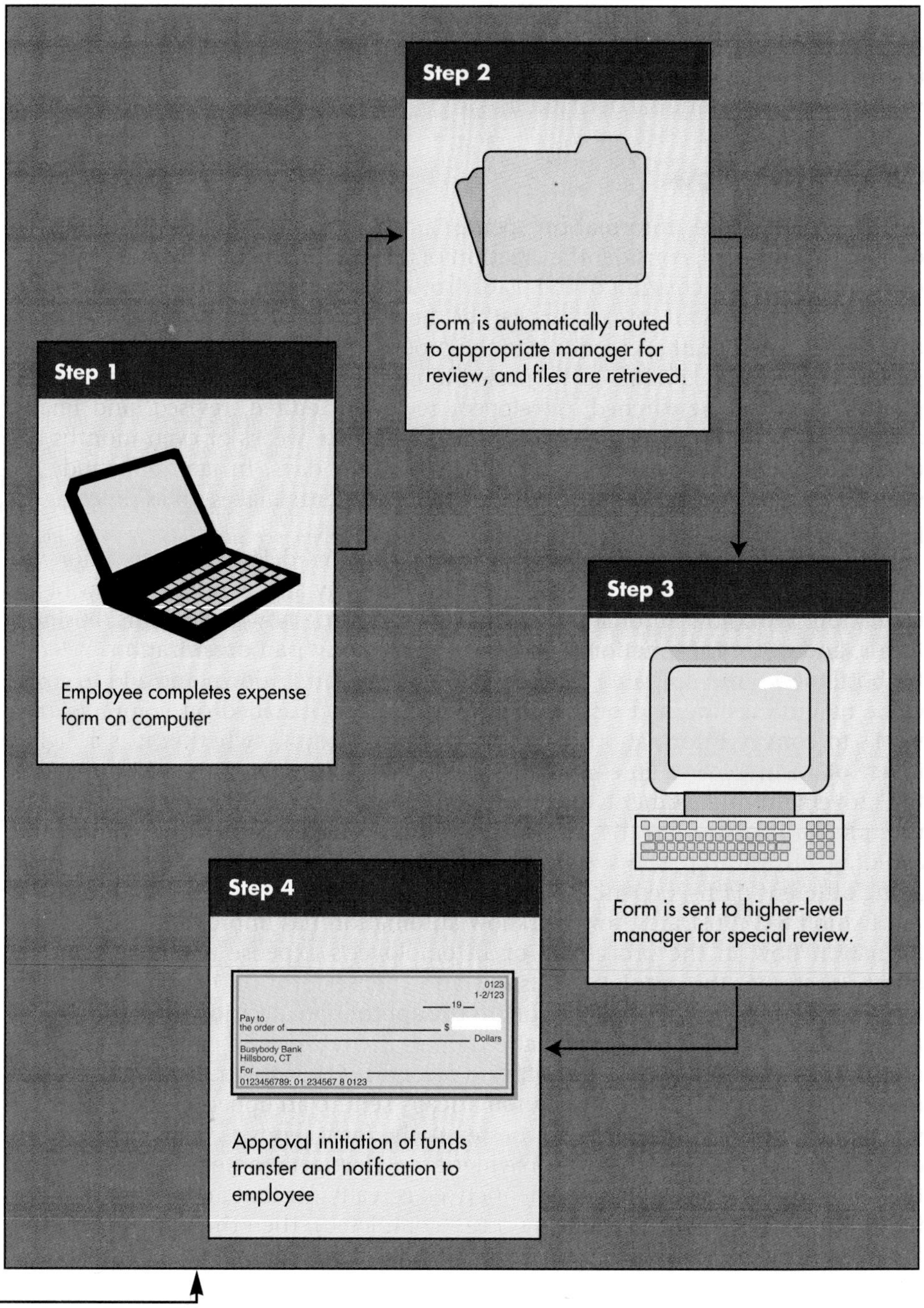

Source: Based on J. W. Verity, "Getting Work to Go with the Flow," *Business Week,* June 21, 1993, p. 156.

EXHIBIT 8-2
Workflow Automation Applied to Expense Reimbursement

aggressively changing all their internal communication systems to the digital format. Why? Analog is slower, less accurate, and prone to interruptions and distortions. Moreover, *any* information can be digitized—numbers, words, voice, or pictures. So, by converting to a completely digital format, organizations will have put in place a system that can permit managers and employees to communicate in any form. Anything can be delivered to any instrument capable of displaying it. A television, for instance, can receive and display computer text, or a radio can receive a phone call.

Now combine digitalization with wireless networks and you have revolutionized internal communications within organizations. Wireless products such as personal digital assistants are going to make it possible for people in organizations to be fully accessible to each other, at any time, regardless of where they are. Employees won't have to be at their desk with their computer plugged in in order to communicate with others in the organization. "I think wireless communications is probably the last communications breakthrough in our lifetimes," says Kenneth Forbes III, president and CEO of MobileDigital Corp. "The ability to reach anyone while I'm mobile in real time without it being intrusive is the closest to thought projection we're going to get."[34] Or, as another executive put it, "The last 100 years have been the wireline century. We have just embarked upon the wireless century."[35]

Wireless products such as personal digital assistants are going to make it possible for people in organizations to be fully accessible to each other, at any time, regardless of where they are.

At the current rate of technological advancement, the digital-wireless organization is not very far away. For some organizations, it exists today. For the rest, we are probably talking about less than 6 or 8 years.

Decision-Making Support

Information technology is providing managers with a wealth of decision support systems. These include expert systems, neural networks, groupware, and specific problem-solving software. **Expert systems** use software programs to encode the relevant experience of a human expert and allow a system to act like that expert in analyzing and solving unstructured problems.[36] The essence of expert systems is that they (1) use specialized knowledge about a particular problem area rather than general knowledge that would apply to all problems, (2) use qualitative reasoning rather than numerical calculations, and (3) perform at a level of competence that is higher than that of nonexpert humans.[37] They guide users through problems by asking them a set of sequential questions about the situation and drawing conclusions based on the answers given. The conclusions are based on programmed rules that have been modeled on the actual reasoning processes of experts who have confronted similar problems before. Once in place, these systems are allowing operative employees and lower-level managers to make high-quality decisions that previously could have been made only by senior managers. Expert systems are being used in such diverse areas as medical diagnosis, mineral and oil exploration, equipment-fault locating, credit approvals, and financial planning.[38] For instance, IDS Financial Services has encoded the expertise of its best financial-planning account managers in an expert-systems program. "Now even the worst of our 6,500 planners is better than our average planner used to be," said the company's chairman.[39]

Neural networks are the next step beyond expert systems.[40] They use computer software to imitate the structure of brain cells and connections among them. Neural networks have the ability to discern patterns and trends too subtle or complex for human beings. For instance, people cannot easily assimilate more than two or three variables at once, but neural networks can perceive correlations among hundreds of variables. As a result, they can perform many operations simultaneously, recognizing patterns, making associations, generalizing about problems they haven't been exposed to before, and learning through experience.

SUMMARY

(This summary is organized by the chapter-opening learning objectives on page 223.)

1. By substituting computerized equipment and machinery for human labor and traditional machinery, technology allows organizations to achieve increased levels of output with less labor, capital, and materials.
2. Computer-aided design has essentially made manual drafting obsolete. It allows designers to create and evaluate alternative designs quickly and dramatically cut the costs of developing prototypes.
3. Flexible manufacturing systems provide management with the technology to meet customers' unique demands by producing nonstandardized products, but with the efficiency associated with standardization.
4. The three key elements of reengineering are: (1) identifying an organization's distinctive competencies—the unique skills and resources that determine an organization's competitive weapons; (2) assessing core processes—these are the processes that customers value; and (3) reorganizing horizontally by process—flattening the structure and relying more on teams.
5. Expert systems, neural networks, groupware, and specific managerial problem-solving software are examples of information technologies that have been created to support and improve organizational decision making.
6. The five key dimensions in a job are skill variety, task identity, task significance, autonomy, and feedback.
7. Managers can design individual jobs to maximize employee performance by combining tasks, creating natural work units, establishing client relationships, expanding jobs vertically, and opening feedback channels.
8. Flextime, job sharing, and telecommuting increase organizational flexibility. Flextime allows employees some discretion in choosing their work hours. Job sharing allows the organization to hire people who might not be available on a full-time basis and gives the organization two heads for the price of one. Telecommuting cuts the costs of maintaining a permanent work area for an employee and increases employee flexibility by cutting out commuting time and allowing workers to better balance work and family responsibilities.

REVIEW AND DISCUSSION QUESTIONS

1. Explain how just-in-time systems improve productivity.
2. Describe how technology can improve an organization's customer service.
3. How might the Internet change organizations and management practice?
4. Contrast reengineering and TQM.
5. How do you think information technology will have reshaped the office by the year 2010?
6. What downside, if any, do you see for (a) the organization and (b) employees from using computerized technology to replace the human element?
7. What are the implications of worker obsolescence on (a) society, (b) management practice, and (c) you, as an individual, planning a career?
8. "Everyone wants a job that scores high on the five JCM dimensions." Build an argument to support this statement. Then negate that argument.
9. What can management do to improve employees' perceptions that their jobs are interesting and challenging?
10. Many managers see job sharing as a burden—something that just makes their job more difficult. Why? What, if anything, can be done to minimize this disadvantage of job sharing?

CASE EXERCISE A
TERRY GALINSKY LOOKS BACK TO THE FUTURE

Terry Galinsky joined Hewlett-Packard in 1982, fresh out of college with her B.S. in electrical engineering. By 1986, she was a production supervisor. Today she heads up a design team. I asked Terry to look back to 1986 and describe how technology had influenced her job and to compare her job then with her job in 1996.

We were a hierarchical company back then. I ran a department with fifteen people. I spent a lot of time in meetings and committees. Communications tended to closely follow the chain of command. We got weekly newsletters from upper management that kept us informed of the lastest happenings. And, since changes came slower in those days, we were better able to prepare for them. For instance, the life of an HP printer model in those days was probably 4 years. Today it's more like 12 to 18 months. We had a lot more time back in the '80s to adjust to anticipated changes. Now they come at us a mile a minute.

Back in '86, I was a department manager. Now I'm a project team leader. Membership on my team is fluid. People come and go. Some months I have twenty people on my team; other months there are only ten or twelve. And the biggest difference is undoubtedly due to the networking of our computers. It was very different back in the '80s. Our individual computers weren't networked. I relied heavily on weekly reports that the centralized systems department created for me. Now I can get that information myself, in less than a minute, by accessing our central databases. And people who worked for me in those days were geographically consolidated together so I could directly supervise them. Today, my team members are spread all over the place. But we are able to communicate as if we're all in the same room because of the development of linking software.

Questions

1. Project into the future. Describe the technological advances you think will realistically develop by the year 2006 that could reshape the manager's job.
2. Now specifically describe how those technological advances in 2006 might likely change Terry Galinsky's job.

CASE EXERCISE B
THE GREYHOUND EXPERIENCE WITH REENGINEERING: A REAL DOG!

Greyhound Lines Inc. benefited greatly when its new management team sought to reengineer the company. But the benefit was not in any fundamental improvement in the organization. The only thing that really benefited was the company's stock and then only in the short term. The following highlights a 3 year period in the life of Greyhound.

Our story begins in October 1991. Greyhound was emerging from bankruptcy brought on by a decline in the bus industry. For instance, because of increased automobile ownership and discounted airline seats, the bus industry's share of interstate travel dropped from 30 percent to 6 percent between 1960 and 1990. The company was now being largely run by CEO Frank Schmieder, a former merchant banker, and the company's chief financial officer, J. Michael Doyle.

Schmieder and Doyle believed that Greyhound could survive only by undertaking a massive reorganization. So that's what they did. They began by cutting the work force, cutting routes and services, and reducing the bus fleet by one-third. Then they committed the company to "Trips," a custom-designed computerized reservation system. Wall Street was so impressed by management's reengineering plan that the company's stock more than doubled in the first month following emergence from bankruptcy.

But there were problems aplenty that Wall Street never saw. (As one observer noted, Wall Street types don't take the bus. They didn't see any problems. All they knew was the rosy picture that management was painting.) What were those problems? Lousy customer service and a failed reservation system top the list. Cutbacks had quickly hurt customer service. Experienced regional executives were being fired and replaced with part-time workers and "customer-service associates," who, whether sweeping floors or selling tickets, were paid about $6 an hour. Management reasoned that if people stayed too long, they would get sour and cynical. The result: Turnover approached 100 percent annually. And customer surveys began regularly identifying employee discourtesy as a major problem. Random checks by management, for instance, found workers making fun of customers and ignoring them.

Meanwhile, as ridership faltered and customer service deteriorated, management and Wall Street analysts spoke as if a turnaround was a sure thing. Trips was the primary source of this optimism. Trips would replace Greyhound's antiquated manual methods for allocating buses and drivers. It would dramatically increase productivity and cut operating costs. At least that's what was promised. But the Trips development team was unable to deal with the program's complexity and management's pressure to bring the system on line. Technicians estimated that the system had to be capable of managing as many as 1,800 vehicle stops a day, more than ten times those of the average airline. And, whereas American Airlines had spent nearly 30 years and several hundred million dollars perfecting its Sabre reservation system, Greyhound's management provided its development team only $6 million to do the job and expected it to be up and running within 2 years, by April 1993. The team did the best it could to meet management's unrealistic deadline. But, not surprisingly, the final product was a disaster. It took far more training than workers were given; it did not include all Greyhound destinations; and, because of the data overload, the system regularly crashed. The typical time it took a worker to issue a ticket doubled.

Meanwhile, during all this chaos, Wall Street analysts were still optimistic—more out of ignorance than anything else. Greyhound stock continued to rise throughout 1992 and into the summer of 1993. The stock's demise began only in August 1993, when the company announced that ridership had fallen 12 percent in the previous month and earnings were down. Schmieder was forced to resign later that month; 3 weeks later Doyle resigned. And from a high of $22.75 a share in May 1993, the company's stock was selling for just over $2 a share by October 1994. As one bondholder put it, "They [Greyhound's management] reengineered that business to hell."

Questions

1. "There is a knee-jerk tendency these days to applaud anything resembling 'reengineering.' Comprehensive change is seen as always good." Relate this comment to the Greyhound case.
2. Are reengineering and first-rate customer service compatible goals? Discuss.
3. If you had been the CEO at Greyhound, would you have done anything differently than Schmieder did? Explain.
4. What implications are there, if any, from this case for implementing reengineering?

Source: R. Tomsho, "How Greyhound Lines Re-Engineered Itself Right into a Deep Hole," *Wall Street Journal,* October 20, 1994, p. A1. Reprinted by permission of the *Wall Street Journal,*

SKILL EXERCISE

Designing Motivating Jobs

Break into groups of four or five. You are a consulting team that has been hired by Citibank to help solve a motivation/performance problem.

Citibank employs several hundred people in its back office. These employees process all the company's financial transactions. Their jobs have been split up so that each person performs a single, routine task over and over again. Employees have become dissatisfied with these mundane jobs, and their dissatisfaction shows in their work. Severe backlogs have developed, and error rates are unacceptably high. Your team's task is to (a) redesign these jobs in order to resolve the problems and (b) identify how your changes are likely to affect the jobs of supervisors in this department.

Your team has 30 minutes to complete this task.

NOTES

1. H. Plotkin, "Riches to Rags," *INC. Technology,* Summer 1995, pp. 62–67.
2. E. E. Adam Jr. and R. J. Ebert, *Production & Operations Management,* 5th ed. (Englewood Cliffs, N.J.: Prentice Hall, 1992), p. 46.
3. P. Engardio, "There's More Than One Way to Play Leapfrog," in *21st Century Capitalism, Business Week,* special issue, November 18, 1994, pp. 162–65.
4. Adam and Ebert, *Production & Operations Management,* 5th ed., p. 137.
5. J. Teresko, "Speeding the Product Development Cycle," *Industry Week,* July 18, 1988, p. 41.
6. G. Bylinsky, "The Digital Factory," *Fortune,* November 14, 1994, pp. 96–100.
7. J. E. Halpert, "One Car, Worldwide, with Strings Pulled from Michigan," *New York Times,* August 29, 1993, p. F7.
8. P. Fuhrman, "New Way to Roll," *Forbes,* April 24, 1995, pp. 180–82.
9. G. Bock, "Limping Along in Robot Land," *Time,* July 13, 1987, p. 55.
10. N. Gross, "Why They Call Japan 'Robot Paradise,'" *Business Week,* August 20, 1990, p. 93.
11. See, for instance, E. H. Hall Jr., "Just-in-Time Management: A Critical Assessment," *The Executive,* November 1989, pp. 315–18.
12. J. Flint, "King Lear," *Forbes,* May 22, 1995, pp. 43–44.
13. See, for instance, O. Port, "Moving Past the Assembly Line," in *Reinventing America, Business Week,* special issue, November 1992, pp. 177–80; D. M. Upton, "The Management of Manufacturing Flexibility," *California Management Review,* Winter 1994, pp. 72–89; Bylinsky, "The Digital Factory"; and N. Gross and P. Coy, "The Technology Paradox," *Business Week,* March 6, 1995, pp. 76–84.
14. S. Moffat, "Japan's New Personalized Production," *Fortune,* October 22, 1990, p. 44.
15. S. M. Silverman, "Retail Retold," *INC. Technology,* Summer 1995, pp. 23–24.
16. B. Ives and R. O. Mason, "Can Information Technology Revitalize Your Customer Service?" *The Executive,* November 1990, pp. 52–69.
17. Ibid.
18. See, for instance, S. Dentzer, "Death of the Middleman?" *U.S. News & World Report,* May 22, 1995, p. 56.
19. See, for instance, J. W. Verity, "Planet Internet," *Business Week,* April 3, 1995, pp. 118–24; and B. Ziegler, "In Cyberspace the Web Delivers Junk Mail," *Wall Street Journal,* June 13, 1995, p. B1.
20. "The Internet: Instant Access to Information," *Canadian Business,* May 1995, pp. 41–43.
21. See, for example, T. H. Berry, *Managing the Total Quality Transition* (New York: McGraw-Hill, 1991); D. Ciampa, *Total Quality* (Reading, Mass.: Addison-Wesley, 1992); W. H. Schmidt and J. P. Finnegan, *The Race without a Finish Line* (San Francisco: Jossey-Bass, 1992); and T. B. Kinni, "Process Improvement," *Industry Week,* January 23, 1995, pp. 52–58.
22. M. Sashkin and K. J. Kiser, *Putting Total Quality Management to Work* (San Francisco: Berrett-Koehler, 1993), p. 44.
23. T. F. O'Boyle, "A Manufacturer Grows Efficient by Soliciting Ideas from Employees," *Wall Street Journal,* June 5, 1992, p. A1.
24. M. Hammer and J. Champy, *Re-engineering the Corporation: A Manifesto for Business Revolution* (New York: HarperBusiness, 1993). See also J. Champy, *Reengineering Management: The Mandate for New Leadership* (New York: HarperBusiness, 1995); and M. Hammer and S. A. Stanton, *The Reengineering Revolution* (New York: HarperBusiness, 1995).
25. R. Karlgaard, "ASAP Interview: Mike Hammer," *Forbes ASAP,* September 13, 1993, p. 70.
26. Ibid.
27. "The Age of Reengineering," *Across the Board,* June 1993, pp. 26–33.
28. Ibid., p. 29.
29. Ibid., p. 33.
30. R. Hotch, "In Touch through Technology," *Nation's Business,* January 1994, pp. 33–35.
31. This section is based on J. W. Verity, "Getting Work to Go with the Flow," *Business Week,* June 21, 1993, pp. 156–61.
32. Study conducted by Delphi Consulting Group and cited in J. W. Verity, "Getting Work to Go with the Flow," p. 156.

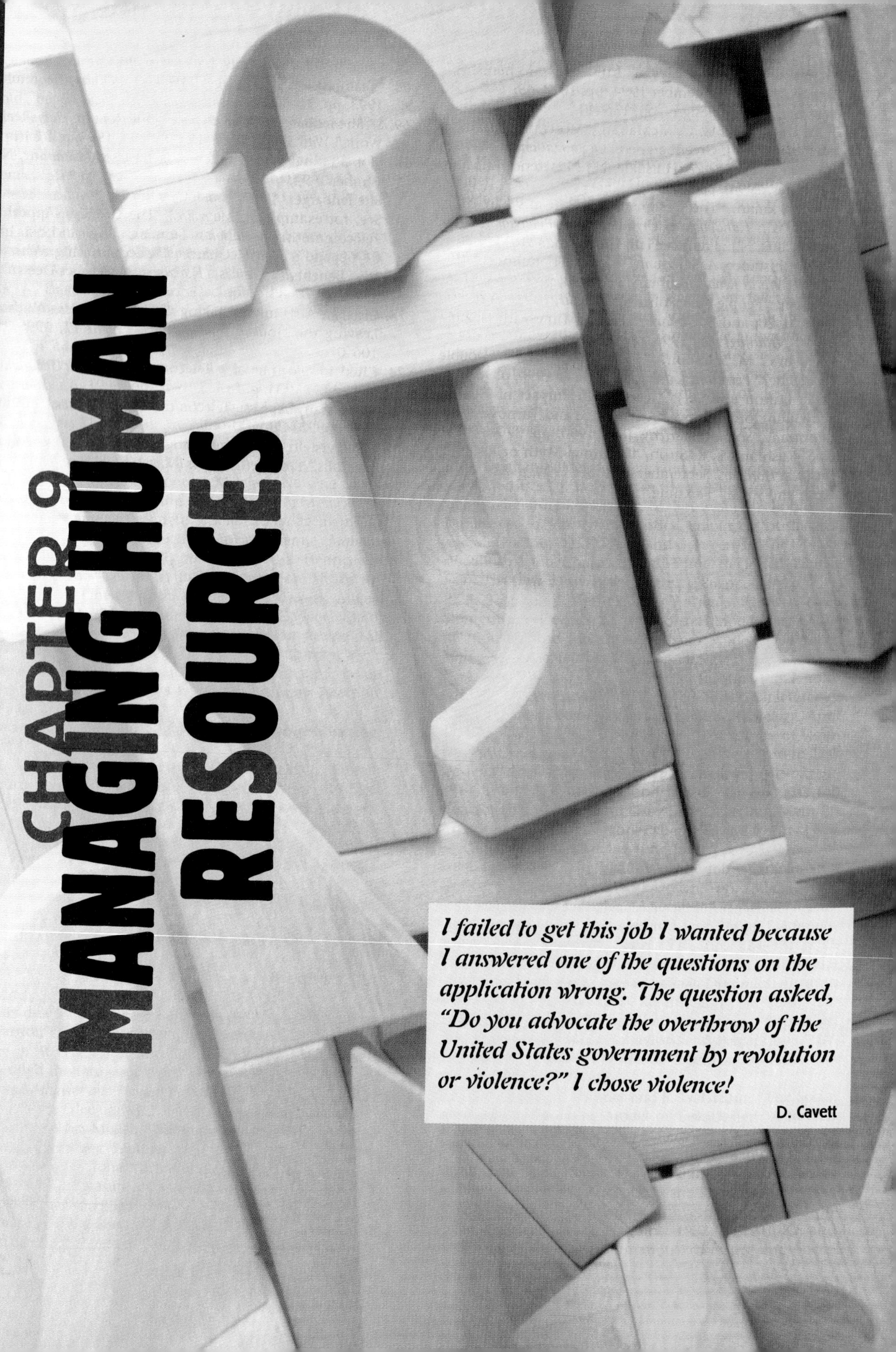

CHAPTER 9
MANAGING HUMAN RESOURCES

I failed to get this job I wanted because I answered one of the questions on the application wrong. The question asked, "Do you advocate the overthrow of the United States government by revolution or violence?" I chose violence!

D. Cavett

LEARNING OBJECTIVES

After studying this chapter, you should be able to:

1. Contrast job analysis, job descriptions, and job specifications
2. Explain why selection devices must be valid and reliable
3. Describe the relationship between IQ and job performance
4. Identify the strengths and weaknesses of the interview as a selection device
5. Describe the four general skills that training can improve
6. Explain the primary methods for appraising employee performance
7. Define sexual harassment and how organizations can limit its occurence

Chris Kerbow, a manager at the Schaumburg (Illinois) Marriott Hotel, rejects 90 percent of the applicants he gets for the job of guest service associate (GSA).[1] The $10 an hour (including tips) position is a multitask job that combines the work that used to be done by four or five people. As one GSA (see photo inset) described his job, "I'm a bellman, a doorman, a front-desk clerk, and a concierge all rolled into one."

"It's not easy finding . . . people" to do the GSA job, according to Kerbow. "But we're willing to be patient." He's looking for candidates who are bright, self-reliant, resourceful, and able to solve problems quickly. "We want associates who can look you in the eye, carry on a conversation, and work well under stress," says another manager. In short, Marriott is looking for a set of skills in its GSAs that once were demanded only of managers.

Marriott not only wants to hire new GSAs with good interpersonal and problem-solving skills; Marriott is also concerned with hiring people who will stay with the company. Marriott historically loses about 60 percent of its frontline staffers at its hotels and resorts every year. And management estimates that it costs as much as $1,100 to recruit and train each replacement. The total bill runs into the millions each year. According to a vice president of human resources, "When someone leaves, it messes up your employee teams, messes up your productivity, and messes up the service you provide to your guests."

To help identify qualified and committed candidates for its service jobs, Marriott is using a specially developed computer software program. Applicants sit down at a company PC and take a 15-minute self-administered test. Why, the computer asks, did you leave your last job? How would you rate your performance? How often do you get frustrated at work? How well do you get along with superiors? How would you rate your organizational skills? Do other people say you're flexible? Answers to these and other questions are then analyzed by the software and generate a set of specific questions for an interviewer to ask the applicant. Marriott's management finds that people seem to be more candid with a computer than they are with real-live interviewers. Says a human resources director, "They might tell me they intend to work here for 3 to 5 years, but they'll tell the computer they plan to leave after 3 months."

Marriott's management attributes its reduction in employee turnover to the computerized selection technique. Before the system was installed, more than 40 percent of new employees who left Marriott departed during the first 3 months on the job. With the help of computerized selection, that proportion has been steadily falling. The net result: Marriott's management believes it now is selecting more-capable service employees, reducing turnover, and cutting its hiring and training costs.

In today's organizations, where 70 percent of workers are engaged in service jobs and management is aggressively redesigning work to expand employee responsibilities, human resource management (HRM) becomes a critical determinant of an organization's effectiveness. Finding, selecting, and keeping highly qualified employees can become a source of sustained competitive advantage.[2] For instance, companies such as Wal-Mart, Southwest Airlines, Mazda, Federal Express, Nordstrom, Lincoln Electric, the Walt Disney Co., W.L. Gore & Associates, and furniture maker Herman Miller have found that well-designed selection and training programs give them a superior work force and a distinct competitive edge against their rivals.

In this chapter we'll describe the HRM process, provide you with some specific guidelines for managing human resources, and discuss a number of contemporary HRM issues currently challenging many managers. First, however, let's look at the role of the everyday manager in HRM.

MANAGERS AND THE HUMAN RESOURCES DEPARTMENT

Some of you may be thinking, "Sure, human resource decisions are important, but aren't they made by people in human resources departments? These aren't decisions that *all* managers are involved in!" It's true that, in large organizations, a number of the activities grouped under the label of HRM often are done by specialists in human resources (or personnel) departments. However, not all managers work in organizations that have formal HR departments, and even those who do still have to be engaged in some human resource activities.

Every manager is involved with human resource decisions in his or her unit.

Small-business managers are an obvious example of individuals who frequently must do their own hiring without the assistance of an HR department. But even managers in billion dollar corporations are involved in recruiting candidates, reviewing application forms, interviewing applicants, inducting new employees, appraising employee performance, and making decisions about employee training. Whether or not an organization has an HR department, *every* manager is involved with human resource decisions in his or her unit.

THE HUMAN RESOURCE MANAGEMENT PROCESS

Exhibit 9-1 depicts the HRM process in organizations. All HRM policies and practices must comply with the laws and regulations of the country, state, or province in which the organization operates. This aspect is shown in Exhibit 9-1 as the regulatory environment, which is an integral part of the organizational boundaries.

The HRM process actually begins with human resource planning. It is here where management learns whether it will need to hire additional employees (recruitment) or, if overstaffed, lay off employees (decruitment). Recruitment leads to attempting to select the best applicant from among those recruited. Decruitment leads to having some people leave the organization.

The need for training tends to be identified in the selection stage ("This candidate appears capable of doing the job but requires some additional training") or as a result of the performance appraisal ("Jason's appraisal indicates that he needs some additional training to bring his performance level up"). Effective managers should link rewards to performance. But we'll leave that issue until Chapter 13, in our discussion of motivation and rewards.

From a manager's standpoint, HRM's primary issues can be seen as answers to seven questions:

1. What laws and regulations shape HRM practices? (Answered by an understanding of the *regulatory environment*).
2. What are our HRM needs? (Answered by a knowledge of *human resource planning*).
3. Where do I find qualified job candidates? (Answered by *recruitment practices*).

EXHIBIT 9-1 HRM Process in Organizations

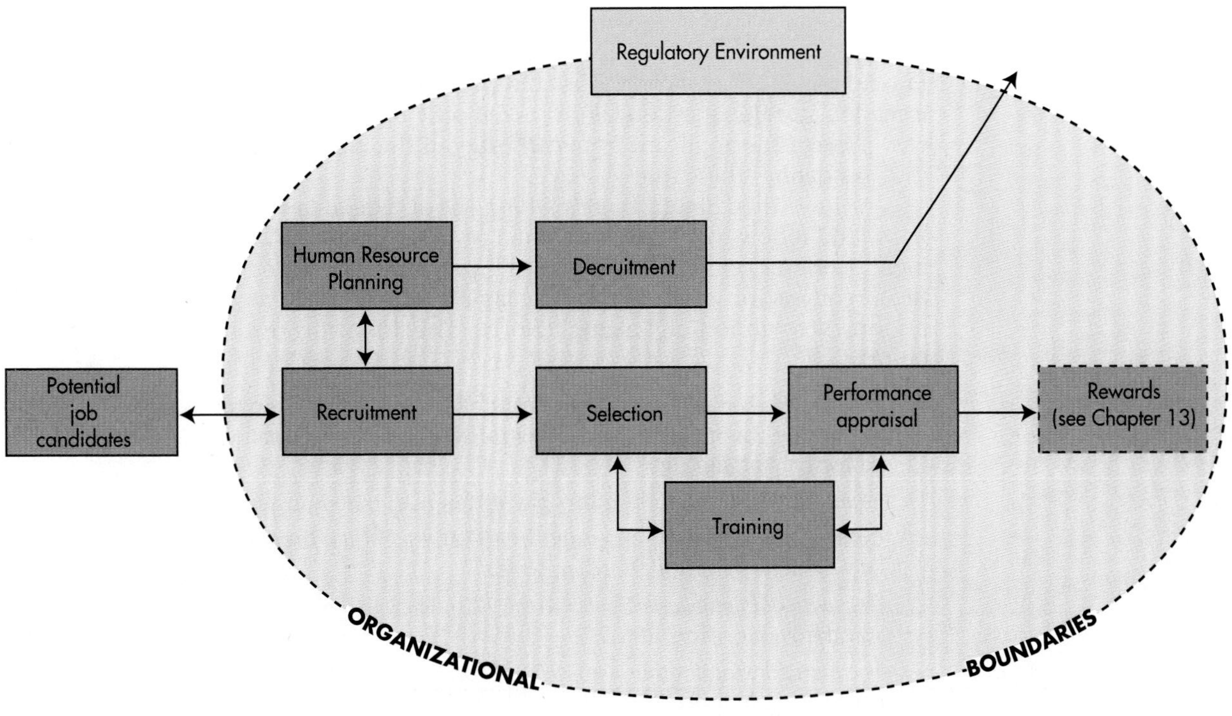

4. How can I choose the best-qualified job candidates? (Answered by *selection techniques*).
5. How can I ensure employee skills are current? (Answered by *training*).
6. What is the best way to evaluate an employee's performance? (Answered by *performance appraisal*).
7. What options exist to handle overstaffing? (Answered by *decruitment* options).

This chapter will provide managers with answers to each of these seven questions. In addition, we'll present a number of contemporary HRM issues with which managers are increasingly being required to deal—sexual harrassment, career development of employees, and unions. Let's begin by reviewing major laws and regulations that guide and shape current HRM practices.

THE REGULATORY ENVIRONMENT: WHAT LAWS AND REGULATIONS SHAPE HRM PRACTICES?

Laws and regulations affecting HRM practices differ from country to country. And, within countries, there are state or provincial and local regulations that further influence specific practices. Consequently, it is impossible to provide you with a full description of the relevant regulatory environment you will face as a manager.

What we can do is remind you that you need to know the laws and regulations that apply in your locale. And, to illustrate our point that laws and regulations shape HRM practices, we can highlight some of the federal legislation that influences HRM practices in the United States, Canada, Australia, and Western Europe.

The United States

You are a manager of a small machine shop operating in Buffalo, New York. Because you're concerned with keeping workers' compensation costs down, you want to know if a job applicant has a history of workers' compensation claims. But did you know you can't ask about previous claims until a conditional job offer is made? And the question can be asked only to determine whether a prior injury may prevent the applicant from carrying out the job. The Americans with Disabilities Act defines these rules.[3]

In the United States, there's a long list of federal laws that managers need to know and follow that apply to human resource practices. They influence management decisions on such issues as hiring procedures, working conditions, pay practices, requests for leaves of absence, lay-off notifications, retirement policies, and responses to union-organizing efforts. The following examples illustrate our point.

National Labor Relations Act (1935). Requires employers to recognize a union chosen by the majority of their employees and established procedures governing collective bargaining.

Equal Pay Act (1963). Prohibits pay differences based on sex for equal work.

Civil Rights Act (1964, amended in 1972). Prohibits discrimination based on race, color, religion, national origin, or sex.

Occupational Safety and Health Act (1970). Establishes mandatory safety and health standards in organizations.

Vocational Rehabilitation Act (1973). Prohibits discrimination on the basis of physical or mental disabilities.

Vietnam-Era Veterans' Readjustment Assistance Act (1974). Prohibits discrimination against disabled veterans and Vietnam-era veterans.

Age Discrimination in Employment Act (1967, amended in 1978 and 1986). Prohibits age discrimination against employees between 40 and 65 years of age and restricts mandatory retirement.

Pregnancy Discrimination Act (1978). Prohibits dismissal of women because of pregnancy alone and protects job security during maternity leaves.

Mandatory Retirement Act (1978). Prohibits the forced retirement of most employees before the age of 70.

Immigration Reform and Control Act (1986). Prohibits employers from knowingly hiring illegal aliens and prohibits employment on the basis of national origin or citizenship.

Worker Adjustment and Retraining Notification Act (1988). Requires employers to provide 60 days' notice before a facility closing or mass layoff.

Employee Polygraph Protection Act (1988). Limits an employer's ability to use lie detectors.

Americans with Disabilities Act (1990). Prohibits employers from discriminating against individuals with physical or mental disabilities or the chronically ill, and requires that "reasonable accommodations" be provided for the disabled.

Civil Rights Act (1991). Reaffirms and tightens prohibition of discrimination; permits individuals to sue for punitive damages in cases of intentional discrimination; and shifts the burden of proof to the employer.

Family and Medical Leave Act (1993). Permits employees in organizations with fifty or more workers to take up to 12 weeks of unpaid leave for family or medical reasons each year.

The above list conveys our point that there are a large number of federal laws that affect HRM practices in the United States. A closer look at this list also reveals that these regulations are in a constate state of flux. New laws and court interpretations continually add to, modify, and delete the list of things managers can and cannot legally do. For instance, in 1995, Congress was beginning to actively discuss the negative ramifications of affirmative action programs on white males and whether some of these programs needed to be dismantled in order to protect this group from discrimination in hiring and promotions.[4] Regardless of whether these changes come about, the message is clear: Organizational practices in the United States relating to personnel issues must be conducted within the laws of the land; there are a large number of these laws, and they change over time; and it is management's responsibility to keep current on these laws and to ensure that they are followed within their organization.

Less than 16 percent of nonagricultural workers in the United States belong to labor unions. In Canada, the comparable figure is 37 percent.

Canada

Canadian laws pertaining to HRM practices closely parallel those in the United States. But Canada's HRM environment is somewhat different from that in the United States. For instance, there is more decentralization of lawmaking to the provincial level in Canada. In addition, unions are more powerful in Canada. Less than 16 percent of nonagricultural workers in the United States belong to labor unions. In Canada, the comparable figure is 37 percent.[5]

The Canadian Human Rights Act provides federal legislation that prohibits discrimination on the basis of race, religion, age, marital status, sex, physical or mental disability, or national origin. This act governs practices throughout the country. Discrimination on the basis of sexual orientation, however, is permissible in Alberta and the Northwest Territories but not in the rest of Canada. Similarly, while employers in Canada cannot discriminate on the basis of marital status, four provinces have laws to limit nepotism. Alberta, New Brunswick, Prince Edward Island, and Newfoundland allow employers to refuse employment to all near relatives except a spouse. And discrimination on the basis of language is not prohibited anywhere in Canada except in Quebec.[6]

Australia

Equal employment opportunity legislation is much more recent in Australia than in the United States.[7] For instance, the United States enacted antidiscrimination legislation with the passage of the Civil Rights Act in 1964. Its origin was essentially to protect American blacks from discriminatory practices, but it also protected women. Australia did not introduce similar antidiscrimination legislation until decades later with the Sex Discrimination Act 1984 and the Affirmative Action (Equal Employment Opportunity for Women) Act 1986. And, although discrimination on racial grounds is outlawed in Australia, the main body of federal laws on discrimination and affirmative action apply only to women. Yet Australia continues to lag behind the United States in widening gender opportunities. As recently as 1990, 59 percent of female workers were employed in only three job categories: clerical, sales/service, and sport/recreation.

As in Canada, labor laws pertaining to unions are more important in Australia than in the United States largely because of the heavy influence of labor unions. Approximately 41 percent of Australian workers are unionized. The high percentage of unionized laborers places increased importance on industrial relations specialists in Australia and reduces the control of line managers over workplace labor issues.

Western Europe

Almost every country in Western Europe has some type of legislation requiring companies to practice **representative participation.** It has been called "the most widely legislated form of employee involvement around the world."[8] The goal of representative participation is to redistribute power within an organization, putting labor on a more equal footing with the interests of management and stockholders.

The two most common forms that representative participation takes are works councils and board representatives. **Works councils** link employees with management. They are groups of nominated or elected employees who must be consulted when management makes decisions involving personnel. For example, in the Netherlands, if a Dutch company is taken over by another firm, the Dutch company's works council must be informed at an early stage, and if the council objects, it has 30 days to seek a court injunction to stop the takeover. **Board representatives** are employees who sit on a company's board of directors and represent the interests of the firm's employees. In some countries, large companies may be legally required to make sure that employee representatives have the same number of board seats as stockholder representatives.

HUMAN RESOURCE PLANNING: WHAT ARE OUR HRM NEEDS?

Human resource planning is the process by which management ensures that it has the right number and kinds of people in the right places, and at the right times, who are capable of effectively and efficiently completing those tasks that will help the organization achieve its overall objectives. Human resource planning, then, translates the organization's objectives into the quantity and mix of workers needed to meet those objectives.[9]

Human resource planning can be condensed into three steps: (1) assessing current human resources, (2) assessing future human resource needs, and (3) developing a program to meet future human resource needs.

Current Assessment

Management typically begins by doing a **job analysis.** This defines the jobs within the organization and the behaviors that are necessary to perform those jobs. For instance, what are the duties of a purchasing specialist, grade 3, who works for International Paper? What minimal knowledge, skills, and abilities are necessary for the adequate performance of a grade 3 purchasing specialist's job? How do the requirements for a purchasing specialist, grade 3, compare with those for a purchasing specialist, grade 2, or a purchasing analyst? These are questions that job analysis can answer.

Information gathering through job analysis allows management to draw up a **job description** and **job specification.** The former is a written statement of what a jobholder does, how it's done, and why it's done. It typically portrays job content, environment, and conditions of employment. The job specification states the minimum acceptable qualifications an incumbent must possess to perform a given job successfully. It identifies the knowledge, skills, and abilities needed to do the job effectively.

The job description and job specification are important documents when managers begin recruiting and selecting new hires. The job description can be used to describe the job to potential candidates. The job specification keeps the manager's attention on the list of qualifications necessary for an incumbent to perform a job and assists in determining whether candidates are qualified.

Future Assessment

Future human resource needs are determined by the organization's objectives and strategies. Demand for human resources is a result of demand for the organization's products or services and levels of productivity. On the basis of its estimate of total revenue, management can attempt to establish the number and mix of human resources needed to reach those revenues. This information is then adjusted to reflect gains or losses in productivity based on changes in technology. For instance, a great deal of the recent personnel cutbacks initiated by large corporations has come about as a result of new technologies. Automated equipment, computerization, reengineering, and process redesign have made it possible for companies to generate greater outputs with less labor input.

Developing a Future Program

After it has assessed both current capabilities and future needs, management is able to estimate shortages—both in number and kind—and to highlight areas in which the organization will be overstaffed. A program can then be developed that matches these estimates with forecasts of future labor supply. So human resource planning not only provides information to guide current staffing needs but also provides projections of future personnel needs and availability.

EXHIBIT 9-2
Major Sources of Potential Job Candidates

Source	Advantages
Current employees	Low cost; build employee morale; candidates are familiar with the organization
Employee referrals	Knowledge about the organization provided by the current employee
Former employees	Rehires know the organization; the organization has historical data about the person's previous performance level
Advertisements	Wide distribution; can be targeted to specific groups
Employment agencies	Wide contacts; careful screening; short-term guarantees often given
College recruiting	Large, centralized body of candidates; good source for entry-level and future-management candidates
Customers and suppliers	Specific industry knowledge; knowledge of your organization; previous contacts might provide insights into candidates' skills and abilities

RECRUITMENT: WHERE DO MANAGERS FIND QUALIFIED JOB CANDIDATES?

If managers find they are understaffed, they need to begin looking for qualified candidates to fill vacancies. **Recruitment** is the process of locating, identifying, and attracting capable applicants.[10]

Where does a manager look to recruit potential candidates? Exhibit 9-2 offers some guidance. Which sources management uses depends on the type or level of the job and the state of the economy.[11] The greater the skill required or the higher the position in the organization's hierarchy, the more the recruitment process will expand to become a regional or national search. And when the unemployment rate is high, organizations find it easier to attract qualified applicants. When unemployment is low, more recruitment sources will typically be needed to fill the applicant pool.

Three recruiting trends have surfaced since the late 1980s. First, organizations are showing more creativity and using more alternative sources in order to increase the diversity of applicants.[12] For instance, to hire more Latinos, Alpine Banks of Colorado ran help-wanted ads printed in Spanish. Other organizations have placed ads in minority papers and magazines, expanded recruiting at women's and historically black colleges, sought the services of minority professional groups, and paid small bonuses to current employees who refer a new minority hire. The second trend is the increased reliance on temporary help firms as a source of new employees.[13] By using temps from companies such as Manpower Inc. to fill positions, an organization increases its flexibility and gets an opportunity to assess a potential permanent employee with minimal commitment.

Organizations are showing more creativity and using more alternative sources in order to increase the diversity of applicants.

Robertshaw Controls, for instance, selects all its permanent hires from its pool of experienced temporaries. Robertshaw's human resources department has taken itself out of the hiring business—anyone walking into the company looking for a job is handed a Manpower application![14] An increasing set of organizations are using temporary positions as the ultimate "job performance test" before hiring anyone as a permanent member of the organization. The final trend is the use of the Internet as a recruiting device. Particularly in the search for candidates with technical and computer-related skills, posting a job vacancy on the Internet can provide wide access to potential candidates. As an illustration, Geometrics Corp., a small imaging-software firm in Wisconsin, posted a job listing for a software engineer on a worldwide electronic-mail bulletin board. The company received 200 résumés—some from as far away as Israel, Germany, and Hong Kong.[15]

Are certain recruiting sources superior to others? More specifically, do certain recruiting sources produce superior candidates? The answer is No. It was long believed that employee referrals were the best candidates because these applicants had more accurate knowledge about organizations and jobs.[16] It was also thought that current employees would only refer others who they were reasonably confident would perform well and thereby make them look good. The most recent research suggests that employee referrals are no more productive or stable than recruits obtained from other sources.[17] At this time, the best advice we can give you, once a final applicant pool has been generated, is to ignore recruitment sources.[18]

SELECTION: HOW CAN MANAGERS CHOOSE THE BEST-QUALIFIED JOB CANDIDATE?

You have developed a set of applicants for your job opening. Now the task before you is to figure out who, among this set, would be the best-qualified candidate so that you can offer him or her a job. This is no easy task. Fortunately, there is a large body of research to help guide you in screening and selecting candidates.[19]

Foundations of Selection

Selection is a prediction exercise. It seeks to predict which applicants will be successful if hired. Successful in this case means performing well on the critieria management uses to evaluate personnel. In filling a sales position, for example, the selection process should be able to predict which applicants will generate a high volume of sales. For a position of software programmer, the criterion might be which applicants will produce the highest quantity of error-free code.

Prediction Consider, for a moment, that any selection decision can result in four possible outcomes. As shown in Exhibit 9-3 on page 266, two of these outcomes would be correct decisions, but two would be errors. A decision is correct when the applicant was accepted and later proved to be successful on the job or when the applicant was rejected and would have performed unsuccessfully if hired.

Problems occur when we make errors by rejecting candidates who would later have performed successfully on the job (reject errors) or by accepting those who subsequently perform poorly (accept errors). These problems are, unfortunately, far from insignificant. Selection techniques that result in reject errors can open the organization to charges of discrimination, especially if applicants from protected groups are disproportionately rejected. Accept errors, on the other hand, have very obvious costs to the organization, including the cost of training the employee, the costs generated or profits forgone because of the employee's incompetence, and the cost of severance and the subsequent costs of further recruiting and selection screening. The major thrust of any selection activity is therefore to

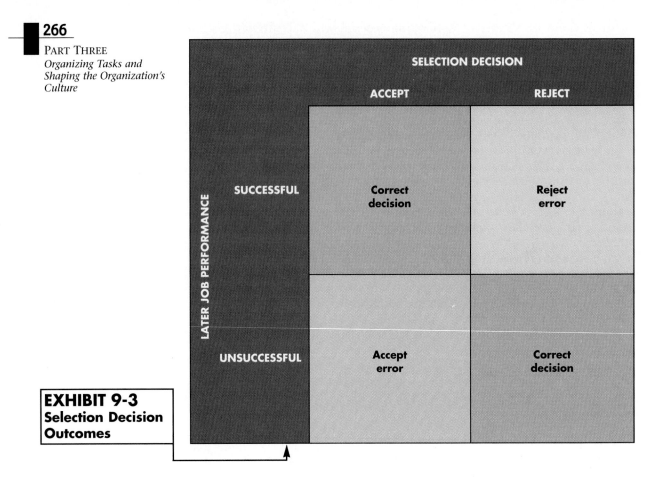

EXHIBIT 9-3
Selection Decision Outcomes

		SELECTION DECISION	
		ACCEPT	REJECT
LATER JOB PERFORMANCE	SUCCESSFUL	Correct decision	Reject error
	UNSUCCESSFUL	Accept error	Correct decision

reduce the probability of making reject errors or accept errors while increasing the probability of making correct decisions.

Validity Any selection device that a manager uses—such as tests or interviews—must demonstrate **validity.** That is, there must be a proven relationship between the selection device and some relevant critierion. For example, U.S. laws prohibit management from using a test score as a selection device unless there is clear evidence that, once on the job, individuals with high scores on this test outperform individuals with low test scores. Thus handwriting analysis is not a valid screening device. Results aren't correlated with job performance criteria![20]

Reliability In addition to being valid, a selection device must also demonstrate reliability. **Reliability** indicates whether the device measures the same thing consistently. For example, if a test is reliable, any single individual's score should remain fairly stable over time, assuming the characteristics it is measuring are also stable.

The importance of reliability should be evident. No selection device can be effective if it is unreliable. Using an unreliable selection device is equivalent to weighing yourself every day on an erratic scale. If the scale is unreliable—randomly fluctuating, say, 5 to 10 pounds every time you step on it—the results won't mean much. To be effective predictors, selection devices must possess an acceptable level of consistency.

Selection Devices

Managers can use a number of selection devices to reduce accept and reject errors. These include application forms, pencil-and-paper tests, performance-simulation

IN THE NEWS

A Good Case for Checking Application Information

THE CONTROLLER AT HATTERAS HAMMOCKS, A $10 MILLION NORTH CAROLINA FIRM, ABRUPTLY QUIT. It fell on the company's executive vice president, Jay Branch, to find a replacement. Branch interviewed several candidates, but one applicant distinguished himself from the others. Recommended by someone Branch knew, he came with a great résumé—B.A. in accounting, M.B.A. from Indiana University, CPA, and several years as controller at a big local corporation.

Branch hired this candidate after a quick call to his previous employer. But after a few months it became obvious that the new controller couldn't do the job. After only 7 months, Branch fired the guy.

The next person Branch hired as controller quickly saw something wrong with the company's books—$60,000 was missing. An audit discovered that the culprit had been the guy with the fancy résumé. A quick background check by Branch turned up no record of either the embezzler's degrees or his CPA credentials.

The embezzler was found, arrested, and confessed. Branch says, "The whole episode taught me the necessity of checking thoroughly, no matter how good a recommendation is."

Source: Based on M. P. Cronin, "This Is a Test," *INC.*, August 1993, p. 64.

tests, and interviews. Let's briefly review each of these devices, giving particular attention to the validity of each in predicting job performance.

The Application Form Almost all organizations require job candidates to fill out an application. It may be only a form on which a prospect gives his or her name, address, and telephone number. At the other extreme, it might be a comprehensive personal history profile, detailing the applicant's education, job experience, skills, and accomplishments.

Hard and relevant biographical data that can be verified—for example, rank in high school graduating class—have shown to be valid measures of performance for some jobs.[21] In addition, when application form items have been appropriately weighted to reflect job relatedness, the device has proved to be a valid predictor for such diverse groups as salesclerks, engineers, factory workers, district managers, clerical employees, and technicians.[22] But, typically, only a couple of items on the application prove to be valid predictors, and then only for a specific job. Use of weighted applications for selection purposes is difficult and expensive because the weights have to be validated for each specific job and must be continually reviewed and updated to reflect changes in weights over time.

Pencil-and-Paper Tests Typical pencil-and-paper tests include tests of intelligence, personality, aptitude, ability, interest, and integrity. Three types of tests arguably have gotten the most attention in recent years—integrity, personality, and intelligence. Integrity tests measure factors such as dependability, carefulness, responsibility, and honesty. But can a pencil-and-paper test really identify people who might, for instance, steal from the organization? The evidence is impressive that these tests are powerful in predicting supervisory ratings of job performance and counterproductive employee behavior on the job such as theft, discipline problems, and excessive absenteeism.[23]

Personality tests are problematic. General personality inventories tend to be weak predictors of an applicant's future job performance when the tests are used with a broad section of jobs.[24] The only personality trait that tends to predict job performance regardless of occupation is *conscientiousness* (reflected in traits such as responsibility, dependability, and persistence).[25] Other personality dimensions can predict job performance, but they need to be used selectively for specific jobs. For instance, an extroverted personality is a valid predictor of job performance in managerial and sales positions; attention to detail has been found to be related to the performance of accountants.[26] Personality inventories that have been carefully validated for specific jobs can be meaningful screening devices.

The issue of intelligence as a job predictor became a headline topic in the fall of 1994 with the publication of Richard Herrnstein and Charles Murray's *The Bell Curve*.[27] This book became one of the most controversial social science books of all time largely because of the authors' claim that economic inequality between racial groups is related to differences in average IQ levels between different races. Unfortunately, that section of the book drowned out the authors' excellent review of the relationship between intelligence and job performance.[28] In the following paragraphs, we'll summarize what we know about this relationship. And as you will see, we know quite a lot!

Smarter employees, on average, are more proficient employees.

Certain facts are beyond significant technical dispute. For instance: (1) IQ scores closely match whatever it is that people mean when they use the word *intelligent* or *smart* in ordinary language; (2) IQ scores are stable, although not perfectly so, over much of a person's life; (3) properly administered IQ tests are not demonstrably biased against social, economic, ethnic, or racial groups; and (4) smarter employees, on average, are more proficient employees.[29]

All jobs require the use of intelligence or cognitive ability. Why? For reasoning and decision making. A high IQ is generally necessary to perform well in jobs that are novel, ambiguous, changing, or multifaceted. This category would include professional occupations such as accountants, engineers, scientists, architects, and physicians. But IQ is also a good predictor in moderately complex jobs such as crafts, clerical, and police work. IQ is a less valid predictor for unskilled jobs that require only routine decision making or simple problem solving.

Intelligence clearly is not the only factor affecting job performance, but it is often the most important! It is, for example, a better predictor of job performance than a job interview, reference checks, or college transcripts. Unfortunately, many U.S. employers have become fearful of using intelligence tests for selecting professional and managerial employees because the courts have generally criticized such tests for lacking job relevance. But the evidence cannot be ignored. As Herrnstein and Murray noted, biographical data, reference checks, and college transcripts are "valid predictors of job performance in part because they imperfectly reflect something about the applicant's intelligence. Employers who are forbidden to obtain test scores nonetheless strive to obtain the best possible work force, and it so happens that the way to get the best possible work force, other things equal, is to hire the smartest people they can find."[30]

Performance-Simulation Tests Performance-simulation tests have increased significantly in popularity during the past two decades. Undoubtedly the enthusiasm for these tests comes from the fact that they are based on job analysis data and, therefore, should more easily meet the requirement of job relatedness than do written tests. Performance-simulation tests are made up of actual job behaviors rather than surrogates, as are written tests. The two best-known performance-simulation tests are work sampling and assessment centers. The former is suited to routine jobs, whereas the latter is relevant for the selection of managerial personnel.

Work sampling is an effort to create a miniature replica of a job. Applicants demonstrate that they possess the necessary talents by actually doing the tasks. Carefully devised work samples based on job analysis data determine the knowledge, skills, and abilities needed for each job. Then each work sample element is matched with a job performance element. For instance, a work sample for a job in which the employee has to use computer spreadsheet software would require the applicant to actually solve a problem using a spreadsheet. The results from work sample experiments are impressive. Studies almost consistently demonstrate that work samples yield validities superior to written aptitude and personality tests.[31]

A more elaborate set of performance-simulation tests, specifically designed to evaluate a candidate's managerial potential, is administered in **assessment centers.** In assessment centers, line executives, supervisors, or trained psychologists evaluate candidates as they go through 2 to 4 days of exercises that simulate real problems that they would confront on the job. Based on a list of descriptive dimensions that the actual job incumbent has to meet, activities might include interviews, in-basket problem-solving exercises, group discussions, and business decision games. For instance, a candidate might be required to play the role of a manager who must decide how to respond to ten memos in his or her in-basket within a 2-hour period.

How valid is the assessment center as a selection device? The evidence on the effectiveness of assessment centers is extremely impressive. They have consistently demonstrated results that accurately predict later job performance in managerial positions.[32]

Interviews In Korea, Japan, and many other Asian countries, employee interviews traditionally have not been part of the selection process. Decisions were made almost entirely on the basis of exam scores, scholastic accomplishments, and letters of recommendation. This is not the case, however, throughout most of the world. It's probably correct to say that most of us don't know anyone who has gotten a job without at least one interview. You may have an acquaintance who got a part-time or summer job through a close friend or relative without having to go through an interview, but such instances are rare. Of all the selection devices that organizations use to differentiate candidates, the interview continues to be the one most frequently used.[33] Even companies in Asian countries have begun to rely on employee interviews as a screening device.[34]

Not only is the interview widely used, it also seems to carry a great deal of weight. That is, its results tend to have a disproportionate amount of influence on the selection decision. The candidate who performs poorly in the employment interview is likely to be cut from the applicant pool, regardless of his or her experience, test scores, or letters of recommendation. Conversely, "all too often, the person most polished in job-seeking techniques, particularly those used in the interview process, is the one hired, even though he or she may not be the best candidate for the position."[35]

These findings are important because of the unstructured manner in which the selection interview is frequently conducted. The unstructured interview—short in duration, casual, and made up of random questions—has been proven to be an ineffective selection device.[36] The data gathered from such interviews are typically biased and often unrelated to future job performance. Without structure, a number of biases can distort results. These biases include interviewers' tending to favor applicants who share their attitudes, giving unduly high weight to negative information, and allowing the order in which applicants are interviewed to influence evaluations.[37] Having interviewers use a standardized set of questions, providing interviewers with a uniform method of recording information, and standardizing the rating of the applicant's qualifications reduce the variability in results among applicants and enhance validity of the interview as a selection device.

The evidence indicates that interviews are most valuable for assessing an applicant's intelligence, level of motivation, and interpersonal skills.[38] When these qualities are related to job performance, the validity of the interview as a selection device is increased. For example, these qualities have demonstrated relevance for performance in upper managerial positions. This relationship may explain why applicants for senior management positions typically undergo dozens of interviews with executive recruiters, board members, and other company executives before a final decision is made. It can also explain why organizations that design work around teams may similarly put applicants through an unusually large number of interviews.

One final benefit from selection interviews needs to be mentioned—they offer the opportunity for management to give prospective employees a realistic preview of the organization and the job vacancy.[39] The typical interviewer tends to paint an overly positive image of a job when he or she is trying to "sell" it to an attractive candidate. Unfortunately, this tendency often builds unrealistic expectations that lead to disappointment and premature resignations. To improve applicants' future job satisfaction and reduce turnover, interviewers should give them a **realistic job preview**—that is, provide candidates with both unfavorable and favorable information before an offer is made. For example, in addition to positive comments, the candidate might be told that there are limited opportunities to talk

SELECTION INTERVIEWING SKILLS

The interview is made up of four stages. *Preparation* is followed by the *opening,* a period of *questioning and discussion,* and a *conclusion.*[40]

1. *Preparation.* Before meeting the applicant, you should review his or her application form and résumé. You also should review the job description and job specification for the position for which the applicant is interviewing.

   Next, structure the agenda for the interview. Specifically, use the standardized questions provided to you, or prepare a set of questions you want to ask the applicant. Choose questions that can't be answered with merely a Yes or a No. Inquiries that begin with *how* or *why* tend to stimulate extended answers. Avoid leading questions that telegraph the desired response (such as "Would you say you have good interpersonal skills?") and bipolar questions that require the applicant to select an answer from only two choices (such as "Do you prefer working with people or working alone?"). Don't ask questions that aren't relevant to the job. In most cases, questions relating to marital and family status, age, race, religion, sex, ethnic background, credit rating, and arrest record are prohibited by law in the United States unless you can demonstrate that they are in some way related to job performance. So avoid them. In place of asking "Are you married?" or "Do you have children?", you might ask "Are there any reasons why you might not be able to work overtime several times a month?" Of course, to avoid discrimination, you have to ask this question of both male and female candidates. Since the best predictor of future behavior is past behavior, the best questions tend to be those that focus on previous experiences that are relevant to the current job. Examples might include: "What have you done in previous jobs that demonstrates your creativity?" "On your last job, what was it that you most wanted to accomplish but didn't? Why didn't you?"
2. *Opening.* Assume that the applicant is tense and nervous. If you're going to get valid insights into what the applicant is really like, you'll need to put him or her at ease. Introduce yourself. Be friendly. Begin with a few simple questions or statements that can break the ice: for example, "Did you run into much traffic coming over?"

   Once the applicant is fairly relaxed, you should provide a brief orientation. Preview what topics will be discussed, how long the interview will take, and explain if you'll be taking notes. Encourage the applicant to ask questions.
3. *Questioning and discussion.* The questions you developed during the preparation stage will provide a general road map to guide you. Make sure you cover them all. Additional questions should arise from the answers to the standardized questions. Select follow-up questions that naturally flow from the answers given.

   Follow-up questions should seek to probe deeper into what the applicant says. If you feel that the applicant's response is superficial or inadequate, seek elaboration. Ask a question such as, "Tell me more about that issue." To clarify information, you could

(continues)

say, "You said working overtime was OK *sometimes*. Can you tell me specifically when you'd be willing to work overtime?" If the applicant doesn't directly answer your question, follow up by repeating the question or paraphrasing it. Finally, never underestimate the power of silence in an interview. One of the biggest errors that inexperienced interviewers make is that they talk too much. You're not learning anything about the candidate when you're doing the talking. Pause for at least a few seconds after the applicant appears to have finished an answer. Your silence encourages the applicant to continue talking.

4. *Concluding*. Once you're through with the questions and discussions, you're ready to wrap up the interview. Let the applicant know this fact with a statement like, "Well, that covers all the questions I have. Do you have any questions about the job or our organization that I haven't answered for you?" Then let the applicant know what's going to happen next. When can he or she expect to hear from you? Will you write or phone? Are there likely to be more follow-up interviews?

   Before you consider the interview complete, write your evaluation while it is fresh in your mind. Ideally, you kept notes or recorded the applicant's answers to your questions and made comments of your impressions. Now that the applicant is gone, take the time to assess the applicant's responses.

with co-workers during work hours or that erratic fluctuations in work load create considerable stress on employees during rush periods. Comparisons of turnover rates between organizations that use the realistic job preview versus either no preview or presentation of only positive job information show that those not using the realistic job preview have, on average, almost 29 percent higher turnover.[41]

TRAINING: HOW CAN MANAGERS ENSURE EMPLOYEE SKILLS ARE CURRENT?

Training can make a real difference in an organization's bottom line. Just ask the executives at Pratt & Whitney's Turbine Airfoils division.[42] In August 1993, when Willie T. Kearney took over as manager of communication, education, and training, the division was barely surviving. Quality and productivity were poor, teamwork among the 1,500 employees was nonexistent, and morale was extremely low. More than $83 million worth of products had been sold but not delivered because of shoddy work practices.

Kearney hit the ground running in his new job. He was determined to improve employee skills, starting with basic literacy. Why? He found that 15 percent of the division's work force read below the fourth-grade level, and another 5 percent spoke English as a second language. Kearney immediately instituted a comprehensive training program. It covered the basic literacy skills of reading, writing, and arithmetic. It also included training in communication, job skills, empowerment, teamwork, company finances, and cross-training for flexibility in job assignments. All the training took place on company time and was individualized to focus on specific employee deficiencies. In little over a year, Kearney could proudly point out some spectacular results from this training effort. Productivity jumped 47 percent; cycle time was reduced by 50 percent; quality improved 89 percent; and inventories were cut by 30 percent. Moreover, the value of products sold but not delivered had plummeted to less than $6 million. Kearney's training programs helped employees feel good about themselves, about their co-workers, and about the company.

The Increasing Importance of Training

As Willie Kearney demonstrated at Pratt & Whitney, money spent on training can provide big returns to management. This may be truer today than at any time in the past century. Intensified competition, technological changes, and the search for improved productivity are increasing skill demands on employees. A recent U.S. study, for instance, found that 57 percent of employers reported that employee skill requirements had increased over a 3-year period and that only 20 percent of employees were fully proficient in their jobs.[43] Skills deteriorate and can become obsolete. Engineers need to update their knowledge of mechanical and electrical systems. Hourly workers, many now working in teams, require problem-solving, quality improvement, and team-building skills. Clerical personnel need to take courses to learn how to fully utilize the latest software programs on their computers. And executives recognize that they have to become more effective leaders and planners. These developments explain why U.S. corporations with 100 or more employees spent $52.2 billion in one recent year on formal training for 47.3 million workers.[44] And why Xerox spent over $300 million a year on training and retraining its employees[45]; and why Motorola has made a commitment to lifelong employee learning, which by the year 2000 will quadruple the current 40 hours a year a typical Motorola employee spends in training.[46]

Assessing Training Needs

Ideally, employees and managers alike should be continually undergoing training to keep their skills current. In reality, few organizations have made a commitment to providing their staff with continual learning, nor do employees voluntarily take the initiative to seek out training opportunities. In most organizations, training is provided on an "as-needed" basis, and the decision as to when that need arises lies with individual managers. So, if you're a manager, what signals do you look for that might suggest an employee is in need of training? Here are a few suggestions:

- New equipment or processes are introduced that may affect an employee's job.
- A change is made in the employee's job responsibilities.
- There is a drop in an employee's productivity or in the quality of his or her output.
- There is an increase in safety violations or accidents.

Workers undergoing training in Tempe, Arizona, at Motorola. In this photo, they're discussing circuits.

- The number of questions employees ask you or their colleagues increases.
- Complaints by customers or co-workers increases.

If you see any of these signs, should you automatically assume that the solution is increased training? Not necessarily! Training is only one response to a performance problem. If the problem is lack of motivation, a poorly designed job, or external conditions, training is not likely to offer much help. For example, training is not likely to be the answer if a performance deficiency is caused by low salaries, inadequate benefits, a lingering illness, or the trauma of layoffs associated with corporate downsizing.

When you have determined that training is necessary, specify training goals.[47] What explicit changes or results do you expect the training to achieve? These goals should be clear to both you and the employee. For instance, the new service assistant at a Kinko's Copy Center is expected to be able to (1) use all photocopying equipment, (2) be able to enlarge and shrink copies, (3) send and receive domestic and international facsimiles, (4) operate the passport photo machine, (5) operate and answer technical questions about the Macintosh computer rentals, (6) answer all technical questions regarding photo processing and differences in paper quality and (7) operate the cash register and make change. These goals then guide the design of the training program and can be used after the program is complete to assess its effectiveness.

Types of Training

Training can include everything from teaching employees basic reading skills to advanced courses in executive leadership. The following summarizes four general skill categories—basic literacy, technical, interpersonal, and problem solving—where most training is focused.

Basic Literacy Skills A recent report by the U.S. Department of Education found that 90 million American adults have limited literacy skills, and about 40 million can read little or not at all![48] Most workplace demands require a tenth- or eleventh-grade reading level, but about 20 percent of Americans between the ages of 21 and 25 can't read at even an eighth-grade level.[49] And in many Third World countries, few workers can read or have gone beyond the equivalent of the third grade.

Organizations are increasingly having to provide basic reading and math skills for their employees. For instance, William Dudek runs a small manufacturing firm on Chicago's north side.[50] His thirty-five employees make metal clips, hooks, and clasps used in household appliances and automotive components. When Dudek tried to introduce some basic quality-management principles in his plant, he noticed that many of his employees seemed to disregard the written instructions. Checking further, he discovered that the workers couldn't read the instructions, and only a few could calculate percentages or plot a simple graph. Dudek conducted a needs assessment, hired an instructor, and had classes in English and mathematics taught to his employees in the firm's cafeteria. Dudek says that this training, which cost him $15,000 in its first year, made his employees more efficient and that they now work better as a team.

Technical Skills Most training is directed at upgrading and improving an employee's technical skills—in both white-collar and blue-collar jobs. Technical training has become increasingly important in the 1990s for two reasons—new technology and new structural designs.

Jobs change as a result of new technologies and improved methods. Postal sorters have had to undergo technical training in order to learn to operate automatic sorting machines. Many auto repair personnel have had to undergo extensive training to fix and maintain recent models with front-wheel drive trains, electronic ignitions, fuel injection, and other innovations. Not many clerical personnel during the past decade have been unaffected by the computer. Literally millions of such employees have had to be trained to operate and interface with a computer terminal.

In addition, technical training has become increasingly important because of changes in organization structures. As organizations flatten their structures, expand their use of teams, and break down traditional departmental barriers, employees need to learn a wider variety of tasks. Management has responded by significantly increasing opportunities for cross-functional training.[51] For instance, Graphic Control Corp. in Buffalo, New York, is using cross-functional training to increase its work force's versatility. By teaching its manufacturing employees to perform the jobs of at least one other person, management can move people around more easily and reduce the need to hire skilled temporary help.[52]

Interpersonal Skills Almost all employees belong to a work unit. To some degree, their work performance depends on their ability to effectively interact with their co-workers and their boss. Some employees have excellent interpersonal skills, but others require training to improve theirs. This includes learning how to be a better listener, how to communicate ideas more clearly, and how to be a more effective team player.[53]

One of the fastest growing areas of interpersonal skill development is diversity training.[54] The two most popular types of this training focus on increasing awareness and building skills. *Awareness training* tries to create an understanding of the need for, and meaning of, managing and valuing diversity. *Skill-building training* educates employees about specific cultural differences in the workplace. Companies leading the way in diversity training include American Express, Avon, Corning, Hewlett-Packard, Monsanto, Motorola, Pacific Gas & Electric, U.S. West, and Xerox.

Problem-Solving Skills Managers, as well as many employees who perform nonroutine tasks, have to solve problems on their job. When people require these skills, but are deficient, they can participate in problem-solving training. This would include activities to sharpen their logic, reasoning, and problem-defining skills, as well as their abilities to assess causation, develop alternatives, analyze alternatives, and select solutions. Problem-solving training has become a basic part of almost every organizational effort to introduce self-managed teams or implement TQM.

What about Ethics Training? Approximately 80 percent of the largest U.S. corporations have formal ethics programs, and 44 percent of these provide ethics training.[55] What do proponents of ethics training expect to achieve? They claim that training can stimulate moral thought, help people recognize ethical dilemmas, create a sense of moral obligation, and help employees learn to tolerate or reduce ambiguity. But the evidence is not clear on whether you can teach ethics.

Critics argue that ethics are based on values, and value systems are fixed at an early age. By the time employers hire people, their ethical values have already been established. The critics also claim that ethics cannot be formally "taught," but must be learned by example. Leaders set ethical examples by what they say and do. If this claim is true, then ethics training is relevant only as part of leadership training.

Supporters of ethics training argue that values can be learned and changed after early childhood. And even if they couldn't, ethics training would be effective because it gets employees to think about ethical dilemmas and become more aware of the ethical issues underlying their actions. Supporters of ethics training point to the research evidence on the last point: A comprehensive analysis of the effectiveness of ethics training programs found that they improved subjects' ethical awareness and reasoning skills.

IN THE NEWS

"Go to School, and I'll Pay for It"

HAMPDEN PAPERS OF HOLYOKE, MASSACHUSETTS, HAS BEEN AROUND FOR MORE THAN A CENTURY. ITS primary business is converting plain paper into gift wrap and greeting card stock. The current president, Bob Fowler, is the fourth generation of the Fowler family to run the company.

When Bob Fowler joined the family business in the early 1970s, the company hired people with minimal skills. Employees didn't have to speak English or work with numbers because the paper-making equipment they worked on was pretty basic. "There was a red button, a yellow button and a green button. You hit the green button to start the machine. If something went wrong, you hit the red button and called a mechanic. The yellow button took the machine out of gear." Today's equipment, however, is highly sophisticated. Machines are as long as a city block, are computerized, and have panels that look like air-traffic control centers. More and more of the equipment at Hampden requires the ability to read detailed instructions, calculate numbers, understand computers, and solve complex problems.

In many companies, this technological transition has not had a happy ending for the employees. Underschooled and underskilled workers are laid off to make way for new faces with high-tech training. Fowler didn't want to go that way. "I don't believe in discardable human beings. I appreciate a 50-year-old worker who comes to work every day and understands responsibility. If that person needs basic skills, we're willing to work with him."

In 1990, Fowler created a new education policy for his company and its 170 employees. Everybody is encouraged to go to school at company expense. Some have learned English. Many have earned their high school equivalency degrees. Several are in college. Fowler, himself, is almost halfway through law school. The program comes with few strings attached. Employees, for instance, can take courses in literature or history or sociology. "Anything that isn't aimed at getting a job somewhere else or isn't a pure hobby," says Fowler.

Fowler is pleased with the program's results as evidenced by how it has changed the work lives of people like Barry Choquette and Tom Mekal. Barry operates some of the plant's sophisticated cutting equipment. "I've been studying math because I use it a lot," he explains. "It gives me extra self-confidence to know that a 41-year-old guy like me can learn new stuff." Tom Mekal, who came to Hampden straight out of high school 25 years ago as a part-time shipping clerk, began by taking computer classes and then started taking courses in order to get his bachelor's degree. His new skills helped him land a position as regional sales manager with the company.

Source: Based on M. Ryan, "'Go to School, and I'll Pay for It,'" *Parade Magazine,* September 18, 1994, pp. 20-21.

Training Methods

Most training takes place on the job. This preference can be attributed to the simplicity and, usually, lower cost of on-the-job training methods. However, on-the-job training can disrupt the workplace and result in an increase in errors as learning proceeds. Also, some skill training is too complex to learn on the job. In such cases, it should take place outside the work setting.[56]

On-the-Job Training Popular on-the-job training methods include job rotation and mentor relationships. *Job rotation* involves lateral transfers that enable employees to work at different jobs. Employees get to learn a wide variety of jobs and gain increased insight into the interdependency between jobs and a wider perspective on organizational activities. New employees frequently learn their jobs under the guidance of a seasoned veteran. In the trades, this is usually called an *apprenticeship.* In white-collar jobs, it is called a *coaching,* or *mentor,* relationship. In each, the new employee works under the observation of an experienced worker, who acts as a model whom the newcomer attempts to emulate.

Both job rotation and mentoring apply to the learning of technical skills. Interpersonal and problem-solving skills are acquired more effectively by training that takes place off the job.

Simple

Written Essays Probably the simplest method of appraisal is to write a narrative describing an employee's strengths, weaknesses, past performance, potential, and suggestions for improvement. The written essay requires no complex forms or extensive training to complete. But the results often reflect the ability of the writer. A good or bad appraisal may be determined as much by the evaluator's writing skill as by the employee's actual level of performance.

Critical Incidents **Critical incidents** focus the appraiser's attention on those behaviors that are key in making the difference between executing a job effectively and executing it ineffectively. That is, the appraiser writes down anecdotes that describe what the employee did that was especially effective or ineffective. The key here is that only specific behaviors, not vaguely defined personality traits, are cited. A list of critical incidents provides a rich set of examples from which the employee can be shown those behaviors that are desirable and those that call for improvement.

Graphic Rating Scales One of the oldest and most popular methods of appraisal is the use of **graphic rating scales.** In this method, a set of performance factors, such as quantity and quality of work, depth of knowledge, cooperation, loyalty, attendance, honesty, and initiative, are listed. The appraiser then goes down the list and rates each on incremental scales. The scales typically specify 5 levels, so a factor such as *job knowledge* might be rated from 1 ("poorly informed about work duties") to 5 ("has complete mastery of all phases of the job").

Why are graphic ratings scales so popular? Though they don't provide the depth of information that essays or critical incidents do, they are less time-consuming to develop and administer. They also allow for quantitative analysis and comparison.

Behaviorally Anchored Rating Scales **Behaviorally anchored rating scales** (BARS) combine major elements from the critical incident and graphic rating scale approaches: The appraiser rates the employees on items along a continuum, but the points are examples of actual behavior on the given job rather than general descriptions or traits.

BARS specify definite, observable, and measurable job behavior. Examples of job-related behavior and performance dimensions are found by asking participants to give specific illustrations of effective and ineffective behavior regarding each performance dimension. These behavioral examples are then translated into a set of performance dimensions, each dimension having varying levels of performance. The results of this process are behavioral descriptions, such as *anticipates, plans, executes, solves immediate problems, carries out orders,* and *handles emergency situations.*

Multiperson Comparisons Multiperson comparisons evaluate one individual's performance against the performance of one or more others. It is a relative rather than an absolute measuring device. The three most popular comparisons are group order ranking, individual ranking, and paired comparisons.

The **group order ranking** requires the appraiser to place employees into a particular classification, such as top one-fifth or second one-fifth. This method is often used in recommending students to graduate schools. Appraisers are asked whether the student ranks in the top 5 percent of the class, the next 5 percent, the next 15 percent, and so forth. But when managers use this method to appraise employees, they deal with all their subordinates. Therefore, if a rater has twenty subordinates, only four can be in the top fifth and, of course, four must also be relegated to the bottom fifth.

The **individual ranking** approach rank-orders employees from best to worst. If the manager is required to appraise thirty subordinates, this approach assumes that the difference between the first and second employee is the same as that between the twenty-first and twenty-second. Even though some of the employees may be closely grouped, this approach allows for no ties. The result is a clear ordering of employees, from the highest performer down to the lowest.

The **paired comparison** approach compares each employee with every other employee and rates each as either the superior or the weaker member of the pair. After all paired comparisons are made, each employee is assigned a summary ranking based on the number of superior scores he or she achieved. This approach ensures that each employee is compared against every other, but it can obviously become unwieldy when many employees are being compared.

Multiperson comparisons can be combined with one of the other methods to blend the best from both absolute and relative standards. For example, a college might use the graphic rating scale and the individual ranking method to provide more-accurate information about its students' performance. The student's relative rank in the class could be noted next to an absolute grade of A, B, C, D, or F. A prospective employer or graduate school could then look at two students who each got a B in their different financial accounting courses and draw considerably different conclusions about each because next to one grade it says "ranked fourth out of twenty-six," while next to the other it says "ranked seventeenth out of thirty." Obviously, the latter instructor gives out a lot more high grades!

Providing Performance Feedback

For many managers, few activities are more unpleasant than providing performance feedback to employees.[67] In fact, unless pressured by organizational policies and controls, managers are likely to ignore this responsibility.[68]

Why the reluctance to give performance feedback? There seem to be at least three reasons. First, managers are often uncomfortable discussing performance weaknesses with employees. Given that almost every employee could stand to improve in some areas, managers fear a confrontation when presenting negative feedback. Second, many employees tend to become defensive when their weaknesses are pointed out. Instead of accepting the feedback as constructive and a basis for improving performance, some employees challenge the evaluation by criticizing the manager or redirecting blame to someone else. Finally, employees tend to have an inflated assessment of their own performance. Statistically speaking, half of all employees must be below-average performers. But the evidence indicates that the average employee's estimate of his or her own performance level generally falls around the seventy-fifth percentile.[69] So even when managers are providing good news, employees are likely to perceive it as not good enough!

The evidence indicates that the average employee's estimate of his or her own performance level generally falls around the seventy-fifth percentile.

The solution to the performance feedback problem is not to ignore it, but to train managers in how to conduct constructive feedback sessions. An effective review—one in which the employee perceives the appraisal as fair, the manager as sincere, and the climate as constructive—can result in the employee's leaving the interview in an upbeat mood, informed about the performance areas in which he or she needs to improve, and determined to correct the deficiencies.[70] In addi-

Source: Dilbert reprinted by permission of United Feature Syndicate, Inc.

EXHIBIT 9-4

tion, the performance review should be designed more as a counseling activity than a judgment process. This can best be accomplished by allowing the review to evolve out of the employee's own self-appraisal.

Team Performance Appraisals

Performance appraisal concepts have been almost exclusively developed with only individual employees in mind. This fact reflects the historical belief that individuals are the core building blocks around which organizations are built. But as we've described throughout this book, more and more organizations are restructuring themselves around teams. How should organizations using teams appraise performance? Four suggestions have been offered for designing a system that supports and improves the performance of teams.[71]

1. *Tie the team's results to the organization's goals.* It's important to find measurements that apply to important goals that the team is supposed to accomplish.
2. *Begin with the team's customers and the work process the team follows to satisfy their needs.* The final product the customer receives can be appraised in terms of the customer's requirements. The transactions between teams can be appraised on the basis of delivery and quality, and the process steps on the basis of waste and cycle time.

3. *Measure both team and individual performance.* Define the roles of each team member in terms of accomplishments that support the team's work process. Then assess each member's contribution and the team's overall performance.
4. *Train the team to create its own measures.* Having the team define its objectives and those of each member ensures that every member understands his or her role on the team and helps the team develop into a more cohesive unit.

DECRUITMENT: WHAT OPTIONS EXIST TO HANDLE OVERSTAFFING?

In the past decade, most large corporations, as well as many government agencies, not-for-profit organizations, and small businesses, have found themselves overstaffed. Because of market changes, implementation of new technologies, foreign competition, mergers, and the like, management concludes that it has a surplus of employees and needs to reduce the labor supply within the organization. These organizations need to engage in **decruitment.**

Decruitment is not a pleasant task for any manager to perform. But as many organizations are forced to shrink the size of their work force or restructure their skill composition, decruitment is becoming an increasingly important part of human resource management.

What are a manager's decruitment options? Obviously, people can be fired. But other choices may be more beneficial to the organization or the employee or both.[72] For instance, Honda of America "rents" some of its engineers to other companies when it finds itself overstaffed.[73] Exhibit 9-5 summarizes a manager's major options.

EXHIBIT 9-5
Decruitment Options

Option	Description
Firing	Permanent involuntary termination
Layoffs	Temporary involuntary termination; may last only a few days or extend to years
Attrition	Not filling openings created by voluntary resignations or normal retirements
Transfers	Moving employees either laterally or downward; usually does not reduce costs but can reduce intraorganizational supply-demand imbalances
External loans	Providing employees' services to other organizations temporarily, on a contract basis, while still keeping them on the payroll
Reduced workweeks	Having employees work fewer hours per week, share jobs, or perform their jobs on a part-time basis
Early retirements	Providing incentives to senior employees for retiring before their normal retirement date

CONTEMPORARY ISSUES IN HUMAN RESOURCES MANAGEMENT

We close this chapter by addressing some specific human resource issues that managers are currently facing.

How Can Managers Limit Sexual Harassment?

Few workplace topics have received more attention in recent years than that of sexual harassment.[74] Since 1980, U.S. courts generally have defined **sexual harassment** as encompassing sexually suggestive remarks, unwanted touching and sexual advances, requests for sexual favors, and other verbal and physical conduct of a sexual nature. Such conduct is illegal in the United States and Canada—a violation of civil rights law. And other countries are quickly moving to enact legislation to protect workers from sexual harassment.[75]

In a 1993 ruling, the U.S. Supreme Court widened the test for sexual harassment under U.S. civil rights law to include comments or behavior in a work environment that "would reasonably be perceived, and is perceived, as hostile or abusive." Now individuals need not show that they have been psychologically damaged to prove sexual harassment in the workplace. They merely need to show that they are working in a hostile or abusive environment.

From a manager's standpoint, sexual harassment is a growing concern because it intimidates employees, interferes with job performance, and exposes the organization to liability. The first step toward reducing an organization's potential liability and limiting sexual harassment behavior is for senior management to establish a written sexual harassment policy (see Exhibit 9-6). This statement should define sexual harassment, make clear that it will not be tolerated, describe disciplinary measures that will be taken if the policy is violated, and tell employees how to make a complaint. The policy should be reinforced by regular discussion sessions in which employees are reminded of the rule and carefully instructed that even the slightest sexual overture to another employee will not be tolerated. At AT&T, for instance, all employees have been specifically advised that they can be fired for making repeated unwelcome sexual advances, using sexually degrading words to describe someone, or displaying sexually offensive pictures or objects at work.

What Role Should Organizations Play in Employee Career Development?

Management's role in career development has undergone significant change in the past decade. It has gone from paternalism—in which the organization took re-

Sexual harassment is complicated by the fact that men and women often perceive behavior differently. A man may think a touch on the hand is innocent, but a woman may view it as a prelude to an assault.

The following guidelines reduce the potential liability of a sexual harassment suit:

- Establish a written policy prohibiting sexual harassment.
- Communicate the policy and train employees in what constitutes sexual harassment.
- Establish an effective organizational complaint procedure.
- Promptly investigate all claims and demonstrate that complaints will be examined fairly and objectively.
- Take remedial action to correct past harassment.
- Follow up to ensure that no further harassment occurs and that retaliation does not occur.

Source: Reproduced with permission from *CCH Sexual Harassment Manual for Managers and Supervisors* published and © by CCH, Inc. 2700 Lake Cook Rd., Riverwoods, Ill. 60016.

EXHIBIT 9-6
Management Guidelines for Reducing Potential Liability for Sexual Harassment

sponsibility for managing its employees' careers—to supporting individuals as they take personal responsibility for their future.[76]

For much of this century, companies recruited young workers with the intent that they would spend their entire career inside that single organization. For those with the right credentials and motivation, they created promotion paths dotted with ever-increasing responsibility. Employers would provide the training and opportunities; and employees would respond by demonstrating loyalty and hard work. The changes we described in Chapter 1 changed those rules. High uncertainty now limits the ability of organizations to accurately forecast future needs. Management seeks flexibility over permanence. Meanwhile, flattened hierarchies have reduced promotion opportunities. The result is that, today, career planning is something increasingly being done by individual employees rather than by their employers. It has become the employee's responsibility to keep his or her skills, abilities, and knowledge current and to prepare for tomorrow's new tasks.

Today, career planning is something increasingly being done by individual employees rather than by their employers.

What, if any, responsibility does management have for career development under these new rules? Amoco Corp.'s career development program is a model for modern companies.[77] It is designed around employee self-reliance and to help employees reflect on their marketability both inside and outside the Chicago-based oil company. All workers are encouraged to participate in a half-day introduction to the program and a full day of self-assessment and self-development sessions. The company supports its employees by providing information—a worldwide electronic job-posting system, a network of career advisers, and a worldwide directory of Amoco employees and their skills from which company managers can search for candidates for job openings. But the whole program is voluntary and assumes that it is the employees' responsibility to maintain their employability.

The essence of a progressive career development program is built on providing support for employees to continually add to their skills, abilities, and knowledge. This support includes:

1. *Clearly communicating the organization's goals and future strategies.* When people know where the organization is headed, they are better able to develop a personal plan to share in that future.
2. *Creating growth opportunities.* Employees should have the opportunity to get new, interesting, and professionally challenging work experiences.
3. *Offering financial assistance.* The organization should offer tuition reimbursement to help employees keep current.
4. *Providing the time for employees to learn.* Organizations should be generous in providing paid time off from work for off-the-job training. In addition, work loads

should not be so demanding that they preclude employees from having the time to develop new skills, abilities, and knowledge.

What if There Is a Labor Union?

Some managers will be working with employees who belong to a labor union. How does unionization affect the manager in the performance of his or her job?

Labor unions are a vehicle by which employees act collectively to protect and promote their interests. They use the collective bargaining process to negotiate wage levels and conditions of employment with management.

Where a union represents a portion of an organization's labor force, many of the management decisions we have discussed in this chapter are spelled out in the collective bargaining contract. For instance, recruitment sources, hiring criteria, work schedules, safety rules, redress procedures, and eligibility for training programs are typical issues addressed in the contract. The most obvious and pervasive area of union influence, of course, is wage rates and working conditions. Where unions exist, performance appraisal systems tend to be less complex than in nonunion organizations because they play a relatively small part in reward decisions. Seniority usually takes priority over performance in decisions regarding job preferences, work schedules, and layoffs. Wage rates, when determined by collective bargaining, also tend to emphasize seniority and downplay performance differences.

The bottom line is that when employees are represented by a union and are covered by a collective bargaining contract, managers need to familiarize themselves with the details of that contract. And if problems surface from the contract that make it difficult to effectively manage unionized members, managers should convey these problems to the organization's labor relations specialist or senior management. This information can then be used to correct those problems in future negotiations.

SUMMARY

(This summary is organized by the chapter-opening learning objectives on page 257.)

1. Job analysis defines the jobs within the organization and the behaviors that are necessary to perform them. Job descriptions and specifications come out of the job analysis. They describe the job and qualifications needed by the jobholder.
2. A selection device must be valid because validity assures that it will be an accurate predictor. If it is not valid, then it will not contribute to identifying effective candidates. Selection devices must be reliable to ensure that results will be consistent over time. If results are erratic, managers can't depend on them in the selection process.
3. The general evidence linking IQ to job performance is impressive. Specifically, the greater a job's ambiguity and complexity, the better IQ is in predicting a candidate's performance in that job.
4. The major strength of the interview as a selection device is that it is reasonably effective for tapping a candidate's intelligence, level of motivation, and interpersonal skills. Unstructured interviews tend to be biased in favor of similar attitudes between interviewer and applicant, biased against negative information, and influenced strongly by the order in which applicants are interviewed.
5. Training can improve an employee's basic literacy, technical, interpersonal, and problem-solving skills.
6. The primary methods for appraising employee performance include written essays, critical incidents, graphic rating scales, behaviorally anchored rating scales (BARS), and multiperson comparisons.
7. Sexual harassment is defined as sexually suggestive remarks, unwanted touching and sexual advances, requests for sexual favors, and other verbal and physical contact of a sexual nature. To reduce its occurrence, management needs a written policy statement that is well communicated; training; specific penalties for breaking the policy; and strong enforcement of the policy.

REVIEW AND DISCUSSION QUESTIONS

1. Give some examples of HRM practices that are governed by laws and regulations in your country.
2. What pluses and minuses for the organization do you see in using temporary employees as a pool from which to select permanent employees? Are there any pluses from the temporary employee's standpoint?
3. What are the costs of reject errors? Of accept errors?
4. What is an assessment center? Why do you think it has proved to be a valid selection predictor?
5. Describe the proper way to conduct a selection interview.
6. Explain why training has gained increased importance in the HRM process during the past decade.
7. Why is it better to appraise employee behaviors rather than traits?
8. Besides firing employees, what other options does management have if it finds its organization overstaffed?
9. Contrast current career development programs in most large organizations with those programs 20 years ago.
10. How does the existence of a labor union affect HRM practices?

CASE EXERCISE
HIRING AT SOUTHWEST AIRLINES

At Southwest Airlines, the People Department is one of the company's most important functions. This 125-member department handles all the company's hiring. And they've been busy lately. Over the past 4 years, Southwest's staff has increased by 97 percent to about 17,000 employees.

Southwest's management favors an informal approach to job interviews. Take, for example, how Rita Bailey, the firm's manager of corporate employment, chose to handle the initial interviews for an opening in the airline's "special marketing" department. This department seeks to attract more businesswomen, elderly, and young people as passengers.

Four female applicants, led by Bailey, sit around talking amicably about everything from their childhoods to tough problems they've faced on the job. For 2 hours, the four applicants chat while Bailey evaluates. In this case, Bailey considers the marketing background of the four women as important. But she is more intent on finding a self-starter who has a willingness to pitch in on any job, even blowing up balloons for festive events. Bailey also is looking for subtler clues—how the candidates interact. "We just want the kind of person who can relate to everybody and everything." For this marketing position, Bailey has already interviewed twenty-two applicants. None of the four candidates in this session quite fits the bill, so there will be no callbacks.

Bailey admits that this is a time-consuming process. But she insists that the company won't compromise quality to speed up its hiring process. Because Southwest is growing so fast and insists on this lengthy hiring process, the People Department's staff is taxed to its limits. In actuality, if Southwest followed more traditional hiring procedures, it might be able to fill positions much more quickly and with a far smaller human resources department.

Questions

1. Contrast Southwest's hiring process with your personal experiences in getting a job.
2. "In a dynamic industry, where firms must respond quickly, Southwest's approach to employment selection is neither effective nor efficient." Do you agree or disagree? Discuss.
3. On the basis of your knowledge of hiring, what suggestions would you make to Bailey to help her increase the probability of finding the right person to fit the marketing vacancy?

Source: Based on W. Zellner, "Southwest," *Business Week*, February 13, 1995, p. 69.

VIDEO CASE EXERCISE
DIVERSITY TRAINING AT THE FAA

Palm Coast, Florida, is home of the Federal Aviation Administration's Center for Management Development. The FAA and other agencies send thousands of managers there each year for training. In fact, every new FAA manager must undergo diversity training before he or she is permanently assigned.

With 50,000 employees and an annual budget of $9 billion, the FAA does a lot of management training. Much of it, even though completed at the Palm Coast facility, is done by outside contractors. For instance, one outside contractor was reportedly paid $1.18 million for programs conducted over a 2-year period. Some diversity training programs put on by outside contractors have become the source of controversy.

In June 1992, an air traffic controller named Douglas Hartman attended an FAA seminar on diversity. He claims that he was forced to run a gauntlet of women who had been encouraged to fondle men inappropriately, supposedly to enable the men to experience what women feel like when they are harassed. In September 1994, Hartman sued the Department of Transportation for sexual harassment. "The FAA is a strange culture," says Hartman. "It's very intimidating. Nothing would be said outright, but I've heard from supervisors who are my friends that I've put my career in the toilet by filing this lawsuit."

In 1991, a union executive representing air traffic controllers filed a complaint against the FAA claiming that during training sessions, men were forced to walk through gauntlets of female employees who fondled and taunted them, and women at sessions were urged to share intimate experiences including childhood molestations.

Between October 1990 and January 1993, senior FAA managers reportedly underwent training that included screaming, sleep deprivation, and name calling at the Palm Coast facility. Although these sessions were run by an outside contractor, workers claimed that they were afraid to complain because they believed that the outside contractor had significant influence on the selection of senior positions within the FAA.

According to official government reports, the questionable training problems have affected other agencies, including employees at the National Transportation Safety Board. The person who now heads the NTSB's Office of Aviation Safety worked for a long time at the FAA, and he picked the contractors who ran that agency's training. The NTSB employees claim they were humiliated to the point of tears during their training. Other attendees had to complete questionnaires about such personal issues as their religious beliefs, fears, sexuality, and experience with unwanted pregnancies and abortions. The answers to these questions were then used to harass them during the training.

Questions

1. "You'll never understand sexual harassment unless you experience it firsthand." Do you agree or disagree with this statement? What are the implications of your answer to the design of training programs to prevent harassment?
2. Where do you draw the line between appropriate and inappropriate practices in a diversity training program?
3. If you were a consultant brought in to advise senior officials at the FAA, what advice would you offer them regarding diversity training?

Source: Based on ABC News 20/20, September 16, 1994.

SKILL EXERCISE

Conducting Effective Interviews

1. Break into groups of three.
2. Take up to 10 minutes to compose five challenging job interview questions that you think would be relevant in the hiring of new college graduates for a sales-management training program at Procter & Gamble. Each hiree will spend 18 to 24 months as a sales representative calling on retail grocers. After this training period, successful candidates can be expected to be promoted to the position of district sales supervisor.
3. Exchange your five questions with another group.
4. Each group should allocate one of the following roles to their three members: interviewer, applicant, and observer. The person playing the applicant should rough out a brief résumé of his or her background and experience, then give it to the interviewer.
5. Role play a job interview. The interviewer should include, but not be limited to, the questions provided by the other group.
6. After the interview, the observer should evaluate the interviewer's behaviors in terms of the selection interviewing skills box presented earlier in the chapter.

NOTES

1. R. Henkoff, "Finding, Training, and Keeping the Best Service Workers," *Fortune,* October 3, 1994, pp. 110–22.
2. J. Pfeffer, "Producing Sustainable Competitive Advantage through the Effective Management of People," *Academy of Management Executive,* February 1995, pp. 55–69.
3. This example is based on L. M. Litvan, "The Disabilities Law: Avoid the Pitfalls," *Nation's Business,* January 1994, pp. 26–27.
4. See, for instance, J. Kaufman, "How Workplaces May Look without Affirmative Action," *Wall Street Journal,* March 20, 1995, p. B1.
5. Cited in P. C. Wright, R. W. Mondy, and R. M. Noe III, *Human Resource Management in Canada* (Scarborough, Ontario: Prentice Hall Canada, 1996).
6. Ibid.
7. This section is based on R. S. Schuler, P. J. Dowling, J. P. Smart, and V. L. Huber, *Human Resource Management in Australia,* 2nd ed. (New South Wales: HarperEducational, 1992), pp. 117, 119, 142.
8. J. L. Cotton, *Employee Involvement* (Newbury Park, Calif.: Sage, 1993), p. 114. See also M. Poole, "Industrial Democracy: A Comparative Analysis," *Industrial Relations,* Fall 1979, pp. 262–72.
9. See, for instance, J. Walker, *Human Resource Management Strategy* (New York: McGraw Hill, 1992).
10. See S. L. Rynes, "Recruitment, Job Choice, and Post–Hire Consequences: A Call for New Research Directions," in M. D. Dunnette and L. M. Hough, eds., *Handbook of Industrial & Organizational Psychology,* 2nd ed. (Palo Alto, Calif.: Consulting Psychologists Press, 1991), pp. 399–444.
11. L. R. Gomez–Mejia, D. B. Balkin, and R. L. Cardy, *Managing Human Resources* (Englewood Cliffs, N.J.: Prentice Hall, 1995), p. 197.
12. See, for example, L. M. Litvan, "Casting a Wider Net," *Nation's Business,* December 1994, pp. 49–51.
13. See, for example, R. Resnick, "Leasing Workers," *Nation's Business,* November 1992, pp. 20–28; T. G. Block, "Brains for Rent," *Forbes,* July 31, 1995, pp. 99–100; and J. Aley, "The Temp Biz Boom: Why It's Good," *Fortune,* October 16, 1995, pp. 53–56.
14. D. L. Boroughs, "Business Gives in to Temptation," *U.S. News & World Report,* July 4, 1994, pp. 56–57.
15. Cited in M. Klimas, "How to Recruit a Smart Team," *Nation's Business,* May 1995, p. 26.
16. See J. C. Ullman, "Employee Referrals: Prime Tool for Recruiting Workers," *Personnel,* May–June 1966, pp. 30–35; and J. P. Kirnan, J. A. Farley, and K. F. Geisinger, "The Relationship between Recruiting Source, Applicant Quality, and Hire Performance: An Analysis by Sex, Ethnicity, and Age," *Personnel Psychology,* Summer 1989, pp. 293–308.
17. C. R. Williams, C. E. Labig Jr., and T. H. Stone, "Recruitment Sources and Posthire Outcomes for Job Applicants and New Hires: A Test of Two Hypotheses," *Journal of Applied Psychology,* April 1993, pp. 163–72.
18. Ibid., p. 171.
19. For instance, see W. F. Cascio, *Applied Psychology in Personnel Management* (Englewood Cliffs, N.J.: Prentice Hall, 1991); and R. L. Dipboye, *Selection Interviews: Process Perspectives* (Cincinnati, Ohio: South-Western Publishing, 1992).
20. See A. Rafaeli and R. J. Klimoski, "Predicting Sales Success through Handwriting Analysis: An Evaluation of the Effects of Training and Handwriting Sample Content," *Journal of Applied Psychology,* May 1983, pp. 212–17; and A. Fowler, "An Even-Handed Approach to Graphology," *Personnel Management,* March 1991, pp. 40–43.
21. J. J. Asher, "The Biographical Item: Can It Be Improved?" *Personnel Psychology,* Summer 1972, p. 266.
22. G. W. England, *Development and Use of Weighted Application Blanks,* rev. ed. (Minneapolis: Industrial Relations Center, University of Minnesota, 1971).

CHAPTER 10

UNDERSTANDING GROUPS AND DEVELOPING EFFECTIVE TEAMS

A lot of athletes say they want to be part of a cohesive team—but they also want their name printed on the back of their jerseys in 6-inch-high block letters.

- S. P. Robbins

LEARNING OBJECTIVES

After studying this chapter, you should be able to:

1. Contrast groups with teams and describe three types of teams
2. Explain how roles and norms shape employee behavior
3. Describe the relationship between group cohesiveness and productivity
4. Explain the work-related implications of social loafing
5. Identify the main characteristics of the grapevine
6. Define groupthink and groupshift and discuss how they can affect group decision making
7. List characteristics of high-performing teams
8. Explain how management can transform individuals into team players

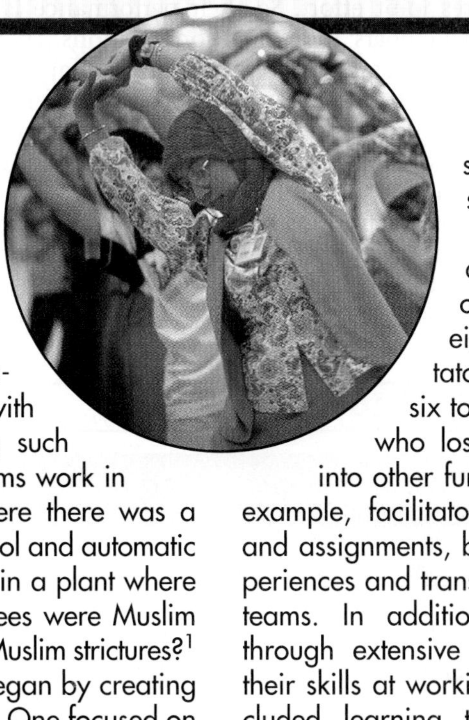

It started as a pilot study in 1989. Managers at Texas Instruments Malaysia (TIM) wanted to improve the productivity and quality of their integrated-circuits plant in Kuala Lumpur. They were aware of Texas Instruments' success in North America with empowered teams for achieving such goals. But would empowered teams work in Malaysia (see photo insert), where there was a long tradition of hierarchical control and automatic deference to authority figures, or in a plant where nearly 90 percent of the employees were Muslim women who observed traditional Muslim strictures?[1]

The experiment with teams began by creating two types of self-managed teams. One focused on maintenance activities. The other sought ways to improve the plant's operation. The success of these teams led to converting the complete plant to teams. Today, all of TIM's production employees are organized into self-managed work teams. They do such varied activities as dealing with suppliers, monitoring productivity and quality, assigning work within teams, and scheduling vacations.

This new team structure has dramatically cut the number of supervisors at TIM—from eighty managers to eight "facilitators." Each facilitator coaches six to twelve teams. The supervisors who lost their jobs were redeployed into other functions, primarily training. For example, facilitators helped teams define tasks and assignments, building on the facilitators' experiences and transferring their knowledge to the teams. In addition, all team members went through extensive training sessions to develop their skills at working on teams. This training included learning team meeting skills, quality-control and problem-solving techniques, cross-training skills, coaching, and peer appraisal skills.

Has the use of teams worked out for TIM? You bet it has! Cycle time has steadily declined and now stands at about half of 1980–1990 levels. Output has more than doubled even though the work force has remained stable. And quality has the employee's behavior and guide you in determining how best to handle situations with that employee.

Norms

Did you ever notice that golfers don't speak while their partners are putting on the green or that employees don't criticize their bosses in public? These behaviors are the result of **norms**—acceptable standards of behavior within a group that are shared by the group's members.[5]

All groups have norms. They tell members what they ought and ought not to do under certain circumstances. When agreed to and accepted by the group, norms act as a means of influencing the behavior of group members with a minimum of external controls. Employees don't need a supervisor to tell them that throwing paper airplanes or gossiping at the water cooler are unacceptable behaviors when the big boss from New York is touring the office. The group norms that are operating tell them. A key point to remember about norms is that groups exert pressure on members to bring members' behavior into conformity with the group's standards. Group members can be expected to act to correct or even punish people in the group who violate its norms.

Because individuals desire acceptance by the groups to which they belong, they are susceptible to conformity pressures. The impact that group pressures for conformity can have on an individual member's judgment and attitudes was demonstrated in the now-classic studies by Solomon Asch.[6] Asch made up groups of seven or eight people, who sat in a classroom and were asked to compare two cards held by the experimenter. One card had one line, the other had three lines of varying length. As shown in Exhibit 10-2, one of the lines on the three-line card was identical to the line on the one-line card. Also as shown in Exhibit 10-2 the difference in line length was quite obvious; under ordinary conditions, subjects made fewer than 1 percent errors. The object was to announce aloud which of the three lines matched the single line. But what would happen if the members in the group began to give incorrect answers? Would the pressures to conform cause an unsuspecting subject (USS) to alter his or her answer to align with the others? That was what Asch wanted to know. He arranged the group so that only the USS was unaware that the experiment was "fixed." The seating was prearranged: The USS was placed so as to be the last to announce his or her decision.

The experiment began with several sets of matching exercises. All the subjects gave the right answers. On the third set, however, the first subject gave an obviously wrong answer—for example, saying that "C" in Exhibit 10-2 matched "X". The next subject gave the same wrong answer, and so did the others. The USS knew that "B" was the same as "X," yet everyone had said "C." The decision confronting the USS was this: Do I publicly state a perception that differs from the preannounced position of the others in the group? Or do I give an answer that I strongly believe is incorrect in order to have my response agree with that of the other group members? Over many experiments and many trials, Asch's subjects con-

EXHIBIT 10-2
Examples of Cards Used in Asch Study

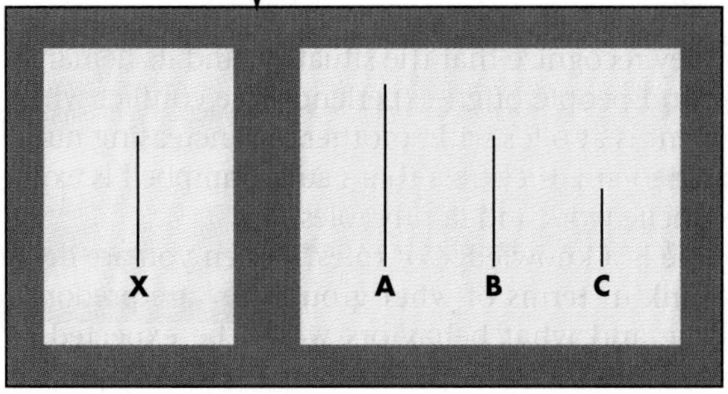

formed in about 35 percent of the trials; that is, the subjects gave answers that they knew were wrong but that were consistent with the replies of other group members.

Asch's findings suggest that people desire to be one of the group, to avoid being visibly different, and thus they feel pressure to conform. We can generalize these findings further to say that when an individual's opinion of objective data differs significantly from that of others in the group, especially if the person has a strong need for acceptance, he or she feels extensive pressure to align his or her opinion to conform with that of the others.

Each group will establish its own set of norms. For instance, group norms might determine appropriate dress, when it's acceptable to goof off, with whom group members each lunch, and friendships on and off the job. However, probably the most widespread norms—and the ones managers tend to be most concerned with—deal with performance-related processes. Work groups typically provide their members with explicit cues on how hard they should work, how to get the job done, their level of output, appropriate communication channels, and the like. These norms are extremely powerful in affecting an individual employee's performance. In fact, it's not unusual to find cases in which an employee with strong abilities and high personal motivation performs at a very modest level because of the overriding influence of group norms that discourage members from producing at high levels.

IN THE NEWS

Ethics in Groups: Cheating Among College Students

A SURVEY ON STUDENT CHEATING WAS CONDUCTED AT THIRTY-ONE PRESTIGIOUS SMALL COLLEGES IN the United States. These colleges have very selective admissions policies. The average SAT score of their elite group of students is 1,241. This small group of prestigious colleges have historically been the undergraduate schools of choice for a disproportionate share of U.S. doctors, lawyers, and corporate executives.

More than 6,000 surveys were returned. In addition to demographic information about the students, the surveys asked questions regarding six specific types of test and exam cheating—using crib notes on a test, having another student allow you to copy during a test, using unfair methods to learn what was on a test before it was given, copying from another student during a test without the person's knowledge, helping someone else to cheat on a test, and cheating on a test in any other way. The survey also sought information on six specific cheating behaviors related to written assignments—copying extensive material and turning it in as your own; falsifying a bibliography; turning in work done by someone else; receiving substantial, unpermitted help on an assignment; collaborating on an assignment when the instructor asked for individual work; and copying a few sentences from a published source without citing it.

The results of this survey confirmed the widespread practice of cheating: The majority (67 percent) of students responding admitted to one or more instances of cheating; 38 percent of the students were "active" cheaters, admitting to at least three incidents of cheating; and 15 percent were "active" test cheaters.

The researchers found that the most important variable predicting cheating behavior was the cheating norms on a campus. If students believe others are cheating, they are likely to follow suit. In addition, the researchers found that responses differed depending on intended occupation. Students aspiring to careers in business consistently reported the highest level of academic dishonesty. Seventy-six percent of those planning to enter business were self-reported cheaters. That compared with 63 percent for law, 68 percent for medicine, and 58 percent for education.

How do students rationalize their behavior? Those planning careers in business seem to have preconceived notions about what is important to success in life and how such success can be achieved in a business career. For example, being well-off financially was a significantly more important life goal for students planning to enter business than for any other occupational group. And the importance respondents attached to financial success was significantly related to cheating behavior. The most common rationalization to explain cheating was the pressure to get good grades in order to get into a top graduate school.

Students also expressed a great deal of concern about needing to cheat in order to maintain their relative advantage. One young woman noted "that students getting ahead by cheating and leaving you behind, would cause you to cheat." Another young man said, "If others [cheat], you're being left behind by not participating." A woman majoring in business, who ranked in the top quarter of her class, philosophized, "When most of the class is cheating on a difficult exam and they will ruin the curve, it influences you to cheat so your grade won't be affected."

Source: Based on D. L. McCabe and L. K. Trevino, "Cheating among Business Students: A Challenge for Business Leaders and Educators," *Journal of Management Education,* May 1995, pp. 205–18.

Cohesiveness

Groups differ in their **cohesiveness:** that is, the degree to which members are attracted to each other and are motivated to stay in the group. For instance, some work groups are cohesive because the members have spent a great deal of time together, or the group's small size facilitates higher interaction, or the group has experienced external threats that have brought members closer together. Cohesiveness is important because it has been found to be related to the group's productivity.[7]

Studies consistently show that the relationship of cohesiveness and productivity depends on the performance-related norms established by the group. The more cohesive the group, the more its members will follow its goals. If performance-related norms are high (for example, high output, quality work, cooperation with individuals outside the group), a cohesive group will be more productive than will a less cohesive group. But if cohesiveness is high and performance norms are low, productivity will be low. If cohesiveness is low and performance norms are high, productivity increases, but less than in the high cohesiveness–high norms situation. Where cohesiveness and performance-related norms are both low, productivity will tend to fall into the low-to-moderate range. These conclusions are summarized in Exhibit 10-3.

What can you, as a manager, do to encourage group cohesiveness? You might try one or more of the following suggestions:[8]

1. Make the group smaller.
2. Encourage agreement with group goals.
3. Increase the time members spend together.
4. Increase the status of the group and the perceived difficulty of attaining membership in the group.
5. Stimulate competition with other groups.
6. Give rewards to the group rather than to members.
7. Physically isolate the group.

Size

Does the size of a group affect the group's overall behavior? The answer is a definite Yes.[9] The evidence indicates, for instance, that smaller groups are faster at completing tasks than are larger ones. However, if the group is engaged in prob-

EXHIBIT 10-3
Relationship between Group Cohesiveness, Performance Norms, and Productivity

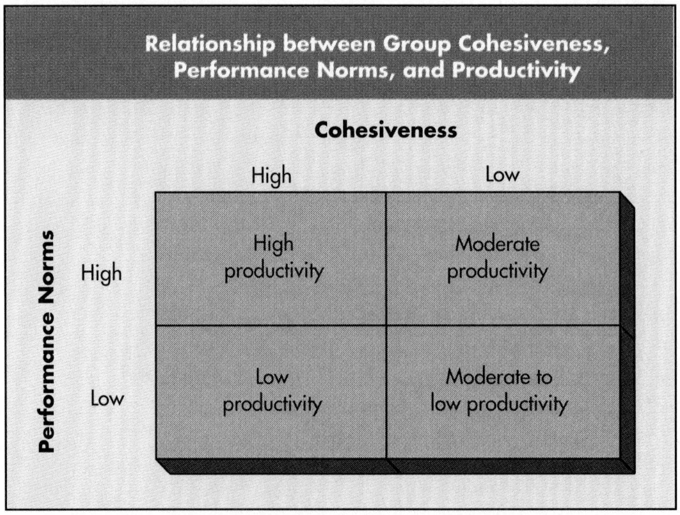

lem solving, large groups consistently get better marks than their smaller counterparts. Translating these results into specific numbers is a bit more hazardous, but we can offer some parameters. Large groups—with a dozen or more members—are good for gaining diverse input. So if the goal of the group is fact finding, larger groups should be more effective. On the other hand, smaller groups are better at doing something productive with that input. Groups of approximately seven members, therefore, tend to be more effective for taking action.

One of the most important findings related to the size of a group has been labeled **social loafing.** Social loafing is the tendency for individuals to expend less effort when working collectively than when working individually. It directly challenges the logic that the productivity of the group as a whole should at least equal the sum of the productivity of all the individuals in that group.

A common stereotype about groups is that the sense of team spirit spurs individual effort and enhances the group's overall productivity. In the late 1920s, a German psychologist named Ringelmann compared the results of individual and group performance on a rope-pulling task.[10] He expected that the group's effort would be equal to the sum of the efforts of individuals within the group. That is, three people pulling together should exert three times as much pull on the rope as one person, and eight people should exert eight times as much pull. Ringelmann's results, however, did not confirm his expectations. Groups of three people exerted a force only two and a half times the average individual performance. Groups of eight collectively achieved less than four times the solo rate.

Replications of Ringelmann's research with similar tasks have generally supported his findings.[11] Increases in group size are inversely related to individual performance. More may be better in the sense that the total productivity of a group of four is greater than that of one or two people, but the individual productivity of each group member declines.

What causes this social loafing effect? It may be due to a belief that others in the group are not carrying their fair share. If you see others as lazy or inept, you can establish equity by reducing your effort. Another explanation is the dispersion of responsibility. Because the results of the group cannot be attributed to any single person, the relationship between an individual's input and the group's output is clouded. In such situations, individuals may be tempted to become "free riders" and coast on the group's efforts. In other words, there will be a reduction in efficiency when individuals think that their contribution cannot be measured.

The implications for managers of this effect on work groups is significant. Managers who utilize collective work situations to enhance morale and teamwork must also provide means by which individual efforts can be identified. If they do not, they must weigh the potential losses in productivity from using groups against any possible gains in worker satisfaction.[12] However, this conclusion has a Western bias. It is consistent with individualistic cultures, such as the United States and Canada, that are dominated by self-interest. It is not consistent with collective societies in which individuals are motivated by in-group goals. For instance, in studies comparing employees from the United States with employees from the People's Republic of China and Israel (both collectivist societies), the Chinese and Israelis showed no propensity to engage in social loafing. In fact, the Chinese and Israelis actually performed better in a group than when working alone.[13]

Managers who utilize collective work situations to enhance morale and teamwork must also provide means by which individual efforts can be identified.

This supervisor and employees at a KFC in Austin, Texas, represent a diverse work team composed of gender, national origin, and racial mix.

Composition

Most group activities require a variety of skills and knowledge. Given this requirement, it would be reasonable to conclude that heterogeneous groups—those composed of dissimilar individuals—would be more likely to have diverse abilities and information and should be more effective than homogeneous groups. Research studies generally substantiate that conclusion.[14]

When a group is heterogeneous in terms of gender, personalities, opinions, abilities, skills, and perspectives, there is an increased probability that the group will possess the needed characteristics to complete its tasks effectively.[15] The group may be more conflict-laden and less expedient as diverse positions are introduced and assimilated, but the evidence generally supports the conclusion that heterogeneous groups perform more effectively than do homogeneous ones.

What are the effects of diversity created by racial or national differences? The evidence indicates that these elements of diversity interfere with group processes, at least in the short term.[16] Cultural diversity seems to be an asset on tasks that call for a variety of viewpoints. But culturally heterogeneous groups have difficulty in learning to work with each other and solving problems. The good news is that these difficulties seem to dissipate with time. Newly formed culturally diverse groups do not perform as well as newly formed culturally homogeneous groups, but the differences disappear after about 3 months. The reason is that it takes diverse groups a while to learn how to work through disagreements and different approaches to solving problems.

The managerial implications here are related to staffing formal groups and using groups to make decisions. To increase the performance of work groups, you should try to choose as members individuals who can bring a diverse perspective to problems and issues. But don't be surprised if these differences negatively affect the group's performance in the short term. Be patient. As members learn to work with these differences, the group's performance will improve.

Informal Communication: The Grapevine

When you put employees into groups, their communication is not limited to the formal channels as defined by their job descriptions or the chains of command. They also develop informal channels to share information. We call these informal channels the **grapevine.** All groups have them. They are a natural phenomenon whenever people get together. Regardless of how conscientious management is in using formal channels—official memos, press releases, supervisory announcements—the grapevine will still flourish. It helps bind people together, lets the powerless blow off steam, conveys concerns of employees, and fills in voids within the formal communication system.

The grapevine has three main characteristics.[17] First, it is not controlled by management. Second, it is perceived by most employees as being more believable and reliable than formal communiqués issued by top management. Third, it is largely used to serve the self-interests of those people within it.

One of the most famous studies of the grapevine investigated the communication pattern among sixty-seven managerial personnel in a small manufacturing firm.[18] The basic approach used was to learn from each communication recipient how he first received a given piece of information and then trace it back to its source. It was found that, although the grapevine was an important source of information, only 10 percent of the executives acted as liaison individuals—that is, passed the information on to more than one other person. For example, when one executive decided to resign to enter the insurance business, 81 percent of the executives knew about it, but only 11 percent had transmitted the information to others.

Two other conclusions from this study are also worth noting. Information on events of general interest tended to flow between the major functional groups (that is, production and sales) rather than within them. Also, no evidence surfaced to suggest that members of any one group consistently acted as liaisons; rather, different types of information passed through different liaison persons.

An attempt to replicate this study among employees in a small state government office also found that only a small percentage (10 percent) acted as liaison individuals.[19] This finding is interesting because the replication contained a wider spectrum of employees—including rank-and-file and managerial personnel—than did the original study. However, the flow of information in the government office took place within, rather than between, functional groups. It was proposed that this discrepancy might be due to comparing an executive-only sample against one that also included rank-and-file workers. Managers, for example, might feel greater pressure to stay informed and thus cultivate others outside their immediate functional group. Also, in contrast to the findings of the original study, the replication found that a consistent group of individuals acted as liaisons by transmitting information in the government office.

Is the information that flows along the grapevine accurate? The evidence indicates that about 75 percent of what is carried is accurate.[20] But what conditions foster an active grapevine? What gets the rumor mill rolling?

It is frequently assumed that rumors start because they make titillating gossip. Such is rarely the case. Rumors have at least four purposes: to structure and reduce anxiety; to make sense of limited or fragmented information; to serve as a vehicle to organize group members, and possibly outsiders, into coalitions; and to signal a sender's status ("I'm an insider and, with respect to this rumor, you're an outsider") or power ("I have the power to make you into an insider").[21] Research indicates that rumors emerge as a response to situations that are important to us, where there is ambiguity, and under conditions that arouse anxiety.[22] Work situations frequently contain these three elements, which explains why rumors flour-

IN THE NEWS

Selecting the Right Compensation Plan for Teams

It is one of the most difficult challenges managers face when they introduce teams: How do you design a pay system that encourages collaboration and spurs the team to produce its utmost but does not ignore the individual's innate desire for personal recognition? There doesn't seem to be any uniform answer to this question, but certain patterns are emerging. For instance, managers are designing the compensation plan to reflect the type of team involved; compensation practices are increasingly one of the last things management changes when organizations introduce teams; and change in compensation is being seen as an ongoing activity.

There are very real differences between groups. On some teams, members participate on only a part-time basis; on others, members work permanently and exclusively on the team. Some organizations designate a loosely connected group of workers a team, even though their work is almost completely independent. Such "teams" aren't teams at all, and most pay systems compensate these workers on an individual basis. Similarly, major changes in compensation practices aren't being made where individuals participate only part-time on teams. It makes the most sense to redo compensation plans for intact work teams, especially where members are cross-trained to do one another's jobs and the jobs themselves are highly interdependent. In practice, organizations typically pay an annual incentive bonus if the team meets certain goals and pay extra for new skills team members acquire and use on the job. Still, in the United States, individual contribution continues to play a major part in almost all organization's pay systems. Management is aware of the need to recognize individual achievement so as not to quash overachievers.

Most organizations delay making changes in their compensation plans until the team structure is well established. Says one expert, "If you try to put together a pay system for teams before workers have firsthand experience with what it means to be part of a team, they look at it and say, 'This is unfair. I should be paid on what I do. I don't have any control over what other people do.'" However, after the team members have learned how to work together toward a common goal, they accept and sometimes even demand more-equitable pay systems. American Express Financial Advisors, Inc., for instance, began to organize its client-services function into teams in 1988 but waited until 1989 to begin tinkering with the compensation system.

Finally, managers have learned that compensation plans need to change over time to reflect team member skills and the team's goals. American Express Financial Advisors originally designed its team pay system to include pay for knowledge in order to encourage people to become generalists. It worked for a time. But after a while, members wanted to go to class whether or not they would use the skills back on the job because they could get compensated more. So the company switched to a system that moves people through salary levels based on what they have learned and *contributed* to the team. Paying for knowledge wasn't as important once the company had achieved its goal of getting people cross-trained.

Source: Based on B. Geber, "The Bugaboo of Team Pay," *Training,* August 1995, pp. 25–34.

tion should be given to individuals for how effective they are as a collaborative team member. This doesn't mean individual contribution is ignored; rather, it is balanced with selfless contributions to the team. Examples of behaviors that should be rewarded include training new colleagues, sharing information with teammates, helping resolve team conflicts, and mastering new skills that your team needs but in which it is deficient.

Unfortunately, in organizations that are undergoing the transformation to teams, there will be some current employees who will resist team training or prove untrainable. Your options with such individuals are essentially two. You can transfer them to another unit within the organization that does not have teams, if this possibility exists. The other choice is obvious and acknowledges that some employees may become casualties of the team approach.

DO YOU HAVE A TEAM MENTALITY?

INSTRUCTIONS Circle the answer that most closely resembles your attitude.

Statement	Strongly Disagree						Strongly Agree
1. Only those who depend on themselves get ahead in life.	1	2	3	4	5	6	7
2. To be superior a person must stand alone.	1	2	3	4	5	6	7
3. If you want something done right, you've got to do it yourself.	1	2	3	4	5	6	7
4. What happens to me is my own doing.	1	2	3	4	5	6	7
5. In the long run the only person you can count on is yourself.	1	2	3	4	5	6	7
6. Winning is everything.	1	2	3	4	5	6	7
7. I feel that winning is important in both work and games.	1	2	3	4	5	6	7
8. Success is the most important thing in life.	1	2	3	4	5	6	7
9. It annoys me when other people perform better than I do.	1	2	3	4	5	6	7
10. Doing your best isn't enough; it is important to win.	1	2	3	4	5	6	7
11. I prefer to work with others in a group rather than working alone.	1	2	3	4	5	6	7
12. Given the choice, I would rather do a job where I can work alone rather than doing a job where I have to work with others in a group.	1	2	3	4	5	6	7
13. Working with a group is better than working alone.	1	2	3	4	5	6	7
14. People should be made aware that if they are going to be part of a group then they are sometimes going to have to do things they don't want to do.	1	2	3	4	5	6	7
15. People who belong to a group should realize that they're not always going to get what they personally want.	1	2	3	4	5	6	7
16. People in a group should realize that they sometimes are going to have to make sacrifices for the sake of the group as a whole.	1	2	3	4	5	6	7
17. People in a group should be willing to make sacrifices for the sake of the group's well-being.	1	2	3	4	5	6	7
18. A group is most productive when its members do what *they* want to do rather than what the group wants them to do.	1	2	3	4	5	6	7
19. A group is most efficient when its members do what *they* think is best rather than doing what the group wants them to do.	1	2	3	4	5	6	7
20. A group is most productive when its members follow their own interests and concerns.	1	2	3	4	5	6	7

Turn to page 561 for scoring directions and key.

***Source:* Adapted from J. A. Wagner III, "Studies of Individualism-Collectivism: Effects on Cooperation in Groups," *Academy of Management Journal,* February 1995, p. 162. With permission.**

CASE EXERCISE B
THE BOEING 777 PROGRAM

As Boeing Corp.'s management prepared to develop its 777 commercial jet, it decided it could no longer do business as usual. Times had changed and so must the development process. The new 777 had to be cost-efficient to compete against Airbus Industrie and McDonnell Douglas. It had to be customer-focused in response to the increasing demands made by airlines. Boeing was still suffering from the disappointing reception given to the company's proposed 150-seat jetliner called the 7J7. It failed to sell in the 1980s.

Senior management wrote up a brief statement of what they wanted in the 777:

> In order to launch on time a truly great airplane we have a responsibility to work together to design, produce and introduce an airplane that exceeds the expectations of flight crews, cabin crews, maintenance and support teams and ultimately our passengers and shippers.
>
> From day one: best dispatch reliability in the industry; greatest customer appeal in the industry and user-friendly and everything works.

To achieve this ambitious goal, management committed itself to designing the plane using the latest computer-aided design technology. Similarly, high-tech manufacturing techniques would be utilized to cut costs and increase quality. For instance, laser beams would be used to align big parts and eliminate costly reworking. But the most significant change would be in the use of teams and the inclusion of customers in the design stage. By getting customer input up front, airlines could select features they wanted, thus allowing Boeing to standardize many items and reduce costly customization.

As development began, Boeing set up about 240 design teams representing every company unit, from engineers, to machinists, to marketing personnel, to suppliers and customers. They dictated open communication among employees who never before had worked together or with customers. But learning to work together instead of maintaining turf was difficult for some. Many were reluctant to share information or mistakes. Financial managers, for instance, who were brought in to consult on costs, had difficulty in being forthright. And there was concern by upper level managers that if too many people knew a lot about a process, design or plan, word would get out to competitors.

Boeing came up with more efficient ways of doing things by bringing together workers from different areas of the company to problem-solve. They learned, for example, that it's faster and better to fill fuselage sections with wires, ducts, tubes, and insulation before joining them together than to do it after. Once the sections are joined, it's easier to connect the systems instead of having a lot of people getting in each other's way trying to install all of the interior parts at once.

The early evidence indicates that the 777 project is going to be a major success for Boeing. It is highly cost-competitive, largely because traditional production time has been cut from 18 months to 10 months. And it is proving to be just what customers want. United Airlines has placed orders or options for sixty-eight planes, and other airlines are rapidly getting in line to place orders.

Questions

1. Why do you think the use of teams was novel for the design of a complex project like an airplane?
2. How valid do you think upper management's concern is that teams could provide competitors with critical information on their new plane, especially with customers actively involved in its design?
3. What happened to the advantages from work specialization? Don't teams undermine the benefits that come from developing planes sequentially—with each department providing its contribution as the project evolves?

Source: Based on P. Lane, "Boeing 777: Delivering on a Promise," *Seattle Times,* May 7, 1995, p. F1.

SKILL EXERCISE

Assessing Team Effectiveness

Think of a team of which you were a part. Did you think it was effective? To objectively assess whether that team was effective, complete the following questionnaire. Using the scale below, rate your assessment of the extent to which each statement is true about your team.

5 = Strongly agree; 4 = Agree; 3 = Neutral; 2 = Disagree; 1 = Strongly disagree

1. Everyone on my team knows exactly why the team does what it does.	5	4	3	2	1
2. The team leader consistently lets the team members know how we're doing on meeting our customers' expectations.	5	4	3	2	1
3. Everyone on my team has a significant amount of say or influence on decisions that affect his or her job.	5	4	3	2	1
4. If outsiders were to describe the way we communicate within our team, they would use words such as "open," "honest," "timely," and "two-way."	5	4	3	2	1
5. Team members have the skills they need to accomplish their roles within the team.	5	4	3	2	1
6. Everyone on the team knows and understands the team's priorities.	5	4	3	2	1
7. As a team, we work together to set clear, achievable, and appropriate goals.	5	4	3	2	1
8. I would rather have the team decide how to do something rather than have the team leader give step-by-step instructions.	5	4	3	2	1
9. As a team, we are able to work together to solve destructive conflicts rather than ignoring conflicts.	5	4	3	2	1
10. The role each member of the team is expected to play makes sense to the whole team.	5	4	3	2	1
11. The team understands how it fits into the organization.	5	4	3	2	1
12. If my team doesn't reach a goal, I'm more interested in finding out why we have failed to meet the goal than I am in reprimanding the team members.	5	4	3	2	1
13. The team has so much ownership of the work that, if necessary, we would offer to stay late to finish a job.	5	4	3	2	1
14. The team leader encourages every person on the team to be open and honest, even if people have to share information that goes against what the team leader would like to hear.	5	4	3	2	1
15. There is a good match between the capabilities and responsibilities of each person on the team.	5	4	3	2	1
16. Everyone on the team is working toward accomplishing the same thing.	5	4	3	2	1
17. The team has the support and resources it needs to meet customer expectations.	5	4	3	2	1
18. The team knows as much about what's going on in the organization as the team leader does, because the team leader always keeps everyone up-to-date.	5	4	3	2	1
19. The team leader believes that everyone on the team has something to contribute that is valuable to all.	5	4	3	2	1
20. Team members clearly understand the team's unwritten rules of how to behave within the group.	5	4	3	2	1

Total up your score. The highest score possible is 100. You can rate your team's effectiveness by how close it comes to achieving the ideal score. Look specifically at items that you rated at 3 or less. These are areas where your team fell down in performance. You can use this twenty-item inventory to help you manage current and future teams of which you're a part.

Source: The questionnaire is from V. A. Hoevemeyer, "How Effective Is Your Team?" *Training & Development Journal,* September 1993, pp. 67–71.

NOTES

1. This vignette is based on "The Language of Teams Can Be Spoken Anywhere" in R. S. Wellins, W. C. Byham, and G. R. Dixon, *Inside Teams: How 20 World-Class Organizations Are Winning through Teamwork* (San Francisco: Jossey-Bass, 1994), pp. 262–71.
2. This section is based on J. R. Katzenbach and D. K. Smith, *The Wisdom of Teams* (Boston: Harvard Business School Press, 1993), pp. 21, 45, 85; and D. C. Kinlaw, *Developing Superior Work Teams* (Lexington, Mass.: Lexington Books, 1991), pp. 3–21.
3. See, for example, R. K. Merton, *Social Theory and Social Structure* (New York: Free Press, 1968); and S. E. Jackson and R. S. Schuler, "A Meta-Analysis and Conceptual Critique of Research on Role Ambiguity and Role Conflict in Work Settings," *Organizational Behavior and Human Decision Processes,* August 1985, pp. 16–78.
4. See M. P. O'Driscoll, D. R. Ilgen, and K. Hildreth, "Time Devoted to Job and Off-Job Activities, Interrole Conflict, and Affective Experiences," *Journal of Applied Psychology,* April 1992, pp. 272–79.
5. D. C. Feldman, "The Development and Enforcement of Group Norms," *Academy of Management Review,* January 1984, pp. 47–53; and J. R. Hackman, "Group Influences on Individuals in Organizations," in M. D. Dunnette and L. M. Hough, eds., *Handbook of Industrial & Organizational Psychology,* 2nd ed., vol. 3 (Palo Alto, Calif: Consulting Psychologists Press, 1992), pp. 235–50.
6. S. E. Asch, "Effects of Group Pressure upon the Modification and Distortion of Judgments," in H. Guetzkow, ed., *Groups, Leadership and Men* (Pittsburgh, Penn.: Carnegie Press, 1951), pp. 177–90.
7. I. Summers, T. Coffelt, and R. E. Horton, "Work-Group Cohesion," *Psychological Reports,* October 1988, pp. 627–36; and B. Mullen and C. Copper, "The Relation between Group Cohesiveness and Performance: An Integration," *Psychological Bulletin,* March 1994, pp. 210–27.
8. Based on J. L. Gibson, J. M. Ivancevich, and J. H. Donnelly Jr., *Organizations* (Burr Ridge, Ill.: Irwin, 1994), p. 323.
9. E. J. Thomas and C. F. Fink, "Effects of Group Size," *Psychological Bulletin,* July 1963, pp. 371–84; A. P. Hare, *Handbook of Small Group Research* (New York: Free Press, 1976); and M. E. Shaw, *Group Dynamics: The Psychology of Small Group Behavior,* 3rd ed. (New York: McGraw Hill, 1981).
10. W. Moede, "Die Richtlinien der Leistungs-Psychologie," *Industrielle Psychotechnik,* 4 (1927), pp. 193–207. See also D. A. Kravitz and B. Martin, "Ringelmann Rediscovered: The Original Article," *Journal of Personality and Social Psychology,* May 1986, pp. 936–41.
11. See, for example, J. A. Shepperd, "Productivity Loss in Performance Groups: A Motivation Analysis," *Psychological Bulletin,* January 1993, pp. 67–81; and S. J. Karau and K. D. Williams, "Social Loafing: A Meta-Analysis Review and Theoretical Integration," *Journal of Personality and Social Psychology,* October 1993, pp. 681–706.
12. S. G. Harkins and K. Seymanski, "Social Loafing and Group Evaluation," *Journal of Personality and Social Psychology,* December 1989, pp. 934–41.
13. See P. C. Earley, "Social Loafing and Collectivism: A Comparison of the United States and the People's Republic of China," *Administrative Science Quarterly,* December 1989, pp. 565–81; and P. C. Earley, "East Meets West Meets Mideast: Further Explorations of Collectivistic and Individualistic Work Groups," *Academy of Management Journal,* April 1993, pp. 319–48.
14. See, for example, P. S. Goodman, E. C. Ravlin, and L. Argote, "Current Thinking about Groups: Setting the Stage for New Ideas," in P. S. Goodman and Associates, eds., *Designing Effective Work Groups* (San Francisco: Jossey-Bass, 1986), pp. 15-16; and R. A. Guzzo and G. P. Shea, "Group Performance and Intergroup Relations in Organizations," in Dunnette and Hough, *Handbook of Industrial & Organizational Psychology,* 2nd ed., vol. 3, pp. 288–90.
15. M. E. Shaw, *Contemporary Topics in Social Psychology* (Morristown, N.J.: General Learning Press, 1976), p. 356.
16. W. E. Watson, K. Kumar, and L. K. Michaelsen, "Cultural Diversity's Impact on Interaction Process and Performance: Comparing Homogeneous and Diverse Task Groups," *Academy of Management Journal,* June 1993, pp. 590–602.
17. See, for instance, J. W. Newstrom, R. E. Monczka, and W. E. Reif, "Perceptions of the Grapevine: Its Value and Influence," *Journal of Business Communication,* Spring 1974, pp. 12–20; and S. J. Modic, "Grapevine Rated Most Believable," *Industry Week,* May 15, 1989, p. 14.
18. K. Davis, "Management Communication and the Grapevine," *Harvard Business Review,* September–October 1953, pp. 43–49.
19. H. Sutton and L. W. Porter, "A Study of the Grapevine in a Governmental Organization," *Personnel Psychology,* Summer 1968, pp. 223–30.
20. K. Davis, cited in R. Rowan, "Where Did That Rumor Come From?" *Fortune,* August 13, 1979, p. 134.
21. L. Hirshhorn, "Managing Rumors," in L. Hirschhorn, ed., *Cutting Back* (San Francisco: Jossey-Bass, 1983), pp. 49–52.
22. R. L. Rosnow and G. A. Fine, *Rumor and Gossip: The Social Psychology of Hearsay* (New York: Elsevier, 1976).
23. See, for instance, J. G. March and G. Sevon, "Gossip, Information and Decision Making," in J. G. March, ed., *Decisions and Organizations* (Oxford: Blackwell, 1988), pp. 429–42; M. Noon and R. Delbridge, "News from behind My Hand: Gossip in Organizations," *Organization Studies*

14, no. 1 (1993), pp. 23–36; N. Difonzo, P. Bordia, and R. L. Rosnow, "Reining in Rumors," *Organizational Dynamics,* Summer 1994, pp. 47–62; and P. LaBarre, "The Other Network," *Industry Week,* September 19, 1994, pp. 33–36.
24. W. F. Whyte, "The Social Structure of the Restaurant," *American Journal of Sociology,* January 1954, pp. 302–08.
25. J. Greenberg, "Equity and Workplace Status: A Field Experiment," *Journal of Applied Psychology,* November 1988, pp. 606–13.
26. See S. P. Robbins, *Managing Organizational Conflict: A Nontraditional Approach* (Englewood Cliffs, N.J.: Prentice Hall, 1974).
27. I. L. Janis, *Groupthink* (Boston: Houghton Mifflin, 1982).
28. Ibid.
29. I. L. Janis and L. Mann, *Decision Making* (New York: Free Press, 1977).
30. I. L. Janis, *Groupthink;* S. Smith, "Groupthink and the Hostage Rescue Mission," *British Journal of Political Science* 15 (1984), pp. 117–23; and G. Moorhead, R. Ference, and C. P. Neck, "Group Decision Fiascoes Continue: Space Shuttle *Challenger* and a Revised Framework," *Human Relations,* May 1991, pp. 539–50.
31. C. R. Leana, "A Partial Test of Janis' Groupthink Model: Effects of Group Cohesiveness and Leader Behavior on Defective Decision Making," *Journal of Management,* Spring 1985, pp. 5–17; G. Moorhead and J. R. Montanari, "An Empirical Investigation of the Groupthink Phenomenon," *Human Relations,* May 1986, pp. 399–410; and C. P. Neck and G. Moorhead, "Groupthink Remodeled: The Importance of Leadership, Time Pressure, and Methodical Decision–Making Procedures," *Human Relations,* May 1995, pp. 537–57.
32. Neck and Moorhead, "Groupthink Remodeled," p. 550.
33. See D. J. Isenberg, "Group Polarization: A Critical Review and Meta-Analysis," *Journal of Personality and Social Psychology,* December 1986, pp. 1141–51; J. L. Hale and F. J. Boster, "Comparing Effect Coded Models of Choice Shifts," *Communication Research Reports,* April 1988, pp. 180–86; and P. W. Paese, M. Bieser, and M. E. Tubbs, "Framing Effects and Choice Shifts in Group Decision Making," *Organizational Behavior and Human Decision Processes,* October 1993, pp. 149–65.
34. See, for example, N. Kogan and M. A. Wallach, "Risk Taking as a Function of the Situation, the Person, and the Group," in N. Kogan and M. A. Wallach, *New Directions in Psychology,* vol. 3 (New York: Holt, Rinehart and Winston, 1967); and M. A. Wallach, N. Kogan, and D. J. Bem, "Group Influence on Individual Risk Taking," *Journal of Abnormal and Social Psychology* 65 (1962), pp. 75–86.
35. R. D. Clark III, "Group-Induced Shift toward Risk: A Critical Appraisal," *Psychological Bulletin,* October 1971, pp. 251–70.
36. A. F. Osborn, *Applied Imagination; Principles and Procedures of Creative Thinking* (New York: Scribner's, 1941).
37. See A. L. Delbecq, A. H. Van deVen, and D. H. Gustafson, *Group Techniques for Program Planning: A Guide to Nominal and Delphi Processes* (Glenview, Ill: Scott, Foresman, 1975); and W. M. Fox, "Anonymity and Other Keys to Successful Problem-Solving Meetings," *National Productivity Review,* Spring 1989, pp. 145–56.
38. R. B. Gallupe, W. H. Cooper, M.-L. Grise, and L. M. Bastianutti, "Blocking Electronic Brainstorms," *Journal of Applied Psychology,* February 1994, pp. 77–86.
39. Cited in "Teams," *Training,* October 1995, p. 72.
40. See, for example, D. Tjosvold, *Team Organization: An Enduring Competitive Advantage* (Chichester, England: Wiley, 1991); J. Lipnack and J. Stamps, *The TeamNet Factor* (Essex Junction, Verm.: Oliver Wight, 1993); and Wellins, Byham, and Dixon, *Inside Teams,* pp. 338–46.
41. Kinlaw, *Developing Superior Work Teams,* p. 43.
42. J. H. Shonk, *Team-Based Organizations* (Homewood, Ill: Business One Irwin, 1992); and M. A. Verespej, "When Workers Get New Roles," *Industry Week,* February 3, 1992, p. 11.
43. See, for example, D. Barry, "Managing the Bossless Team," *Organizational Dynamics,* Summer 1991, pp. 31–47; and J. R. Barker, "Tightening the Iron Cage: Concertive Control in Self-Managing Teams," *Administrative Science Quarterly,* September 1993, pp. 408–37.
44. M. A. Verespej, "Workers-Managers," *Industry Week,* May 16, 1994, p. 30.
45. J. S. Lublin, "Trying to Increase Worker Productivity, More Employers Alter Management Style," *Wall Street Journal,* February 13, 1992, p. B1.
46. "A Conversation with Charles Dull," *Organizational Dynamics,* Summer 1993, pp. 57–70.
47. T. B. Kirker, "Edy's Grand Ice Cream," *Industry Week,* October 18, 1993, pp. 29–32.
48. R. Zemke, "Rethinking the Rush to Team Up," *Training,* November 1993, pp. 55–61.
49. See, for instance, T. D. Wall, N. J. Kemp, P. R. Jackson, and C. W. Clegg, "Outcomes of Autonomous Workgroups: A Long-Term Field Experiment," *Academy of Management Journal,* June 1986, pp. 280–304; and J. L. Cordery, W. S. Mueller, and L. M. Smith, "Attitudinal and Behavioral Effects of Autonomous Group Working: A Longitudinal Field Study," *Academy of Management Journal,* June 1991, pp. 464–76.
50. Lipnack and Stamps, *The TeamNet Factor,* pp. 14–17.
51. D. Woodruff, "Chrysler's Neon: Is This the Small Car Detroit Couldn't Build?" *Business Week,* May 3, 1993, pp. 116–26.
52. T. B. Kinni, "Boundary-Busting Teamwork," *Industry Week,* March 21, 1994, pp. 72–78.
53. "Cross-Functional Obstacles," *Training,* May 1994, pp. 125–26.
54. The suggestions in this discussion come from K. Hess, *Creating the High-Performance Team* (New York: Wiley, 1987); Katzenbach and Smith, *The Wisdom of Teams,* pp. 43–64; Wellins, Byham, and Dixon, *Inside Teams,* pp. 299–337; and K. D. Scott and A. Townsend, "Teams: Why Some Succeed and Others Fail," *HRMagazine,* August 1994, pp. 62–67.
55. B. Dumaine, "Payoff from the New Management," *Fortune,* December 13, 1993, pp. 103–10.
56. S. T. Johnson, "Work Teams: What's Ahead in Work Design and Rewards Management," *Compensation & Benefits Review,* March–April 1993, pp. 35–41; and A. M. Saunier and E. J. Hawk, "Realizing the Potential of Teams through Team-Based Rewards," *Compensation & Benefits Review,* July–August 1994, pp. 24–33.
57. D. Harrington-Mackin, *The Team Building Tool Kit* (New York: AMACOM, 1994), p. 53.
58. T. D. Schellhardt, "To Be a Star among Equals, Be a Team Player," *Wall Street Journal,* April 20, 1994, p. B1.
59. Ibid.
60. Ibid.

CHAPTER 11

CREATING AND SUSTAINING THE ORGANIZATION'S CULTURE

Cult-like cultures are great places to work, but only for those who buy into the core ideology. Those who don't fit with the ideology are ejected like a virus.

- J. C. Collins and J. I. Porras

LEARNING OBJECTIVES

After studying this chapter, you should be able to:

1. Define organizational culture
2. Identify the seven primary characteristics that describe an organization's culture
3. Define the qualities that characterize a strong culture
4. Explain the ultimate source of an organization's culture
5. Describe how employees learn their organization's culture
6. Explain the primary forces that sustain a culture
7. Identify the situational factors that favor cultural change
8. Describe how to minimize cultural clash in mergers and acquisitions

In the early summer of 1995, IBM made a surprise offer to buy software powerhouse Lotus Development Corp. After some bargaining, IBM agreed to pay $3.5 billion for Lotus, and the marriage was soon consummated. But just as in personal relationships, not all corporate marriages are happy ones. For instance, a few years back, BankAmerica bought Charles Schwab & Co., the big discount brokerage firm. The acquisition looked terrific on paper—allowing BA to diversify into a broader range of financial products and giving Schwab access to BA's deep pockets. The only problem was that the cultures of the two companies were dramatically different. BankAmerica is conservative. Schwab is an aggressive risk taker. They tried to live together, but it just would not work. After 4 years, Charles Schwab bought his company back from BankAmerica, and the two firms went their separate ways.

Source: Chip Bok, reprinted with permission of the *Akron Beacon Journal* and creators syndicate.

How do things look for the IBM-Lotus marriage?[1] You be the judge. IBM has a long conservative tradition, although it has tried hard in the last few years to change. This is a company that, until very recently, was elitist and extremely rigid, tolerated a narrow range of "acceptable behaviors" from its employees (including a regulation dress code), and was obsessively focused on the prerogatives of authority. It was the corporate equivalent of the U.S. Marine Corps. New management has tried to change the culture, but IBM continues to be tradition-bound. In contrast, Lotus is technology-driven. Its main assets are the brilliant and often eccentric people who have developed products such as Lotus 1-2-3 and Lotus Notes. The work environment is extemely egalitarian, casual, and idiosyncratic. The office of John Landy, Lotus's senior vice president and chief technology officer, for instance, is a high-tech playground. It is full of computer docking stations, hand-held computers, video phones, and voice synthesizers embedded in plastic toys. All of Lotus's offices look more like college dorm rooms than corporate suites. But that's the way Lotus people like it. And Lotus's culture relishes the "strange and unusual." As a case in point, thousands of Lotus Notes users never even blinked when Landy gave a conference presentation dressed in a "Spiderman" suit!

Can Lotus's creative-type employees live happily and productively inside IBM? Will the marriage lead to a "brain drain," with Lotus employees exiting the company for more compatible surroundings? IBM's CEO, Louis Gerstner, acknowledged the potential problem when he told a news conference that he wanted to maintain Lotus's "entrepreneurial spirit" and would allow the company to retain its Cambridge, Massachusetts, base.

Organizational cultures differ. The right culture for one organization may be totally inappropriate for another. Moreover, these cultures have a powerful influence on organizational members. In this chapter, we define organizational culture, show how cultures differ, describe how they are created and transmitted, and offer some techniques for managing them.

WHAT IS ORGANIZATIONAL CULTURE?

A few years back, I asked an executive to tell me what he thought *organizational culture* meant. He gave me essentially the same answer that a Supreme Court justice once gave in attempting to define pornography: "I can't define it, but I know it when I see it." This executive's approach to defining organizational culture is not acceptable for our purposes. We need a basic definition to provide a point of departure for our quest to better understand the phenomenon. In this section, we will propose a specific definition and review several peripheral issues that revolve around that definition.

A Definition

There seems to be wide agreement that **organizational culture** refers to a system of shared meaning held by members that distinguishes the organization from other organizations.[2] This system of shared meaning is, on closer examination, a set of key characteristics that the organization values. The most recent research suggests that there are seven primary characteristics that, in aggregate, capture the essence of an organization's culture.[3]

1. *Innovation and risk taking.* The degree to which employees are encouraged to be innovative and take risks.
2. *Attention to detail.* The degree to which employees are expected to exhibit precision, analysis, and attention to detail.
3. *Outcome orientation.* The degree to which management focuses on results or outcomes rather than on the techniques and processes used to achieve those outcomes.
4. *People orientation.* The degree to which management decisions take into consideration the effect of outcomes on people within the organization.
5. *Team orientation.* The degree to which work activities are organized around teams rather than individuals.
6. *Aggressiveness.* The degree to which people are aggressive and competitive rather than easygoing.

7. *Stability*. The degree to which organizational activities emphasize maintaining the status quo in contrast to growth.

Each of these characteristics exists on a continuum from low to high. Appraising the organization on these seven characteristics, then, gives a composite picture of the organization's culture. This picture becomes the basis for feelings of shared understanding that members have about the organization, how things are done in it, and the way members are supposed to behave. Exhibit 11-1 demonstrates how these characteristics can be mixed to create highly diverse organizations.

Do Organizations Have Uniform Cultures?

Organizational culture represents a common perception held by the organization's members. This aspect of a culture was made explicit when we defined a culture as a system of *shared* meaning. We should expect, therefore, that individuals with different backgrounds or at different levels in the organization will tend to describe the organization's culture in similar terms.[4]

EXHIBIT 11-1
Contrasting Organizational Cultures

Organization A

This organization is a manufacturing firm. Managers are expected to fully document all decisions, and "good managers" are those who can provide detailed data to support their recommendations. Creative decisions that incur significant change or risk are not encouraged. Because managers of failed projects are openly criticized and penalized, they try not to implement ideas that deviate much from the status quo. One lower-level manager quoted an often-used phrase in the company: "If it ain't broke, don't fix it."

There are extensive rules and regulations in this firm that employees are required to follow. Managers supervise employees closely to ensure there are no deviations. Management is concerned with high productivity, regardless of the impact on employee morale or turnover.

Work activities are designed around individuals. There are distinct departments and lines of authority, and employees are expected to minimize formal contact with other employees outside their functional area or line of command. Performance evaluations and rewards emphasize individual effort, although seniority tends to be the primary factor in the determination of pay raises and promotions.

Organization B

This organization is also a manufacturing firm. Here, however, management encourages and rewards risk taking and change. Decisions based on intuition are valued as much as those that are well rationalized. Management prides itself on its history of experimenting with new technologies and its success in regularly introducing innovative products. Managers or employees who have a good idea are encouraged to "run with it," and failures are treated as "learning experiences." The company prides itself on being market-driven and rapidly responsive to the changing needs of its customers.

There are few rules and regulations for employees to follow, and supervision is loose because management believes that its employees are hardworking and trustworthy. Management is concerned with high productivity but believes that this comes through treating its people right. The company is proud of its reputation as being a good place to work.

Job activities are designed around work teams, and team members are encouraged to interact with people across functions and authority levels. Employees talk positively about the competition between teams. Individuals and teams have goals, and bonuses are based on achievement of outcomes. Employees are given considerable autonomy in choosing the means by which the goals are attained.

Acknowledgment that organizational culture has common properties does not mean, however, that there cannot be subcultures within any given culture. Most large organizations have a dominant culture and numerous sets of subcultures.[5] A **dominant culture** expresses the core values that are shared by a majority of the organization's members. When we talk about an *organization's culture,* we are referring to its dominant culture. It is this macro view of culture that gives an organization its distinct personality. **Subcultures** tend to develop in large organizations to reflect common problems, situations, or experiences that members face. These subcultures are likely to be defined by department designations and geographical separation. The purchasing department, for example, can have a subculture that is uniquely shared by members of that department. It will include the **core values** of the dominant culture plus additional values unique to members of the purchasing department. Similarly, an office or unit of the organization that is physically separated from the organization's main operations may take on a different personality. Again, the core values are essentially retained but modified to reflect the separated unit's distinct situation.

It is the "shared meaning" aspect of culture that makes it such a potent device for guiding and shaping behavior.

If organizations had no dominant culture and were composed only of numerous subcultures, the importance of organizational culture would be significantly lessened because there would be no uniform interpretation of what represented appropriate and inappropriate behavior. It is the "shared meaning" aspect of culture that makes it such a potent device for guiding and shaping behavior. But we cannot ignore the reality that many organizations also have subcultures that can influence the behavior of members.

Strong versus Weak Cultures

It has become increasingly popular to differentiate between strong and weak cultures.[6] The argument is that strong cultures have a greater impact on employee behavior and a more positive effect on the organization's performance.

In a **strong culture,** the organization's core values are both intensely held and widely shared.[7] The more members who accept the core values and the greater their commitment to those values, the stronger the culture is. Consistent with this definition, a strong culture will have a great influence on the behavior of its members because the high degree of sharedness and intensity creates an internal climate of high behavioral control. For example, Seattle-based Nordstrom has developed one of the strongest service cultures in the retailing industry. Nordstrom employees know in no uncertain terms what is expected of them, and these expectations go a long way in shaping their behavior. This message is communicated on a single 5-by-8-inch card that the company distributes (see Exhibit 11-2).

An increasing body of evidence indicates that strong cultures are associated with high organizational performance.[8] For instance, a study comparing eighteen high-performing companies—which included Procter & Gamble, Nordstrom, Citicorp, Hewlett-Packard, and Walt Disney—against a control group of eighteen lesser-performing firms found that a strong culture was the key factor in explaining the high-performers' long-term success.[9]

Culture as the Organization's Personality

In many organizations, especially those with strong cultures, one cultural dimension will rise above the others and essentially shape the organization. 3M Co., for instance, is dominated by its focus on innovation. The company "lives and breathes" new product generation. Let's take a look at how different organizations

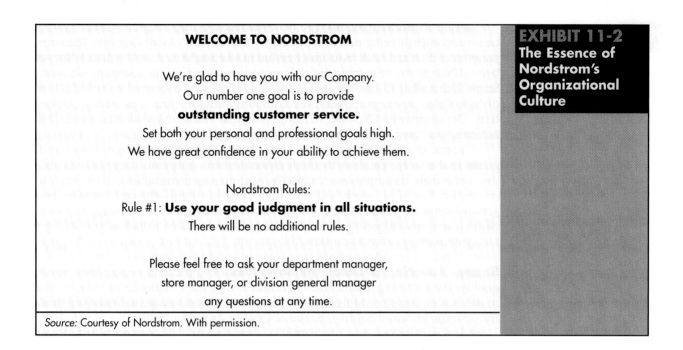

EXHIBIT 11-2
The Essence of Nordstrom's Organizational Culture

WELCOME TO NORDSTROM

We're glad to have you with our Company.
Our number one goal is to provide
outstanding customer service.
Set both your personal and professional goals high.
We have great confidence in your ability to achieve them.

Nordstrom Rules:
Rule #1: **Use your good judgment in all situations.**
There will be no additional rules.

Please feel free to ask your department manager,
store manager, or division general manager
any questions at any time.

Source: Courtesy of Nordstrom. With permission.

have chosen different cultural themes. This discussion will illustrate that strong cultures don't have to be similar to be successful.

Strong Risk-Taking Personalities Companies such as Microsoft, Coca-Cola, and Broderbund pride themselves on risk taking and tolerance (even encouragement) of failure. Microsoft wants people who have taken chances and failed.[10] But management looks to see whether people have learned from their mistakes. In hiring, for instance, interviewers always ask: What was a major failure you had? What did you learn from it? Microsoft wants employees who are willing to take risks, fail, and learn from their mistakes. Bill Gates, the company's CEO, says, "The way people deal with things that go wrong is an indicator of how they deal with change."[11]

Recognize failure

Most computer games have a shelf life of less than a year. But Broderbund's Carmen Sandiego is into its 11th year and still going strong. The company continues to add new and creative products to its line-up. In 1994, Broderbund overtook Microsoft to become the leading publisher of CD-ROM software.

Carmen Sandiego and the Logo Design are trademarks of Broderbund Software, Inc. Used with permission.

BUILDING SELF-AWARENESS • BUILDING SELF-AWARENESS

BUILDING SELF-AWARENESS • BUILDING SE

WHICH KIND OF CULTURE FITS YOU BEST?

INSTRUCTIONS

Read through the list of the following seven statements. Which of the statements do you *most* agree with? Put a 1 next to that statement. Which of the statements would you next most agree with? Put a 2 next to that statement. Continue this ranking until you place a 7 next to the statement you *least* agree with. Even though you may agree with many of these statements, think hard about your preferences as you rank order them.

a. I like being part of a team and having my performance assessed in terms of my contribution to the team. _____

b. No person's needs should be compromised in order for a department to achieve its goals. _____

c. I like the thrill and excitement of taking risks. _____

d. If a person's job performance is inadequate, it doesn't matter how much effort he or she made. _____

e. I like things to be stable and predictable. _____

f. I prefer managers who provide detailed and rational explanations for their decisions. _____

g. I like to work where there isn't a great deal of pressure and where people are essentially easygoing. _____

Turn to page 561 for scoring directions and key.

How do these two concepts compare in terms of strength? More specifically, does national culture override an organization's culture? Is an IBM facility in Germany, for example, more likely to reflect German ethnic culture or IBM's corporate culture?

The research indicates that national culture has a greater impact on employees than does their organization's culture.[24] German employees at an IBM facility in Munich, therefore, will be influenced more by German culture than by IBM's culture. This means that as influential as organizational culture is in shaping managerial practices and employee behavior, national culture is even more influential.

The above conclusion has to be qualified to reflect the self-selection that goes on at the hiring stage. IBM, for example, may be less concerned with hiring the "typical Italian" for its Italian operations than in hiring an Italian who fits within the IBM way of doing things.[25] Italians who have a high need for autonomy are more likely to go to Olivetti than IBM. Why? Because Olivetti's organizational culture is informal and nonstructured. It allows employees considerably more freedom than IBM does.[26] In fact, Olivetti seeks to hire individuals who are impatient, risk taking, and innovative—qualities in job candidates that IBM's Italian operations would purposely seek to exclude in new hires.

HOW IS CULTURE CREATED?

An organization's current customs, traditions, and general way of doing things are largely due to what it has done before and the degree of success it has had with those endeavors. This principle leads us to the ultimate source of an organization's culture: its founders.[27]

The founders of an organization traditionally have a major impact on that organization's early culture. They have a vision of what the organization should be. They are unconstrained by previous customs or ideologies. The small size that typically characterizes new organizations further facilitates the founders' imposition of their vision on all organizational members.

McDonald's founder, Ray Kroc, died in 1984. But his philosophy of providing customers with quality, service, cleanliness, and value continue to shape managerial decisions. Other contemporary examples of founders who have had an immeasurable impact on their organization's culture are Akio Morita at Sony, Ted Turner at Turner Broadcasting Systems, Bill Gates at Microsoft, Fred Smith at Federal Express, Mary Kay at Mary Kay Cosmetics, Chung Ju Yung at Hyundai, Steve Jobs at Apple Computer, David Packard at Hewlett-Packard, and Richard Branson at the Virgin Group.

IN THE NEWS

Patagonia Has Been Shaped in the Image of Its Founder

PATAGONIA INC. IS A $125 MILLION COMPANY THAT MAKES AND SELLS OUTDOOR GEAR. IT DOESN'T LOOK OR act much like your typical business firm. And that's because its founder and owner, Yvon Chouinard, doesn't look or act much like your typical chief executive.

Chouinard started his business out of the back of his car in the early 1960s. An avid "extreme adventurer," Chouinard lived to participate in sports such as mountain climbing and surfing (see photo). Beginning with one product—disposable iron pitons used by rock climbers—his company today sells a full line of outdoor gear through its retail stores and catalogue. "I never intended for my craft to become a business, but every time I returned from the mountains, my head was spinning with ideas for improving the tools of climbing," says Chouinard.

As the company grew, Chouinard hired people in a most unorthodox way. He chose people, not because of any specific business skills, but because he climbed, fished, or surfed with them. Employees were friends, and work was treated as something fun to do.

Patagonia now has 520 employees at its two main facilities in Ventura, California ("only minutes from the surf"), and Bozeman, Montana, and it has nineteen retail stores worldwide. Despite its size, the company continues to reflect Chouinard's casual approach to business and his strongly held values. Employees at the company's headquarters in Ventura think nothing of abandoning the office in midday to hop on a mountain bike, go rollerblading, or disappear to the beach. And Chouinard's strong belief in protecting the environment has had a pervasive influence on Patagonia's culture. For instance, as we noted in Chapter 6 and in our discussion on strategy, Patagonia has chosen to pursue a no-growth strategy because it considered its growth a threat to the environment. In 1991, Chouinard became very concerned that his company's rapid sales growth and expanded product lines were inconsistent with what was good for society. So he decided to use the company as a tool for social change. He downsized the company by 20 percent, cut the clothing line by more than 30 percent, and reduced the issuance of its popular catalogue from four to two times a year. In Patagonia's Fall 1991 catalogue, Chouinard told his customers, "We are limiting Patagonia's growth in the United States with the eventual goal of halting growth altogether." And he explained Patagonia's reduced product line: "Last fall you had a choice of five ski pants; now you may choose between two. This is, of course, un-American, but two styles of ski pants are all that anyone needs."

Patagonia has cut out a unique market niche and created a unique culture to match. And both are largely a reflection of the company's founder, Yvon Chouinard. Ask a Patagonia employee what his or her company is about, and you're likely to hear a common theme: simplicity, dedication to employees and community, pursuit of the highest quality, and commitment to the environment. Not surprisingly, these are the values that have guided Chouinard throughout his career.

Source: P. LaBarre, "Patagonia Comes of Age," reprinted with permission from *Industry Week,* April 3, 1995, pp. 42–48. © Penton Publishing Inc., Cleveland, Ohio

HOW DO EMPLOYEES LEARN THEIR ORGANIZATION'S CULTURE?

Culture is transmitted to employees in a number of forms. The most potent are stories, rituals, material symbols, and language.

Stories

During the days when Henry Ford II was chairman of the Ford Motor Co., one would have been hard-pressed to find a manager who hadn't heard the story about Mr. Ford's reminding his executives, when they got too arrogant, that "it's my name that's on the building." The message was clear: Henry Ford II ran the company!

Nordstrom employees are fond of the following story. It strongly conveys the company's policy toward customer returns: When this specialty retail chain was in its infancy, a customer came in and wanted to return a set of automobile tires. The salesclerk was a bit uncertain how to handle the problem. As the customer and salesclerk were speaking, Mr. Nordstrom walked by and overheard the conversation. He immediately interceded, asking the customer how much he had paid for the tires. Nordstrom then instructed the clerk to take the tires back and provide a full cash refund. After the customer had received his refund and left, the perplexed clerk looked at the boss. "But, Mr. Nordstrom, we don't sell tires!" "I know," replied the boss, "but we do whatever we need to do to make the customer happy. I mean it when I say we have a no-questions-asked return policy." Nordstrom then picked up the telephone and called a friend in the auto parts business to see how much he could get for the tires.

Stories such as these circulate through many organizations. They typically contain a narrative of events about the organization's founders, rule breaking, rags-to-riches successes, reductions in the work force, relocation of employees, reactions to past mistakes, and organizational coping.[28] These stories anchor the present in the past and provide explanations and legitimacy for current practices.[29]

Rituals

Rituals are repetitive sequences of activities that express and reinforce the key values of the organization, what goals are most important, which people are important and which are expendable.[30] College faculty members undergo a lengthy ritual in their quest for permanent employment—tenure. Typically, the faculty member is on probation for 6 years. At the end of that period, the member's colleagues must make one of two choices: extend a tenured appointment or issue a 1-year terminal contract. What does it take to obtain tenure? It usually requires satisfactory teaching performance, service to the department and university, and scholarly activity. But, of course, what satisfies the requirements for tenure in one department at one university may be appraised as inadequate in another. The key is that the tenure decision, in essence, asks those who are tenured to assess whether the candidate has demonstrated, on the basis of 6 years of performance, whether he or she fits in. Colleagues who have been socialized properly will have proved themselves worthy of being granted tenure. Every year, hundreds of faculty members at colleges and universities are denied tenure. In some cases, this action is a result of poor performance across the board. More often, however, the decision can be traced to the faculty member's not doing well in those areas that the tenured faculty believe are important. The instructor who spends dozens of hours each week preparing for class and achieves outstanding evaluations by students but neglects his or her research and publication activities may be passed over for tenure. What has happened, simply, is that the instructor has failed to adapt to the norms set by the department. The astute faculty member will assess early on in the probationary period what attitudes and behaviors his or her colleagues want and will then proceed to give them what they want. And, of course, by demanding certain attitudes and behaviors, the tenured faculty have made significant strides toward standardizing tenure candidates.

One of the best-known corporate rituals is Mary Kay Cosmetics' annual award meeting.[31] Looking like a cross between a circus and a Miss America pageant, the meeting takes place over a couple of days in a large auditorium, on a stage in front of a large, cheering audience, with all the participants dressed in glamorous evening clothes. Saleswomen are rewarded with an array of flashy gifts—gold and diamond pins, fur stoles, pink Cadillacs—in recognition of their success in achieving sales goals. This "show" acts as a motivator by publicly acknowledging outstanding sales performance. In addition, the ritual aspect reinforces Mary Kay's determination and optimism, which enabled her to overcome personal hardships, found her own company, and achieve material success. It conveys to her salespeople that reaching their sales goals is important and that through hard work and encouragement they too can achieve success.

Material Symbols

Fullers and Lampreia are two of Seattle's most highly rated and expensive restaurants. Geographically, they are less than ten blocks apart, but culturally the two restaurants are miles apart. Fullers is formal to the point of being "stuffy." It has a museum-level decor. The staff is formally attired, serious, focused, and stiff. In contrast, Lampreia is casual and low-key. It has a stylish but minimalist decor. The staff's casual dress and style are consistent with the decor.

Both Fullers and Lampreia consistently receive honors for their food and service; they both require reservations days, and sometimes weeks, ahead of time; and they both cost at least $80 for dinner for two. Yet the restaurants' distinct cultures, as reflected in material symbols such as the decor and the attire worn by employees, are conveyed to customers, new employees, and current employees. At Fullers, that message is that we're serious, formal, and conservative. The message at Lampreia is that we're relaxed and open.

Did you ever notice that some corporations provide their top executives with chauffeur-driven limousines and, when they travel by air, unlimited use of the corporate jet? Executives at other firms may not get to ride in limousines or private jets, but they might still get a car and air transportation paid for by the company. The car, however, is a Chevrolet (with no driver), and the jet seat is in the economy section of a commercial airliner.

The layout of an organization's facilities, dress attire, the types of automobiles top executives are given, and the presence or absence of corporate aircraft are examples of material symbols. Others include the size of offices, the elegance of furnishings, executive perks, the existence of employee lounges or on-site dining facilities, and the presence of reserved parking spaces for certain employees. These material symbols convey to employees who is important, the degree of egalitarianism desired by top management, and the kinds of behavior (for example, risk-taking, conservative, authoritarian, participative, individualistic, social) that are appropriate.

Language

Many organizations and units within organizations use language as a way to identify members of a culture or subculture. By learning this language, members attest to their acceptance of the culture and, in so doing, help to preserve it.

Many organizations and units within organizations use language as a way to identify members of a culture or subculture.

The following are examples of terminology used by employees at Knight-Ridder Information, a Cali-

ate culture, (2) change a culture that is no longer compatible with the organization's direction, and (3) successfully blend their culture with the cultures of other organizations in response to mergers, strategic alliances, or other interorganizational arrangements.

Sustaining an Organization's Culture

Once a culture is in place, there are practices within the organization that act to maintain and reinforce it by giving employees a set of similar experiences.[35] For example, many of the human resource practices discussed in Chapter 10 reinforce the organization's culture. The selection process, performance appraisal criteria, training activities, and promotion procedures ensure that those hired fit in with the culture, reward those who support it, and penalize (and even expel) those who challenge it. Three forces, controllable by management, play a particularly important part in sustaining an appropriate culture—selection practices, the actions of top management, and socialization methods.

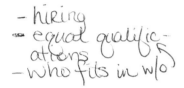

Selection Practices The explicit goal of the selection process is to identify and hire individuals who have the knowledge, skills, and abilities to perform the jobs within the organization successfully. But, typically, more than one candidate will be identified who meets any given job's requirements. It would be naive to ignore the fact that, when that point is reached, the final decision as to who is hired will be significantly influenced by the decision maker's judgment of how well the candidates will fit into the organization. This attempt to ensure a proper match, whether purposely or inadvertently, results in the hiring of people who have values essentially consistent with those of the organization.[36] In addition, the selection process provides information to applicants about the organization. Candidates learn about the organization, and, if they perceive a conflict between their values and those of the organization, they can self-select themselves out of the applicant pool. Selection, therefore, becomes a two-way street, allowing either employer or applicant to refuse a marriage if there appears to be a mismatch. In this way, the selection process sustains an organization's culture by selecting out those individuals who might attack or undermine its core values.

Applicants for entry-level positions in brand management at Procter & Gamble undergo an exhaustive application and screening process. Their interviewers are part of an elite cadre who have been selected and trained extensively via lectures, videotapes, films, practice interviews, and role plays to identify applicants who will successfully fit in at P&G. Applicants are interviewed in depth for such qualities as their ability to "turn out high volumes of excellent work," "identify and understand problems," and "reach thoroughly substantiated and well-reasoned conclusions that lead to action." P&G values rationality and seeks applicants who think rationally. College applicants receive two interviews and a general knowledge test on campus before being flown to Cincinnati for three more one-on-one interviews and a group interview at lunch. Each encounter seeks corroborating evidence of the traits that the firm believes are highly correlated with "what counts" for success at P&G.[37] Applicants for positions at Compaq Computer are carefully chosen for their ability to fit into the company's teamwork-oriented culture. As one executive put it, "We can find lots of people who are competent. . . . The No. 1 issue is whether they fit into the way we do business."[38] At Compaq, that means job candidates who are easy to get along with and who feel comfortable with the company's consensus management style. Compaq's screening process increases the likelihood that loners and people with big egos will be weeded out. It's not unusual for an applicant to be interviewed by fifteen people who represent all departments of the company and a variety of seniority levels.[39]

leading by examples

Top Management Behavior The actions of top management also have a major impact on the organization's culture.[40] Through what they say and how they behave, senior executives establish norms that filter down through the organization as to whether risk taking is desirable; how much freedom managers should give their subordinates; what is appropriate dress; what actions will pay off in terms of pay raises, promotions, and other rewards; and the like.

For example, look at Xerox Corp.[41] Its chief executive from 1961 to 1968 was Joseph C. Wilson. An aggressive, entrepreneurial type, he oversaw Xerox's staggering growth on the basis of its 914 copier, one of the most successful products in American history. Under Wilson, Xerox had an entrepreneurial environment, with an informal, high-camaraderie, innovative, bold, risk-taking culture. Wilson's replacement as CEO was C. Peter McColough, a Harvard MBA with a formal management style. He instituted bureaucratic controls and a major change in Xerox's culture. By the time McColough stepped down in 1982, Xerox had become stodgy and formal, with lots of politics and turf battles and layers of watchdog managers. His replacement was David T. Kearns. He believed that the culture he had inherited hindered Xerox's ability to compete. To increase the company's competitiveness, Kearns trimmed Xerox down by cutting 15,000 jobs, delegating decision making downward, and refocusing the organization's culture around a simple theme: boosting the quality of Xerox products and services. By his actions and those of his senior managerial cadre, Kearns conveyed to everyone at Xerox that the company valued and rewarded quality and efficiency. When Kearns retired in 1990, Xerox still had its problems. The copier business was mature and Xerox had fared badly in developing computerized office systems. The current CEO, Paul Allaire, has again sought to reshape Xerox's culture. Specifically, he has reorganized the corporation around a worldwide marketing department, has unified product development and manufacturing divisions, and has replaced half of the company's top-management team with outsiders. Allaire seeks to reshape Xerox's culture to focus on innovative thinking and out-hustling the competition.

Denny's Inc. is aggressively moving to root out racism at the restaurant chain, led by the company's CEO. He is sending a clear warning to employees and franchisees alike: "If you discriminate, you're history." In 1994, only one of Denny's 512 franchises was minority-owned. By 1996, 27 were black-owned. New Syracuse, N.Y. franchisee Charles E. Davis (seated in photo), has aggressively sought black customers and has doubled his black business.

Socialization Methods No matter how good a job the organization does in recruiting and selection, new employees are not fully indoctrinated in the organization's culture. Maybe most important, because they are unfamiliar with the organization's culture, new employees are potentially likely to disturb the beliefs and customs that are in place. The organization will, therefore, want to help new employees adapt to its culture. This adaptation process is called **socialization.**[42]

All U.S. Marines must go through boot camp, where they "prove" their commitment. Of course, at the same time, the Marine trainers are indoctrinating new recruits in the "Marine way." New Sanyo employees go through an intensive 5-month training program (trainees eat and sleep together in company-subsidized dorms and are required to vacation together at company-owned resorts), in which they learn the Sanyo way of doing everything—from how to speak to superiors to proper grooming and dress.[43] The company considers this program essential for transforming young employees, fresh out of school, into dedicated *kaisha senshi,* or corporate warriors.

As we discuss socialization, keep in mind that the most critical socialization stage is at the time of entry into the organization. This is when the organization seeks to mold the outsider into an employee "in good standing." Those employees who fail to learn the essential or pivotal role behaviors risk being labeled "nonconformists" or "rebels," labels that often lead to expulsion. But the organization will be socializing every employee, though maybe not as explicitly, throughout his or her entire career in the organization. This continued socialization further contributes to sustaining the culture.

Socialization can be conceptualized as a process made up of three stages: prearrival, encounter, and metamorphosis.[44] The first stage encompasses all the learning that occurs before a new member joins the organization. In the second stage, the new employee sees what the organization is really like and confronts the possibility that expectations and reality may diverge. In the third stage, the relatively long-lasting changes take place. The new employee masters the skills required for his or her job, successfully performs his or her new roles, and makes the adjustments to his or her work group's values and norms.[45]

The **prearrival stage** explicitly recognizes that each individual arrives with a set of values, attitudes, and expectations. These cover both the work to be done and the organization. For instance, in many jobs, particularly professional work, new members will have undergone a considerable degree of prior socialization in training and in school. One major purpose of a business school, for example, is to socialize business students to the attitudes and behaviors that business firms want. If business executives believe that successful employees value the profit ethic, are loyal, will work hard, desire to achieve, and willingly accept directions from their superiors, they can hire individuals out of business schools that are known to premold students in that pattern. But prearrival socialization goes beyond the specific job. The selection process is used in most organizations to inform prospective employees about the organization as a whole. In addition, as noted previously, the selection process also acts to ensure the inclusion of the "right type"—those who will fit in. "Indeed, the ability of the individual to present the appropriate face during the selection process determines his ability to move into the organization in the first place. Thus, success depends on the degree to which the aspiring member has correctly anticipated the expectations and desires of those in the organization in charge of selection."[46]

Upon entry into the organization, the new member enters the **encounter stage.** In this stage, the individual confronts the possible dichotomy between her expectations—about her job, her co-workers, her boss, and the organization in general—and reality. If expectations prove to have been more or less accurate, the encounter stage merely provides for a reaffirmation of the perceptions gained earlier. Expectations, however, are not always accurate. When expectations and reality differ, the new employee must undergo socialization that will detach her from her previous assumptions and replace them with another set that the organization deems desirable. At the extreme, a new member may become totally disillusioned with the actualities of her job and resign. Proper selection should significantly reduce the probability of the latter occurrence.

Finally, the new member must work out any problems discovered during the encounter stage. This process may mean going through changes—hence, we call this the **metamorphosis stage.** The options presented in Exhibit 11-3 on page 342 are alternatives designed to bring about the desired metamorphosis. Note, for example, that the more management relies on socialization programs that are formal, collective, fixed, serial, and that emphasize divestiture, the greater the likelihood that newcomers' differences and perspectives will be stripped away and replaced by standardized and predictable behaviors. Careful selection by management of newcomers' socialization experiences can—at the extremes—create rigid conformists who maintain traditions and customs or creative individualists who consider no organizational practice to be sacred.

We can say that metamorphosis and the entry socialization process are complete when the new member has become comfortable with the organization and his or her job. She has internalized the norms of the organization and her work group, and she understands and accepts those norms. The new member feels accepted by her peers as a trusted and valued individual, is self-confident that she has the competence to complete the job successfully, and understands the system—not only her own tasks, but the rules, procedures, and informally accepted practices as well. Finally, she knows how she will be appraised, that is, what criteria will be used to measure and evaluate her work. She knows what is expected and what constitutes a job "well done."

Changing an Organization's Culture

The fact that an organization's culture is made up of relatively stable and permanent characteristics—and is reinforced by its selection process, top management behavior, and socialization methods—tends to make most cultures very resistant to change.[47] A culture takes a long time to form, and once it has been established it tends to become entrenched. Strong cultures at firms such as General Motors, AT&T, IBM, Westinghouse Electric, Eastman Kodak, and Ciba-Geigy have been found to be particularly resistant to change because employees have become so committed to them. If, over time, a given culture becomes inappropriate to an organization and a handicap to management, there might be little management can do to change it, especially in the short run. Even in the most favorable conditions, cultural changes have to be measured in years, not in weeks or months.

A culture takes a long time to form, and once it has been established it tends to become entrenched.

Understanding the Situational Factors What "favorable conditions" *might* facilitate cultural change? The evidence suggests that cultural change is most likely to take place when most or all of the following conditions exist:

A dramatic crisis occurs. This is the shock that undermines the status quo and calls into question the relevance of the current culture.[48] Examples might be a surprising financial setback, the loss of a major customer, a serious decline in market share, or a dramatic breakthrough by a competitor. Executives at Pepsi-

Real or perceived

Read!

EXHIBIT 11-3
Entry Socialization Options

Formal vs. Informal The more a new employee is segregated from the ongoing work setting and differentiated in some way to make explicit his or her newcomer's role, the more formal socialization is. Specific orientation and training programs are examples. Informal socialization puts the new employee directly into his or her job, with little or no special attention.

Individual vs. Collective New members can be socialized individually, as in many professional offices. They can also be grouped together and processed through an identical set of experiences, as in military boot camp.

Fixed vs. Variable This refers to the time schedule in which newcomers make the transition from outsider to insider. A fixed schedule establishes standardized stages of transition. This schedule characterizes rotational training programs. It also includes probationary periods, such as the 8-to-10 year "associate" status used by accounting and law firms before deciding on whether a candidate is made a partner. Variable schedules give no advanced notice of their transition timetable. Variable schedules describe the typical promotion system, in which one is not advanced to the next stage until he or she is "ready."

Serial vs. Random Serial socialization is characterized by the use of role models who train and encourage the newcomer. Apprenticeship and mentoring programs are examples. In random socialization, role models are deliberately withheld. The new employee is left on his or her own to figure things out.

Investiture vs. Divestiture Investiture socialization assumes that the newcomer's qualities and qualifications are the necessary ingredients for job success, so those qualities and qualifications are confirmed and supported. Divestiture socialization tries to strip away certain characteristics of the recruit. Fraternity and sorority "pledges" go through divestiture socialization to shape them into the proper role.

Sources: Based on J. Van Maanen, "People Processing: Strategies of Organizational Socialization," *Organizational Dynamics,* Summer 1978, pp. 19–36; and E. H. Schein, "Organizational Culture," *American Psychologist,* February 1990, p. 116.

Cola and Ameritech even admit to creating crises in order to stimulate change in their cultures.[49]

Turnover in leadership. New top leadership, which can provide an alternative set of key values, may be perceived as being needed to respond to the crisis. New leadership would definitely include the organization's chief executive but also might need to include all senior management positions. The hiring of outside CEOs at IBM (Louis Gerstner), General Motors (Jack Smith), Kodak (George Fisher), and Westinghouse (Michael Jordan) illustrates attempts to introduce new leadership.

Young and small organization. The younger the organization is, the less entrenched its culture will be. Similarly, it is easier for management to communicate its new values when the organization is small. This relationship helps explain the difficulty that multibillion-dollar corporations have in changing their cultures.

Weak culture. The more widely held a culture is and the higher the agreement among members on its values, the more difficult it will be to change. Weak cultures are more amenable to change than strong ones.

These situational factors help to explain why companies such as IBM and General Motors have had such difficulty in reshaping their cultures. For the most part, employees didn't see their company's day-to-day problems as being of crisis proportions. Until just a couple of years ago, top management positions were always filled by internal candidates who were steeped in the company's established culture. And, finally, both IBM and GM are neither young nor small, and their cultures are not weak.

How Can Cultural Change Be Accomplished? If the situational factors are favorable, how does management go about enacting the cultural change? The challenge is to "unfreeze" the current culture. No single action is likely to have the impact necessary to unfreeze something that is entrenched and highly valued. Therefore there needs to be a comprehensive and coordinated strategy for managing culture.

The best place to begin is with a cultural analysis.[50] This would include a cultural audit to assess the current culture, a comparison of the present culture with the culture that is desired, and a gap evaluation to identify what cultural elements specifically need changing.

Next, management needs to make it clear to employees that the organization's survival is legitimately threatened if change is not forthcoming. This is where exploiting a dramatic crisis comes in. If a crisis exists but isn't visible to all members of the organization, then management needs to raise the alarm. If there isn't any crisis to exploit, it may be necessary to invent one. Remember, if employees don't see the urgency for change, apathy is likely to win out over any change efforts.

The appointment of a new top executive is likely to dramatize that major changes are going to take place. He or she can offer a new role model, a new vision, and new standards of behavior. The change effort is more likely to succeed if the new executive moves quickly to introduce his or her new vision and to staff key management positions with individuals who are similarly committed to this vision.

IN THE NEWS

Trying to Remake Eastman Kodak's Culture

After the first year in his new job, George Fisher had laid the initial groundwork for changing Eastman Kodak's lethargic, centralized, authority-conscious culture. But, even he would admit, it has been slow going. He's finding Kodak's plodding operating mentality tough to change.

Fisher had been instrumental in leading Motorola to "world-class" status. In December 1993, Kodak's board hired the 53-year-old Fisher away from Motorola to do the same thing for the photography and imaging giant.

As the new CEO at Kodak, Fisher was clearly aware of the problems he was taking on. Although the company had annual sales of $20 billion, it continued to lose ground to foreign competitors such as Fuji Photo Film Co., and it risked further losses to newer rivals in the fast-paced digital arena.

The Kodak culture that Fisher inherited reflected decades of success and complacency. Kodak was "fat and happy," with layers of bureaucrats. Decisions moved through numerous management levels and got slowed down along the way. Fisher sought to replace this culture with a new vision. Kodak would lead the way into a new electronic age, meshing traditional photography with wireless communication. Key decisions would be made at the operating unit level. And managers would be encouraged to get products to market faster and shed their old superstar egos when dealing with customers and joint-venture partners. Finally, Fisher planned to introduce Total Customer Satisfaction as a new objective at Kodak—a direct throwback to a similar program he had championed at Motorola.

Fisher recognized that he could not shake up Kodak's culture with the management team that was in place on his arrival. So he quickly moved to bring in new blood. For instance, he brought in Harry Kavetas from IBM as chief financial officer. He wooed Carl Gustin away from Digital Equipment Corp. to help run Kodak's digital business. And former Apple Computer CEO John Sculley was brought on board to help revitalize Kodak's marketing efforts.

Fisher's battle to change Kodak's culture is just beginning. As he noted, "The mind-sets here have to be worked on—but you can't change a culture just by decree." In Fisher's defense, his first steps seem to be in the right direction.

Source: Based on W. Bounds, "Kodak under Fisher: Upheaval in Slow Motion," *Wall Street Journal,* December 22, 1994, p. B1.

Mellon Bank Corp. chairman and CEO Frank Cahouet has had considerable difficulty trying to mesh Boston Co.'s aggressive culture into his company's risk-aversive, cost-conscious culture.

The new leadership will want to move quickly to create new stories, symbols, and rituals to replace those that were previously used to convey to employees the organization's dominant values. This change needs to be done rapidly. Delays will allow the current culture to become associated with the new leadership, thus closing the window of opportunity for change.

Finally, management will want to change the selection and socialization processes and the appraisal and reward systems to support employees who espouse the new values that are sought.

These suggestions, of course, provide no guarantee that change efforts will succeed. Organizational members do not quickly let go of values that they understand and that have worked well for them in the past. Managers must therefore show patience. Change, if it comes, will be painfully slow. And management must keep on constant alert to protect against reversion to old, familiar practices and traditions. Yet, there is an expanding set of success stories. For instance, Bankers Trust, British Airways, First Chicago, Nissan, and GE have effectively achieved dramatic cultural change.[51] Three points about these success stories are worth noting. First, these turnarounds tended to take 7 to 10 years, confirming our call for patience. Second, in every case of successful cultural change, the CEOs who provided the leadership were essentially outsiders. They were brought in either from outside the organization or from a division not in the corporate mainstream. And, finally, all of the CEOs started their new jobs by trying to create an atmosphere of perceived crisis.

Blending Organizational Cultures

The Lotus acquisition by IBM, described at the opening of this chapter, represents an example of blending organizational cultures. In this section, our objective is to see if we can derive some lessons from previous experiences with mergers, acquisitions, and joint ventures that can guide managers in making future interorganizational linkage decisions.

A review of major mergers and acquistions leads us to the obvious conclusion that not all marriages are made in heaven! In fact, studies repeatedly indicate that, at best, only half of all mergers and acquistions meet initial financial expectations.[52]

The motive behind almost all corporate marriages is to gain positive synergy by merging financial, marketing, or strategic advantages. For instance, AT&T bought McCaw Cellular as part of its strategy to become a power in wireless communications.[53] Consistent with this synergy motive, when assessing marriage partners, acquirers have historically focused the bulk of their attention on financial and strategic factors. The evidence, however, suggests that cultural incompatibility breaks up more marriages than those traditional factors.[54] For instance, a survey of more than 200 European chief executives found that the ability to integrate the new company was ranked as the most important factor for acquisition success.[55] Cultural fit is probably the most important determinant of whether mergers, acqusitions, or joint ventures succeed.

The landscape is littered with corporate marriages in which management failed to accurately assess the downside from culture clash. The staid Mellon Bank's acquisition in 1993 of the freewheeling money-management firm Boston Co. created one big unhappy family.[56] By 1995, key Boston Co. money managers were leaving in droves, unable to adapt to Mellon's cautious, penny-pinching ways. The joint venture to develop a revolutionary computer memory chip by Siemens AG, Toshiba Corp., and IBM has been plagued with problems as researchers try, unsuccessfully, to reconcile disparate organizational and national cultures.[57] Waterford Crystal's takeover of Wedgwood China, billed originally as "the perfect marriage," has been a financial disaster.[58] And some culture clashes seem to never mellow, even after decades of living together. McDonnell Douglas, the result of merging McDonnell Co. and Douglas Aircraft in 1967, continues to be a company characterized by internal bickering created by efforts to blend two disparate cultures.[59]

The landscape is littered with corporate marriages in which management failed to accurately assess the downside from culture clash.

What can management do to improve its odds when acquiring another firm?[60] First, consistent with our previous discussion of cultural change, management should conduct a cultural audit of the acquisition candidate. This is *in addition to* the more traditional financial and strategic analysis. The results of the cultural analysis should be used to determine the degree of integration the acquiring firm will introduce and to guide communication with the takeover candidate.

Corporate marriages fall into one of three types based upon the degree of integration and culture change necessary. The least disruptive are *extension mergers,* in which the acquiring organization takes a relatively "hands-off" approach. The newly acquired firm is allowed to operate essentially independently of the acquirer. *Collaborative mergers* integrate operations or involve exchange of technology or other expertise. Collaborative efforts should be pursued only when the different organizational cultures are highly compatible. The final category encompasses *redesign mergers.* This type characterizes organizations that intend to introduce widescale change in the firm they are acquiring. The acquired firm is expected to totally adopt the practices, procedures, and culture of the dominant merger partner.

Any of these three typologies *can* be successful. The key factor is gaining consensus between the combining organizations and their members as to the desired mode of acculturation. When corporate marriages fail because of cultural incompatibility, the typical culprit is that the parties did not recognize, share, or accept each other's perception of the marriage terms. It is important, therefore, to invite employees of the acquired company or both merger partners to participate in a series of group meetings so that they can discuss results of the culture analysis and expectations. This effort to open communications, of course, provides no guarantee that cultural clashes can be avoided, but it improves the odds.

THREATS TO DIVERSITY: THE DOWNSIDE OF STRONG CULTURES

We conclude this chapter by acknowledging one additional drawback to strong cultures: They create a real barrier to achieving workforce diversity and capitalizing on its benefits. Hiring new employees who, because of race, gender, ethnicity, or other differences, are not like the majority of the organization's members creates a paradox.[61] Management wants new employees to accept the organization's core cultural values. Otherwise, these employees are unlikely to fit in or be accepted. But at the same time, management wants to openly acknowledge and demonstrate support for the differences these employees bring to the workplace.

Strong cultures put considerable pressure on employees to conform. They limit the range of values and styles that are acceptable. Obviously, this emphasis creates a dilemma. Organizations hire diverse individuals because of the alternative strengths these people bring to the workplace. Yet these diverse behaviors and strengths are likely to diminish in strong cultures as people attempt to fit in. Strong cultures, therefore, can be liabilities when they effectively eliminate those unique strengths that people of different backgrounds bring to the organization.

SUMMARY

(This chapter summary is organized by the chapter-opening learning objectives on page 325.)

1. Organizational culture is a system of shared meaning held by members that distinguishes the organization from other organizations.
2. The seven primary characteristics that define an organization's culture are: (1) innovation and risk taking, (2) attention to detail, (3) outcome orientation, (4) people orientation, (5) team orientation, (6) aggressiveness, and (7) stability.
3. A strong culture is characterized by core values that are intensely held and widely shared.
4. The ultimate source of an organization's culture is the organization's founder. He or she is unconstrained by previous ideologies, and the organization's typical small size in its early years facilitates communication of the founder's vision.
5. Employees learn their organization's culture through stories, rituals, material symbols, and language.
6. The primary forces that sustain a culture are the organization's selection practices, top management behavior, and socialization methods.
7. The situational factors that favor cultural change are a dramatic crisis, turnover in top leadership, a young and small organization, and a weak culture.
8. To minimize cultural clash in mergers and acquisitions, management of the acquiring organization should conduct a cultural audit, choose a degree of integration consistent with compatibility, and use open communications to share expectations.

REVIEW AND DISCUSSION QUESTIONS

1. Contrast *dominant* and *sub* cultures and compare their influence on shaping the behavior of organizational members.
2. Demonstrate how one individual dimension of organizational culture can rise above the others and essentially shape the organization.
3. Contrast the strength of organizational culture with that of national culture. Explain your conclusion.
4. How do stories shape cultures?
5. What do the material symbols in offices and classrooms at your college convey about its culture?
6. Think of a large organization you know. Develop a list of jargon used in that organization that would differentiate its members and the organization from other organizations.
7. How do you read and assess an organization's culture?
8. Describe various socialization options and how they shape new organizational members.
9. "To survive in today's dynamic environment, organizations need to have an innovative, risk-taking, team-oriented, and aggressive culture." Do you agree or disagree with this statement? Support your answer.
10. "You can't change an organization's culture." Build an argument to support this statement; then negate your argument.

CASE EXERCISE A
A DISCRIMINATORY AND HARASSING CULTURE: THE CIA

Strong cultures are not always positive. The U.S. Central Intelligence Agency is an example of an organization with a strong culture but some of whose core values adversely affect the organization's performance. Several of the people's names in this case have been changed at their request.

By the time "Janet" finished her training in Virginia, she looked like the perfect spy. Outgoing and affable, she slipped easily into foreign cultures—a legacy from having grown up overseas. In college in Tokyo, Janet became fluent in Japanese. Now, skilled in picking locks and servicing film drops, the 26-year-old spy eagerly awaited her first assignment abroad. But the old boys of the CIA were not eager to have Janet among their ranks. Women spies have never been fully accepted in the hard-drinking, macho world of the agency's clandestine service, known as the Directorate of Operations, or DO. Janet quit the agency in 1988 out of frustration.

Today, the women of the CIA refuse to quit. Angered by a male-dominated climate and inequality in promotions and assignments, the CIA's female spies are demanding changes. Such reform is one of the many challenges facing newly appointed CIA director John Deutch.

To many, the issue goes beyond money and fairness. The agency's old-boy mentality wastes some of its most talented people, many CIA women say, while it hampers the basic mission of the CIA. "They really protect their own," says Lynne Larkin, a 7-year veteran who recently resigned over a job discrimination issue. The old-boy network, Larkin says, contributes to an atmosphere in which people feel they can break the rules without repercussion. "They have this idea that they're not really held accountable," says Larkin. "Abuse not only continues but tends to get worse."

For Janet, the discrimination was blatant. Her first assignment in Tokyo became the joke of the CIA station. She was assigned as a "port caller," an officer who recruits sailors, usually off of Third World ships, to photograph Chinese ports and North Korean vessels when they sail into "denied areas"—places U.S. spies cannot gain access to. Usually, the port caller job is reserved for swaggering jocks, not a 5-foot-6-inch, 125-pound female officer. For Janet, the station chief slapped on a special restriction: She was forbidden to go into bars or to drink while recruiting sailors. The job was a recipe for failure. "He clearly felt that if I was given a hard enough time, maybe they wouldn't send in another woman for a while," she says. Janet wouldn't be outsmarted, however. With some ingenuity, she devised a scheme to phone a ship's radio operator when a new vessel docked. Then, pretending to work for a publishing company, she invited the sailors ashore. Face to face, Janet persuaded them to take photos for pay. Within a year, Janet became the station's top recruiter. But her bosses didn't appreciate her efforts. After failing to win another overseas posting, Janet claimed that the station chief had altered her performance report, in violation of CIA policy. Today, some 300 women have threatened a class action suit against the CIA, citing similar discriminatory practices.

Sexual harassment has been an even bigger problem at the CIA. Nearly 50 percent of all white women have reported being sexually harassed. Like a throwback to the 1950s, a fixation with nude photographs and crude sexual jokes is common among some male case officers. Women complain of a hostile work environment rife with insensitive or derogatory comments, jokes, signs, and posters.

Women who try to fight the old boys through offical channels often encounter a fierce backlash. There is a strong perception within the DO that those who complained received no help or, worse, jeopardized their careers. "Jennifer," who had an otherwise stellar career in the DO, found her promotion path blocked after she officially complained that a male boss, at a staff meeting, had referred to "minorities, women and other two-headed animals." "If you complain, you are seen as betraying the system," she says.

Questions

1. Describe the CIA's culture in as much detail as you can.
2. What specific forces have shaped and sustained this culture?
3. Many police departments have similar macho cultures. Research your local police organization to see to what degree women feel harassed or discriminated against. What policies did you find that contribute to discouraging or encouraging a macho culture?
4. If you were John Deutch, what actions would you take to deal with the problems of discrimination and sexual harassment at the CIA?

Source: Adapted from D. Stanglin, "The Angry Women of the CIA," *U.S. News & World Report,* April 10, 1995, pp. 47–49. Reprinted with permission.

CASE EXERCISE B
CABLETRON SYSTEMS, INC.

In 1994, S. Robert Levine, CEO of Cabletron Systems Inc., paid his company more than it paid him! Levine, 36, draws only $52,000 a year in salary—ridiculous compensation for a company with 4,900 employees and sales of over $800 million. Yet in 1994 he wrote the company a personal check for more than $70,000 to cover his business expenses that were not reimbursable by Cabletron. What's going on?

Levine and his partner, Craig Benson, founded the company in 1983. They have made more than $500 million from selling some of their stock, and together they still hold Cabletron stock worth some $927 million. Clearly, Levine doesn't rely on his annual salary. Levine wrote that check for symbolic purposes. Along with his low salary, it's a statement of his disgust with out-of-control executive pay, and it conveys his company's frugal corporate culture. Both Levine and Benson sit at used metal desks in spartan offices at the company's headquarters in Rochester, New Hampshire. And there are strict limits on expenses: no first-class air travel, no hotel bills of more than $70 a night, and a maximum meal allowance of $35 a day.

Levine is driven to keep his company efficient, fast, and lean. And he believes that it's important for him to be a positive role model.

Questions

1. Is Levine just being foolish? An outside compensation consultant says that Levine is "naive" and should pay himself at least what it would cost to hire someone to do his job. Do you agree or disagree? Explain.
2. How have the company's founders shaped their culture?
3. How do you think new employees learn Cabletron's culture?

Source: Based on J. A. Byrne, "Are You Guys Crazy or Something?" *Business Week,* April 24, 1995, p. 92.

SKILL EXERCISE

Reading an Organization's Culture

Select an organization where you have worked. If you have no work experience, choose an organization with which you have had regular contact and to which you can gain access.

Visit the organization and take the time to talk with as many people as possible and observe employees executing their jobs. Ask pertinent questions. The answers will give you insights into the organization's culture.

After gathering your data: (a) describe the organization's culture using the seven characteristics described in the chapter, and (b) list some probable preferred employee behaviors in this organization based on your data.

NOTES

1. C. Wilson, "Would IBM-Lotus Deal Lead to Clash of Cultures?" *Seattle Times,* June 11, 1995, p. E3.
2. See, for example, H. S. Becker, "Culture: A Sociological View," *Yale Review,* Summer 1982, pp. 513–27; and E. H. Schein, *Organizational Culture and Leadership* (San Francisco: Jossey-Bass, 1985), p. 168.
3. C. A. O'Reilly III, J. Chatman, and D. F. Caldwell, "People and Organizational Culture: A Profile Comparison Approach to Assessing Person-Organization Fit," *Academy of Management Journal,* September 1991, pp. 487–516; and J. A. Chatman and K. A. Jehn, "Assessing the Relationship between Industry Characteristics and Organizational Culture: How Different Can You Be?" *Academy of Management Journal,* June 1994, pp. 522–53.
4. The view that there will be consistency among perceptions of organizational culture has been called the "integration" perspective. For a review of this perspective and conflicting approaches, see D. Meyerson and J. Martin, "Cultural Change: An Integration of Three Different Views," *Journal of Management Studies,* November 1987, pp. 623–47; and P. J. Frost, L. F. Moore, M. R. Louis, C. C. Lundberg, and J. Martin, eds., *Reframing Organizational Culture* (Newbury Park, Calif.: Sage, 1991).
5. See J. M. Jermier, J. W. Slocum Jr., L. W. Fry, and J. Gaines, "Organizational Subcultures in a Soft Bureaucracy: Resistance behind the Myth and Facade of an Official Culture," *Organization Science,* May 1991, pp. 170–94; and S. A. Sackmann, "Culture and Subcultures: An Analysis of Organizational Knowledge," *Administrative Science Quarterly,* March 1992, pp. 140–61.
6. See, for example, G. G. Gordon and N. DiTomaso, "Predicting Corporate Performance from Organizational Culture," *Journal of Management Studies,* November 1992, pp. 793–98; and J. P. Kotter and J. L. Heskett, *Corporate Culture and Performance* (New York: Free Press, 1992), pp. 15–27.
7. Y. Wiener, "Forms of Value Systems: A Focus on Organizational Effectiveness and Cultural Change and Maintenance," *Academy of Management Review,* October 1988, p. 536.
8. See, for example, D. R. Denison, *Corporate Culture and Organizational Effectiveness* (New York: Wiley, 1990); Gordon and DiTomaso, "Predicting Corporate Performance from Organizational Culture," pp. 784–98; and J. C. Collins and J. I. Porras, *Built to Last* (New York: HarperBusiness, 1994).
9. Collins and Porras, *Built to Last.*
10. B. McMenamin, "The Virtue of Making Mistakes," *Forbes,* May 9, 1994, pp. 192–94; and B. Gates, "Failure Is a Part of the Game and Should Be Used," *Seattle Post-Intelligence,* April 26, 1995, p. B5.
11. B. Gates, "Failure Is a Part of the Game and Should Be Used."
12. P. Sellers, "So You Fail . . . Now Bounce Back!" *Fortune,* May 1, 1995, p. 49.
13. M. A. Verespej, "Managing for Creativity," *Industry Week,* April 17, 1995, pp. 24–26.
14. T. P. Pare, "Rebuilding a Lost Reputation," *Fortune,* May 30, 1994, p. 176.
15. B. Rogers, "Serious about Its Code of Ethics," *HRMagazine,* September 1994, pp. 46–48.
16. Collins and Porras, *Built to Last,* pp. 207–08.
17. R. Osborne, "Company with a Soul," *Industry Week,* May 1, 1995, pp. 21–27.
18. R. S. Wellins, W. C. Byham, and G. R. Dixon, *Inside Teams: How 20 World-Class Organizations Are Winning through Teamwork* (San Francisco: Jossey-Bass, 1994), pp. 164–78.
19. Ibid., pp. 234–47.
20. See, for example, P. Elmer-Dewitt, "Mine, All Mine," *Time,* June 5, 1995, pp. 49–54.
21. K. L. Miller, "Siemens Shapes Up," *Business Week,* May 1, 1995, pp. 52–53.
22. See J. Castro, T. McCarroll, J. Moody, and W. McWhirter, "Jack in the Box," *Time,* October 3, 1994, pp. 56–58.
23. S. Glain, "Korea's Samsung Plans Very Rapid Expansion into Autos, Other Lines," *Wall Street Journal,* March 2, 1995, p. A1.
24. See N. J. Adler, *International Dimensions of Organizational Behavior,* 2nd ed. (Boston: PWS-Kent, 1991), pp. 58–60.

PART FOUR: Leading and Empowering People

CHAPTER 12

UNDERSTANDING THE BASICS OF HUMAN BEHAVIOR

You can observe a lot by just watching.
- Y. Berra

LEARNING OBJECTIVES

After studying this chapter, you should be able to:

1. Identify the personality dimensions in the Myers-Briggs Type Indicator
2. Describe the personality-job fit model
3. Explain attribution theory
4. Discuss the implications of the self-fulfilling prophecy
5. Contrast the three components of an attitude
6. Explain the theory of cognitive dissonance
7. Describe the relationship between satisfaction and productivity
8. Contrast operant conditioning and social-learning theory

Today's "politically correct" management style includes being sensitive to others' needs and treating people with respect. But not all managers follow this model. For some, showing sensitivity and respect for others is not part of their personality. One such manager is Linda Wachner (standing in photo), chief executive of the Warnaco Group.[1]

Wachner is one of the few female chief executives at a Fortune 500 company. And her somewhat abrasive personality hasn't seemed to deter her from doing her job. Her record at Warnaco, in fact, is sterling. Since becoming head of the giant apparel maker (the company's annual sales now exceed $800 million) in 1986, she has increased the value of stockholder equity by more than $140 million. In one recent 3-year period, the company's stock price rose 60 percent. But would you want to work for her? You decide.

"I've been called controlling in my business style—and I am," Wachner admits. But then she quickly adds: "That's what delivers 43 percent [return on equity] for shareholders, not laissez-faire."

Former employees describe Wachner as a smart boss, but someone who is so impatient to achieve results that she will do almost anything, including frequently humiliating employees in front of their peers. She has a fiery temper, which she readily admits to. "I'm not very long on patience. I've yelled at people," she says, "and I'm not ashamed of it. We have to run this company efficiently and without a bunch of babies who say, 'Mommy yelled at me today.' If you don't like it, leave. It's not a prison."

How does Wachner see herself? "Effective and good, with an excellent record. You don't achieve that without focus, strategy, and having people do it your way."

For people who have to work with Linda Wachner, having insights into her personality can help them better understand and predict her behavior. But this is true for all of us since our personality goes a long way in shaping our behavior. In this chapter, we look at five psychological concepts—personality, perception, expectations, attitudes, and learning—and demonstrate how these concepts can help managers to better understand the behavior of those people with whom they have to work.

PERSONALITY: CLASSIFYING INDIVIDUAL DIFFERENCES

Some people are quiet and passive; others are loud and aggressive. When we describe people in terms such as *quiet, passive, loud, aggressive, ambitious,* or *persistent,* we are categorizing them in terms of *personality traits*. An individual's **personality** is the combination of the psychological traits we use to classify that person.

Predicting Behavior from Personality Traits

There are literally dozens of personality traits, but a small number have been found to be particularly valuable in providing insights into employee behavior. We review those traits in this section.

Locus of Control Some people believe that they are masters of their own fate. Other people see themselves as pawns of fate, believing that what happens to them in their lives is due to luck or chance. The first type, those who believe that they control their destinies, have been labeled **internals**, whereas the latter, who see their lives as being controlled by outside forces, have been called **externals**.[2]

Comparisons of internals with externals have consistently shown that individuals who rate high in externality are less satisfied with their jobs, have higher absenteeism rates, are more alienated from the work setting, and are less involved in their jobs than are internals.[3] Why are externals more dissatisfied? The answer is probably because they perceive themselves as having little control over those organizational outcomes that are important to them. Internals, facing the same situation, attribute organizational outcomes to their own actions. If the situation is unattractive, they believe that they have no one to blame but themselves. Also, the dissatisfied internal is more likely to quit a dissatisfying job.

The effect of **locus of control** on absenteeism is an interesting one. Internals believe that health is substantially under their own control through proper habits, so they take more responsibility for their health and have better health habits. Consequently, internals have lower incidences of sickness and, hence, lower absenteeism than externals.[4]

The overall evidence indicates that internals generally perform better on their jobs, but that conclusion should be moderated to reflect differences in jobs. Internals search more actively for information before making a decision, are more motivated to achieve, and make a greater attempt to control their environment. Externals, however, are more compliant and willing to follow directions. Therefore, internals do well on jobs that involve sophisticated tasks—which include most managerial and professional positions—that require complex information processing and learning. In addition, internals are more suited to jobs that require initiative and independence of action. In contrast, externals should do well on jobs that are well structured and routine and in which success depends heavily on complying with the direction of others.

BUILDING SELF-AWARENESS • BUILDING SELF-AWARENESS •

ASSESS YOUR LOCUS OF CONTROL

INSTRUCTIONS Read the following statements and indicate whether you agree more with choice A or choice B.

A	B	Choice
1. Making a lot of money is largely a matter of getting the right breaks.	1. Promotions are earned through hard work and persistence.	_____
2. I have noticed that there is a direct connection between how hard I study and the grades I get.	2. Often, the reactions of teachers seem haphazard to me.	_____
3. The number of divorces indicates that more and more people are not trying to make their marriages work.	3. Marriage is largely a gamble.	_____
4. It is silly to think that one can really change another person's basic attitudes.	4. When I am right I can convince others.	_____
5. Getting promoted is really a matter of being a little luckier than the next person.	5. In our society, a person's future earning power is dependent upon his or her ability.	_____
6. If one knows how to deal with people, they are really quite easily led.	6. I have little influence over the way other people behave.	_____
7. The grades I make are the result of my own efforts; luck has little or nothing to do with it.	7. Sometimes I feel that I have little to do with the grades I get.	_____
8. People like me can change the course of world affairs if we make ourselves heard.	8. It is only wishful thinking to believe that one can readily influence what happens in our society at large.	_____
9. A great deal that happens to me is probably a matter of chance.	9. I am the master of my fate.	_____
10. Getting along with people is a skill that must be practiced.	10. It is almost impossible to figure out how to please some people.	_____

Turn to page 561 for scoring directions and key.

***Source*: Adapted from J. B. Rotter, "External Control and Internal Control," *Psychology Today*, June 1971, p. 42. Copyright 1971 by the American Psychological Association. Adapted with permission.**

Achievement Orientation We noted that internals are motivated to achieve. This achievement orientation has also been singled out as a personality characteristic that varies among employees and that can be used to predict certain behaviors.

People with a **high need to achieve** (nAch) continually strive to do things better.[5] They want to overcome obstacles, but they want to feel that their successes (or failures) are due to their own actions. This means that they like tasks of intermediate difficulty. If a task is very easy, it will lack challenge. High achievers receive no feelings of accomplishment from doing tasks that fail to challenge their abilities. Similarly, they avoid tasks that are so difficult that the probability of success is very low and where, even if they do succeed, it's more apt to be due to luck than to ability. Given the high achiever's propensity for tasks where the outcome can be attributed directly to his or her efforts, the high-*nAch* person looks for challenges having approximately a 50-50 chance of success.

What can we say about high achievers on the job? In jobs that provide intermediate difficulty and rapid performance feedback and that give the employee control over his or her results, the high-*nAch* individual will perform well.[6] So high achievers should do better in sales or professional sports than on an assembly line or in clerical tasks. That is, those individuals with a high *nAch* will not *always* outperform those who are low or intermediate in this characteristic. The tasks that high achievers undertake must provide the challenge, feedback, and responsibility they look for if the high-*nAch* personality is to be positively related to job performance.

Machiavellianism The personality characteristic of **Machiavellianism** (Mach) is named after Niccolo Machiavelli, who wrote in the sixteenth century on how to gain and manipulate power. An individual high in Machiavellianism is pragmatic, maintains emotional distance, and believes that ends can justify means.

A considerable amount of research has been directed toward relating high and low-Mach personalities to certain behavioral outcomes.[7] High-Machs manipulate more, win more, are persuaded less, and persuade others more than do low-Machs.[8] Yet these high-Mach outcomes are moderated by situational factors. It has been found that high-Machs flourish (1) when they interact face to face with others rather than indirectly; (2) when the situation has a minimum number of rules and regulations, thus allowing latitude for improvisation; and (3) when emotional involvement with details irrelevant to winning distracts low-Machs.[9]

Should we conclude that high-Machs make good employees? That answer depends on the type of job and whether you consider ethical implications in evaluating performance. In jobs that require bargaining skills (such as labor negotiation) or that offer substantial rewards for winning (as in commissioned sales), high-Machs will be productive. But if ends can't justify the means, if there are *absolute* standards of behavior, or if the three situational factors noted in the preceding paragraph are not in evidence, our ability to predict a high-Mach's performance will be severely curtailed.

Self-Esteem People differ in the degree to which they like or dislike themselves. This trait is called **self-esteem**.[10] The research on self-esteem (SE) offers some interesting insights into employee behavior. For example, self-esteem is directly related to expectations for success. High-SEs believe that they possess the ability they need in order to succeed at work. Individuals with high SEs will take more risks in job selection and are more likely to choose unconventional jobs than people with low SEs.

The most generalizable finding on self-esteem is that low-SEs are more susceptible to external influence than are high-SEs. Low-SEs depend on positive evaluations from others. As a result, they are more likely to seek approval from others and more prone to conform to the beliefs and behaviors of those they respect than are high-SEs. In managerial positions, low-SEs will tend to be concerned with pleasing others and, therefore, are less likely to take unpopular stands than are high-SEs.

Not surprisingly, self-esteem has also been found to be related to job satisfaction. A number of studies confirm that high-SEs are more satisfied with their jobs than are low-SEs.[11]

Self-Monitoring A personality trait that has recently received increased attention is called **self-monitoring.**[12] It refers to an individual's ability to adjust his or her behavior to external, situational factors. Individuals high in self-monitoring show considerable adaptability in adjusting their behavior to external situational factors. They are highly sensitive to external cues and can behave differently in different situations. High self-monitors are capable of presenting striking contradictions between their public persona and their private self. Low self-monitors can't disguise themselves in this way. They tend to display their true dispositions and attitudes in every situation; hence, there is high behavioral consistency between who they are and what they do.

The research on self-monitoring is in its infancy, so predictions must be guarded. However, preliminary evidence suggests that high self-monitors tend to pay closer attention to the behavior of others and are more capable of conforming than are low self-monitors.[13] High self-monitors also seem to get more promotions than individuals who score low on this characteristic.[14] We might additionally hypothesize that high self-monitors will be more successful in managerial positions, in which individuals are required to play multiple, and even contradicting, roles. This correlation is because the high self-monitor is capable of putting on different "faces" for different audiences.

Risk Taking People differ in their willingness to take chances. This propensity to assume or avoid risk has been shown to have an impact on how long it takes managers to make a decision and how much information they require before making their choice. For instance, seventy-nine managers worked on simulated personnel exercises that required them to make hiring decisions.[15] High-risk-taking managers made decisions more rapidly and used less information in making their choices than did the low-risk-taking managers. Interestingly, the decision accuracy was the same for both groups.

Antonio Hui, 45, has been a risk-taker all his life. While others fled El Salvador because of its ongoing civil war, Hui stayed and created El Dragon Industries, a retailer with sales of $8.6 million. "There was little competition and great demand . . . The war left a place for small- to medium-size companies because large industries left the country." Now that the 12-year war is over, he's well positioned for growth. It looks as if his risk-propensity and determination is about to pay off.

EXHIBIT 12-1
Holland's Typology of Personality and Sample Occupations

Type	Description	Personality Characteristics	Sample Occupations
Realistic	Prefers physical activities that require skill, strength, and coordination	Shy, genuine, persistent, stable, conforming, practical	Mechanic, drill press operator, assembly-line worker, farmer
Investigative	Prefers activities involving thinking, organizing, and understanding	Analytical, original, curious, independent	Biologist, economist, mathematician, news reporter
Social	Prefers activities that involve helping and developing others	Sociable, friendly, cooperative, understanding	Social worker, teacher, counselor, clinical psychologist
Conventional	Prefers rule-regulated, orderly, unambiguous activities	Conforming, efficient, practical, unimaginative, inflexible	Accountant, corporate manager, bank teller, file clerk
Enterprising	Prefers verbal activities where there are opportunities to influence others and attain power	Self-confident, ambitious, energetic, domineering	Lawyer, real estate agent, public relations specialist, small business manager
Artistic	Prefers ambiguous and unsystematic activities that allow creative expression	Imaginative, disorderly, idealistic, emotional, impractical	Painter, musician, writer, interior decorator

ing this procedure, research strongly supports the hexagonal diagram in Exhibit 12-2.[25] This figure shows that the closer two fields or orientations are in the hexagon, the more compatible they are. Adjacent categories are quite similar, whereas those diagonally opposite are highly dissimilar.

What does all this mean? The theory argues that satisfaction is highest and turnover lowest when personality and occupation are in agreement. Social individuals should be in social jobs, conventional people in conventional jobs, and so forth. A realistic person in a realistic job is in a more congruent situation than is a realistic person in an investigative job. A realistic person in a social job is in the most incongruent situation possible.

Implications for Managers

Because personality characteristics create the parameters for people's behavior, they give us a framework for predicting behavior.

A review of the personality literature offers general guidelines that can lead to effective job performance. As such, it can improve hiring, transfer, and promotion decisions. Because personality characteristics create the parameters for people's behavior, they give us a framework for predicting behavior. For example, individuals who are shy, introverted, and uncomfortable in social situations would probably be ill suited as salespeople. Individuals who are submissive and conforming might not be effective as advertising "idea" people.

Can we predict which people will be high performers in sales, research, or assembly-line work on the basis of their personality characteristics alone? The answer is No. But a knowledge of an individual's personality can aid in reducing

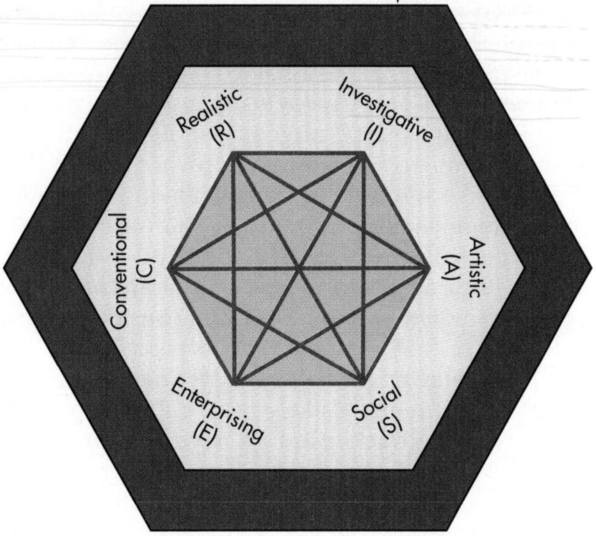

EXHIBIT 12-2
Hexagonal Diagram of the Relationship among Occupational Personality Types

Source: Reproduced by special permission of the Publisher, Psychological Assessment Resources, Inc., from "Making Vocational Choices," © 1973, 1985, 1992 by Psychological Assessment Resources, Inc. All rights reserved.

mismatches, which, in turn, can lead to greater job stability and higher job satisfaction.

We can look at certain personality characteristics that tend to be related to job success, test for those traits, and use the data to make selection more effective. A person who accepts rules, conformity, and dependence and rates low on risk taking is likely to feel more comfortable in, say, a structured assembly-line job, as an admittance clerk in a hospital, or as an administrator in a large public agency than as a researcher or an employee whose job requires a high degree of creativity.

PERCEPTION AND ATTRIBUTIONS: INTERPRETING THE WORLD AROUND US

One of the basic tenets of human behavior is that people act on their perceptions, not on reality. The world as it is perceived is the world that is behaviorally important. And because there are a number of forces acting to distort perceptions, people often misinterpret events and activities. As we will show, the message for managers is if you are going to try to explain or predict someone's behavior, it is important to try to see the world the way he or she sees it.

Perception can be defined as a process by which individuals organize and interpret their sensory impressions in order to give meaning to their environment. However, as we have noted, what one perceives can be substantially different from objective reality. It need not be, but there is often disagreement. For example, it's possible that all employees in a firm may view it as a great place to work—favorable working conditions, interesting job assignments, good pay, an understanding and responsible management—but, as most of us know, it is very unusual to find such agreement.

attitude that affects behavior ultimately

Factors Influencing Perception

How do we explain the fact that people can perceive the same thing differently? A number of factors operate to shape and sometimes distort perception. These factors can reside in the *perceiver*; in the object, or *target*, being perceived; or in the context of the *situation* in which the perception is made.

perceiver = individual

When an individual looks at a target and attempts to interpret what he or she sees, the individual's personal characteristics are going to heavily influence the interpretation. These personal characteristics include attitudes, personality, motives, interests, past experiences, and expectations. For instance, it shouldn't surprise you that a plastic surgeon is more likely to notice an imperfect nose than is a plumber. Similarly, the supervisor who has just been reprimanded by her boss for the excessive amount of tardiness among her staff is more likely to notice lateness by an employee tomorrow than she was last week. And if you are preoccupied with a personal problem, you may find it hard to be attentive in class. These examples illustrate that the focus of our attention is influenced by our interests. Because our individual interests differ considerably, what one person notices in a situation can differ from what others perceive.

The characteristics of the target being observed can affect what is perceived. Loud people are more likely than quiet people to be noticed in a group. So, too, are extremely attractive or unattractive individuals. Because targets are not looked at in isolation, the relationship of a target to its background also influences perception (see Exhibit 12-3), as does our tendency to group close things together and similar things together. Employees in a specific department, for example, are seen as a group. If two people in a four-member department suddenly resign, we tend to assume that their departures were related when, in fact, they may have been totally unrelated.

The context in which we see objects or events is also important. The time at which an object or event is seen can influence attention, as can location, light, heat, and any number of other situational factors. For instance, you probably wouldn't take particular notice of a couple in formal evening attire at an exclusive London club on a Saturday night. But that same couple, dressed similarly, walking down a residential street in London at 10 A.M. the following Monday morning would undoubtedly turn your head. Notice that the only thing that changed was the situational context in which you saw the couple.

Attribution Theory

Our perceptions of people differ from our perceptions of inanimate objects such as desks, machines, or buildings because we make inferences about the actions of people that we don't make about inanimate objects. Nonliving objects are subject to the laws of nature, but they have no beliefs, motives, or intentions. People do. The result is that when we observe people, we attempt to develop explanations of why they behave in certain ways. Our perception and judgment of a person's ac-

EXHIBIT 12-3
Perception Illustration

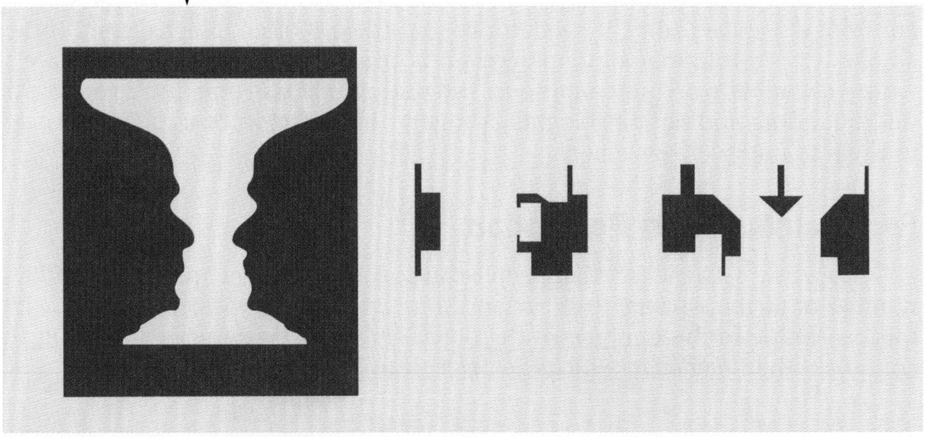

The object on the left may at first look like a beige vase. However, if beige is taken as the background, we see two purple profiles. Similarly, at first observation, the group of objects on the right appears to be some modular figure against a beige background. Closer inspection will reveal the word "FLY" once the background is defined as purple.

tions, therefore, will be significantly influenced by the assumptions we make about the person's internal state.

Attribution theory has been proposed to develop explanations of the ways in which we judge people differently, depending on what meaning we attribute to a given behavior.[26] Basically, the theory suggests that when we observe an individual's behavior, we attempt to determine whether it was internally or externally caused. Internally caused behaviors are those that are believed to be under the personal control of the individual. Externally caused behavior results from outside causes; that is, the person is seen as having been forced into the behavior by the situation. That determination, however, depends largely on three factors: distinctiveness, consensus, and consistency.

Distinctiveness refers to whether an individual displays different behaviors in different situations. Is the employee who arrives late today also the source of complaints by co-workers for being a "goof-off"? What we want to know is whether this behavior is unusual. If it is, the observer is likely to give the behavior an external attribution. If this action is not unusual, it will probably be judged as internal.

If everyone who is faced with a similar situation responds in the same way, we can say the behavior shows *consensus*. Our late employee's behavior would meet this criterion if all employees who took the same route to work were also late. From an attribution perspective, if consensus is high, you would be expected to give an external attribution to the employee's tardiness, whereas if other employees who took the same route made it to work on time, you would conclude that the cause was internal.

Finally, an observer looks for *consistency* in a person's actions. Does the person respond the same way over time? Coming in 10 minutes late for work is not perceived in the same way for an employee who is rarely late (she hasn't been late for several months) as it is for an employee who is routinely late (she is late two or three times a week). The more consistent the behavior, the more the observer is inclined to attribute it to internal causes.

Exhibit 12-4 summarizes the key elements in attribution theory. It would tell us, for instance, that if your employee—Kim Randolph—generally performs at

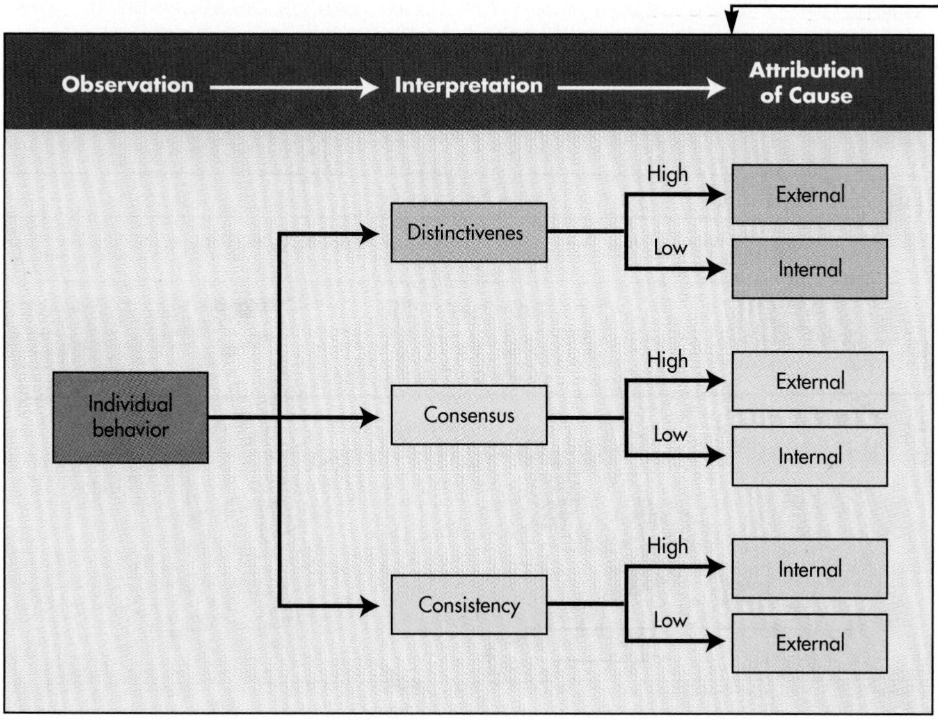

EXHIBIT 12-4
Attribution Theory

about the same level on other related tasks as she does on her current task (low distinctiveness), if other employees frequently perform differently—better or worse—than Kim does on that current task (low consensus), and if Kim's performance on this current task is consistent over time (high consistency), you or anyone else who is judging Kim's work is likely to hold her primarily responsible for her task performance (internal attribution).

One of the more interesting findings from attribution theory is that there are errors or biases that distort attributions. For instance, there is substantial evidence that when we make judgments about the behavior of other people, we have a tendency to underestimate the influence of external factors and overestimate the influence of internal or personal factors.[27] This is called the **fundamental attribution error** and can explain why a sales manager is prone to attribute the poor performance of her sales agents to laziness rather than to the innovative product line introduced by a competitor. There is also a tendency for individuals to attribute their own successes to internal factors such as ability or effort while putting the blame for failure on external factors such as luck. This is called the **self-serving bias** and suggests that feedback provided to employees in performance reviews will be predictably distorted by recipients depending on whether it is positive or negative.

Perceptual Shortcuts or Errors We Make in Judging Others

We use a number of shortcuts when we judge others. Perceiving and interpreting what others do is burdensome. As a result, we all develop techniques for making the task more manageable. These techniques are frequently valuable—they allow us to make accurate perceptions rapidly and provide valid data for making predictions. But they are not foolproof. They can and do get us into trouble. An understanding of these shortcuts can be helpful toward recognizing when they can result in significant distortions.

Individuals cannot assimilate all they observe, so they engage in **selectivity.** They take in bits and pieces. These bits and pieces are not chosen randomly; rather, they are selectively chosen depending on the interests, background, experience, and attitudes of the observer. Selective perception allows us to "speed read" others, but not without the risk of drawing an inaccurate picture.

EXHIBIT 12-5

Source: Non Sequitur, by Wiley, © 1996, Washington Post Writers Group. Reprinted with permission.

It's easy to judge others if we assume that they are similar to us. In **assumed similarity,** or the "like-me" effect, the observer's perception of others is influenced more by the observer's own characteristics than by those of the person observed. For example, if you want challenge and responsibility in your job, you will assume that others want the same. People who assume that others are like them can, of course, be right, but most of the time they are wrong.

When we judge someone on the basis of our perception of a group to which he or she belongs, we are using the shortcut called **stereotyping**. "Married people are more stable employees than singles" and "union people expect something for nothing" are examples of stereotyping. To the degree that a stereotype is based on fact, it may produce accurate judgments. However, many stereotypes have no foundation in fact. In such cases, they distort judgments.

When we form a general impression about an individual on the basis of a single characteristic such as intelligence, appearance, or sociability, we are being influenced by the **halo effect.** This effect frequently occurs when students evaluate their classroom instructor. Students may isolate a single trait such as enthusiasm and allow their entire evaluation to be tainted by their perception of this one trait. An instructor might be quiet, assured, knowledgeable, and highly qualified, but if his style lacks zeal, he will be rated lower on a number of other characteristics.

distort or cause errors in perception

Implications for Managers

Managers need to recognize that their employees react to perceptions, not to reality. So whether a manager's appraisal of an employee is *actually* objective and unbiased or whether the organization's salary levels are *actually* among the highest in the industry is less relevant than what employees perceive them to be. If individuals perceive appraisals as biased or salary levels as low, they'll behave as if those conditions actually exist. Employees organize and interpret what they see; and this becomes *their reality*.

The message to managers should be clear: Close attention needs to be paid to how employees perceive their jobs and management practices. Remember, the valuable employee who quits because of an *incorrect perception* is just as great a loss to an organization as the valuable employee who quits for a *valid reason*.

EXPECTATIONS: WHAT YOU SEE IS WHAT YOU GET

Expectations exert a powerful force on behavior. Take the case of 105 Israeli soldiers who were participating in a combat command course.[28] The four course instructors were told that one-third of the specific incoming trainees had high potential, one-third had normal potential, and the potential of the rest was unknown. In reality, the trainees were randomly placed into these categories by researchers conducting the study. Consistent with the power of expectations, those trainees whom instructors were told had high potential scored significantly higher on objective achievement tests, exhibited more positive attitudes, and held their leaders in higher regard than did the others. The instructors of the supposedly high-potential trainees got better results from them because the instructors expected it!

The terms **self-fulfilling prophecy** and *pygmalion effect* have evolved to characterize the fact that an expectation about how someone is likely to act *causes* that person to fulfill the expectation.[29] From an organizational standpoint, managers get the performance they expect.

How does the self-fulfilling prophecy work in manager-employee relations? Exhibit 12-6 provides an explanation. First, a manager forms an impression of the

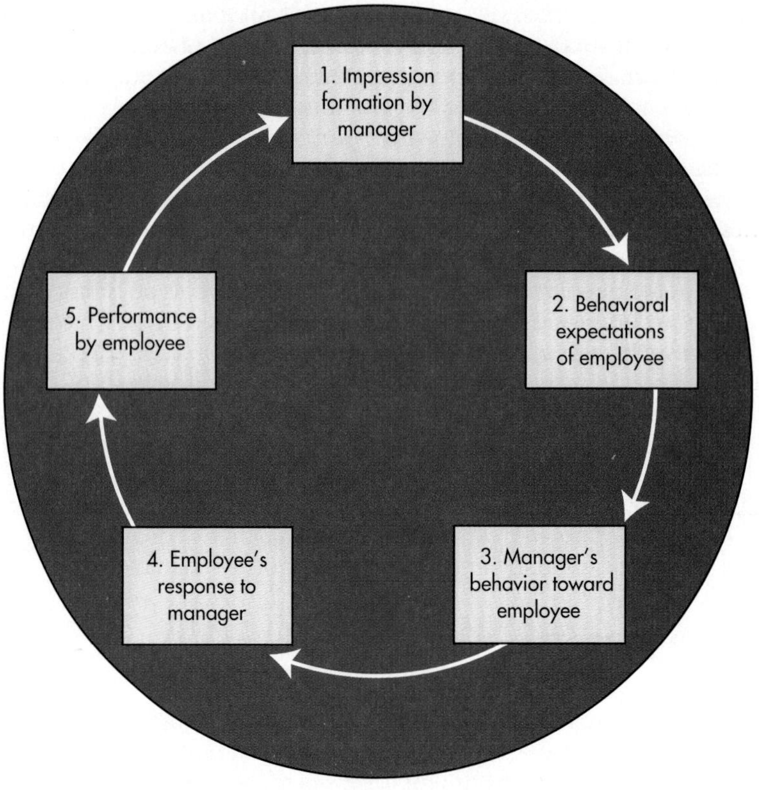

EXHIBIT 12-6
Development of the Self-Fulfilling Prophecy

employee. From this perception, the manager further develops expectations about the employee's future behavior. When those expectations are high, the manager will behave in ways consistent with high expectations. For instance, the manager will tend to be supportive, friendly, offer helpful feedback, and provide more opportunities for the employee. The employee, in turn, responds positively to his or her manager's behavior. He or she will take advantage of the support and opportunities offered. In addition, the confidence that the manager exhibits toward the employee builds that employee's self-esteem, and the employee then behaves in ways that fulfill the manager's high expectations.

We can draw two conclusions from the self-fulfilling prophecy: (1) Misperceptions of a situation can evoke actions that make the original misperception come true; and (2) managers who set high expectations for their employees—but not so high as to be intimidating or impossible—will initiate a process that can lead to the fulfillment of those high expectations.

ATTITUDES: FEELINGS INFLUENCE BEHAVIOR

BP Exploration conducts annual attitude surveys among its 12,000 employees. And it's not alone. Many organizations regularly survey their employees to learn how they feel about their job, their bosses, company pay practices, and the like. Why do organizations do this? Because managers recognize that attitudes have a significant bearing on employee behavior. An increase in complaints about working conditions or benefits, for instance, is often followed by an increase in resignations.

Attitudes are evaluative statements—either favorable or unfavorable—concerning objects, people, or events. They reflect how one feels about something. When I say "I like my job," I am expressing my attitude about work.

To better understand the concept of attitudes, we should look at an attitude as being made up of three components: cognition, affect, and behavior.[30] The **cognitive component of an attitude** makes up the beliefs, opinions, knowledge, or information held by a person. The belief that "discrimination is wrong" illustrates a cognition. It sets the stage for the more critical part of an attitude—the **affective component of an attitude**. Affect is the emotional, or feeling, segment of an attitude and is reflected in the statement "I don't like Jon because he discriminates against minorities." Finally, affect can lead to behavioral outcomes. The **behavioral component of an attitude** refers to an intention to behave in a certain way toward someone or something. So, to continue our example, I might choose to avoid Jon because of my feelings about him.

Viewing attitudes as made up of three components—cognition, affect, and behavior—is helpful toward understanding their complexity and the potential relationship between attitudes and behavior. But for clarity's sake, keep in mind that the term *attitude* essentially refers to the affect part of the three components.

Popular Work-Related Attitudes

A person can have thousands of attitudes, but managers aren't interested in every attitude an employee might hold. They are interested in job-related attitudes. The three most popular of these are job satisfaction, job involvement, and organizational commitment.[31]

Job Satisfaction The term **job satisfaction** refers to an individual's general attitude toward his or her job. A person with a high level of job satisfaction holds positive attitudes toward the job, while a person who is dissatisfied with his or her job holds negative attitudes about the job. When people speak of employee attitudes, more often than not they mean job satisfaction. In fact, the two terms are frequently used interchangeably.

Job Involvement Although there is not complete agreement over what the term **job involvement** means, a workable definition states that it measures the degree to which a person identifies psychologically with his or her job and considers his or her perceived performance level to be important to self-worth.[32] Employees with a high level of job involvement strongly identify with and really care about the kind of work they do.

IN THE NEWS

U.S. Employees Express Declining Satisfaction

THE MOOD OF THE U.S. WORKPLACE IS RESTLESS AND FRUSTRATED, BUT MOST PEOPLE ARE STILL COMMITTED to their employers. That at least is the conclusion drawn from a government-sponsored telephone survey of 2,408 workers in private companies employing twenty-five or more employees. The following highlights some of the findings:

- Lack of trust was one of the most dominant concerns expressed by employees. Sixty-two percent said they didn't feel they could trust their management to keep its promises.
- A mere 18 percent of workers said employee-management relations in their company were excellent; 32 percent said they were fair or poor.
- Worker satisfaction declined with length of service. Workers aged 35 to 54 had the most negative attitudes toward management.
- Despite the anxiety expressed by workers, 54 percent said they were committed to their current employer, and 60 percent regarded their present job as either long-term or a stepping stone to something better with the same company.

Source: R. Taylor, "Anxious Times," *Financial Times*, February 3, 1995, p. 3.

IN THE NEWS

A Happy Work Force Can Make for Good Financial Returns

TERRY DIAMOND, A MONEY MANAGER AT TALON ASSET MANAGEMENT, BELIEVES THAT A HAPPY WORK force adds to the bottom line. For instance, he decided to buy shares of Starbucks, the gourmet coffee chain, the minute he heard the company's chairman, Howard Shultz, speak at a conference. "Shultz didn't even mention one financial number. Instead, he talked about how all employees, even temporary employees, got health insurance," recalls Diamond. And that decision to buy Starbucks stock proved a good one. The stock has since nearly tripled in price.

Starbucks' progressive personnel policies help it keep its employee turnover low. It loses about 50 to 65 percent of its workers each year, compared with average rates ranging between 100 and 400 percent at other retail and fast-food outlets.

Other companies also get high marks from investors for both their financial returns and the way they treat their employees. These include Wal-Mart, Herman Miller, and steel producer Nucor.

Temporary workers at this Starbucks in Los Angeles enjoy the same benefits that the company provides its full-time employees.

At Nucor, workers get full credit for their contribution to the bottom line. The company's annual report displays the names of all employees every year with a thank you from management. The company has also built a reputation for listening to employee suggestions and generously rewarding workers for their efforts. The results have been high productivity, low turnover, and little fear of strikes. Says one steel analyst, "It's a nonunion shop and they make sure their employees are happy so that they won't bring in a union and strike. In the steel industry, if you strike you don't have revenue, but you still have costs."

Source: M. Gonzalez, "Happy Staff May Mean Happy Stock," reprinted by permission of the *Wall Street Journal*, March 27, 1995, p. C1. © 1995 Dow Jones & Co. Inc. All rights reserved worldwide.

relationship.[43] For example, the relationship is stronger when the employee's behavior is not constrained or controlled by outside factors. An employee's productivity on machine-paced jobs, for instance, is going to be much more influenced by the speed of the machine than by his or her level of satisfaction. Similarly, a stockbroker's productivity is largely constrained by the general movement of the stock market. When the market is moving up and volume is high, both satisfied and dissatisfied brokers are going to ring up lots of commissions. Conversely, when the market is in the doldrums, the level of broker satisfaction is not likely to mean much. Job level also seems to be an important moderating variable. The satisfaction-performance correlations are stronger for higher-level employees. Thus, we might expect the relationship to be more relevant for individuals in professional, supervisory, and managerial positions.

Another point of concern in the satisfaction-productivity issue is the direction of the causal arrow. Most of the studies on the relationship used research designs that could not prove cause and effect. Studies that have controlled for the direction of the relationship indicate that the more valid conclusion is that productivity leads to satisfaction rather than the other way around.[44] If you do a good job, you intrinsically feel good about it. In addition, assuming that the organization rewards productivity, your higher productivity should increase verbal recognition, your pay level, and probabilities for promotion. These rewards, in turn, increase your level of satisfaction with the job.

The most recent evidence provides renewed support for the original satisfaction-productivity relationship.[45] When satisfaction and productivity data are gathered for the organization as a whole, rather than at the individual level, we find that organizations with more-satisfied employees tended to be more effective than organizations with less-satisfied employees. If this conclusion can be reproduced in additional studies, it may well be that the reason we haven't gotten strong support for the *satisfaction causes productivity thesis* is that studies have focused on individuals rather than on the organization and that individual-level measures of productivity don't take into consideration all the interactions and complexities in the work process.

Implications for Managers

Managers should be interested in their employees' attitudes because attitudes give warnings of potential problems and because they influence behavior. Satisfied and committed employees, for instance, have relatively low rates of turnover and absenteeism. Given that managers want to keep resignations and absences down—especially among their more productive employees—they will want to do those things that will generate positive job attitudes.

Managers should recognize that employees will try to reduce cognitive dissonance. More important, dissonance can be managed. If employees are required to engage in activities that appear to be inconsistent or are at odds with their attitudes, the pressures to reduce the resulting dissonance are lessened when the employee perceives the dissonance as being externally imposed and beyond his or her control or if the rewards are significant enough to offset the dissonance.

LEARNING: HOW PEOPLE ADAPT

No basic review of human behavior would be complete without a discussion of learning. Why? Because almost all complex behavior is learned. If we want to understand human behavior, we need to understand how people learn.

What is learning? It's more than "what we did when we went to school." Learning occurs all the time. We continually learn from our experiences. So we'll define **learning** as any relatively permanent change in behavior that occurs as a result of experience.

Almost all complex behavior is learned. If we want to understand human behavior, we need to understand how people learn.

Ways People Learn

How do we learn such varied skills as riding a bicycle, writing a memo, or using a computer spreadsheet? Psychologists have developed two explanations for how we learn—*operant conditioning* and *social learning theory*.

Operant Conditioning **Operant conditioning** argues that behavior is a function of its consequences. People learn to behave to get something they want or avoid something they don't want. Operant behavior means voluntary or "learned" behavior in contrast to reflexive or "unlearned" behavior. The tendency to repeat such behavior is influenced by the reinforcement or lack of reinforcement brought about by the consequences of the behavior. Reinforcement, therefore, strengthens a behavior and increases the likelihood that it will be repeated.[46]

positive + negative reinforcement

Operant conditioning proposes that behavior is determined from "without"—that is, it is learned—rather than from "within"—reflexive or unlearned. Creating pleasing consequences that follow specific forms of behavior increases the frequency of that behavior. People will most likely engage in desired behaviors if they are positively reinforced for doing so. Rewards, for example, are most effective if they immediately follow the desired response. In addition, behavior that isn't rewarded, or is punished, is less likely to be repeated.

You see illustrations of operant conditioning everywhere. For example, any situation in which it is either explicitly stated or implicitly suggested that reinforcements are contingent on some action on your part involves the use of operant learning. Your instructor says that if you want a high grade in the course you must supply correct answers on the test. A commissioned salesperson wanting to earn a sizable income finds that this is contingent on generating high sales in her territory. Of course, the linkage can also work to teach the individual to engage in behaviors that work against the best interests of the organization. Assume that your boss tells you that if you will work overtime during the next 3-week busy season, you will be compensated for it at the next performance appraisal. However, when performance appraisal time comes, you find that you are given no positive reinforcement for your overtime work. The next time your boss asks you to work overtime, what will you do? You'll probably decline! Your behavior can be explained by operant conditioning: If a behavior fails to be positively reinforced, the probability that the behavior will be repeated declines.

Social Learning Individuals can also learn by observing what happens to other people and just by being told about something, as well as by direct experiences. So, for example, much of what we have learned comes from watching models—parents, teachers, peers, motion picture and television performers, bosses, and so forth. This view that we can learn through both observation and direct experience has been called **social-learning theory**.[47]

Although social-learning theory is an extension of operant conditioning—that is, it assumes that behavior is a function of consequences—it also acknowledges the existence of observational learning and the importance of perception in learning. People respond to how they perceive and define consequences, not to the objective consequences themselves.

The influence of models is central to the social-learning viewpoint. Four processes have been found to determine the influence that a model will have on an individual:

1. *Attentional processes*. People learn from a model only when they recognize and pay attention to its critical features. We tend to be most influenced by models that are attractive, repeatedly available, important to us, or similar to us in our estimation.
2. *Retention processes*. A model's influence will depend on how well the individual remembers the model's action after the model is no longer readily available.
3. *Motor reproduction processes*. After a person has seen a new behavior by observing the model, the watching must be converted to doing. This process then demonstrates that the individual can perform the modeled activities.
4. *Reinforcement processes*. Individuals will be motivated to exhibit the modeled behavior if positive incentives or rewards are provided. Behaviors that are reinforced will be given more attention, learned better, and performed more often.

Managing Learning through Shaping

Because learning takes place on the job as well as before it, managers will be concerned with how they can teach employees to behave in ways that most benefit the organization. When managers attempt to mold individuals by guiding their learning in graduated steps, they are **shaping behavior**.

Consider the situation in which an employee's behavior is significantly different from that sought by management. If management reinforced the individual only when he or she showed desirable responses, there might be very little reinforcement taking place. In such a case, shaping offers a logical approach toward achieving the desired behavior.

Managers *shape* behavior by systematically reinforcing each successive step that moves the employee closer to the desired response. If an employee who has chronically been a half-hour late for work comes in only 20 minutes late, we can reinforce this improvement. Reinforcement would increase as responses more closely approximate the desired behavior.

Methods of Shaping Behavior There are four ways in which to shape behavior: through positive reinforcement, negative reinforcement, punishment, and extinction.

Following a response with something pleasant is called *positive reinforcement*. This would describe, for instance, the boss who praises an employee for a job well done. Following a response by the termination or withdrawal of something unpleasant is called *negative reinforcement*. If your college instructor asks a question and you don't know the answer, looking through your lecture notes is likely to preclude your being called on. This is a negative reinforcement because you have learned that looking busily through your notes prevents the instructor from calling on you. *Punishment* is causing an unpleasant condition in an attempt to eliminate an undesirable behavior. Giving an employee a 2-day suspension without pay for showing up drunk is an example of punishment. Eliminating any reinforcement that is maintaining a behavior is called *extinction*. When the behavior is not reinforced, it tends to gradually be extinguished. College instructors who wish to discourage students from asking questions in class can eliminate this behavior by ignoring students who raise their hands to ask questions. Hand raising will become extinct when it is invariably met with an absence of reinforcement.

Both positive and negative reinforcement result in learning. They strengthen a response and increase the probability of repetition. In the preceding illustrations, praise strengthens and increases the behavior of doing a good job because praise is desired. The behavior of "looking busy" is similarly strengthened and increased by its terminating the undesirable consequence of being called on by the teacher. Both punishment and extinction, however, weaken behavior and tend to decrease its subsequent frequency.

Reinforcement, whether it is positive or negative, has an impressive record as a shaping tool. Our interest, therefore, is in reinforcement rather than in punishment or extinction. A review of the evidence on the impact of reinforcement upon behavior in organizations has concluded that:

1. Some type of reinforcement is necessary to produce a change in behavior.
2. Some types of rewards are more effective for use in organizations than others.
3. The speed with which learning takes place and the permanence of its effects will be determined by the timing of reinforcement.[48]

Point 3 is extremely important and deserves elaboration.

Schedules of Reinforcement The two major types of reinforcement schedules are *continuous* and *intermittent*. A **continuous reinforcement** schedule reinforces the desired behavior each and every time it is demonstrated. For example, in the case of someone who has historically had trouble arriving at work on time, every time he is not tardy his manager might compliment him on his desirable behavior. In an intermittent schedule, on the other hand, not every instance of the desirable behavior is reinforced, but reinforcement is given often enough to make the behavior worth repeating. This latter schedule can be compared to the workings of a slot machine, which people will continue to play even when they know that it is adjusted to give a considerable return to the gambling house. The intermittent payoffs occur just often enough to reinforce the behavior of slipping in coins and pulling the handle. Evidence indicates that the intermittent or varied form of reinforcement tends to promote more resistance to extinction than does the continuous form.[49]

An **intermittent reinforcement** can be of a ratio or interval type. *Ratio schedules* depend upon how many responses the subject makes. The individual is reinforced after giving a certain number of specific types of behavior. *Interval schedules*

EXHIBIT 12-8
Learning-Style Types

Because em
learn on the
is whether m
to let emplo
randomly o
going to
through the r
and the ex

The United States Americans score high on individualism, below average on power distance, well below average on uncertainty avoidance, well above average on quantity of life, and they have a short-term orientation. These results are not inconsistent with the world image of the United States.

The below-average score on power distance aligns with what one might expect in a country with a representative type of government with democratic ideals. The well-below-average ranking on uncertainty avoidance is also consistent with a democracy. Americans perceive themselves as being relatively free from threats of uncertainty. The individualistic ethic is one of the most frequently used stereotypes to describe Americans, and that stereotype seems well founded. In one contrast of forty countries, the United States ranked as the single most individualistic.[56] Finally, the well-above-average score on quantity of life and the short-term focus are not surprising. Capitalism—which values aggressiveness, materialism, and immediate gratification—is consistent with quantity of life and short-term characteristics.

Japan Japanese workers like being part of a group. They prefer to sublimate their individual contribution to that of the group or team of which they are a part. Their high score on collectivism is consistent with this preference.[57]

The Japanese culture has long valued lifetime employment security. Employees were traditionally hired right out of school. These employees were expected to show absolute loyalty to their employer, and the employer responded reciprocally. Until very recently, it was unusual for a worker to switch employers. And Japanese managers are expected to show patience. Promotions come slowly. It's not uncommon for an employee to wait 10 years or more for his or her first promotion. All these organizational practices fit with trying to offset a society that scores high on uncertainty avoidance.

The Japanese also practice a form of consultative decision making that fits well with their moderate score on power distance. Japanese managers are not autocratic. But they also do not actively involve their employees in the decision-making process. What they do is informally discuss and consult with all those people who may be affected by the decision. When all are familiar with the proposal, a formal request for a decision is made, and, as a result of the previous informal preparations, it is almost always ratified. The key is not so much agreement with a decision but that those concerned are advised about it and have their views fairly heard.

Australia Much of the world's impression of Australians is based on the *Crocodile Dundee* character. His words—"put another shrimp on the barbee" and "You call that a knife? THIS is what we call a knife!"—gave the image of Australians as down-to-earth, straightforward, no-frills, honest people, with a wry sense of humor.[58] Is this characterization accurate? Partly. Australians are very casual and direct. They are also competitive, especially in sports, and they are leisure-oriented and known for betting on almost anything.[59]

Contrasts between U.S. and Australian managers reveal that, while there are wide similarities, there are also a few interesting differences.[60] Australian managers are less extroverted, tend to be more dominating and assertive, and are more forthright and moralistic.

The above descriptions can be reconciled with research on Australian attitudes. For instance, Australians score high on both individualism and quantity of life. This score would suggest a population of people who are competitive, risk-taking, and assertive—which Australians are.

Implications for Managers

Differences in employees' cultural backgrounds have wide implications for many, if not most, managerial practices. As a result, managers need to make sure they consider cultural differences when they choose a leadership or communication style, select motivation techniques, design a compensation system, decide on training methods, or consider the redesign of jobs.

This chapter introduced a number of principles and concepts that can be applied to people in general. But we also underscored the importance of acknowledging individual differences. Managers, for instance, who do not recognize the existence of personality differences and use that information in making hiring or job-placement decisions are going to be less effective than their counterparts who do. Similarly, people from different cultures present challenges to managers. In a world where workforce diversity has become the norm, effective managers are increasing their knowledge of different cultures and using that information to better lead their work units.

In a world where workforce diversity has become the norm, effective managers are increasing their knowledge of different cultures and using that information to better lead their work units.

SUMMARY

(This summary is organized by the chapter-opening learning objectives on page 353.)

1. The personality dimensions in the Myers-Briggs Type Indicator (MBTI) are: extroverted or introverted, sensing or intuitive, thinking or feeling, and perceiving or judging.
2. The personality-job fit model identifies six personality types—realistic, investigative, social, conventional, enterprising, and artistic. The better the fit between an individual's personality type and occupational environment, the higher will be the individual's satisfaction and the less likely he or she will be to quit.
3. Attribution theory proposes that we judge people differently depending on whether we attribute their behavior to internal or external causes. We hold people responsible in internal attributions.
4. As a result of the self-fulfilling prophecy, managers should set high expectations for their employees because doing so will initiate a process that leads to the fulfillment of those high expectations.
5. The *cognitive* component of an attitude makes up the beliefs, opinions, knowledge, or information held by a person. The *affective* component is the emotional or feeling segment of an attitude. The *behavioral* component is the intent to behave in a certain way.
6. The theory of cognitive dissonance says that people will try to reduce inconsistencies that might arise between multiple attitudes or between behavior and attitudes.
7. At the individual level, findings on the relationship between satisfaction and productivity report a positive but low correlation. It may well be that satisfaction does not lead to productivity but the other way around. At the organizational level, the evidence indicates that more-satisfied employees tend to be more effective.
8. Operant conditioning states that learning occurs as a result of reinforcement or lack of reinforcement after a given behavior. Social-learning theory states that learning can take place as a result of observation as well as direct experience.

REVIEW AND DISCUSSION QUESTIONS

1. What work-related predictions would you make about an employee who had each of the following: (a) an internal locus of control, (b) a high *nAch*, (c) a high Mach score, (d) low SE, (e) a high self-monitoring score, or (f) a Type A personality?
2. Which personality type would fit best in the job of (a) management professor? (b) Physician? (c) Aerobics instructor?
3. How is it possible for two people to see the same phenomenon, yet perceive it differently?
4. The acquisition editor at Simon & Schuster was frustrated because one of her authors was extremely late in turning in a highly prized book manuscript. Assume that you are that author. Using attribution theory, develop a plausible explanation that might satisfy your editor.
5. What is the self-serving bias? What are its implications for managers?
6. You strongly dislike large cities. However, you have been offered a promotion by your employer that requires you to move to Chicago. How might you reconcile your attitude toward large cities and the decision to accept the move to Chicago?
7. Is a happy worker a productive worker?
8. Using social-learning theory, how could you maximize the effectiveness of an employee training program?
9. Contrast schedules of reinforcement.
10. You are a manager with Honda, born and raised in Japan. You have been transferred to the United States to run one of your company's plants in Ohio. What adjustments, if any, do you think you will have to make in your management style?

CASE EXERCISE
JACK WELCH'S PERSONALITY

Jack Welch, Jr., has successfully reshaped General Electric since he became CEO in 1981. He has bought and sold dozens of companies, fired tens of thousands of employees, and fine-tuned the company's strategy. He is widely regarded as one of the world's toughest managers, but you can't argue with his track record at GE.

Welch joined GE right out of graduate school and quickly rose through the ranks. His appointment to the CEO job when he was only 45 made him the youngest chief executive in the company's history. Since taking the top spot, he has bought companies worth $19 billion, notably RCA, and sold operations worth $10 billion. He has refocused GE's product lines, trimmed corporate staff by 40 percent, and turned America's most diversified corporation into a growth machine. Between 1981 and 1994, GE's annual revenues went from under $25 billion to more than $60 billion. Its return on equity and earnings per share far outpaced most Fortune 500 firms.

What makes Jack Welch the kind of executive he is? Here are some clues. He was an only child whose main source of inspiration was his dominant mother. "She always felt I could do anything. It was my mother who trained me, taught me the facts of life. She wanted me to be independent. Control your own destiny—she always had that idea. Saw reality. No mincing words. Whenever I got out of line she would whack me one. But always positive. Always constructive. Always uplifting." Jack Welch's philosophy of business was also strongly influenced by his mother's values: Face reality, even when doing so is uncomfortable, and communicate candidly, even when doing so may sting. His mother believed that these values were the necessary means to achieve what was to her the all-important end: control of one's destiny. As she regularly told her son, "If you don't control your destiny, someone else will control it for you."

Questions

1. Describe Jack Welch's personality using the MBTI.
2. Do you think the qualities that have made Welch a success at GE were discernible when he was a teenager? Defend your answer.
3. Do you think Welch could be an effective CEO at a small entrepreneurial firm? At a company that operates solely in India? Explain your answer.

Sources: Based on S. P. Sherman, "Inside the Mind of Jack Welch," *Fortune*, March 27, 1989, pp. 38–50; T. A. Stewart, "GE Keeps Those Ideas Coming," *Fortune*, August 12, 1991, pp. 41–49; and A. J. Michels, "Now for Jack Welch's Second Act," *Fortune*, January 13, 1992, p. 12.

LEARNING OBJECTIVES

After studying this chapter, you should be able to:

1. Explain why a highly motivated worker may not necessarily be a high-performing employee
2. Define motivation
3. Contrast the hierarchy of needs with ERG theory
4. Describe the motivational implications of Theory X-Theory Y
5. Explain the motivational implications of motivation-hygiene theory
6. Identify how goals motivate
7. Describe the motivation implications of inequitable rewards
8. Explain expectancy theory
9. Define employee involvement and describe why it can increase motivation
10. Contrast variable- and skill-based pay programs

Anyone who thinks that "people are the same, no matter where they come from" or that *everybody* wants more money should contrast the work lives of two people who have comparable jobs for comparable pay at two department stores—one is from the United States, and the other is from Germany.[1]

Angie Clark is a 50-year-old merchandising manager at a JC Penney store in suburban Washington, D.C. She earns $32,000 a year plus bonus. Andreas Drauschke is a 29-year-old floor supervisor at Karstadt, Germany's largest department-store chain. Drauschke works at the chain's Berlin store, earning $28,000 a year plus bonus and holiday pay. Clark and Drauschke have very different attitudes toward work and leisure. But their attitudes essentially reflect those of their countrymen.

Clark puts in 44 hours a week on her job, including evening shifts and frequent Saturdays and Sundays. Her typical workday wraps up at about 7 P.M., then she brings a couple of hours of paperwork home with her. She never takes more than a week of vacation at a time. In contrast, Drauschke works only 37 hours a week. He has no extended hours. His store, like all stores in Germany, closes for weekends at 2 P.M. on Saturday and is open only one evening, Thursday. He comes in 20 minutes earlier than the rest of his staff, but otherwise he has no interest in working beyond his 37 hours, even if it means more money. "Free time can't be paid for," he says.

The desire to keep short hours is an obsession in Germany. For instance, Drauschke finds it hard to staff the extra 2 hours on Thursday evening, even though the late shift is rewarded with an hour less overall on the job. He can't relate to the American habit of taking a second job to earn extra money, "I already get home at 7. When should I work?" he asks. Clearly, Drauschke reflects the German attitude that leisure comes first and work second.

Clark has no problem staffing her store on weekends or evenings. Her employees reflect the American attitude that work is more important than leisure. In fact, she estimates that between 25 and 35 percent of her Penney's sales staff hold second jobs. When given the chance to earn more money or have more free time, her workers are quick to take the money.

While Americans often marvel at German industriousness, the reality is that Americans work far longer hours. The weekly U.S. average among manufacturing workers is 37.7 hours and rising. In Germany, it is 30 hours and has been falling steadily for decades. In addition, all German workers are guaranteed by law a minimum of 5 weeks' annual vacation. While an increasing number of American workers are putting in 60 or more hours a week counting overtime and second jobs, Germans hold firm to their preference for leisure over work. Germans continue to fiercely resist any intrusions on their leisure hours.

The cultural differences between the United States and Germany toward the work-leisure trade-off can largely explain why Clark spends far more time than Drauschke interviewing job candidates and training new workers. The annual turnover rate at the German store is negligible. At Clark's Penney's store, it is 40 percent a year!

The above example explodes the misconception that everybody wants more money. Interestingly, there is no shortage of erroneous notions when it comes to the subject of motivation and rewards. There are probably more misconstrued ideas on this subject than any other in management, with the possible exception of leadership. So let's start our discussion by debunking a few of these myths.

SOME POPULAR MISCONCEPTIONS ABOUT MOTIVATION AND REWARDS

We offer the following to open your mind to the challenges in motivating today's work force and to show you how preconceived notions can limit your ability to get the most out of your people.

Myth: Motivation is individual-specific.
Fact: Motivation is situation-specific.

Few of us are highly motivated all the time, regardless of the task.

Many people assume that some people are highly motivated and others are lazy. Managers who follow this assumption spend a lot of time in the selection process trying to find job candidates who are "motivated." The fact is, few of us are highly motivated all the time, regardless of the task. Similarly, almost everyone is highly motivated occasionally.

If you want to get the most out of people, stop looking for the "super" individual. Your time will be better spent, and employee motivation will increase, if you learn what is important to each individual and (recognizing that this will change with times and conditions) match people to jobs that fit their interests and personality. You should also ensure that rewards are linked to performance and focus on similar situational factors.

Myth: A motivated worker is a high-performing employee.
Fact: High employee performance requires ability and support as well as motivation.

Motivation is only one element in getting employees to perform at their highest level. Just as important are ability and support.[2] Individuals need to have the skills and talent necessary to do the job properly. If they are underskilled or undertrained, their performance will suffer. They also need to have the tools, equipment, supplies, favorable working conditions, helpful colleagues, sufficient information, and similar supportive resources so that they can do their best work. Nothing is more demotivating than to want to do a good job but to be incapable of it because you have outdated computer software, a poorly designed workstation, shabby tools, or unqualified co-workers.

Myth: Young people today aren't motivated.
Fact: Young people today are more unorthodox, rebellious, and have different values than baby boomers; but they aren't necessarily less motivated.

Young workers today, the so-called Generation X, have different work values than baby boomers.[3] Generation X workers value flexibility, job satisfaction, and loyalty to relationships. They are much more individualistic than boomers. They value family and relationships. Money is important as an indicator of career performance, but they are willing to trade off salary increases, titles, security, and promotions for expanded lifestyle options and work that challenges them. And Xers are not loyal to a single employer. Consistent with the growth of the contingent work force, they want to build a diverse set of skills that will maintain their marketability.

Young people today can be highly motivated workers. But managers have to accommodate their needs.

Myth: Most people are interested in absolute rewards.
Fact: People are more sensitive to relative differences than to absolute differences.

Beginning salaries, pay increases, and office furnishings are important factors in motivation. But not in the way that most people think. Most employees are sensitive to inequities.[4] They compare what they get from the organization with what others get. And even though the absolute amount might be considerable, if it is relatively less than what others receive, it acts as a demotivator. Think of the professional basketball player who, although earning $2 million a year, refuses to report to his team until his contract is renegotiated. His agent's argument is never that the player can't live on $2 million a year. Rather, the argument is that other players, of lesser or equal qualifications, have more lucrative contracts.

Myth: Everyone wants a challenging job.
Fact: Not everyone values a challenging job.

Behavioral scientists, consultants, professors, and many others who study organizations have been arguing, for years, that employees want jobs that are interesting and challenging and that allow them to experience meaningfulness and responsibility. Well, not *everyone* wants a job like that. There are still a lot of people who prefer jobs that make minimal psychological demands. Work to them is merely a means to some other end; it is not an end in itself. They use their hours off the job to fulfill their needs for responsibility, achievement, growth, and recognition.

The belief that everyone wants a challenging job has been promoted by individuals who have projected their own needs onto the work population as a whole. Work for most behavioral scientists, consultants, and professors is their central life interest. And they value challenging jobs. But they have projected their values onto others. Certainly an increasing portion of the labor force is seeking work that is interesting and that challenges them.[5] But you can't generalize to the entire work force.

Having cleared up some misconceptions about motivation and rewards, let's now make sure we have a uniform understanding of just what we mean by the term *motivation*.

DEFINING MOTIVATION

What is motivation? What does a motivated worker look like? **Motivation** is the willingness to exert a persistent and high level of effort toward organizational goals, conditioned by the effort's ability to satisfy some individual need.[6] General motivation is concerned with effort toward *any* goal; we narrow the focus to *organizational* goals in order to reflect our singular interest in work-related behaviors. The key elements in our definition are intensity of effort, persistence, direction toward organizational goals, and needs.

The effort element is a measure of intensity. Someone who is motivated tries hard. Persistence is follow-through, or stick-to-itiveness. People who are persistent sustain their high level of effort despite barriers or difficulties. Of course, persistence and effort are unlikely to lead to favorable job performance outcomes unless the effort is channeled in a direction that benefits the organization. Therefore, we must consider the quality of the effort as well. Effort that is directed toward, and consistent with, the organization's goals is the kind of effort we should be seeking. Finally, we treat motivation as a need-satisfying process. A **need**, in our terminology, means some internal state that makes certain outcomes appear attractive. An unsatisfied need creates tension that stimulates drives within the individual. These drives generate a search behavior to find particular goals that, if attained, will satisfy the need and lead to the reduction of tension.

EXHIBIT 13-1

Source: Harley Schwadron

SCHWADRON
"I RESENT BEING CALLED 'LAZY.' THE CORRECT TERM IS 'MOTIVATIONALLY IMPAIRED.'"

So we can say that motivated employees are in a state of tension. To relieve this tension, they exert effort. The greater the tension, the higher the effort level. If this effort successfully leads to the satisfaction of the need, tension is reduced. But since we are interested in work behavior, this tension-reduction effort must also be directed toward organizational goals. Therefore, inherent in our definition of motivation is the requirement that the individual's needs be compatible and consistent with the organization's goals. When they are not, individuals might exert high levels of effort that actually run counter to the interests of the organization. This, incidentally, is not so unusual. For example, some employees regularly spend a lot of time talking with friends at work in order to satisfy their social needs. There is a high level of effort, only it's being unproductively directed.

BASIC MOTIVATION AND REWARD ISSUES

In this section, we address in a question format some of the basic issues managers need to address if they are going to design motivation and reward systems that will maximize employee performance. We begin by considering the different needs that drive human behavior.

What Basic Needs Do People Seek to Satisfy?

Four specific theoretical frameworks have sought to identify basic needs that individuals seek to satisfy. The common theme among these frameworks is that motivation is caused by deficiencies in one or more needs or need groups.

Maslow's Hierarchy of Needs Probably the best-known approach to motivation is Abraham Maslow's **hierarchy of needs**.[7] He hypothesized that within every human being there exists a hierarchy of the following five sets of needs.

1. *Physiological needs*. Includes hunger, thirst, shelter, sex, and other survival needs.
2. *Safety needs*. Includes security, stability, and protection from physical and emotional harm.
3. *Belongingness needs*. Includes the need for social interaction, affection, companionship, and friendship.
4. *Esteem needs*. Includes internal esteem factors such as self-respect, autonomy, and achievement; and external esteem factors such as status, recognition, and attention.
5. *Self-actualization needs*. Includes growth, self-fulfillment, and achieving one's potential.

Maslow described the first three sets as *deficiency needs* because they must be satisfied if the individual is to be healthy and secure. The last two were called *growth needs* because they are related to the development and achievement of one's potential. These groups are also frequently referred to as *lower-order* and *higher-order needs,* respectively.

Maslow proposed that these needs were inherent in all people, that they were genetically determined, and that the five need-sets existed in a hierarchy (see Exhibit 13-2). Although all people have the same need structure, according to Maslow, they can be at different levels on the hierarchy. And as each of these needs becomes substantially satisfied, the next higher need becomes dominant. From the standpoint of motivation, Maslow was arguing that, although no need is ever fully gratified, a substantially satisfied need no longer motivates. So if you want to motivate someone, you need to understand what level of the hierarchy that person is currently on and focus on satisfying the needs at or above that level.

EXHIBIT 13-2
Maslow's Hierarchy of Needs

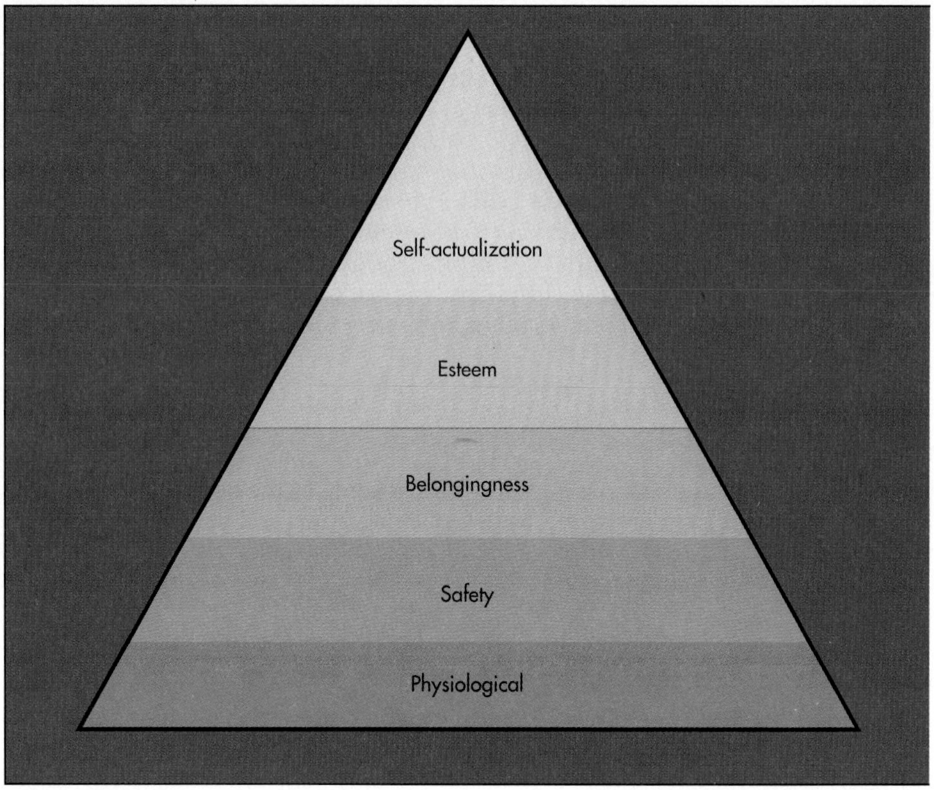

Source: Data for diagram based on "Hierarchy of Needs" from *Motivation and Personality,* 3rd Ed. by Abraham H. Maslow. Revised by Robert Frager, James Fadiman, Cynthia McReynolds, and Ruth Cox. © 1954, © 1987 by Harper & Row. © 1970 by Abraham H. Maslow. Reprint by permission of HarperCollins Publishers, Inc.

ERG Theory Despite the popularity of Maslow's hierarchy of needs framework, efforts to support it with substantive research evidence have met with little success.[8] In an attempt to deal with some of its limitations, Clayton Alderfer proposed a condensed version with some modified assumptions.[9] As you will see, this modification of Maslow's framework has proved to more accurately describe the relationship between needs and motivation.

Alderfer argued that there are three groups of core needs—existence, relatedness, and growth—hence the label **ERG theory**. The *existence* group is concerned with providing our basic material existence requirements. It includes the items that Maslow considered physiological and safety needs. The second group includes needs of *relatedness*—the desire we have for maintaining interpersonal relationships. These social and status desires require interaction with others if they are to be satisfied, and they align with Maslow's belongingness need and the external component of his esteem classification. Finally, Alderfer isolated *growth* needs—an intrinsic desire for personal development. These include the internal component from Maslow's esteem category and the characteristics included under self-actualization.

In contrast to Maslow's rigid steplike progression, ERG theory does not assume a rigid hierarchy where a lower need must be substantially gratified before one can move on. A person can, for instance, be working on growth even though existence or relatedness needs are unsatisfied, or all three need categories could be operating at the same time.

ERG theory also contains a frustration-regression dimension. Essentially, Alderfer argued that the frustration of higher-order needs prompts demands for greater satisfaction of lower-order needs. Inability to satisfy a relatedness need such as social interaction, for instance, tends to increase the desire for more money or better working conditions.

Tests have demonstrated far more support for ERG theory than for Maslow's theory.[10] ERG theory has been particularly helpful in explaining why so many people become singularly focused on lower-order needs such as pay and benefits.[11] Frustrated by unsatisfied higher-order needs, they demand greater satisfaction of lower-order needs. Because pay and benefits—which substantially gratify lower-order needs—are visible and relatively easy for management to administer, managers rely on them too much to motivate employees. And this overreliance on lower-order needs creates a vicious circle of deprivation, regression, and temporary gratification—deprived of higher-order need gratification, employees come to expect more and more lower-order–focused rewards.

Theory of Manifest Needs Sixty years ago, Henry Murray developed his **theory of manifest needs.**[12] Despite the passing of years, Murray's work still provides us with some important insights into the link between needs and motivation.

First, Murray gets credit for identifying needs as having two components—direction and intensity. You will remember those terms as part of our earlier definition of motivation. Second, he identified more than twenty needs that individuals can possess. Some of his examples included the need for achievement, affiliation, autonomy, change, order, and power. Third, in direct contrast to Maslow, Murray argued that most needs were learned, rather than inherited, and that they are activated by cues from an individual's environment. So an employee with a high need for achievement would pursue that need only when the environmental conditions were appropriate (such as when he or she was assigned a challenging job). Only then would the need surface or become manifest. If not cued, the need would be latent. Finally, Murray's theory provides more flexibility in describing people. Unlike Maslow, Murray didn't assume that people were at a single level on a rigid hierarchy. He proposed that multiple needs motivate behavior simultaneously rather than in some preset order. So people could have high needs for achievement and affiliation and a low need for power—all at the same time.

How well has the theory of manifest needs held up in terms of providing managers with insights into employee motivation? Specific tests of the full theory do not exist. But certain elements seem valid. For instance, many needs appear to be learned; and individuals regularly demonstrate the capability of pursuing multiple needs at the same time. Murray's work is also important for providing the foundation for research conducted by David McClelland in the 1960s through the 1970s. As we show in the next section, McClelland extended and expanded on Murray's ideas, with specific focus on the needs for achievement, affiliation, and power.

Learned Needs Theory David McClelland spent much of his career studying three learned needs that he considered to be particularly important sources of motivation.[13] As noted, they are achievement, affiliation, and power. He defined them as follows:

- **Need for achievement *(nAch)*.** The drive to excel, to achieve in relation to a set of standards, to strive to succeed
- **Need for affiliation *(nAff)*.** The desire for friendly and close interpersonal relationships
- **Need for power *(nPow)*.** The need to make others behave in a way that they would not have behaved otherwise

McClelland believed that these needs are acquired from the culture of a society—hence, the label **learned needs theory.** For instance, he argued that the *nAch* is nurtured early in life through children's books, parental styles, and social norms. Some societies stimulate it a lot more in their young than do others. In fact, McClelland has had considerable success in making people from low-achievement cultures exhibit high-achievement behaviors.

As previously noted in Chapter 12, McClelland found that high achievers differentiate themselves from others by their desire to do things better.[14] They seek situations in which: they can attain personal responsibility for finding solutions to problems; they can receive rapid feedback on their performance so that they can tell easily whether they are improving; and they can set moderately challenging goals. High achievers are not gamblers; they dislike succeeding by chance. They prefer the challenge of working at a problem and accepting the personal responsibility for success or failure rather than leaving the outcome to chance or the actions of others. Importantly, they avoid what they perceive to be very easy or very difficult tasks. They want to overcome obstacles, but they want to feel that their success (or failure) is due to their own actions. This means they like tasks of intermediate difficulty.

The need for power is the desire to have impact, to be influential, and to control others. Individuals high in *nPow* enjoy being "in charge," strive for influence over others, prefer to be placed into competitive and status-oriented situations, and tend to be more concerned with prestige and gaining influence over others than with effective performance.

The third need considered by McClelland is affiliation. This need has received the least attention from researchers. Affiliation can be likened to Dale Carnegie's goals—the desire to be liked and accepted by others. Individuals with a high affiliation motive strive for friendship, prefer cooperative situations rather than competitive ones, and desire relationships involving a high degree of mutual understanding.

Relying on an extensive amount of research, we can make some reasonably well-supported predictions on the basis of the relationship between achievement need and job performance. Although less research has been done on power and affiliation needs, there are consistent findings on those dimensions, too.

First, as shown in Exhibit 13-3, individuals with a high need to achieve prefer job situations with personal responsibility, feedback, and an intermediate degree of risk. When these characteristics are prevalent, high achievers will be strongly motivated. The evidence consistently demonstrates, for instance, that high achievers are successful in entrepreneurial activities such as running their own businesses and managing a self-contained unit within a large organization.[15]

EXHIBIT 13-3
Matching Achievers and Jobs

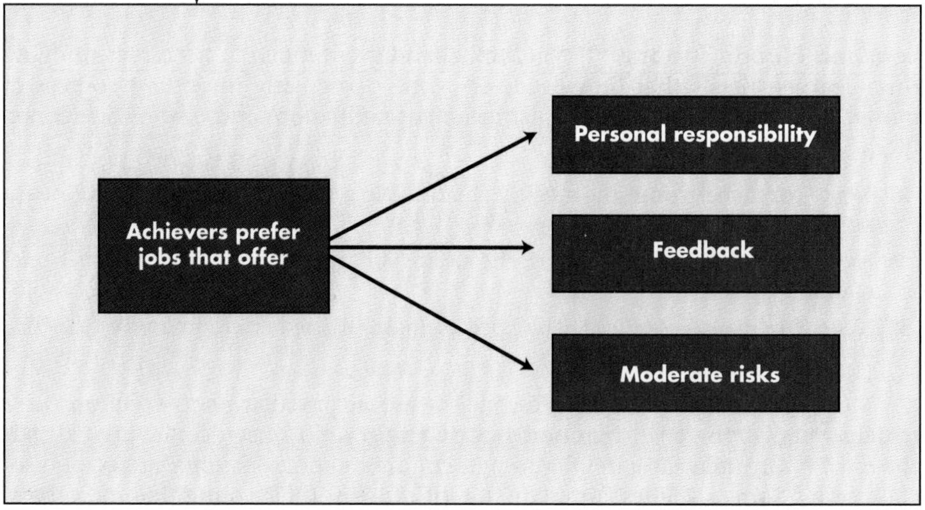

WHAT MOTIVATES YOU?

INSTRUCTIONS For each of the following fifteen statements, circle the number that most closely agrees with how you feel. Consider your answers in the context of your current job or past work experience.

	Strongly Disagree				Strongly Agree
1. I try very hard to improve on my past performance at work.	1	2	3	4	5
2. I enjoy competition and winning.	1	2	3	4	5
3. I often find myself talking to those around me about nonwork matters.	1	2	3	4	5
4. I enjoy a difficult challenge.	1	2	3	4	5
5. I enjoy being in charge.	1	2	3	4	5
6. I want to be liked by others.	1	2	3	4	5
7. I want to know how I am progressing as I complete tasks.	1	2	3	4	5
8. I confront people who do things I disagree with.	1	2	3	4	5
9. I tend to build close relationships with co-workers.	1	2	3	4	5
10. I enjoy setting and achieving realistic goals.	1	2	3	4	5
11. I enjoy influencing other people to get my way.	1	2	3	4	5
12. I enjoy belonging to groups and organizations.	1	2	3	4	5
13. I enjoy the satisfaction of completing a difficult task.	1	2	3	4	5
14. I often work to gain more control over the events around me.	1	2	3	4	5
15. I pay a good deal of attention to the feelings of others at work.	1	2	3	4	5

Turn to page 561 for scoring directions and key.

***Sources:* Based on R. Steers and D. Braunstein, "A Behaviorally Based Measure of Manifest Needs in Work Settings," *Journal of Vocational Behavior,* October 1976, p. 254; and R. N. Lussier, *Human Relations in Organizations: A Skill Building Approach* (Homewood, Ill: Richard D. Irwin, 1990), p. 120.**

Second, a high need to achieve does not necessarily lead to being a good manager, especially in large organizations. People with a high achievement need are interested in how well they do personally and not in influencing others to do well. High-*nAch* salespeople do not necessarily make good sales managers, and the good general manager in a large organization does not typically have a high need to achieve.[16]

Third, the needs for affiliation and power tend to be closely related to managerial success. The best managers are high in their need for power and low in their need for affiliation.[17] In fact, a high power motive may be a requirement for managerial effectiveness.[18] Of course, what is the cause and what is the effect is arguable. It has been suggested that a high power need may occur simply as a function of one's level in a hierarchical organization.[19] The latter argument pro-

IN THE NEWS

Lower-Order Needs Dominate in Eastern Europe

If employees don't have some basic job security, other needs are not likely to be very important to them. This fact has become evident as executives try to turn around inefficient, formerly state-owned businesses in Eastern Europe.

Take the case of boiler manufacturer Alstrom Fakop in Poland. Managers of the 400-employee company initially tried to increase motivation and morale by offering employees incentive pay. It didn't work. So management tried something different. It offered to maintain staffing at current levels if sales targets were met. To management's pleasant surprise, this commitment resulted in an increase in morale and sales.

Because of the chaos inherent in changing to a market economy, many Eastern European employees are more concerned with keeping their jobs than with getting a bonus. And, while this may be an obvious point, notes Ted Snyder of the University of Michigan, it's one most Western managers just don't get. Western managers rush in with new incentives, downsizing targets, and cost-accounting systems, but that isn't enough, says Snyder: "There's real fear. You need a growth strategy. You need to say, 'If we achieve this, we won't have to cut.'"

Ironically, this advice may have more relevance to managing in the West than many managers want to admit. Cost-cutting, downsizing, and reengineering efforts in the United States, Canada, and Western Europe have left many employees feeling insecure about their jobs. People whose jobs are in jeopardy are not likely to be motivated by efforts to redesign work into teams or by offers of more-flexible work schedules.

Employees at this boiler plant in Poland want job security, not incentive pay.

Source: R. Jacob, "Secure Jobs Trump Higher Pay," *Fortune*, March 20, 1995, p. 24.

poses that the higher the level an individual rises to in the organization, the greater is the incumbent's power motive. As a result, powerful positions would be the stimulus to a high power motive.

Conclusions What conclusions can we draw from these studies of needs that might help you better motivate others? Despite its popularity, Maslow's hierarchy of needs seems to offer little of value for managers. There is no evidence, for instance, that there is a rigid hierarchy of needs that would be applicable to a diverse work force. Which needs dominate in an individual seem to change with the situation and time. So managers need to become adept at "reading" their employees' needs. How? Ask and pay attention to employee behaviors. Don't be afraid to ask people what would motivate them to do a good job. And watch what on-the-job activities employees choose to do when they have free time. This is a window into what currently interests them and drives their actions.

On a more positive note, there does appear to be value in differentiating lower-order and higher-order need sets. Why? If lower-order needs are not substantially met, employees are unlikely to respond to management efforts to stimulate higher needs. For instance, employees are unlikely to respond positively to the introduction of self-managed teams (which can help satisfy autonomy, achievement, and recognition needs) if they are afraid of layoffs and losing their jobs.

Are People Basically Responsible or Irresponsible?

After watching the way managers dealt with employees, Douglas McGregor made an interesting observation.[20] Managers, he said, hold either of two sets of assumptions about human nature. And those assumptions shape the way the managers treat their employees. He then proceeded to list the assumptions. The first set McGregor called **Theory X,** which basically sees people as irresponsible and lazy. Theory X assumes that:

1. Employees inherently dislike work and, whenever possible, will attempt to avoid it.
2. Since employees dislike work, they must be coerced, controlled, or threatened with punishment to achieve goals.
3. Employees will avoid responsibilities and seek formal direction whenever possible.
4. Most workers place security above all other factors associated with work and will display little ambition.

The second set of assumptions McGregor called **Theory Y,** which basically views people as responsible and conscientious. Theory Y assumes that:

1. Employees can view work as being as natural as rest or play.
2. People will exercise self-direction and self-control if they are committed to the objectives.
3. The average person can learn to accept, even seek, responsibility.
4. The ability to make innovative decisions is widely dispersed throughout the population and is not necessarily the sole province of those in management positions.

What are the motivational implications of McGregor's analysis? Theory X assumes that lower-order needs dominate individuals. Theory Y assumes that higher-order needs dominate individuals. And, because McGregor himself held to the belief that Theory Y assumptions were more valid, he proposed such ideas as participative decision making, responsible and challenging jobs, and good group relations as approaches that would maximize an employee's job motivation.

Unfortunately, there is no evidence to confirm that either set of assumptions is universally valid or that managers who accept Theory Y assumptions and alter their actions accordingly have more-motivated workers. Either Theory X or Theory Y assumptions may be appropriate depending on the particular situation.

The lack of supporting evidence does not negate the value of McGregor's analysis. Quite the contrary. You should familiarize yourself with his terminology because it is frequently used (or misused) by people in organizations. Autocratic executives, for instance, are frequently described as Theory X managers. Although this is not the correct usage of McGregor's terminology—remember, he was describing assumptions about human nature, not management styles—it has nonetheless become a popular way to describe how managers relate to their employees.

What Leads to Satisfaction or Dissatisfaction?

What do people want from their jobs? That was the question psychologist Frederick Herzberg asked that led to one of the most frequently cited theories of motivation.

Herzberg asked people to describe, in detail, situations in which they felt exceptionally *good* and *bad* about their jobs. The responses were tabulated and categorized. His findings, shown in Exhibit 13-4, represent the essence of what he called **motivation-hygiene theory.**[21]

EXHIBIT 13-4
Comparison of Satisfiers (Motivators) and Dissatisfiers (Hygiene Factors)

Source: F. Herzberg, "One More Time, How Do You Motivate Employees?" Adapted and reprinted by permission of *Harvard Business Review,* September–October, 1987. Copyright © 1987 by the President and Fellows of Harvard College; all rights reserved.

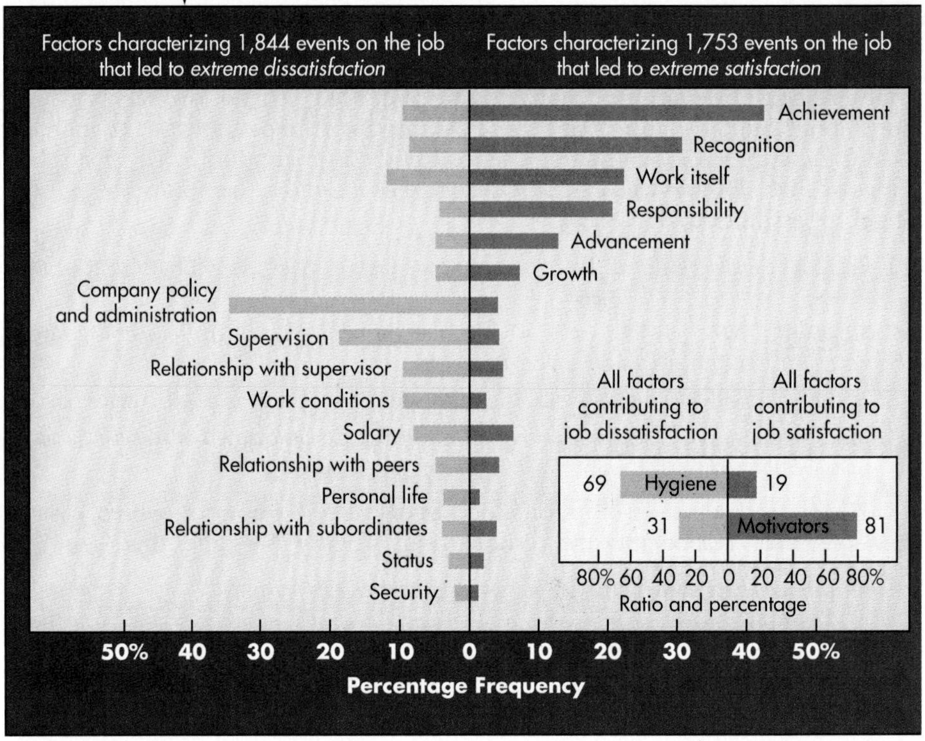

Herzberg found that the replies people gave when they felt good about their jobs were significantly different from the replies given when they felt bad. This finding led to motivation-hygiene theory's primary conclusion: Intrinsic factors are related to job satisfaction, whereas extrinsic factors are associated with dissatisfaction.

According to Herzberg, the factors leading to job satisfaction are separate and distinct from those that lead to job dissatisfaction. Therefore, managers who seek to eliminate factors that create job dissatisfaction can bring about peace, but not necessarily motivation. They will be placating their work force rather than motivating them. As a result, such characteristics as company policy and administration, supervision, interpersonal relations, working conditions, and salary have been characterized by Herzberg as *hygiene factors*. When they are adequate, people will not be dissatisfied; however, neither will they be satisfied. If we want to motivate people on their jobs, Herzberg suggests emphasizing achievement, recognition, the work itself, responsibility, and growth. These are the characteristics that people find intrinsically rewarding.

This theory has had more than its fair share of criticism.[22] The most relevant of these criticisms, at least from our perspective, is that it is actually more a theory of job satisfaction than of motivation. Yet Herzberg's findings have been widely used by managers to justify efforts at job enrichment (see Chapter 9). Many organizations have combined job tasks, expanded employee responsibility, and introduced work teams with the intention of increasing employee satisfaction and motivation.

If you want a more accurate and comprehensive explanation of what leads to employee satisfaction, we would offer four recommendations based on an extensive review of the job satisfaction literature.[23] But there is no assurance that these recommendations will automatically lead to increased motivation or employee performance.

1. *Give employees mentally challenging jobs.* Consistent with Herzberg's recommendations, employees tend to prefer jobs that give them opportunities to use their skills and abilities and offer a variety of tasks, freedom, and feedback on how well they're doing. These characteristics make work mentally challenging.
2. *Provide equitable rewards.* Employees want pay systems and promotion policies that they perceive as being just, unambiguous, and in line with their expectations. When pay or other rewards are seen as fair, satisfaction is likely to result.
3. *Offer supportive working conditions.* Employees are concerned with their work environment for both personal comfort and facilitating doing a good job. They prefer physical surroundings, for instance, that are not dangerous or uncomfortable. Most employees also prefer working relatively close to home, in clean and relatively modern facilities, and with adequate tools and equipment.
4. *Encourage supportive colleagues.* People get more out of work than merely money or tangible achievements. For most employees, work also fills the need for social interaction. Not surprisingly, therefore, having friendly and supportive co-workers leads to increased job satisfaction. Satisfaction is also increased when employees perceive that their immediate supervisor is understanding and friendly, offers praise for good performance, listens to employees' opinions, and shows a personal interest in them.

Does Having "Specific Goals" Improve Motivation?

Dawn Sanders felt she was being honest and supportive with her employees when she told them, "Just do your best. That's all anyone can ask from you." But would Dawn have been more effective if she had substituted specific goals for the generalized goal of "do your best"? The answer is probably Yes. Let's look at why.

There is now an extensive body of evidence that demonstrates that goals are a major source of work motivation.[24] More to the point, we can say that specific goals increase performance; that difficult goals, when accepted, result in higher performance than do easy goals; and that goal feedback leads to higher performance than does lack of feedback.[25] We call these principles **goal-setting theory.**

Specific hard goals produce a higher level of output than does the generalized goal of "do your best." The specificity of the goal itself acts as an internal stimulus. For instance, when a trucker commits to making twelve round-trip hauls between Toronto and Buffalo, New York, each week, this intention gives him a specific objective to reach for. We can say that, all things being equal, the trucker with a specific goal will outperform his counterpart operating with no goals or the generalized goal of "do your best."

Specific hard goals produce a higher level of output than does the generalized goal of "do your best."

If factors such as ability and acceptance of the goals are held constant, we can also state that the more difficult the goal, the higher the level of performance. It is logical to assume that easier goals are more likely to be accepted. But once an employee accepts a hard task, he or she will exert a high level of effort until it is achieved, lowered, or abandoned.

People do best when they get feedback on how well they are progressing toward their goals, because feedback helps to identify discrepancies between what they have done and what they want to do; that is, feedback acts to guide behavior. But all feedback is not equally potent. Self-generated feedback—in which the employee is able to monitor his or her own progress—has been shown to be a more powerful motivator than externally generated feedback.[26]

If employees have the opportunity to participate in the setting of their own goals, will they try harder? The evidence is mixed regarding the superiority of participative over assigned goals.[27] In some cases, participatively set goals elicited superior performance; in other cases, individuals performed best when assigned goals by their boss. But a major advantage of participation may be in increasing acceptance of the goal itself as a desirable one to work toward.[28] As we noted, resistance is greater when goals are difficult. If people participate in goal setting, they are more likely to accept even a difficult goal than if they are arbitrarily assigned it by their boss. The reason is that individuals are committed to choices in which they have a part. Thus, although participative goals may have no superiority over assigned goals when acceptance is taken as a given, participation does increase the probability that more difficult goals will be agreed to and acted upon.

Are there any contingencies in goal-setting theory, or can we take it as a universal truth that difficult and specific goals will always lead to higher performance? In addition to feedback, three other factors have been found to influence the goals-performance relationship. These are goal commitment, adequate self-efficacy, and national culture. Goal-setting theory presupposes that an individual is *committed* to the goal; that is, is determined not to lower or abandon the goal. Commitment is most likely to occur when goals are made public, when the individual has an internal locus of control, and when the goals are self-set rather than assigned.[29] **Self-efficacy** refers to an individual's belief that he or she is capable of performing a task.[30] The higher your self-efficacy, the more confidence you have in your ability to succeed in a task. So, in difficult situations, we find that people with low self-efficacy are likely to lessen their effort or give up altogether, whereas those with high self-efficacy will try harder to master the challenge.[31] In addition, individuals high in self-efficacy seem to respond to negative feedback with increased effort and motivation, whereas those low in self-efficacy are likely to lessen their effort when given negative feedback.[32] Lastly, goal-setting theory is culture-bound. It is well adapted to countries such as the United States and Canada because its key components align reasonably well with North American cultures. It assumes that subordinates will be reasonably independent (not too high a score on power distance), that managers and subordinates will seek challenging goals (low in uncertainty avoidance), and that performance is considered important by both (high in quantity of life). So don't expect goal setting to necessarily lead to higher employee performance in countries such as Portugal or Chile, where the opposite conditions exist.

How Does Reinforcement Affect Motivation?

A counterpoint to goal-setting theory is **reinforcement theory**. The former is a cognitive approach, proposing that an individual's purposes direct his or her action. Reinforcement theory is a behavioristic approach that argues that reinforcement conditions behavior. The two are clearly at odds philosophically. Reinforcement theorists see behavior as being environmentally caused. You needn't be concerned, they would argue, with internal cognitive events; what controls behavior are reinforcers—any consequence that, when immediately following a response, increases the probability that the behavior will be repeated.

Reinforcement theory ignores the inner state of the individual and concentrates solely on what happens to a person when he or she takes some action. Because it doesn't concern itself with what initiates behavior, it is not, strictly speaking, a theory of motivation. But it does provide a powerful means of analysis of what controls behavior, and it is for this reason that it is typically considered in discussions of motivation.[33]

In the previous chapter, we discussed the reinforcement process in detail. We showed how using reinforcers to condition behavior gives us considerable insight into how people learn. Yet we can't ignore the fact that reinforcement has a wide following as a motivational device. In its pure form, however, reinforcement theory ignores feelings, attitudes, expectations, and other cognitive variables that are known to affect behavior.

Reinforcement is undoubtedly an important influence on behavior, but it is not the only influence. The behaviors employees engage in at work and the amount of effort they allocate to each task are affected by the consequences that follow from those behaviors and efforts. So, for instance, if an employee's colleagues consistently reprimand him for outproducing them, he is likely to reduce his productivity. But the lower productivity may also be explained in terms of goals, inequity, or expectancies.

What Happens When Employees Believe That They Are Being Unfairly Rewarded?

Do the concepts of *fairness* and *equity* have relevance to employee motivation? Absolutely! As we noted early in this chapter, in our discussion of popular misconceptions, people are sensitive to relative differences in rewards. Specifically, they make comparisons of their job inputs and outcomes relative to those of others. They perceive what they get from a job situation (outcomes) in relation to what they put into it (inputs), then they compare their outcome-input ratio with the outcome-input ratio of relevant others. As shown in Exhibit 13-5, there are three possible perceptions. If the ratio is equal to that of the relevant others, a state of equity exists. That is, an individual would perceive the situation as fair. But when the ratio is unequal, there is equity tension. **Equity theory** proposes that this state of negative tension provides the motivation to do something to correct it.[34]

use in game

Evidence indicates that the referent chosen is an important element in equity theory.[35] There are four referent comparisons an employee can use:

1. *Self-inside.* An employee's experiences in a different position inside his or her current organization
2. *Self-outside.* An employee's experiences in a situation or position outside his or her current organization
3. *Other-inside.* Another individual or group of individuals inside the employee's organization
4. *Other-outside.* Another individual or group of individuals outside the employee's organization

So employees might compare themselves with friends, neighbors, co-workers, colleagues in other organizations, or past jobs they themselves have had. Which referent an employee chooses will be influenced by the information the employee holds about referents as well as by the attractiveness of the referent.

Equity theory predicts that, when employees perceive an inequity, they will make one of six choices:[36]

1. Change their inputs (for example, don't exert as much effort)
2. Change their outcomes (for example, individuals paid on a piece-rate basis can increase their pay by producing a higher quantity of units of lower quality)
3. Distort perceptions of self (for example, "I used to think I worked at a moderate pace but now I realize that I work a lot harder than everyone else.")

EXHIBIT 13-5
Equity Theory

Outcome-Input Ratio Comparison Employee		Relevant Others	Perception
O/I_A	<	O/I_B	Inequity due to being underrewarded
O/I_A	=	O/I_B	Equity
O/I_A	>	O/I_B	Inequity due to being overrewarded

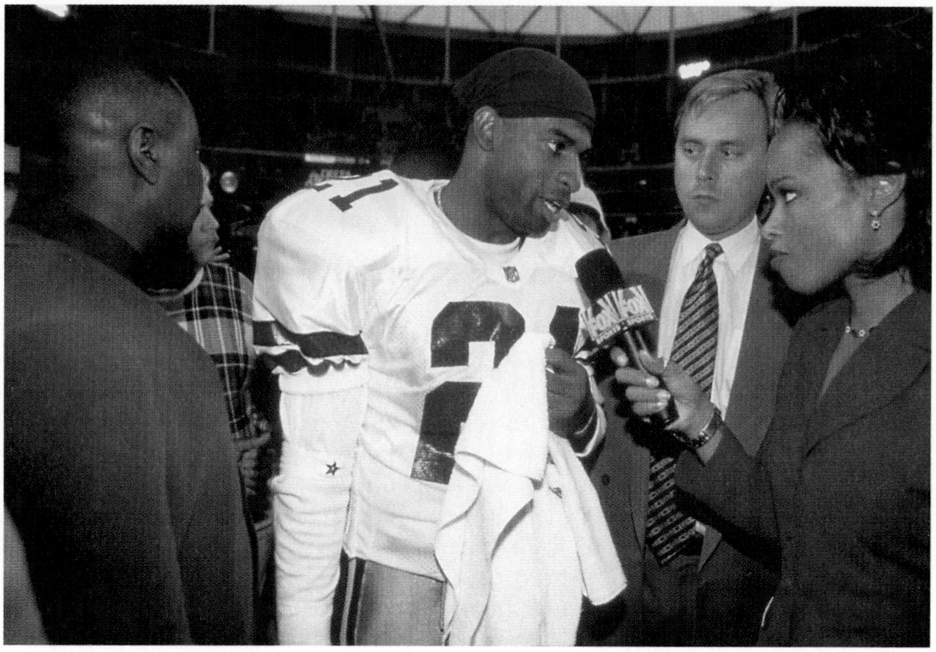

Deion Sanders was paid more than a million dollars a year with the San Francisco 49ers. But, disgruntled with his pay relative to other defensive backs, Sanders signed with the Dallas Cowboys for more than $5 million a year. Consistent with equity theory, Sanders sought a pay package that he thought more fairly matched his performance on the field and his star status off the field.

4. Distort perceptions of others (for example, "Mike's job isn't as desirable as I previously thought it was.")
5. Choose a different referent (for example, "I may not make as much as my brother-in-law, but I'm doing a lot better than my dad did when he was my age.")
6. Leave the field (for example, quit the job)

Equity theory recognizes that individuals are concerned not only with the absolute amount of rewards they receive for their efforts but also with the relationship of that amount to what others receive. They make judgments as to the relationship between their inputs—such as effort, experience, education, and competence—and outcomes—such as salary levels, raises, recognition, and other factors—and the inputs and outcomes of others. When people perceive an imbalance in their outcome-input ratio relative to others, tension is created. This tension provides the basis for motivation, as people strive for what they perceive as equity and fairness.

Specifically, the theory establishes four propositions relating to inequitable pay:

1. *Given payment by time, overrewarded employees will produce more than will equitably paid employees.* Hourly and salaried employees will generate high quantity or quality of production in order to increase the input side of the ratio and bring about equity.
2. *Given payment by quantity of production, overrewarded employees will produce fewer, but higher-quality, units than will equitably paid employees.* Individuals paid on a piece-rate basis will increase their effort to achieve equity, which can result in greater quality or quantity. However, increases in quantity will only increase inequity since every unit produced results in further overpayment. Therefore, effort is directed toward increasing quality rather than increasing quantity.
3. *Given payment by time, underrewarded employees will produce less or poorer quality of output.* Effort will be decreased which brings about lower productivity or poorer quality output than equitably paid subjects.
4. *Given payment by quantity of production, underrewarded employees will produce a large number of low-quality units in comparison with equitably paid employees.* Employees

on piece-rate pay plans can bring about equity because trading off quality of output for quantity will result in an increase in rewards with little or no increase in contributions.

These propositions have generally been supported, with a few minor qualifications.[37] First, inequities created by overpayment do not seem to have a very significant impact on behavior in most work situations. Apparently, people have a great deal more tolerance of overpayment inequities than of underpayment inequities, or they are better able to rationalize them. Second, not all people are equity-sensitive. For example, there is a small part of the working population who actually prefer that their outcome-input ratio be less than the referent comparison. Predictions from equity theory are not likely to be very accurate with these "benevolent types."

It's also important to note that, although most studies on equity theory have focused on pay, employees seem to look for equity in the distribution of other organizational rewards. For instance, it has been shown that the use of high-status job titles as well as large and lavishly furnished offices may function as outcomes for some employees in their equity equation.[38]

How Do Expectations Influence Motivation?

Currently, one of the most widely accepted explanations of motivation is provided by **expectancy theory.**[39] This theory argues that the strength of a tendency to act in a certain way depends on the strength of an expectation that the act will be followed by a given outcome and on the attractiveness of that outcome to the individual. In more practical terms, expectancy theory says that an employee will be motivated to exert a high level of effort when he or she believes that the effort will lead to a good performance appraisal; that a good appraisal will lead to organizational rewards such as a bonus, a salary increase, or a promotion; and that the rewards will satisfy the employee's personal goals. The theory, therefore, focuses on three relationships (see Exhibit 13-6).

1. *Effort-performance relationship.* The probability perceived by the individual that exerting a given amount of effort will lead to performance
2. *Performance-rewards relationship.* The degree to which the individual believes that performing at a particular level will lead to the attainment of a desired outcome

EXHIBIT 13-6
Expectancy Theory

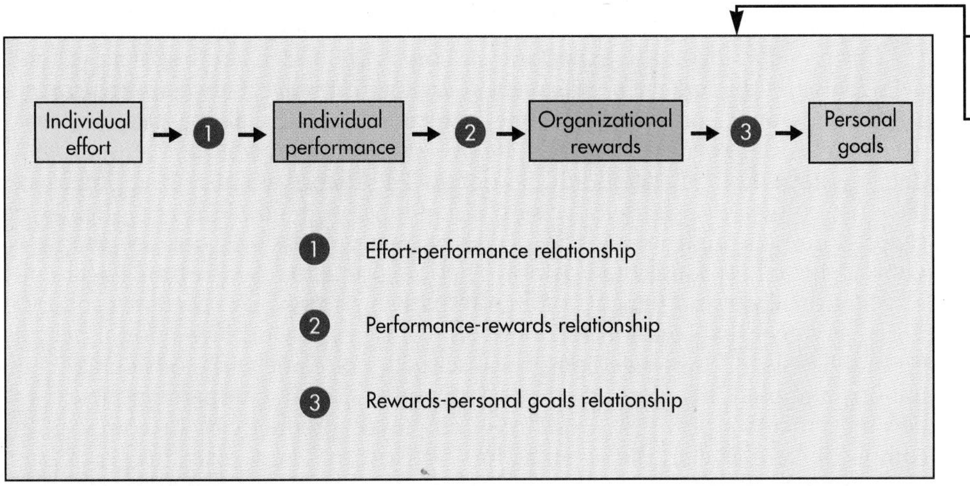

3. *Rewards-personal goals relationship.* The degree to which organizational rewards satisfy an individual's personal goals or needs and the attractiveness of those potential rewards for the individual

Expectancy theory helps explain why a lot of workers aren't motivated on their jobs and merely do the minimum necessary to get by.

Expectancy theory helps explain why a lot of workers aren't motivated on their jobs and merely do the minimum necessary to get by. This attitude is evident when we look at the theory's three relationships in a little more detail. We present them as questions employees need to answer in the affirmative if their motivation is to be maximized.

First, *if I give a maximum effort, will it be recognized in my performance appraisal?* For a lot of employees, the answer is No. Why? Their skill level may be deficient, which means that no matter how hard they try, they are not likely to be high performers. Or, if the organization's performance appraisal system is designed to assess nonperformance factors such as loyalty, initiative, or courage, more effort won't necessarily result in a higher evaluation. Still another possibility is that the employee, rightly or wrongly, perceives that her boss doesn't like her. As a result, she expects to get a poor appraisal regardless of her level of effort. These examples suggest that one possible source of low employee motivation is the employee's belief that no matter how hard she works, the likelihood of getting a good performance appraisal is low.

Second, *if I get a good performance appraisal, will it lead to organizational rewards?* Many employees see the performance-rewards relationship in their job as weak. The reason is that organizations reward a lot of things besides just performance. For example, when pay is allocated to employees on the basis of factors such as seniority, being cooperative, or "kissing up" to the boss, employees are likely to see the performance-rewards relationship as being weak and demotivating.

Last, *if I'm rewarded, are they the rewards that I find personally attractive?* The employee works hard in hope of getting a promotion, but gets a pay raise instead. Or the employee wants a more interesting and challenging job, but receives only a few words of praise. Or the employee puts in extra effort to be relocated to the company's Paris office but instead is transferred to Chicago. These examples illustrate the importance of the rewards' being tailored to individual employee needs. Unfortunately, many managers are limited in the rewards they can distribute, so it is difficult for them to individualize rewards. Moreover, some managers incorrectly assume that all employees want the same thing and thus overlook the motivational effects of differentiating rewards. In either case, employee motivation is not maximized.

In summary, the key to expectancy theory is the understanding of an individual's goals and the linkage between effort and performance, between performance and rewards, and, finally, between the rewards and individual goal satisfaction.

Does expectancy theory work? The overall evidence is generally supportive.[40] But one important caveat should be noted. The theory assumes that employees have few constraints on their decision discretion. For major decisions, such as accepting or resigning from a job, expectancy theory works well because people do not rush into those kinds of decisions. They are prone to take the time to carefully consider the costs and benefits of all alternatives. However, expectancy theory is not a very good explanation for more typical types of work behavior, especially for individuals in lower-level jobs, because such jobs come with considerable limitations imposed by work methods, supervisors, and company policies. Expectancy theory's power in explaining employee productivity increases as the complexity and level in the organization increase; that is, as discretion increases.

What Are the Motivation Implications of the New Employee-Employer Covenant?

As introduced in Chapter 1 and reiterated in many subsequent chapters, today's employee-employer relationship is very different from the one that existed just 20 years ago. In most organizations, the "loyalty-for-security" bond has been irreparably broken.[41] *Security* and *stability* are increasingly something that "my father and grandfather had" but that "don't relate much to me." The majority of employees today face a working world characterized by temporariness, little job security, and limited promotion opportunities (created by flatter structures). Our question is: What are the motivation implications for this new employee-employer covenant?

There's no simple answer to that question. To better focus the issue, let's look at some of the fastest-growing segments of the new work force. These include independent contractors, contingent workers, professionals, minimum-wage service workers, and people required to do highly repetitive tasks.

Independent Contractors An increasing number of employees are acting as independent contractors. They have no permanent ties to a specific organization. Rather, they contract on an individual basis to work on a specific project or set of projects. Some examples of these jobs include an accounting expert who *contracts* with a small trucking firm to install a cost-control system; an electrical engineer who *contracts* with Intel to help in the design of the next generation of microchips; or a training specialist who *contracts* with Boeing to provide an in-house course to improve diversity awareness.

The common characteristics of these "employees" is that, because of the temporary nature of their work, they have no loyalty to the organization. So how can managers who have to work with these people motivate them? Money should be one factor that is important. Since the "relationship" is designed to be short-lived, good pay can be a meaningful and sustainable stimulus to high performance. Other factors that should provide motivation to these people are challenging assignments and opportunities to develop new skills. An independent contractor's future employment is essentially determined by his or her ability to meet employers' needs. Doing so requires keeping skills highly tuned and current. Managers who can provide independent contractors with jobs that fulfill this requirement should have motivated workers.

Contingent Workers Temporary and part-time workers, especially those who choose this status voluntarily, tend to place a high value on flexibility. They should be particularly receptive to flexible work schedules and other options that increase their autonomy. For instance, companies such as Lancaster Laboratories and Ridgeview Hosiery find that they can cut turnover and improve motivation by providing employees with on-site day care.[42] For single parents and dual-career parents, quality day care may make the difference between staying home or being able to come to work. It also allows employees to concentrate on their job once they're at work.

Starbucks Coffee, Hemmings Motor News, and G.T. Water Products have found that they can get more out of part-time employees by providing them with the same benefits offered full-timers.[43] For instance, Starbucks offers health and dental insurance, stock options, and matching retirement plan benefits to part-timers as well as full-timers.

Other motivators for contingent workers include company-paid training and opportunities for permanent status.

IN THE NEWS

Empowered Plumbers Who Make Six Figures a Year

TOM WARNER RUNS A PLUMBING, HEATING, AND AIR-CONDITIONING REPAIR BUSINESS IN MONTGOMERY County, Maryland. In 1990, he faced a dilemma. The company's primary target audience—commercial property-management firms—was cutting costs and increasingly hiring handymen to do work in-house. Though the competition would be stiff, Warner decided to refocus his firm on the residential market. But how could his business, with more than 250 people, successfully compete against little mom-and-pop operators who had built personal relationships with many clients? Warner's answer: Turn his plumbers, electricians, and technicians into empowered businesspeople.

Warner divided huge Montgomery County into territories of approximately 10,000 households. Each of his technicians—he calls them "area technical directors" (ATDs)—was given a territory, Then the ATDs were trained in how to run their territory as if it were their own business. They learned sales techniques, budgeting, negotiating, cost estimating, and how to handle customer complaints. Warner's idea was to field a corps of technically superb, friendly, and ambitious mechanics who operate like small-town tradesmen despite the big-city reality.

The program has proved to be an unqualified success. ATDs have developed a strong sense of pride and ownership in their territory. The average ATD puts in 63 hours a week. They not only fix pipes and repair heaters, but they generate referrals, schedule their own work, do their own estimates, handle their own equipment, develop their own advertising campaigns, and collect their own receivables. Warner provides training, trucks, tools, phones, pagers, dispatchers, and an all-night answering service. He also performs such chores as payroll and taxes. His ATDs are then free to run their businesses the best way they see fit. In 1993, Warner's company earned $544,000 on revenues of $15.6 million. In 1994, he made $1.3 million on $20.3 million in revenues. In 1995, he was estimating revenues of over $31 and profits of $4.8 million. Maybe more startling has been the program's effect on employee income. Ron Inscoe, for instance, is a 34-year-old ATD with a high school education. Before joining Warner's firm, he never made more than $60,000 a year as a heating, ventilation, and air-conditioning technician. In his first year as an ATD he made $103,000. In his second, he made $126,000! But why shouldn't he be making the big bucks? He's no longer just a technician; he's an empowered businessman!

Tom Warner has created a system that motivates his plumbers by turning them into empowered businesspeople.

Source: J. Finegan, "Pipe Dreams," *INC.*, August 1994, pp. 64–70.

performance, earnings recognize contribution rather than being a form of entitlement. Low performers find, over time, that their pay stagnates; high performers enjoy pay increases commensurate with their contribution.

Skill-Based Pay Plans

The highest pay that machine operators at Polaroid Corporation can earn is $14 an hour. But if they can broaden their competencies to include additional skills such as material accounting, equipment maintenance, and quality inspection, they can earn up to 10 percent more.[54] At Xel Communications, a maker of telecommunications transmission equipment, its 300 employees can earn an additional 50 cents an hour for each new task they master.[55] Workers at American Steel & Wire

EXHIBIT 13-9
Popular Variable-Pay Programs

Type	Description
Piece-rate wages	Long used to compensate production employees. Workers are paid a fixed sum for each unit of production completed.
Bonuses	One-time payments that can be paid on the basis of individual, group, or organization-wide performance variables.
Profit-sharing	Organizationwide programs that distribute compensation based on some established formula designed around a company's profitability. These can be direct cash outlays, or, particularly popular for compensating top executives, they can be allocated as stock options.
Gainsharing	A formula-based group incentive plan. Improvements in group productivity—from one period to another—determine the total amount of money allocated. Typically, the division of productivity savings is split 50-50 between the company and employees.

can boost their annual salaries by up to $12,480 by acquiring as many as ten skills. And new employees at a Quaker Oats' pet food plant in Topeka, Kansas, start at $8.75 an hour, but they can reach a top rate of $14.50 when they master ten to twelve skills such as operating lift trucks and factory computer controls.[56]

The above examples illustrate **skill-based pay.** Rather than having an individual's job title define his or her pay category, skill-based pay rewards employees for the job skills and competencies they can demonstrate.[57] It provides an incentive for individuals to learn new tasks and broaden their skills. It facilitates communication across the organization because people gain a better understanding of others' jobs. And it helps meet the needs of ambitious employees who confront minimal advancement opportunities. These people can increase their earnings and knowledge without a promotion in job title.

Skill-based pay meshes nicely with the new world of work. As one expert noted, "Slowly, but surely, we're becoming a skill-based society where your market value is tied to what you can do and what your skill set is. In this new world where skills and knowledge are what really count, it doesn't make sense to treat people as jobholders. It makes sense to treat them as people with specific skills and to pay them for those skills."[58]

"In this new world where skills and knowledge are what really count, it doesn't make sense to treat people as jobholders. It makes sense to treat them as people with specific skills and to pay them for those skills."

Family-Friendly Workplaces

Forty-six percent of the U.S. work force is now female. More and more fathers want to actively participate in the care and raising of their children. As the baby boom generation ages, many are finding themselves having to care for elderly parents. These three facts translate into an increasing number of employees who are attempting to juggle family obligations along with their job responsibilities. In response, companies such as AT&T, Aetna Life & Casualty, Corning, Du Pont, Hewlett-Packard, Johnson & Johnson, Merck, The Prudential, Quaker Oats, and

U.S. West are leading the way in establishing themselves as **family-friendly workplaces**. They offer an umbrella of work-family programs such as paid paternity and adoption leave, on-site day care, child-care and elder-care referrals, use of sick leave for children's illnesses, flexible work hours, 4-day workweeks, job sharing, telecommuting, temporary part-time employment, and relocation assistance for employees' family members.[59]

Creating a family-friendly work climate was initially introduced by management because of concern with improving employee morale and productivity and to reduce absenteeism. It has been estimated that the cost to U.S. businesses of time lost through breakdowns in child-care arrangements alone is about $3 billion annually.[60] At Quaker Oats, for instance, 60 percent of employees admitted being absent at least 3 days a year because of children's illnesses, and 56 percent said they were unable to attend company-related functions or to work overtime because of child-care problems.[61]

Has it worked? Yes and no! There are few data to support any significant increase in productivity. But the evidence does indicate that creating a family-friendly workplace makes it easier for employers to recruit and retain first-class workers.[62] There are also substantial observational data to suggest that it limits family-related distractions and reduces absenteeism.[63]

Bob Schlesinger, owner and president of Bookman's Used Books, Arizona's largest used entertainment stores, was recently recognized as one of the USA's top bosses by 9 to 5 National Association of Working Women. *He was commended for creating a family-friendly environment for his 150 employees. All employees, for instance, are provided health insurance, a 401(k) retirement plan, and four weeks' paid vacation after their third year. Schlesinger also works to accommodate individual employee needs by providing part-time work, flexible hours, and telecommuting.*

Employee Recognition Programs

A few years back, 1,500 employees were surveyed in a variety of work settings to find out what they considered to be the most powerful workplace motivator. Their response? Recognition, recognition, and more recognition![64]

In today's highly competitive global economy, most organizations are under severe cost pressures. That makes recognition programs particularly attractive. In contrast to most other motivators, recognizing an employee's superior performance often costs little or no money. Maybe that's why a recent survey of 3,000 employers found that two-thirds use or plan to use special recognition awards.[65]

Consistent with reinforcement theory, rewarding a behavior with recognition immediately following that behavior is likely to encourage its repetition. How can managers use this technique? They can personally congratulate an employee in private for a good job. They can send a handwritten note or an e-mail message acknowledging something positive that the employee has done. For employees with a strong need for social acceptance, managers can publicly recognize accomplishments. And to enhance group cohesiveness and motivation, managers can celebrate team successes. They can use meetings to recognize the contributions and achievements of successful work teams.

EXHIBIT 13-10

Source: Scott Adams. *Dilbert* reprinted by permission of United Feature Syndicate, Inc.

SUMMARY

(This summary is organized by the chapter-opening learning objectives on page 385.)

1. High performance is not just a function of high motivation. It also requires that an employee have the requisite *ability* to do a job and the necessary *supportive resources*.
2. Motivation is the willingness to exert a persistent and high level of effort toward organizational goals, conditioned by the effort's ability to satisfy some individual need.
3. The hierarchy of needs identifies five needs categories—physiological, safety, belongingness, esteem, and self-actualization—that exist in a hierarchy of steps. As a need is substantially satisfied, the individual moves on to the next. ERG theory condenses these into three groups of core needs—existence, relatedness, and growth. Existence equals physiological and safety needs. Relatedness equals belongingness and the external component of esteem. Growth equals the internal component of esteem and self-actualization. ERG theory proposes that individuals can be working on all three core needs at the same time and can regress from higher-order needs to lower-order needs.
4. Theory X assumes that lower-order needs dominate individuals. So a manager who holds Theory X assumptions is likely to motivate by focusing on physiological and safety needs. This manager is likely to believe that "fear is a great motivator." Theory Y assumes that higher-order needs dominate. Managers holding Theory Y assumptions will try to motivate employees through using participation, creating challenging jobs, and developing good group relations.
5. According to motivation-hygiene theory, extrinsic hygiene factors such as company policy, supervision, pay, and working conditions don't motivate workers. They only placate them. Motivation comes from achievement, growth, responsibility, and similar intrinsic factors in a job.
6. Goals motivate by providing individuals with specific and challenging targets to reach for. Goal feedback further tells a person how well he or she is progressing so adjustment can be made.
7. For people who are equity-sensitive, inequitable rewards (specifically, underrewarding) create tension. People compare the rewards (outcomes) they receive with their inputs; then they compare their outcome-input ratio with the ratios of relevant others. If they perceive inequity, they will try to reestablish equity through actions such as exerting less effort, reducing quality of work, increasing absences, distorting perceptions of self or others, changing referents, or quitting their jobs.
8. Expectancy theory essentially says that for employees to exert high levels of effort, they must believe that the effort will result in a favorable performance appraisal; that the favorable appraisal will lead to increased organizational rewards; and that those rewards will satisfy their personal goals or needs.
9. Employee involvement is a participative process that uses the entire capacity of employees and is designed to encourage increased commitment to the organization's success. Employees are more likely to work hard on a task or job if they have more control over it.
10. Variable-pay programs tie pay to performance. Skill-based programs tie pay to the number of skills or competencies an employee masters. The former focuses on outcomes, the latter on means. Skill-based pay encourages learning, growth, and teamwork. Variable pay encourages individuals to do whatever is necessary to achieve the individual, group, and organizational criteria used for measuring performance.

REVIEW AND DISCUSSION QUESTIONS

1. Contrast the belief that motivation is individual-specific with the belief that it is situation-specific.
2. "Everyone wants a challenging job." Build an argument in favor of this statement. Then build an argument negating the statement.
3. Integrate the two components of a need—direction and intensity—identified by Murray with this chapter's definition of motivation.
4. What characteristics do high achievers prefer in a job?
5. What can managers do to increase employee satisfaction?
6. Does employee participation in goal setting lead to higher performance? Explain your answer.
7. In what ways can you use reinforcement theory to improve employee motivation?
8. How can you motivate (a) contingent workers? (b) Professionals? (c) Minimum-wage service workers?
9. Explain Exhibit 13-7 in terms of how it can help a manager motivate his or her staff.
10. What are "family-friendly workplaces"? How might they influence employee motivation?

CASE EXERCISE A
LANTECH: INCENTIVE PAY IGNITES GANG WARFARE

Lantech is a privately owned company of 325 employees that manufactures packaging machinery in Louisville, Kentucky. Founded in 1972, the company was a pioneer in incentive pay.

In the mid-1970s, workers were asked to rate one another's job performance, and bonuses were distributed accordingly. That program caused too much anxiety and was scrapped. But the company's CEO, Pat Lancaster, was still determined to make incentive pay work. So he sought other incentive ideas.

At one point, each of the company's five manufacturing divisons was given a bonus determined by how much profit it made. Employees could earn up to 10 percent of their regular pay in bonus money. But the divisions are interdependent, so it was very difficult to sort out which was entitled to what profits. "That led to so much secrecy, politicking, and sucking noise that you wouldn't believe it," says the present CEO, Jim Lancaster, Pat's son. For example, the division that built standard machines and the one that added custom design features to those machines depended on each other for parts, engineering expertise, and such. So inevitably the groups clashed, each one trying to assign costs to the other and claim credit.

Pat recalls that by the early 1990s, "I was spending 95 percent of my time on conflict resolution instead of on how to serve our customers." The divisions fought so long over who would get charged for overhead cranes to haul heavy equipment around the factory floor that Lantech couldn't install those useful machines until 1992, several years later than planned. At the end of each month, the divisons would rush to fill orders from other parts of the company. Such actions created profits for the divisions filling the order but generated piles of costly and unnecessary inventory in the receiving division. Some employees even argued over who would pay for the toilet paper in the common restrooms. One person suggested that toilet paper costs should reflect the gender makeup of the division, on the questionable theory that one gender uses more tissue than the other.

Given all these problems, Lantech has abandoned individual and division performance pay.

Questions

1. What, if anything, did Lantech do wrong in setting up its incentive pay plan?
2. What suggestions would you make for a new incentive system?
3. What lessons could managers draw from this case?

Source: P. Nulty, "Incentive Pay Can Be Crippling," *Fortune*, November 13, 1995, p. 235.

CASE EXERCISE B
MAKING THE SALES NUMBERS AT PIER 1'S STORE NO. 398

The managers at Pier 1's store number 398, in Nashville, Tennessee—Paula Hankins and Eva Goldyn—are obsessed with improving their unit's sales during the Christmas season. Since the 1995 fiscal year began on March 1, the store has posted sales gains of 36 percent against the previous year. This gain contrasts very favorably with an average of only 4.5 percent gain at the 650 other Pier 1 stores. But Hankins and Goldyn are not resting on their laurels. They are determined to maintain their percentage gain through year-end.

On the first day of the store's 5-week Christmas season, Hankins tells her staff that she wants to beat last year's comparable day's business of $3,159 by 36 percent. "We can do it, I know we can," she tells the troops. And part of her strategy is to keep her employees fully informed on how well the store is doing, which has both positive and negative effects.

Letting the store staff in on financial objectives and detailed results can transform an 8-hour shift of clock-watching into an enthralling race. "The more information you give the associates, the more ownership they feel in the store's performance," says a Pier 1 regional manager. On the selling floor, many agree. "It adds to the excitement," says an assistant manager at store 398. All day, as customers come and go, the store's employees take turns consulting a backroom computer for an up-to-the-moment sales tally. On the downside, however, employees tend to get dejected when the numbers are weak.

It has been a roller-coaster ride for the people at store 398 on this first week of the Christmas season. November 26th, a Sunday, goes well. The store rings up $4,409 in sales, up 40 percent from last year. Any elation proves premature as Monday's sales increase only 24 percent over 1994. And Tuesday proves a real bummer. The store has a 40 percent increase in-hand late in the day, but a customer walks in and returns a $500 furniture set purchased days earlier. This customer single-handedly knocks Tuesday's increase down to 20 percent. Wednesday's sales climb only 19 percent, and Thursday's actually drop 12 percent. "The weather is too nice," Hankins tells her staff. "With that full weekend before Christmas, people are waiting to do their shopping this year." Friday is another disaster: Sales drop 22 percent.

This roller-coaster week has been rough on managers and employees. Noting that only 33 percent of people who enter Pier 1 actually purchase something, managers constantly encourage employees to pay close attention to those who come in. And because salespeople receive a bonus based on the sales gain in their store, failing to achieve the sales goal that management has established can hurt morale.

Questions

1. Contrast the positive and negative effects on motivation from providing employees with specific goals and detailed feedback on results.
2. In regard to store 398, do you think the benefits exceed the cost?
3. What suggestions might you make to Hankins and Goldyn for improving employee motivation and performance?

Source: K. Helliker, "Pressure at Pier 1: Beating Sales Numbers of Year Earlier Is a Storewide Obsession," *Wall Street Journal,* December 7, 1995, p. B1. Reprinted by permission of the *Wall Street Journal,* © 1995. Dow Jones & Co., Inc. All rights reserved worldwide.

SKILL EXERCISE

Motivating a Team of Professionals

Dawn Pizaro had to laugh. She was sitting at her desk, looking at a list of company stock options held by her Microsoft team. No one on her nine-person team was older than 33. Yet everyone was a millionaire, at least on paper. The value of their options, on this given day, ranged from $1.7 million to $18.4 million.

Her team wasn't unusual. More than 2,000 of Microsoft's 18,000 employees are millionaires—all created by the incredible rise in the value of the company's stock. So Dawn's problem isn't unique at Microsoft or, for that matter, at a number of fast-growing, high-tech companies. Her problem? How do you motivate multimillionaires to come to work every day?

Assume that you're Dawn. What can you do to increase your employees' motivation?

NOTES

1. D. Benjamin and T. Horwitz, "German View: 'You Americans Work Too Hard—and For What?'" *Wall Street Journal,* July 14, 1994, p. B1.
2. See, for instance, M. Blumberg and C. D. Pringle, "The Missing Opportunity in Organizational Research: Some Implications for a Theory of Work Performance," *Academy of Management Review,* October 1982, pp. 560–69; and J. Hall, "Americans Know How to Be Productive If Managers Will Let Them," *Organizational Dynamics,* Winter 1994, pp. 33–46.
3. S. Ratan, "Generational Tension in the Office: Why Busters Hate Boomers," *Fortune,* October 4, 1993, pp. 56–70; B. Filipczak, "It's Just a Job: Generation X at Work," *Training,* April 1994, pp. 21–27; and P. Sellers, "Don't Call Me Slacker!" *Fortune,* December 12, 1994, pp. 181–96.
4. See E. W. Miles, J. D. Hatfield, and R. C. Huseman, "The Equity Sensitive Construct: Potential Implications for Worker Performance," *Journal of Management,* December

CHAPTER 14
BASIC ISSUES IN LEADERSHIP

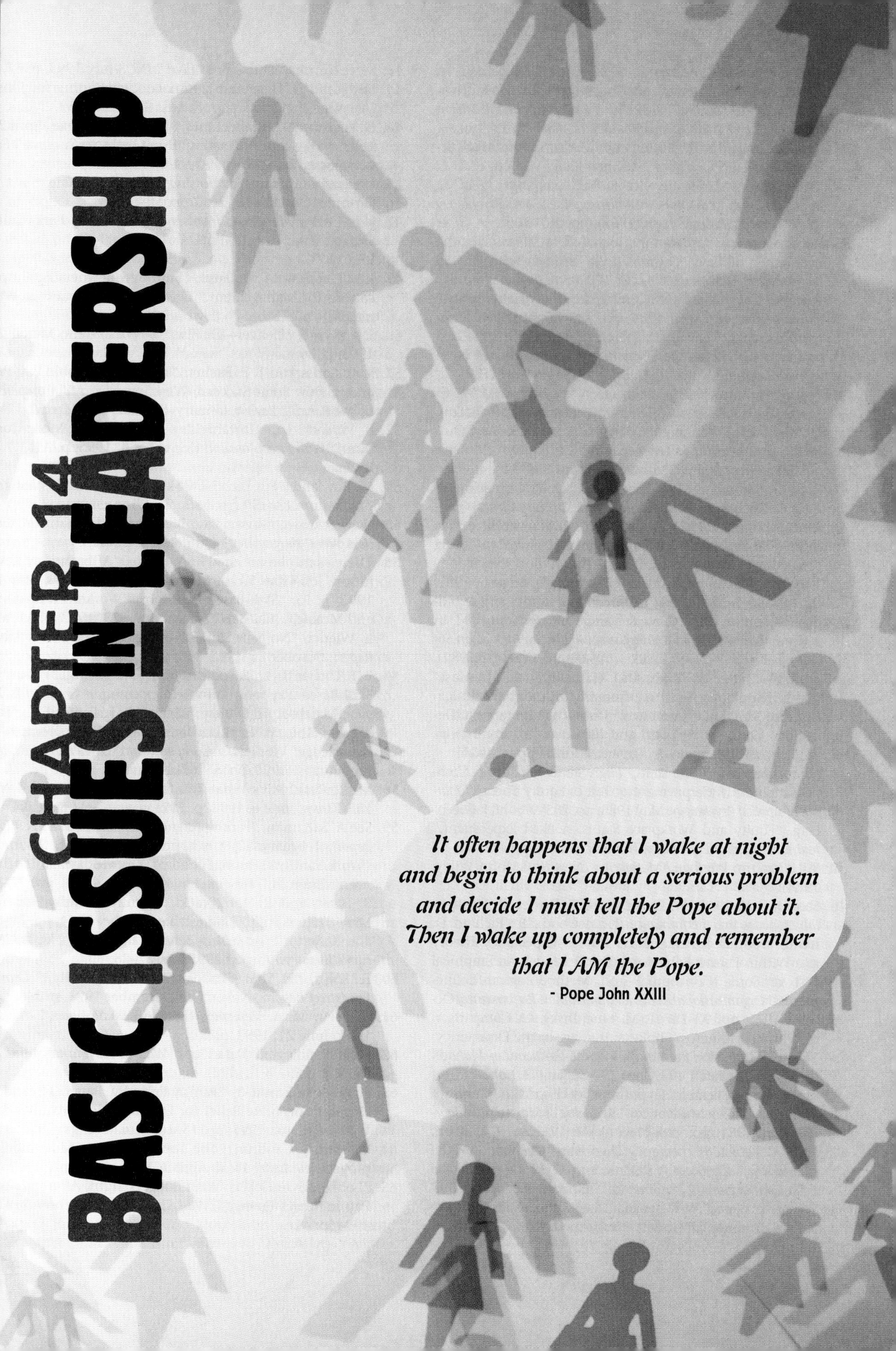

*It often happens that I wake at night
and begin to think about a serious problem
and decide I must tell the Pope about it.
Then I wake up completely and remember
that I AM the Pope.*

- Pope John XXIII

LEARNING OBJECTIVES

After studying this chapter, you should be able to:

1. Contrast leadership and management
2. Identify the five key variables that have shaped our understanding of leadership
3. Explain what is meant by leadership effectiveness
4. List the traits that have been found to regularly explain perceptions of leadership
5. Describe the three primary leadership styles
6. Explain the leader-participation model
7. Describe the leader-member exchange model and its implications
8. Contrast the Fiedler and path-goal models of leadership

Lee Kun-Hee took over the chairmanship of the Samsung Group in 1987, upon the death of his father, who founded the Seoul-based corporation. With its 200,000 employees and sales of $50 billion, the thirty companies that make up the Samsung Group form Asia's largest non-Japanese conglomerate.[1]

During his first few years as chairman, Lee continued the policies and practices established by his father. But by 1993, it had become clear to Lee that things had to change. Sales were stagnant and profits were minimal. The company had historically competed on the basis of cheap labor and a cheap Korean currency. Those no longer existed. If Samsung was to successfully compete against the likes of Sony, General Electric, and Philips, it would have to create cutting-edge technology. In addition, Lee wanted his executives to reorder Samsung's priorities, refocus its product-development and marketing strategies, and radically improve quality. Lee's goal was to become one of the world's ten largest technology companies. To achieve this goal, Lee realized he needed to launch a sweeping remake of his company. And that is precisely what he has been doing. He is turning upside down the hierarchical, inward-looking management installed by his father.

To force managers to make their own decisions, Lee often works from his guest house in central Seoul, refusing to take calls or accept visitors. To convey the urgency for change, he summoned hundreds of Samsung executives in batches of twenty to forty for intensive, often round-the-clock meetings. Over a 2-month period, he convened groups of all 850 of his senior executives. The purpose of these sessions was to attack complacency. Executives were shown how poorly Samsung products were positioned in the marketplace and the urgent need to improve competitiveness and quality.

Lee is convinced that his executive group is too inward-looking. He believes that they have lost touch with their foreign markets. To attack this parochialism, he has significantly increased the company's commitment to training. In September 1993, for instance, he launched what he calls "the CEO School." This program is aimed to put all 850 top group executives through 6 months of reeducation, including 3 months overseas. Lee forbids CEO School students to travel by plane while abroad. They have to travel by car, bus, or train to more closely experience the country they are visiting. In addition, Lee now selects 400 managers each year to go abroad for 12 months and do whatever they want, no questions asked. Lee expects them to return with initimate knowledge of their host country's language and culture. After a few years back in Korea, they will return to their country of specialization to push Samsung products.

It's too early to tell if Lee's internal management revolution will have the positive changes he hopes for. But, as an executive at Toshiba Corp. remarked, "I respect the speed and foresight of his leadership."

Great organizations almost always have great leaders. But what is leadership? What differentiates effective leaders from ineffective leaders? In this and the next chapter, we will review what we have come to learn about leadership and provide you with some specific guidelines for selecting and training leaders.

WHAT IS LEADERSHIP?

Few terms have stimulated as much debate about definition as *leadership* has. Everyone seems to agree about its importance. And experts generally agree that Bill Gates at Microsoft, Linda Wachner of Warnaco, Michael Eisner at Disney, and Richard Branson of the Virgin Group are effective leaders. But are leaders born or made? Do leaders have common personality characteristics? On questions such as these, there is little agreement.

A review finds that common to all definitions of **leadership** is the notion that leaders are individuals who, by their actions, facilitate the movement of a group of people toward a common or shared goal.[2] This definition implies that leadership is an influence process.

The distinction between *leader* and *leadership* is important, but potentially confusing. The leader is the individual; leadership is the function or activity the individual performs. Do all leaders exercise leadership? It depends on what *you* mean by the term *leader.* The word *leader* is often used (interchangeably with the word *manager*) to describe those individuals in an organization who have positions of formal authority, regardless of how they actually act in those jobs. But just because someone is supposed to be a formal leader in an organization might not mean that he or she exercises leadership.

The distinction between *leader* and *leadership* is important, but potentially confusing.

In fact, one of the most debated issues related to this topic is whether leadership is a different function and activity from management.[3] Do some formal leaders exercise leadership while others exercise management? Arguably, the best analysis of this question has been provided by Harvard's John Kotter.[4] He says that management is about coping with complexity. Good management brings about order and consistency by drawing up formal plans, designing rigid organization structures, and monitoring results against the plans. Leadership, in contrast, is about coping with change. Leaders establish direction by developing a vision of the future; then they align people by communicating this vision and inspiring them to overcome hurdles. Kotter sees both strong leadership and strong management as necessary for optimum organizational effectiveness. But he believes that most organizations are underled and overmanaged. He claims we need to focus more on developing leadership in organizations because the people in charge today are too concerned with keeping things on time and on budget and with doing what was done yesterday, only doing it 5 percent better.

In contrasting management and leadership, it may also help to think of the latter as involving the ability to inspire people. Management focuses on inanimate objects, whereas leadership focuses on raising human potential. Or, as the late Admiral Grace Murray Hopper put it, "You cannot manage men into battle. You manage things; you lead people."[5]

So we have learned that formal leaders—those in positions of authority—may exhibit behaviors that we would call leadership, but not in every case. On the other hand, we often use the word *leader* to describe people in organizations who are exhibiting leadership, even though they don't hold formal leader positions. These people are typically referred to as informal, or **emergent, leaders.** Our discussion in this and the next chapter will encompass both formal and emergent leaders.

IDENTIFYING THE BASIC ISSUES IN LEADERSHIP

Leadership can best be understood by looking at its key variables: *leadership effectiveness, leader characteristics and style, follower characteristics, leader behavior,* and *leadership context* (see Exhibit 14-1). As you will see, all the basic issues that have shaped the direction of leadership study throughout the twentieth century can be subsumed within these five variables.

Our discussion begins with leadership effectiveness. This, after all, is the final test of whether a leader is successfully doing his or her job. Much of the difficulty in making generalizations about leadership is directly due to different definitions given to the term *leadership effectiveness.*

Then we move to the individual leader—specifically, his or her characteristics and style. This variable is central to almost all leadership frameworks because it is

EXHIBIT 14-1
Key Leadership Variables

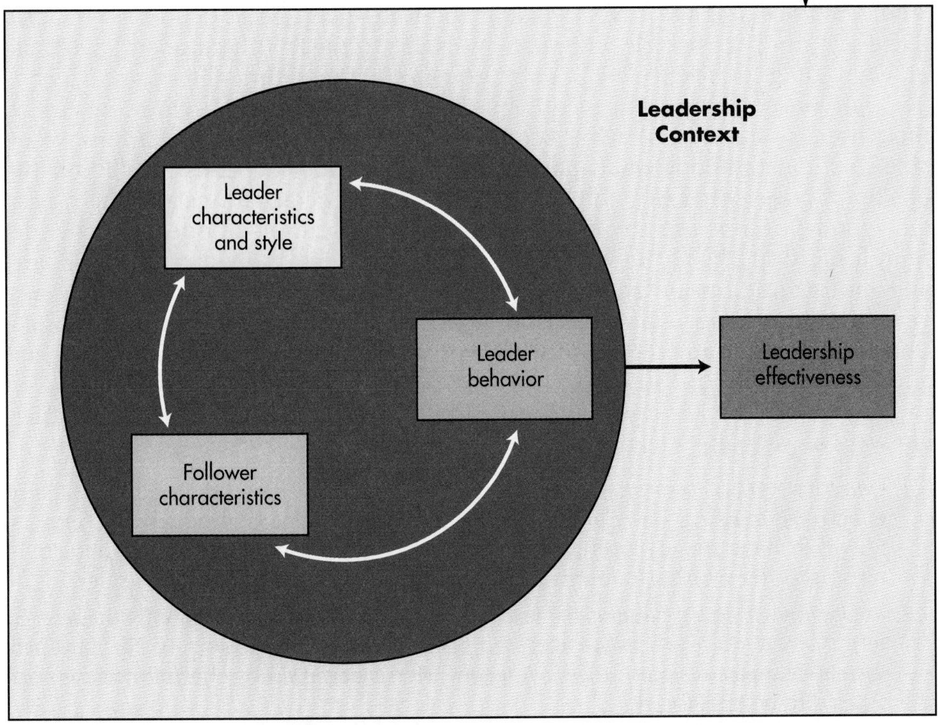

the individual leader who is at the heart of any leadership effort. Two issues directly address *leader characteristics*. First, do effective leaders have common traits that differentiate them from others? Second, does experience make leaders more effective? Two issues focus on *leader style:* Do effective leaders use a common leadership style? And are leadership styles fixed, or can leaders change them to fit the situation? We also deal with the role of perceptions. Specifically, we answer the question, If someone can't *be* a leader, can he or she at least *look* like one?

Leaders can't be leaders without *followers*. Surprisingly, this self-evident truth was ignored until somewhat recently. So we need to take a look at the role of followership. Do followers matter? What characteristics of followers seem to be important? Can great leadership overcome mediocre followers? Do leaders treat all followers alike?

The next variable brings leader characteristics and style and follower characteristics together to discuss choices leaders face about the *behaviors* they should exhibit. Our focus is trying to find if there is something unique in the way effective leaders behave. How do follower characteristics influence the effectiveness of a leader's style? How much should leaders involve followers in their decisions? Answers to these questions look more closely at interaction—and fit—*between* the leader and the follower.

Finally, the *leadership context* influences not only what leadership characteristics and style, follower characteristics, and leader behavior emerge, but it also affects whether a particular leader will be effective. An overwhelming amount of evidence demonstrates that leader actions that work well under *some* circumstances don't necessarily work well under *all* circumstances. And in some situations, leadership doesn't seem to have much effect at all on a group's goal efforts. Specifically, we'll address two issues: What situational variables might make a leader effective sometimes and ineffective other times? And under what conditions are leaders relatively unimportant?

LEADERSHIP EFFECTIVENESS

In Chapter 2, we described the problems in defining organizational effectiveness. Studies of leadership too have been guilty of using inconsistent definitions of effectiveness. Part of the trouble, undoubtedly, is due to the fact that leaders have to do different things to be effective. It may also reflect different interests of researchers.

Our concern may seem inconsequential—relevant to researchers but not to practitioners—but it isn't! Why? Because the quality of any generalizations we are able to stipulate about what makes an effective leader depends heavily on the quality of leadership research used to draw those generalizations and the consistency of definitions used by those researchers. For example, if one researcher defines leadership effectiveness in terms of how satisfied individual followers are, and another in terms of group productivity, it becomes very difficult to make any generalizations about what makes an effective leader. Productivity and satisfaction are different outcomes. And what works with individuals may not be generalizable to groups.

A review of the leadership literature finds researchers using at least five different ways of assessing effectiveness.

1. *Objective versus perceptual measures.* Some studies have defined leadership effectiveness using hard and objective measures such as productivity. Others, however, have merely been concerned with perceptions of leadership effectiveness. In other words, do followers say that an individual *looks* like a leader?
2. *Acceptance versus rejection of the leader.* Some studies have defined effectiveness in terms of whether leaders are accepted or rejected by their followers. No hard performance measures are utilized. A leader who is accepted by the followers is considered to be effective.

3. *Individual versus group performance measures.* Although most studies emphasize performance outcomes, they are not uniform in whether they measure the leader's effect on individual performance or on group performance. The focus on different levels can create very different and noncomparable outcomes.
4. *Productivity versus satisfaction.* Some studies have emphasized follower or group satisfaction rather than productivity. The actions a leader takes to increase productivity may be very different from the actions that would increase satisfaction.
5. *Level of analysis.* Most studies focus on the leader's influence on his or her group. Others, however, focus on the organization or even on specific societies. When we say that a Jack Welch at GE, an Elizabeth Dole at the American Red Cross, or a Newt Gingrich in the U.S. House of Representatives is an effective leader, we are using organizational-level measures of effectiveness. And when the discussion centers on the effectiveness of presidents or prime ministers, the level of analysis jumps to how well they lead their countries.

It isn't our intention to suggest an easy synthesis of these differences. Rather, we have introduced the issue to make two points. First, leadership effectiveness is important. It is the ultimate critierion upon which we determine whether a leader succeeds or fails. Second, the people who study leadership have not defined effectiveness in a consistent manner. So care needs to be taken in making generalizations about what contributes to leadership effectiveness.

As you proceed through this and the following chapter, we'll repeatedly refer to leadership effectiveness. And when we do, we'll attempt to clarify how the researchers defined the term, along with their research evidence.

LEADER CHARACTERISTICS AND STYLE

Every 4 years, Americans vote to elect a president. Since 1960, these elections have been preceded by widely televised debates. Presidential candidates spend 90 minutes or so discussing issues, responding to questions, and trying to "look presidential." Looking good in this "beauty contest" is viewed by the candidates and their staffs as critical to a campaign's success. The losses by Richard Nixon (1960), Gerald Ford (1976), and Michael Dukakis (1988) are often attributed to their inability to project the leadership traits that the television audience was looking for in their next president.[6] Voters seem to look for certain leader characteristics in their presidents—such as confidence, determinedness, decisiveness, and trustworthiness—and they use the debates as an important indicator of whether candidates have those characteristics.

Debates may be a poor means for assessing leadership traits, but the question still remains: Do effective presidents have common traits? The American voting public seems to think so. Since presidents are chosen for their leadership qualities, let's broaden the question to look at all leaders. Specifically, what traits, if any, differentiate leaders from nonleaders or effective from ineffective leaders?

Do effective presidents have common traits? The American voting public seems to think so.

Do Leaders Have Common Traits?

The media have long believed that leaders share common traits. They identify people such as Margaret Thatcher, Ronald Reagan, Nelson Mandela, Ted Turner, and Colin Powell as leaders and then describe them in terms such as *charismatic, enthusiastic,* and *courageous.* Well, the media aren't alone. The search for personality, social, physical, and intellectual attributes that would describe leaders and differentiate them from nonleaders has been going on among management and leadership researchers for more than half a century.[7]

A full review of the evidence leads us to the familiar good news–bad news scenario. First the good news. Six traits seem to regularly appear that differentiate leaders from others. They are ambition and energy, the desire to lead, honesty and integrity, self-confidence, intelligence, and job-relevant knowledge.[8] In addition, a seventh trait has recently emerged. There is strong evidence that people who are high self-monitors (see Chapter 12)—that is, are highly flexible in adjusting their behavior in different situations—are much more likely to emerge as leaders in groups than are low self-monitors.[9] Overall, it appears that these traits are relatively powerful at explaining people's perceptions of leadership.[10]

IN THE NEWS

One Leader Who Made a Difference: Roger Penske at Detroit Diesel

IN 1987, DETROIT DIESEL CORP. WAS OWNED BY GENERAL MOTORS. THE COMPANY HAD A PALTRY 3 PERCENT of the market for heavy-truck engines. Between 1982 and 1987, the company had lost $600 million. Then, in 1988, former auto racer turned transportation tycoon Roger Penske bought control of the firm. Keeping the same senior management team and hourly work force that had floundered under GM, Penske has demonstrated that a dynamic leader can make a real difference.

Penske's greatest knack as a leader has been his ability to obtain his employees' loyalty. His respect for workers' personal needs and desires is what seems to make the difference. He treats them like valued players on a winning team.

After taking over Detroit Diesel, Penske quickly determined that the company's problem was not a lack of good products but a lack of motivation. The sales force had been rendered slow and lazy by GM's bureaucracy, and the blue-collar workforce was demoralized.

Penske began meeting regularly with union leaders to regain their trust. He gave the union veto power over outside contractors and suppliers. "I don't agree with them all the time, but we're not in a confrontation mode, we're in a solution mode," says Penske. Agrees Jim Brown, chairman of the United Auto Workers' local: "Roger has developed a lot of credibility with us."

Penske also initiated a marathon series of small-group meetings with the entire work force. His goal? To get employees to understand what the business was about. He laid out information on earnings, productivity, and capital investments. Penske introduced profit sharing and economic incentives for attendance. He convinced workers that, although the company had a superior product, the highest quality standards had to be achieved if the company was to beat the competition. Further, Penske made Detroit Diesel a leaner, more responsive firm by cutting nearly a quarter of the company's white-collar work force and eliminating some departments. He also pushed authority down to lower levels in the organization; this flatter structure allowed for much faster decision making. And he used his reputation as an Indy racing hero to win back customers. Fleet owners, disgruntled with GM, listened in awe as Penske described the changes taking place at Detroit Diesel under his leadership.

Under Penske's guidance, Detroit Diesel's sales have doubled to $1.7 billion a year. It now commands 25 percent of the heavy-truck engine market. And the company is back making money. Recent profits have been running at better than $35 million a year.

Source: D. Woodruff, "Talk about Life in the Fast Lane," *Business Week*, October 17, 1994, pp. 155–66.

Roger Penske does everything from running the pits at Indy to building relations with the UAW.

Now for the bad news. First, traits provide no guarantees. Some traits seem to be associated with success as a leader, but none of the traits *guarantee* success.[11] Second, the evidence is unclear in separating cause from effect. For example, are leaders self-confident, or does success as a leader build self-confidence? Finally, traits do a better job at predicting the *appearance* of leadership than in actually distinguishing between *effective* and *ineffective* leaders.[12] The facts that an individual exhibits the traits and others consider that person to be a leader does not necessarily mean that the "leader" is successful at getting his or her group to achieve its goals. Remember, as we noted earlier, having a leader doesn't automatically mean having effective leadership.

Does Experience Make Leaders More Effective?

Those same American voters who are looking for leadership traits also assume that there is a relationship between experience and effectiveness. Presidential candidates typically have been U.S. senators or state governors. Why? Voters tend to believe that these jobs prepare individuals to be effective presidents.

This belief in the power of experience is very strong and widespread. Organizations, for instance, carefully screen outside candidates for senior management positions on the basis of their experience. Similarly, organizations usually require several years of service at one managerial level before a person can be considered for promotion. And have you ever filled out an employment application that *didn't* ask about previous experience or job history? In many instances, experience is the single most important factor in hiring and promotion decisions.[13] Obviously, organizations attribute considerable importance to experience. But does experience translate into leader effectiveness? The answer may surprise you.

Experience per se doesn't seem to necessarily contribute to leadership effectiveness. "Some inexperienced leaders have been outstandingly successful, while many experienced leaders have been outstanding failures. Among the most highly regarded former presidents are Abraham Lincoln and Harry Truman, who had very little previous leadership experience, while the highly experienced Herbert Hoover and Franklin Pierce were among the least successful."[14] Studies of military officers, research and development teams, shop supervisors, post office administrators, and school principals indicate that experienced managers tend to be no more effective than the managers with little experience.[15] How could this be? Doesn't experience create learning opportunities that would translate into improved on-the-job leadership skills? This logic is intuitively appealing, but the problem appears to be in the variability of situations.

The situation in which experience is obtained is rarely comparable to new situations. But this fact is rarely taken into account. It's true that past behavior is the best predictor of future behavior; perhaps that is why experience is so popular as a selection criterion. But it is critical to take into consideration the *relevance* of past experience to a new situation. Jobs differ, support resources differ, organizational cultures differ, follower characteristics differ, and so on. The primary reason that leadership experience isn't strongly related to leadership performance is variability of situations. However, where previous experience has been in substantially similar situations, successful past leadership experience should be a reasonably good predictor of future leadership performance.

Do Effective Leaders Use a Common Leadership Style?

Robert Crandall, chairman of American Airlines, and Paul B. Kazarian, the former chairman of Sunbeam-Oster, both have been very successful in leading their companies through difficult times.[16] And they both rely on a common leadership style—tough-talking, intense, autocratic. Does this suggest that autocratic behavior is a preferred style for *all* leaders? Maybe not! Bob Eaton, CEO at Chrysler, uses a very different style.[17] This soft-spoken leader purposely avoids making major product decisions. He delegates those decisions to teams. The result has been a string of hot cars and record earnings.

How many behavioral options do leaders have? And what is the relationship between these various options and leadership effectiveness?

Style Options Numerous efforts have been made to identify the primary dimensions of leader behavior. Studies typically emphasize just a few, and rarely does the list extend beyond four. A careful review finds that there seems to be considerable convergence around two dimensions: task behavior and people behavior. And, as we will show, there is encouraging new evidence indicating the importance of a third dimension—development-oriented behavior.

The case for a **two-dimensional view of leadership behavior**—one focusing on tasks and the other on people—can be traced back to the late 1940s. Independent work at Ohio State University and the University of Michigan found that two categories substantially accounted for most of the leadership behavior described by subordinates.[18] The *task* dimension refers to actions such as emphasizing the accomplishment of group goals, defining and structuring group-member work assignments, and emphasizing the meeting of deadlines. The *people* dimension encompasses actions such as developing good interpersonal relationships, being friendly and approachable, and being concerned with workers' personal problems.

Looking at leadership style along two dimensions was popularized for leadership training in the 1960s by way of a graph called the **managerial grid.**[19] As shown in Exhibit 14-2, the managerial grid depicts "concern for people" and

EXHIBIT 14-2
The Managerial Grid

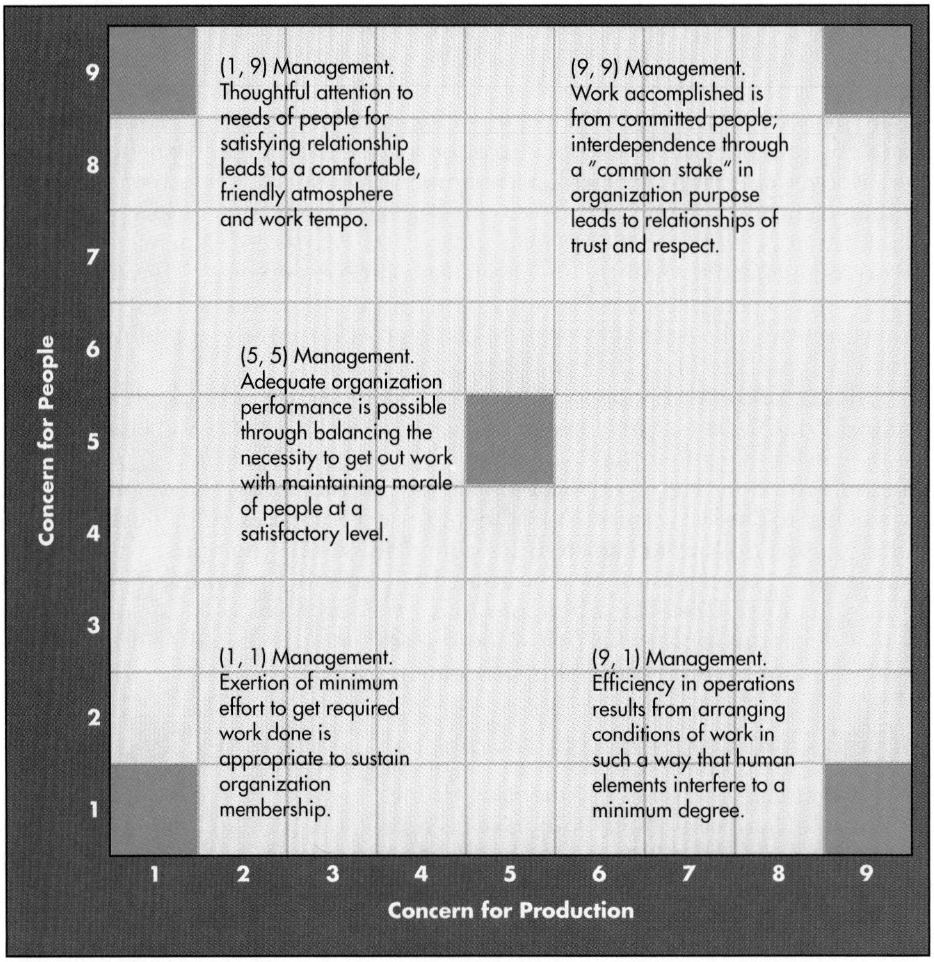
(1, 9) Management.
Thoughtful attention to needs of people for satisfying relationship leads to a comfortable, friendly atmosphere and work tempo.
(9, 9) Management.
Work accomplished is from committed people; interdependence through a "common stake" in organization purpose leads to relationships of trust and respect.
(5, 5) Management.
Adequate organization performance is possible through balancing the necessity to get out work with maintaining morale of people at a satisfactory level.
(1, 1) Management.
Exertion of minimum effort to get required work done is appropriate to sustain organization membership.
(9, 1) Management.
Efficiency in operations results from arranging conditions of work in such a way that human elements interfere to a minimum degree.
Concern for People
1 2 3 4 5 6 7 8 9
Concern for Production

Source: R. R. Blake, J. S. Mouton, L. B. Barnes, and L. E. Greiner, "Breakthrough in Organization Development," *Harvard Business Review,* November–December 1964, p. 136. Copyright © 1964 by the President and Fellows of Harvard College; all rights reserved. Adapted and reprinted by permission of *Harvard Business Review.*

"concern for production" (which is synonymous with a task focus) on separate axes. The grid has nine possible positions along each axis, creating eighty-one different positions in which a leader's style may fall. Proponents of the grid focus their attention at its extremes—1,1; 1,9; 9,1; and 9,9—and claim that the most ef-

BUILDING SELF-AWARENESS • BUILDING SELF-AWARENESS

WHAT IS YOUR TWO-DIMENSIONAL LEADERSHIP STYLE?

INSTRUCTIONS

The following questions analyze your two-dimensional leadership style. Read each item carefully. Think about how you usually behave when you are the leader. Then circle the letter that most closely describes your style. Circle only one choice for each question. Use the following key for your answers:

A = Always
O = Often
? = Sometimes
S = Seldom
N = Never

1.	I take time to explain how a job should be carried out.	A O ? S N
2.	I explain the part that members are to play in the team.	A O ? S N
3.	I make clear the rules and procedures for others to follow in detail.	A O ? S N
4.	I organize my own work activities.	A O ? S N
5.	I let people know how well they are doing.	A O ? S N
6.	I let people know what is expected of them.	A O ? S N
7.	I encourage the use of uniform procedures to get things accomplished.	A O ? S N
8.	I make my attitudes clear to others.	A O ? S N
9.	I assign others to particular tasks.	A O ? S N
10.	I make sure that others understand their part in the group.	A O ? S N
11.	I schedule the work that I want others to do.	A O ? S N
12.	I ask that others follow standard rules and regulations.	A O ? S N
13.	I make working on the job more pleasant.	A O ? S N
14.	I go out of my way to be helpful to others.	A O ? S N
15.	I respect others' feelings and opinions.	A O ? S N
16.	I am thoughtful and considerate of others.	A O ? S N
17.	I maintain a friendly atmosphere in the team.	A O ? S N
18.	I do little things to make it pleasant for others to be a member of my team.	A O ? S N
19.	I treat others as equals.	A O ? S N
20.	I give others advance notice of change and explain how it will affect them.	A O ? S N
21.	I look out for others' personal welfare.	A O ? S N
22.	I am approachable and friendly toward others.	A O ? S N

Turn to page 562 for scoring directions and key.

***Source:* C. A. Schriesheim, *Leadership Questionnaire.* Reprinted by permission.**

U.S. President Bill Clinton is often criticized for his lack of leadership. Part of this criticism can undoubtedly be attributed to the perception that President Clinton is inconsistent on policy issues.

What are the practical implications of these findings for individuals who want to be leaders? Do what you can to help foster the perception that you are smart, personable, verbally adept, aggressive, understanding, and hard-working. Focus your behavior on emphasizing both tasks and people. And maintain the appearance of consistency.

FOLLOWER CHARACTERISTICS

When someone was once asked what it took to be a great leader, he responded, "Great followers!" While this response may have seemed sarcastic, it has some truth.

Do Followers Matter?

Followers are important in the leadership equation because: (1) They differ in the qualities they bring to the job and therefore require adjustments by leaders; and (2) there is evidence that "good" followers exhibit common characteristics that make it easier for leaders to succeed. In addition, focusing on followers makes increasing sense today, as organizations flatten hierarchies and introduce self-managed teams. Followers have become more important as they have gained increased autonomy and accountability.[33]

What Characteristics of Followers Seem to Be Important?

Studies have found that certain follower characteristics influence the actions of leaders. These include the follower's locus-of-control personality dimension, experience, and perceived ability.[34] For instance:

- Followers with an internal locus of control (those who believe that they control their own destiny) will be most satisfied with a particpative leadership style. Those with an external locus of control will be most satisfied with a directive style.
- A task-oriented style of leadership is likely to be perceived negatively by followers with considerable experience. They already know what needs to be done and how to do it, so they see the task-oriented behavior as redundant or even insulting. Conversely, followers with minimal experience tend to appreciate the structure and guidance provided by task-oriented leadership.
- Followers who perceive that they have strong abilities are likely to view task-oriented leadership negatively. They consider such behavior as demeaning to their abilities.
- Followers who lack both ability and motivation need clear and specific directions. Followers who have ability but lack motivation will perform best with a supportive, nondirective, participative style of leadership.

In addition, the quality of the leader-member relationship has been found to be important.[35] For instance, when followers have a high degree of confidence, trust, and respect for their leader, they are more willing to accept a task-oriented approach. When leader-member relations are poor, a task-oriented approach is very likely to lead to reduced group performance.

Since leadership is the process of helping people achieve a common goal, to the degree that followers have certain qualities, leaders are more likely to be effective. We find that effective followers have these common qualities:[36]

1. *They manage themselves well.* Effective followers are able to think for themselves. They can work independently and without close supervision.
2. *They are committed to a purpose outside themselves.* Effective followers are committed to something—a cause, a product, a work team, an organization, an idea—in addition to the care of their own lives. Most people like working with colleagues who are emotionally, as well as physically, committed to their work.
3. *They build their competence and focus their efforts for maximum impact.* Effective followers master skills that will be useful to their organizations, and they hold higher performance standards than their job or work group requires.
4. *They are courageous, honest, and credible.* Effective followers establish themselves as independent, critical thinkers whose knowledge and judgment can be trusted. They hold high ethical standards, give credit where credit is due, and aren't afraid to admit their mistakes.

Can Great Leadership Overcome Mediocre Followers?

Even if we acknowledge that effective followers can make effective leaders, we still run into cause-and-effect issues. It may be that effective followers *result from* effective leaders. In fact, leaders who are development-oriented might be likely to turn mediocre followers into effective followers over time!

The attitudes and behaviors of followers are not fixed. Followers can and do respond to the actions of their leaders. So individuals with superior leadership skills—what we call transformational or outstanding leadership in the next chapter—can successfully inspire mediocre followers and transform them into effective followers.

Do Leaders Treat All Followers Alike?

Think about your experiences in groups. Did you notice that leaders often act very differently toward different subordinates? Did the leader tend to have favorites who made up his or her "in" group? If you answered yes to these ques-

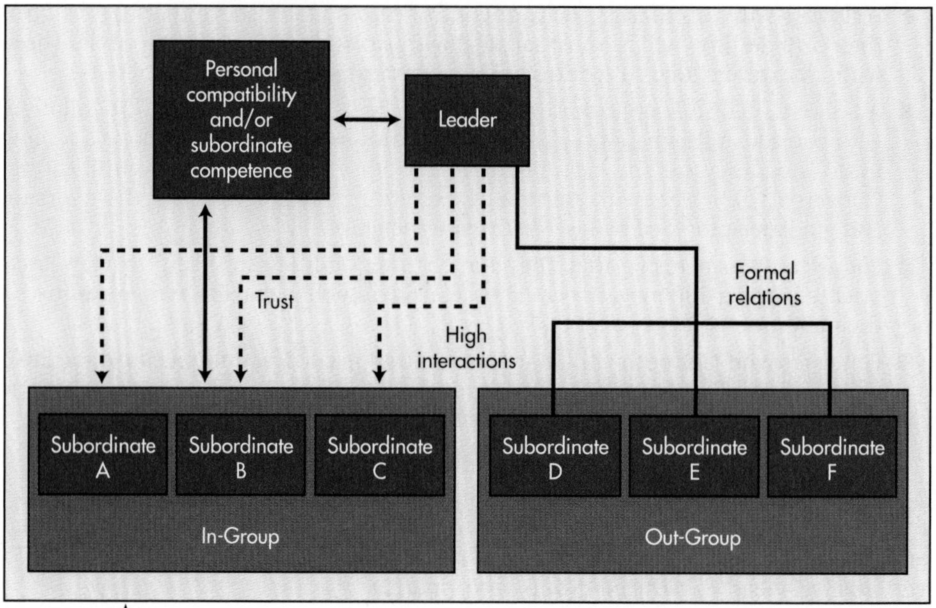

EXHIBIT 14-3
Leader-Member Exchange Model

tions, you are confirming what an increasing amount of evidence supports—leaders *don't* treat everyone alike![37]

Leaders almost always differentiate among subordinates. The result is a dichotomization of in-group and out-group members.[38] Leaders establish a special relationship with a small set of their subordinates who make up the in-group—they are trusted, get a disproportionate amount of the leader's attention, and are likely to receive special privileges. Other subordinates fall into the out-group. They get less of the leader's time, fewer of the preferred rewards that the leader controls, and have superior-subordinate relations based on formal authority interactions. This is called the **leader-member exchange model.**

Apparently, early in the history of the interaction between a leader and a given subordinate, the leader implicitly categorizes the subordinate as an "in" or an "out," and that relationship holds relatively steady over time.[39] Just precisely how the leader chooses who falls into each category is unclear, but there is evidence that leaders tend to choose in-group members because they have personal characteristics (for example, age, gender, attitudes) that are similar to the leader's, a higher level of competence than out-group members, or an extroverted personality.[40] (See Exhibit 14-3.) A key point to note here is that even though it is the leader who is doing the choosing, it is the follower's characteristics that are driving the leader's categorizing decision.

Overall, there is substantial evidence that leaders do differentiate among subordinates; that these disparities are far from random; and that subordinates with in-group status will have higher performance ratings, less turnover, and greater satisfaction with their superior than will the out-group.[41] These positive findings for in-group members shouldn't be totally surprising given our knowledge of the self-fulfilling prophecy (see Chapter 12). Leaders invest their resources with those they expect to perform best. And "knowing" that in-group members are most competent, leaders treat them as such and unwittingly fulfill their prophecy.[42]

LEADER BEHAVIOR

In addition to traits and experience, the behavior of a leader is a critical factor in determining overall leadership effectiveness. Let's begin our look at leader behavior by considering the various styles that leaders can exhibit.

How Do Follower Characteristics Influence the Effectiveness of a Leader's Style?

We have already shown how follower characteristics influence the effectiveness of a leader's style. We identified three styles that leaders tended to exhibit: task-oriented, people-oriented, development-oriented, or some combination of the three. We also said that these styles might not be fixed, but rather that leaders could make decisions about which style to use. As also previously noted, studies have found that certain follower characteristics appear to influence the leader's choice of style. These include the follower's personality, experience, ability, and motivation.[43]

How Much Involvement Should Followers Be Given?

Leaders need to determine how much involvement they should allow followers to have in the group's decision-making process. For instance, at one extreme, the leader can make the decision by herself, without any consultation with others in the group. Or, at the other extreme, she could turn the decision over completely to the group and empower them to make the choice.

The most comprehensive and meaningful framework for dealing with this issue is the **leader-participation model.**[44] It provides a set of rules for leaders to follow in determining the amount and form of participative decision making that should be encouraged in different situations.

The model identifies five leadership behaviors. As we describe each, note that they progressively trade off leader control for increased group involvement (see Exhibit 14-4).

1. The leader makes the decision alone.
2. The leader asks for information from group members but makes the decision alone. Group members may or may not be informed as to what the situation is.

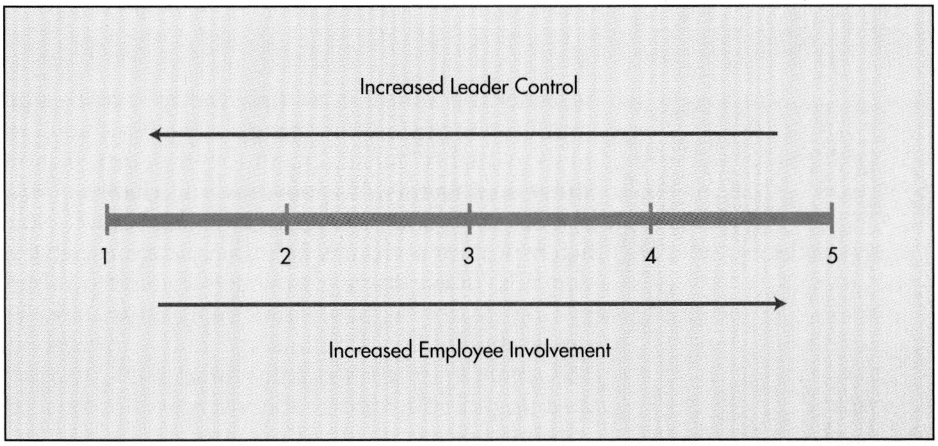

EXHIBIT 14-4
Employee-Involvement Continuum

3. The leader shares the situation with each group member individually and asks for information and evaluation. Members do not meet as a group, and the leader alone makes the decision.
4. The leader and group members meet to discuss the situation, but the leader makes the decision.
5. The leader and group members meet to discuss the situation, and the group makes the decision.

Which of the five styles should a leader use? The evidence indicates that eight situational variables should guide the leader: the quality of the decision; the importance of subordinate commitment to the decision; whether the leader has sufficient information; how well-structured the problem is; whether subordinates would still be committed to the decision if the leader made the decision alone; the degree to which subordinates share the organizational goals to be attained in solving the problem; whether there is conflict among subordinates over preferred solutions; and whether subordinates have sufficient information to make a high-quality decision.

A substantial amount of evidence supports the following general propositions.[45] Leaders should increase group participation when:

- They lack sufficient information to solve a problem by themselves.
- The problem is unclear, and help is needed to clarify the situation.
- Acceptance of the decision by others is necessary for its successful implementation.
- Adequate time is available to allow for true participation.

On the other hand, leaders should give up less control and rely on more unilateral behaviors when:

- They personally have the expertise needed to solve the problem.
- They are confident and capable of acting alone.
- Others are likely to accept the decision they make.
- Little or no time is available for discussion.

In summary, since leaders actually lead followers, leadership effectiveness is influenced by how well the two parties interact. Leaders have to make decisions about the style they will exhibit to the followers, along with the amount of interaction in decision making they will promote. Understanding how the follower's characteristics influence those leader-behavior choices brings leaders a step closer to being effective.

LEADERSHIP CONTEXT

The effect of a leader's traits and behavior, as well as follower characteristics, on a group's performance almost always depends on the context in which leadership is happening.

It seems as if almost every time we try to make a definitive conclusion on some leadership issue, we have to qualify our statement to reflect one or more situational factors. It is obvious that the effect of a leader's traits and behavior, as well as follower characteristics, on a group's performance almost always depends on the context in which leadership is happening. Many of these situational factors have already shown up at numerous points throughout this chapter, since it's almost impossible to draw meaningful conclusions about leadership concepts without taking the situation into account. In this section, we identify the more potent elements of this context and also consider those conditions under which formal leaders take on minimal importance.

What Situational Factors Influence Leader Effectiveness?

Two primary streams of research have sought to identify the key situational factors in leadership effectiveness. In actuality, each offers more than just inclusion of situational factors. Because they also include follower characteristics and contextual factors, they represent integrative approaches to understanding leadership effectiveness. Let's look at each of these research programs, then briefly review several additional studies that suggest other pertinent situational factors.

The Fiedler Model The first comprehensive attempt to develop a situational approach to leadership was presented by Fred Fiedler in the mid-1960s.[46] The **Fiedler leadership model** proposed that effective group performance depends on the proper match between the leader's style and the degree to which the situation gives control and influence to the leader. From our perspective, we are specifically interested in the situational variables he identified that provided control to the leader.

Fiedler identified three variables that, he argued, determine leadership effectiveness. The first variable, leader-member relations, we have discussed already. Fiedler combined this variable with task structure and position power. They are all defined as follows:

1. *Leader-member relations*. The degree of confidence, trust, and respect subordinates have in their leader. (Rated as either *good* or *poor*.)
2. *Task structure*. The degree to which the subordinate's job assignments are structured. (Rated as either *high* or *low*.)
3. *Position power*. The degree of influence a leader has over variables such as hiring, firing, discipline, promotions, and salary increases. (Rated as either *strong* or *weak*.)

Fiedler stated that the better the leader-member relations, the more highly structured the job, and the stronger the position power, the more control or influence the leader will have. For example, a very favorable situation (in which the leader would have a great deal of control) might involve a payroll manager who is well respected and whose subordinates have confidence in her (good leader-member relations); where the activities to be done—such as wage computation, check writing, report filing—are specific and clear (high task structure); and the job provides considerable freedom for her to reward and punish her subordinates (strong position power). On the other hand, an unfavorable situation might be the disliked chairman of a voluntary United Way fund-raising team. In this job, the leader has very little control. Altogether, by mixing the three contingency variables, there are potentially eight different situations or categories in which leaders can find themselves.

Fiedler studied over 1,200 groups. He compared people- versus task-oriented leadership styles in each of the eight situational categories, and he concluded that task-oriented leaders tend to perform better than people-oriented leaders in situations that are *very favorable* to them and in situations that are *very unfavorable* (see Exhibit 14-5). So Fiedler would predict that when faced with a category I, II, III, VII, or VIII situation, task-oriented leaders perform better. People-oriented leaders, however, perform better in moderately favorable situations—categories IV through VI.

Many studies have tested Fiedler's model, and the overall evidence is generally supportive.[47] Although Fiedler may not have definitively identified all the situational variables that affect leadership, the ones he did identify do seem to contribute substantially to our understanding of situational factors.

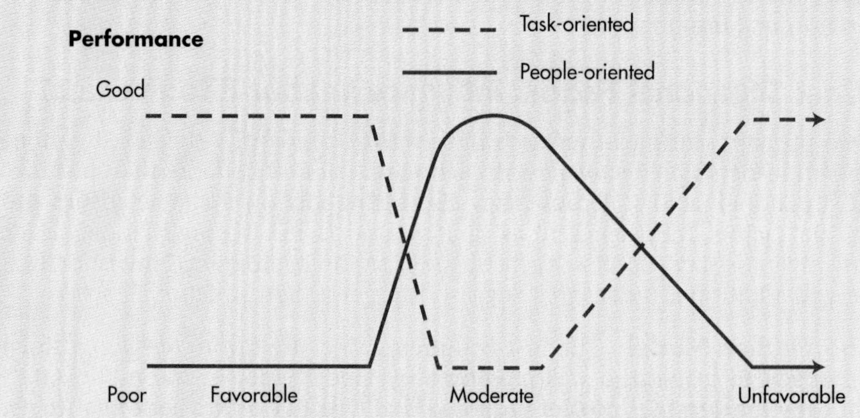

Category	I	II	III	IV	V	VI	VII	VIII
Leader-member relations	Good	Good	Good	Good	Poor	Poor	Poor	Poor
Task structure	High	High	Low	Low	High	High	Low	Low
Position power	Strong	Weak	Strong	Weak	Strong	Weak	Strong	Weak

EXHIBIT 14-5
The Fiedler Model

The Path-Goal Model The other major situational approach to leadership is the path-goal model.[48] The essence of the **path-goal model of leadership** is that it is the leader's job to assist his or her followers in attaining their goals and to provide the necessary direction and support to ensure that their goals are compatible with the overall objectives of the group or organization. The term *path-goal* is derived from the belief that effective leaders clarify the path to help their followers get from where they are to the achievement of their work goals and make the journey along the path easier by reducing roadblocks.

The path-goal model proposes two classes of so-called situational variables—those in the environment that are outside the control of the subordinates (task structure, the formal authority system, and the work group) and those that are part of the personal characteristics of the subordinate (locus of control, experience, and perceived ability). (Note that these "situational variables" are respectively synonymous with what we have called "leadership context" and "follower characteristics.") Environmental factors determine the type of leader behavior required as a complement if the subordinate outcomes are to be maximized; personal characteristics of the subordinate determine how the environment and leader behavior are interpreted (see Exhibit 14-6). So the model proposes that leader behavior will be ineffective when it's redundant with sources of environmental structure or incongruent with subordinate characteristics. For example, the following are illustrations of predictions based on the path-goal model (note that because the path-goal model takes into consideration characteristics of the subordinate, some of these predictions repeat findings previously discussed in Follower Characteristics):

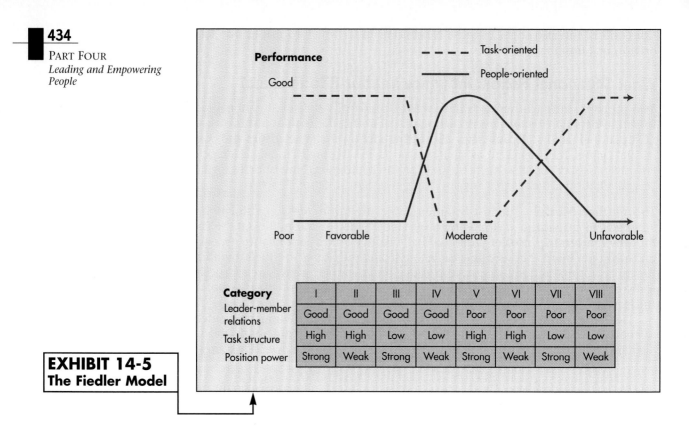

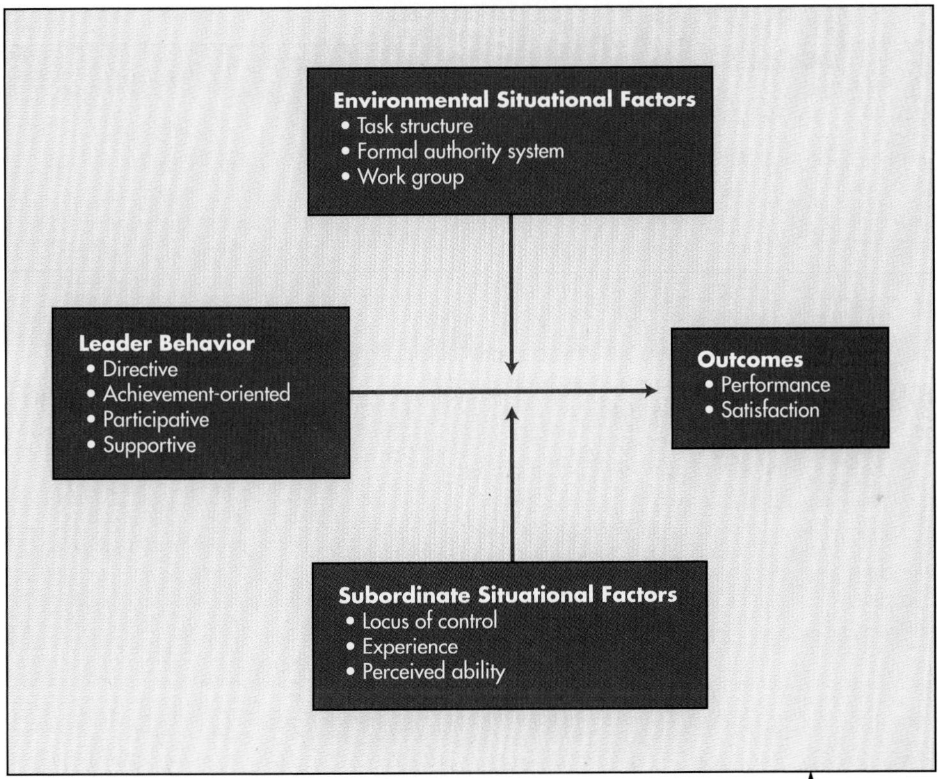

EXHIBIT 14-6
Path-Goal Model

- Task-oriented leadership leads to greater employee satisfaction when tasks are ambiguous than when they are highly structured and well laid out.
- People-oriented leadership results in high employee performance and satisfaction when subordinates are performing structured tasks.
- Task-oriented leadership is likely to be perceived as redundant among subordinates with high perceived ability or with considerable experience.
- The clearer and more structured the formal authority relationships, the more leaders should exhibit people-oriented behavior and deemphasize task-oriented behavior.
- Task-oriented leadership will lead to higher employee satisfaction when there is substantial conflict within a work group.
- Subordinates with an external locus of control will be more satisfied with a directive style.

The evidence generally supports the logic underlying the path-goal model.[49] That is, employee performance and satisfaction are likely to be positively influenced when the leader compensates for things lacking in either the employee or the work setting. However, the leader who spends time explaining tasks when those tasks are already clear or when the employee has the ability and experience to handle them without interference is likely to be ineffective because the employee will see such task-oriented behavior as redundant or even insulting.

Does the path-goal model contradict Fiedler? No. In fact, there is considerable overlap. For instance, both directly recognize the importance of the employee's

IN THE NEWS

Esprit Asia Chairman Michael Ying

MICHAEL YING LEE YUEN IS AN ASIAN LEADER WHO IS TAKING ON THE WORLD. AT THE AGE OF 44, HE IS chairman of Esprit Asia Holdings. The company employs 2,000 people and has 110 stores in Hong Kong, Japan, South Korea, and Taiwan. Ying is also a major shareholder of Esprit in San Francisco and Esprit in Europe. As the following excerpts from a recent interview reveal, he is currently attempting to merge his Asian and European operations.

Interviewer: What took you to Germany?

Ying: Germany is our headquarters for Europe, which is now our biggest business in the world. I went there to try to integrate the European and Asian operations, which have been handled quite independently.

Interviewer: Are there major differences in the two operations in terms of managing people and the business?

Ying: The Europeans are quite territorial and nationalistic. Look at France for instance. They don't want to deal with any foreigners. You go to Germany or Holland and each country is quite rigid in its ways. But Asians, because they are like students trying to catch up with the Western world, are a lot more open-minded, humble, and willing to learn.

I now realize that in Europe I must get into the thick of things. I must learn more about their structure and reporting lines. My feeling is that it's too complex—too many different jobs and authority levels. There is a lot of confusion. I told them my approach is very simple: Street smarts, common sense.

Interviewer: Were the Europeans receptive to your ideas?

Ying: Surprisingly, yes. When I started speaking my mind on the common sense approach to problem solving, it was quite refreshing to them. It was interesting to see how they are feeling the weight and burden of the structure they have created. They feel paralyzed by it. They spend more time in meetings, debating and talking, rather than managing the business itself.

Interviewer: What do you wish to achieve by greater integration?

Ying: The United States, Europe, and Asia should be operating as a company rather than duplicating overheads. Activities should be shifted to the most appropriate regions. The professionals are still coming from the West. Asia can provide buying, sourcing, manufacturing, and retail software functions. And Europe is our source for fashion. Everybody goes to Milan and Paris for fashion. People don't come to Bangkok or Taipei to look for fashion ideas.

Source: Based on "Street Smarts and Common Sense," *Asian Business*, December 1994, pp. 49-50.

task in determining the best leadership behavior, and both recognize the moderating influence of the leader's formal position power.

Cultural Variables We conclude our discussion of situational variables by mentioning two additional factors that seem to play an important role in determining leadership effectiveness—national and organizational culture.

National culture affects leadership style in two ways. It shapes the preferences of leaders. It also defines what is acceptable to subordinates.[50] Leaders cannot choose their styles at will. They are constrained by the cultural conditions in which they have been socialized and that their subordinates have come to expect. For example, a manipulative or autocratic style is compatible with high power distance, and we find high power distance scores in Arab, Far Eastern, and Latin countries. Power distance rankings should also be good indicators of employee willingness to accept participative leadership. Participation is likely to be most effective in such low power distance cultures as exist in Norway, Finland, Denmark, and Sweden. Not incidentally, the participation–low power distance relationship may explain (1) why a number of leadership approaches implicitly favor the use of a participative or people-oriented style; (2) the emergence of development-oriented leader behavior found in Scandinavian organizations; and (3) the recent enthusiasm in North America for empowerment. Remember that most leadership theories were developed by North Americans, using North American subjects, and the United States, Canada, and Scandinavian countries all rate below average on power distance.

An organization's culture shapes a leader's behavior by influencing the selection of leaders and the values that effective leaders are expected to exhibit.[51] When organizations seek to fill leadership positions, they look for individuals whose traits and behaviors are compatible with the organization's culture. In fact, a good part of the selection process, particularly interviews, attempts to identify and reject mismatches. Similarly, the culture conveys to leaders what behaviors are acceptable and unacceptable. The result is that leadership styles in organizations tend to be more alike than different; and "effective leadership" is often assessed in terms of how well a leader's traits and behaviors align with the values that the organization holds. For instance, an autocratic leader may be successful in getting high performance out of his work group. But if the organization's culture values and encourages people-oriented leadership, this autocratic leader is likely to be assessed as ineffective merely because of his incompatible style. So a good culture-leader fit would seem to be important in determining leader effectiveness; and leaders whose style clashes with the organization's culture don't tend to last too long.

When Are Formal Leaders Relatively Unimportant?

Formal leaders may not always be important. Data from numerous studies collectively demonstrate that, in many situations, whatever behaviors leaders exhibit are irrelevant. Certain individual, job, and organizational variables can act as *substitutes* for formal leaders or can *neutralize* the leader's ability to influence his or her subordinates.[52]

Formal leaders may not always be important.

Neutralizers make it impossible for leader behavior to make any difference to subordinate outcomes. They negate the leader's influence. Substitutes, on the other hand, make a leader's influence not only impossible but also unnecessary. They act as a replacement for the leader's influence. For instance, characteristics of subordinates such as their experience, training, "professional" orientation, or indifference toward organizational rewards can substitute for, or neutralize the effect of, leaders. Experience and training, for example, can replace the need for a leader's support or ability to create structure and reduce task ambiguity. Jobs that are inherently unambiguous and routine or that are intrinsically satisfying may require little direct attention from formal leaders. Organizational characteristics such as explicit formalized goals, rigid rules and procedures, and cohesive work groups can replace formal leaders (see Exhibit 14-7). However, if we go back to our original definition of *leadership* as "a process that influences a group of people toward a common goal," we could argue that although *formal leaders* can be re-

EXHIBIT 14-7
Substitutes and Neutralizers for Formal Leaders

Defining Characteristic	Effect on People-Oriented Leadership	Effect on Task-Oriented Leadership
Individual		
Experience/training	No effect on	Substitutes for
Professionalism	Substitutes for	Substitutes for
Indifference to rewards	Neutralizes	Neutralizes
Job		
Highly structured task	No effect on	Substitutes for
Provides its own feedback	No effect on	Substitutes for
Intrinsically satisfying	Substitutes for	No effect on
Organization		
Explicit formalized goals	No effect on	Substitutes for
Rigid rules and procedures	No effect on	Substitutes for
Cohesive work groups	Substitutes for	Substitutes for

Source: Based on S. Kerr and J. M. Jermier, "Substitutes for Leadership: Their Meaning and Measurement," *Organizational Behavior and Human Performance,* December 1978, p. 378.

placed, *leadership* can't be. Instead of formal leaders' exercising leadership, the process of leadership might be happening through informal leaders, through group norms, and so on, rather than being the formal responsibility of one person. In fact, we propose that often, when formal leaders are ineffective, these other forms of leadership emerge to help the organization continue to survive.

THE LEADERSHIP JOURNEY: WHERE WE HAVE BEEN

Our understanding of leadership has focused on five variables—(1) leader effectiveness, (2) leader characteristics and style, (3) follower characteristics, (4) leader behavior, and (5) leadership context. Let's try to summarize where our journey has taken us in terms of what we currently know about leadership.

1. Leadership effectiveness is problematic. In many cases, leadership effectiveness is defined in terms of perception. And that perception may not align with any objective measure of effectiveness.

2a. Certain traits do seem to be related to the perception of leadership. But possession of these traits is no guarantee of success. The power of traits to predict is undoubtedly enhanced by matching traits to specific organizational cultures. The leader characteristics that one organization values are not necessarily transferrable to another organization.

2b. Prior experience—both in terms of time in a leadership position and past successes or failures—does not mean much in predicting leadership effectiveness, because of incompatibility of situations. However, the more that a new situation mirrors a past situation, the greater the likelihood that prior experience will predict future performance.

2c. Regardless of actual effectiveness, people characterize individuals as "leaders" when they have traits such as intelligence, outgoing personality, strong verbal skills, aggressiveness, understanding, and industriousness and when they exhibit high-people and high-task behaviors.

2d. Some people—those who are low self-monitors—tend to meet every leadership challenge with the same response. People who are high self-monitors are more flexible. They're able to adjust their style to the situation, thus increasing the likelihood of achieving the proper leader-situation match.

3a. Leader effectiveness is enhanced by having followers who exhibit "good follower" behaviors.

3b. Leaders play favorites. They give preferential treatment to those followers in the "in" group. In response, those with favored status tend to have higher performance ratings, less turnover, and greater satisfaction with their leader.

4a. The actions of a leader are influenced by a follower's personality, experience, ability, and motivation.

4b. The proper amount of employee participation in decision making has been found to be heavily influenced by situational factors such as quality requirements, subordinate commitment, and conflict over options.

5a. There is no leadership style that is consistently effective. Contextual factors and follower characteristics must be taken into consideration in the selection of the "best" leadership style.

5b. Key situational variables determining leadership effectiveness include task structure, position power, leader-member relations, the work group, subordinate characteristics, organizational culture, and national culture.

5c. Formal leaders don't always make a difference. There are substitutes for leadership and neutralizers that can negate the formal leader's influence.

SUMMARY

(This summary is organized by the chapter-opening learning objectives on page 417.)

1. Leadership is about coping with change, whereas management is concerned with bringing about order and consistency. Organizations need both leadership and management. Leadership provides a vision and helps people to move toward that vision; management puts together the plans and structure to achieve specific goals.
2. The five key variables that have shaped our understanding of leadership are leadership effectiveness, the leader's characteristics and style, follower characteristics, leader behavior, and leadership context.
3. Leadership effectiveness essentially refers to success in moving a group to the achievement of a common goal. But success can be an objective outcome or a perception. Moreover, researchers haven't used consistent factors as outcomes. Examples of outcomes used by researchers include group performance, follower satisfaction, and acceptance of the leader. This lack of consistency makes conclusions about what makes an effective leader somewhat dubious since these conclusions are based on different effectiveness criteria. The result is that we need to specify the effectiveness criteria when we make leadership predictions.
4. The following traits have been found to regularly explain perceptions of leadership: ambition and energy, the desire to lead, honesty and integrity, self-confidence, intelligence, job-relevant knowledge, and a high self-monitoring personality.
5. The three primary leadership styles are *task-oriented* (emphasizes accomplishing group goals and defining and structuring group-member work assignments); *people-oriented* (develops good interpersonal relationships; is friendly and approachable); and *development-oriented* (experiments and encourages change).
6. The leader-participation model provides a set of rules for leaders to follow in determining the degree of participation subordinates should have in decision making. It identifies five leadership behaviors and projects the most effective behavior based on eight situational variables.
7. The leader-member exchange model recognizes that leaders differentiate among subordinates and place them into either an "in" or an "out" group. In-group members are trusted, get more of the leader's attention, and are more likely to receive special privileges. Consistent with the self-fulfilling prophecy, in-group members respond positively, so leaders appear to be more effective with in-group members.

8. Both Fiedler's model and the path-goal model recognize that the "right" leadership style depends on the situation, and both identify the situational variables of task structure and the leader's formal position. Fiedler's model emphasizes leader-member relations. The path-goal model adds the work group and directly recognizes that leaders need to adjust their style to reflect the characteristics of the followers.

REVIEW AND DISCUSSION QUESTIONS

1. What role do you think traits play in the selection process for filling most management jobs?
2. What is the managerial grid? What are its implications for leadership?
3. When might leaders be irrelevant?
4. Would you give different recommendations to a person who wanted to be an effective leader than you would to a person who wanted others to think he was a good leader?
5. What is the attribution theory of leadership?
6. How might the leader-member exchange model provide insights into problems that women and minorities often have in being accepted and promoted in organizations?
7. Do you think most managers use a situational approach to increase leader effectiveness? Discuss.
8. When average people on the street are asked to explain why a given individual is a leader, they tend to describe the person in terms such as *competent, consistent, self-assured,* and *supportive* of his or her followers. Can you reconcile this description with the variables illustrated in Exhibit 14-1?
9. "The essence of effective leadership is matching the leader's personality with the dominant leadership style in the organization." Do you agree or disagree with this statement? Discuss.
10. What does the phrase "organizations are overmanaged and underled" mean?

CASE EXERCISE
CHRISTOPHER STEFFEN: LEADER OR SCOREKEEPER?

Christoper Steffen has played in the big leagues for many years. He's held senior management positions at Chrysler, Honeywell, Eastman Kodak, and Citicorp. But in spite of having developed an impressive track record in finance and cost-control, he seems to get into trouble everywhere he goes.

Steffen was born in 1942. After graduating from Wayne State University with an MBA, he worked for Ford Motor Co., Unarco Industries, Price Waterhouse, and IC Industries. He joined Chrysler in 1981 and played a major role in that company's turnaround. A former colleague at Chrysler described him as "a very good organized individual and a very good delegator" who put together a "good, integrated financial-management system." Another former Chrysler executive says Steffen "wrung a lot of money out of the company by squeezing on receivables and inventories." But others aren't so kind with their appraisal. His former boss at Chrysler criticized Steffen's ability to understand the company's operations or think strategically. He says Steffen is "a good administrator, a great scorekeeper, but he's not a great leader." Steffen resigned from Chrysler in 1989. He says he wanted a higher-level job. His former boss says he was demoted and encouraged to leave.

From Chrysler, Steffen moved to Honeywell as chief financial officer. He helped engineer thousands of layoffs and shed assets. His reputation for financial sophistication was further enhanced, but again he met with criticism. He was said to have interpersonal problems and a limited grasp of Honeywell operations. After failing to be selected for the top spot at Honeywell, he resigned in late 1992.

With great fanfare, in January 1993, Steffen joined Eastman Kodak as their top financial executive. On the day of the announcement, Kodak stock surged more than $4 billion! But almost immediately, Steffen clashed with Kodak's CEO over issues such as the appropriate number of layoffs, how fast some assets should be sold, and his managerial role. After just eleven weeks at Kodak, Steffen resigned. While

Kodak's CEO might not have thought very much of Steffen's contribution to the company, the stock market thought otherwise. The value of Kodak's stock dropped $1.7 billion on the day of his resignation.

Steffen was then hired by Citicorp as senior executive vice president and chief financial officer. Citicorp's CEO, John Reed, wanted Steffen to focus on improving the company's weak financial controls and on enhancing productivity through reengineering its operations. By almost every account, Steffen made real contributions to Citicorp. For instance, he identified the cost of performing various processes so that Citicorp executives could better define standards and goals. But, as had happened before in his career, Steffen ran into problems. Just exactly what those problems were are unclear. His supporters depict him as a brilliant executive with piercing intelligence, sophisticated financial acumen and an aura of supreme self-confidence. His detractors call him abrasive, confrontational and lacking in interpersonal skills. Reed decided in December 1995 that the company was better off without Steffen. Reed had an announcement drafted of Steffen's resignation, then walked over to Steffen's office and handed it to him.

People close to Reed say that he felt Steffen lacked the credibility or people skills to further improve the company's productivity. Said one official, "John felt Chris had made a contribution but that he didn't have the leadership skills to take us to the next level."

Questions

1. In spite of Christopher Steffen's successes, he isn't seen as a leader. Why?
2. Why do you think he was hired at Citicorp if he lacked leadership qualities?
3. What does this case say about leadership?

Source: Based on G. B. Knecht, "Steffen's Departure From Citicorp Shows Reed's Dominant Role," *Wall Street Journal*, December 20, 1995, p. A1.

VIDEO CASE EXERCISE
DR. DAVID KESSLER AT THE F.D.A.

Dr. David Kessler was trained as a pediatrician. He also holds a law degree from Harvard. This unusual background uniquely equipped him for his appointment, in 1990, as head of the U.S. Food and Drug Administration.

Kessler has built a "folk hero" reputation by taking on powerful constituencies. For instance, in 1991, he sent in U.S. marshals to seize thousands of crates of orange juice which Procter & Gamble called fresh. Kessler disagreed. He felt the label was false and misleading and confusing to consumers. He has also taken on the drug industry and medical device manufacturers for misleading labels.

It is undoubtedly Kessler's views on smoking that have gotten him the most publicity and criticism. "Every day, 3,000 additional kids start smoking," says Kessler. "Every year, a million kids begin to smoke cigarettes. We need to focus our efforts on reducing the number of kids who are going to become hooked for life." This obsession with young people is based on statistics, which Kessler cites, that show if someone doesn't start smoking by the age of 20, it is very unlikely that he or she will ever start smoking. He continually repeats the phrase "hooked for life" in his campaign to regulate the production and sale of cigarettes. And he is targeting young people for his message. "Everyone knows that cigarettes are not good for you," he says. "But I'm not sure that everybody really understands how bad they really are. And I think that especially with regard to kids and teenagers."

Many in the tobacco industry think his objective is to ban smoking, but Kessler says he simply doesn't want the tobacco companies to have any new customers.

Questions

1. What characteristics have made some people call Dr. Kessler a leader?
2. How does "the situation" play into the perception that Kessler is a leader?
3. Contrast Kessler's actions with those of the CEO of a major tobacco company. Is the latter a leader? Why or why not?

Source: Based on "Person of the Week—Dr. David Kessler," World News Tonight; ABC News; aired on June 24, 1994.

SKILL EXERCISE

Choosing an Effective Leadership Style

You are a manufacturing manager in a large electronics plant. The company's management is always searching for ways to increase efficiency. They recently installed new machines and set up a new simplified work system, but to the surprise of everyone—including you—the expected increase in productivity was not realized. In fact, production has begun to drop, quality has fallen off, and the number of employee resignations has risen.

You don't think that there is anything wrong with the machines. You have had reports from other companies that are using them, and they confirm your opinion. You have also had representatives from the firm that built the machines go over them, and they report that the machines are operating at peak efficiency.

You know that some aspect of the new work system must be responsible for the change, but you are getting no help from your immediate subordinates—four first-line supervisors, each in charge of a section, and your supply manager. The drop in production has been variously attributed to poor training of the operators, lack of an adequate system of financial incentives, and poor morale. All of the individuals involved have deep feelings about this issue. Your subordinates do not agree with you or with each other.

This morning you received a phone call from your division manager. He had just received your production figures for the last 6 months and was calling to express his concern. He indicated that the problem was yours to solve in any way that you think best but that he would like to know within a week what steps you plan to take.

You share your division manager's concern with the falling productivity and know that your employees are also concerned. Using your knowledge of leadership concepts, which leadership style would you choose? Justify your choice.

Source: Based on V. H. Vroom, "A New Look at Managerial Decision Making," *Organizational Dynamics,* Spring 1973, pp. 66–80. With permission.

NOTES

1. Based on L. Nakarmi and R. Neff, "Samsung's Radical Shakeup," *Business Week,* February 28, 1994, pp. 74–76; "Improved Efficiency and Enhanced Corporate Image," *Business Korea,* November 1994, pp. 24–25; and P. Klebnikov, "'Chairman Lee Is a Very Young Man,'" *Forbes,* September 25, 1995, pp. 66–70.
2. R. J. House and P. M. Podsakoff, "Leadership Effectiveness: Past Perspectives and Future Directions for Research," in J. Greenberg, ed., *Organizational Behavior: The State of the Science* (Hillsdale, N.J.: Lawrence Erlbaum Associates, 1994), p. 46.
3. G. Capowski, "Anatomy of a Leader: Where Are the Leaders of Tomorrow?" *Management Review,* March 1994, pp. 12–15.
4. J. P. Kotter, "What Leaders Really Do," *Harvard Business Review,* May–June 1990, pp. 103–11; and J. P. Kotter, *A Force for Change: How Leadership Differs from Management* (New York: Free Press, 1990).
5. Cited in Capowski, "Anatomy of a Leader," p. 13.
6. See, for instance, W. Shapiro, "What Debates Don't Tell Us," *Time,* October 19, 1992, pp. 32–33.
7. See, for instance, early reviews in C. A. Gibb, "The Principles and Traits of Leadership," *Journal of Abnormal and Social Psychology,* July 1947, pp. 267–84; R. M. Stogdill, "Personal Factors Associated with Leadership: A Survey of the Literature," *Journal of Psychology,* January 1948, pp. 35–71.
8. See S. A. Kirkpatrick and E. A. Locke, "Leadership: Do Traits Matter?" *The Executive,* May 1991, pp. 48–60.
9. G. H. Dobbins, W. S. Long, E. J. Dedrick, and T. C. Clemons, "The Role of Self-Monitoring and Gender on Leader Emergence: A Laboratory and Field Study," *Journal of Management,* September 1990, pp. 609–18; and S. J. Zaccaro, R. J. Foti, and D. A. Kenny, "Self-Monitoring and Trait-Based Variance in Leadership: An Investigation of Leader Flexibility across Multiple Group Situations," *Journal of Applied Psychology,* April 1991, pp. 308–15.

10. R. G. Lord, C. L. DeVader, and G. M. Alliger, "A Meta-Analysis of the Relation between Personality Traits and Leadership Perceptions: An Application of Validity Generalization Procedures," *Journal of Applied Psychology,* August 1986, pp. 402–10.
11. G. Yukl and D. D. Van Fleet, "Theory and Research on Leadership in Organizations," in M. D. Dunnette and L. M. Hough, eds., *Handbook of Industrial & Organizational Psychology,* 2nd ed., vol. 3 (Palo Alto, Calif.: Consulting Psychologists Press, 1992), p. 150.
12. Lord, DeVader, and Alliger, "A Meta-Analysis of the Relation between Personality Traits and Leadership Perceptions."
13. F. E. Fiedler, "Time-Based Measures of Leadership Experience and Organizational Performance: A Review of Research and a Preliminary Model," *Leadership Quarterly,* Spring 1992, p. 5.
14. Ibid., p. 7.
15. F. E. Fiedler, "Leadership Experience and Leadership Performance: Another Hypothesis Shot to Hell," *Organizational Behavior and Human Performance,* January 1970, pp. 1–14.
16. See T. Mulligan, "It's All a Matter of How to Crack the Whip," *Los Angeles Times,* April 3, 1993, p. D1.
17. M. Loeb, "Empowerment That Pays Off," *Fortune,* March 20, 1995, pp. 145–46.
18. R. M. Stogdill and A. E. Coons, eds., *Leader Behavior: Its Description and Measurement,* Research Monograph No. 88 (Columbus: Ohio State University, Bureau of Business Research, 1951); R. Kahn and D. Katz, "Leadership Practices in Relation to Productivity and Morale," in D. Cartwright and A. Zander, eds., *Group Dynamics: Research and Theory,* 2nd ed. (Elmsford, N.Y.: Row, Peterson, 1960); and R. Likert, *New Patterns of Management* (New York: McGraw Hill, 1961).
19. R. R. Blake and J. S. Mouton, *The Managerial Grid* (Houston: Gulf, 1964).
20. See G. Ekvall and J. Arvonen, "Change-Centered Leadership: An Extension of the Two-Dimensional Model," *Scandinavian Journal of Management* 7, no. 1 (1991), pp. 17–26; M. Lindell and G. Rosenqvist, "Is There a Third Management Style?" *The Finnish Journal of Business Economics* 3 (1992), pp. 171–98; and M. Lindell and G. Rosenqvist, "Management Behavior Dimensions and Development Orientation," *Leadership Quarterly,* Winter 1992, pp. 355–77.
21. See Stogdill and Coons, *Leader Behavior*; and S. Kerr, C. A. Schriesheim, C. J. Murphy, and R. M. Stogdill, "Toward a Contingency Theory of Leadership Based upon the Consideration and Initiating Structure Literature," *Organizational Behavior and Human Performance,* August 1974, pp. 62–82.
22. See references cited in note 18.
23. E. Van Velsor and J. B. Leslie, "Why Executives Derail: Perspective across Time and Culture," *The Executive,* November 1995, pp. 62–72.
24. See, for example, L. L. Larson, J. G. Hunt, and R. N. Osborn, "The Great Hi-Hi Leader Behavior Myth: A Lesson from Occam's Razor," *Academy of Management Journal,* December 1976, pp. 628–41; and P. C. Nystrom, "Managers and the Hi-Hi Leader Myth," *Academy of Management Journal,* June 1978, pp. 325–31.
25. This position is probably most adamantly argued by Fred Fiedler in his contingency theory. See F. Fiedler, *A Theory of Leadership Effectiveness* (New York: McGraw Hill, 1967).
26. This position is probably best articulated in the Vroom-Yetton-Jago leader-participation model. See V. H. Vroom and A. G. Jago, *The New Leadership: Managing Participation in Organizations* (Englewood Cliffs, N.J.: Prentice Hall, 1988).
27. See references cited in note 9.
28. See, for instance, J. C. McElroy, "A Typology of Attribution Leadership Research," *Academy of Management Review,* July 1982, pp. 413–17; J. R. Meindl and S. B. Ehrlich, "The Romance of Leadership and the Evaluation of Organizational Performance," *Academy of Management Journal,* March 1987, pp. 91–109; J. C. McElroy and J. D. Hunger, "Leadership Theory as Causal Attribution of Performance," in J. G. Hunt, B. R. Baliga, H. P. Dachler, and C. A. Schriesheim, eds., *Emerging Leadership Vistas* (Lexington, Mass.: Lexington Books, 1988); B. Shamir, "Attribution of Influence and Charisma to the Leader: The Romance of Leadership Revisited," *Journal of Applied Social Psychology,* March 1992, pp. 386–407; and J. R. Meindl, "The Romance of Leadership as a Follower-Centric Theory: A Social Constructionist Approach," *Leadership Quarterly,* Fall 1995, pp. 329–41.
29. Lord, DeVader, and Alliger, "A Meta-Analysis of the Relation between Personality Traits and Leadership Perceptions."
30. G. N. Powell and D. A. Butterfield, "The 'High-High' Leader Rides Again!" *Group and Organization Studies,* December 1984, pp. 437–50.
31. J. R. Meindl, S. B. Ehrlich, and J. M. Dukerich, "The Romance of Leadership," *Administrative Science Quarterly,* March 1985, pp. 78–102.
32. B. M. Staw and J. Ross, "Commitment in an Experimenting Society: A Study of the Attribution of Leadership from Administrative Scenarios," *Journal of Applied Psychology,* June 1980, pp. 249–60; J. Pfeffer, *Managing with Power* (Boston: Harvard Business School Press, 1992), p. 194; and M. Loeb, "An Interview with Warren Bennis: Where Leaders Come From," *Fortune,* September 19, 1994, p. 241.
33. T. Brown, "Great Leaders Need Great Followers," *Industry Week,* September 4, 1995, p. 30.
34. R. J. House and T. R. Mitchell, "Path-Goal Theory of Leadership," *Journal of Contemporary Business,* Autumn 1974, pp. 81–97.
35. Fiedler, *A Theory of Leadership Effectiveness.*
36. R. E. Kelley, "In Praise of Followers," *Harvard Business Review,* November–December 1988, pp. 142–48; and I. Chaleff, *The Courageous Follower: Standing Up To and For Our Leaders* (San Francisco: Berrett-Koehler, 1995).
37. F. Dansereau, J. Cashman, and G. Graen, "Instrumentality Theory and Equity Theory as Complementary Approaches in Predicting the Relationship of Leadership and Turnover among Managers," *Organizational Behavior and Human Performance,* October 1973, pp. 184–200; and G. Graen, M. Novak, and P. Sommerkamp, "The Effects of

Leader-Member Exchange and Job Design on Productivity and Satisfaction: Testing a Dual Attachment Model," *Organizational Behavior and Human Performance,* August 1982, pp. 109–31.

38. R. M. Dienesch and R. C. Liden, "Leader-Member Exchange Model of Leadership: A Critique and Further Development," *Academy of Management Review,* July 1986, pp. 618–34.
39. R. Liden and G. Graen, "Generalizability of the Vertical Dyad Linkage Model of Leadership," *Academy of Management Journal,* September 1980, pp. 451–65; and R. C. Liden, S. J. Wayne, and D. Stilwell, "A Longitudinal Study of the Early Development of Leader-Member Exchanges," *Journal of Applied Psychology,* August 1993, pp. 662–74.
40. D. Duchon, S. G. Green, and T. D. Taber, "Vertical Dyad Linkage: A Longitudinal Assessment of Antecedents, Measures, and Consequences," *Journal of Applied Psychology,* February 1986, pp. 56–60; Liden, Wayne, and Stilwell, "A Longitudinal Study of the Early Development of Leader-Member Exchanges"; R. J. Deluga and J. T. Perry, "The Role of Subordinate Performance and Ingratiation in Leader-Member Exchanges," *Group & Organization Management,* March 1994, pp. 67–86; and A. S. Phillips and A. G. Bedeian, "Leader-Follower Exchange Quality: The Role of Personal and Interpersonal Attributes," *Academy of Management Journal,* August 1994, pp. 990–1001.
41. See, for example, R. P. Vecchio and B. C. Gobdel, "The Vertical Dyad Linkage Model of Leadership: Problems and Prospects," *Organizational Behavior and Human Performance,* August 1984, pp. 5–20; T. M. Dockery and D. D. Steiner, "The Role of the Initial Interaction in Leader-Member Exchange," *Group and Organization Studies,* December 1990, pp. 395–413; and G. B. Graen and M. Uhl-Bien, "Relationship-Based Approach to Leadership: Development of Leader-Member Exchange (LMX) Theory of Leadership over 25 Years: Applying a Multi-Level Multi-Domain Perspective," *Leadership Quarterly,* Summer 1995, pp. 219–47.
42. D. Eden, "Leadership and Expectations: Pygmalion Effects and Other Self-Fulfilling Prophecies in Organizations," *Leadership Quarterly,* Winter 1992, pp. 278–79.
43. See specifically House and Mitchell, "Path-Goal Theory of Leadership"; Fiedler, *A Theory of Leadership Effectiveness;* and P. Hersey and K. H. Blanchard, *Management of Organizational Behavior: Utilizing Human Resources,* 5th ed. (Englewood Cliffs, N.J.: Prentice Hall, 1988).
44. Vroom and Jago, *The New Leadership.*
45. Ibid.; and R. H. G. Field and R. J. House, "A Test of the Vroom-Yetton Model Using Manager and Subordinate Reports," *Journal of Applied Psychology,* June 1990, pp. 362–66; and V. H. Vroom and A. G. Jago, "Situation Effects and Levels of Analysis in the Study of Leader Participation," *Leadership Quarterly,* Summer 1995, pp. 169–81.
46. Fiedler, *A Theory of Leadership Effectiveness;* and F. E. Fiedler, M. M. Chemers, and L. Mahar, *Improving Leadership Effectiveness: The Leader Match Concept* (New York: John Wiley, 1977).
47. L. H. Peters, D. D. Hartke, and J. T. Pohlmann, "Fiedler's Contingency Theory of Leadership: An Application of the Meta-Analysis Procedures of Schmidt and Hunter," *Psychological Bulletin,* March 1985, pp. 274–85; C. A. Schriesheim, B. J. Tepper, and L. A. Tetrault, "Least Preferred Co-Worker Score, Situational Control, and Leadership Effectiveness: A Meta-Analysis of Contingency Model Performance Predictions," *Journal of Applied Psychology,* August 1994, pp. 561–73; and R. Ayman, M. M. Chemers, and F. Fiedler, "The Contingency Model of Leadership Effectiveness: Its Levels of Analysis," *Leadership Quarterly,* Summer 1995, pp. 147–67.
48. R. J. House, "A Path-Goal Theory of Leader Effectiveness," *Administrative Science Quarterly,* September 1971, pp. 321–38; House and Mitchell, "Path-Goal Theory of Leadership"; and R. J. House, "Retrospective Comment," in L. E. Boone and D. D. Bowen, eds., *The Great Writings in Management and Organizational Behavior,* 2nd ed. (New York: Random House, 1987), pp. 354–64.
49. See J. Indik, "Path-Goal Theory of Leadership: A Meta-Analysis," paper presented at the National Academy of Management Conference, Chicago, August 1986; R. T. Keller, "A Test of the Path-Goal Theory of Leadership with Need for Clarity as a Moderator in Research and Development Organizations," *Journal of Applied Psychology,* April 1989, pp. 208–12; and J. C. Wofford and L. Z. Liska, "Path-Goal Theories of Leadership: A Meta-Analysis," *Journal of Management,* Winter 1993, pp. 857–76.
50. For a review of the cross-cultural applicability of the leadership literature, see R. S. Bhagat, B. L. Kedia, S. E. Crawford, and M. R. Kaplan, "Cross-Cultural Issues in Organizational Psychology: Emergent Trends and Directions for Research in the 1990s," in C. L. Cooper and I. T. Robertson, eds., *International Review of Industrial and Organizational Psychology,* vol. 5 (Chichester, England: John Wiley & Sons, 1990), pp. 79–89.
51. E. H. Schein, *Organizational Culture and Leadership* (San Francisco: Jossey-Bass, 1985); and H. M. Trice and J. M. Beyer, *The Cultures of Work Organizations* (Englewood Cliffs, N.J.: Prentice Hall, 1993), pp. 254–98.
52. S. Kerr and J. M. Jermier, "Substitutes for Leadership: Their Meaning and Measurement," *Organizational Behavior and Human Performance,* December 1978, pp. 375–403; J. P. Howell and P. W. Dorfman, "Substitutes for Leadership: Test of a Construct," *Academy of Management Journal,* December 1981, pp. 714–28; J. P. Howell, P. W. Dorfman, and S. Kerr, "Leadership and Substitutes for Leadership," *Journal of Applied Behavioral Science* 22, no. 1 (1986), pp. 29–46; J. P. Dorfman, P. W. Dorfman, and S. Kerr, "Moderator Variables in Leadership Research,"

Academy of Management Review, January 1986, pp. 88–102; N. J. Pitner, "Leadership Substitutes: Their Factorial Validity in Educational Organizations," *Educational & Psychological Measurement,* Summer 1988, pp. 307–15; J. P. Howell, D. E. Bowen, P. W. Dorfman, S. Kerr, and P. M. Podsakoff, "Substitutes for Leadership: Effective Alternatives to Ineffective Leadership," *Organizational Dynamics,* Summer 1990, pp. 21–38; P. M. Podsakoff, B. P. Niehoff, S. B. MacKenzie, and M. L. Williams, "Do Substitutes for Leadership Really Substitute for Leadership? An Empirical Examination of Kerr and Jermier's Situational Leadership Model," *Organizational Behavior and Human Decision Processes,* February 1993, pp. 1–44; and P. M. Podsakoff and S. B. MacKenzie, "An Examination of Substitutes for Leadership within a Levels-of-Analysis Framework," *Leadership Quarterly,* Fall 1995, pp. 289–328.

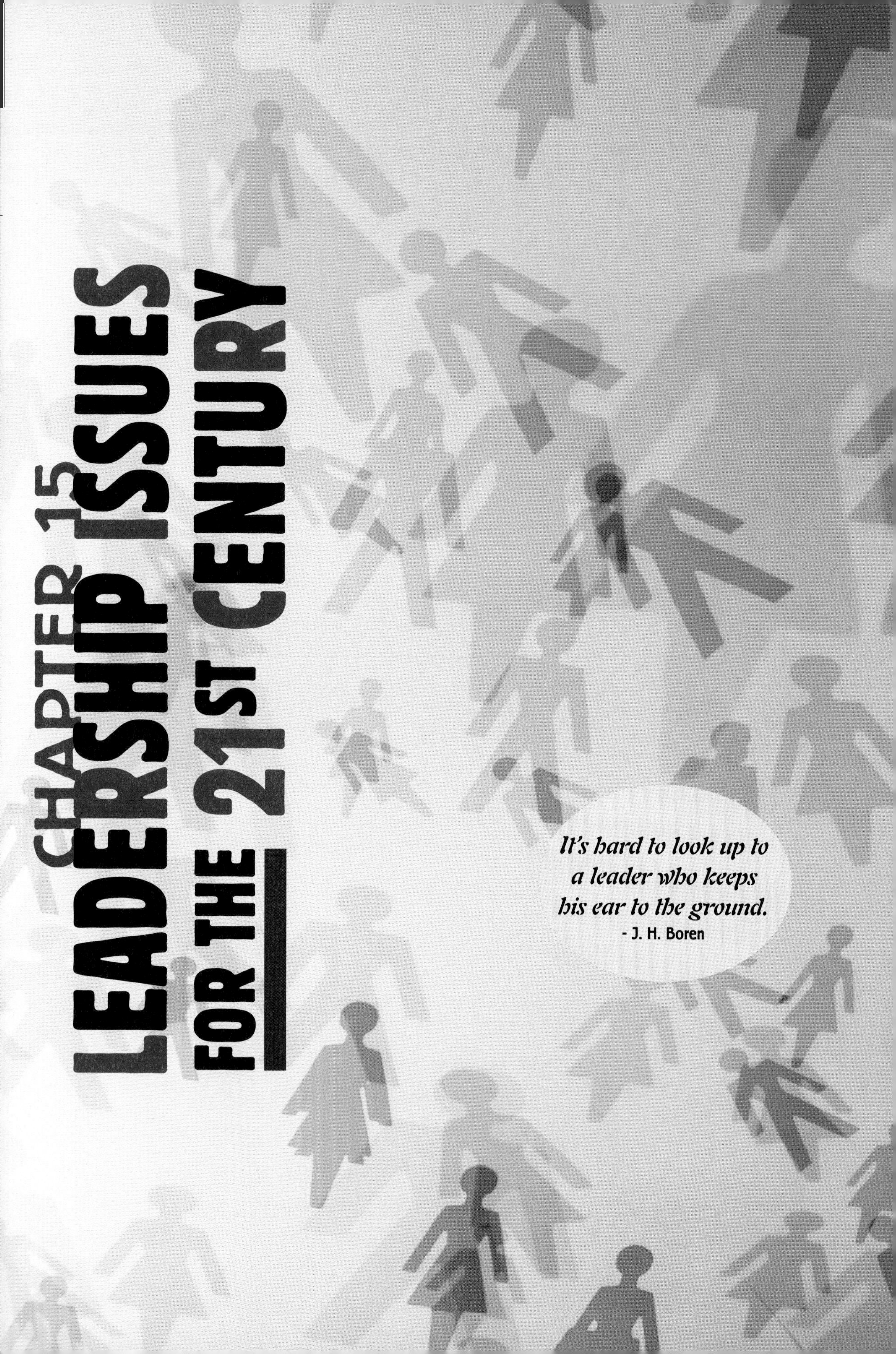

CHAPTER 15
LEADERSHIP ISSUES FOR THE 21ST CENTURY

It's hard to look up to
a leader who keeps
his ear to the ground.
- J. H. Boren

LEARNING OBJECTIVES

After studying this chapter, you should be able to:

1. Contrast transactional with transformational leadership
2. Define the qualities of a charismatic leader
3. Identify the skills visionary leaders exhibit
4. List the five dimensions that underlie the concept of trust
5. Describe how a leader can make others dependent upon him or her
6. Identify the four roles that team leaders perform
7. Explain the role of a mentor
8. Define what coaching is
9. Explain whether men and women lead differently
10. Describe the implications of leadership concepts to management practice

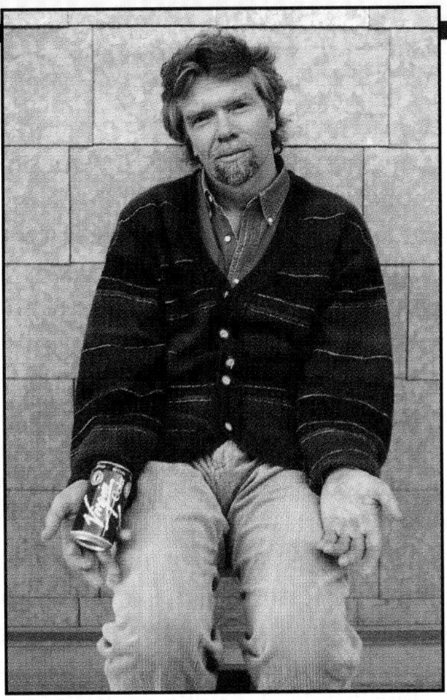

Richard Branson marches to the beat of a different drummer.[1] He's brash, confident, unconventional, a self-promoter, a bold risk taker, and a man with big ideas. A born maverick, the charismatic Branson has raised establishment bashing to an art form and built a business with close to $2 billion in revenues in the process. His Virgin brand can be found on records, entertainment megastores, an airline, and now even soda pop.

Branson never graduated from high school. But lack of a diploma hasn't stopped him from becoming the eleventh-richest person in Britain. He understood the taste of music consumers, created Virgin Records, built it into a megacorporation, then sold it for nearly a billion dollars. Then he started Virgin Atlantic Airlines. With only eight 747s, it has redefined trans-Atlantic service. First class was replaced with upper class—which includes free limo service. Branson's airline has aggressively captured a large share of the trans-Atlantic business-traveler market by merging technology with service. For instance, he was the first to install multichannel video monitors for every seat on his planes.

Branson's latest venture is a Coca-Cola clone—Virgin Cola. Why take on Coke? "I believe that if you're going to take someone on, you might as well take on the biggest brand in the world," says Branson. "Besides, most people who have been around as long as Coke have become quite fat. I believe they've got very vulnerable skin." In only its first few months on the market, Virgin Cola captured 9 percent of the cola business in British supermarkets. Branson claims that the product generated profits almost immediately.

overarching goal, to communicate high performance expectations, to exhibit confidence in the ability of subordinates to meet those expectations, and to empathize with the needs of their subordinates. They learned to project a powerful, confident, and dynamic presence, and they practiced using a captivating and engaging voice tone. To further capture the dynamics and energy of charisma, the leaders were trained to evoke charismatic nonverbal characteristics: They alternated between pacing and sitting on the edges of their desks, leaned toward the subordinates, maintained direct eye contact, and had a relaxed posture and animated facial expressions. These researchers found that these students could learn how to project charisma. Moreover, subordinates of these leaders had higher task performance, task adjustment, and adjustment to the leader and to the group than did subordinates who worked under groups led by noncharismatic leaders.

When Charisma Is a Liability One last word on this topic: Charismatic leadership may not always be needed to achieve high levels of employee performance. It may be most appropriate when the follower's task has an ideological component.[18] This may explain why, when charismatic leaders surface, it is most likely to be in politics, religion, wartime, or when a business firm is introducing a radically new product or facing a life-threatening crisis. Such conditions tend to involve ideological concerns. Franklin D. Roosevelt offered a vision to get Americans out of the Great Depression. Steve Jobs achieved unwavering loyalty and commitment from the technical staff he oversaw at Apple Computer during the late 1970s and early 1980s by articulating a vision of personal computers that would dramatically change the way people lived. General "Stormin' Norman" Schwarzkopf's blunt, passionate style, absolute confidence in his troops, and a vision of total victory over Iraq made him a hero in the free world after Operation Desert Storm in 1991. A charismatic leader, in fact, may become a liability to an organization once the crisis and need for dramatic change subside.[19] Why? Because when there is no crisis the charismatic leader's overwhelming self-confidence probably isn't needed. Nor is unconventional behavior needed. And a charismatic leader often is unable to listen to others, becomes uncomfortable when challenged by aggressive subordinates, and holds a rigid belief in his or her "rightness" on issues. Philippe Kahn's charismatic style, for instance, was an asset in his position as CEO during the rapid-growth years of software-database company Borland International. But he became a liability as the company matured. His dictatorial style, arrogance, and reckless decision making have put the company's future in jeopardy.[20]

When charismatic leaders surface, it is most likely to be in politics, religion, wartime, or when a business firm is introducing a radically new product or facing a life-threatening crisis.

Visionary Leadership

The term *vision* has recurred throughout our discussion of charismatic leadership. But visionary leadership goes beyond charisma. In this section, we review recent revelations about the importance of visionary leadership.

Defining Visionary Leadership **Visionary leadership** is the ability to create and articulate a realistic, credible, attractive vision of the future that grows out of and improves upon the present.[21] This vision, if properly selected and implemented, is so energizing that it "in effect jump-starts the future by calling forth the skills, talents, and resources to make it happen."[22]

A review of various definitions finds that a vision differs from other forms of direction setting in several ways: "A vision has clear and compelling imagery that offers an innovative way to improve, which recognizes and draws on traditions, and connects to actions that people can take to realize change. Vision taps people's emotions and energy. Properly articulated, a vision creates the enthusiasm that people have for sporting events and other leisure-time acitivites, bringing the energy and commitment to the workplace."[23]

Keep in mind what a vision is *not*. It's not a dream, it's not a mission statement, and it's not synonymous with goals. A vision is not some nebulous prophecy—it is a reality that has yet to come into existence. A mission statement conveys an organization's purpose, not its direction. A well-designed vision provides direction; that is, it offers means as well as ends. Finally, a vision is not a statement of goals. Goals point to a desired end and rarely consider values. They don't contain an innovative solution possibility that shows the way with a clear and compelling picture of the future. A vision contains values and the actions to take to achieve the desired result.

The Case For and Against Visionary Leadership The case for visionary leadership has been made by many writers. For instance: "The twenty-first-century organization virtually demands visionary leadership. It cannot function without it, for an organization driven by accelerating technological change, staffed by a diverse, multicultural mix of highly intelligent knowledge workers, facing global complexity, a vast kaleidoscope of individual customer needs, and the incessant demands of multiple constituencies would simply self-destruct without a common sense of direction."[24] Another article argues that vision is "the glue that binds individuals into a group with a common goal. . . . When shared by employees, [it] can keep an entire company moving forward in the face of difficulties, enabling and inspiring leaders and employees alike."[25]

A survey of 1,500 senior leaders, 870 of them CEOs from twenty different countries, additionally attests to the growing importance of visionary leadership.[26] The leaders were asked to describe the key traits or talents desirable for a CEO in the year 2000. The dominant characteristic most frequently mentioned was that the CEO convey a "strong sense of vision." Ninety-eight percent rated this trait as "most important." Another study contrasted eighteen visionary companies with eighteen comparable nonvisionary firms over a 65-year period.[27] The visionary companies were found to have outperformed the comparison group by six times on standard financial criteria, and their stocks outperformed the general market by fifteen times.

But not *everyone* buys into the importance of visionary leadership.[28] Louis Gerstner, after taking over the top job at IBM, said that a vision was the last thing IBM needed at the moment. Robert Eaton, CEO of Chrysler, said that inside his company they don't use the word *vision*. He sees the concept as too vague and esoteric and wants Chrysler people to focus on quantifiable short-term results. Microsoft's Bill Gates says "being a visionary is trivial."

Gerstner, Eaton, and Gates are in the minority. And Gates is clearly a visionary leader, regardless of whether he accepts the title or thinks it is trivial. Why? Because Gates has created a direction for Microsoft that is defining the future of information technology.

The debate on the importance of vision can best be reconciled by recognizing that visionary leadership needs to be supported by detailed plans. An outstanding organization needs both a vision and a high level of attention to daily operations. A strong vision can't substitute for good day-to-day management. Both are necessary.

Qualities of a Vision The key properties of a vision seem to be inspirational possibilities that are value-centered, realizable, and communicated with superior imagery and articulation.[29] Visions should be able to create possibilities that are inspirational, unique, and offer a new order that can produce organizational distinction. A vision is likely to fail if it doesn't offer a view of the future that is clearly and demonstrably better for the organization and its members than is the status quo. Desirable visions fit the times and circumstances and reflect the uniqueness of the organization. People in the organization must also believe that the vision is attainable. It should be perceived as challenging yet doable. Visions that have clear articulation and powerful imagery are easily grasped and accepted.

What do visions look like? They are typically easier to talk about than to actually create. In practice, they often lack the direction that differentiates them from mere mission statements. But, given this caveat, here are a few examples: "To be the single source software provider to the financial services industry." "To be the leading African-American-owned promotional and public relations firm in the USA." "To become the most customer-responsive producer of automobile interior trim in North America."[30] Here are some additional organization-specific examples.[31] Walt Disney single-handedly reinvented the idea of an amusement park went he described his vision of Disneyland in the early 1950s. Rupert Murdoch was one of the first people to see the future of the communications industry by combining entertainment and news media. Through his News Corporation, Murdoch has successfully integrated a broadcast network, TV stations, movie studio, publishing, and global satellite distribution. Mary Kay Ash's vision of women as entrepreneurs selling products that improved their self-image gave impetus to her cosmetics company. Scandinavian Airlines CEO Jan Carlzon used the notion of "50,000 daily moments of truth" to depict the emphasis to be placed on customer service. Carlzon wanted every employee to ensure that each "moment of truth"—those instances when customers come into contact with employees—would be a positive experience for SAS customers. H. Wayne Huizenga began picking up garbage with a beat-up old truck, envisioned potential in waste disposal, and built Waste Management (now WMX); then bought into a small Dallas video-store chain, saw the future was in big stores, and turned the small chain into Blockbuster Video (now part of Viacom). Steve Jobs created a vision for Apple Computer that energized employees around the idea of not just building computers but dramatically changing the world. Charles Schwab is currently attempting to redefine financial services by combining discount prices with comprehensive offerings.

Rupert Murdoch was one of the first people to see the future of the communications industry by combining entertainment and news media.

Qualities of a Visionary Leader What skills do visionary leaders exhibit? Once the vision is identified, these leaders appear to have three qualities that are related to effectiveness in their visionary roles.[32]

First is the ability to explain the vision to others. The leader needs to make the vision clear in terms of required actions and aims through clear oral and written communication. The best vision is likely to be ineffective if the leader isn't a strong communicator. Ronald Reagan—the so-called Great Communicator—used his years of acting experience to help him articulate a simple vision for his presidency: a return to happier and more prosperous times through less government, lower taxes, and a strong military.

Second is to be able to express the vision not just verbally but also through the leader's behavior. The leader must behave in ways that continually convey and reinforce the vision. Herb Kelleher, CEO at Southwest Airlines, lives and breathes his commitment to customer service. He is famous within the company for jumping in, when needed, to help check in passengers, load baggage, fill in for flight attendants, or do anything else to make the customer's experience more pleasant.

The third skill is being able to extend the vision to different leadership contexts. This is the ability to sequence activities so that the vision can be applied in a variety of situations. For instance, the vision has to be as meaningful to the people in accounting as to those in marketing, to employees in Prague as well as in Pittsburgh.

CONTEMPORARY LEADERSHIP ROLES

Let's now move to important issues that every effective leader in the 1990s and beyond is, and will continue to be, concerned about. How do I build credibility and trust with the people I work with? How do I acquire power? What demands does team leadership place on me? And how can I be an effective mentor and coach?

Building Credibility and Trust

Willie Williams, Chief of Police for the City of Los Angeles, has been widely criticized within his organization for lack of leadership.[33] Officers acknowledge the challenges he faced coming into his job as an outsider—he was previously the police chief in Philadelphia—and his success at reducing crime, but they claim that he has lost their trust. "He lied, and that's unforgivable," said one officer. The main issue in question is whether Williams and his wife accepted free room and gratuities while staying in Las Vegas. He first denied the charge, then changed his story. As another officer put it, "I don't care if he got the freebies or not. That's not the issue. The issue is he lied about it."

Clarifying Terminology Followers want leaders who are credible and whom they can trust. But what do the terms *credibility* and *trust* mean?

The most dominant component of credibility is honesty. Surveys have found that honesty is consistently singled out as the number one characteristic of admired leaders.[34] "Honesty is absolutely essential to leadership. If people are going to follow someone willingly, whether it be into battle or into the boardroom, they first want to assure themselves that the person is worthy of their trust."[35] In addition to being honest, credible leaders have been found to be competent and inspiring.[36] They are personally able to effectively communicate their confidence and enthusiasm. So followers judge a leader's **credibility** in terms of his or her honesty, competence, and ability to inspire.

Trust is so closely entangled with the concept of credibility that the two terms are frequently used interchangeably. For instance, the authors of the definitive work on credibility state that "the credibility check can reliably be simplified to just one question: 'Do I trust this person?'"[37]

We define **trust** as the belief in the integrity, character, and ability of a leader. When followers trust a leader, they are willing to be vulnerable to the leader's actions because they are confident that their rights and interests will not be abused.[38] Recent evidence has identified five dimensions that underlie the concept of trust:[39]

Integrity. Honesty and truthfulness

Competence. Technical and interpersonal knowledge and skills

Consistency. Reliability, predictability, and good judgment in handling situations

Loyalty. Willingness to protect and save face for a person

Openness. Willingness to share ideas and information freely

Consistent with the work on credibility, the evidence indicates that integrity and competence are the most critical characteristics that an individual looks for in determining another's trustworthiness. Integrity seems to be rated highest because "without a perception of the other's 'moral character' and 'basic honesty,' other dimensions of trust [are] meaningless."[40]

You don't have to be a manager or have formal authority to have power. You can influence others through personal characteristics such as your expertise or personal charisma. In today's high-tech world, expertise has become an increasingly powerful source of influence. As jobs have become more specialized and complex, organizations and members have become dependent on experts with special skills or knowledge to achieve goals. Specialists such as software analysts, tax accountants, environmental engineers, and industrial psychologists are examples of individuals in organizations who can wield power as a result of their expertise. If you are director of human resources in your firm and you need valid selection tests to help you identify high-potential candidates—and you rely on your industrial psychologist to provide these valid tests—that industrial psychologist has expert power. Of course, as we have already discussed earlier in this chapter, charisma is a powerful source of influence. If you possess charismatic traits, you can use this power to get others to do what you want.

Creating Dependency We said earlier that probably the most important aspect of power is that it is a function of dependence. When you possess a resource that others require but you alone control, you make them dependent on you, and, therefore, you gain power over them. That resource could be information, money, status, expertise, friends in high places, or anything else that others desire. Dependence is increased when the resource you control is important, scarce, and nonsubstitutable.[46]

If nobody wants what you have, it is not going to create dependency. To create dependency, therefore, the thing(s) you control must be perceived as being *important*. It has been found, for instance, that organizations actively seek to avoid uncertainty.[47] We should, therefore, expect that those individuals or groups who can absorb an organization's uncertainty will be perceived as controlling an important resource. For instance, a study of industrial organizations found that the marketing departments in these firms were consistently rated as the most powerful.[48] It was concluded by the researcher that the most critical uncertainty facing these firms was selling their products. This finding might suggest that, during a labor strike, the organization's negotiating representatives have increased power, or that engineers, as a group, would be more powerful at Intel than at Procter & Gamble. These inferences appear to be generally valid. Labor negotiators do become more powerful within the human resources area and the organization as a whole during periods of labor strife. An organization such as Intel, which is heavily technologically oriented, is highly dependent on its engineers to maintain its products' technical advantages and quality. And, at Intel, engineers are clearly a powerful group. At Procter & Gamble, marketing is the name of the game, and marketers are the most powerful occupational group. These examples support not only the view that the ability to reduce uncertainty increases a group's importance and, hence, its power but also that what is important is situational. It varies between organizations and undoubtedly also varies over time within any given organization.

When you possess a resource that others require but you alone control, you make them dependent on you, and, therefore, you gain power over them.

As noted previously, if something is plentiful, possession of it will not increase your power. A resource needs to be perceived as *scarce* to create dependency. Scarcity can help to explain how low-ranking members in an organization who have important knowledge not available to high-ranking members gain power over the high-ranking members. Possession of a scarce resource—in this case, important knowledge—makes the high-ranking member dependent on the low-ranking member. The scarcity-power relationship also helps make sense out of behaviors of low-ranking members that otherwise might seem illogical, such as

BUILDING SELF-AWARENESS • BUILDING SELF-AWARENES

HOW POWER-ORIENTED ARE YOU?

INSTRUCTIONS For each statement, circle the number that most closely resembles your attitude.

	Disagree		Neutral	Agree	
Statement	**A Lot**	**A Little**		**A Little**	**A Lot**
1. The best way to handle people is to tell them what they want to hear.	1	2	3	4	5
2. When you ask someone to do something for you, it is best to give the real reason for wanting it rather than giving reasons that might carry more weight.	1	2	3	4	5
3. Anyone who completely trusts anyone else is asking for trouble.	1	2	3	4	5
4. It is hard to get ahead without cutting corners here and there.	1	2	3	4	5
5. It is safest to assume that all people have a vicious streak, and it will come out when they are given a chance.	1	2	3	4	5
6. One should take action only when it is morally right.	1	2	3	4	5
7. Most people are basically good and kind.	1	2	3	4	5
8. There is no excuse for lying to someone else.	1	2	3	4	5
9. Most people more easily forget the death of their father than the loss of their property.	1	2	3	4	5
10. Generally speaking, people won't work hard unless they're forced to do so.	1	2	3	4	5

Turn to page 562 for scoring directions and key.

destroying the procedure manuals that describe how a job is done, refusing to train people in their jobs or even to show others exactly what they do, creating specialized language and terminology that inhibits others from understanding their jobs, or operating in secrecy so that an activity will appear more complex and difficult than it really is. Interestingly, technology has both increased and decreased the power of information in today's organizations. As previously noted, expertise has become an increasingly potent power base in organizations. At the same time, computerized networks have widened the availability of information and, ironically, have thereby reduced leader power. When the leaders were the ones who knew things, they could use that knowledge to control followers. They no longer can. The democratization of information has lessened the power of many leaders by making information more plentiful.

The fewer viable *substitutes* a resource has, the more power control over that resource provides. This relationship is illustrated in a concept we will call the **elasticity of power.**

In economics, considerable attention is focused on the elasticity of demand, which is defined as the relative responsiveness of quantity demanded to change in price. This concept can be modified to explain the strength of power. Elasticity of power is defined as the relative responsiveness of power to change in available alternatives. A leader's ability to influence others is viewed as being dependent on how those others perceive their alternatives.

Looking at Exhibit 15-3, assume that there are two individuals. A's power elasticity curve is relatively inelastic. This curve would describe, for example, an employee who believed that he had a large number of employment opportunities outside his current organization. Fear of being fired would have only a moderate impact on A, for he perceives that he has other alternatives. A's boss finds that threatening A with termination has only a minimal impact on influencing his behavior. A reduction in alternatives (from *X* to *X* – 1) increases the power of A's boss only slightly (A' to A"). However, B's curve is relatively elastic. She sees few other job opportunities. Her age, education, present salary, or lack of contacts may severely limit her ability to find a job somewhere else. As a result, B is dependent on her present organization and boss. If B loses her job (*Y* to *Y* – 1), she may face prolonged unemployment, so B's boss has considerable power over her. As long as B perceives her options as limited and her boss holds the power to terminate her employment, B's boss will hold considerable power over her.

Implications For managers, the message behind an understanding of power is that it is more than formal authority. As a manager of a group, you are not the only one with power. Your ability to get things accomplished depends, to a considerable degree, on learning who has power in your group and working to get

EXHIBIT 15-3
Elasticity of Power

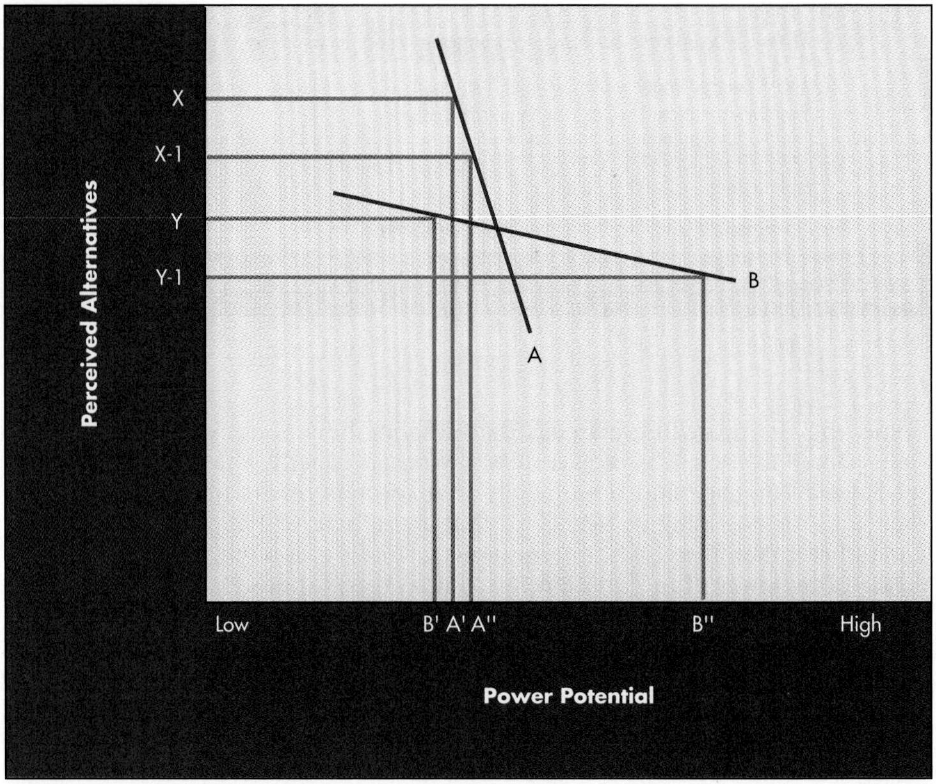

them to use their power in ways that will help the group achieve its goals. A subordinate whom others admire or who has skills that your work group needs has the capacity to have power over you. Many managers have found themselves captive to subordinates who have no formal authority but who have power and who have learned to use it in ways to make their managers dependent upon them. As one young supervisor told me, "I'm very careful how I treat Sharon. She's been in the department longer than anyone. She knows everyone's job, backwards and forwards. People in the department look up to her. They follow her example. If Sharon didn't think I was treating her right, she could turn the whole department against me. And make my life miserable." In addition, our discussion of power tells us that managers within an organization can expand their own power by increasing their alternatives, gaining control over specific scarce resources, or some combination of both.

Providing Team Leadership

Leadership is increasingly taking place within a team context. As teams grow in popularity, the role of the leader in guiding team members takes on heightened importance. And the role of team leader is different from the traditional leadership role performed by first-line supervisors. J. D. Bryant, a supervisor at Texas Instruments' Forest Lane plant in Dallas, found that out.[49] One day he was happily overseeing a staff of fifteen circuit-board assemblers. The next day he was informed that the company was moving to teams and that he was to become a "facilitator." "I'm supposed to teach the teams everything I know and then let them make their own decisions," he said. Confused about his new role, he admitted, "There was no clear plan on what I was supposed to do." In this section, we consider the challenge of being a team leader, review the new roles that team leaders take on, and offer some tips on how to increase the likelihood that you can perform effectively in this position.

The Challenge of Team Leadership Many leaders are not equipped to handle the change to teams. As one prominent consultant noted, "Even the most capable managers have trouble making the transition because all the command-and-control type things they were encouraged to do before are no longer appropriate. There's no reason to have any skill or sense of this."[50] This same consultant estimated that "probably 15 percent of managers are natural team leaders; another 15 percent could never lead a team because it runs counter to their personality. [They're unable to sublimate their dominating style for the good of the team]. Then there's that huge group in the middle: Team leadership doesn't come naturally to them, but they can learn it."[51]

The challenge for most managers, then, is to learn how to become an effective team leader. They have to learn skills such as sharing information, trusting others, giving up authority, and understanding when to intervene. Effective leaders have mastered the difficult balancing act of knowing when to leave their teams alone and when to intercede. New team leaders may try to retain too much control at a time when team members need more autonomy, or they may abandon their teams at times when the team needs support and help.[52]

Team Leadership Roles A recent study of twenty organizations that had reorganized around teams found certain common responsibilities that all leaders had to assume. These included coaching, facilitating, handling disciplinary problems, reviewing team and individual performance, training, and communication.[53] Many of these responsibilities apply to managers in general. A more meaningful way to describe the team leader's job is to focus on two priorities: managing the team's external boundary and facilitating the team process.[54] We have broken these priorities down into four specific roles.

First, team leaders are *liaisons with external constituencies.* These include upper management, other internal teams, customers, and suppliers. The leader represents the team to other constituencies, secures needed resources, clarifies others' expectations of the team, gathers information from the outside, and shares this information with team members.

Second, team leaders are *trouble-shooters.* When the team has problems and asks for assistance, team leaders sit in on meetings and help try to resolve the problems. This role is rarely related to technical or operation issues. Why? Because the team members typically know more about the tasks being done than does the team leader. The leader is most likely to contribute by asking penetrating questions, helping the team talk through problems, and getting needed resources from external constituencies. For instance, when a team in an aerospace firm found itself short-handed, its team leader took responsibility for getting more staff. He presented the team's case to upper management and got the approval through the company's human resources department.

Third, team leaders are *conflict managers.* When disagreements surface, they help process the conflict. What is the source of the conflict? Who is involved? What are the issues? What resolution options are available? What are the advantages and disadvantages of each? By getting team members to address questions such as these, the leader minimizes the disruptive aspects of intrateam conflicts.

Finally, team leaders are *coaches.* They clarify expectations and roles, teach, offer support, cheerlead, and do whatever else is necessary to help team members improve their work performance.

Suggestions for Being an Effective Team Leader If you want to be an effective team leader, what can you do?[55] Let's begin with the obvious: You need to develop your team-leadership skills. Specifically, these include coaching, conflict resolution, listening, feedback, and oral persuasion.

You need to overcome any fears you may have about admitting ignorance. Accept the reality that you don't have, and are unlikely to acquire, the level of technical skills held by the people on your team. The skills you bring are of another sort. Your job is to get people to focus on goals, provide motivation, and reduce barriers that the team may come across. A team leader at Honeywell's defense avionics division in Albuquerque quickly made this discovery: "My most important task was not trying to figure out everybody's job. It was to help this team feel as if they owned the project by getting them whatever information, financial or otherwise, they needed."[56]

EXHIBIT 15-4

Source: Dilbert, by Scott Adams. *Dilbert* reprinted by permission of United Feature Syndicate, Inc.

You need to learn to share authority. You need to empower your team. Doing so is a lot easier said than done. Most experienced managers have come to link responsibility and authority. If they are going to be held responsible for their team's performance, they want control over the decisions that will shape that performance. But effective leaders understand their teams' need to be given autonomy and that giving it to them won't necessarily result in disaster. Quite the contrary. Team norms can be powerful devices to control slackers and maintain high levels of performance.

Effective team leaders do not associate empowerment with abdication. The leader monitors the team's progress and lets the team solve its own problems. But as one consultant noted, "Too little help and direction is just as paralyzing as too much."[57] When the team is struggling, the effective leader knows when to let the team find its own solution and when to intervene. This distinction requires leaders to maintain ongoing communication and feedback on the team's progress.

Mentoring

Many leaders create mentoring relationships. A **mentor** is a senior employee who sponsors and supports a less-experienced employee (a protégé). The mentoring role includes coaching, counseling, and sponsorship.[58] As a coach, mentors help to develop their protégés' skills. As counselors, mentors provide support and

IN THE NEWS

Saint June Provides Strong Team Leadership at Lotus

JUNE ROKOFF ISN'T FOND OF NICKNAMES. BUT AT LOTUS DEVELOPMENT CORPORATION, WHERE SHE IS senior vice president for software development and a cult hero, Rokoff is known as Saint June. When projects are in trouble, they call in Rokoff. And the soft-spoken 44-year-old leader has consistently shown her skill at turning problems into successes.

Rokoff is credited, for instance, with saving the critical follow-on Release 3 to the company's 1-2-3 spreadsheet package in 1989 by leading a disastrous development project to success. More recently, her strong support and leadership brought 1-2-3 for Windows to a highly successful debut and kept key team members from leaving.

How Rokoff works can be seen with Release 3, the follow-on to Lotus's original 1-2-3 spreadsheet for DOS. She volunteered to take over the development team because she saw that it was in trouble. The product was late, and the team was disorganized. If that wasn't bad enough, six managers had come and gone as the project dragged along, and the team had come to distrust all Lotus managers. Rokoff immediately set and clarified objectives and made sure they were communicated clearly and often. She set interim goals to test the progress of the new software and had daily "bug" meetings in which quality-assurance engineers and programmers discussed problems and took immediate action if needed. Knowing that programmers hate meetings, she created a rule limiting them to an hour. Rokoff began ensuring that team members were recognized for their work—for example, posters were tailor-made for individual achievements. She also got the company chairman and other senior executives to stop in regularly and to congratulate team members who had made some important breakthroughs. In 8 months, Rokoff had turned the team around and had Release 3 moving out the door.

What's the secret to Saint June's leadership successes? She knows how to make sure team needs are met and has the ability to build trust and commitment within groups of tempermental software programmers. "Technologists don't generally like to take directions, but they like to take direction from June," said Don McLagan, a former boss of hers. Rokoff sums up her skill simply: "When things are crazy, I tend to be a calming influence."

Source: G. Rifkin, "The 'Iron Lady' Keeping Lotus on Track," *New York Times*, January 23, 1994, p. F10.

help bolster protégés' self-confidence. And as sponsors, mentors actively intervene on behalf of their protégés, lobby to get their protégés visible assignments, and politic to get their protégés rewards such as promotions and salary increases.

Some organizations have formal mentoring programs. New employees or young managers for whom the organization has high expectations are assigned to senior managers who play mentoring roles. More typically, senior managers informally select an employee and take that employee on as a protégé. The most effective mentoring relationships exist *outside* the immediate boss-subordinate interface.[59] The boss-subordinate context has an inherent conflict of interest and tension, mostly attributable to managers' directly evaluating the performance of subordinates, that limit openness and meaningful communication.

Successful mentors are good teachers. They can present ideas clearly, listen well, and empathize with the problems of their protégés. They also share experiences with the protégé, act as role models, share contacts, and provide guidance through the political maze of the organization. They provide advice and guidance on how to survive and get ahead in the organization and act as a sounding board for ideas that a protégé may be hesitant to share with his or her direct supervisor. A mentor vouches for a protégé, answers for him or her in the highest circles within the organization, and makes appropriate introductions.

Gloria A. McDowell is director of human resources at Golden State Mutual Life Insurance. She worked her way up in the company from an accounting-clerk position. Today, recognizing her visibility as a role model, she spends a large part of her time mentoring young women in her organization.

Why would a leader want to be a mentor? There are personal benefits to the leader as well as benefits for the organization. The mentor-protégé relationship gives the mentor unfiltered access to the attitudes and feelings of lower-ranking employees. Protégés can be an excellent source of potential problems by providing early warning signals. They provide timely information to upper managers that short-circuits the formal channels. So the mentor-protégé relationship is a valuable communication channel that allows mentors to have news of problems before they become common knowledge to others in upper management. In addition, in terms of leader self-interest, mentoring can provide personal satisfaction to senior executives. In the latter stages of their career, managers are often allowed the luxury of playing the part of elder statesperson. They are respected for their judgment, built up over many years and through varied experiences. The opportunity to share this knowledge with others can be personally rewarding for the mentor.

A major organizational benefit of mentoring is its influence in shaping and sustaining the organization's culture.[60] Mentors play a critical role in the socialization process, especially for new and inexperienced employees. They help reinforce strong cultures by conveying those stories, myths, and rituals that identify the organization's core values. In addition, mentors provide a support system for high-potential employees. Where mentors exist, protégés are often more motivated, better politically grounded, and less likely to quit. For instance, one study found that where a significant mentoring relationship existed, the protégés had more favorable and frequent promotions, were paid significantly more than those who were not mentored, had a greater level of commitment to the organization, and had greater career success.[61]

Are all employees in an organization equally likely to participate in a mentoring relationship? Unfortunately the answer is No.[62] Evidence indicates that minorities and women are less likely to be chosen as protégés than are white males and thus are less likely to accrue the benefits of mentorship. Mentors tend to select protégés who are similar to themselves on criteria such as background, education, gender, race, ethnicity, and religion. "People naturally move to mentor and can more easily communicate with those with whom they most closely identify."[63] In the United States, for instance, upper-management positions in most organizations have been traditionally staffed by white males, so it is hard for minorities and women to be selected as protégés. In addition, in terms of cross-gender mentoring, senior male managers may select male protégés to minimize problems such as sexual attraction or gossip. Organizations have responded to this dilemma by increasing formal mentoring programs and providing training and coaching for potential mentors of special groups such as minorities and women.

Coaching

We first introduced the topic of *coaching* in Chapter 1 when we described how the "manager as boss" is changing to the "manager as coach." In this section, we want to offer some suggestions on how managers can improve their coaching skills.

What Is Coaching? **Coaching** is a day-to-day hands-on process of helping employees recognize opportunities to improve their work performance.[64] A coach analyzes the employee's performance, provides insights as to how that performance can be improved, and offers the leadership to help the employee achieve that improvement. As a coach, you provide instruction, guidance, advice, and encouragement to help employees improve their job performance.

Coaching requires you to suspend judgment and evaluation. Managers, in the normal routine of carrying out their jobs, regularly express judgments about performance against previously established goals. As a coach, you focus on accepting employees the way they are and help them to make continual improvement toward the goal of developing their full potential.

The Transition from "Boss" to "Coach" Jim Chartrand, a plant manager with International Paper, provides some interesting insights into the transformation from "boss" to "coach."[65] Chartrand took over IP's Philadelphia liquid-packaging plant in 1984. The 130-person plant was struggling when he came in. His natural autocratic style—"I was a kick-ass-and-take-names manager whose job it was to tell people what they were doing wrong"—only made the situation worse. In 2 years, under his leadership, the plant's costs were excessive, quality was substandard, union relations were terrible, and customers were unhappy. Something had to change. Chartrand decided the changes had to begin with him.

"He had absolutely no empathy for employees," says Pat Kerner, a plate-room operator. Added Dennis Hughes, supervisor of the converting department, "Jim used to go to the supervisors and pound the heck out of them, leaving them no choice but to do the same to others." Chartrand's change program touched almost every part and person in the liquid-packaging plant. He reorganized the plant around teams. He empowered the teams to make operating decisions. Chartrand began regular strolls around the plant floor, looking for examples of workers doing positive things—so that he could provide recognition. He initiated an open-door policy and encouraged people to come into his office at any time and discuss anything. He reconfigured his office, replacing the visitor's chair in front of his desk with a round table. Now he could talk with people more informally, face to face. But, maybe most important, Chartrand changed the way he managed his people. He considers his transition from autocrat to coach as critical to his plant's success:

> Almost every individual in the organization, myself included, is capable and willing to perform at a higher level. To do that, we need coaching.
>
> A good coach listens to what people are saying, trying to get all the information available about a situation. The good coach then asks questions, prompting the person to work through the possibilities and come up with solutions. After all, the person closest to the problem likely has a better feel than I do for what will handle the problem. It's also important not to confuse being an expert with being a good coach. Many great athletic coaches weren't particularly good athletes, but they know how to build on others' successes.
>
> To become a great coach, I have to overcome my own ego and the feeling that no one else can do something as well as I can. I can never withhold knowledge or worry that helping someone else succeed will somehow threaten me.[66]

The results speak for themselves. After 3 years under the "new" Jim Chartrand, production quality at the Philadelphia plant has greatly improved while the scrap rate has dropped more than 15 percent; labor productivity is up significantly; cost per ton produced has dropped to one of the lowest in the industry; and customer complaints have decreased by 20 percent. Chartrand's performance recently resulted in his being promoted to facility manager at IP's folding-cartons plant in Richmond, Virginia.

General Coaching Skills There are three general coaching skills that leaders can apply to help their employees generate breakthroughs in performance.[67]

1. *Ability to analyze ways to improve an employee's performance and capabilities.* A coach looks for opportunities for an employee to expand his or her capabilities and improve performance. To do this you need to observe your employee's behavior on a day-to-day basis. You can also ask questions of the employee: Why do you do a task this way? Can it be improved? What other approaches might be used? Then listen to the employee. You need to understand the world from the employee's perspective. Finally, show genuine interest in the person as an individual, not merely as an employee. Respect his or her individuality. More important than any technical expertise you can provide about improving job performance is the insight you have into the employee's uniqueness.
2. *Ability to create a supportive climate.* It is the coach's responsibility to reduce barriers to development and to foster a climate that encourages performance improvement. Through intensive listening and empowering employees to implement appropriate ideas they suggest, you can create a climate that contributes to a free and open exchange of ideas. You can also offer help by being available for assistance, guidance, or advice if asked. By being positive and upbeat, you can encourage your employees. Effective coaches do not use threats because they create a climate of fear and inhibition. Focus on mistakes as learning opportunities. Change implies risk, and employees must not feel that mistakes will be punished. When failure occurs, ask: "What did we learn that can help us in the future?"

   Analyze the factors that you control and reduce all obstacles that you can to help the employee to improve his or her job performance. Validate employees' efforts when they succeed, and point to what was missing when they fail. But never blame employees for poor results. Express to the employee the value of his or contribution to your unit's goals.
3. *Ability to influence employees to change their behavior.* The ultimate test of coaching effectiveness is whether an employee's performance improves. But this is not a static concept. The concern is for ongoing growth and development. Consequently, you should help employees continually work toward improvement and encourage them by recognizing and rewarding even small improvements. Continual improvements, however, means that there are no absolute upper limits to an employee's job performance.

Your concern as a coach is to enable your employees to accomplish tasks independently at a high level of effectiveness when you're not there to assist. Your task is education or training so that employees can solve their own problems and perform effectively independently in the future.

THE GENDER ISSUE: DO MEN AND WOMEN LEAD DIFFERENTLY?

An extensive review of the evidence suggests two conclusions regarding gender and leadership.[68] First, the similarities between men and women tend to outweigh the differences. Second, what differences there are seem to be that women prefer a more democratic leadership style, while men feel more comfortable with a directive style.

The similarities among men and women leaders should not be completely surprising. Almost all the studies looking at this issue have used managerial positions as being synonymous with leadership. Consequently, gender differences apparent in the general population do not tend to be evident. Why? Because of career self-selection and organization selection. Just as people who choose careers in law enforcement or civil engineering have a lot in common, individuals who choose managerial careers also tend to have commonalities. People with traits associated with leadership—such as intelligence, confidence, and sociability—are likely to be perceived as leaders and encouraged to pursue careers in which they can exert leadership. This is true regardless of gender. Similarly, organizations tend to recruit and promote people into leadership positions who project leadership attributes. The result is that, regardless of gender, those who achieve formal leadership positions in organizations tend to be more alike than different.

Despite the previous conclusion, studies indicate some differences in the inherent leadership styles between women and men. Women tend to adopt a more democratic leadership style. They encourage participation, share power and information, and attempt to enhance followers' self-worth. They prefer to lead through inclusion and rely on their charisma, expertise, contacts, and interpersonal skills to influence others. Men, on the other hand, are more likely to use a directive command-and-control style. They rely on the formal authority of their position for their influence base. However, consistent with our first conclusion, these findings need to be qualified. The tendency for female leaders to be more democratic than males declines when women are in male-dominated jobs. Apparently, group norms and masculine stereotypes of leaders override personal preferences so that women abandon their feminine styles in such jobs and act more autocratically.

Given that men have historically held the great majority of leadership positions in organizations, it is tempting to assume that the existence of the noted differences between men and women would automatically work to favor men. It doesn't. In today's organizations, flexibility, teamwork, trust, and information sharing are replacing rigid structures, competitive individualism, control, and secrecy. The best managers listen, motivate, and provide support to their people. And many women seem to do those things better than men. As a specific example, the expanded use of cross-functional teams in organizations means that effective managers must become skillful negotiators. The leadership styles women typically use can make them better at negotiating, as they are less likely than men to focus on wins, losses, and competition. They tend to treat negotiations in the context of a continuing relationship—trying hard to make the other party a winner in his own and others' eyes.

The best managers listen, motivate, and provide support to their people. And many women seem to do those things better than men.

THE ETHICS ISSUE: IS THERE A MORAL DIMENSION TO LEADERSHIP?

The topic of leadership and ethics has surprisingly received little attention. Only very recently have ethicists and leadership researchers begun to consider the ethical implications in leadership.[69] Why now? One reason may be the growing general interest in ethics throughout the field of management. Another reason may be the discovery by probing biographers that many of our past leaders—such as

Martin Luther King, Jr., John Kennedy, and Franklin D. Roosevelt—suffered from ethical shortcomings. Regardless, no contemporary discussion of leadership is complete without addressing its ethical dimension.

Ethics touches on leadership at a number of junctures. Transformational leaders, for instance, have been described by one authority as fostering moral virtue when they try to change the attitudes and behaviors of followers.[70] Charisma, too, has an ethical component. Unethical leaders are likely to use their charisma to enhance *power over* followers, directed toward self-serving ends. Ethical leaders are considered to use their charisma in a socially constructive way to *serve* others.[71] There is also the issue of abuse of power by leaders, for example, when they give themselves large salaries and bonuses while, at the same time, they seek to cut costs by laying off long-time employees. And, of course, the topic of trust explicitly deals with honesty and integrity in leadership.

Leadership effectiveness needs to address the *means* that a leader uses in trying to achieve goals as well as the content of those goals. Jack Welch, for instance, is consistently described as a highly effective leader because he has succeeded in achieving outstanding returns for shareholders. But Welch is also widely regarded as one of the world's toughest managers. He is regularly listed high on *Fortune*'s annual list of the most hated and reviled executives. Similarly, Bill Gates's success in leading Microsoft to domination of the world's software business has been achieved by means of an extremely demanding work culture. Microsoft's culture demands long work hours by employees and is intolerant of individuals who want to balance work and their personal life. In addition, ethical leadership must address the content of a leader's goals. Are the changes that the leader seeks for the organization morally acceptable? Is a business leader effective if he builds his organization's success by selling products that damage the health of its users? This question might be asked of tobacco executives. Or is a military leader successful if he wins a war that should not have been fought in the first place?

Leadership is not value-free. Before we judge any leader as effective, we should consider both the means used by the leader to achieve his or her goals and the moral content of those goals.

FINDING AND CREATING EFFECTIVE LEADERS

We have covered a lot of ground in these two chapters on leadership. But the ultimate goal of our review is to answer this question: How can organizations find or create effective leaders? Let's use our review to try to answer that question.

Selection

The entire process that organizations go through to fill management positions is essentially an exercise in trying to identify individuals who will be effective leaders. You might begin by reviewing the job specification for the position to be filled. What knowledge, skills, and abilities are needed to do the job effectively? You should try to analyze the situation in order to find candidates who will make a proper match.

Testing is useful for identifying and selecting leaders. Personality tests can be used to look for traits associated with leadership—intelligence, aggressiveness, industriousness, self-confidence, persistence. Testing to find a leadership-candidate's score on self-monitoring also makes sense. High self-monitors are likely to outperform their low-scoring counterparts because the former are better at reading situations and adjusting their behavior accordingly. You can additionally use simulation tests such as the assessment-center exercises described in Chapter 9.

Having candidates act out leadership situations, and observing their behavior in those situations, has been found to be an effective selection device.[72]

Interviews additionally provide an opportunity to evaluate leadership candidates. For instance, we know that experience, per se, is a poor predictor of leader effectiveness, but situation-specific experience is relevant. You can use the interview to determine if a candidate's prior experience fits with the situation you are trying to fill. Similarly, the interview is a reasonably good vehicle for identifying the degree to which a candidate has leadership traits such as an outgoing personality, strong verbal skills, a vision, or a charismatic physical presence.

We know the importance of situational factors in leadership success. And we should use this knowledge to match leaders to situations. Does the situation require a change-focused leader? If so, look for transformational qualities. If not, look for transactional qualities. You might also ask: Is leadership actually important in this specific position? There may be situational factors that substitute for or neutralize leadership. If there are, then the leader essentially performs a figurehead or symbolic role, and the importance of selecting the "right" person is not particularly crucial.

Training

Organizations, in aggregate, spend billions of dollars, yen, and marks on leadership training and development. And these efforts take many forms—from $20,000 executive leadership programs offered by universities such as Harvard, to the hiring of executive coaches, to rock-climbing experiences at the Outward Bound School. Although much of the money spent on training may pro-

An increasing number of organizations are participating in Outward Bound's five-day program that helps leaders build skills such as risk-taking, communication, and teamwork. "I saw my teammates do it and thought, I can do it too," says this rock-climbing manager.

vide dubious benefits, our review suggests that there are some things management can do to get the maximum effect from their leadership-training budgets.

First, let's recognize the obvious. People are not equally trainable. Leadership training of any kind is likely to be more successful, for instance, with individuals who are high self-monitors than with low self-monitors. Such individuals have the flexibility to change their behavior.

What kinds of things can individuals learn that might be related to higher leader effectiveness? It may be a bit optimistic to believe that we can teach "vision-creation," but we can teach implementation skills. We can train people to develop "an understanding about content themes critical to effective visions."[73] We also can teach skills such as coaching and mentoring, and we can teach people to exhibit behaviors associated with credibility and trust. The evidence is mixed on whether we can teach people to have a greater need for power, but we can certainly train individuals on how to use power, especially in a positive way. And leaders can be taught situational-analysis skills. They can learn how to evaluate situations, how to modify situations to make them fit better with their style, and how to assess which leader behaviors might be most effective in given situations.

On an optimistic note, there is evidence suggesting that behavioral training through modeling exercises can increase individuals' ability to exhibit charismatic leadership qualities. The success of the researchers mentioned earlier (see Are Charismatic Leaders Born or Made?) in actually scripting undergraduate business students to "play" charismatic is a case in point.[74]

SUMMARY

(This summary is organized by the chapter-opening learning objectives on page 447.)

1. Transactional leaders guide and motivate their followers in the direction of established goals by clarifying role and task requirements. Transformational leaders provide outstanding leadership by inspiring followers to transcend their self-interests for the good of the organization. Transformational leaders are capable of having a profound and extraordinary effect on followers.
2. Charismatic leaders have self-confidence, a vision, ability to articulate the vision, strong convictions about the vision, and behavior that is out of the ordinary. They are perceived as change agents and are environmentally sensitive.
3. Visionary leaders have the ability to express the vision through their behavior, to explain the vision to others, and to extend the vision in a variety of situations.
4. Trustworthy individuals are perceived as having integrity, competence, consistency, loyalty, and openness.
5. Leaders increase follower dependence by controlling resources that are important, scarce, and nonsubstitutable.
6. Team leaders play four roles: liasions with external constituencies, trouble-shooters, conflict managers, and coaches.
7. Mentors coach, counsel, and support a protégé who is lower in the organization.
8. Coaching is a day-to-day hands-on process of helping employees recognize opportunities to improve their work performance.
9. The leadership styles of men and women are more alike than different. However, in general, men are more comfortable with a directive style, and women prefer a more democratic style.
10. Leadership concepts can help practicing managers make selection decisions and design training programs that will increase the effectiveness of managers.

REVIEW AND DISCUSSION QUESTIONS

1. Are transformational leaders always more effective than transactional leaders?
2. What could you do if you wanted others to perceive you as a charismatic leader?
3. "Great leaders have a vision." Do you agree or disagree? Explain.
4. How does a leader build trust?
5. Contrast positional and personal sources of power.
6. Explain the "elasticity of power" concept.
7. How does one become an effective team leader?
8. As a new employee in an organization, why might you want to acquire a mentor? Why might women and minorities have more difficulty in finding a mentor than would white males?
9. Describe general coaching skills.
10. Why do you think successful leaders of both genders in specific organizations tend to have a common leadership style?

CASE EXERCISE A
STANLEY GAULT AT GOODYEAR

Stanley Gault has quite a resumé. Before assuming the job as CEO at Goodyear Tire & Rubber Co. in 1991, he ran a major part of General Electric and was a strong candidate to run the whole company. He built a mundane manufacturer—Rubbermaid—into one of America's most admired companies. Upon retiring from Rubbermaid as CEO, he decided to come out of retirement to try to turn around Goodyear.

Central casting would never pick Gault to play the part of the successful CEO. His style is low-key. He speaks rather matter of factly, often with some care, and without a great deal of emotion. No one has ever called him charismatic.

Stanley Gault is all substance. And lots of it. In the first 3 years since taking over the CEO job, he has engineered a turnaround that has been nothing short of spectacular. The company is again profitable, and he has increased the company's value from $1 billion to $6.5 billion.

In his first two and a half years on the job, Gault did "what the vast majority of people felt could not be done." Says Gault, "And that's what substantiates the conviction I have expressed about Goodyear associates [the only word he uses to describe his colleagues] the very day I arrived—that we were capable of far greater performance." Goodyear associates, their CEO explains, not only have taken on difficult objectives, but they also have challenged conventional wisdom by tackling several of them almost at once. "Because of the status of the enterprise at the time, we didn't have the benefit of going through them sequentially," Gault says.

How did Gault turn Goodyear around? First he focused on reducing the $3.7 billion in debt he inherited. This was costing Goodyear more than $1 million each day in interest costs alone. He cut that figure to $2 billion by issuing new stock and using the proceeds to reduce debt. Then he sold off assets not essential to the tire-and-rubber-products business, and he made significant cost reductions and initiated productivity-improvement programs. He also set a goal of improving operating margins to a 10 percent level on a sector basis within 3 years. "That was an extremely ambitious objective," he says, "for we were standing there with *no* margin because of a loss for the first time in 58 years." And Gault brought to Goodyear the same talent he displayed at Rubbermaid—a focus on bringing new products to market. "We have really strengthened the entire line," he says. "Aquatred was one example. We have others, but they haven't earned the notoriety."

Questions

1. Describe Gault's leadership style.
2. Why has it worked?
3. What, if anything, does this case suggest about tranformational leadership?

Source: C. R. Day Jr., "A Little Style, Tons of Substance," *Industry Week*, February 7, 1994, pp. 18–23.

CASE EXERCISE B
IS SHERM HAYES A LEADER?

It's hard to find anyone who doesn't like Sherm Hayes. Hired as plant manager for ESS Plastics' facility in Parkersburg, West Virginia, Hayes immediately won over the plant's 330 employees by learning everyone's name after he had worked there only a week. Friendly, outgoing, and upbeat, Sherm Hayes is a charmer. The problem is, he doesn't seem to get much done.

Workers regularly describe Hayes in terms such as "charismatic," "visionary," and "inspiring." They appreciate his informality, his friendliness, and his availability to even the lowest ranking employees. As one machine operator put it, "Mr. Hayes has been here only a year but he's really changed this place. The previous plant manager was aloof and autocratic. He didn't care about his people. But Mr. Hayes cares. He's always walking around the plant, answering questions, and talking with everyone. He's a regular guy."

In spite of Hayes' popularity, two facts suggest that there are problems that many don't see. First, three of the four department heads who oversee operations and report directly to Hayes have resigned recently. All three complained about Hayes' tendency to procrastinate and his inability to make decisions. They also felt that his "hands-on" style of managing preempted their own attempts to run their departments. Second, ESS Plastics division manager Ian Campbell—the person to whom Sherm Hayes reports—has been very disappointed with the performance of the Parkersburg plant. Month-to-month comparisons of this year's productivity figures against the previous year's show declines of between 2.3 and 7.7 percent. Meanwhile, the other five plants under Campbell have all shown consistent month-to-month productivity improvements.

Questions

1. Is Sherm Hayes an effective leader? Explain your answer.
2. If you were Ian Campbell, what would you do?

SKILL EXERCISE

Coaching

You work for a large mortgage brokering company. The company has thirty offices in California. You are supervisor of the Napa Valley office and have seven mortgage brokers, an assistant, and a secretary reporting to you. Your business entails helping home buyers find mortgages and acting as a link between lenders and borrowers in getting loans approved and processed.

Todd Corsetti is one of your brokers. He has been in the Napa Valley office for two and a half years. Before that, he sold commercial real estate. You have been in your Napa Valley job for 14 months; before that you supervised a smaller office for the same company.

You have not been pleased with Todd's job performance. So you decide to review his personnel file. His first 6-month review stated: "Todd is enthusiastic. He is a bit disorganized but willing to learn. Seems to have good potential." After a year, his previous supervisor had written, "Todd seems to be losing interest. Seems frequently disorganized. Often rude to clients. Did not mention these problems to him. Hope he'll improve. His long-term potential now much more in question."

You have not spent much time with Todd, perhaps because your offices are far apart. But probably the real reason is that he is not easy to talk to and you have little in common. When you took the Napa Valley job, you decided that you would wait some time before attacking any problems to make sure you had a good grasp of the people and the situation.

But Todd's problems have gotten too visible to ignore. He is consistently missing his quarterly sales projections. On the basis of mortgages processed, he is your lowest performer. In addition, his reports are constantly late. After reviewing last month's performance reports, you made an appointment yesterday to meet him today at 9:00 A.M. But he didn't show up and wasn't in his office. You waited 15 minutes and gave up. Your secretary tells you that Todd regularly comes in late for work in the morning and takes extra-long coffee breaks. Last week, Valerie Oleata, who has the office next to Todd's, complained to you that Todd's behavior was demoralizing for her and some of the other brokers.

You don't want to fire Todd. It wouldn't be easy to find a replacement. Moreover, he has a lot of contacts with new-home builders, which brings in a number of borrowers to your office. In fact, maybe 60 percent of the business generated by your entire office comes from builders who have personal ties to Todd. If Todd were to leave your company and go to a competitor, he would probably be able to convince the builders to take their business somewhere else.

Directions: Break into groups of two. One person plays the role of the supervisor. The other plays the role of Todd. You have up to 15 minutes to simulate how a supervisor could use his or her coaching skills to deal with Todd's problem.

NOTES

1. See J. Fierman, "Winning Ideas from Maverick Managers," *Fortune,* February 6, 1995, p. 80.
2. See, for example, B. M. Bass, *Leadership and Performance Beyond Expectations* (New York: Free Press, 1985); B. M. Bass, "From Transactional to Transformational Leadership: Learning to Share the Vision," *Organizational Dynamics,* Winter 1990, pp. 19–31; F. J. Yammarino, W. D. Spangler, and B. M. Bass, "Transformational Leadership and Performance: A Longitudinal Investigation," *Leadership Quarterly,* Spring 1993, pp. 81–102; B. J. Avolio and B. M. Bass, "Individual Consideration Viewed at Multiple Levels of Analysis: A Multi-Level Framework for Examining the Diffusion of Transformational Leadership," *Leadership Quarterly,* Summer 1995, pp. 199–218; and P. Bycio, R. D. Hackett, and J. S. Allen, "Further Assessments of Bass's (1985) Conceptualization of Transactional and Transformational Leadership," *Journal of Applied Psychology,* August 1995, pp. 468–78.
3. R. J. House and P. M. Podsakoff, "Leadership Effectiveness: Past Perspectives and Future Directions for Research," in J. Greenberg, *Organizational Behavior: The State of the Science* (Hillsdale, N.J.: Lawrence Erlbaum Associates, 1994), p. 55.
4. Ibid.
5. B. M. Bass, "Leadership: Good, Better, Best," *Organizational Dynamics,* Winter 1985, pp. 26–40; and J. Seltzer and B. M. Bass, "Transformational Leadership: Beyond Initiation and Consideration," *Journal of Management,* December 1990, pp. 693–703.
6. Cited in B. M. Bass and B. J. Avolio, "Developing Transformational Leadership: 1992 and Beyond," *Journal of European Industrial Training,* January 1990, p. 23.
7. J. J. Hater and B. M. Bass, "Supervisors' Evaluation and Subordinates' Perceptions of Transformational and Transactional Leadership," *Journal of Applied Psychology,* November 1988, pp. 695–702.
8. Bass and Avolio, "Developing Transformational Leadership."
9. J. A. Conger and R. N. Kanungo, "Behavioral Dimensions of Charismatic Leadership," in J. A. Conger, R. N. Kanungo and Associates, *Charismatic Leadership* (San Francisco: Jossey-Bass, 1988), p. 79.
10. R. J. House, "A 1976 Theory of Charismatic Leadership," in J. G. Hunt and L. L. Larson, eds., *Leadership: The Cutting Edge* (Carbondale: Southern Illinois University Press, 1977), pp. 189–207.
11. W. Bennis, "The Four Competencies of Leadership," *Training and Development Journal,* August 1984, pp. 15–19.
12. Conger and Kanungo, "Behavioral Dimensions of Charismatic Leadership," pp. 78–97; and J. A. Conger and R. N. Kanungo, "Charismatic Leadership in Organizations: Perceived Behavioral Attributes and Their Measurement," *Journal of Organizational Behavior,* September 1994, pp. 439–52.
13. B. Shamir, R. J. House, and M. B. Arthur, "The Motivational Effects of Charismatic Leadership: A Self-Concept Theory," *Organization Science,* November 1993, pp. 577–94.
14. R. J. House, J. Woycke, and E. M. Fodor, "Charismatic and Noncharismatic Leaders: Differences in Behavior and Effectiveness," in Conger, Kanungo, et al. *Charismatic Leadership,* pp. 103–04; and D. A. Waldman, B. M. Bass, and F. J. Yammarino, "Adding to Contingent-Reward Behavior: The Augmenting Effect of Charismatic Leadership," *Group & Organization Studies,* December 1990, pp. 381–94.
15. J. A. Conger and R. N. Kanungo, "Training Charismatic Leadership: A Risky and Critical Task," in Conger, Kanungo, et al., *Charismatic Leadership,* pp. 309–23.
16. R. J. Richardson and S. K. Thayer, *The Charisma Factor: How to Develop Your Natural Leadership Ability* (Englewood Cliffs, N.J.: Prentice Hall, 1993).
17. J. M. Howell and P. J. Frost, "A Laboratory Study of Charismatic Leadership," *Organizational Behavior and Human Decision Processes,* April 1989, pp. 243–69.
18. House, "A 1976 Theory of Charismatic Leadership."
19. J. A. Conger, *The Charismatic Leader: Behind the Mystique of Exceptional Leadership* (San Francisco: Jossey-Bass, 1989); R. Hogan, R. Raskin, and D. Fazzini, "The Dark Side of Charisma," in K. E. Clark and M. B. Clark, eds., *Measures of Leadership* (West Orange, N.J.: Leadership Library of America, 1990); and D. Sankowsky, "The Charismatic Leader as Narcissist: Understanding the Abuse of Power," *Organizational Dynamics,* Spring 1995, pp. 57–71.

20. G. P. Zachary, "How 'Barbarian' Style of Philippe Kahn Led Borland into Jeopardy," *Wall Street Journal,* June 2, 1994, p. A1.
21. This definition is based on M. Sashkin, "The Visionary Leader," in Conger, Kanungo, et al., eds., *Charismatic Leadership,* pp. 124–25; B. Nanus, *Visionary Leadership* (New York: Free Press, 1992), p. 8; and N. H. Snyder and M. Graves, "Leadership and Vision," *Business Horizons,* January–February 1994, p. 1.
22. Nanus, *Visionary Leadership,* p. 8.
23. P. C. Nutt and R. W. Backoff, "Crafting Vision." A working paper. College of Business; Ohio State University, July 1995, p. 4.
24. Nanus, *Visionary Leadership,* pp. 178–79.
25. Snyder and Graves, "Leadership and Vision," p. 2.
26. Cited in L. B. Korn, "How the Next CEO Will Be Different," *Fortune,* May 22, 1989, p. 157.
27. J. C. Collins and J. I. Porras, *Built to Last: Successful Habits of Visionary Companies* (New York: HarperBusiness, 1994).
28. See, for instance, D. Lavin, "Robert Eaton Thinks 'Vision' Is Overrated and He's Not Alone," *Wall Street Journal,* October 4, 1993, p. A1.
29. Nutt and Backoff, "Crafting Vision," pp. 5–7.
30. Cited in L. Larwood, C. M. Falbe, M. P. Kriger, and P. Miesing, "Structure and Meaning of Organizational Vision," *Academy of Management Journal,* June 1995, pp. 740–69.
31. Cited in Nanus, *Visionary Leadership,* pp. 141, 173, 178; and Nutt and Backoff, "Crafting Vision," pp. 1, 3.
32. Based on Sashkin, "The Visionary Leader," pp. 128–30.
33. Based on a CBS *60 Minutes* segment, September 24, 1995.
34. J. M. Kouzes and B. Z. Posner, *Credibility: How Leaders Gain and Lose It, and Why People Demand It* (San Francisco: Jossey-Bass, 1993), p. 14.
35. Ibid.
36. Ibid.
37. Ibid., p. 24.
38. Based on L. T. Hosmer, "Trust: The Connecting Link between Organizational Theory and Philosophical Ethics," *Academy of Management Review,* April 1995, p. 393; and R. C. Mayer, J. H. Davis, and F. D. Schoorman, "An Integrative Model of Organizational Trust," *Academy of Management Review,* July 1995, p. 712.
39. P. L. Schindler and C. C. Thomas, "The Structure of Interpersonal Trust in the Workplace," *Psychological Reports,* October 1993, pp. 563–73.
40. J. K. Butler Jr. and R. S. Cantrell, "A Behavioral Decision Theory Approach to Modeling Dyadic Trust in Superiors and Subordinates," *Psychological Reports,* August 1984, pp. 19–28.
41. See Kouzes and Posner, *Credibility,* pp. 278–83.
42. This section is based on F. Bartolome, "Nobody Trusts the Boss Completely—Now What?" *Harvard Business Review,* March–April 1989, pp. 135–42; and J. K. Butler Jr., "Toward Understanding and Measuring Conditions of Trust: Evolution of a Conditions of Trust Inventory," *Journal of Management,* September 1991, pp. 643–63.
43. See, for instance, H. Mintzberg, *Power In and Around Organizations* (Englewood Cliffs, N.J.: Prentice Hall, 1983); J. Pfeffer, *Managing with Power* (Boston: Harvard Business School Press, 1992); and R. I. Dilenschneider, *On Power* (New York: HarperBusiness, 1994).
44. R. E. Emerson, "Power-Dependence Relations," *American Sociological Review* 27 (1962), pp. 31–41.
45. Based on J. R. P. French Jr. and B. Raven, "The Bases of Social Power," in D. Cartwright, ed., *Studies in Social Power* (Ann Arbor: University of Michigan, Institute for Social Research, 1959), pp. 150–67; and N. W. Biggart and G. G. Hamilton, "The Power of Obedience," *Administrative Science Quarterly,* December 1984, pp. 540–49.
46. Mintzberg, *Power In and Around Organizations,* p. 24.
47. R. M. Cyert and J. G. March, *A Behavioral Theory of the Firm* (Englewood Cliffs, N.J.: Prentice Hall, 1963).
48. C. Perrow, "Departmental Power and Perspective in Industrial Firms," in M. N. Zald, ed., *Power in Organizations* (Nashville, Tenn.: Vanderbilt University Press, 1970).
49. S. Caminiti, "What Team Leaders Need to Know," *Fortune,* February 20, 1995, pp. 93–100.
50. Ibid., p. 93.
51. Ibid., p. 100.
52. N. Steckler and N. Fondas, "Building Team Leader Effectiveness: A Diagnostic Tool," *Organizational Dynamics,* Winter 1995, p. 20.
53. R. S. Wellins, W. C. Byham, and G. R. Dixon, *Inside Teams: How 20 World-Class Organizations Are Winning through Teamwork* (San Francisco: Jossey-Bass, 1994), p. 318.
54. Steckler and Fondas, "Building Team Leader Effectiveness," p. 21.
55. This is largely based on Caminiti, "What Team Leaders Need to Know," pp. 94–98.
56. Ibid., p. 94.
57. Ibid.
58. See, for example, K. E. Kram, *Mentoring at Work: Developmental Relationships in Organizational Life* (Glenview, Ill.: Scott, Foresman, 1985).
59. J. A. Wilson and N. S. Elman, "Organizational Benefits of Mentoring," *The Executive,* November 1990, p. 90.
60. Ibid., p. 89; and A. H. Geiger-DuMond and S. K. Boyle, "Mentoring: A Practitioner's Guide," *Training & Development Journal,* March 1995, pp. 51–54.
61. G. F. Dreher and R. A. Ash, "A Comparative Study of Mentoring among Men and Women in Managerial, Professional, and Technical Positions," *Journal of Applied Psychology,* October 1990, pp. 539–46.
62. See, for example, J. Clawson and K. Kram, "Managing Cross-Gender Mentoring," *Business Horizons,* May–June 1984, pp. 22–32; and D. A. Thomas, "The Impact of Race on Managers' Experiences of Developmental Relationships: An Intra-Organizational Study," *Journal of Organizational Behavior,* November 1990, pp. 479–92.
63. Wilson and Elman, "Organizational Benefits of Mentoring," p. 90.
64. See S. P. Robbins and P. L. Hunsaker, *Training in InterPersonal Skills: TIPS for Managing People at Work,* 2nd ed. (Upper Saddle River, N.J.: Prentice Hall, 1996), p. 151.
65. R. Wellins and J. Worklan, "The Philadelphia Story," *Training,* March 1994, pp. 93–100.
66. Ibid., p. 95.
67. C. D. Orth, H. E. Wilkinson, and R. C. Benfari, "The Manager's Role as Coach and Mentor," *Organizational Dynamics,* Spring 1987, p. 67.
68. The material in this section is based on J. Grant, "Women as Managers: What They Can Offer to Organizations," *Organizational Dynamics,* Winter 1988, pp. 56–63; S. Helge-

sen, *The Female Advantage: Women's Ways of Leadership* (New York: Doubleday, 1990); A. H. Eagly and B. T. Johnson, "Gender and Leadership Style: A Meta-Analysis," *Psychological Bulletin,* September 1990, pp. 233–56; A. H. Eagly and S. J. Karau, "Gender and the Emergence of Leaders: A Meta-Analysis," *Journal of Personality and Social Psychology,* May 1991, pp. 685–710; J. B. Rosener, "Ways Women Lead," *Harvard Business Review,* November–December 1990, pp. 119–25; "Debate: Ways Men and Women Lead," *Harvard Business Review,* January–February 1991, pp. 150–60; A. H. Eagly, M. G. Makhijani, and B. G. Klonsky, "Gender and the Evaluation of Leaders: A Meta-Analysis," *Psychological Bulletin,* January 1992, pp. 3–22; A. H. Eagly, S. J. Karau, and B. T. Johnson, "Gender and Leadership Style among School Principals: A Meta-Analysis," *Educational Administration Quarterly,* February 1992, pp. 76–102; L. R. Offermann and C. Beil, "Achievement Styles of Women Leaders and Their Peers," *Psychology of Women Quarterly,* March 1992, pp. 37–56; T. Melamed and N. Bozionelos, "Gender Differences in the Personality Features of British Managers," *Psychological Reports,* December 1992, pp. 979–86; G. N. Powell, *Women & Men in Management,* 2nd ed. (Thousand Oaks, Calif.: Sage, 1993), pp. 158–80; C. Lee, "The Feminization of Management," *Training,* November 1994, pp. 25–31; and H. Collingwood, "Women as Managers: Not Just Different—Better," *Working Woman,* November 1995, p. 14.

69. This section is based on J. B. Ciulla, "Leadership Ethics: Mapping the Territory," *Business Ethics Quarterly,* January 1995, pp. 5–28; E. P. Hollander, "Ethical Challenges in the Leader-Follower Relationship," *Business Ethics Quarterly,* January 1995, pp. 55–65; and J. C. Rost, "Leadership: A Discussion about Ethics," *Business Ethics Quarterly,* January 1995, pp. 129–42.
70. J. M. Burns, *Leadership* (New York: Harper & Row, 1978).
71. J. M. Howell and B. J. Avolio, "The Ethics of Charismatic Leadership: Submission or Liberation?" *Academy of Management Executive,* May 1992, pp. 43–55.
72. B. J. Avolio, D. A. Waldman, and W. O. Einstein, "Transformational Leadership in a Management Game Simulation," *Group & Organization Studies,* March 1988, pp. 59–80.
73. Sashkin, "The Visionary Leader," p. 150.
74. Howell and Frost, "A Laboratory Study of Charismatic Leadership."

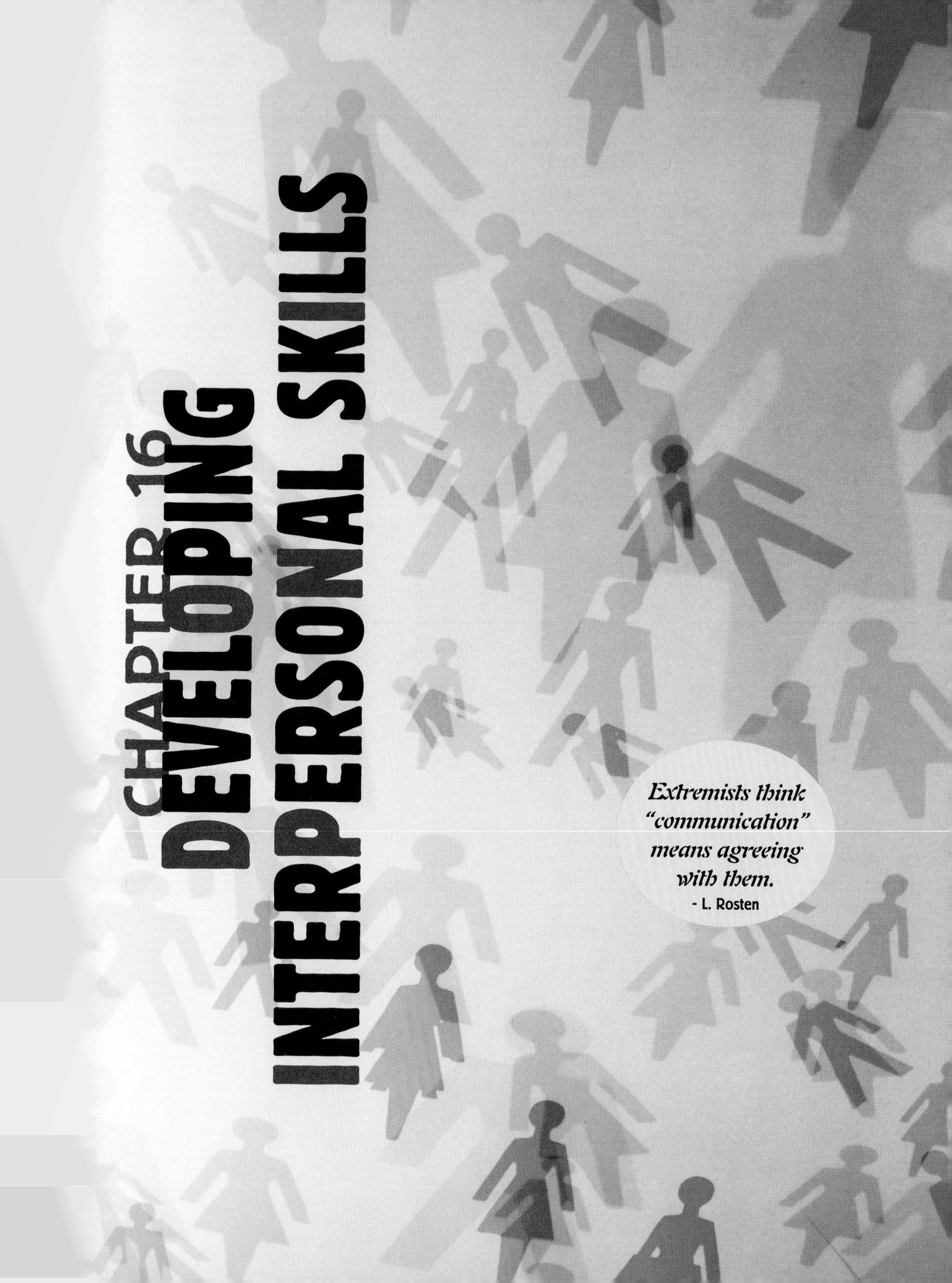

CHAPTER 16
DEVELOPING INTERPERSONAL SKILLS

Extremists think "communication" means agreeing with them.
- L. Rosten

LEARNING OBJECTIVES

After studying this chapter, you should be able to:

1. Describe the communication process
2. Contrast gender differences in interpersonal communications
3. List behaviors associated with effective active listening
4. Identify behaviors related to providing effective performance feedback
5. Describe five conflict resolution behaviors
6. Contrast distributive and integrative bargaining
7. Identify skills associated with effective negotiation
8. List steps to take in delegating authority
9. Contrast directive, nondirective, and participative counseling
10. Describe how a manager can become more politically adept

Deborah S. Kent's rise in the automotive industry is a success story built on strong people skills.[1] It's also a striking example of a manager who breaks stereotypes.

Kent entered the auto industry, first with General Motors and then with Ford Motor Co., after finishing her master's degree in industrial psychology from Washington University in St. Louis. Unlike many of her contemporaries who chose careers in marketing or accounting, Kent sought out manufacturing management. Dave Gorman, her boss and Ford's vehicle operations manager, said "three things stood out" when he hired her in 1988: "She was a female, she had great people skills, and she worked in production. . . . We were extremely impressed with her floor savvy, and she had come from a plant that had a reputation as being difficult to run and she had been good at it."

In September 1994, at age 41, Deborah Kent became the plant manager of Ford's Avon Lake, Ohio, 3.3 million–square foot assembly plant. The first woman to head a vehicle assembly plant at Ford, and the only African-American woman ever to rise to this post, she oversees 3,700 workers. In 1994, more than 216,000 Ford Econoline vans and 115,000 Mercury Villager and Nissan Quest minivans were produced along her plant's 19.5 miles of assembly line.

Kent is aware she doesn't fit the stereotype of the typical auto plant manager. A petite woman, with horn-rimmed glasses and a preference for white silk blouses, she's a white-collar woman in a brawny blue-collar man's world. But don't let her

Our focus in this chapter is on **interpersonal communication.** That is, communication between two people, either one-to-one or in face-to-face or group settings, in which the parties are treated as individuals rather than as objects. This type is in contrast to **organizational communication,** which encompasses communication among several individuals or groups. Because our interest here is in interpersonal skills, our attention will be directed at interpersonal communication.

The Communication Process

Exhibit 16-1 depicts the **communication process.** This model is made up of seven parts: (1) the communication source, (2) encoding, (3) the message, (4) the channel, (5) decoding, (6) the receiver, and (7) feedback. The source is the sender. He or she initiates the communication process by converting a thought or message to symbolic form. We call this conversion **encoding.** The **message** is the actual physical product from the source encoding. "When we write, the writing is the message. When we paint, the picture is the message. When we gesture, the movements of our arms, the expressions on our faces are the messages."[7] In interpersonal communication, the message is typically words and nonverbal cues. The **channel** is the medium through which the message travels. Interpersonal communications rely heavily on face-to-face talk, the telephone, and increasingly e-mail as primary channels. The receiver is the object to whom the message is directed. But before the message can be received, the symbols in it must be translated into a form that can be understood by the receiver. This is the **decoding** of the message. The final link in the communication process is a **feedback** loop. Feedback is the check on how successful we have been in transferring our messages as originally intended. It seeks to determine whether understanding has been achieved.

If communication were perfect, messages would be transferred so that the receiver understood them *exactly* as they were envisioned in the mind of the sender. Unfortunately that rarely happens, because there are deviations or blockages in the flow of the communication process. Most of the seven components in Exhibit 16-1 have the potential to create distortion and, therefore, impinge on the goal of communicating perfectly. If the encoding is done carelessly, the message encoded by the sender will be distorted. The message itself can also cause distortion. The poor choice of symbols and confusion in the content of the message are frequent problem areas. The channel can distort communication if a poor one is selected or if the "noise level" is high. And, of course, the receiver represents a potential source for distortion. His or her prejudices, knowledge gaps, perceptual skills, attention span, and care in decoding are all factors that can result in interpreting the message somewhat differently than intended by the sender.

Contemporary Communication Issues

In this section, we address five contemporary issues: (1) Contrary to what some people think, not *all* problems in organizations are caused by poor communication. (2) Sometimes communication distortions are purposeful and even func-

EXHIBIT 16-1
The Communication Process

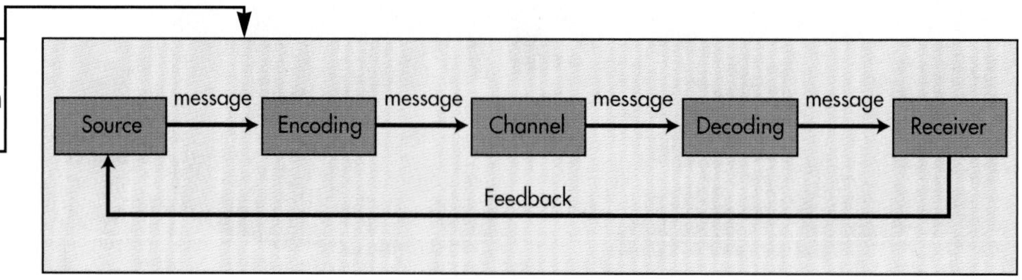

tional. (3) Nonverbal communications may be more powerful than the verbal variety. (4) Men and women generally use talk for different reasons, thus creating cross-gender communication difficulties. (5) And cross-cultural communication is becoming a major challenge to managers in today's global environment.

The "Blame Game" Poor communication is an obvious problem in organizations. But poor communication gets blamed for a lot of problems that aren't its doing.[8] If a TQM program fails, inevitably someone is going to attribute it to lack of communication. When work teams have trouble developing positive synergy, it's likely to be blamed on a communication problem. If a manager has trouble motivating his or her work group, it's probably a communication problem. When conflicts arise between two employees, we tend to assume that the culprit, again, is poor communication. Well, communication isn't necessarily the source of all these problems. It *may* be, but not necessarily!

Communication is a convenient, all-encompassing source of blame for organizational problems. Why? We can offer three possible explanations. First, many people call everything under the sun a communication problem because they find it too painful to confront what is often the real problem—competence. It's difficult to tell someone that he or she is incompetent in doing the job. So we say the person has a communication problem, which is a far less sweeping indictment. Second is the growing credibility problem in organizations. For instance, a recent study found that 61 percent of U.S. employees don't believe that management tells them the truth, and this number has been increasing in recent years.[9] In this distrustful climate, employees aren't likely to believe that management is open or honest in what it says, so what appear to be communication problems develop. Finally, many so-called communication problems are really value differences. Interpersonal conflicts, for example, are often called communication problems but are actually caused by basic differences in beliefs. If a manager believes that fair compensation means tying pay to productivity, but a union member believes that fair compensation means linking pay to seniority, discussions between the two parties may seem to be one of communication problems. In reality, the parties fully understand each other. It's just that they disagree as to what characterizes "fair compensation."

The above shouldn't be construed as suggesting that communication problems aren't real or that they don't create serious problems for managers. Poor communications *do* frequently undermine a manager's or unit's effectiveness. Our point, however, is to emphasize that a lot of dilemmas that masquerade as communication problems are, under closer scrutiny, caused by something else.

Purposeful Miscommunication A basic fact about communication is often overlooked: It is frequently in the interest of one or both parties to a communication to avoid clarity.[10] While rarely admitted in public, most of us recognize that ambiguity in communication has its benefits. Keeping communications fuzzy can cut down on questions, permit faster decision making, minimize objections, reduce opposition, make it easier to deny one's earlier statements, preserve freedom to change one's mind, help to preserve mystique and hide insecurities, allow one to say several things at the same time, permit one to say No diplomatically, and help to avoid confrontation and anxiety.

It is frequently in the interest of one or both parties to a communication to avoid clarity.

If you want to see the fine art of ambiguous communication up close, all you have to do is watch a television interview with a politician who is running for office. The interviewer attempts to get specific information; the politician tries to retain multiple possible interpretations. Such ambiguous communications allow the politician to approach his or her ideal image of being "all things to all people."

Nonverbal Communication Your boss can tell you that his office door is always open and that he wants you to come to him with any problem any time. Yet every time you take him up on his offer he fidgets with his pen, seems to be distracted by papers on his desk, and constantly glances at his watch. Are you getting a different message than the one he verbally conveyed? Probably. What you are experiencing is the power of nonverbal communication. You are learning that actions frequently speak louder (and more accurately) than words. Or, as so aptly put by the industrialist Andrew Carnegie, "As I grow older, I pay less attention to what men say. I just watch what they do."[11]

The telephone, voice mail, e-mail, electronic meetings, faxes, and personal communicators have lessened the importance of nonverbal communication. But the majority of interpersonal communication in organizations still takes place through face-to-face interaction. This means that every verbal message also comes with a nonverbal component. And, if you are going to be an effective communicator, you need to make sure that your verbal and nonverbal messages are in alignment.

Receivers interpret messages by taking in meaning from all channels that are available to them. So when they are communicating face to face with someone, they listen to words, interpret symbols such as appearance, and watch for facial expressions, body positions, eye contact, physical distancing, and other nonverbal cues in their effort to extract meaning.[12] To the degree that your nonverbal cues are consistent with your verbal message, they act to reinforce the message. But when they are inconsistent, they create confusion for the receiver. And, as we noted, most of us tend to put more stock in the nonverbal messages we receive than the words we hear.

Cross-Gender Communication Differences in speech styles are not always related to gender. But there is increasing evidence of general differences between men and women in terms of their conversational styles.[13] And these differences can create real barriers when men and women attempt to communicate with each other.

The most interesting finding is that men use talk to emphasize status, whereas women use it to create connection. You can think of communication as a continual balancing act, juggling the conflicting needs for intimacy and independence. Intimacy emphasizes closeness and commonalities. Independence emphasizes separateness and differences. Interestingly, the sexes tend to give different emphasis to these two forces. Women speak and hear a language of connection and intimacy; men speak and hear a language of status and independence. So, for many men, conversations are primarily a means to preserve independence and maintain status in a hierarchical social order. For many women, conversations are negotiations for closeness in which people try to seek and give confirmation and support.

For example, men frequently complain that women talk on and on about their problems. Women criticize men for not listening. What's happening is that when men hear a problem, they frequently assert their desire for independence and control by offering solutions. Many women, however, view telling a problem as a means to promote closeness. The women present the problem to gain support and connection, not to get the male's advice. Mutual understanding is symmetrical. But giving advice is asymmetrical—it sets the advice giver up as more knowledgeable, more reasonable, and more in control. This attitude contributes to distancing men and women in their efforts to communicate.

Cross-Cultural Communication Effective communication is difficult under the best of conditions. Cross-cultural factors clearly create potential for increased communication problems. Four specific problems have been identified that are related to language difficulties in cross-cultural communications.[14]

First, there are *barriers caused by semantics.* Words mean different things to different people, particularly people from different national cultures. Some words, for instance, don't translate between cultures. Understanding the word *sisu* will help you in communicating with people from Finland, but this word is untranslatable into English. It means something akin to "guts" or "dogged persistence." Similarly, the new capitalists in Russia may have difficulty communicating with their British or Canadian counterparts because English terms such as *efficiency, free market,* and *regulation* are not directly translatable into Russian.

Second, there are *barriers caused by word connotations.* Words imply different things in different languages. Negotiations between American and Japanese executives, for instance, are made more difficult because the Japanese word *hai* translates as "yes," but its connotation may be "yes, I'm listening," rather than "yes, I agree."

Third are *barriers caused by tone differences.* In some cultures, language is formal, in others it's informal. In some cultures, the tone changes depending on the context: People speak differently at home, in social situations, and at work. Using a personal, informal style in a situation where a more formal style is expected can be embarrassing and off-putting.

Fourth, there are *barriers caused by differences among perceptions.* People who speak different languages actually view the world in different ways. Eskimos perceive snow differently from people in milder climates because they have many words for it. Thais perceive "no" differently from Americans because Thais have no such word in their vocabulary.

When communicating with people from different cultures, what can you do to minimize misperceptions, misinterpretations, and misevaluations? Following these four rules can be helpful:[15]

1. Assume differences until similarity is proved. You are far less likely to make an error if you assume that others are different from you rather than assuming they are similar.
2. Emphasize description of what someone has said or done rather than interpretation or evaluation. Interpretations are highly culture-sensitive. So delay judgment until you have had sufficient time to observe and interpret the situation from the differing perspectives of all the cultures involved.
3. Practice empathy. Before sending a message, put yourself in the recipient's shoes. Try to see the other person as he or she really is.
4. Treat your interpretations as a working hypothesis. Once you have developed an explanation for a new situation or think you empathize with someone from a foreign culture, treat your interpretation as a hypothesis that needs further testing rather than as a certainty. And be ready to modify your interpretation as new information arises.

Key Communication Skills

Two of the most important skill elements for effective communication are the ability to be an active listener and the ability to provide feedback. Each of these skills is associated with a set of specific behaviors. In this section, we review those specific behaviors.

Active Listening Most people take listening skills for granted.[16] They confuse hearing with listening. What's the difference? Hearing is merely picking up sound vibrations. Listening is making sense of what we hear. Listening requires paying attention, interpreting, and remembering sound stimuli.

Effective listening is active rather than passive. In passive listening, you are like a tape recorder. You absorb the information given. **Active listening,** in contrast, requires you to "get inside" the speaker's head so that you can understand the communication from his or her point of view.

Listening to customers and employees has helped Ted Kauffman, left, and Jim Berluti grow their Boston-based courier service, Eastern Connection, to annual sales of $27 million. Employees came up with the "Driven to Deliver" motto.

The average person normally speaks at the rate of 125 to 200 words per minute. However, the average listener can comprehend up to 400 words per minute. This difference leaves a lot of time for idle mind wandering while listening. The active listener works to fill in this idle time. The active listener concentrates intensely on what the speaker is saying and tunes out the thousands of miscellaneous thoughts (about money, sex, vacations, parties, friends, bills, getting the car fixed, and the like) that create distractions. As an active listener, you try to understand what the speaker wants to communicate rather than what you want to understand. You also demonstrate acceptance of what is being said. You listen objectively without judging content. Finally, as an active listener, you take responsibility for completeness. You do whatever is necessary to get the full intended meaning from the speaker's communication.

The following eight behaviors are associated with effective active-listening skills. If you want to improve your listening skills, look to these behaviors as guides:

1. *Make eye contact.* How do you feel when somebody doesn't look at you when you're speaking? If you're like most people, you're likely to interpret this behavior as aloofness or lack of interest. We may listen with our ears, but others tend to judge whether we're really listening by looking at our eyes.
2. *Exhibit affirmative head nods and appropriate facial expressions.* The effective listener shows interest in what is being said. How? Through nonverbal signals. Affirmative head nods and appropriate facial expressions, when added to good eye contact, convey to the speaker that you're listening.
3. *Avoid distracting actions or gestures.* The other side of showing interest is avoiding actions that suggest that your mind is somewhere else. When listening, don't look at your watch, shuffle papers, or engage in similar distractions. They make the speaker feel as if you're bored or uninterested. Maybe more important, they indicate that you aren't fully attentive and may be missing part of the message the speaker wants to convey.
4. *Ask questions.* The critical listener analyzes what he or she hears and asks questions. This behavior provides clarification, ensures understanding, and assures the speaker that you're listening.

5. *Paraphrase.* Paraphrasing means restating what the speaker has said in your own words. The active listener uses phrases such as "What I hear you saying is . . ." or "Do you mean . . .?" Why rephrase what has already been said? Two reasons! First, it's an excellent control device to check on whether you're listening carefully. You can't paraphrase accurately if your mind is wandering or if you're thinking about what you're going to say next. Second, it's a control for accuracy. By rephrasing what the speaker has said in your own words and feeding it back to the speaker, you verify the accuracy of your understanding.
6. *Avoid interrupting the speaker.* Let the speaker complete his or her thought before you try to respond. Don't try to second-guess where the speaker's thoughts are going. When the speaker is finished, you'll know it!
7. *Don't overtalk.* Most of us would rather speak our own ideas than listen to what someone else says. Too many of us listen only because it's the price we have to pay to get people to let us talk. Although talking may be more fun and silence may be uncomfortable, you can't talk and listen at the same time. The active listener recognizes this fact and doesn't overtalk.
8. *Make smooth transitions between the roles of speaker and listener.* In most situations, you're continually shifting back and forth between the roles of speaker and listener. The active listener makes transitions smoothly from speaker to listener and back to speaker. From a listening perspective, this means concentrating on what a speaker has to say and practicing not thinking about what you're going to say as soon as you get your chance.

Providing Feedback There are abundant data that indicate that managers do a pretty poor job of providing employees with performance feedback. For instance, a recent survey found that 60 percent of U.S. and European companies identified poor or insufficient performance feedback as a primary cause of deficient employee performance—by far the highest percentage of any response in the study.[17]

We can make six specific suggestions to help you be more effective in providing feedback.[18] Since our focus is on management, these suggestions, for the most part, are directed at performance issues in work situations. However, you can modify them to improve feedback on any type of communication.

1. *Focus on specific behaviors.* Feedback should be specific rather than general. Avoid such statements as "You have a bad attitude" or "I'm really impressed with the good job you did." They are vague, and, although they do provide information, they do not tell the recipient enough to correct the "bad attitude" or *on what basis* you concluded that a "good job" had been done.

   Suppose you said something like, "Todd, I'm concerned with your attitude toward your work. You were a half-hour late to yesterday's staff meeting and then told me you hadn't read the preliminary report we were discussing. Today you tell me you're taking off 3 hours early for a dental appointment." Or, "Laura, I was really pleased with the job you did on the Phillips account. They increased their purchases from us by 22 percent last month, and I got a call a few days ago from Dan Phillips complimenting me on how quickly you responded to those specification changes for the MJ-4 microchip." Both of these statements focus on specific behaviors. They tell the recipient *why* you are being critical or complimentary.
2. *Keep feedback impersonal.* Feedback, particularly the negative variety, should be descriptive rather than judgmental or evaluative. No matter how upset you are, keep the feedback job-related and never criticize someone personally because of an inappropriate action. Telling people they're "stupid," "incompetent," or the like is almost always counterproductive. It provokes such an emotional reaction that the performance deviation itself is apt to be overlooked. When you are criticizing, remember that you are censuring a job-related behavior, not the person. You might

BUILDING SELF-AWARENESS • BUILDING SELF-AWARENESS

WHAT IS YOUR UNDERLYING CONFLICT-HANDLING STYLE?

INSTRUCTIONS Indicate how often you rely on each of the following tactics by circling the number that you feel is most appropriate.

	Rarely				Always
1. I argue my case with my co-workers to show the merits of my position.	1	2	3	4	5
2. I negotiate with my co-workers so that a compromise can be reached.	1	2	3	4	5
3. I try to satisfy the expectations of my co-workers.	1	2	3	4	5
4. I try to investigate an issue with my co-workers to find a solution acceptable to us.	1	2	3	4	5
5. I am firm in pursuing my side of the issue.	1	2	3	4	5
6. I attempt to avoid being "put on the spot" and try to keep my conflict with my co-workers to myself.	1	2	3	4	5
7. I hold on to my solution to a problem.	1	2	3	4	5
8. I use "give and take" so that a compromise can be made.	1	2	3	4	5
9. I exchange accurate information with my co-workers to solve a problem together.	1	2	3	4	5
10. I avoid open discussion of my differences with my co-workers.	1	2	3	4	5
11. I accommodate the wishes of my co-workers.	1	2	3	4	5
12. I try to bring all our concerns out in the open so that the issues can be resolved in the best possible way.	1	2	3	4	5
13. I propose a middle ground for breaking deadlocks.	1	2	3	4	5
14. I go along with the suggestions of my co-workers.	1	2	3	4	5
15. I try to keep my disagreements with my co-workers to myself in order to avoid hard feelings.	1	2	3	4	5

Turn to page 562 for scoring directions and key.

***Source:* This is an abbreviated version of a thirty-five-item instrument described in M. A. Rahim, "A Measure of Styles of Handling Interpersonal Conflict," *Academy of Management Journal,* June 1983, pp. 368–76.**

Evaluate the Conflict Players If you choose to manage a conflict situation, it's important that you take the time to get to know the players. Who is involved in the conflict? What interests does each party represent? What are the players' values, personalities, feelings, and resources? Your chances of success in managing a conflict will be greatly enhanced if you can view the conflict situation through the eyes of the conflicting parties.

Assess the Source of the Conflict Conflicts don't pop out of thin air. They have causes. Because your approach to resolving a conflict is likely to be determined largely by its causes, you need to determine the source of the conflict. Sources of conflict can generally be separated into three categories: communication differences, structural differences, and personal differences.[25]

Communication differences are disagreements arising from semantic difficulties, misunderstandings, and noise in the communication channels. People are often quick to assume that most conflicts are caused by lack of communication, but there is usually plenty of communication going on in most conflicts. The mistake many people make is equating good communication with having others agree with their views. As noted earlier in this chapter, what might at first look like an interpersonal conflict based on poor communication is usually found, upon closer analysis, to be a disagreement caused by different value systems, role requirements, unit goals, personalities, or other factors. As a source of conflict for managers, poor communication probably gets more attention than it deserves.

As we discussed in Chapter 7, organizations are typically horizontally differentiated through specialization and departmentalization and vertically differentiated by creation of management levels. This *structural differentiation* creates problems of integration. The frequent result is conflict. Individuals disagree over goals, responsibilities, decision alternatives, performance criteria, and resource allocations. These conflicts are not due to poor communication or personal animosities. Rather, they are rooted in the structure of the organization itself.

The third conflict source is *personal differences*. Conflicts can evolve out of individual idiosyncrasies and personal value systems. The chemistry between some people makes it hard for them to work together. Factors such as background, education, experience, and training mold each individual into a unique personality with a particular set of values. The result is people who may be perceived by others as abrasive, untrustworthy, strange, or difficult to work with. These personal differences can create conflict.

Know Your Options What resolution tools or techniques can a manager call upon to reduce conflict when it's too high? Managers essentially can draw upon five conflict resolution options: avoidance, accommodation, forcing, compromise, and collaboration.[26] Each has particular strengths and weaknesses, and no one option is ideal for every situation. You should consider each a "tool" in your conflict management "tool chest." You will have a preferred style and might be better at using some tools than others, but the skilled manager knows what each tool can do and when each is likely to be most effective.

As previously noted, not every conflict requires an assertive action. Sometimes **avoidance**—just withdrawing from or suppressing the conflict—is the best solution. When is avoidance a desirable strategy? When the conflict is trivial, when emotions are running high and time is needed to cool them down, or when the potential disruption from a more assertive action outweighs the benefits of resolution.

The goal of **accommodation** is to maintain harmonious relationships by placing another's needs and concerns above your own. You might, for example, yield to another person's position on an issue. This option is most viable when the issue under dispute isn't that important to you or when you want to build up credits for later issues.

In **forcing,** you attempt to satisfy your own needs at the expense of the other party. In organizations this is most often illustrated by a manager's using his or her formal authority to resolve a dispute. Forcing works well when you need a quick resolution on important issues, when unpopular actions must be taken, and when commitment by others to your solution is not critical.

A **compromise** requires each party to give up something of value. Typically this is the approach taken by management and labor in negotiating a new labor contract. Compromise can be an optimum strategy when conflicting parties are about equal in power, when it is desirable to achieve a temporary solution to a complex issue, or when time pressures demand an expedient solution.

Collaboration is the ultimate win-win solution. All parties to the conflict seek to satisfy their interests. It is typically characterized by open and honest discussion among the parties, active listening to understand differences, and careful deliberation over a full range of alternatives to find a solution that is advantageous to all. When is collaboration the best conflict option? When time pressures are minimal, when all parties seriously want a win-win solution, and when the issue is too important to be compromised.

Don't Forget about Conflict Stimulation

What about the other side of conflict management—situations that require managers to *stimulate* conflict? The notion of stimulating conflict is often difficult to accept. For almost all of us the term *conflict* has a negative connotation, and the idea of purposely creating conflict seems to be the antithesis of good management. Few of us personally enjoy being in conflict situations. Yet the evidence demonstrates that there are situations in which an increase in conflict is constructive.[27] Given this reality and the fact that there is no clear demarcation between "good" conflicts and "bad" ones, we have listed in Exhibit 16-2 a set of questions that might help you. Although there is no definitive method of assessing the need for more conflict, an affirmative answer to one or more of the questions in Exhibit 16-2 suggests a need for conflict stimulation.

We know a lot more about resolving conflict than about stimulating it. That's only natural, since human beings have been concerned with the subject of conflict reduction for hundreds, maybe thousands, of years. The dearth of ideas on conflict stimulation techniques reflects the relatively recent interest in the subject. The following are some preliminary suggestions that managers might want to utilize.[28]

Change the Organization's Culture The initial step in stimulating conflict is for managers to convey to subordinates the message, supported by actions, that conflict has its legitimate place. Individuals who challenge the status quo, suggest innovative ideas, offer divergent opinions, and demonstrate original thinking need to be rewarded visibly with recognition, promotions, salary increases, and other positive reinforcers.

EXHIBIT 16-2
Is Conflict Stimulation Needed?*

1. Are you surrounded by "yes" people?
2. Are subordinates afraid to admit ignorance and uncertainties to you?
3. Is there so much concentration by managers on reaching a compromise that they lose sight of values, long-term objectives, or the organization's welfare?
4. Do managers believe that it's in their best interest to maintain the impression of peace and cooperation in their unit, regardless of the price?
5. Is there an excessive concern by decision makers for not hurting the feelings of others?
6. Do managers believe that popularity is more important for obtaining organizational rewards than competence and high performance?
7. Are managers unduly enamored of obtaining consensus for their decisions?
8. Do employees show unusually high resistance to change?
9. Is there a lack of new ideas?
10. Is there an unusually low level of employee turnover?

Source: From S. P. Robbins, "'Conflict Management' and 'Conflict Resolution' Are Not Synonymous Terms," *California Management Review,* Winter 1978, p. 71. Copyright 1978 by The Regents of the University of California. Reprinted from *California Management Review,* Vol. 21, No. 2. By permission of The Regents.

*An affirmative answer to any or all of these questions suggests the need for conflict stimulation.

Use Communication In the United States, as far back as Franklin Roosevelt's administration (in the 1930s), and probably before, the White House consistently has used communication to stimulate conflict. Senior officials "plant" possible decisions with the media through the infamous "reliable source" route. For example, the name of a prominent judge is "leaked" as a possible Supreme Court appointment. If the candidate survives the public scrutiny, his or her appointment will be announced by the president. However, if the candidate is found lacking by the media and public, the president's press secretary or other high-level official will make a formal statement such as, "At no time was this candidate under consideration." Regardless of party affiliation, occupants of the White House have regularly used the reliable source as a conflict stimulation technique. It's all the more popular because of its handy escape mechanism. If the conflict level gets too high, the source can be denied and eliminated.

Ambiguous or threatening messages also encourage conflict. Information that a plant might close, that a department is likely to be eliminated, or that a layoff is imminent can reduce apathy, stimulate new ideas, and force reevaluation—all positive outcomes that result from increased conflict.

Another way communication can stimulate conflict is to draw attention to differences of opinion that individuals themselves didn't previously recognize. People often cover up or sublimate potential differences in order to "keep the peace." When these differences are overtly addressed, parties are forced to confront conflicts.

Bring in Outsiders A widely used method for shaking up a stagnant unit or organization is to bring in—either by hiring from outside or by internal transfer—individuals whose backgrounds, values, attitudes, or managerial styles differ from those of present members. Many large corporations have used this technique during the last several decades in filling vacancies on their boards of directors. Women, minority group members, consumer activists, and others whose backgrounds and interests differ significantly from those of the rest of the board have been purposely selected to add a fresh perspective.

Restructure the Organization We know that structural variables are a source of conflict. It is therefore only logical that managers look to structure as a conflict stimulation technique. Centralizing decisions, realigning work groups, introducing teams into a highly individualistic culture, increasing formalization, and increasing interdependencies between units are all structural devices that disrupt the status quo and can act to increase conflict levels.

Appoint a Devil's Advocate A **devil's advocate** is a person who purposely presents arguments that run counter to those proposed by the majority or against current practices. He or she plays the role of the critic, even to the point of arguing against positions with which he or she actually agrees.

A devil's advocate acts as a check against groupthink and practices that have no better justification than "that's the way we've always done it around here." When thoughtfully listened to, the advocate can improve the quality of group decision making. On the other hand, others in the group often view advocates as time wasters, and their appointment is almost certain to delay any decision process.

NEGOTIATION SKILLS

Managers often need to negotiate. For instance, they may have to negotiate salaries for incoming employees, cut deals with superiors, work out differences with associates, and resolve conflicts with subordinates. For our purposes, we'll

Managers find themselves engaged in negotiation almost on a daily basis. This photo pictures the closing of a long and formal bargaining process between representatives of management and a group of investment bankers. Most negotiations that managers participate in, however, are much more informal; conducted with subordinates, peers, or bosses; and resolved in minutes rather than days.

define **negotiation** as a process in which two or more parties exchange goods or services and attempt to agree on the exchange rate for them.[29] Note that we use the terms *negotiation* and *bargaining* interchangeably.

Bargaining Strategies

There are two general approaches to negotiation—*distributive bargaining* and *integrative bargaining*.[30] These are compared in Exhibit 16-3.

Distributive Bargaining You see a used car advertised for sale in the newspaper. It appears to be just what you've been looking for. You go out to see the car. It's great and you want it. The owner tells you the asking price. You don't want to pay that much. The two of you then negotiate over the price. The negotiating strategy you're engaging in is called **distributive bargaining.** Its most identifying feature is that it operates under zero-sum conditions. That is, any gain I make is at

EXHIBIT 16-3
Distributive vs. Integrative Bargaining

Bargaining Characteristic	Distributive Bargaining	Integrative Bargaining
Available resources	Fixed amount of resources to be divided	Variable amount of resources to be divided
Primary motivations	I win, you lose	I win, you win
Primary interests	Opposed to each other	Convergent or congruent with each other
Focus of relationships	Short-term	Long-term

Source: Based on R. J. Lewicki and J. A. Litterer, *Negotiation* (Homewood, Ill.: Irwin, 1985), p. 280.

your expense, and vice versa. Referring to the used car example, every dollar you can get the seller to cut from the car's price is a dollar you save. Conversely, every dollar more he can get from you comes at your expense. So the essence of distributive bargaining is negotiating over who gets what share of a fixed pie.

Probably the most widely cited example of distributive bargaining is in labor-management negotiations over wages. Typically, labor's representatives come to the bargaining table determined to get as much money as possible out of management. Since every cent more that labor negotiates increases management's costs, each party bargains aggressively and treats the other as an opponent who must be defeated.

The essence of distributive bargaining is depicted in Exhibit 16-4. Parties A and B represent two negotiators. Each has a *target point* that defines what he or she would like to achieve. Each also has a *resistance point,* which marks the lowest outcome that is acceptable—the point below which they would break off negotiations rather than accept a less-favorable settlement. The area between these two points makes up the aspiration range of each. As long as there is some overlap between A and B's aspiration ranges, there exists a settlement range where each one's aspirations can be met.

When engaged in distributive bargaining, your negotiation tactics should focus on trying to get your opponent to agree to your specific target point or to get as close to it as possible. Examples of such tactics are persuading your opponent of the impossibility of getting to his or her target point and the advisability of accepting a settlement near yours; arguing that your target is fair, while your opponent's isn't; and attempting to get your opponent to feel emotionally generous toward you and thus accept an outcome close to your target point.

Integrative Bargaining A sales representative for a women's sportswear manufacturer has just closed a $15,000 order from a small clothing retailer. The sales rep calls in the order to her firm's credit department. She is told that the firm can't approve credit to this customer because of a past slow-pay record. The next day, the sales rep and the firm's credit manager meet to discuss the problem. The sales rep doesn't want to lose the business. Neither does the credit manager, but he also doesn't want to get stuck with an uncollectible debt. The two openly review their options. After considerable discussion, they agree on a solution that meets both their needs: The credit manager will approve the sale, but the clothing store's owner will provide a bank guarantee that will assure payment if the bill isn't paid within 60 days.

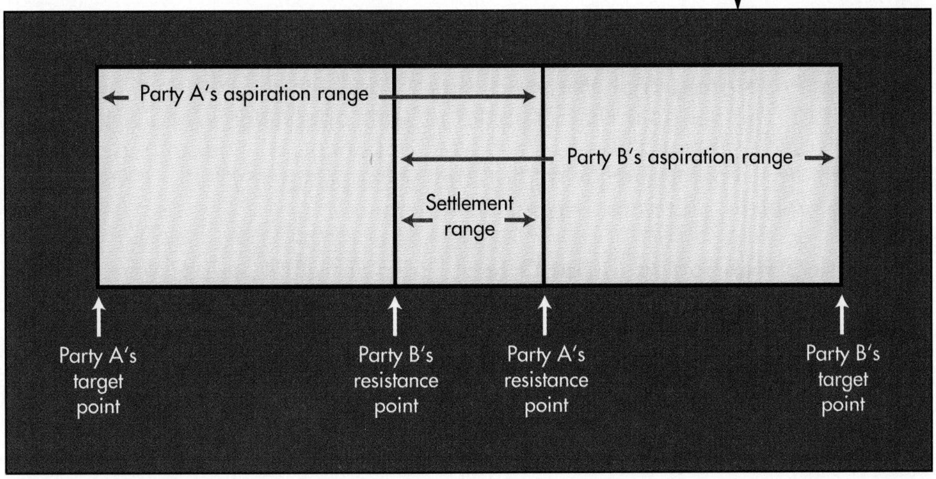

EXHIBIT 16-4
Staking Out the Bargaining Zone

This sales–credit negotiation is an example of **integrative bargaining.** In contrast to distributive bargaining, integrative problem solving operates under the assumption that there exists one or more settlements that can create a win-win solution.

In general, integrative bargaining is preferable to distributive bargaining. Why? Because it builds long-term relationships and facilitates working together in the future. It bonds negotiators and allows each to leave the bargaining table feeling that he or she has achieved a victory. Distributive bargaining, in contrast, leaves one party a loser. It tends to build animosities and deepen divisions when people have to work together on an ongoing basis.

Why, then, don't we see more integrative bargaining in organizations? The answer lies in the conditions necessary for this type of negotiation to succeed. These conditions include parties who are open with information and candid about their concerns, a sensitivity by both parties to the other's needs, the ability to trust one another, and a willingness by both parties to maintain flexibility.[31] Because many organizational cultures and interpersonal relationships aren't characterized by openness, trust, and flexibility, it is not surprising that negotiations often take the approach of "win-at-any-cost."

Developing Effective Negotiation Skills

The essence of effective negotiation can be summarized in the following seven recommendations.[32]

Research Your Opponent Jerry Anderson, president of Apogee Enterprises, a Minneapolis-based architectural-glass fabricator, is constantly negotiating with architects, engineers, and building contractors—three groups whose agendas clash more often than not. Yet he's consistently successful at reaching a consensus.[33] He attributes a large amount of his success to forethought. "Always try to figure out where the other guy is coming from," he says. "If you think enough about it, you can usually come up with a reading."

Start negotiations by acquiring as much information as you can about your opponent's interests and goals. What constituencies must he or she appease? What is his or her strategy? Understanding your opponent's position will help you to better understand his or her behavior, to predict his or her responses to your offers, and to frame solutions in terms of his or her interests.

Begin with a Positive Overture A substantial amount of evidence shows that concessions tend to be reciprocated and lead to agreements. So begin bargaining with a positive overture—perhaps a minor concession—and then reciprocate your opponent's concessions.

Address Problems, Not Personalities Concentrate on the negotiation issues, not on the personal characteristics of your opponent. When negotiations get tough, avoid the tendency to attack your opponent. It's your opponent's ideas or position that you disagree with, not him or her personally. Separate the people from the problem, and don't personalize differences.

Pay Little Attention to Initial Offers Treat an initial offer as merely a point of departure. Everyone has to have an initial position. Such positions tend to be extreme and idealistic. Treat them as such.

Emphasize Win-Win Solutions Inexperienced negotiators often assume that their gain must come at the expense of the other party. As noted with integrative bargaining, that needn't be the case. There are often win-win solutions. But assuming a zero-sum game means missed opportunities for trade-offs that could benefit both sides. So if conditions are supportive, look for an integrative solution. Frame options in terms of your opponent's interests and look for solutions that can allow your opponent, as well as yourself, to declare a victory.

Create an Open and Trusting Climate Skilled negotiators are good listeners, ask questions, focus their arguments directly, are not defensive, and have learned to avoid words and phrases that can irritate an opponent (e.g., "generous offer," "fair price," "reasonable arrangement"). In other words, they are adept at creating the open and trusting climate necessary for reaching an integrative settlement.

Be Open to Accepting Third-Party Assistance When stalemates are reached, consider using a neutral third party. *Mediators* can help parties come to an agreement, but they don't impose a settlement. *Arbitrators* hear both sides of the dispute and then impose a solution. *Conciliators* are more informal and act as a communication conduit, passing information between the parties, interpreting messages, and clarifying misunderstandings.

DELEGATION SKILLS

Managers get things done through other people. This statement recognizes that there are limits to any manager's time and knowledge. Effective managers, therefore, need to understand the value of delegating and know how to do it.[34]

What Is Delegation?

Delegation is the assignment of authority to another person to carry out specific activities. It allows a subordinate to make decisions—that is, it is a shift of decision-making authority from one organizational level to another, lower one.[35]

Delegation should not be confused with participation. In participative decision making, there is a sharing of authority. With delegation, subordinates make decisions on their own.

Barriers to Delegation

Many managers, especially inexperienced ones and those new to the managerial ranks, have a tough time delegating. They would rather do the work themselves, then complain about how overworked they are. Why don't managers delegate more often? Five reasons have been suggested:[36]

> **Many managers, especially inexperienced ones and those new to the managerial ranks, have a tough time delegating.**

1. Managers think they are giving up power and control when they delegate. But they aren't. By delegating, managers increase their influence through their employees' efforts. Managers who delegate widen their span of control, and by doing so ultimately have more people reporting to them and become more powerful.
2. A lot of managers think delegation is abdication. When properly done, it isn't. The key word here is *properly.* If a manager dumps tasks on a subordinate without clarifying the exact job to be done, the range of the subordinate's discretion, the expected level of performance, the time the tasks are to be completed, and similar concerns, he or she is abdicating responsibility and inviting trouble. Proper delegation also includes establishing controls that will quickly advise the manager if a subordinate acts outside his or her delegated authority.
3. Many managers lack confidence in their subordinates or fear that they will be criticized for their subordinates' mistakes. So they try to do everything themselves.

It's often true that a manager is capable of doing tasks better, faster, or with fewer mistakes. The catch is that a manager's time and energy are limited. It is not possible for managers to do everything themselves. What effective managers do is determine the acceptable level of performance in a task, then delegate that task to someone who can achieve that level. And they accept some mistakes by their subordinates. Mistakes are part of delegation. As long as their costs aren't excessive, mistakes are often good learning experiences for subordinates.

4. Many managers tend to do those things that are interesting, quick, and easy. They take the "fun tasks" for themselves. Ironically, these are the tasks that often are easiest to delegate. If a manager insists on doing all the interesting or easy tasks, he or she will never get to the important work managers are supposed to be doing.
5. A lot of managers are insecure and fear that delegation could undermine their own job. They think that if they delegate important tasks to their subordinates, those subordinates will become better skilled, more experienced, and eventually steal their jobs from them. Quite the contrary is typically true. The best managers, and the ones who get promoted fastest, are often the ones who build a reputation for developing the people below them.

Developing Effective Delegating Skills

If you're a manager and want to delegate some of your authority to someone else, how do you go about it? The following summarizes the primary steps you need to take.[37]

Clarify the Assignment The place to begin is to determine *what* is to be delegated and to *whom*. You need to identify the person best capable of doing the task, then determine if he or she has the time and motivation to do the job.

Assuming you have a willing and able subordinate, it is your responsibility to provide clear information on what is being delegated, the results you expect, and any time or performance expectations you hold.

Unless there is an overriding need to adhere to specific methods, you should delegate only the end results. That is, get agreement on what is to be done and the end results expected, but let the subordinate decide on the means.

Are there any activities that managers should *never* delegate? Yes![38] Don't delegate feedback. Feedback should be given only by the direct manager. Don't delegate disciplinary action. Reprimands, suspensions, dismissals, and similar disciplinary actions should be made and conveyed by the direct manager. And never delegate politically sensitive matters. It's not fair to subordinates to burden them with decisions that are certain to be highly controversial.

Specify the Subordinate's Range of Discretion Every act of delegation comes with constraints. You are delegating authority to act, but not *unlimited* authority. What you are delegating is authority to act on certain issues and, on those issues, within certain parameters. You need to specify what those parameters are so that subordinates know, in no uncertain terms, the range of their discretion. When this has been successfully communicated, both you and the subordinate will have the same idea of the limits to the latter's authority and how far he or she can go without further approval.

Allow the Subordinate to Participate One of the best sources for determining how much authority will be necessary to accomplish a task is the subordinate who will be held accountable for that task. If you allow employees to participate in determining what is delegated, how much authority is needed to get the job done, and the standards by which they'll be judged, you increase employee motivation, satisfaction, and accountability for performance.

Be aware, however, that participation can present its own set of potential problems as a result of subordinates' self-interest and biases in evaluating their own abilities. Some subordinates might be personally motivated to expand their authority beyond what they need and beyond what they are capable of handling. Allowing such people too much participation in deciding what tasks they should take on and how much authority they must have to complete those tasks can undermine the effectiveness of the delegation process.

Inform Others That Delegation Has Occurred Delegation should not take place in a vacuum. Not only do you and the subordinate need to know specifically what has been delegated and how much authority has been granted, but anyone else who may be affected by the delegation act also needs to be informed. The people affected include those outside the organization as well as those inside it. Essentially, you need to convey what has been delegated (the task and the amount of authority) and to whom. Failure to inform others makes conflict likely and decreases the chances that your subordinate will be able to accomplish the delegated task efficiently.

When Problems Surface, Insist on Recommendations from the Subordinate Many managers fall into the trap of letting subordinates reverse the delegation process: The subordinate runs into a problem and then comes back to the manager for advice or a solution. Avoid being sucked into reverse delegation by insisting from the beginning that when subordinates want to discuss a problem with you, they come prepared with a recommendation. When you delegate downward, the subordinate's job includes making necessary decisions. Don't allow the subordinate to push decisions back upward to you.

Establish Feedback Controls To delegate without instituting feedback controls is to invite problems. There is always the possibility that a subordinate will misuse the discretion that he or she has been delegated. The establishment of controls to monitor the subordinate's progress increases the likelihood that important problems or expensive mistakes will be identified early and that the task will be completed on time and to the desired performance level.

Ideally, controls should be determined at the time of the initial assignment. Agree on a specific time for completion of the task and then set progress dates when the subordinate will report back on how well he or she is doing and any major problems that have surfaced. These controls can be supplemented with periodic spot checks to ensure that authority guidelines are not being abused, organization policies are being followed, proper procedures are being met, and the like.

Too much of a good thing can be dysfunctional. If the controls are too constraining, the subordinate will be deprived of the opportunity to build self-confidence and much of the motivational aspect of delegation will be lost. A well-designed control system permits your subordinates to make small mistakes but quickly alerts you when big mistakes are imminent.

COUNSELING SKILLS

Counseling is discussion of a problem (usually one with emotional content) with an employee in order to resolve the problem or, at a minimum, to help the employee to cope with it better.[39] Examples of problems that might require you to counsel an employee include divorce, serious illness, difficulty in getting along with a co-worker, a drinking problem affecting work performance, or frustration over a lack of career progress in the organization.

A manager (right), engaged in participative counseling, helps an employee deal with personal problems that are adversely affecting her job performance.

Counseling is not the same thing as *coaching*. Coaching, as discussed in the preceding chapter, addresses ability issues. As a coach, you provide instruction, guidance, advice, and encouragement to help employees improve their job performance. Counseling deals with personal problems. When employee personality or attitudes are the problem, you need to provide counseling.

Types of Counseling How much direction should a manager provide during a counseling session? The answer to this question reveals three types of counseling: directive, participative, and nondirective. As you move to the right along the continuum shown in Exhibit 16-5, you will find yourself doing more of the talking and taking a more assertive role in solving the problem.

Directive Counseling Historically, many managers used **directive counseling.** They listened to employee problems, decided what should be done, and then told employees what to do. In directive counseling, the manager is in control. However, directive counseling has fallen out of favor in recent years. It assumes that managers fully understand the employee's problem, the options, and what is best for the employee. Clearly, these assumptions are unrealistic. And even if they were realistic, a manager's telling employees what they should do is no guarantee that they will follow that manager's advice. Most employees today prefer to have a say in decisions that directly affect them. They don't look kindly on managers

EXHIBIT 16-5
Three Types of Counseling

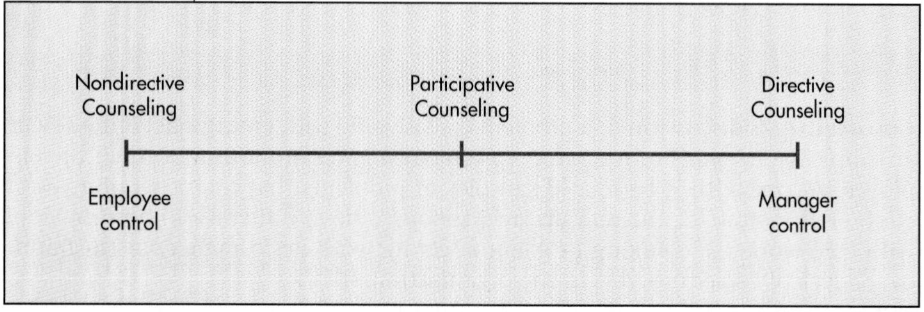

who tell them what they should do. When confronted by such a boss, they aren't likely to accept his or her advice with much enthusiasm or conviction.

Nondirective Counseling Whereas directive counseling gives control to the manager, nondirective counseling puts control in the hands of the employee. That is why the latter is also known as client-centered counseling.[40]

Nondirective counseling is based on the belief that people can solve their own problems with the aid of a sympathetic listener. The manager listens, repeats, synthesizes, understands, and gives feedback; however, the employee determines the alternatives and makes the decision. Most important, the manager avoids passing judgment.

When an employee is frustrated, nondirective counseling can help in two ways: First, the employee has the opportunity to vent frustrations; second, when frustrations are not reduced, the employee can still improve his or her ability to adjust to the problems when they are stated and listened to and solutions are formulated.

Participative Counseling The middle ground between the two extremes of directive and nondirective counseling is called **participative counseling.** In this approach, the manager is an active listener but plays a more assertive role than in nondirective counseling by offering insights and advice. For example, because of the knowledge and experience you have acquired, you can often discuss the situation from a broader perspective and give your employee a different view of the problem.

In terms of management practice, the participative approach tends to be more widely used nowadays than either directive or nondirective counseling. Directive counseling has become increasingly inconsistent with the needs of today's employees and the values of today's organization. And nondirective counseling ignores the insights that an experienced manager can contribute as a result of his or her knowledge of the organization. Participative counseling fills an important place in the 1990s because it is consistent with the view that managers empower their people rather than boss them.

Effective Counseling Skills

The following twelve points provide you with specific guidelines to make you more effective in counseling employees.[41]

1. *Create a nonthreatening and supportive atmosphere for discussion.* The first thing you need to do is create a climate in which the employee will be comfortable and that will encourage him or her to be open and honest. Pick a time and place that provides privacy and where you won't be interrupted. Then greet the employee in a friendly and open manner.
2. *Emphasize confidentiality.* Convey early in the counseling session that everything the employee says will be treated in confidence. Effective counseling requires that the employee trust you.
3. *Listen patiently.* Listen to what the employee has to say before making any comments on your own.
4. *Avoid offering hasty advice.* Hold your tongue. Let the employee get his or her concerns and frustrations out on the table.
5. *Use your active-listening skills.* Paraphrase. Ask questions such as "Tell me about . . ." Avoid questions that can be answered with a mere Yes or No. Watch for negative nonverbal messages. And don't interrogate the employee.
6. *Provide supportive responses.* Show empathy rather than sympathy. By your comments and gestures, show your support and concern. Withhold criticism. Don't argue with the employee, even if you disagree with what he or she is saying. And

display confidence in the employee. Show that you believe that he or she can solve the problem.

7. *Focus on job performance expectations.* The purpose of the counseling session is to deal with some problem or problems that are affecting the employee's job performance. Keep the focus on those attitudes or behaviors that are undesirable. Don't pry into your employee's personal life. And don't moralize. Explain in very specific terms your job performance expectations.
8. *Help the employee to identify and articulate the problem.* It is not your role to define the problem. You should focus on job expectations. Make the employee responsible for identifying the problem. Don't allow yourself to be distracted or swayed by emotional pleas or hard-luck stories.
9. *Help the employee to look at several alternatives for solving the problem.* Individuals frequently limit their search for alternatives. In many cases, they quickly focus on a single option and discontinue the search for other alternatives. Encourage the employee to search for a wide range of possible solutions to his or her problem.
10. *Don't solve the problem for the employee.* It is the employee's problem, and he or she needs to take responsibility for it. If you provide a solution, the employee is not likely to accept ownership for it. Moreover, if your solution doesn't work out, you are the natural person for the employee to blame.
11. *Encourage the employee to articulate an action plan.* Conclude the counseling session by encouraging the employee to describe, in clear and specific language, the course of action he or she plans to take to solve the problem.
12. *Refer problems that are beyond your expertise.* You are not a trained therapist. Severe emotional or behavioral problems should be referred to a professional.

POLITICKING SKILLS

In the real world of organizations, the "good guys" don't always win. Demonstrating openness, trust, objectivity, support, and similar humane qualities in relationships with others doesn't always lead to improved managerial effectiveness. There will be times when, to get the resources you want or to have decisions go your way, you will need to engage in politics. This section can help you develop your politicking skills.

What Is Politicking?

Politicking is the actions you can take to influence, or attempt to influence, the distribution of advantages and disadvantages within your organization.

Politics is related to who gets what, when, and how. **Politicking** is the actions you can take to influence, or attempt to influence, the distribution of advantages and disadvantages within your organization.[42]

Politics is closely intertwined with the concept of power. When managers (or any organizational members, for that matter) convert their power into action, they are engaging in politics. Those with good political skills have the ability to use their power bases effectively.

Why Is There Politics in Organizations?

Can you conceive of an organization that is politics-free? It's possible, but not likely. Organizations are made up of individuals and groups with different values, goals, and interests. Therefore they have the potential for conflict over resources.

Department budgets, space allocations, project responsibilities, and salary adjustments are just a few examples of the resources about whose allocation organizational members will disagree.

Resources in organizations are also limited, so potential conflict often turns into real conflict. If resources were abundant, then all the various internal constituencies within the organization could satisfy their goals. But because resources are limited, not everyone's interests can be provided for. Further, whether true or not, gains by one individual or group are often *perceived* as being at the expense of others within the organization. These factors create a competition among members for the organization's limited resources.

Maybe the most important factor leading to politics within organizations is the realization that most of the "facts" that are used to allocate the limited resources are open to interpretation. What, for instance, is *good* performance? What's a *good* job? What's an *adequate* improvement? The manager of any major league baseball team knows that a .400 hitter is a high performer and a .125 hitter is a poor performer. You don't need to be a baseball genius to know that you should play your .400 hitter and send the .125 hitter back to the minors. But what if you have to choose between players who hit .280 and .290? Then other factors—less objective ones—come into play: fielding, attitude, potential, ability to perform in the clutch, and so on. Most managerial decisions in organizations more closely resemble choosing between a .280 and a .290 hitter than deciding between a .125 hitter and a .400 hitter. It's in this large and ambiguous middle ground of organizational life—where the facts *don't* speak for themselves—that politics takes place.

Finally, because most decisions have to be made in a climate of ambiguity—where facts are rarely fully objective, and thus are open to interpretation—people within organizations will use whatever influence they can to taint the facts to support their goals and interests. That tendency, of course, creates the activities we call *politicking.*

Effective Politicking Skills

Forget, for a moment, the ethics of politicking and any negative impressions you may have of people who engage in organizational politics. If you wanted to be more politically adept in your organization, what could you do? The following suggestions are likely to improve your political effectiveness.[43]

Frame Arguments in Terms of Organizational Goals Effective politicking requires covering up self-interest. No matter that your objective is self-serving; all the arguments you marshal in support of it must be framed in terms of the benefits that will accrue to the organization. People whose actions appear to blatantly further their own interests at the expense of the organization's are almost universally denounced, are likely to lose influence, and often suffer the ultimate penalty of being expelled from the organization.

Develop the Right Image If you know your organization's culture, you understand what the organization wants and values from its managers—in terms of dress, associates to cultivate and those to avoid, whether to appear to be risk-taking or risk-aversive, the preferred leadership style, the importance placed on getting along with others, and so forth. Then you are equipped to project the appropriate image.

Because effectiveness in an organization is not a fully objective outcome, style as well as substance must be attended to. **Impression management**—that is, attempting to shape the image you project during an interaction—is an important part of political success.[44] People who are good at impression management tend to favorably shape how others see and evaluate them. Exhibit 16-6 summarizes some impression management techniques and provides an example of each.

EXHIBIT 16-6
Impression Management Techniques

Conformity Agreeing with someone else's opinion in order to gain his or her approval.

Example: A manager tells his boss, "You're absolutely right on your reorganization plan for the western regional office. I couldn't agree with you more."

Excuses Explanations of a predicament-creating event aimed at minimizing the apparent severity of the predicament.

Example: Sales manager to boss, "We failed to get the ad in the paper on time, but no one responds to those ads anyway."

Apologies Admitting responsibility for an undesirable event and simultaneously seeking to get a pardon for the action.

Example: Employee to boss, "I'm sorry I made a mistake on the report. Please forgive me."

Acclaiming Explanation of favorable events to maximize the desirable implications for oneself.

Example: A salesperson informs a peer, "The sales in our division have nearly tripled since I was hired."

Flattery Complimenting others about their virtues in an effort to make oneself appear perceptive and likable.

Example: New sales trainee to peer, "You handled that client's complaint so tactfully! I could never have handled that as well as you did."

Favors Doing something nice for someone to gain that person's approval.

Example: Salesperson to prospective client, "I've got two tickets to the theater tonight that I can't use. Take them. Consider it a thank-you for taking the time to talk with me."

Association Enhancing or protecting one's image by managing information about people and things with which one is associated.

Example: A job applicant says to an interviewer, "What a coincidence. Your boss and I were roommates in college."

Sources: Based on B. R. Schlenker, *Impression Management: The Self-Concept, Social Identity, and Interpersonal Relations* (Monterey, Calif.: Brooks/Cole, 1980); W. L. Gardner and M. J. Martinko, "Impression Management in Organizations," *Journal of Management,* June 1988, p. 332; and R. B. Cialdini, "Indirect Tactics of Image Management: Beyond Basking," in R. A. Giacalone and P. Rosenfeld, eds., *Impression Management in the Organization* (Hillsdale, N.J.: Lawrence Erlbaum Associates, 1989), pp. 45–71.

Gain Control of Organizational Resources The control of organizational resources that are scarce and important is a source of power. Knowledge and expertise are particularly effective resources to control. They make you more valuable to the organization and therefore more likely to gain security, advancement, and a receptive audience for your ideas.

Make Yourself Appear Indispensable Since we are dealing with appearances rather than objective facts, you can enhance your power by appearing to be indispensable. That is, you don't have to really be indispensable as long as key people in the organization believe that you are. If the upper management believes that there is no ready substitute for what you are giving the organization, they are likely to go to great lengths to ensure that your desires are satisfied. How do you make yourself appear indispensable? The most effective means is to develop expertise through experience, contacts, secret techniques, natural talents, and the like—that is, attributes that are perceived as critical to the organization's operations and that upper management believes no one else possesses to the extent that you do. In today's competitive climate, where managers are increasingly overseeing teams, the ability to display team leadership and build strong team loyalty can be seen as indispensable qualities.

It can also help for others in your organization to perceive you as mobile and to believe you have ready employment options available at other organizations. Combining perceived mobility with perceived indispensability lessens the likelihood that your rise in your present organization will be stalled by the excuse that "we can't promote you right now because your current unit can't afford to lose your expertise."

Be Visible Because the evaluation of managerial effectiveness has a substantial subjective component, it is important that your boss and those in power in the organization be made aware of your contribution. If you are fortunate enough to have a job that brings your accomplishments to the attention of others, it may not be necessary to take direct measures to increase your visibility. But your job may require you to handle activities that are low in visibility, or your specific contribution may be indistinguishable because you are part of a team. In such cases—without creating the image of a braggart—you will want to call attention to yourself by giving progress reports to your boss and others, being seen at social functions, being active in professional associations, developing powerful allies who speak positively about your accomplishments, and similar tactics. Of course, the skilled politician actively and successfully lobbies to get those projects that will increase his or her visibility.

Get a Mentor We discussed the benefits of mentors in the preceding chapter on leadership. From a political perspective, they offer two very positive benefits. First, they are a valuable communication source. A mentor can relay inside information that you might otherwise not have access to. And second, they send a message to others in the organization. Just the fact that you have a mentor provides a signal to others that you have the resources of a powerful higher-up behind you. Obviously, the more powerful your mentor, the stronger the signal.

But how do you get a mentor? Typically, at least where mentoring is an informal process, the mentors do the choosing. They spot someone lower in the organization with whom they identify and take that person on as a protégé. The more contacts you make with higher-ups—both formally and informally—the greater chance you have of being singled out as someone's protégé. Participating in company sports tournaments, going out with colleagues after work, taking on visible projects, and assignments to cross-functional teams are examples of activities that are likely to bring you to the attention of a potential mentor.

Develop Powerful Allies It helps to have powerful people in your camp. In addition to a mentor, you can cultivate contacts with potentially influential people above you, at your level, and in the lower ranks. They can provide you with important "grapevine" information not available through formal channels. In addition, there will be times when decisions will be made by those with the greatest support. Sometimes—though not always—there is strength in numbers. Having powerful allies can provide you with a coalition of support if and when you need it.

Avoid "Tainted" Members In almost every organization, there are fringe members whose status is questionable. Their performance or loyalty is under close scrutiny. Such individuals, while they are under the microscope, are "tainted." Carefully keep your distance from them. We all tend to judge others by the company they keep. Given the reality that effectiveness has a large subjective component, your own effectiveness might be called into question if you are perceived as being too closely associated with tainted people.

Support Your Boss Your immediate future is in the hands of your current boss. Since he or she evaluates your performance, you will typically want to do whatever is necessary to have your boss on your side.

You should make every effort to help your boss succeed, make her look good, support her if she is under siege, and spend the time to find out what criteria she will be using to assess your effectiveness. Don't undermine your boss. Don't speak negatively of her to others. If she is competent, visible, and in possession of a power base, she is likely to be on the way up in the organization. By being perceived as supportive, you increase the likelihood of being pulled along too. At the worst, you will have established an ally higher up in the organization. If your boss's performance is poor and her power low, it is difficult to distance yourself from her without her perceiving you as a traitor. The most effective solution in such a situation is to quietly lobby for a transfer. It's better to switch than fight.

Is It Unethical to Act Politically?

We conclude our discussion of politics by providing some ethical guidelines for political behavior. While there are no clear-cut ways to differentiate ethical from unethical politicking, there are some questions you should consider.

Exhibit 16-7 illustrates a decision tree to guide ethical actions. The first question you need to answer addresses self-interest versus organizational goals. Ethical actions are consistent with the organization's goals. Spreading untrue rumors about the safety of a new product introduced by your company, in order to make that product's design group look bad, is unethical. However, there may be nothing unethical if a department head exchanges favors with her division's purchasing manager in order to get a critical contract processed quickly.

The second question concerns the rights of other parties. If the department head described in the previous paragraph went down to the mailroom during her lunch hour and read through the mail directed to the purchasing manager—with the intent of "getting something on him" so he will expedite her contract—she would be acting unethically. She would have violated the purchasing manager's right to privacy.

The final question that needs to be addressed is related to whether the political activity conforms to standards of equity and justice. The department head who inflates the performance evaluation of a favored employee and deflates the evaluation of a disfavored employee—then uses those evaluations to justify giving the former a big raise and nothing to the latter—has treated the disfavored employee unfairly.

Unfortunately, the answers to the questions in Exhibit 16-7 are often argued in ways to make unethical practices seem ethical. Powerful people, for example, can become very good at explaining self-serving behaviors in terms of the organization's best interests. Similarly, they can persuasively argue that unfair actions are really fair and just. Our point is that immoral people can justify almost any behavior. Those who are powerful, articulate, and persuasive are most vulnerable because they are likely to be able to get away with unethical practices. When faced with an ethical dilemma regarding organizational politics, try to answer the questions in Exhibit 16-7 truthfully. And if you have a strong power base, recognize the ability of power to corrupt. Remember, it's a lot easier for the powerless to act ethically, for no other reason than that they typically have very little political discretion to exploit.

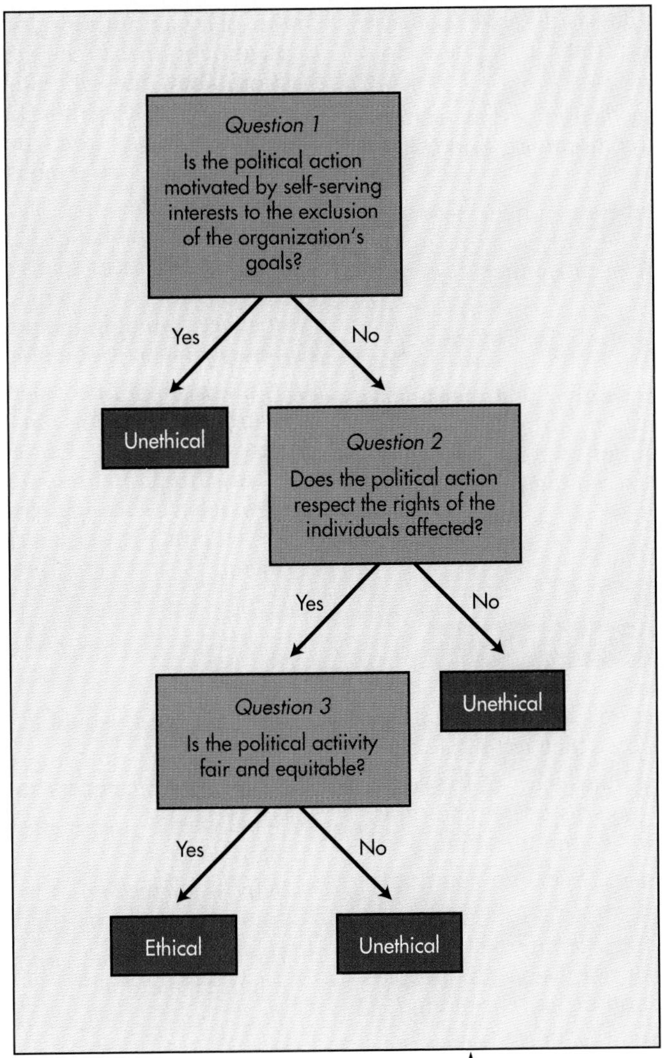

Source: Adapted from G. Cavanagh, D. Moberg, and M. Valasquez, "The Ethics of Organizational Politics," *Academy of Management Review,* July 1981, p. 368.

EXHIBIT 16-7
Is a Political Action Ethical?

SUMMARY

(This summary is organized by the chapter-opening learning objectives on page 477.)

1. The communication process is made up of seven parts: (1) the source, (2) encoding, (3) the message, (4) the channel, (5) decoding, (6) the receiver, and (7) feedback.
2. Men and women tend to use talk differently. For women, conversation provides intimacy and connection. For men, it is primarily a means to preserve independence and maintain status.
3. Effective active listening is characterized by eye contact, affirmative head nods and appropriate facial expressions, an absence of distracting actions or gestures, the asking of questions, paraphrasing, avoiding interrupting the speaker, an absence of overtalking, and smooth transitions between the roles of speaker and listener.
4. Effective performance feedback is characterized by focusing on specific behaviors and keeping feedback impersonal. It is goal-oriented and well-timed, en-

sures understanding, and directs negative feedback toward behavior that is controllable by the recipient.

5. Five conflict resolution behaviors are avoidance, accommodation, forcing, compromise, and collaboration.
6. Distributive bargaining operates under zero-sum conditions. Any gain for one party is a loss to the other. In contrast, integrative bargaining seeks win-win solutions.
7. Effective negotiation is characterized by researching the opponent, beginning with a positive overture, focusing on problems rather than personalities, paying little attention to initial offers, emphasizing win-win solutions, creating an open and trusting climate, and accepting third-party assistance when needed.
8. To delegate authority, you should clarify the assignment, specify the subordinate's range of discretion, allow the subordinate to participate, inform others that delegation has occurred, insist on recommendations from the subordinate when problems surface, and establish feedback controls.
9. Directive counseling places control for solving the problem in the hands of the manager. Nondirective counseling places that control with the employee. Participative counseling is a compromise, with the manager listening and providing advice and insights but relying on the employee to solve the problem.
10. A manager can become more politically adept by framing arguments in terms of organizational goals, developing the right image, gaining control of organizational resources, appearing to be indispensable, increasing visibility, getting a mentor, developing powerful allies, avoiding "tainted" members, and supporting the boss.

REVIEW AND DISCUSSION QUESTIONS

1. Why do you think interpersonal skills may be more important to a manager's success than technical skills?
2. Explain how each of the various parts of the communication process can cause distortion and limit the ability to achieve perfect communication.
3. "The medium is the message." What do you think this phrase means?
4. How can you improve your listening skills, at the same time recognizing that not everything people have to say is worth the effort of active listening?
5. What are the three sources of conflict? Which one do you think is most prevalent in organizations? In families? Explain your answers.
6. When, if ever, would a manager want to increase conflict?
7. Why might managers be reluctant to delegate?
8. What could you do to improve your counseling skills?
9. Why is there politics in organizations? Can it be completely eliminated? Explain.
10. How can you assess whether a political action you might take is unethical?

CASE EXERCISE
STAN WHITLEY'S PROBLEM

Stan Whitley had been a bit nervous about accepting the job at ProElecTronix. Although he had an engineering degree and quite a bit of summer work experience, he was only 23 years old and his entry-level job would be as the line supervisor of the assembly production unit. But he took the job and made it a high priority to gain the respect and trust of the older workers he was supervising.

Stan started his job four months ago. So far, everything has gone well. Just last week, in fact, he was praised by his boss for the good job he was doing with building morale in his unit. That is, everything went well until this morning's staff meeting.

Company policy states that workers have to use their annual vacation by December 31 or lose it.

Stan knew this policy. He was also aware that in past years many workers timed their vacations to coincide with holidays. So, during the past two months, as employees brought their vacation cards to him for his signature, he approved a number of requests for December vacations. He even gave verbal approvals to several requests. He didn't run any of these requests by his boss, since approving vacations was an area where he had full authority.

You can imagine Stan's surprise at the morning staff meeting, when his boss said in an off-handed way that the company would need to maintain full production in December, and that "it will be Stan's responsibility to make sure line scheduling is balanced." Stan left the meeting in a daze. Even ignoring the verbal agreements he had approved, over one-third of his line was going to be out on vacation at different times during the month of December. For at least one week, almost half the line could potentially be gone.

Trying to keep his cool, Stan first went to the human resources department to find out exactly what the rules were about vacations. Tina Chen, the HR manager, explained that it was a long-standing company policy not to allow vacations to be carried over. "What's the logic of that?" Stan asked. He learned management was concerned about the potential impact to scheduling production if people were permitted to take vacations lasting more than four weeks. Tina also told Stan that his particular Christmas scheduling problem had happened not only last year, but the year before as well. Apparently, it was common practice for management to promise too many vacations and leave the employees and human resources to pick up the mess. Tina obviously wasn't too excited about the news that it might happen again.

Tina's information on past practices made Stan feel as if he had been blind-sided. Why hadn't his boss warned him earlier about this problem? Why hadn't the employees said anything as they asked for their vacations?

Stan is now sitting at his desk pondering his dilemma. It's the middle of November. If he turns the problem over to his boss and admits defeat, he thinks he would undermine his credibility with both management and his work group. But he needs to do something.

Questions

1. Discuss Stan's dilemma in political terms.
2. What do you think Stan should do?

Source: Adapted, with permission, from "Vacation Blues," prepared by Dr. P. S. Heath.

VIDEO CASE EXERCISE
DOES WOMEN'S COMMUNICATION STYLE HINDER THEM IN BUSINESS?

Deborah Tannen says there's a distinct difference between the genders in the way they communicate. She calls them male and female rituals and she says they can get in the way of achieving work-related goals.

One of Tannen's findings relates to directness. Tannen says women often tend to avoid directness and cast themselves in an inferior light. This is seen in this conversation between two *Money Magazine* writers—Lesley Alderman and Gary Belsky:

Gary: Well, do you have anything that you're considering?

Lesley: Here are things we . . . we were . . . that we've been thinking about. I'm just throwing things up.

Gary: Go on.

Lesley: So that's good. Then this one's really out, but . . . you're going to think I'm completely insane . . . but you know, there's like this whole like spiritual kind of drive thing. I can see you . . . like you're saying, 'Oh, no.'

I don't even know if that's the angle, exactly. I'm not sure if that's the angle. All I'm saying is . . . I'm sort of throwing that out as something . . .

Gary: OK.

Lesley: Maybe there's something in that. It's a little way out, perhaps.

Another gender-related ritual is apologizing. Women tend to apologize when they haven't done anything wrong. Why? They use it as a ritual way to get into the interaction. Men, on the other hand, seem to apologize only when they absolutely need to.

Tannen says women use a communication style that allows others to save face. They avoid directness and prefer subtlety. But this can create real problems in organizations. Female managers may appear to be lacking in confidence. They may also appear to be tentative when giving orders. According to Tannen, these conversational rituals can be the basis for underestimating a woman's capabilities. She can be seen as incompetent, whereas she thinks she's being considerate. She can be seen as lacking in confidence, whereas she feels she's simply being a good person by not flaunting her authority.

Women may be in a "can't win" situation. If they try to be considerate through indirectness, they may receive lower performance evaluations. Their bosses may assume they are not aggressive or confident enough to handle their jobs. But if they talk too much like men, they suffer because their bosses and subordinates may see them as too aggressive.

Questions

1. Do you think gender stereotypes of communication styles can be generalized to the entire workforce?
2. Do you think these gender styles are influenced by national culture? Explain.
3. Do you think adults can unlearn specific gender-related commmunication styles? Defend your position.
4. What suggestions would you make so women can communicate more effectively at work?
5. What suggestions would you make for men?

Source: Based on "He Says She Says," *20/20;* ABC News; aired on October 21, 1994.

SKILL EXERCISE

Active Listening

This exercise is a debate. Break into groups of two. Party A can choose any contemporary issue. Some examples: business ethics, value of unions, prayer in schools, stiffer college grading policies, gun control, money as a motivator. Party B then selects a position on that issue and presents his or her argument. Party A must automatically take the counterposition. The debate is to proceed, with only one catch. Before Party A speaks, he or she must first summarize, in his or her *own* words and without notes, what Party B said. If the summary doesn't satisfy Party B, it must be corrected until it does. Then Party A presents the counterposition, and Party B must summarize Party A's argument. This format should be continued until both parties have made all their points.

This exercise should not exceed 10 minutes in length. Remember that each debater has to paraphrase the other's statements until acknowledged as correct before stating his or her own points.

NOTES

1. L. Williams, "A Silk Blouse on the Assembly Line? (Yes, the Boss's)," *New York Times,* February 5, 1995, p. F7.
2. See, for instance, J. D. Pettit Jr., B. C. Vaught, and R. L. Trewatha, "Interpersonal Skill Training: A Prerequisite for Success," *Business,* April–June 1990, pp. 8–14; D. Milbank, "Managers Are Sent to 'Charm Schools' to Discover How to Polish Up Their Acts," *Wall Street Journal,* December 14, 1990, p. B1; and E. Van Velsor and J. B. Leslie, "Why Executives Derail: Perspectives across Time and Cultures," *Academy of Management Executive,* November 1995, pp. 62–72.
3. Milbank, "Managers Are Sent to 'Charm Schools' to Discover How to Polish Up Their Acts."
4. C. Hymowitz, "Five Main Reasons Why Managers Fail," *Wall Street Journal,* May 2, 1988, p. 25.
5. L. W. Porter and L. E. McKibbin, *Future of Management Education and Development: Drift or Thrust into the Twenty-First Century?* (New York: McGraw-Hill, 1988).
6. B. Filipczak, "Obfuscation Resounding: Corporate Communication in America," *Training,* July 1995, p. 36.
7. D. K. Berlo, *The Process of Communication* (New York: Holt, Rinehart and Winston, 1960), p. 54.

8. Filipczak, "Obfuscation Resounding," p. 30
9. Ibid.
10. See, for instance, C. O. Kursh, "The Benefits of Poor Communication," *The Psychoanalytic Review,* Summer–Fall 1971, pp. 189–208; and E. M. Eisenberg and M. G. Witten, "Reconsidering Openness in Organizational Communication," *Academy of Management Review,* July 1987, pp. 418–26.
11. Cited in L. E. Boone, *Quotable Business* (New York: Random House, 1992), p. 60.
12. See, for instance, M. L. Kapp and J. A. Hall, *Nonverbal Communication in Human Interaction* (Fort Worth: Holt, Rinehart & Winston, 1992).
13. This section is based on D. Tannen, *You Just Don't Understand: Women and Men in Conversation* (New York: Ballantine Books, 1991); D. Tannen, *Talking from 9 to 5* (New York: William Morrow, 1994); and D. Tannen, "The Power of Talk: Who Gets Heard and Why," *Harvard Business Review,* September–October 1995, pp. 138–48.
14. See M. Munter, "Cross-Cultural Communication for Managers," *Business Horizons,* May–June 1993, pp. 69–77.
15. N. Adler, *International Dimensions of Organizational Behavior,* 2nd ed. (Boston: PWS-Kent, 1991), pp. 83–84.
16. This section is based on S. P. Robbins and P. L. Hunsaker, *Training in InterPersonal Skills: TIPS for Managing People at Work,* 2nd ed. (Upper Saddle River, N.J.: Prentice Hall, 1996), pp. 33–39; and data in R. C. Husman, J. M. Lahiff, and J. M. Penrose, *Business Communication: Strategies and Skills* (Chicago: Dryden Press, 1988), pp. 380, 425.
17. Cited in M. Hequet, "Giving Good Feedback," *Training,* September 1994, p. 72.
18. This section is based on Robbins and Hunsaker, *Training in InterPersonal Skills,* pp. 70–75.
19. See S. P. Robbins, *Managing Organizational Conflict: A Nontraditional Approach* (Englewood Cliffs, N.J.: Prentice Hall, 1974).
20. K. W. Thomas and W. H. Schmidt, "A Survey of Management Interests with Respect to Conflict," *Academy of Management Journal,* June 1976, pp. 315–18.
21. Ibid.
22. J. Graves, "Successful Management and Organizational Mugging," in J. Papp, ed., *New Directions in Human Resource Management* (Englewood Cliffs, N.J.: Prentice Hall, 1978).
23. M. A. Rahim and N. R. Magner, "Confirmatory Factor Analysis of the Styles of Handling Interpersonal Conflict: First-Order Factor Model and Its Invariance across Groups," *Journal of Applied Psychology,* February 1995, pp. 122–32.
24. L. Greenhalgh, "Managing Conflict," *Sloan Management Review,* Summer 1986, pp. 45–51.
25. Robbins, *Managing Organizational Conflict,* pp. 31–55.
26. K. W. Thomas, "Conflict and Negotiation Processes in Organizations," in M. D. Dunnette and L. M. Hough, eds., *Handbook of Industrial and Organizational Psychology,* 2nd ed., vol. 3 (Palo Alto, Calif.: Consulting Psychologists Press, 1992), pp. 666–77.
27. See, for instance, E. van de Vliert and C. K. W. de Dreu, "Optimizing Performance by Conflict Stimulation," *International Journal of Conflict Management,* July 1994, pp. 211–22.
28. Robbins, *Managing Organizational Conflict,* pp. 78–89.
29. J. A. Wall Jr., *Negotiation: Theory and Practice* (Glenview, Ill.: Scott, Foresman, 1985).
30. R. E. Walton and R. B. McKersie, *A Behavioral Theory of Labor Negotiations: An Analysis of a Social Interaction System* (New York: McGraw-Hill, 1965).
31. Thomas, "Conflict and Negotiation Processes in Organizations."
32. These suggestions are based on J. A. Wall Jr. and M. W. Blum, "Negotiations," *Journal of Management,* June 1991, pp. 278–82.
33. D. J. McConville, "The Artful Negotiator," *Industry Week,* August 15, 1994, p. 40.
34. B. K. Hackman and D. C. Dunphy, "Managerial Delegation," in C. L. Cooper and I. T. Robertson, eds., *International Review of Industrial and Organizational Psychology,* vol. 5 (Chichester, England: Wiley, 1990), pp. 35–57.
35. C. R. Leana, "Predictors and Consequences of Delegation," *Academy of Management Journal,* December 1986, pp. 754–74.
36. Adapted from S. Caudron, "Delegate for Results," *Industry Week,* February 6, 1995, pp. 27–28.
37. This section is adapted from Robbins and Hunsaker, *Training in InterPersonal Skills,* pp. 93–95.
38. Caudron, "Delegate for Results," p. 30.
39. See, for example, R. Walsh, "Basic Counseling Skills," *Supervisory Management,* July 1977, pp. 2–9; G. D. Cook, "Employee Counseling Session," *Supervision,* August 1989, pp. 3–5; and J. Wisinski, "A Logical Approach to a Difficult Employee," *HR Focus,* January 1992, pp. 15–18.
40. C. Rogers, *Counseling and Psychotherapy* (Boston: Houghton Mifflin, 1942).
41. Based on R. L. Knowdell and E. N. Chapman, *Personal Counseling,* rev. ed. (Los Altos, Calif.: Crisp Publications, 1986).
42. D. Farrell and J. C. Petersen, "Patterns of Political Behavior in Organizations," *Academy of Management Review,* July 1982, p. 405.
43. This section is from Robbins and Hunsaker, *Training in InterPersonal Skills,* pp. 131–34.
44. See, for example, B. R. Schlenker, *Impression Management: The Self-Concept, Social Identity, and Interpersonal Relations* (Monterey, Calif.: Brooks/Cole, 1980); J. Tedeschi and V. Melburg, "Impression Management and Influence in the Organization," in S. Bacharach and E. J. Lawler, eds., *Research in the Sociology of Organizations,* vol. 3 (Greenwich, Conn.: JAI Press, 1984), pp. 31–58; M. R. Leary and R. M. Kowalski, "Impression Management: A Literature Review and Two-Component Model," *Psychological Bulletin,* January 1990, pp. 34–47; and B. R. Schlenker and M. F. Weigold, "Interpersonal Processes Involving Impression Regulation and Management," in M. R. Rosenzweig and L. W. Porter, eds., *Annual Review of Psychology,* vol. 43 (Palo Alto, Calif.: Annual Reviews Inc., 1992), pp. 133–68.

PART FIVE: Organizational Renewal

CHAPTER 17

MANAGING CHANGE:

REVISITING THE CHANGING WORLD OF WORK

Ten popular explanations for avoiding change:
(1) We've never done it before;
(2) nobody else has ever done it before;
(3) it can't be done;
(4) it won't work in a small company;
(5) it won't work in a large company;
(6) it won't work in our company;
(7) we're not ready for it;
(8) why change—it's working OK;
(9) we've been doing it this way for 25 years; and
(10) you can't teach an old dog new tricks.

- L. E. Boone

LEARNING OBJECTIVES

After studying this chapter, you should be able to:

1. List sources of individual and organizational resistance to change
2. Contrast first-order and second-order change
3. Identify strategies for reducing resistance to change
4. List tactics for reducing resistance to change
5. Describe what it is that managers can change
6. Define organizational development
7. Identify techniques for reducing employee stress
8. Explain how managers can increase innovation
9. Describe a learning organization

Encyclopedia Britannica. It's a brand name that is known throughout the world. Yet it is a product that is currently in big trouble. Why? Executives at Encyclopedia Britannica have been slow to adapt to changes in the reference business.[1]

The product goes back to 1768, the year it was first published in Edinburgh, Scotland, by a group of scholars known as the Society of Gentlemen. By the early 1920s, Britannica had come under the ownership of Sears, Roebuck. In 1943, Sears sold it to William Benton, a former advertising executive. Today, the William Benton Foundation of Chicago continues ownership but is looking for a buyer. Sales are down. In 1990, for instance, 117,000 sets of the Encylopedia Britannica were sold. Sales in 1994 had plunged to 51,000. No one questions the breadth or depth of its thirty-two-volume set. But it costs $1,500 and consumes four feet of shelf space. In today's digital age, the traditional encyclopedia set is a dinosaur. It is being rapidly replaced by far less expensive CD-ROM–based multimedia products. Competitors such as Grolier, Compton (see photo insert), and Funk & Wagnalls have developed CD-ROM versions of their products that contain the text, graphics, and photos of an entire set of books on a single silicon disk. And electronic publishers can sell their products at a fraction of the price that hardbound volumes commanded. For instance, Encarta, Microsoft's CD-ROM encyclopedia, which is based on Funk & Wagnalls, sells for only $99.

The management at Encyclopedia Britannica appear to have been lulled into a false belief in the permanence of their product. When you have been around for more than 225 years, you begin

IN THE NEWS

Compaq Computer: Building Creative Destruction

ECKHARD PFEIFFER, HEAD OF COMPAQ COMPUTER, IS OVERSEEING A TRANSFORMATION OF HIS COMPANY. He is taking on new risks and shaking up the global computer business. The Compaq story can be depicted as a drama in three acts:

Act I, October 1991. Compaq, which has prospered by producing high-quality, high-priced personal computers for business users, hits its first crisis. Customers, trying to cut costs, turn to lower-priced, almost-as-good clones. Compaq sales and profits plummet. Rod Canion, the company's CEO, is ousted. Pfeiffer, head of Compaq's highly successful international business, is promoted to replace Canion. Pfeiffer cuts the worldwide work force from about 12,000 to 10,000, expands the number of dealers from 3,500 to 38,000, and presses suppliers for better terms. He expands into the PC markets for home, education, and small business uses and introduces numerous production efficiencies.

Act II, January 1995. Compaq replaces IBM as the world's top PC vendor. In just 2 years, Compaq's share of the worldwide market has risen from 4.8 percent to 10 percent. Sales reach $10.9 billion. Pfeiffer sets a goal of doing $30 billion a year in sales by 2000.

Act III, March 1995. Pfeiffer proudly describes the "new" Compaq. The old company introduced no more than eight new models a year. Pfeiffer announces 118 new PCs. He also announces price cuts of 5 to 23 percent. Compaq is now seen as a feisty competitor—aggressively grabbing market share from IBM and Apple.

Eckhard Pfieffer, head of Compaq Computer.

Pfeiffer is reinventing Compaq to compete effectively in a rapidly growing and fiercely competitive market. His strategy can be summed up as: By cutting costs, you can cut prices. By reducing prices, you can build market share. As share rises, you can negotiate lower prices from suppliers—and cut your own prices further. And this circular process continues indefinitely. Meanwhile, the market for PCs explodes. In the United States alone, 60 million families don't have PCs. Compaq wants to fill this need as prices fall and the PC replaces the television set as the all-in-one device for work, education, and entertainment.

Pfeiffer describes his actions at Compaq as all part of "building creative destruction" into his company. "Nothing is harder than casting aside the thinking, strategies, and biases that propelled a business to its current success," says Pfeiffer. "Companies need to learn how to unlearn, to slough off yesterday's wisdom."

Source: M. Loeb, "Leadership Lost—And Regained," *Fortune*, April 17, 1995, pp. 217–18.

elements to successful change. The more affirmative answers a manager gives to the following questions, the greater the likelihood that change efforts will succeed.

1. Is the sponsor of change high up enough to have power to effectively deal with resistance?
2. Is day-to-day leadership supportive of the change and committed to it?
3. Is there a strong sense of urgency from senior management about the need for change, and is it shared by the rest of the organization?
4. Does management have a clear vision of how the future will look different from the present?
5. Are there objective measures in place to evaluate the change effort, and are reward systems explicitly designed to reinforce them?
6. Is the specific change effort consistent with other changes going on within the organization?
7. Are functional managers willing to sacrifice their personal self-interest for the good of the organization as a whole?
8. Does management pride itself on closely monitoring changes and actions taken by competitors?

9. Is the importance of the customer and a knowledge of customer needs well accepted by everyone in the work force?
10. Are managers and employees rewarded for taking risks, being innovative, and looking for new solutions?
11. Is the organization structure flexible?
12. Are communication channels open both downward and upward?
13. Is the organization's hierarchy relatively flat?
14. Has the organization successfully implemented major changes in the recent past?
15. Are employee satisfaction and trust in management high?
16. Is there a high degree of cross-boundary interactions and cooperation between units in the organization?
17. Are decisions made quickly, taking into account a wide variety of suggestions?

Strategies for Reducing Resistance Given that the climate supports change, managers need to prepare a strategy for change. Six suggestions have been offered as crucial in preparing the organization and its members for the trauma of seismic change.[15]

1. *Conduct an organizational identity audit before undertaking any major change.* This audit should include all departments and levels affected by the change, and it should focus on members' beliefs about the organization. What do they see as the organization's core beliefs—current and ideal states?
2. *Tailor the change to fit the organization.* Different organizations and subunits within organizations have different concerns and identities. One size *doesn't* fit all! Use the audit to identify those differences, then use change tactics that fit best.
3. *Present the change as significant (to overcome organizational inertia) while tying it to valued aspects of organizational identity.* The change agent needs to convince employees of the critical importance and need for change. This phase is essentially the task of providing visionary leadership.
4. *Introduce change in a series of midrange steps.* Comprehensive changes are very threatening to people. They are less likely to resist if changes are presented in steps. And each successful step increases momentum and widens the distance to the past.
5. *Take the path of least resistance.* In complex organizations, members in separate units are likely to have distinct identity beliefs that are held with varying levels of conviction. This diversity of beliefs creates entry points at which change can be implemented with relative ease. Managers should select those units in which the probability that change will be readily accepted is highest. Then, successes in these units can be leveraged to build momentum for expanding the change to more resistant units.
6. *Know how much change your organization can handle.* Organizations differ in their willingness to accept change. So do subunits within a large organization. What is perceived as radical and threatening in one organization or subunit may be viewed as incremental in others. There is an upper limit to how much change is acceptable. You need to keep this limit in mind as a constraint on how much change your organization can absorb at any one time.

Tactics for Reducing Resistance Six specific tactics have been suggested for use by change agents in dealing with resistance to change.[16]

1. *Education and communication.* Resistance can be reduced through communicating with employees to help them see the logic of a change. This tactic basically assumes that the source of resistance lies in misinformation or poor

communication: If employees receive the full facts and get any misunderstandings cleared up, resistance will subside. Communication can be achieved through one-on-one discussions, memos, group presentations, or reports. Does it work? It does, provided that the source of resistance is inadequate communication and that management-employee relations are characterized by mutual trust and credibility. If these conditions don't exist, the change is unlikely to succeed.

2. *Participation.* It's difficult for individuals to resist a change decision in which they participated. Before a change is made, those opposed can be brought into the decision process. If the participants have the expertise to make a meaningful contribution, their involvement can reduce resistance, obtain commitment, and increase the quality of the change decision. However, against these advantages are the negatives: potential for a poor solution and great time consumption.
3. *Facilitation and support.* Change agents can offer a range of supportive efforts to reduce resistance. When employee fear and anxiety are high, employee counseling and therapy, new-skills training, or a short paid leave of absence may facilitate adjustment. The drawback of this tactic is that, as with the others, it is time-consuming. If addition, it is expensive, and its implementation offers no assurance of success.
4. *Negotiation.* Another way for the change agent to deal with potential resistance to change is to exchange something of value for a lessening of the resistance. For instance, if the resistance is centered in a few powerful individuals, a specific reward package can be negotiated that will meet their individual needs. Negotiation as a tactic may be necessary when resistance comes from a powerful source. Yet one cannot ignore its potentially high costs. There is also the risk that, once a change agent negotiates with one party to avoid resistance, he or she is open to the possibility of being blackmailed by other individuals in positions of power.
5. *Manipulation and cooptation.* Manipulation refers to covert influence attempts. Twisting and distorting facts to make them appear more attractive, withholding undesirable information, and creating false rumors to get employees to accept a change are all examples of manipulation. If corporate management threatens to close down a particular manufacturing plant if that plant's employees fail to accept an across-the-board pay cut, and if the threat is actually untrue, management is using manipulation. Cooptation, on the other hand, is a form of both manipulation and participation. It seeks to "buy off" the leaders of a resistance group by giving them a key role in the change decision. The leaders' advice is sought, not to seek a better decision, but to get their endorsement. Both manipulation and cooptation are relatively inexpensive and easy ways to gain the support of adversaries, but the tactics can backfire if the targets become aware that they are being tricked or used. Once discovered, the change agent's credibility may drop to zero.
6. *Coercion.* Last on the list of tactics is coercion: that is, the application of direct threats or force upon the resisters. If the corporate management mentioned in item 5 really is determined to close a manufacturing plant if employees don't acquiesce to a pay cut, then coercion would be the label attached to its change tactic. Other examples of coercion are threats of transfer, loss of promotions, negative performance evaluations, and a poor letter of recommendation. The advantages and drawbacks of coercion are approximately the same as those mentioned for manipulation and cooptation.

The Politics of Change

No discussion of resistance to change would be complete without a brief mention of the politics of change. Because change invariably threatens the status quo, it inherently implies political activity.[17]

Internal change agents typically are managers high in the organization who have a lot to lose from change. They have, in fact, risen to their positions of authority by developing skills and behavioral patterns that have, so far, been favored by the organization. Change is a threat to those skills and patterns. What if they are no longer the ones the organization values? Any change creates the potential for others in the organization to gain power at their expense.

Politics suggests that the impetus for change is most likely to come from individuals who are new to the organization (and have less invested in the status quo) or from executives slightly removed from the main power structure. Those managers who have spent their entire careers with a single organization and eventually achieve a senior position in the hierarchy are often major impediments to change. Change, itself, is a very real threat to their status and position. Yet they may be expected to implement changes to demonstrate that they are not merely caretakers. By acting as change agents, they can symbolically convey to various constituencies—stockholders, suppliers, employees, customers—that they are on top of problems and adapting to a dynamic environment. Of course, as you might guess, when forced to introduce change, these long-time power holders tend to implement first-order changes. Radical change is too threatening.

Power struggles within the organization will determine, to a large degree, the speed and quantity of change. You should expect that long-time career executives will be sources of resistance. This, incidentally, explains why boards of directors who recognize the imperative for the rapid introduction of second-order change in their organizations frequently turn to outside candidates for new leadership.[18]

The above suggests that all managers should tread carefully in their roles as change agents. It's a good idea, for instance, to assess how much support you have from above. For top executives, this means having the board in your corner. For mid- and lower-level managers, you need to know that you will be backed up by the people above you. Once you have support, you should consider who will have a vested interest in the change. This group might include specific departments and teams, staff units, suppliers, key customers, unions, and informal employee leaders. Then focus on these vested interests. Winning their support will be crucial to the change effort's success or failure. The techniques discussed previously for dealing with resistance—education and communication, participation, facilitation, negotiation, manipulation and cooptation, and coercion—can be used to build this support.

WHAT CAN MANAGERS CHANGE?

What can managers change? The options essentially fall into five categories: structure, culture, technology, the physical setting, and people.[19] (See Exhibit 17-3 on page 524.) Changing *structure* involves making an alteration in authority relations, coordination mechanisms, job redesign, or similar structural variables. Changing *culture* requires reshaping the organization's core values. Changing *technology* encompasses modifications in the way work is processed and in the methods and equipment used. Changing the *physical setting* covers altering the space and layout arrangements in the workplace. Changing *people* refers to changes in employee attitudes, skills, expectations, perceptions, or behavior.

Changing Structure

In Chapter 7, we discussed structural issues such as work specialization, span of control, and various organizational designs. But organizational structures are not set in concrete. Changing conditions demand structural changes. As a result, managers might need to modify the organization's structure.

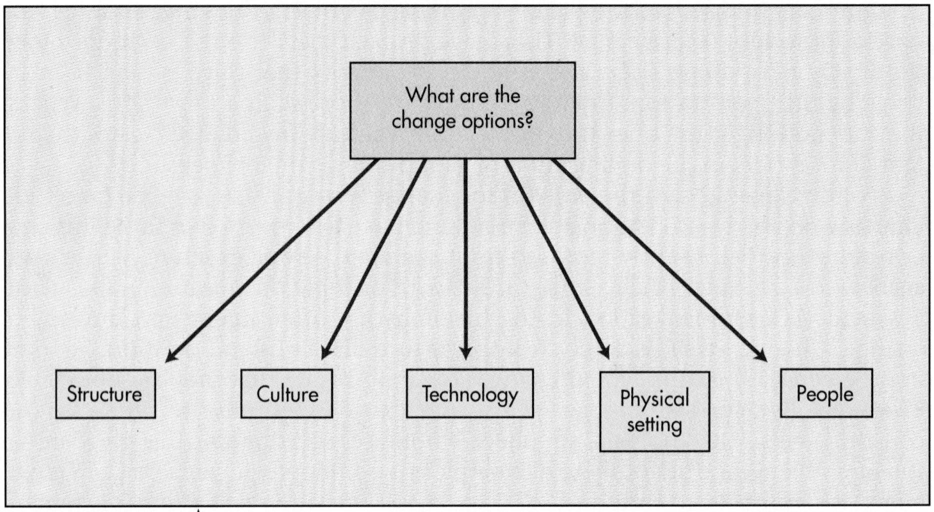

EXHIBIT 17-3
Change Options

An organization's structure is defined as how tasks are formally divided, grouped, and coordinated. Managers can alter one or more of the key elements in an organization's design. For instance, departmental responsibilities can be combined, vertical layers removed, and spans of control widened to make the organization flatter and less bureaucratic. More rules and procedures can be implemented to increase standardization. An increase in decentralization can be made to speed up the decision-making process.

Management can also introduce major modifications in the actual structural design. Modifications might include a shift from a simple structure to a team-based structure or the creation of a matrix design. Managers might also consider redesigning jobs or work schedules; jobs can be redefined or enriched, or flexible work hours can be introduced. Still another option is to modify the organization's compensation system. Employee motivation could be increased by, for example, introducing performance bonuses or profit sharing.

Changing Culture

We discussed cultural change in Chapter 11. In that discussion, we drew on a number of studies to conclude that cultures are highly resistant to change. And when change does come, it comes slowly. Jack Welch, CEO at General Electric, characterized his company's cultural transformation as a 7-to-10-year effort.[20] It is probably accurate to say that it is a lot easier to change an organization's structure or technology than it is to transform its culture.

The above doesn't mean that culture can't be changed. Again, as we noted in Chapter 11, certain conditions increase the likelihood that cultural change can be successfully accomplished. These include a dramatic crisis, new top leadership, a fairly new and small organization, and a weak dominant culture.

The typical challenges management faces in trying to change its organization's culture are captured in the experiences of IBM Canada.[21] Like its parent, IBM Canada had become cocky, arrogant, and removed from its customers. The company was oblivious to its environment and rewarded its employees for conformity. Between 1991 and 1993, IBM Canada lost $125 million. The company brought in a new CEO who reduced the work force by almost one-third and did away with the company's practice of promoting exclusively from within. But change has come very slowly. This isn't completely surprising given that fourteen of the company's current top fifteen executives are long-time IBM veterans, still enmeshed in the company's old country-club mentality. You can understand the problem when the most visible and most talked-about evidence of cultural change in the company is the dumping of its rigid, dark suit and white shirt dress code.

Changing Technology

Most of the early studies in management dealt with efforts aimed at technological change. At the turn of the century, for example, scientific management sought to implement changes based on time-and-motion studies that would increase production efficiency (see Appendix A). Today, major technological changes usually involve the introduction of new equipment, tools, or methods; automation; or computerization.

Most of the early studies in management dealt with efforts aimed at technological change.

Competitive factors or innovations within an industry often require managers to introduce new equipment, tools, or operating methods. For example, many aluminum companies have significantly modernized their plants in recent years to compete more effectively. More efficient handling equipment, furnaces, and presses have been installed to reduce the cost of manufacturing a ton of aluminum.

Automation is a technological change that replaces people with machines. It began in the Industrial Revolution and continues as a change option today. Examples of automation are the introduction of automatic mail sorters by the U.S. Postal Service, robots on automobile assembly lines, and flexible manufacturing systems in production operations.

As noted in previous chapters, the most visible technological change in recent years has been expanding computerization. Many organizations now have sophisticated management information systems. Large supermarkets have converted their cash registers into input terminals and linked them to computers to provide instant inventory data. The office of 1997 is dramatically different from the office of 1977, predominantly because of computerization. Now desktop microcomputers can run hundreds of business software packages, and network systems allow these computers to communicate with one another.

Changing the Physical Setting

The layout of work space should not be a random activity. Typically, management thoughtfully considers work demands, formal interaction requirements, and social needs when making decisions about space configurations, interior design, equipment placement, and the like.

For example, when an office design is opened up by eliminating walls and partitions, employees can easily communicate with each other. Similarly, management can change the quantity and types of lights, the level of heat or cold, the levels and types of noise, the cleanliness of the work area, and interior design dimensions such as furniture, decorations, and color schemes.

The evidence indicates that changes in the physical setting, in and of themselves, do not have a substantial impact on organizational or individual performance.[22] But they can make certain employee behaviors easier or harder to perform. In this way, employee and organizational performance may be enhanced or reduced.[23]

Changing People

The final area in which management or change agents operate is in helping individuals and groups within the organization to work more effectively together. This category typically involves changing the attitudes and behaviors of organizational members through processes of communication, decision making, and problem solving. A good part of our discussion of learning, in Chapter 12, reflects efforts to understand the most effective ways to change employee attitudes and behaviors.

TECHNIQUES FOR CHANGING PEOPLE

In the 1990s, practicing managers and academics have tended to focus their attention on three variables: structure, culture, and people. Structural change has been subsumed within the reengineering movement. We will return to reengineering later in this chapter. We have already discussed cultural change in Chapter 11. So that leaves the topic of people change. In this section we will review the most popular techniques for changing employee attitudes and behaviors.

Organizational Development

The umbrella term used most frequently to encompass methods for changing employees is **organizational development (OD).** Essentially, this term refers to a collection of techniques for understanding, changing, and developing an organization's work force in order to improve its effectiveness.[24] It builds on humanistic, democratic values. It emphasizes confronting problems and conflicts between individuals in work groups and between work groups.

OD techniques emphasize a set of underlying values. OD places a high degree of importance on human and organizational growth, collaborative and participative processes, and a spirit of inquiry.[25] For example, OD techniques assume that individuals are responsible and conscientious; that effective relationships are based on trust and equality; that problems should be openly confronted; and that the more people participate in the decisions surrounding a change, the more they will be committed to implementing those decisions. Popular OD techniques include survey feedback, team building, and intergroup development.

Survey Feedback

A tool for assessing attitudes held by organizational members, identifying discrepancies among member perceptions, and solving these differences is the **survey feedback** approach. Everyone in an organization can participate in survey feedback, but of key importance is the organizational family—the manager of any given unit and those employees who report directly to him or her. A questionnaire is usually completed by all members in the organization or unit. Organization members may be asked to suggest questions or may be interviewed to determine what issues are relevant. The questionnaire typically asks members for their perceptions and attitudes on a broad range of topics, including decision-making practices; communication effectiveness; coordination between units; and satisfaction with the organization, job, peers, and their immediate supervisor.

The data from this questionnaire are first cross-tabulated with data pertaining to an individual's specific "family" and to the entire organization and then distributed to employees. These data then become the springboard for identifying problems and clarifying issues that may be creating difficulties for people. In some cases, the manager may be counseled by an external change agent about the meaning of the responses to the questionnaire and may even be given suggested guidelines for leading the organizational family in group discussion of the results.

Particular attention is given to the importance of encouraging discussion and ensuring that discussions focus on issues and ideas and not on attacking individuals.

Finally, group discussion in the survey feedback approach should result in members' identifying possible implications of the questionnaire's findings. Are people listening? Are new ideas being generated? Can decision making, interpersonal relations, or job assignments be improved? Answers to questions such as these, it is hoped, will result in the group's agreeing upon commitments to various actions that will remedy the problems that are identified.

Team Building

As we have noted in numerous places throughout this book, organizations are increasingly relying on teams to accomplish work tasks. **Team building** utilizes high-interaction group activities to increase trust and openness among team members.[26]

Team building can be applied within groups or at the intergroup level where activities are interdependent. For this discussion, we'll emphasize the intragroup level and leave intergroup development to the next section. So our interest concerns applications to organizational families (command groups), as well as to committees, project teams, self-managed teams, and task groups.

Not all group activity has interdependence of functions. For example, consider a football team and a track team:

> Although members on both teams are concerned with the team's total output, they function differently. The football team's output depends synergistically on how well each player does his particular job in concert with his teammates. The quarterback's performance depends on the performance of his linemen and receivers, the end's on how well the quarterback throws the ball, and so on. On the other hand, a track team's performance is determined largely by the mere addition of the performances of the individual members.[27]

Team building is applicable to the case of interdependence, such as in football. The objective is to improve coordinative efforts of members in such a way that the team's performance will also improve.

The activities considered in team building typically include goal setting, development of interpersonal relations among team members, role analysis to clarify each member's role and responsibilities, and team process analysis. Of course, team building may emphasize or exclude certain activities depending on the purpose of the development effort and the specific problems with which the team is confronted. Basically, however, team building attempts to use high interaction among members to increase trust and openness.

It may be beneficial to begin by having members attempt to define the goals and priorities of the team. This exercise will bring to the surface different perceptions of what the team's purpose may be. Next, members can evaluate the team's performance—how effective are they in structuring priorities and achieving their goals? This step should identify potential problem areas. This self-critique discussion of means and ends can be done with all members of the team present, or, if large size impinges on a free interchange of views, it may initially take place in smaller groups, which can later share their findings with the total team.

Team building can also address itself to identifying and clarifying each member's role on the team. Previous ambiguities can be brought to the surface. It may offer one of the few opportunities some individuals have had to think through thoroughly what their job is all about and what specific tasks they are expected to carry out if the team is to optimize its effectiveness.

Still another team-building activity is to analyze key processes that go on within the team to identify the way work is performed and how these processes might be improved to make the team more effective.

Intergroup Development

A major area of concern in OD is the dysfunctional conflict that exists between groups. This has been a subject to which change efforts have been directed.

Intergroup development seeks to change the attitudes, stereotypes, and perceptions that groups have of each other. For example, in one company, the engineers saw the accounting department as composed of shy and conservative types and the human resources department as having a bunch of "ultra-liberals, who are more concerned that some protected group of employees might get their feelings hurt than with the company's making a profit." Such stereotypes can have an obvious negative impact on the coordinative efforts between the departments.

Although there are several approaches for improving intergroup relations,[28] one popular method emphasizes problem solving.[29] In this method, each group meets independently to develop lists of its perception of itself and of the other group and how it believes the other group perceives it. The groups then share their lists and discuss similarities and differences. Differences are clearly articulated, and the groups look for the causes of the disparities.

Are the groups' goals at odds? Were perceptions distorted? On what basis were stereotypes formulated? Have some differences been caused by misunderstandings of intentions? Have words and concepts been defined differently by each group? Answers to questions such as these clarify the exact nature of the conflict. Once the causes of the difficulty have been identified, the groups can move to the integration phase—working to develop solutions that will improve relations between the groups. Subgroups, with members from each of the conflicting groups, can now be created for further diagnosis and to begin to formulate possible alternative actions that will improve relations.

CONTEMPORARY ISSUES IN MANAGING CHANGE

We wrap up this chapter, and the text itself, by discussing some contemporary issues related to managing change. These are: the importance of adjusting change practices to reflect national differences; the reengineering revolution; employee stress; building innovative organizations; and creating a learning organization.

Managing Change Needs to Reflect National Culture

A number of the issues addressed in this chapter are culture-bound. To illustrate, let's briefly look at four questions: (1) Do people believe that change is possible? (2) If it is possible, how long will it take to bring it about? (3) Is resistance to change greater in some cultures than in others? (4) Does culture influence how change efforts will be implemented?

Do people believe change is possible? Remember that cultures vary in terms of beliefs about their ability to control their environment. In cultures in which people believe that they can dominate their environment, individuals will take a proactive view of change. This would describe the United States and Canada. In other countries, such as Iran and Saudi Arabia, people see themselves as subjugated to their environment and thus will tend to take a passive approach toward change.

If change is possible, how long will it take to bring it about? A culture's time orientation can help us answer this question. Societies that focus on the long term, such as Japan, will demonstrate considerable patience while waiting for positive outcomes from change efforts. In societies with a short-term focus, such as the United States and Canada, people expect quick improvements and will seek change programs that promise fast results.

Is resistance to change greater in some cultures than in others? Resistance to change will be influenced by a society's reliance on tradition. Italians, as an example, focus on the past, whereas Americans emphasize the present. Italians, therefore, should generally be more resistant to change efforts than are Americans.

Does culture influence how change efforts will be implemented? Power distance can help answer this question. In high power distance cultures, such as the Philippines or Venezuela, change efforts will tend to be autocratically implemented by top management. In contrast, low power distance cultures value democratic methods. We would predict, therefore, a greater use of participation in countries such as Denmark and Israel than in the Philippines or Venezuela.

The Reengineering Revolution

Reengineering was recently described as "the favored management tool for implementing change."[30] If it is, it is favored only in second-order change. Reengineering, as you remember, refers to redesigning the organization's core processes by essentially starting with a blank sheet of paper. It entails ignoring the way things have historically been done and completely redesigning everything the organization does—from product development to customer service. But it has little relevance for first-order or incremental change efforts.

Reengineering has been widely applied in tens of thousands of U.S. and European organizations. In fact, it is the unusual organization today whose management *hasn't* tried reengineering. However, not surprisingly, given the magnitude of change inherent in reengineering and our knowledge of resistance pressures, many of these efforts have failed or at least fallen well short of original expectations. Many companies undertook reengineering efforts "only to abandon them with little or no positive result."[31] One of the original founders of the reengineering movement has said, "The revolution we started has gone, at best, only halfway."[32]

Reengineering has a high failure rate because it tries to do so much and because it has such broad-sweeping implications for employees and managers alike. As the CEO of Aetna Life & Casualty noted, reengineering is "agonizingly, heartbreakingly tough."[33] Lots of people typically lose their jobs, and those who don't find that their jobs aren't the ones they used to do. Most successful reengineering efforts leave little intact. Such drastic change is extremely threatening to everyone in the organization.

Some experts say that reengineering will eliminate between 1 million and 2.5 million jobs each year in the United States for the foreseeable future.[34] The impact, however, won't be uniform across the organization. Staff support jobs, especially middle managers, will be most vulnerable. So, too, will clerical jobs in service industries. For instance, one knowledgeable observer has predicted that reengineering will reduce employment in commercial banks and thrift institutions by 30 to 40 percent between 1993 and 2000.[35]

Reengineering will reduce employment in commercial banks and thrift institutions by 30 to 40 percent.

Reengineered jobs typically require a wider range of skills, include more interaction with customers and suppliers, offer greater challenge, contain increased responsibilities, and provide higher pay than the original jobs did. For many managers, reengineering requires a complete revision of their managerial roles. For instance, at Engelhard, a New Jersey specialty chemicals company, the greatest problems during reengineering were encountered in middle management, where people felt very threatened by loss of control.[36] In a reengineered organization, managers empower and collaborate rather than direct and control.[37]

Reengineering isn't going away. And getting people to buy into the radical changes it dictates isn't easy. Senior executives find themselves selling something to a group of people who don't want to buy,[38] especially among the middle-management ranks. Their resistance is often greatest because their jobs are frequently the most threatened.

The massive changes that typically come with reengineering are going to be resisted. That is a fact. It is naive to assume that changes of this magnitude can be introduced without significant resistance. Given this reality, senior management's skills at overcoming this resistance are likely to be tested. On the basis of an assessment of reengineering successes and failures, two factors appear to be important in gaining acceptance to change.[39] First, participation is critical. When the managers and employees who will be affected are involved in the reengineering effort, they can criticize from the inside rather than resist from the outside. Second, rely on team building to get people working together on implementing changes. The creation of cohesive and trusting teams allows members to rely on each other in moments of stress and confusion.

Reducing Employee Stress

Today's new work environment is increasingly characterized by employees' assuming larger work loads, putting in longer hours, having fewer resources to work with, confronting more day-to-day ambiguities, and facing less job security. And these changes are a major cause of employee stress. In a recent sample of 600 U.S. workers, 46 percent said that their jobs were highly stressful, and 34 percent reported that the stress was so bad they were thinking of quitting.[40] What, if anything, can management do to help employees reduce stress or better cope with it?

Not all sources of stress are controllable by management.[41] Some people, for instance, are naturally high-strung and stress-prone. And employees often have dilemmas outside their work—such as financial and family problems—that management can't control but that employees bring with them to their jobs. The good news is that stress isn't necessarily all bad. Low levels of stress can make work more interesting for employees and stimulate higher performance.

Yet there are things management can do to lessen the negative impact of work stress on employees. They include improved personnel selection and job placement, the use of realistic goal setting, training in time management, redesign of jobs, increased employee involvement, expanded social support networks, improved organizational communication, and creation of organizationally supported wellness programs.[42]

Certain jobs are more stressful than others, and individuals differ in their response to stress situations. For example, individuals with little experience in their job tend to be more stress-prone than are experienced jobholders. Similarly, people with a highly anxious personality are not likely to do well in jobs, such as air traffic controllers and emergency-room physicians, that are inherently stressful. *Selection and placement* decisions should take these factors into consideration.

We discussed *goal setting* in Chapter 5. On the basis of an extensive amount of research, we concluded that individuals perform best when they have specific and challenging goals and receive feedback on how well they are progressing toward those goals. The use of goals can reduce stress. Specific goals that are perceived as attainable clarify performance expectations. In addition, goal feedback reduces uncertainties as to actual job performance. The results are less employee frustration, less job uncertainty, and less stress.

A frequent cause of stress is poor use of time. So management should consider providing *time-management* training. The well-organized employee can often accomplish twice as much as the person who is poorly organized. An understanding and utilization of time-management principles can help individuals better cope with job demands.

BUILDING SELF-AWARENESS • BUILDING SELF-AWARENESS

BUILDING SELF-AWARENESS • BUILDING SELF-AWARENESS • BUILDING

WHAT IS YOUR STRESS LEVEL?

INSTRUCTIONS

Using the following numerical scale, indicate how strongly you agree with each of the following statements.

4 = All the time
3 = Often
2 = Sometimes
1 = Never

Turn to page 563 for scoring directions and key.

1. I'm exhaused by daily demands at work, college, and home. ______
2. My stress is caused by outside forces beyond my control. ______
3. I'm trapped by circumstances that I just have to live with. ______
4. No matter how hard I work to stay on top of my schedule, I can't get caught up. ______
5. I have financial obligations I can't seem to meet. ______
6. I dislike my work, but I can't take the risk of making a career change (or, if not working: I dislike college, but I can't take the risk of of dropping out). ______
7. I'm dissatisfied with my personal relationships. ______
8. I feel responsible for the happiness of people around me. ______
9. I'm embarrassed to ask for help. ______
10. I do not know what I want out of life. ______
11. I'm disappointed that I have not achieved what I had hoped for. ______
12. No matter how much success I have, I feel empty. ______
13. If the people around me were more competent, I would feel happier. ______
14. People let me down. ______
15. I stew in my anger rather than express it. ______
16. I become enraged and resentful when I am hurt. ______
17. I can't take criticism. ______
18. I'm afraid I'll lose my job (or fail out of school). ______
19. I don't see the value of expressing sadness or grief. ______
20. I don't trust that things will work out. ______

Source: Adapted from *From Stress to Strength,* Robert S. Eliot, M.D. © 1994 by Robert S. Eliot, M.D. Used by permission of Bantam Books, a division of Bantam Doubleday Dell Publishing Group, Inc.

Redesigning jobs to give employees more responsibility, more-meaningful work, more autonomy, and increased feedback can reduce stress, because these factors give the employee greater control over work activities and lessen dependence on others. But as we noted in our discussion of work design, not all employees want enriched jobs. The right job redesign, then, for employees with a low need for growth might be less responsibility and increased specialization. If individuals prefer structure and routine, reducing skill variety should also reduce uncertainties and stress levels.

Job stress occurs to a large extent because employees feel uncertain about goals, expectations, how they will be evaluated, and the like. By giving these employees a voice in those decisions that directly affect their job performances, management can increase employee control and reduce this cause of stress. So managers should consider increasing *employee involvement* in decision making.

Having friends, family, or colleagues to talk to provides an outlet when stress levels become excessive. Helping employees expand their *social support networks* can be a means of reducing tension. Having someone else to hear a problem can provide an objective perspective on a given situation. Interestingly, the value of social support in lessening stress may be an important, but rarely mentioned, advantage provided by work teams.

Increasing formal *organizational communication* with employees reduces uncertainty by lessening ambiguity. If uncertainty creates stress, then improving internal communication and lessening uncertainty and ambiguity can reduce it.

Our final suggestion is to offer organizationally supported *wellness programs*. These programs focus on the employee's total physical and mental condition. For example, they typically provide workshops to help people quit smoking, control alcohol use, lose weight, eat better, and develop a regular exercise program. The assumption underlying most wellness programs is that employees need to take personal responsibility for their physical and mental health. The organization is merely a vehicle to facilitate this end.

Organizations, of course, aren't altruistic. They expect a payoff from their investment in wellness programs. And most of those firms that have introduced wellness programs have found that the benefits exceed the costs. For instance, Du Pont saw a 14 percent decline in sick days among employees at forty-one plants; nonhospital health-care costs shrank 43 percent at Tenneco Inc.; and the average annual employee health claim at Steelcase Inc. fell from $1,155 to $537.[43]

Building an Innovative Organization

Innovativeness stimulates opportunities and growth. Without it, organizations "eventually wither and die."[44] But how does an organization become innovative?

The standard toward which many organizations strive is that achieved by the 3M Co.[45] It has built a reputation as one of the most innovative organizations in the world by consistently developing new products over a very long period of time. The company currently markets some 60,000 different products. 3M has historically sought to have 25 percent of its annual sales come from products developed in the previous 5 years. And it always reached that goal. More recently, top management challenged the company by increasing the goal to 30 percent for products introduced in the previous *4* years and 10 percent for those introduced in the *last year.*

3M is obviously doing something right. What can other organizations do to achieve 3M's track record for innovation? There is no guaranteed formula, but certain characteristics surface again and again when researchers study innovative organizations. We have grouped them into structural, cultural, and human resource categories. Our message to top management is that they should consider introducing these characteristics into their organization if they want to create an innovative climate. Before we look at these characteristics, however, let's clarify what we mean by innovation.

Definition Innovation is a special kind of change. Whereas *change* refers to making things different, **innovation** refers to a new idea applied to initiating or improving a product, process, or service.[46] So all innovations involve change, but not all changes necessarily involve new ideas or lead to significant improvements. Innovations in organizations can range from small incremental improvements, such as RJR Nabisco's extension of the Oreo product line to include double stuffs and chocolate-covered Oreos, up to radical breakthroughs, such as McGraw-Hill's recent creation of customized textbooks that utilize computer networks to link bookstore laser printers to McGraw's central database of text material. Keep in mind that, although our examples are mostly of product innovations, the concept of innovation also encompasses new production process technologies, new structures or administrative systems, and new plans or programs pertaining to organizational members.

Sources of Innovation *Structural variables* have been the most-studied potential source of innovation.[47] A comprehensive review of the structure-innovation relationship leads to the following conclusions.[48] First, organic structures positively influence innovation. Because they are low in vertical differentiation, formalization, and centralization, organic organizations have the flexibility, adaptiveness, and cross-fertilization that facilitate the adoption of innovations. Second, long tenure in management is associated with innovation. Managerial tenure apparently provides legitimacy and knowledge of how to accomplish tasks and obtain desired outcomes. Third, innovation is nurtured where resources are abundant. Having an abundance of resources allows an organization to afford to purchase innovations, bear the cost of instituting innovations, and absorb failures. Finally, interunit communication is high in innovative organizations.[49] These organizations are high users of committees, task forces, new-venture teams and other mechanisms that facilitate interaction across departmental lines.

Innovative organizations tend to have similar *cultures*. They encourage experimentation. They reward both successes and failures. They celebrate mistakes. At Hewlett-Packard, for instance, CEO Lewis Platt has successfully built a corporate culture that supports people who try something that doesn't work out.[50] Platt, himself, protects people who stick their necks out, fearful that to do otherwise

Hewlett Packard CEO Lew Platt has successfully built a corporate culture that encourages risk taking and innovation. H-P, for instance, has become the dominant player in the market for laser printers by consistently developing higher quality and more reliable products at prices that undercut those of its competitors.

would stifle the risk-taking culture he encourages among his managers. Unfortunately, in too many organizations, people are rewarded for the absence of failures rather than for the presence of successes. Such cultures extinguish risk taking and innovation. People will suggest and try new ideas only when they feel that such behaviors will exact no penalties. Managers in innovative organizations recognize that failures are a natural by-product of venturing into the unknown. When Babe Ruth set his record for home runs in one season, he also led the league in strikeouts. And he is remembered for the former, not the latter!

Within the *human resources* category, we find that innovative organizations actively train and develop their members so that they can keep current. They offer high job security so that employees won't fear getting fired for making mistakes, and they encourage individuals to become champions of change. Once a new idea

IN THE NEWS

Rubbermaid Knows How to Innovate

IT MAKES SOME OF THE MOST MUNDANE PRODUCTS YOU CAN IMAGINE—THINGS SUCH AS DUSTPANS, spatulas, ice cube trays, dish strainers, food-storage containers, and mailboxes. Yet this company, Rubbermaid, is one of the most powerful brands in the United States. A recent consumer survey rated it ahead of such well-known firms as Kellogg, Johnson & Johnson, Walt Disney, General Mills, and Quaker Oats.

The secret of Rubbermaid's success can be summarized in one word: innovation. Year-in and year-out, Rubbermaid has continued to develop new products and make small improvements to its line-up of more than 5,000 products. In 1994, as an example, the company introduced 400 new (not just improved) products. That's more than one a day! Just as important, few of these products failed in the marketplace. Nine out of every 10 product introductions are rated as commercial successes. Top management has recently set goals of entering a completely new market every 12 to 18 months (most recently this includes hardware cabinets and garden sheds), achieving one-third of its sales from products introduced in the previous 5 years, and increasing non-U.S. sales from 18 percent to 30 percent of total revenues.

How does Rubbermaid consistently chalk up its impressive innovation successes? It has created a culture that values and rewards risk taking and the constant search for ways to improve products. But management attributes most of its new product ideas to a structural device: cross-functional teams. It allows the company to have the advantages of a large company without losing the entrepreneurial drive, focus, intensity, and ownership that comes with very small groups. Twenty-one of these teams, each made up of five to seven members from marketing, manufacturing, R&D, finance, and other departments, focus on specific product lines such as bathroom accessories. Dick Gates, head of Rubbermaid business development, says "If we weren't organized that way [around teams], who would be thinking about ice cube trays? Who would be thinking about johnny mops?"

Source: Based on A. Farnham, "America's Most Admired Company," *Fortune,* February 7, 1994, pp. 50–54; and T. Stevens, "Where the Rubbermaid Meets the Road," *Industry Week,* March 20, 1995, pp. 14–18.

The Little Tikes Co., a division of Rubbermaid, makes toys and playground equipment. Following Rubbermaid's proven innovation formula of identifying trends, use of cross-functional teams, and exploiting the latest technology, Little Tikes recently introduced the Play Center 2 for the day-care industry. It is a runaway success.

is developed, **idea champions** actively and enthusiastically promote the idea, build support, overcome resistance, and ensure that the innovation is implemented.[51] Recent research finds that idea champions have common personality characteristics: extremely high self-confidence, persistence, energy, and a tendency to take risks. Idea champions also display characteristics associated with transformational leadership. They inspire and energize others with their vision of the potential of an innovation and through their strong personal conviction in their mission. They are also good at gaining the commitment of others to support their mission. In addition, idea champions have jobs that provide considerable decision-making discretion. This autonomy helps them introduce and implement innovations in organizations.[52]

Given the status of 3M as a premier product innovator, we would expect it to have most or all of the properties we have identified. It does. The company is so highly decentralized that it has many of the characteristics of small, organic organizations. All of 3M's scientists and managers are challenged to "keep current." Idea champions are created and encouraged by allowing scientists and engineers to spend up to 15 percent of their time on projects of their own choosing. The company encourages its employees to take risks—and rewards the failures as well as the successes. 3M management exhibits high patience. The company invests nearly 7 percent of its sales revenue (more than $1 billion a year) in research and development, yet management tells its R&D people that *not everything is going to work*. And very important, 3M doesn't hire and fire with the business cycle. For instance, during the most recent recession, while nearly all major companies cut costs by firing employees, 3M initiated no layoffs. When reductions in staff have been necessary, 3M has averted layoffs by relying on early retirement incentives and transfers of full-time employees to jobs filled by temporary or part-time workers.

Creating a Learning Organization

What TQM was to the 1980s and reengineering was to the early 1990s, the learning organization has become to the mid-1990s. It has developed a groundswell of interest from managers looking for new ways to successfully respond to a world of interdependence and change.[53] In this section, we describe what a learning organization looks like and methods for managing learning.

What Is a Learning Organization? A **learning organization** is an organization that has developed the continuous capacity to adapt and change. Just as individuals learn, so too do organizations. "All organizations learn, whether they consciously choose to or not—it is a fundamental requirement for their sustained existence."[54] However, some organizations—such as Xerox, Corning, Federal Express, Ford, General Electric, Motorola, Wal-Mart—just do it better than others.

Most organizations engage in what has been called **single-loop learning.**[55] When errors are detected, the correction process relies on past routines and present policies. In contrast, learning organizations use **double-loop learning.** When an error is detected, it is corrected in ways that involve the modification of the organization's objectives, policies, and standard routines. Like second-order change, double-loop learning challenges deep-rooted assumptions and norms within an organization. In this way, it provides opportunities for radically different solutions to problems and dramatic jumps in improvement.

Learning organizations use double-loop learning.

Exhibit 17-4 on page 536 summarizes the five basic characteristics of a learning organization. It is an organization in which people put aside their old ways of thinking, learn to be open with each other, understand how their organization really works, form a plan or vision that everyone can agree upon, and then work together to achieve that vision.[56]

Proponents of the learning organization envision it as a remedy for the three fundamental problems inherent in traditional organizations: fragmentation, competition, and reactiveness.[57] First, *fragmentation* based on specialization creates "walls" and "chimneys" that separate different functions into independent and often warring fiefdoms. Second, an overemphasis on *competition* often undermines collaboration. Members of the management team compete with one another to show who is right, who knows the most, or who is most persuasive. Divisions compete with one another when they ought to cooperate to share knowledge. Team project leaders compete to show who is the best manager. And third, *reactiveness* misdirects management's attention to problem solving rather than to creation. The problem solver tries to make something go away, whereas a creator tries to bring something new into being. An emphasis on reactiveness pushes out innovation and continuous improvement and, in its place, encourages people to run around "putting out fires."

It may help to better understand what a learning organization is if you think of it as an *ideal* model that builds on a number of contemporary management concepts. No company has successfully achieved (or probably ever will achieve) all the characteristics described in Exhibit 17-4. You should think of a learning organization as an ideal to strive toward rather than a realistic description of structured activity. Notice, too, how learning organizations draw on previous concepts such as TQM, organizational culture, the boundaryless organization, functional conflict, and transformational leadership. For instance, the learning organization adopts TQM's commitment to continuous improvement. Learning organizations are also characterized by a specific culture that values risk taking, openness, and growth. It seeks "boundarylessness" through breaking down barriers created by hierarchical levels and fragmented departmentalization. A learning organization supports the importance of disagreements, constructive criticism, and other forms of functional conflict. And transformational leadership is needed in a learning organization to implement the shared vision.

Managing Learning How do you change an organization to make it into a continual learner? What can managers do to make their firms learning organizations?

Establish a strategy. Management needs to make explicit its commitment to change, innovation, and continuous improvement.

Redesign the organization's structure. The formal structure can be a serious impediment to learning. Flattening the structure, eliminating or combining departments, and increasing the use of cross-functional teams reinforce interdependence and reduce boundaries between people.

EXHIBIT 17-4
Characteristics of a Learning Organization

1. There exists a shared vision upon which everyone agrees.
2. People discard their old ways of thinking and the standard routines they use for solving problems or doing their jobs.
3. Members think of all organizational processes, activities, functions, and interactions with the environment as part of a system of interrelationships.
4. People openly communicate (across vertical and horizontal boundaries) without fear of criticism or punishment.
5. People sublimate their personal self-interest and fragmented departmental interests to work together to achieve the organization's shared vision.

Source: Based on P. M. Senge, *The Fifth Discipline* (New York: Doubleday, 1990).

Reshape the organization's culture. As noted earlier, learning organizations are characterized by risk taking, openness, and growth. Management sets the tone for the organization's culture both by what it says (strategy) and what it does (behavior). Managers need to demonstrate by their actions that taking risks and admitting failures are desirable traits. That means rewarding people who take chances and make mistakes. And management needs to encourage functional conflict. "The key to unlocking real openness at work," says one expert on learning organizations, "is to teach people to give up having to be in agreement. We think agreement is so important. Who cares? You have to bring paradoxes, conflicts, and dilemmas out in the open, so collectively we can be more intelligent than we can be individually."[58]

An Application: The U.S. Army? The U.S. Army isn't the typical example that comes to mind when you think of what a learning organization might look like. But think again.[59] The Army's environment has changed dramatically since the days of the Vietnam conflict. For one thing, the Soviet threat, which was a major justification for the Army's military buildup, is largely gone. Army soldiers are more likely to be involved in feeding children in Somalia, keeping peace in Haiti, or helping put out forest fires in the Pacific Northwest than fighting a war. And its new mission is reflected in its budget. The Army's annual appropriation dropped from $90 billion in 1989 to $60 billion in 1994. Meanwhile, the number of troops in uniform has been downsized from 780,000 to less than 500,000. Clearly, it's no longer "business as usual" in the U.S. Army.

The Army's high command has redesigned its structure to reflect its new mission. The old Army was said to be an organization "designed by geniuses to be run by idiots."[60] That rigid, hierarchical, command-and-control structure was fine when the Army's single purpose was combat-related. Authority was centralized at the Pentagon, and orders were passed down to the field. Officers weren't expected

Soldiers in the U.S. Army rehearse for an uncertain real world where civilians are sometimes trapped by combat. While the blood in this photo is fake, the training provides a dress rehearsal for what these soldiers might face on the job.

to innovate or make adjustments. But that type of structure doesn't fit with the changing role of the military. The new Army is putting into place an adaptive and flexible structure to match its more-varied objectives.

Along with the new structure is a major program to make the Army's culture more egalitarian. Everyone, from PFCs to brigadier generals, has gone through team training to learn how to make decisions in the field and even to question authority (a previously unheard-of idea). Senior officers are required to go through something called the After Action Review—a public performance appraisal—where decisions are openly critiqued by subordinates. The potential for public embarrassment in an AAR would never have been allowed in the old Army.

The bottom line is that the U.S. Army is becoming a learning organization. It is developing soldiers, especially officers, who can adapt rapidly to different tasks and missions. The new Army seeks to be able to quickly improvise in complex and ambiguous situations. Its soldiers will be prepared to play a multiple set of changing roles—fighting, peacekeeping, peacemaking, humanitarian rescue, nation building, or whatever—and be able to change those roles quickly as needed.

SUMMARY

(This summary is organized by the chapter-opening learning objectives on page 511.)

1. Sources of individual resistance to change include habit, security, economic factors, fear of the unknown, and selective information processing. Sources of organizational resistance include structural and group inertia, limited focus, and threats to expertise, power relationships, and established resource allocations.
2. First-order change involves minor incremental improvements. Second-order change is a multidimensional, multilevel, discontinuous, radical change involving a reframing of assumptions.
3. Strategies for reducing resistance to change include conducting an identity audit, identifying key differences so change will fit properly, presenting the change as significant and tying it to valued aspects of the organization's identity, introducing the change as a series of midrange steps, taking the path of least resistance, and keeping the amount of change within tolerable limits.
4. Tactics for reducing resistance include education and communication, participation, facilitation and support, negotiation, manipulation and cooptation, and coercion.
5. Change options available to a manager include structure, culture, technology, the physical setting, and people.
6. Organizational development refers to a collection of techniques for understanding, changing, and developing an organization's work force to improve its effectiveness.
7. Stress reduction techniques include improved personnel selection and job placement, use of realistic goals, time management, job redesign, increased employee involvement, expanded social support networks, improved organizational communication, and wellness programs.
8. Managers can increase innovation by implementing an organic structure; facilitating long tenure in the management ranks; providing abundant resources; expanding interunit communication; creating cultures that reward risk-taking and tolerate mistakes; and promoting employee training and development; offering job security; and encouraging idea champions.
9. A learning organization is one that has developed the continuous capacity to adapt and change.

REVIEW AND DISCUSSION QUESTIONS

1. What are the forces reshaping the changing world of work?
2. "Resistance to change isn't all bad." Build an argument to support this statement.
3. It is commonly assumed that an individual's resistance to change increases with age. Do you think this is true? Defend your position.
4. What is the transformational leader's role in planned change? What is the role of the transactional leader?
5. As a low-level manager acting as a change agent, what can you do to deal with the political aspects of implementing change?
6. How can managers get people to more readily accept a major organizational change—such as the redesign of jobs from individual work activities to teams?
7. How does national culture influence change agents?
8. Do you think it is unethical for managers to try to help employees deal with stress that is nonwork-related? Explain.
9. Describe the characteristics of a learning organization. Relate the learning organization to the concepts of reengineering, TQM, team building, and organization design.
10. Organizations typically have limits to how much change they can absorb. As a senior manager, what signs would you look for that might suggest that your organization has exceeded its change capacity?

CASE EXERCISE A
CHANGE COMES SLOWLY AT WESTINGHOUSE

Michael Jordan, a veteran PepsiCo executive, took the job as chief executive at Westinghouse Electric in the summer of 1993. He knew he had a challenge when he took the Westinghouse job, but it is proving to be more than even he reckoned for.

For example, one of his early objectives was to cut costs. He blanched when he saw that the company was spending $14 to process a single lunch-expense voucher. A team of Westinghouse executives, told to trim that figure, set a target of $7 a voucher. Unfortunately, other companies in the industry could do it for about $2. This difference only confirmed what Jordan suspected: Westinghouse had a mentality that did not insist on top performance.

Westinghouse's board chose Jordan specifically for his past experience in consumer goods and marketing. He was, after all, the first outside chief executive at Westinghouse in 64 years. They hoped he could transform a company fixated on manufacturing old industrial products into a more flexible and market-driven firm.

Upon arriving, Jordan immediately began trying to shake things up. He brought in a new financial team from the outside. He quickly sold off two units for $1.4 billion. He cut 4,300 jobs, or 8 percent of the work force. And in his grandest gesture, he paid more than $8 billion to buy CBS Inc.

Despite all his efforts, Jordan has had trouble getting his people to adapt a leaner operating style. "None of this 'let's change' attitude has filtered down," complains an engineer at the company's Florida-based power-generation unit. "The top guys may be scurrying, but it is still hard to get support from midlevel managers for new ideas."

Jordan also is facing a culture clash. His consensus approach runs counter to Westinghouse's more bureaucratic style, where managers rarely tried to outperform financial goals. Indeed, senior executives used to carry wallet cards—Jordan calls them "death cards"—listing their retirement dates. "People are used to getting into their foxholes. It was better to promise 10 percent [growth] and deliver 12 percent, than promise 30 percent and get 28 percent," he says.

Questions

1. Analyze the sources of resistance to change.
2. If you were Jordan, what would you do?

Source: Based on R. Narisetti, "Jordan Finds Change Comes Slowly at Westinghouse," *Wall Street Journal*, March 2, 1995, p. B4.

CASE EXERCISE B
THE GERMANS COME TO ALABAMA

One day in the spring of 1994, two Mercedes managers participated in an Outward Bound–type of team-building exercise in the Austrian Alps. This exercise was just one of Andreas Renschler's ideas on how to shake up the culture at Mercedes-Benz.

Renschler is the fast-rising, 37-year-old executive who has been given the challenging task of overseeing the development of Mercedes' first mass-market sport-utility vehicle (the All Activity Vehicle, or AAV), which will be produced at the company's first big foreign plant in Vance, Alabama. As president of Mercedes-Benz U.S. International Inc., Renschler is trying to do in the company's U.S. operations what his bosses are trying to do in Germany—to transform the once-ponderous luxury-car maker into an efficient worldwide competitor.

Renschler's relative youth was a major reason he was selected for his job. He's not steeped in the Mercedes culture, which has always put engineering excellence ahead of costs. In his 6 years with the company, as assistant to the CEO, he helped plan the current corporate turnaround and became known as a creative problem solver and idea generator. He also planned strategies for light trucks in Europe and Latin America and ran the feasibility study for the AAV. But he has a tough job ahead of him. Japanese transplants typically copy plants back home and assemble existing models. But, at first, Renschler will have to simultaneously debug a product, a manufacturing process, and a work force. "It's a prescription for disaster," says one manufacturing consultant. "There are too many variables."

As part of a plan to adapt the best operating techniques of other companies, Renschler has hired managers from Chrysler, Ford, Mitsubishi, and Sony. Unfortunately, their diverse backgrounds make it hard to mesh their styles. For instance, one Toyota alum spent Thanksgiving weekend of 1993 in an Alabama motel with a dozen German and American colleagues, debating a factory layout. German engineers wanted a sprawling E-shaped building with departments linked by complex conveyors. After endless wrangling, those with Japanese experience prevailed, and the group settled on a compact, rectangular design.

To shape his diverse group into a team, Renschler is going all-out to erase Mercedes' stiff formality and to encourage bonds. The team-building exercise in the Alps, for instance, was designed to help meet that objective. Renschler is also pushing changes in Mercedes' traditional product-development process. To save time and money, Renschler will have only 100 primary suppliers for the AAV—versus 1,000 for the just-introduced E-class sedan. In addition, suppliers get a freer hand in designing parts, sometimes adapting off-the-shelf components rather than always starting from scratch as in the past. And rather than make suppliers bid for business annually, as Mercedes usually does, Renschler has been offering multi-year contracts in return for annual 5 percent price cuts.

Renschler's aggressive change program has won him his share of enemies within the company. "Lots of people are envious" of his rise or are threatened by the changes he's pushing, says one insider, and some are quietly hoping for him to fail.

Questions

1. "If it ain't broke, don't fix it." Why doesn't Renschler accept this adage?
2. Is Renschler trying to implement too much change, too fast? Support your position.
3. Do you think Renschler's innovations at Vance will succeed? Explain your position.

Source: Based on D. Woodruff, "Mercedes' Maverick in Alabama," *Business Week,* September 11, 1995, pp. 64–65.

SKILL EXERCISE

Managing Resistance to Change

Almost from its inception, Prentice Hall's college division (which produces textbooks and educational materials for use in colleges and universities) had been located in Englewood Cliffs, New Jersey. This location proved convenient for a wide range of employees. City types were only 20 minutes from the upper west side of New York City. Suburbanites could choose from dozens of small New Jersey communities that were only minutes from the office. And employees who preferred a rural lifestyle could have it and still be less than a 40-minute commute to work.

Prentice Hall's senior management decided in the early 1990s that the company had outgrown its present Englewood Cliffs facility, but local officials resisted management's efforts to expand on its current site. After much analysis, management bought the former headquarters of Western Union in Upper Saddle River, New Jersey. After remodeling of the Upper Saddle River location, all Prentice Hall operations were to be moved by June 1995.

Upper Saddle River repositioned Prentice Hall in terms of hiring and retaining employees. The major difference between Upper Saddle River and Englewood Cliffs was proximity to New York City. The latter was just a few miles away and a short commute by car or bus. The former was 35 miles from the city—taking nearly an hour each way to commute and accessible only by car.

The relocation had little impact on managers in the production area, because most production employees lived in New Jersey and drove to work. But it caused problems for managers of creative departments such as advertising and design. Most employees in those departments lived in New York City, had no desire to live anywhere else, and did not own cars.

Linda Wilson manages a small group at Prentice Hall that exclusively works on designing books. All six of her people live in New York City. When Linda learned in the summer of 1994 of the move to Upper Saddle River, she informed her people. No one immediately resigned. But as the official moving date got closer, she was hearing more and more rumors that most of her people were looking for jobs in the city.

Assume that you are Linda Wilson. It's spring 1995. You don't want to lose any of the skilled and talented people you have in your group. What will you do? Be specific.

NOTES

1. M. Landler, "Slow-to-Adapt Encyclopedia Britannica Is For Sale," *New York Times,* May 16, 1995, p. C1.
2. Cited in T. Peters, "The Peters Principles," *Forbes ASAP,* October 9, 1995, p. 184.
3. Ibid.
4. E. Appelbaum and R. Batt, *The New American Workplace: Transforming Work Systems in the United States* (Ithaca, N.Y.: ILR Press, 1994).
5. D. Bottoms, "Facing Change or Changing Face?" *Industry Week,* May 1, 1995, p. 17.
6. D. Miller, "What Happens after Success: The Perils of Excellence," *Journal of Management Studies,* May 1994, pp. 325–58; and E. E. Lawler III and J. R. Galbraith, "Avoiding the Corporate Dinosaur Syndrome," *Organizational Dynamics,* Autumn 1994, pp. 5–17.
7. See, for instance, A. B. Fisher, "Making Change Stick," *Fortune,* April 17, 1995, pp. 121–29.
8. D. Katz and R. L. Kahn, *The Social Psychology of Organizations,* 2nd ed. (New York: Wiley, 1978), pp. 714–15.
9. H. Lancaster, "Quick-Change Artists May Find Fast Route to Executive Positions," *Wall Street Journal,* May 9, 1995, p. B1.
10. See A. Levy, "Second-Order Planned Change: Definition and Conceptualization," *Organizational Dynamics,* Summer 1986, pp. 4–20; J. H. Want, "Managing Radical Change," *Journal of Business Strategy,* May–June 1993, pp. 21–28; and D. A. Nadler, R. B. Shaw, and A. E. Walton, *Discontinuous Change* (San Francisco: Jossey-Bass, 1995).
11. K. L. Miller, "The Factory Guru Tinkering with Toyota," *Business Week,* May 17, 1993, pp. 95–97.
12. R. Pascale, cited in T. Brown, "Re-Invent Yourself," *Industry Week,* November 21, 1994, pp. 21–26.
13. D. J. Yang and A. Rothman, "Reinventing Boeing: Radical Change and Crisis," *Business Week,* March 1, 1993, pp. 60–67.

14. As described in T. A. Stewart, "Rate Your Readiness to Change," *Fortune,* February 7, 1994, pp. 106–10.
15. R. K. Reger, J. V. Mullane, L. T. Gustafson, and S. M. DeMarie, "Creating Earthquakes to Change Organizational Mindsets," *The Executive,* November 1994, pp. 38–41.
16. J. P. Kotter and L. A. Schlesinger, "Choosing Strategies for Change," *Harvard Business Review,* March–April 1979, pp. 106–14.
17. See J. Pfeffer, *Managing with Power: Politics and Influence in Organizations* (Boston: Harvard Business School Press, 1992), pp. 7, 318–20.
18. See, for instance, W. Ocasio, "Political Dynamics and the Circulation of Power: CEO Succession in U.S. Industrial Corporations, 1960–1990," *Administrative Science Quarterly,* June 1994, pp. 285–312.
19. Based on H. J. Leavitt, "Applied Organization Change in Industry," in W. Cooper, H. Leavitt, and M. Shelly, eds., *New Perspectives on Organization Research* (New York: Wiley, 1964); and P. J. Robertson, D. R. Roberts, and J. I. Porras, "Dynamics of Planned Organizational Change: Assessing Empirical Support for a Theoretical Model," *Academy of Management Journal,* June 1993, pp. 619–34.
20. Cited in T. D. Jick, "Accelerating Change for Competitive Advantage," *Organizational Dynamics,* Summer 1995, p. 78.
21. T. Tillson, "Be It Ever So Humble," *Canadian Business,* Special Technology Issue, June 1995, pp. 26–32.
22. F. Steele, *Making and Managing High-Quality Workplaces: An Organizational Ecology* (New York: Teachers College Press, 1986).
23. J. I. Porras and P. J. Robertson, "Organizational Development: Theory, Practice, and Research," in M. D. Dunnette and L. M. Hough, eds., *Handbook of Industrial & Organizational Psychology,* 2nd ed., vol. 3 (Palo Alto, Calif.: Consulting Psychologists Press, 1992), p. 734.
24. This definition is adapted from T. G. Cummings and C. G. Worley, *Organizational Change and Development,* 5th ed. (St. Paul, Minn.: West, 1993).
25. L. D. Brown and J. G. Covey, "Development Organizations and Organization Development: Toward an Expanded Paradigm for Organization Development," in R. W. Woodman and W. A. Pasmore, eds., *Research in Organizational Change and Development,* vol. 1 (Greenwich, Conn.: JAI Press, 1987), p. 63; and W. A. Pasmore and M. R. Fagans, "Participation, Individual Development, and Organizational Change: A Review and Synthesis," *Journal of Management,* June 1992, pp. 375–97.
26. See, for instance, P. F. Buller, "The Team Building–Task Performance Relation: Some Conceptual and Methodological Refinements," *Group and Organization Studies,* September 1986, pp. 147–68; and D. Eden, "Team Development: Quasi-Experimental Confirmation among Combat Companies," *Group and Organization Studies,* September 1986, pp. 133–46.
27. N. Margulies and J. Wallace, *Organizational Change: Techniques and Applications* (Glenview, Ill.: Scott, Foresman, 1973), pp. 99–100.
28. See, for example, E. H. Neilsen, "Understanding and Managing Intergroup Conflict," in J. W. Lorsch and P. R. Lawrence, eds., *Managing Group and Intergroup Relations* (Homewood, Ill.: Irwin-Dorsey, 1972), pp. 329–43.
29. R. R. Blake, J. S. Mouton, and R. L. Sloma, "The Union-Management Intergroup Laboratory: Strategy for Resolving Intergroup Conflict," *Journal of Applied Behavioral Science,* no. 1 (1965), pp. 25–57.
30. M. A. Verespej, "Reengineering Isn't Going Away," *Industry Week,* February 20, 1995, p. 42.
31. M. Hammer and S. A. Stanton, "Beating the Risks of Reengineering," *Fortune,* May 15, 1995, p. 106.
32. J. Champy, *Reengineering Management: The Mandate for New Leadership* (New York: HarperBusiness, 1995).
33. Hammer and Stanton, "Beating the Risks of Reengineering," p. 106.
34. A. Ehrbar, "'Re-Engineering' Gives Firms New Efficiency, Workers the Pink Slip," *Wall Street Journal,* March 16, 1993, p. A1.
35. Ibid.
36. Hammer and Stanton, "Beating the Risks of Reengineering," p. 114.
37. Champy, *Reengineering Management.*
38. Hammer and Stanton, "Beating the Risks of Reengineering," p. 106.
39. M. Hammer and S. A. Stanton, *The Reengineering Revolution* (New York: HarperBusiness, 1995).
40. Cited in A. Farnham, "Who Beats Stress Best—and How," *Fortune,* October 7, 1991, p. 71.
41. S. Parasuraman and J. A. Alutto, "Sources and Outcomes of Stress in Organizational Settings: Toward the Development of a Structural Model," *Academy of Management Journal,* June 1984, pp. 330-50; and R. L. Kahn and P. Byosiere, "Stress in Organizations," in Dunnette and Hough, eds., *Handbook of Industrial & Organizational Psychology,* 2nd ed., vol. 3, pp. 573–80.
42. Adapted from J. M. Ivancevich and M. T. Matteson, "Organizational Level Stress Management Interventions: A Review and Recommendations," *Journal of Organizational Behavior Management,* Fall–Winter 1986, pp. 229–48; and J. M. Ivancevich, M. T. Matteson, S. M. Freedman, and J. S. Phillips, "Worksite Stress Management Interventions," *American Psychologist,* February 1990, pp. 252–61.
43. C. E. Beadle, "And Let's Save 'Wellness.' It Works," *New York Times,* July 24, 1994, p. F9.
44. D. L. Day, "Raising Radicals: Different Processes for Championing Innovative Corporate Ventures," *Organization Science,* May 1994, p. 148.
45. Discussions of the 3M Co. in this section are based on K. Labich, "The Innovators," *Fortune,* June 6, 1988, p. 49; R. Mitchell, "Masters of Innovation," *Business Week,* April 10, 1989, p. 58; K. Kelly, "The Drought Is Over at 3M," *Business Week,* November 7, 1994, pp. 140–41; T. Stevens, "Tool Kit for Innovators," *Industry Week,* June 5, 1995, pp. 28–31; and T.A. Stewart, "3M Fights Back," *Fortune,* February 5, 1996, pp. 94–99.
46. See, for instance, A. Van de Ven, "Central Problems in the Management of Innovation," *Management Science* 32 (1986), pp. 590–607; R. M. Kanter, "When a Thousand Flowers Bloom: Structural, Collective, and Social Conditions for Innovation in Organizations," in B. M. Staw and L. L. Cummings, eds., *Research in Organizational Behavior,* vol. 10 (Greenwich, Conn.: JAI Press, 1988), pp. 169–211; and R. A. Wolfe, "Organizational Innovation: Review, Critique, and Suggested Research Directions," *Journal of Management Studies,* May 1994, pp. 405–29.
47. F. Damanpour, "Organizational Innovation: A Meta-Analysis of Effects of Determinants and Moderators," *Academy of Management Journal,* September 1991, p. 557.

48. Ibid., pp. 555–90.
49. See also C. K. Bart, "New Venture Units: Use Them Wisely to Manage Innovation," *Sloan Management Review,* Summer 1988, pp. 35–43; and P. R. Monge, M. D. Cozzens, and N. S. Contractor, "Communication and Motivational Predictors of the Dynamics of Organizational Innovation," *Organization Science,* May 1992, pp. 250–74.
50. J. H. Sheridan, "Lew Platt: Creating a Culture for Innovation," *Industry Week,* December 19, 1994, pp. 26–30.
51. J. M. Howell and C. A. Higgins, "Champions of Change," *Business Quarterly,* Spring 1990, pp. 31–32; and Day, "Raising Radicals."
52. Howell and Higgins, "Champions of Change."
53. See, for example, P. M. Senge, *The Fifth Discipline* (New York: Doubleday, 1990); G. P. Huber, "Organizational Learning: The Contributing Processes and the Literatures," *Organization Sciences,* February 1991, pp. 88–115; M. Dodgson, "Organizational Learning: A Review of Some Literatures," *Organization Studies* 14, no. 3 (1993), pp. 375–94; J. W. Slocum, Jr., M. McGill, and D. T. Lei, "The New Learning Strategy: Anytime, Anything, Anywhere," *Organizational Dynamics,* Autumn 1994, pp. 33–47; and F. J. Barrett, "Creating Appreciative Learning Cultures," *Organizational Dynamics,* Autumn 1995, pp. 36–49.
54. D. H. Kim, "The Link between Individual and Organizational Learning," *Sloan Management Review,* Fall 1993, p. 37.
55. C. Argyris and D. A. Schon, *Organizational Learning* (Reading, Mass.: Addison-Wesley, 1978).
56. B. Dumaine, "Mr. Learning Organization," *Fortune,* October 17, 1994, p. 148.
57. F. Kofman and P. M. Senge, "Communities of Commitment: The Heart of Learning Organizations," *Organizational Dynamics,* Autumn 1993, pp. 5–23.
58. Dumaine, "Mr. Learning Organization," p. 154.
59. L. Smith, "New Ideas from the Army (Really)," *Fortune,* September 19, 1994, pp. 203–12.
60. Ibid., p. 203.

APPENDIX A
THE HISTORICAL ROOTS OF CURRENT MANAGEMENT PRACTICE

When I want to understand what is happening today or try to decide what will happen tomorrow, I look back.

– O. W. Holmes Jr.

Hans Becherer, chief executive of John Deere & Co., thinks he has introduced some innovative changes at his company. When he took over the top spot at Deere in 1990, sales and profits were both falling. He needed to cut costs, reduce design time, and increase productivity. He decided to reach out to his work force for solutions.[1] "It's often the people at the root of the company, on the shop floor, who will provide the best answers," said Becherer. He believed that employees would be more receptive to improving efficiency if they felt part of the process.

So Becherer restructured jobs around teams and brought Deere's blue-collar workers into the decision-making process. Hourly workers now routinely offer advice on everything from cutting production costs to improving product quality. Cost-reduction teams composed of production workers at Deere's Davenport, Iowa, plant, for example, meet weekly to figure out ways to simplify parts or eliminate production problems. One of these teams found that two engine brackets could be eliminated from a new line of earth-moving equipment. The savings? Sixteen dollars per vehicle. Suggestions such as these have cut Deere's design times by 33 percent over 3 years. Another work team in the company's East Moline, Illinois, factory helped overhaul assembly-line methods. That team cut assembly costs by over 10 percent. Overall, Becherer's innovations are paying big dividends. In 1991, the company lost $20 million on sales of $7 billion. In 1994, Deere made $385 million profits on sales of $8 billion.

Although Becherer may think that the changes he has made at Deere are innovative, the truth is that his ideas were being advocated more than 75 years ago by a prominent Boston business philosopher and lecturer.[2] Her name was Mary Parker Follett.

As early as 1918, Follett was extolling the benefits of participative management and teams. Follett advocated tapping into workers' firsthand experience. She warned that in most large organizations, one loses "what we might learn from the man actually on the job." She also argued that command-style, hierarchical organizations "ignore one of the fundamental facts of human nature, namely, the wish to govern one's own life." Follett advocated what she called "cross-functioning," in which "a horizontal rather than a vertical authority" would foster a freer exchange of knowledge within organizations. Her cross-functioning groups are essentially the same thing that we, today, call cross-functional work teams.

The purpose of this appendix is twofold. First, it illustrates, as we showed with the John Deere example, that things that may seem new and innovative often aren't. Second, it can help you better understand current management practices. This appendix will introduce you to the origins of many contemporary management concepts and demonstrate how they evolved, over time, to reflect the changing needs of organizations and society as a whole.

THE PREMODERN ERA

Organized endeavors and management have existed for thousands of years. The Egyptian pyramids and the Great Wall of China are current evidence that projects of tremendous scope, employing tens of thousands of people, were undertaken well before modern times. The pyramids are a particularly interesting example. The construction of a single pyra-

Scene from Sistine Chapel ceiling fresco. While this work is attributed to Michelangelo, in reality it was done by others under his managerial leadership.

mid occupied over 100,000 people for 20 years.[3] Who told each worker what he or she was supposed to do? Who ensured that there would be enough stones at the site to keep workers busy? The answer to questions such as these is management. Regardless of what managers were called at the time, someone had to plan what was to be done, organize people and materials to do it, and provide direction for the workers.

When you hear the name Michelangelo, what comes to your mind? *Renaissance artist*? *Genius*? How about *manager*? Recent evidence tells us that the traditional image of Michelangelo—the lonely genius trapped between agony and ecstasy, isolated on his back on a scaffold, single-handedly painting the ceiling of the Sistine Chapel—is not exactly accurate.[4] Some 475 years ago, Michelangelo was actually running a medium-sized business. Thirteen people helped him paint the Sistine ceiling; about twenty helped carve the marble tombs in the Medici Chapel in Florentine, and he supervised a crew of at least 200 to build the Laurentian Library in Florence. Michelangelo personally selected his workers, trained them, and assigned them to one or more teams. And he kept detailed employment records. For example, he recorded the names, days worked, and wages of every employee, every week. Meanwhile, Michelangelo played the role of the trouble-shooting manager. He would daily dart in and out of the various work areas under his supervision, check on workers' progress, and handle any problems that arose.

These examples from the past demonstrate that organized activities and managers have been with us since ancient times. However, it has been only in the past several hundred years, particularly in the last century, that management has undergone systematic investigation, acquired a common body of knowledge, and become a formal discipline of study.

Organized activities and managers have been with us since ancient times.

Adam Smith's name is typically cited in economics courses for his contributions to classical economic doctrine, but his discussion in *The Wealth of Nations*, published in 1776, included a brilliant argument on the economic advantages that organizations and society would reap from division of labor.[5] He used the pin-manufacturing industry for his examples. Smith noted that ten individuals, each doing a specialized task, could produce about 48,000 pins a day among them. However, if each were working separately and independently, those ten workers would be lucky to make 200—or even ten—pins in one day. If each worker had to draw the wire, straighten it, cut it, pound heads for each pin, sharpen the point, and solder the head and pin shaft, it would be quite a feat to produce ten pins a day!

Smith concluded that division of labor increased productivity by increasing each worker's skill and dexterity, by saving time that is commonly lost in changing tasks, and by the creation of labor-saving inventions and machinery. The wide application today of job specialization—in service jobs such as teaching and medicine as well on assembly lines in manufacturing plants—is undoubtedly due to the economic advantages cited over 200 years ago by Adam Smith.

Possibly the most important pre-twentieth-century influence on management was the **Industrial Revolution.** Begun in the eighteenth century in Great Britain, the Revolution had crossed the Atlantic to America by the end of the Civil War. Machine power was rapidly being substituted for human power. This change, in turn, made it more economical to manufacture goods in factories than in homes. For instance, before the Industrial Revolution, an item such as a blanket was made by one person, typically at home. The worker would shear wool from his or her sheep, twist the wool into yarn, dye the yarn, weave the blanket manually on a home loom, and then sell the finished product to merchants who would travel to farms buying merchandise that then would be sold at regional fairs or markets. The introduction of machine power, combined with the division of labor, made it possible to have large, efficient factories using power-driven equipment. A blanket factory with 100 people doing specialized tasks—some making wool into yarn, some dyeing, others working on the looms—could manufacture large numbers of blankets at a fraction of their previous cost. But these factories required managerial skills. Managers were needed to forecast demand, ensure that enough wool was on hand to make the yarn, assign tasks to people, direct daily activities, coordinate the various tasks, ensure that the machines were kept in good working order and that output standards were maintained, find markets for the finished blankets, and so forth. When blankets were made individually at home, there was little concern with efficiency. Suddenly, however, when the factory owner had 100 people working for him or her and a regular payroll to meet, it became important to keep workers busy. The performing of management skills became necessary.

The advent of machine power, mass production, the reduced transportation costs that followed the rapid expansion of the railroads, and almost no governmental regulation also fostered the development of big corporations. John D. Rockefeller was putting together the Standard Oil monopoly. Andrew Carnegie was gaining control of two-thirds of the steel industry, and similar entrepreneurs were creating other large businesses that would require formalized management practices. The need for a formal theory to guide managers in running their organizations had arrived. However, it was not until the early 1900s that the first major step toward developing such a theory was taken.

CLASSICAL CONTRIBUTIONS

The roots of modern management lie with a group of practitioners and writers who sought to create rational principles that would make organizations more efficient. Because they set the theoretical foundation for a discipline of management, we call their contributions the **classical approach** to management. We can break the classical approach down into two subcategories: scientific management and general administrative theorists.

Scientific Management

If you had to pick a specific year that modern management theory was born, you could make a very strong case for 1911. That was the year that Frederick Winslow Taylor's book *The Principles of Scientific Management* was published.[6] Its contents would become widely accepted by managers throughout the world. The book described the theory of **scientific management**—the use of the scientific method to define the "one best way" for a job to be done. The studies conducted before and after the book's publication would establish Taylor as the father of scientific management.

Frederick Taylor Frederick Taylor did most of his work at the Midvale Steel Company in Pennsylvania. As a mechanical engineer with a Quaker-Puritan background, he was consistently appalled at the inefficiency of workers. Employees used vastly different techniques to do the same job. They were prone to "take it easy" on the job. Taylor believed that worker output was only about one-third of what was possible. Therefore, he set out to correct the situation by applying the scientific method to jobs on the shop floor. He spent more than two decades pursuing with a passion the "one best way" for each job to be done.

It is important to understand what Taylor saw at Midvale that aroused his determination to improve efficiency in the plant. At the time, there were no clear concepts of worker and management responsibilities. Virtually no effective work standards existed. Workers purposely worked at a slow pace. Management decisions were of the "seat-of-the-pants" nature, based on hunch and intuition. Workers were placed on jobs with little or no concern for matching their abilities and aptitudes with the tasks they were required to do. Most important, management and workers considered themselves to be in continual conflict. Rather than cooperating to their mutual benefit, they perceived their relationship as a zero-sum game—any gain by one would be at the expense of the other.

Taylor sought to create a mental revolution among both the workers and management by defining clear guidelines for improving production efficiency. He defined four principles of management, listed in Exhibit A-1. He argued that following these principles would result in the prosperity of both management and workers. That is, workers would earn more pay, and management more profits.

Probably the most widely cited example of scientific management has been Taylor's pig iron experiment. Workers loaded "pigs" of iron, weighing 92 pounds each, onto rail cars. Their average daily output was 12.5 tons. Taylor believed that scientifically analyzing the job to determine the one best way to load pig iron could increase the output to between 47 and 48 tons per day.

EXHIBIT A-1
Taylor's Principles of Management

1. Develop a science for each element of an individual's work, which replaces the old rule-of-thumb method.
2. Scientifically select and then train, teach, and develop the worker. (Previously, workers chose their own work and trained themselves as best they could.)
3. Heartily cooperate with the workers so as to ensure that all work is done in accordance with the principles of the science that has been developed.
4. Divide work and responsibility almost equally between management and workers. Management takes over all work for which it is better suited than the workers. (Previously, almost all the work and the greater part of the responsibility were thrown upon the workers.)

Taylor began his experiment by looking for a physically strong subject who placed a high value on the dollar. The individual Taylor chose was a big, strong Dutch immigrant, whom he called Schmidt. Schmidt, like the other loaders, earned $1.15 a day, which even at the turn of the century was barely enough for a person to survive on. Taylor offered Schmidt $1.85 a day if he would do exactly what Taylor told him.

Using money to motivate Schmidt, Taylor then went about having him load the pig irons, alternating various job factors to see what impact the changes had on Schmidt's daily output. For instance, on some days Schmidt would lift the pig irons by bending his knees; on other days he would keep his legs straight and use his back. Taylor experimented with rest periods, walking speed, carrying positions, and other variables. After a long period of scientifically trying various combinations of procedures, techniques, and tools, Taylor succeeded in obtaining the level of productivity he thought possible. By putting the right person on the job with the correct tools and equipment, by having the worker follow his instructions exactly, and by motivating the worker through the economic incentive of a significantly higher daily wage, Taylor was able to reach his 48-ton objective.

Using scientific management techniques, Taylor was able to define the one best way for doing each job. He could then, after selecting the right people for the job, train them to do it precisely in this one best way. To motivate workers, he favored incentive wage plans. Overall, Taylor achieved consistent improvements in productivity in the range of 200 percent or more. And he reaffirmed the role of managers to plan and control and that of workers to perform as they were instructed.

The impact of Taylor's work cannot be overstated.[7] During the first decade of the century, Taylor delivered numerous public lectures to convey scientific management to interested industrialists. Between 1901 and 1911, at least eighteen firms adopted some variants of scientific management. In 1908, the Harvard Business School declared Taylor's approach the standard for modern management and adopted it as the core around which all courses were to be organized. Taylor, himself, began lecturing at Harvard in 1909. Between 1910 and 1912, two events catapulted scientific management into the limelight. In 1910, the Eastern Railroad requested a rate increase from the Interstate Commerce Commission. Appearing before the commission, an efficiency expert claimed that railroads could save a million dollars a day (equivalent to about $16 million a day in 1997 dollars) through the application of scientific management. This claim became the centerpiece of the hearings and created a national audience for Taylor's ideas. Then in 1911, Taylor published *The Principles of Scientific Management.* It became an instant best seller. By 1914, Taylor's principles had become so popular that an "efficiency exposition" held in New York City, with Taylor as the

By 1914, Taylor's principles had become so popular that an "efficiency exposition" held in New York City, with Taylor as the keynote speaker, drew a crowd estimated at 69,000!

Frederick Taylor was the father of scientific management. His ideas were instrumental in redefining the roles of workers and managers, and in leading to huge increases in production efficiency.

keynote speaker, drew a crowd estimated at 69,000! And, although Taylor spread his ideas not only in the United States but also in France, Germany, Russia, and Japan, his greatest influence was on U.S. manufacturing. It gave U.S. companies a comparative advantage over foreign firms that made U.S. manufacturing efficiency the envy of the world—at least for 50 years or so.

Frank and Lillian Gilbreth Taylor's ideas inspired others to study and develop methods of scientific management. His most prominent disciples were Frank and Lillian Gilbreth.[8]

A construction contractor by background, Frank Gilbreth gave up his contracting career to study scientific management after hearing Taylor speak at a professional meeting. Along with his wife Lillian, a psychologist, he studied work arrangements to eliminate wasteful hand-and-body motions. The Gilbreths also experimented in the design and use of the proper tools and equipment for optimizing work performance. Frank Gilbreth is probably best known for his experiments in reducing the number of motions in bricklaying.

By carefully analyzing the bricklayer's job, he reduced the number of motions in the laying of exterior brick from eighteen to four and one-half. On interior brick, the eighteen motions were reduced to two. He developed a new way to stack bricks, utilized the scaffold to reduce bending, and even devised a different mortar consistency that reduced the need for bricklayers to level the brick by tapping it with a trowel. The importance of these productivity improvements become meaningful when you recognize that most quality buildings at that time were constructed of brick, that land was cheap, and that the major cost of a factory or home was the cost of the materials (bricks) and the labor cost to lay them.

The Gilbreths were among the first to use motion picture films to study hand and body motions. They devised a microchronometer that recorded time to $\frac{1}{2000}$ second, placed it in the field of study being photographed, and thus determined how long a worker spent enacting each motion. Wasted motions missed by the naked eye could be identified and eliminated. The Gilbreths also devised a classification system to label seventeen basic hand motions—such as "search," "select," "grasp," "hold"—which they called **therbligs** (*Gilbreth* spelled backward with the *th* transposed). This system allowed the Gilbreths a more precise way of analyzing the exact elements of any worker's hand movements.

General Administrative Theorists

The **general administrative theorists** were individuals who looked at the subject of management from the perspective of the entire organization. They are important because they developed early general theories of what managers do and what constitutes good management practice. The most prominent of the general administrative theorists were Henri Fayol and Max Weber.

Henri Fayol Henri Fayol wrote during the same time as Taylor.[9] However, whereas Taylor was concerned with management at the shop level (or what we today would describe as the job of a supervisor) and used the scientific method, Fayol's attention was directed at the activities of *all* managers, and he wrote from personal experience. Taylor was a scientist. Fayol, the managing director of a large French coal-mining firm, was a practitioner.

Fayol described the practice of management as something distinct from accounting, finance, production, distribution, and other typical business activities. He argued that management was an activity common to all human undertakings in business, in government, and even in the home. He then proceeded to state fourteen principles of management—fundamental or universal truths—that could be taught in schools and universities. These principles are listed in Exhibit A-2.

Max Weber Max Weber (pronounced *Vay-ber*) was a German sociologist. Writing in the early 1900s, Weber developed a theory of authority structures and described organizational activity based on authority relations.[10] He described an ideal type of organization that he called a bureaucracy. It was a system characterized by division of labor, a clearly defined hierarchy, detailed rules and regulations, and impersonal relationships. It also acknowledged a separation of owners from managers, thus legitimizing the status of career or professional managers. The detailed features of Weber's ideal bureaucratic structure are outlined in Exhibit A-3.

Weber recognized that this "ideal bureaucracy" didn't exist in reality but, rather, represented a selective reconstruction of the real world. He meant it as a basis for theorizing about work and how work could be done in large groups. But Weber sincerely believed that his model could remove the ambiguity, inefficiencies, and patronage that characterized most organizations at that time. This model became the design prototype for most large organizations until less than a decade ago.

EXHIBIT A-2
Fayol's 14 Principles of Management

1. *Division of work.* This principle is the same as Adam Smith's "division of labor." Specialization increases output by making employees more efficient.
2. *Authority.* Managers must be able to give orders. Authority gives them this right.
3. *Discipline.* Employees must obey and respect the rules that govern the organization.
4. *Unity of command.* Every employee should receive orders from only *one* superior.
5. *Unity of direction.* Each group of organizational activities that have the same objective should be directed by one manager using one plan.
6. *Subordination of individual interests to the general interest.* The interests of any one employee or group of employees should not take precedence over the interests of the organization as a whole.
7. *Remuneration.* Workers must be paid a fair wage for their services.
8. *Centralization.* Whether decision making is centralized with management or decentralized to subordinates is a question of proper proportion. The task is to find the optimum degree of centralization for each situation.
9. *Scalar chain.* Communication should follow the line of authority from top management to the lowest ranks. However, if following this chain creates delays, cross-communications can be allowed if agreed to by all parties and superiors are kept informed.
10. *Order.* People and materials should be in the right place at the right time.
11. *Equity.* Managers should be kind and fair to their subordinates.
12. *Stability of tenure of personnel.* High employee turnover is inefficient. Management should provide orderly personnel planning and ensure that replacements are available to fill vacancies.
13. *Initiative.* Employees who are allowed to originate and carry out plans will exert high levels of effort.
14. *Esprit de corps.* Promoting team spirit will build harmony and unity within the organization.

Bureaucracy, as described by Weber, is not unlike scientific management in its ideology. Both emphasize rationality, predictability, impersonality, technical competence, and authoritarianism. Although Weber's writings were less operational than Taylor's, the fact that his "ideal type" still describes many contemporary organizations attests to the importance of his work.

EXHIBIT A-3
Weber's Ideal Bureaucracy

1. *Division of labor.* Jobs are broken down into simple, routine, and well-defined tasks.
2. *Authority hierarchy.* Offices or positions are organized in a hierarchy, each lower one being controlled and supervised by a higher one.
3. *Formal selection.* All organizational members are to be selected on the basis of technical qualifications demonstrated by training, education, or formal examination.
4. *Formal rules and regulations.* To ensure uniformity and to regulate the actions of employees, managers must depend heavily on formal organizational rules.
5. *Impersonality.* Rules and controls are applied uniformly, avoiding involvement with personalities and personal preferences of employees.
6. *Career orientation.* Managers are professional officials rather than owners of the units they manage. They work for fixed salaries and pursue their careers within the organization.

HUMAN RESOURCES APPROACH

Job selection tests. Pay-for-performance reward systems. Benefit programs. Designing jobs to improve employee motivation. Participative leadership. Using teams to increase productivity. These contemporary management concepts have evolved out of ideas and research efforts contributed by followers of the **human resources approach** to management. This approach looks at management by focusing on factors that influence and explain human behavior at work.

Early Contributors

There were undoubtedly a number of people in the nineteenth and early part of the twentieth century who recognized the importance of the human factor to an organization's success, but four individuals stand out as early advocates of the human resources approach. They were Robert Owen, Hugo Münsterberg, Mary Parker Follett, and Chester Barnard.

Robert Owen Robert Owen was a successful Scottish businessman who bought his first factory in 1789 when he was just 18. Repulsed by the harsh practices he saw in factories across Scotland—such

APPENDIX B
SCORING KEYS FOR "BUILDING SELF-AWARENESS" BOXES

Chapter 3: What's Your Decision-Making Style?

Scoring the decision-style inventory:

1. Add the points in each of the four columns—I, II, III, IV.
2. The sum of the four columns should be 300 points. If your sum does not equal 300 points, check your addition and your answers.
3. Place your score for each column—I, II, III, IV—into the box of the corresponding number.

Analytic II ___	___ **Conceptual III**
Directive I ___	___ **Behavioral IV**

4. The box with the highest score reflects your dominant style. The closer the distribution is to a score of 75 in each category, the greater flexibility you show.

Chapter 7: How Well Suited Are You to Working in a Bureaucracy?

Give yourself one point for each answer that matches the answers below.

1. Mostly agree
2. Mostly agree
3. Mostly disagree
4. Mostly agree
5. Mostly disagree
6. Mostly disagree
7. Mostly agree
8. Mostly agree
9. Mostly disagree
10. Mostly agree
11. Mostly agree
12. Mostly disagree
13. Mostly disagree
14. Mostly agree
15. Mostly disagree
16. Mostly agree
17. Mostly disagree
18. Mostly agree
19. Mostly agree
20. Mostly disagree

A very high score (15 or over) suggests that you would enjoy working in a bureaucracy. A very low score (5 or lower) suggests that you would be frustrated by working in a bureaucracy.

Chapter 8: Is an Enriched Job for You?

This questionnaire taps the degree to which you have a strong versus weak desire to obtain growth satisfaction from your work. Each item on the questionnaire yields a score from 1 to 7 (that is, "Strongly prefer A" is scored 1; "Neutral" is scored 4; and "Strongly prefer B" is scored 7). To obtain your individual growth need strength score, average the twelve items as follows:

Numbers 1, 2, 7, 8, 11, 12 (direct scoring)

Numbers 3, 4, 5, 6, 9, 10 (reverse scoring)

Average scores for typical respondents are close to the midpoint of 4.0. Research indicates that if you score high on this measure, you will respond positively to an enriched job. Conversely, if you score low, you will tend *not* to find enriched jobs satisfying or motivating.

Chapter 10: Do You Have a Team Mentality?

Reverse the ratings for items 1–10, 12, and 18–20. (That is, 1 = 7, 2 = 6, 3 = 5, 5 = 3, and so forth.) Now add your answers to calculate your score. Your total score will be between 20 and 140.

The higher your score, the higher your collectivist-orientation, so high scores are more compatible with being a team player. For comparative purposes, 492 undergraduate students enrolled in an introductory management course at a large U.S. university scored an average of approximately 89. We might speculate that scores below 69 indicate a strong individualistic ethic, and scores above 109 indicate a strong team mentality.

Chapter 11: Which Kind of Culture Fits You Best?

Each statement describes a cultural theme. Look at your highest-rated responses (1–3). These provide insights into the type of culture that fits you best. Similarly, those statements with which you least agreed (5–7) provide guidance as to cultures you should stay away from. Cultural theme key: (a) strong team orientation; (b) strong people orientation; (c) strong risk-taking culture; (d) strong outcome orientation; (e) high stability orientation; (f) strong attention-to-detail culture; and (g) low aggressiveness culture.

Chapter 12: Assess Your Locus of Control

Give yourself 1 point for each of the following selections: 1B, 2A, 3A, 4B, 5B, 6A, 7A, 8A, 9B, and 10A. Scores can be interpreted as follows:

8–10	=	High internal locus of control
6–7	=	Moderate internal locus of control
5	=	Mixed
3–4	=	Moderate external locus of control
1–2	=	High external locus of control

Chapter 13: What Motivates You?

To determine your dominant needs—and what motivates you—place the number (1 through 5) that you circled for each statement next to the number for that statement.

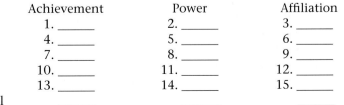

	Achievement	Power	Affiliation
	1. ______	2. ______	3. ______
	4. ______	5. ______	6. ______
	7. ______	8. ______	9. ______
	10. ______	11. ______	12. ______
	13. ______	14. ______	15. ______
Total	______	______	______

PHOTO CREDITS

Chapter 1
page 2, Letraset Phototone
page 3, Doug Menuez/SABA Press Photos, Inc.
page 6, Jon Feingersh/The Stock Market
page 14, Mike Mazzaschi/Stock Boston
page 21, Brian Palmer
page 24, Bob Sacha Photography

Chapter 2
page 30, Letraset Phototone
page 31, David Butow/SABA Press Photos, Inc.
page 34, Peter Sibbald Photography
page 37, Quidu/Gamma–Liaison, Inc.
page 41, Rick Friedman/Black Star
page 50, Caroline Baird/AP/Wide World Photos

Chapter 3
page 60, Letraset Phototone
page 61, Pete Leabo/AP/Wide World Photos
page 75, George Widman/AP/World Wide Photos
page 88, Imke Lass
page 91, Richard Shock/Gamma–Liaison, Inc.

Chapter 4
page 96, Letraset Phototone
page 97, Mike Greenlar
page 102, Alan Solomon/AP/Wide World Photos
page 113, Berlinger/Gamma–Liaison, Inc.
page 120, Jeffery MacMillan
page 121, T. Michael Keza/Nation's Business Magazine

Chapter 5
page 128, Letraset Phototone
page 129, Neil Shoebridge/Gary Ede
page 134, Rubbermaid Incorporated
page 140, Peter Sibbald Photography
page 143, Teri Stratford
page 145, Jim Lo Scalzo

Chapter 6
page 158, Letraset Phototone
page 159, AP/Wide World Photos
page 163, Robert Holmgren
page 171, Laura Arsie
page 175, John Greenleigh/Apple Computer Inc.

Chapter 7
page 190, Letraset Phototone
page 191, John Madere/Stock Market
page 205, Brian Smith, Photographer
page 212, Seth Resnick
page 213, Paul Barker/AP/Wide World Photos

Chapter 8
page 222, Letraset Phototone
page 223, Brian Leng Photography
page 226, Raghu Rai/Magnum Photo, Inc.
page 229, Photo courtesy Ross Controls, Troy, MI.
page 240, Lizzie Himmel
page 248, Andy Freeberg Photography

Chapter 9
page 256, Letraset Phototone
page 257, Kenneth Jarecke/Contact Press Images
page 272, David Butow/SABA Press Photos, Inc.
page 276, Internal & External Communication Inc./Courtesy Lexus
page 279, Andy Freeberg Photography
page 284, Mug Shots/Stock Market

Chapter 10
page 292, Letraset Phototone
page 293, Greg Girard/Contact Press Images
page 300, Bob Daemmrich/Stock Boston
page 308, Ron Garrison/Zoological Society of San Diego
page 311, Courtesy Chrysler Corporation

Chapter 11
page 324, Letraset Phototone
page 329, Broderbund Software, Inc.
page 333, Lauren Espeillac/Patagonia
page 339, Mike Greenlar
page 344, Mark Bolster

Chapter 12
page 352, Letraset Phototone
page 353, John Abbott Photography
page 357, Jamie Tanaka
page 370, Mark Richards/Contact Press Images
page 375, Billy E. Barnes/Stock Boston

Chapter 13
page 384, Letraset Phototone
page 385, Thomas Meyer, Hanover, Germany
page 394, Tomas Muscionico/Contact Press Images
page 400, Giboux/Gamma–Liaison, Inc
page 408, Tom Salyer
page 410, Courtesy Bookman's Used Books

Chapter 14
page 416, Letraset Phototone
page 417, Ki Ho Park/Kistone Photography
page 422, David Fields Photography
page 428, Karl Gehring/Gamma–Liaison, Inc.
page 436, H. Lagerway

Chapter 15
page 446, Letraset Phototone
page 447, Chris Buck
page 450, Suzanne Opton
page 463, Lotus Development Corp.

page 464, Courtesy Golden State Mutual Life Insurance Company, Los Angeles
page 469, Litz/Monkmeyer Press

Chapter 16 page 476, Letraset Phototone
page 477, Courtesy Ford Motor Company
page 479, David Butow/SABA Press Photos, Inc.
page 484, Richard Howard Photography
page 492, J. Pickerell/The Image Works
page 498, Esbin-Anderson/The Image Works

Chapter 17 page 510, Letraset Phototone
page 511, Compton's NewMedia
page 520, Wyatt McSpadden Photography
page 533, William Mercer McLeod
page 534, Courtesy Rubbermaid Incorporated. Used with permission.
page 537, Fritz Hoffmann/JB Pictures Ltd.

Appendix page 544, Deere & Company
page 545, The Granger Collection
page 547, Courtesy Stevens Institute of Technology, Hoboken, NJ.
page 551, Courtesy Western Electric

A

B

C

D

E

F

G

S

T

U

V

A

ABC system *An inventory control system that prioritizes items by importance,* 170

Ability, team skills, 312

Accommodation *Maintaining harmonious relationships by placing another's needs and concerns above your own,* 489

Achievement, need for, 355–56

Active listening *Listening so as to understand the communication from a speaker's point of view,* 483–85

Activities *The time or resources required to progress from one event to another on a PERT network,* 181

Activity-based budgeting *Allocates costs for producing a good or service based on the activities performed and services employed,* 179

Advertising, as a strategy to manage the environment, 112

Affective component of an attitude *The emotional or feeling segment of an attitude,* 367

Affiliation, need for, 355–56, 391–93

Agriculture-based society, 7

Application forms, 267

Apprenticeships, 275

Asia-Pacific Economic Cooperation, 6

Assessment centers *A set of performance simulation tests designed to evaluate a candidate's managerial potential,* 269

Assignable causes *Sources of nonchance variation in a process; capable of being identified and controlled,* 184

Assumed similarity *Observers perceive others as being like themselves,* 365

Assumptions about human nature, 395

Attitudes *Evaluative statements or judgments concerning objects, people, or events,* 366
- components, 367
- job involvement, 367–68
- job satisfaction, 367, 369–71, 395–97
- managerial implications of, 371
- organizational commitment, 368

Attribute charts *Measures a product characteristic in terms of whether it is good or bad,* 183

Attribute listing, 66

Attribution
- model of leadership *Proposes that leadership is merely an attribution that people make about other individuals; and that effective leaders are generally considered consistent in their decisions,* 427–28
- theory *When individuals observe behavior, they attempt to determine whether it is internally or externally caused,* 362–64

Audit *A formal verification of an organization's accounts, records, operating activities, or performance,* 167

Authority *The rights inherent in a managerial position to give orders and expect the orders to be obeyed,* 196

Autonomous internal units *A structural form characterized by decentralized business units with their own products, clients, competitors, and profit goals; these units behave as free-standing companies,* 211–12

Availability heuristic *The tendency for people to base their judgments on information that is readily available to them,* 79

Avoidance *Withdrawing from or suppressing a conflict,* 489

B

Bargaining (*see* Negotiation)

Basic corrective action *Seeks how and why performance has deviated and then corrects the source of the deviation,* 164

Behavioral
- component of an attitude *An intention to behave in a certain way toward someone or something,* 367
- science theorists *Individuals who use objective research in the study of human behavior in organizations,* 553–54

Behaviorally anchored rating scales (BARS) *An evaluation method where actual job-related behaviors are rated along a continuum,* 280

Benchmarking *The practice of comparing, using some measurable scale, how well a key business operation is performed in-house vis-à-vis like operations in other organizations,* 107–08

Benefits, family-friendly, 12

Bi-modal work force *A workforce composed of two separate classes of employees—high skilled and low skilled,* 22

Board representatives *A form of representative participation; employees sit on a company's board of directors and represent the interests of the firm's employees,* 262

Bonus pay, 409

Boss, manager as, 42–43, 465

Bottom-up budgeting *The initial budget requests are prepared by those who must implement them and then forwarded up to higher levels of management for modification and approval,* 179

Boundaryless organization *Seeks to eliminate the chain of command, create limitless spans of control, replace departments with empowered teams, and minimize other vertical and horizontal boundaries,* 215–16

Bounded rationality *Individuals make decisions by constructing simplified models that extract the essential features from problems without capturing all their complexity,* 73–75

Brainstorming *An idea-generation process that specifically encourages any and all alternatives, while withholding any criticism of those alternatives,* 306

Break-even analysis *A quantitiative technique to determine whether a particular sales volume will result in losses or profits,* 67–68

Broadbanding compensation *Reducing the number of job levels or salary grades into a few wide bands,* 18

Budgets *A numerical plan for allocating resources to specific activities,* 166
- activity-based, 179
- as control devices, 178–80
- incremental *Each period's budget begins by using the last period as a reference point,* 178
- zero-base *The entire budget begins from scratch and each budget item must be justified,* 178–79

Buffering *A strategy to manage the environment by reducing the possibility that the organization's operations will be disturbed by insuring supplies and/or absorption of outputs,* 110

Bureaurcracy *A structure characterized by highly standardized operating tasks achieved through specialization, very formalized rules and regulations, tasks that are grouped into functional departments, centralized authority, narrow spans of control, and decision making that follows the chain of command,* 206–08, 548–49

C

Career(s)
- planning, 284–86
- self-directed, 23, 285

D

E

F

Objectives (*cont.*)
individuals, groups, or entire organizations, 149
as control mechanism, 165
downside of, 151–52
management by, 151
motivators, as, 397–98
multiple, 149
real *What members of the organization actually do*, 150
stated *Official statements of what an organization says are its objectives*, 149–50
team, 313
value of, 150–51
Obsolescence, worker, 239–40
Open systems *Systems that interact dynamically with their environment*, 554–55, 557
Operant conditioning *A type of conditioning in which desired voluntary behavior leads to a reward or prevents a punishment*, 371–72
Operational plans *Plans that specify the details of how the overall objectives are to be achieved*, 130
Operations
management, 168–70
research (*see* Quantitative Analysis *and* Quantitative approaches to management)
technology, 225–34
Operatives *Employees who work directly on a job or task and have no responsibility for overseeing the work of others*, 32
Organic organization *A highly adaptive form that is loose and flexible; characterized by limited levels, teams, low formalization, a comprehensive information network, and decentralization*, 200–01, 204
Organization *A systematic arrangement of two or more people who fulfill formal roles and share a common purpose*
defined, 35
purpose of, 35–36
Organization design, 199–201, 204–16
Organization structure *Defines how job tasks are formally divided, grouped, and coordinated*, 192
autonomous internal units, 211–12
boundaryless, 215–16
bureaucratic, 206–08
change, 523–24
conflict-creation through, 491
contingency view of, 199–204
dimensions of, 192–99
dismantling, 16–17
environment and, 192, 203–04
matrix, 209–10
mechanistic, 199–201
organic, 200–01, 204
redesigning, 192
simple, 204–06
size and, 201–02
strategy and, 201
team-based, 210–11
technology and, 202–03
virtual, 213–15
Organizational behavior *The systematic study of how people behave in organizations*, 36
Organizational commitment *The degree to which an employee identifies with a particular organization and its goals, and wishes to maintain membership in the organization*, 368
Organizational communication *Communication among several individuals or groups*, 235–37
Organizational culture *A system of shared meaning held by members that distinguishes the organization from other organizations*, 326
blending diverse, 325–26, 344–46
changing, 341–44, 490
characteristics of, 326–27
core values of, 328
creation of, 332–33
dominant, 328
downside of a strong, 346
founders, impact on, 332–33
language, 335–36
leadership, influence on, 436–37
learning, 334–36
managing, 337–46, 537
material symbols, 335
vs. national culture, 331–32
personality, 328–31
perspective on management, 555–56, 557
process of creating, 332–33
reading, 336–37
rituals, 334–35
socialization, 340–41, 342
stories, 334
strong vs. weak, 328, 346
subcultures, 328
sustaining, 338–41
uniformity of, 327–28
Organizational development (OD) *A collection of techniques for understanding, changing, and developing an organization's work force in order to improve its effectiveness*, 526
Organizing *The management function that includes the determination of what tasks are to be done, who is to do them, how the tasks are to be grouped, who reports to whom, and where decisions are to be made*, 37
Orientation, employee, as control mechanism, 165
Outsourcing *Contracting with outside firms to provide resources or services*, 16–17, 214

P

Paired comparison *An evaluation method that compares each employee with every other employee and assigns a summary ranking based on the number of superior scores that the employee achieves*, 281
Participative counseling *Listen to an employee's problem, ask questions, offer insights and advice, and participate with the employee in seeking a solution*, 499
Participative management, 407 (*see also* Empowerment)
Path-goal model of leadership *The leader's job is to assist his or her followers in attaining their goals and to provide the necessary direction and/or support to ensure their goals are compatible with the overall objectives of the group or organization*, 434–36
Pay-for-performance, 18
Pay, equity, 387, 399–401
PDCA cycle, 231–32
Perception *A process by which individuals organize and interpret their sensory impressions in order to give meaning to their environment*, 361
errors in, 364–65
factors influencing, 361–62
job dimensions, 243–44
managerial implications of, 365
reality vs., 361
selective, 364, 515–16
Performance appraisal
appraisers, 278–79
as control mechanism, 166
criteria, 277–78
as decision making constraint, 85–86
feedback, 281–82
importance of, 277
methods, 279–81
team, 282–83, 314
Permanent employment, 23, 403–05
Personal digital assistants (PDAs), 174–75
Personality *The combination of the psychological traits we use to classify individuals*, 354
entrepreneurial, 146–47
-job fit model *Identifies six personality types and proposes that the fit between personality type and occupational environment determines satisfaction and turnover*, 359–60, 361
managerial implications of, 360–61
matching with jobs, 359–60
organizational, 328–31
tests for employment, 267–68
traits, 278, 354–59, 421–23
Personnel management (*see* Human Resource Management)

PERT network *A flowchartlike diagram that depicts the sequence of activities needed to complete a project and the time or costs associated with each activity*, 181

Piece-rate wages, 409

Planned change *Change activities that are intentional and goal-oriented*, 518

Planning *The management function that encompasses defining an organization's goals, establishing an overall strategy for achieving these goals, and developing a comprehensive hierarchy of plans to integrate and coordinate activities*, 37, 130
- commitment concept of *The more current plans affect future commitments, the longer the time frame for which managers need to plan*, 131
- criticisms of, 132–33
- human resource, 262–63
- length of, 131
- and performance, 133–34
- project, 143–45
- types of, 130–31
- in uncertainty, 131–34
- value of, 132

Politicking *Actions a person takes to influence, or attempt to influence, the distribution of advantages and disadvantages within his or her organization*, 500–04, 522–23

Power *The capacity to influence the behavior of another individual or group of individuals, so that individual or group does something it wouldn't otherwise do*, 457
- authority and, 457–58
- dependency, 458–60
- elasticity of, 460
- need for, 391–93
- and politics, 503
- source of, 457–58

Prearrival stage *The period of learning in the socialization process that occurs before a new employee joins the organization*, 340

Principles of management, 548, 549

Problem
- identification, 76–78
- -solving teams *Groups of 5 to 12 employees from the same department who meet for a few hours each week to discuss ways of improving quality, efficiency, and the work environment*, 309

Process
- departmentalization, 195
- value analysis *A key element of reengineering; assess core processes to identify the value each adds to the organization's distinctive competencies*, 232

Product departmentalization, 195, 209–10

Production technology, 227–29

Productivity and technology, 224–25

Productivity (*see* Efficiency)

Professional employees, 404

Profit-sharing, 409

Program Evaluation and Review Technique (PERT) *A technique for scheduling complex projects*, 181–82

Programmed decisions *Recurring and routine decisions*, 71–72

Project *A one-time-only set of activities with a definite beginning and ending point in time*, 143–45

Project management *The task of getting activities done on time, within budget, and according to specifications*, 143–45

Purchasing controls, 168–70

Pygmalion effect, 365

Q

Qualitative forecasts *The use of judgment and opinions of knowledgeable individuals to predict future outcomes*, 105, 106

Quality (*see also* Total quality management), 48, 122

Quality circles, 407

Quantitative
- analysis, 66–70, 73
- approaches to management *Mathematical applications that help managers improve resource allocation choices*, 554, 557
- forecasts *A set of mathematical rules to a series of past data to predict future outcomes*, 105, 106

Queuing theory *A mathematical technique for balancing the cost of having a waiting line against the cost of service to maintain that line*, 70

R

Rational *Consistent, value-maximizing choices within specified constraints*, 62

Rational decision making process, 62–64

Rationing *A strategy to manage the environment by allocating output according to some priority system*, 111

Realistic job preview *Providing job candidates with both unfavorable and favorable information before an offer is made*, 270–71

Recognition programs, 410

Recruitment *The process of locating, identifying, and attracting capable applicants*, 109–110, 264–65

Reengineering *How work would be done and the organization structured if it were started from scratch*, 15–16
- change and, 529–30
- defined, 15–16
- elements, 232–33
- value of, 15–16, 233
- vs. TQM, 233

Regulations, as control mechanism, 165

Reinforcement
- schedules, 373–75
- theory *Behavior is a function of its consequences*, 371–72, 398–99

Reliability *For selection devices; an indication that the device measures the same thing consistently*, 266

Representative
- heuristic *Assessing the likelihood of an occurrence by drawing analogies and seeing identical situations where they don't exist*, 80
- participation *Workers participate in organizational decision making through a small group of representative employees*, 262, 407

Return on investment *Profits computed as a percentage of capital invested in an organization*, 68

Revenue forecasting *Predicting future organizational revenues*, 104–05

Reward systems
- as control mechanism, 166
- as decision making constraint, 85
- equitable, 387, 397, 399–401
- as motivators, 387, 399–402, 405–06, 407–09, 410
- performance and, 401–02
- performance evaluation and, 401–02
- team-based, 314

Risk *Those conditions in which a decision maker is able to estimate the likelihood of alternatives or outcomes*, 64

Risk taking, 357–58

Rituals, 334–35

Robots *Machines that act like human beings*, 227

Roles *A set of expected behavior patterns that are attributed to occupying a given position in a social unit*, 295–96
- leadership, 455–66
- management (*see also* Management roles), 37–38
- team, 312–13

S

Satisfaction (*see* Job satisfaction)

Satisfaction, employee, 48, 395–97

T

U

V

Visionary leadership *The ability to create and articulate a realistic, credible, attractive vision of the future for an organization or organizational unit, that grows out of and improves upon the present*, 452–55

W

Women (*see* Diversity, gender)
Work councils *Groups of nominated or elected employees who must be consulted when management makes decisions involving personnel*, 262
Work design
 as control mechanism, 165
 group, 245
 individual, 245
 job dimensions, 241–44
Work force diversity (*see* Diversity, work force)
Work group *A group whose members interact primarily to share information and to make decisions to help each other perform within their area of responsibility*, 294
Work sampling *Creating a miniature replica of a job to evaluate the performance abilities of job candidates*, 268
Work schedules, 247–49
Work specialization *Division of labor; the degree to which tasks in the organization are subdivided into separate jobs*, 193–94, 545
Work team(s) *A group whose individual efforts result in a performance that is greater than the sum of those individual inputs*, 294
 appraisal of, 314
 common purpose, 313
 compensating, 314, 316
 cross-functional, 196, 310–11
 flexibility device, 17
 goals, 313
 high-performance, 311–14
 individualists on, 314–17
 leadership of, 461–63
 membership, 23–24
 performance appraisals, 282–83
 popularity of, 308
 problem-solving, 309
 rewarding, 314, 316
 self-managed, 205, 309–10
 types of, 309–11
Workflow automation *Eliminating workflow bottlenecks and outdated procedures; replacing them with software that improves efficiency*, 235, 236

Z

Zero-base budget (ZBB) *The entire budget begins from scratch and each budget item must be justified*, 178–79